The Elgar Companion to Marxist Economics

Edited by

Ben Fine

Professor of Economics, SOAS, University of London, UK

Alfredo Saad-Filho

Professor of Political Economy, SOAS, University of London, UK

with editorial assistance from

Marco Boffo

PhD Candidate, SOAS, University of London, UK

Edward Elgar
Cheltenham, UK • Northampton, MA, USA

Published by
Edward Elgar Publishing Limited
The Lypiatts
15 Lansdown Road
Cheltenham
Glos GL50 2JA
UK

Edward Elgar Publishing, Inc.
William Pratt House
9 Dewey Court
Northampton
Massachusetts 01060
USA

Paperback edition 2013
Paperback edition reprinted 2015

A catalogue record for this book
is available from the British Library

Library of Congress Control Number: 2011932881

MIX
Paper from
responsible sources
FSC   FSC® C013056
www.fsc.org

ISBN 978 1 84844 537 6 (cased)
ISBN 978 1 78100 198 1 (paperback)

Typeset by Servis Filmsetting Ltd, Stockport, Cheshire
Printed and bound in Great Britain by T.J. International Ltd, Padstow

Contents

Contributors

Greg Albo is Associate Professor of Political Science, York University, Canada.

Robert Albritton is Professor Emeritus, Department of Political Science, York University, Canada.

Daniel Ankarloo is Senior Lecturer of Social Work and Social Policy, Department of Health and Society, Malmö University, Sweden.

Sam Ashman is Post-Doctoral Research Fellow, University of Johannesburg, and Visiting Senior Researcher, University of the Witwatersrand, South Africa.

Alison J. Ayers is Assistant Professor, Departments of Political Science, Sociology and Anthropology, Simon Fraser University, Canada.

Radhika Balakrishnan is Professor of Women's and Gender Studies, Rutgers, The State University of New Jersey, United States of America.

Jairus Banaji is Professorial Research Associate, Department of Development Studies, School of Oriental and African Studies, University of London, United Kingdom.

Savitri Bisnath is Senior Policy Advisor for the Center for Women's Global Leadership, Rutgers University, United States of America.

Marco Boffo is a PhD Candidate in Economics, School of Oriental and African Studies, University of London, United Kingdom.

Terence J. Byres is Emeritus Professor of Political Economy, School of Oriental and African Studies, University of London, United Kingdom.

Al Campbell is Professor Emeritus of Economics, University of Utah, United States of America.

Paula Cerni MPhil, University of Sussex, United Kingdom, is an independent writer and a foreign languages teacher in the United States of America.

Paresh Chattopadhyay is Professor of Political Economy, Faculty of Human Sciences, University of Québec, Montreal, Canada.

Simon Clarke is Emeritus Professor of Sociology, University of Warwick, United Kingdom.

Alejandro Colás is Senior Lecturer in International Politics, Birkbeck College, University of London, United Kingdom.

George C. Comninel is Associate Professor and Chair of the Department of Political Science at York University, Canada.

Mauro Di Meglio is Associate Professor of Sociology, Department of Social Sciences, University of Naples L'Orientale, Italy.

Paulo L. dos Santos is Lecturer in Economics, School of Oriental and African Studies, University of London, United Kingdom.

Gérard Duménil is former Research Director, Centre National de la Recherche Scientifique, France.

Ben Fine is Professor of Economics, School of Oriental and African Studies, University of London, United Kingdom.

Jayati Ghosh is Professor, Centre for Economic Studies and Planning, Jawaharlal Nehru University, India.

Hugh Goodacre is Senior Lecturer at University of Westminster, Affiliate Lecturer at Birkbeck College, University of London, and Teaching Fellow at University College London, United Kingdom.

Branwen Gruffydd Jones is Senior Lecturer in International Political Economy, Department of Politics, Goldsmiths, University of London, United Kingdom.

Barbara Harriss-White is Professor of Development Studies and Senior Research Fellow in the Contemporary South Asian Studies Programme in the School of Interdisciplinary Area Studies, Oxford University, United Kingdom.

Keith Hart is Professor Emeritus, Department of Anthropology, Goldsmiths, University of London, United Kingdom, and Honorary Professor of Development Studies, University of Kwazulu-Natal, South Africa.

Gong Hoe Gimm is Lecturer at Kookmin University and Korea University, South Korea.

Makoto Itoh is Professor Emeritus of Economics, University of Tokyo, Japan, and a Member of the Japan Academy.

Heesang Jeon is a PhD Candidate in Economics, School of Oriental and African Studies, University of London, United Kingdom.

Bob Jessop is Distinguished Professor of Sociology, Lancaster University, United Kingdom.

Deborah Johnston is Senior Lecturer in Development Economics, School of Oriental and African Studies, University of London, United Kingdom.

Ray Kiely is Professor of International Politics, Queen Mary University of London, United Kingdom.

Samuel Knafo is Lecturer in International Relations, University of Sussex, United Kingdom.

David Laibman is Emeritus Professor of Economics, City University of New York, United States of America, and Editor of *Science & Society*.

Dominique Lévy is Researcher in Economics, Centre National de la Recherche Scientifique, France.

Dic Lo is Senior Lecturer in Economics, School of Oriental and African Studies, University of London, United Kingdom, and Co-Director of the Center of Research in Comparative Political Economy, Renmin University of China.

Thomas Marois is Lecturer in Development Studies, School of Oriental and African Studies, University of London, United Kingdom.

Pietro Masina is Associate Professor of International Political Economy, Department of Social Sciences, University of Naples L'Orientale, Italy.

Stavros D. Mavroudeas is Associate Professor of Political Economy, Department of Economics, University of Macedonia, Greece.

Dimitris Milonakis is Associate Professor of Political Economy and Director of Postgraduate Studies at the Department of Economics, University of Crete, Greece.

Simon Mohun is Emeritus Professor of Political Economy, Queen Mary University of London, United Kingdom.

Susan Newman is Lecturer in International Economics, International Institute of Social Studies, Erasmus University of Rotterdam, the Netherlands.

Prabhat Patnaik has retired from the Sukhamoy Chakravarty Chair, Centre for Economic Studies and Planning, Jawaharlal Nehru University, and is Vice-Chairman of the Planning Board in the State of Kerala, India.

Utsa Patnaik has retired as Professor of Economics, Centre for Economic Studies and Planning, Jawaharlal Nehru University, New Delhi, India.

Lucia Pradella is a PhD student in Philosophy, University of Naples Federico II, Italy, and Paris X Nanterre, France, and Researcher, Jan van Eyck Academie, the Netherlands.

Hugo Radice is a Life Fellow of the School of Politics and International Studies, University of Leeds, United Kingdom.

Alfredo Saad-Filho is Professor of Political Economy, School of Oriental and African Studies, University of London, United Kingdom.

Sungur Savran is a founding member of the Revolutionary Workers' Party (DIP) of Turkey.

Gary Slater is Senior Lecturer in Economics, University of Bradford, United Kingdom.

Tony Smith is Professor of Philosophy, Iowa State University, United States of America.

Erik Swyngedouw is Professor of Geography, School of Environment and Development, University of Manchester, United Kingdom.

Bruno Tinel is Maître de Conferences in Economics, University of Paris 1 Panthéon-Sorbonne, France.

Alberto Toscano is Senior Lecturer in Sociology, Goldsmiths, University of London, United Kingdom.

John Weeks is Professor Emeritus of Development Economics, School of Oriental and African Studies, University of London, United Kingdom.

Ellen Meiksins Wood is Professor Emerita of Political Science, York University, Canada.

Alfred Zack-Williams is Professor of Sociology, University of Central Lancashire, United Kingdom.

Paul Zarembka is Professor of Economics, State University of New York at Buffalo, United States of America.

Yu Zhang is Professor of Economics, Renmin University of China.

Acknowledgements

We are grateful to Alan Sturmer, Alexandra Mandzak and Laura Seward, from Edward Elgar Publishing, for their unflinching support for this project even after several deadlines had been missed. They have made this volume possible. Several contributors have supported the editors as reviewers. We are grateful to them for their optimism, scholarship, professionalism and forbearance.

Introduction

Ben Fine and Alfredo Saad-Filho

Marxist political economy experiences a rhythm and evolution in terms of both its prominence and (perceptions of) its substantive content. There can be no doubt, for example, that the global crisis that broke from the end of 2007 has raised the profile and the perceived relevance of Marxism, but this is necessarily different from the Marxisms that were prominent before 1917, in the interwar period, after 1956 or post-1968. Influential social theories are moulded by, just as they mould, their own social and historical context. But, in contrast with mainstream approaches, Marxism offers a theoretical and conceptual apparatus that can be used to review its own evolution and historical experiences, and that can support the emergence of new generations of progressive movements and thought.

Nevertheless, there are also some ways in which the dynamic and content of Marxist political economy are unique, uniquely influenced and uniquely influential. First and foremost, given its principled attachment to working-class social and political perspectives, the revolutionary abolition of capitalism and the transition to communism (all of which have been conceptualized in different ways within the Marxist tradition, and over time), the fortunes of Marxism are, inevitably, closely tied to the strength, balance and composition of progressive forces across the globe. Over the past 40 years, these have been unfavourable for several well-known reasons: the rise under US hegemony of neoliberalism and financialization however understood, the global restructuring of production, regressive shifts in economic policy, the collapse of eastern European socialism and the rapid transformations in China, the historical hiatus and limitation in outcomes of national liberation movements, the fragmentation and decline of left political parties, and the shrinking membership and influence of (industrial) trade unions. Consequently, there has been a noticeable lack of a significant impulse to Marxism in the 'age of neoliberalism', despite the renewal of radicalism in Latin America and elsewhere.

Second, and closely related to the factors listed above, Marxist political economy has become increasingly confined within academic life and scholarship, where it has been rejected by mainstream economists for its presumably flawed economics, and by non-economists for its presumed economism and reductionism. At the same time, the relentless consolidation of disciplinary boundaries has fragmented and reduced Marxist political economy, while also increasing its vulnerability to the growing intolerance of 'mainstream' academic disciplines – especially economics – to any heterodoxy, Marxist or otherwise. Even within the heterodoxy, critiques of Marxian political economy often proceed on the basis of facile, stylized or even ignorant understandings of Marxism's substantive content. In short, Marxism and its political economy are often revealed to be subject to a careless reconstruction at the hands of those who both criticize and deploy it, thereby being far removed from its original content and intent.

Yet, those more faithfully interpreted and retained elements of Marxism that have often led to its being rendered more marginal have also withstood the tests of both hard times and intellectual prejudice. For example, because of its emphasis on modes of production, class and the historical, and its attention to, but not intellectual monopoly on, considerations of power, conflict and the systemic, Marxism is genuinely interdisciplinary, with Marx himself offering the richest of contributions across an impressively wide range of fields within (and beyond) the social sciences. These not only provide a fertile body of work upon which continuing scholarship can draw but also the opportunity for the rediscovery and renewal of interpretations of the classics of Marx and Marxism and their application to, or rejection under, changing circumstances. This allows Marxist political economy to sustain an insightful, critical and constructive presence within and across many disciplines and topics, and to retain its appeal on a broader front. This is true for objects of study ranging from the economic to the ideological, and from the most detailed at the local level to the fate of the contemporary world.

Third, and of uneven significance across place, discipline and topic, Marxism has a generational rhythm based most recently in the West on the continuing impact of the radicalized generation of the 1960s. Now, a new generation of scholars and activists must fill their intellectual and professional places, although the scope for doing so has become sharply reduced because of the economic, social, political and intellectual developments examined above.

This discussion offers some explanation for the range and content of the contributions that are represented in this Companion. Having put this volume together across the various entries, and we could have solicited as many again, the most striking aspect of the collection is the breadth and depth of the coverage in terms of subject matter and substantive contribution. These reflect a balance between the views of the editors, the intellectual context in which they are located, the intellectual priorities of the authors, and the willingness or otherwise of those contacted to agree to contribute (and to deliver on their agreement). In inviting entries and in steering those that we received, our guiding principle has been demonstrable depth of understanding of, and commitment, to Marxism: this is a book by Marxists. It takes stock of the trajectory, achievements, shortcomings and prospects of Marxist political economy; it reflects a shared commitment to bringing the methods, theories and concepts of Marx himself to bear across a wide range of topics and perspectives, and it provides a statement about the purpose and vitality of Marxist political economy. Within these limits, there is no single Marxist 'line' across the entries and, inevitably, they fall into three categories. The first concerns the longstanding issues of method and basic concepts, which address Marx's own contributions and continuing debate and controversy over these. Second are those relatively concrete topics that could not be systematically addressed by Marx or his most immediate followers because the passage of time has introduced new material and new historical and intellectual developments and challenges. Third are those topics that lie in between these two extremes, including issues over which Marx has much insight to offer but which remain underdeveloped in his own work, although the range of his coverage and insight never fails to astonish.

This structure is undoubtedly a consequence of that central aspect of Marxist economics, value theory. And, unsurprisingly, it is represented here by a large number of entries. Some of these are focused on exposition of the basic categories of Marx's and Marxist analysis, inevitably accompanied by further discussion of controversies over both these categories themselves and, not quite the same thing, their continuing relevance for, or application to, contemporary capitalism. Others have the opposite emphasis – addressing the conditions of contemporary capitalism as a way of interrogating the continuing salience of value theory.

Its centrality is indicative of the rich content with which value theory is endowed, although this requires that value theory is rejected as simply a theory or price based on a technical definition of the quantity of labour embodied in a commodity. Rather, with value taken as a social relationship between producers expressed, through the market, as a physical relationship between things, value theory both traces the structures, agencies and processes by which market forms emerge, evolve and are reproduced and seeks to locate them in their historically and socially specific contexts. Of course, to a large extent, focus upon the market forms within capitalism offers the opportunity for general analysis of the mode of production in terms of its economic categories. Such abstract analysis is also extended in the entries to a wide range of aspects of economic and social reproduction.

The connection of value theory to the economic and the social, and to the dynamics of change, is a central aspect of Marxist political economy that inevitably raises questions of method and methodology which are directly addressed across a number of entries. Such questions loom large within Marxism and in its disputes with, and distinction from, other schools of thought. Marxism adopts a holistic or systemic approach, certainly placing it outside the orbit of neoclassical economics. This is not only because of the latter's methodological individualism of a special type but because of its constituting the economic as a fetishised category in its own right, independent of its social and historical location. The latter is also what distinguishes Marxist political economy from much heterodox economics.

Put another way, Marxist political economy derives from its analysis of the category of capital (and of capitalism) as central. It does not proceed from the economy or the economic in abstract as ideal and universal categories (attached, for example, as in neoclassical economics, to scarcity or to 'fundamentals' such as technology, endowments and preferences). But locating the social and historical specificity of the capitalist mode of production – whether and how value relations prevail – draws Marxist political economy into a broader terrain concerning periodization *within* capitalism and *between* capitalism and other modes of production. For the periodization of capitalism, we necessarily include contributions over the nature of the world economy and what are its (shifting) defining characteristics. And for the transitions to and from capitalism, there are issues over what consists a mode of production, how many there are, what are the natures and causes of the transitions between them, and how do they mutually co-exist. Across these entries, we find considerable variation of position, hardly surprising given the grand sweep of material that they cover, with differences over method, its application and the historical processes themselves, with correspondingly distinct (re-)interpretations and refinements of Marx's own work and the historical record.

In this respect, and others, Marxist political economy has much to offer in two further directions. One is in the critique of economics in all of its versions, recalling that Marx's own magnus opus, *Capital*, is subtitled *A Critique of Political Economy*, with himself covering, in the *Theories of Surplus Value* and elsewhere, the degradation of classical economics (most closely associated with Ricardo) into the vulgar economics that prevails today. Further, Marxist political economy establishes a presence within, influence on and critique of each of the social science disciplines as well as of specific topics that straddle disciplinary boundaries (how we understand the state or globalization, for example, as well as the political, the sociological, the historical and the anthropological).

This Companion offers a rich mix of contributors but the single most important criterion, as indicated above, is level of expertise in, and commitment to, Marxism. At the outset, the editors imposed standard conditions on our authors. For reasons of space, the entries are limited in length, have no footnotes and include only a limited number of references to the literature. Wherever possible and appropriate, quotes from Marx's works and the classics of Marxism are sourced from http://www.marxists.org, in order to make the original sources more transparent and widely accessible. Emphasis (shown in italics) is in the original quote unless otherwise indicated. Each entry offers, first, an exposition of basic concepts and contributions, accessible to the general reader, and laying out Marx's own contribution, its significance and the subsequent positions within Marxist political economy. Second, the author's assessment of past and continuing material, and the relevant developments within capitalism.

These requirements have inevitably skewed the mix of contributors towards more established scholars. This has allowed for certain advantages, not least deep, often long-standing, knowledge of Marxism and its critical application both to the historical and to contemporary capitalism, and also to scholarship and intellectual thought as these have evolved. For example, the current crisis that erupted as this volume was being prepared potentially looks very different to those who lived through both the radicalism of the 1960s and the collapses of the post-war boom and, subsequently, of 'actually existing socialism'. This offers the opportunity for self-reflection upon the (in)stabilities of capitalism, and alternatives to it, as lived experiences. A large number of younger scholars has also been invited to submit entries for this Companion, demonstrating the relevance of their research at the frontier of Marxist political economy, as well as the continuing vitality of the topics and approaches examined in this book. These younger contributors confront events that belong to the past, as opposed to developments that heavily influenced the older contributors as they formed their commitment to, and understanding of, Marxism. This is not to privilege the old over the new as wiser from having drunk from the fount of age. As Marx himself put it, 'The tradition of all dead generations weighs like a nightmare on the brains of the living' (*The Eighteenth Brumaire of Louis Bonaparte*). Applying this insight to Marxism itself, it is imperative to acknowledge that Marxism in general, and its political economy in particular, is neither a fixed attachment to a more or less conventional wisdom nor is it immune from incorporating the material and intellectual dynamism that is characteristic of our age. In this light, our volume will have served its purpose if it inspires a new generation of scholars to use it both as a resource and as a critical point of departure.

1. Accumulation of capital

Paul Zarembka

In 1847, Marx published *The Poverty of Philosophy* as a critique of Proudhon. It represents an important initial step in his theoretical development regarding conceptual categories. In it, Marx argues that the categories of classical political economy have been applied to all modes of production: 'Economists express the relations of bourgeois production, the division of labour, credit, money, etc., as fixed, immutable, eternal categories . . . [W]hat they do not explain is how these relations themselves are produced'. All economists 'represent the bourgeois relations of production as eternal categories'. This weakness of bourgeois economists regarding eternalization of categories would become basic to all of Marx's subsequent work. In his earlier and unpublished *The Economic and Philosophic Manuscripts of 1844*, Marx had not challenged the economic conceptions of classical political economy. Only in 1845 does he begin to introduce new concepts – mode of production, relations of production and productive forces. Further progress on Marx's conceptual categories, at least from written evidence in the *Grundrisse*, awaited a dozen years.

Marx uses the word 'capital' to refer fundamentally to the relationship of the capitalist class and the class of wage-labourers. If 'capital' is to refer to a class relation, surely, one would think that it would also apply in the case of discussing the accumulation of that class relation. Indeed, Marx's chapters in *Capital I* on 'Simple reproduction' and 'Conversion of surplus-value into capital' are summarized in his following chapter by writing that accumulation 'reproduces the capital relation on a progressive scale, more capitalists or larger capitalists at this pole, more wage workers at that' and thus it is 'increase of the proletariat'. Yet, in Marx the concept of accumulation of capital remains ambiguous, perhaps a result of inheriting the usage of the classical political economists. As indicated below, Lenin, on the one hand, pushed the definition in a misleading direction by moving away from social relations of production towards the production of means of production; on the other hand, Luxemburg's criticism of Marx's schemes of extended reproduction turns out to be helpful in pushing discussion of accumulation back towards emphasis on class relations.

As the accumulation of capital moves through Marx's works, the *1844 Manuscripts* are found to have a nine-page section on 'The accumulation of capital and the competition among the capitalists', and six of these pages consist of quotations from the classical political economists focusing on competition versus concentration of capitals. Marx's concerns at this time were that 'competition among capitalists increases the accumulation of capital' while 'accumulation, where private property prevails, is the *concentration* of capital in the hands of a few . . . With the increase of capital the profit on capital diminishes, because of competition. The first to suffer, therefore, is the small capitalist'. There are earlier passages in his section on wages that mention the relationship between accumulation of capital and the increase in the division of labour. Both discussions are within the purview of bourgeois political economy. The first evidence that Marx considered as problematic the classicals' use of accumulation is found in the *Grundrisse* (setting aside references to primitive, or original, accumulation), but it was not pursued at the time.

Accumulation of capital becomes defined in the chapter of *Capital I* entitled 'Conversion of surplus value into capital', and it represents a significant departure from classical political economy. This chapter begins immediately with the main point: 'Hitherto we have investigated how surplus-value emanates from capital; we have now to see how capital arises from surplus-value. Employing surplus-value as capital, reconverting it into capital, is called accumulation of capital.' It reads simply enough and Marx proceeds directly with a numerical example for an individual capitalist. The illustration captures a conception Marx uses throughout most of his work, that accumulation of capital entails increases in *both* the value of the means of production used in production processes *and* in the value expended on labour power, that is, increases in both constant capital and variable capital. Marx continues:

> To accumulate it is necessary to convert a portion of the surplus-product into capital. But we cannot, except by a miracle, convert into capital anything but such articles as can be employed in the labour process (*i.e.*, means of production), and such further articles as are suitable for the sustenance of the labourer (*i.e.*, means of subsistence) . . . Now in order to allow of these elements actually functioning as capital, the capitalist class requires additional labour. If the exploitation of the labourers already employed do not increase, either extensively or intensively, then additional labour-power must be found. For this the mechanism of capitalist production provides beforehand, by converting the working class into a class dependent on wages, a class whose ordinary wages suffice, not only for its maintenance, but for its increase. It is only necessary for capital to incorporate this additional labour-power, annually supplied by the working class in the shape of labourers of all ages, with the surplus means of production comprised in the annual produce, and the conversion of surplus-value into capital is complete.

No account is taken of technological changes, which could cheapen the cost to capital of goods consumed by workers with their wages, that is, no account of the production of relative surplus-value discussed in an earlier part of *Capital I* is included. Note, also, for reasons to become apparent when we discuss Lenin, that increases in production resulting from accumulation are not mentioned.

The next chapter, 'The general law of capitalist accumulation', after briefly discussing the meaning of composition of capital, begins by summarizing what had been learned from the prior chapter. The language is concise and not really subject to much ambiguity: a fuller portion of the passage we have already mentioned reads, 'As simple reproduction constantly reproduces the capital relation itself, *i.e.*, the relation of capitalists on the one hand, and wage workers on the other, so reproduction on a progressive scale, *i.e.*, accumulation, reproduces the capital relation on a progressive scale, more capitalists or larger capitalists at this pole, more wage workers at that. . . . Accumulation of capital is, therefore, increase of the proletariat.' The text is clear, the essential factor of accumulation of capital is the increase in wage-labour, not an increase in constant capital, even though the latter is required for the increase of employed labour power. Note Marx's reference to either 'more capitalists' or 'larger capitalists', but when the issue comes to labour it is simply 'more wage-workers' – only the number is important.

At the very beginning of the chapter on accumulation in *Capital II*, in which his schemes of reproduction are developed, Marx indicates a distinction between the material on accumulation in *Capital I* and the discussion to be undertaken in *Capital II*: the former deals with the individual capitalist while the discussion in *Capital II* deals with reproduction as a whole. However, Marx does not make an argument that the very meaning of 'accumulation of capital' would be affected by whether the individual capitalist or the capitalist economy as a whole is being discussed. In any case, a remarkable aspect of the schemes of *Capital II* is that Marx always holds both the rates of surplus value and the organic compositions of capital fixed, even though technological improvements could be expected to be associated with accumulation of capital. Thus, the schemes in *Capital II* fully correspond to that opening of the chapter on 'The general law of capitalist accumulation' from *Capital I*, discussed above.

Returning to *Capital I* and going further into the chapter 'The general law of capitalist accumulation', Marx's second section raises the issue of a rising composition of capital as accumulation progresses. Along with his next section, this indicates how the number of workers employed could decline as constant capital grows, not only in relative terms but also possibly absolutely. Indeed, as we progress, Marx first seems to define accumulation necessarily to include an increase in the number of workers under the domination of capital, as both constant capital and variable capital increase. Then, accumulation seems to include a case where the number of workers stays the same or even declines. But another passage suggests that accumulation could take place without a change in constant capital. So, what is accumulation of capital? Could accumulation of capital be any increase in variable capital v and/or constant capital c, with both at the same time being the most typical case? In other words, could accumulation of capital be simply $c+v$ increasing with the proportions between c and v unimportant for the definition? Is this broad range of possibilities a way out? Or is it a way of saying so much that we wind up saying very little or nothing at all? Most importantly, is it consistent with the very concept of 'capital' in Marx? These questions are unresolved in Marx's writing and led to an ambiguity embedded in twentieth-century Marxism insofar as accumulation of capital as a concept fails to be precise in its meaning.

Vladimir Lenin had a far-reaching influence on Marxist political economy, since he insisted that his own understanding was clearly the Marxist one, and he did lead the October revolution. None of his leading contemporaries, such as Karl Kautsky, Rosa Luxemburg, Nicolai Bukharin and Henryk Grossmann, challenged him on economic issues. In 1897 Lenin wrote a long pamphlet on the Swiss economist J.-C.-L. Simonde de Sismondi, focusing particularly on issues surrounding accumulation of capital. This was much before Marx's *Theories of Surplus Value* was published and thus Lenin was taking a gamble against what Marx had written about Sismondi. As it turned out Lenin was much more critical of Sismondi than Marx, even as Lenin claimed Marx's mantle. Lenin (*A Characterisation of Economic Romanticism*, ch. 1, section V) writes:

> Accumulation is indeed the excess of production over revenue (articles of consumption). To expand production (to 'accumulate' in the categorical meaning of the term) it is first of all necessary to produce means of production, and for this it is consequently necessary to expand that department of social production which manufactures means of production, it is necessary *to draw into it* workers who immediately *present a demand for articles of consumption, too*. Hence, 'consumption' develops *after* 'accumulation', or *after* 'production'; strange though it may seem, it cannot be otherwise in capitalist society.

In other words, to accumulate – for Lenin – is to expand production, and a market for consumption goods develops after accumulation. As his argument proceeds, Lenin even concludes, contrary to Sismondi, that accumulation 'opens a new market *for means of production without correspondingly expanding the market for articles of consumption, and even contracting this market*' (*A Characterisation of Economic Romanticism,* ch. 1, section V). The demand for consumer goods is a demand derived from the expansion of production and thus expansion of means of production.

Such an interpretation of Marx opens the avenue for analysing accumulation of capital centred around expansion of Marx's Department I, the production of means of production. In the next two years, Lenin published a number of other works in political economy, most importantly, *The Development of Capitalism in Russia* but does not change significantly his approach to the accumulation of capital. Indeed, when in 1915 Lenin surveys Marx's political economy he writes: 'New and important in the highest degree is Marx's analysis of the *accumulation of capital*—i.e., the transformation of a part of surplus value into capital, and its use, not for satisfying the personal needs of whims of the capitalist, but for new production' (Lenin, *Karl Marx: A Brief Biographical Sketch with an Exposition of Marxism,* ch. 3). This rendering of accumulation of capital has widespread influence to this day, particularly around discussions of the falling tendency of the rate of profit (although Lenin did not discuss that tendency at all and it was not a focus for early Marxist political economists). Lenin's rendering is connected to his separate discussion of Taylorism, his emphasis in early Soviet history upon socialism entailing accounting and control of production, and his subsequent emphasis on electrification as the basis of communism.

Luxemburg's *Accumulation of Capital* was published in 1913 and offers an unintended counterpose to Lenin as she focuses on critiquing Marx. Indeed, she is the only Marxist to have devoted a full book to the subject of accumulation of capital. Luxemburg notes that Marx wrote *Capital* theoretically characterizing an economy as only capitalist without other social classes than capitalists and workers (albeit landlords in some places). This delimitation of the theoretical project to be a theory of a purely capitalist structure (reviewed by Luxemburg, *The Accumulation of Capital*) was only a posture to understand capitalism. However, according to Luxemburg, this delimitation got Marx into trouble in analysing the accumulation of capital and she proceeds by logical deduction. Capitalist society is characterized by 'an increase in capital by means of a progressive capitalisation of surplus value, or, as Marx has put it, by the accumulation of capital'. After the capitalist has put together the needs of production, 'still his task is not completely done . . . It is absolutely essential to the accumulation of capital that a sufficient quantity of commodities created by the new capital should win a place for itself on the market and be realised' (*The Accumulation of Capital,* ch. 1). In other words, the realization of the additional surplus-value must somehow obtain. She finds no answer in workers' consumption needs which the capitalists want to keep as low as possible, nor in capitalists' luxury consumption. Nor can it be found in expanding the production of means of production since that itself would only lead to a further restatement of the problem. She suggests that expansion into new areas of capitalist conquest does offer an answer, at least so long as considerable portions of the global are non-capitalist.

Luxemburg's work received a statement from Lenin that she was 'wrong' on accumulation of capital. She was criticized by Otto Bauer, Nicolai Bukharin, Henryk Grossmann,

Paul Sweezy and Roman Rosdolsky, among others. While she herself thought that her criticisms of Marx's schemes of reproduction might be obvious and not subject to challenge, she turned out to be incorrect on that score. She was forced to respond in a pamphlet, fortunately completed before her January 1919 murder, but unfortunately before Bukharin was to offer his criticism in 1924.

In any case, tensions remain within Marxist political economy over the conceptualization of accumulation of capital and related issues such the falling tendency of the rate of profit, imperialism and crises. 'Accumulation of capital' is often invoked without clarity as to its meaning. Yet, surely, Marx meant something important when he wrote in *Capital I*, 'Accumulate, accumulate! That is Moses and the prophets! . . . Accumulation for accumulation's sake, production for production's sake: by this formula classical economy expressed the historical mission of the bourgeoisie . . . Political Economy takes the historical function of the capitalist in bitter earnest.'

Accumulation of capital considerations have considerable influence on modern discussions of the tendency of the rate of profit. Marx had described the rate of profit as the ratio of surplus-value s to constant capital c plus variable capital invested v, that is, $s/(c + v)$. c should be understand to include the values of circulating capital as well as of total fixed capital in structures and machinery, the latter being considerably more than depreciation expenses. Since there would be no investment in variable capital v if workers are paid out of sales receipts for operations involving a short turnover of capital, often little in other cases, most investment in v can be left out as insignificant. If we can divide both the numerator and resulting denominator – now simply c – by the expenditure on variable capital v, we obtain $s/v \div c/v$. With an emphasis, such as Lenin's, on Department I production of means of production, one might causally expect the denominator c/v to be rising and the profit rate falling, if s/v is not changing. (If we would want to go further and explicitly abstract from the influence of changes in paid portion of the working day v relative to the total workday $v + s$, this can be accomplished by rewriting the denominator c/v by its equivalent $(1 + s/v) \cdot c/(v + s)$ while placing aside any consideration the transformation problem of values into prices of production. Taking the rate of surplus-value s/v to be constant, the importance of a rising constant capital c on the denominator term $c/(v + s)$ would still seem apparent, implying that the denominator as a whole rises and the rate of profit falls.)

A falling rate of profit would be particularly indicated if discussion of the influences of technological changes towards reducing the time required to produce means of production failed to be considered. Magaline's (1975) little known work is an excellent basis for deeper consideration of this issue.

2.   The agrarian question and the peasantry

Terence J. Byres

Marx and Engels were acutely aware of the historical significance of peasantries in Europe and their importance in the Europe of their own time. Both, moreover, stressed the need to consider peasantries that were socially differentiated. Marx did so, for example, when considering the 'genesis of capitalist ground rent', and analysing the transition from feudalism to capitalism in England, in *Capital III*, ch. 47. For Engels, this was fundamental to his treatment of *The Peasant Question in France and Germany*, written in 1894 not long before he died.

By the late nineteenth century, European Marxists saw the prolonged existence in Europe (apart from England and Prussia) of peasantries as constituting what Engels termed the 'peasant question', which quickly became known as the 'agrarian question'. These continuing peasantries were symptomatic of an incomplete transition to capitalism. Central to the agrarian question was the fact of differentiated peasantries, composed of distinct social strata, with differing class interests.

In 1899, two remarkable Marxist analyses of the agrarian question appeared: Kautsky's *The Agrarian Question* (English translation, 1988), which was European in scope; and Lenin's *Development of Capitalism in Russia*, focusing exclusively on Russia. The latter, unlike the former, was from the 1930s translated into several languages and had a far greater impact. Lenin provided a treatment of the Russian peasantry distinguished by its power and clarity. It was to prove very influential in subsequent Marxist treatment of differentiation of the peasantry, both among historians and those concerned with contemporary poor countries. The strata have been variously identified but, following Lenin, came to be seen as a rich, a middle and a poor peasantry.

In contemporary poor countries, peasantries that are socially differentiated loom large. Such countries, then, may be seen as having an agrarian question, in the aforementioned sense. Among contemporary Marxists, Utsa Patnaik (1987) has contributed powerfully and originally to the analysis of differentiation. To grasp the nature of the problem, it is necessary to explore the conceptual apparatus used to treat it.

PEASANTS AND THE PEASANTRY

The term 'peasantry' is commonly used in Marxist discourse to identify a variety of forms of non-capitalist or non-socialist agricultural production. But it is, in such usage, a descriptive rather than an analytical category. Thus, attempts to identify a distinct 'peasant mode of production', to be added to those commonly employed (feudalism, capitalism, socialism and so on.), have not found an accepted place in Marxism. The first such attempt, that of the important Russian neo-populist theorist of the peasantry, A.V. Chayanov, was not couched in Marxist terms, and cannot be so accommodated, not least because of the fundamental difference between Marxist and neo-populist conceptions. Marxists argue that inequality is socio-economic in nature, encompassing cumulative possession of the means of production, irrespective of family size, that is, is based on class. Neo-populists, such as Chayanov, however, stress demographic rather than social differentiation. For them, in a 'peasant society', it is family size that explains variations in farm size and wealth. Inequality derives from the family cycle, from the growth and decay of families. Farms will be at different stages of the family cycle and will have different family sizes; over the cycle, as the size of family varies, so the size of farm will simultaneously grow and decline. This has been tested and rebutted for a variety of countries.

In Marxist terms, peasant farming is defined as production by petty producers, using their own means of production and their own labour (although not necessarily exclusively so). Peasantries with such characteristics, not themselves constitutive of a distinct mode of production, have existed within a variety of modes of production since the dawn of recorded history. In a materialist treatment, they are to be analysed in terms of the mode of production in which they are located, and via consideration of the distinguishing forces and relations of production of that mode. They are not autonomous entities, but are part of the existing rural class structure.

Peasant agriculture is, then, in Marxist analytical terms, an example of petty commodity production. This distinguishes it from capitalist production and is an illuminating way of treating peasantries in contemporary poor countries, and in a range of historical situations, where peasants produce commodities for exchange.

In a dynamic view, a poor peasantry may be identified as showing signs of movement towards proletarian status; a rich peasantry as containing the possibility of transformation into a capitalist class; and a middle peasantry as tending towards an 'archetypal' peasant condition. Such tendencies may be weak or strong. Differentiated peasantries may well reproduce themselves over long periods of time. There is no necessary guarantee that peasant production will be transformed into a fully developed capitalist agriculture: that the processes underpinning and reproducing differentiation will generate qualitative change.

Peasants, then, are distinguished from wage labourers and capitalist farmers. A peasantry may, ultimately, where a transition to capitalism, or 'capitalist road' (see below), is traversed, disintegrate irrevocably and be distributed across these two classes. But, in conditions of continuing economic backwardness, it will persist quite distinctly from them. It is also distinguished from a landlord class. Marxism pursues these distinctions to identify the likely nature of peasantries in a variety of historical situations; and to establish some preliminary notion of what a socially differentiated peasantry entails.

A pure wage labourer has been separated from the means of production and is free in Marx's double sense: free to 'dispose of his labour-power as his own commodity', and free of the means of production. (*Capital I*, ch. 6). She or he has no possession of the means of production, and no access to the means of subsistence. To survive, she or he must, therefore, sell her or his labour-power.

It is the mark of the peasant, by contrast, that she or he is not separated from the means of production in this complete sense. The peasant may have lost land, and may face the prospect of losing yet more. She or he may, in other words, have become, or be in the process of becoming, a poor peasant. But, for so long as she or he possesses land and possesses the instruments of production she or he is a peasant. She or he may own land, or may rent it or may do both. Whatever the means of access to land, a crucial distinguishing characteristic of a peasant is possession of that land.

She or he may have been forced into selling her or his labour-power to others, to ensure survival: again, a characteristic feature of a poor peasantry. But, for so long as this is not her or his sole means of survival, she or he is a peasant.

Among the characteristics of capitalist farmers are that they are 'the owners of money, means of production, means of subsistence, who are eager to increase the sum of values they possess, by buying other people's labour power' (*Capital I*, ch. 26). It is one of the prerequisites of a fully formed capitalist agriculture that 'the actual tillers of the soil are wage labourers employed by a capitalist, the capitalist farmer who is engaged in agriculture merely as a particular field of exploitation for capital' (*Capital III*, ch. 37). The capitalist farmer appropriates surplus value exclusively via the wage relation: via the purchase and setting to work of the labour power of others. That is a necessary, though not a sufficient, condition for the existence of capitalist agriculture. A capitalist may own the land worked or rent it as a tenant farmer.

A peasant will use family labour. One may, ideally, conceive of an 'archetypal' peasant using only family labour. Where, further, the peasantry is socially differentiated, a poor peasant or middle peasant may have this as a characteristic. But a peasant – even a poor or middle peasant – may well use non-family labour. She or he may hire labour, as well as selling her or his own labour: in peak seasons (for example, at harvest time, or, say, in rice cultivation, at the time of transplanting) to release tight labour constraints; or even in a more prolonged way. Part of the peasantry – a rich peasantry – may be a class that appropriates surplus. The major proportion of labour input on a rich peasant's land may, indeed, be wage labour. What marks the peasant off from the capitalist farmer is, however, the continuing recourse to family, manual labour.

A landlord class is one that owns land and rents it out to tenants, appropriating surplus via rent. A landlord may have some of her or his land cultivated, whether by peasants supplying labour in the form of labour rent, or by bonded labour, or via wage labour. Where, however, the predominant form of exploitation is rent we confront a landlord class, in essence. We may distinguish a feudal landlord class, which appropriates rent coercively from immobile, unfree tenants (feudal rent); and a capitalist landlord class which appropriates market-determined rent from free tenants, with unfettered right of movement (capitalist ground rent).

A peasant may well own her or his land, cultivate some of it and let some of it out for rent. She or he is not, however, thereby to be considered a landlord, or part of the land-lord class. To the extent that she or he still cultivates it, that this constitutes a major part of her or his activity, and that she or he has the other distinguishing characteristics of a peasant, she or he must be designated a peasant – a rich peasant, or *kulak* – and not a member of the landlord class. The same logic applies to those peasants who lend money at usurious interest.

The evolving nature of agriculture in a country, whether deliberately so or not, will hinge upon variations in the extent and nature of differentiation of the peasantry. The distinction between countries embarking upon separate roads derives, in part, from the very different role ascribed to differentiation in each road. For a successful capitalist road, unchecked processes of social differentiation may be essential. Under socialism, attempts to eradicate it, in favour of collective structures, may be made. Where populist strategies are followed, efforts to minimize it, or replace it with small, individual holdings, may be pursued.

THE AGRARIAN QUESTION

The notion of 'the agrarian question' has acquired different layers of meaning since first identified by Marxists in the late nineteenth century. Each connotation continues to be an important part of contemporary Marxist discourse. Each relates to economic backwardness. For an unresolved agrarian question is a central characteristic of economic backwardness. In its broadest meaning, the agrarian question may be defined as the continuing existence in the countryside of a poor country of substantive obstacles to an unleashing of the forces capable of generating economic development, both inside and outside agriculture. Originally formulated with respect to incomplete capitalist transition, and certain political consequences of that incompleteness, the agrarian question also became part of the debate on the possibility of socialist transition in poor countries.

In the late nineteenth century, the notion of an agrarian question bore a particular connotation. Our broader current usage has developed from that initial rendering. Three early but distinct senses of the agrarian question may be distinguished, those associated with: (a) Engels, (b) Kautsky-Lenin and (c) Preobrazhensky.

Engels's formulation derived from an explicitly political concern: how to capture political power in European countries in which capitalism was developing but had not yet replaced pre-capitalist social relations, overwhelmingly agrarian, with the expected stark division between capitalist farmer and wage labour. Had capitalism done its work, a strategy similar to that pursued in urban areas, and geared to mobilization of the rural proletariat, would have been broached. Otherwise, there was the 'agrarian question'. For Engels, and other Marxists of his time, 'the agrarian question' was 'the peasant question': the challenge posed by the continuing existence, throughout Europe, of large peasantries. The agrarian/peasant question was one of which strata of the peasantry could be won over by Marxist parties, given practical difficulties of mobilization and differentiation of the constituency. This was a critical matter for immediate, careful analysis and was subject to intense political debate. It continues to be a burning issue in contemporary poor countries. The ultimate resolution of the agrarian question was seen to be the development and dominance of capitalist agriculture; and its accompanying fully developed capitalist relations of production, with a rural proletariat free in Marx's double sense.

With Kautsky and Lenin, the agrarian question is broken into its component parts, and this brings a shift of emphasis, as one of these parts becomes the focus. The issue is the extent to which capitalism has developed in the countryside, the forms that it takes and the barriers that may impede it. This rendering of the agrarian question is now detached from the more explicitly political sense used by Engels, and becomes central and widely accepted as such thereafter. But the agrarian question remains the peasant question in view of a differentiated and differentiating peasantry. For Lenin, even more than for Kautsky, it is the key to understanding the nature of the agrarian question, and this is how it is understood after prolonged debate in today's poor countries. More specifically, Lenin distinguished two broad paths of agrarian capitalist development: capitalism from above (the Prussian path), where a class of capitalist farmers emerges from the feudal landlord class; and capitalism from below (the American path), where the source is out of a differentiated peasantry. These roads, in theory and historical practice, and their possible relevance to contemporary poor countries are explored at length by Byres (1996).

Preobrazhensky is associated with discussion of the agrarian question in light of early Soviet socialist experience. For, in the Soviet Union, in the aftermath of the Revolution, the essence of the agrarian question continued to be a differentiated and differentiating peasantry, with attention directed towards the possibly disruptive role of the kulaks (the rich peasantry). This had important political implications: an Engels's sense of the agrarian question in the socialist context. The agrarian question also had a parallel Kautsky-Lenin reading: the manner and forms of, and the obstacles to, the development of socialism in the countryside. But then the agrarian question was not limited specifically to the development of socialism in agriculture. This new preoccupation derived from the needs of overall socialist transformation: needs dictated by difficulties in securing accumulation outside of agriculture. In particular, this related to the resources required for socialist industrialization. The countryside was cast as an essential source of the necessary surplus for industrial investment. The agrarian question became, in part, the degree to which agriculture could supply that surplus, the means by which the fledgling socialist state might appropriate such surplus, and the speed and smoothness of transfer. The most cogent and sophisticated exponent of this position was Preobrazhensky, whose celebrated work, *The New Economics,* appeared in 1926 (published in English in 1965). This new layer of meaning is now a central part of discourse on the agrarian question and the transition to socialism. But it has also broadened, fruitfully, the notion of the agrarian question as it relates to capitalism (as a source of agrarian surplus for capitalist industrialization). In the socialist case, collectivization has been seen as a way of resolving the agrarian question, in each of the three indicated senses.

The broad sense of the agrarian question, then, in both the capitalist and the socialist cases, encompasses urban/industrial as well as rural/agricultural transformation. By an agrarian transition broadly construed is envisaged those changes in the countryside of a poor country necessary to the overall development of either capitalism or socialism and the ultimate dominance of either of those modes of production in a particular national social formation. This is not to abandon either the Engels or the Kautsky-Lenin renderings. On the contrary, it remains essential to explore, with the greatest care, the agrarian question in each of their senses. For example, the important possibility arises in the capitalist case, that the agrarian question in the broad sense may be partly, and even fully, resolved without the dominance of capitalist relations of production in the countryside. This is historically illustrated by the remarkable absence of wage labour in North American and in Japanese agriculture, and the staying power of the peasantry in France. There are also those who currently argue that socialism is possible without collective agriculture: that is, that the agrarian question in the broad sense may be resolved without socialist relations of production in the countryside.

THE NEW AGRARIAN QUESTION

There are, then, disagreements and ambiguities, and even renewed debate. Marxists have assumed that the agrarian question, in its various meanings, is critical in today's poor countries. But Bernstein has argued (first in a paper of 1996–97) that, while an agrarian question has existed in the past and this may be a fruitful way of analysing historical situations, this is no longer the case: the 'agrarian question now' is very different from the 'agrarian question then', because of imperialism and globalization. What imperialism in its classic phase failed to do, that is, industrialize the periphery, it will deliver in its globalization phase. It is imperialism and globalization that may industrialize backward, agrarian formations, and *without* reference to agriculture, albeit with an effective 'developmental state' as a necessary condition. For global capital there is no (national) agrarian question. We have 'the end of the agrarian question without its resolution' (Bernstein, 1996–97, p. 50). So the agrarian question is dead, agrarian transition is impossible in any form disclosed by history, and there are no lessons of any kind to be disclosed by history in this respect.

This has been contested (Byres, 2003, pp. 206–9). There is a danger of 'world system determinism', whereby one reads from the global a series of conclusions with respect to national social formations without substantive treatment of those social formations. To take the two largest of these, India and China, one can argue that their respective industrializations have always been contingent upon the need to overcome obstacles to capitalist transformation in the countryside; while the prospects continue to exist, in each case, of agrarian transitions constituting a route to comprehensive industrialization – a route along which China has progressed significantly further than India. Thus, the home market is crucial, and it needs to have a large agricultural component. Then, in large economies, at least, if comprehensive industrialization is to proceed the necessary accumulation cannot, in any full sense, be external. It must be based largely upon domestic sources, and these, in part, will need to be financial flows from the countryside. The sheer size of these economies means that, within their borders, even global capital will have to confront an agrarian question in all three senses. Moreover, this argument is likely to have some validity, too, in smaller economies where industrialization has made more limited progress.

The debate continues.

3. Analytical Marxism

Marco Boffo

Analytical Marxism (AM) is an approach to Marxism that stands at the crossroads of Anglo-Saxon analytical philosophy, neoclassical economics and a (partly) Marxian research agenda. Its most distinctive feature is its *method*, the deployment of both neoclassical economics' mathematical modelling and analytical political and moral philosophy's reliance on formal logic. Embracing the epistemological foundation of the mainstream social sciences and 'analytical' reasoning, AM rejects dialectical materialism, distancing itself from traditional forms of Marxism, attempting 'to reconstruct Marxism upon methodological foundations previously assumed to be antithetical to the Marxist tradition' (Roberts, 1996, p. ix).

AM represents the culmination of a renewal of interest in 'Marxist themes' within Anglo-American analytical philosophy during the 1970s, in the wake of 'the descending trajectory of structuralist Marxism and the renaissance of liberal egalitarianism' (Veneziani, 2009, p. 236). The publication in 1978 of G.A. Cohen's *Karl Marx's Theory of History: A Defence*, with second edition of 2000, are commonly identified as its founding stone. Cohen set about defending and reconstructing historical materialism through the techniques of analytical philosophy, purposefully respecting two constraints, 'what Marx wrote' and the 'standards of clarity and rigour which distinguish twentieth-century analytical philosophy' (Cohen, 2000, p. ix). Nonetheless, and despite the aim of constructing 'a tenable theory of history . . . in broad accord with what Marx said on the subject', Cohen's 'defence' is far from a faithful account of a classic interpretation of Marx's theory of the forces and relations of production. Ultimately, his failings in conceptualizing Marxian theory and his rejection of it, rather than his own contribution as such, mark Cohen's indirect contribution to AM, as well as his own personal trajectory.

Cohen's 'defence' initiated a search for alternative foundations for Marxian theory, and a dissociation from those of 'traditional' Marxism, that gained momentum first through the work of John Roemer and Jon Elster, and later through a group of like-minded researchers under the umbrella of their 'September Group' and the motto '*Marxismus sine stercore tauri*' (Roemer, 1988, p. viii) – that is, 'bullshit-free Marxism' – hinting at the denial of dialectics characteristic of the group. According to Roemer, this 'search for foundations', 'which led to asking . . . perhaps heretical questions, and use state-of-the-art methods of analytical philosophy and "positivist" social science to study them', was a product of 'the chequered success of socialism and the dubious failure of capitalism . . . unquestionably *the* serious challenges to Marxism, as it was inherited from the nineteenth century' (Roemer, 1986, pp. 3–4). Nonetheless, other factors were essential in shaping the intellectual climate that allowed AM, temporarily, to flourish. These follow from the broader historical background that has allowed the progressive marginalization of

Marxism, heterodoxy, and radicalism within economics. Due to both external influences and internal idiosyncrasies, such marginalization has not been a linear or unidimensional process, nor has it been successful in completely eradicating Marxism and Marxian political economy (MMPE), but it has certainly succeeded in affecting their path and the conditions for their survival.

In particular, the advent of Sraffianism proved extremely influential in pushing heterodoxy towards increasing formalism and adopting the methods and methodologies of mainstream economics and social sciences. Indeed, on the basis of the same analytical framework used to criticize neoclassical economics, Sraffianism also advocated the rejection of Marx's value theory. Eventually, with the Sraffian critique being immanent within neoclassical economics (Rowthorn, 1974), its cultural effect was not a 'radical rupture' with the neoclassical mainstream, rather its reabsorption into it through a '*reconstruction* [of its theory of production] by a generalization of the simple one-sector model to many sectors' (Fine, 1980b, p. 111). With its acceptance of the 'categories of capitalist society', left 'unexplained together with their specific historical origin' (Fine, 1980b, p. 112), with its rejection of value theory, and its emphasis on modelling to construct a theory of production, Sraffianism instrumentally paved the way for more formalism, thus setting the origin and continuing character of the move of heterodoxy towards more affinity with the mainstream. Not surprisingly, some see Sraffa as a precursor of AM (Bertram, 2008, p. 123, note 1).

The process of dissociation from Marx's method being *the* foundational aspect of AM, it is doubtful whether AM should be categorized as Marxism at all. Such a question has been raised by many AMists and Marxists, and it is revealing that Roemer's answer to it is: 'I am not sure that it should; but the label does convey at least that certain fundamental insights are viewed as coming from Marx' (Roemer, 1986, p. 4). What warrants the 'Marxism' in AM is, in the opinion of AMists, the perpetuation of a research programme seen as descending from Marx, and, ultimately, a commitment to socialism. Nonetheless, AM's uncritical acceptance of the mainstream method, its conception of what is to be considered 'bullshit' Marxism and its rejection of any methodological specificity of MMPE (Cohen, 2000, pp. xxv–xxviii), rest soundly on a positivist understanding of change in the social sciences as a harmonious, frictionless, progressive and cumulative rather than competitive process. This conception of change also informs AM's conception of socialism, and the transition to it.

As far as economic analysis is concerned, AM's trajectory has been heavily influenced by the work of John Roemer. Characterized by a search for a 'general' theory of exploitation developed in opposition to the classical Marxian reliance on the labour theory of value, Roemer's contribution has had a pioneering effect similar to Cohen's work on historical materialism (from which Roemer also derived inspiration). Judging MMPE and their tools as outdated for the standards of contemporary social sciences, Roemer set out 'to use mathematics to turn Marxism into a science', largely basing himself on Morishima's mathematical reading of Marxian economics (Tarrit, 2006, p. 605). Redefining Marxism, in his *Analytical Foundations of Marxian Economic Theory* (1981), 'as a hypothetico-deductive model', 'a set of theorems and premises subjected to rigorous examination', Roemer blamed 'Marxists for being frequently guilty of functionalist mistakes' (Tarrit, 2006, p. 605). As a result, Roemer deemed necessary to provide Marxism with strong microfoundations. To do so he resorted to the mathematical modelling apparatus of neoclassical economics and the equilibrium method. Though 'less confident' about the latter than about the validity of mathematical modelling and microfoundations, intellectual fascination for it as analytical ideal type, identification of precedents in Marx's thought (equalization of profit rates among capitals, models of balanced growth exemplifying reproduction), and 'knowing no other method' lead Roemer to embrace it totally (Roemer, 1981, p. 10).

Roemer's theory of exploitation and class formation takes as starting point differently endowed optimizing individuals in a competitive setting, and shows, generally on the basis of linear models of exchange, prices and profits, how unequal distribution of assets produces inequitable results, especially in the distribution of income, even without transfer of labour and with growth added to show how exploitation may or may not persist. On this basis, Roemer derives a general equilibrium framework in which to embed different types of exploitation (Marxian, feudal, socialist and neoclassical), with the aim of comparing antithetical ideologies (Marxian versus. neoclassical) on ethical grounds and understanding better the different types of inequalities and class formation processes in building socialism. Arguing, on the basis of his modelling, that 'one can define corn values or energy values of commodities instead of labor values, and show that corn is exploited or energy is exploited if there are positive profits' (Roemer, 1981, p. 204), that is, that any commodity can be 'exploited' and thus replace labour in constructing a theory of value, Roemer could claim that Marx's choice of labour as 'numéraire' rested on normative reasoning, and was 'mandated' by a 'historical-materialist hypothesis' (Roemer, 1981, p. 207). Abandoning the scientific and objective aspect of exploitation resting on the labour theory of value on behalf of an ethical approach to the issue of exploitation, Roemer reinterpreted the Marxian theory of exploitation as best conceived in normative terms, and the issue of exploitation as needing normative justification. Ultimately, Roemer's contribution was fundamental in setting AM's trajectory on a conception of exploitation understood primarily in terms of property rights, reflected in exchange rather than derived from the production process, and of class as income stratification, with no attention to the development of methods of production nor the extraction of surplus value. Furthermore, ignoring the various critiques of neoclassical economics and general equilibrium elaborated during the 1960s and 1970s, as well as the problematic aspect of microfoundations resting on general equilibrium, Roemer's contributions mark a clear and strong difference between AM and radical economics, as Roemer uses neoclassical economics as a neutral instrument, while radical economics, perceiving it as ideological, clearly defines itself in opposition to it (Tarrit, 2006, pp. 606–10).

Thus, AM rests on two methodological pillars. First of all, its game-theoretic rational choice approach to social theory originates partly in the hegemonizing mainstream of its time, a particular approach within neoclassical economics characterized by the aggressive extension of its methods and analysis to the other social sciences as best represented by authors such as Buchanan, Downs, Olson and Becker. Although sharing the same origins and many similarities, AM and Rational Choice Marxism (RCM) are distinct from one another, with RCM being a narrower approach within AM based on fine-grained causal microfounded explanation, the main difference between them residing in whether aligning to methodological individualism and rational choice explanation or not (see Veneziani, 2009). Nonetheless, despite being more general, less reductionist and less aggressive towards MMPE than RCM, AM remains influenced in principle by formalism, and by standard select methods from mainstream economics in practice (especially linear growth models). Turning to methodological individualism and rational choice was a strong reaction against the hegemony of Althusserian Structuralism, the dominant school of Marxism during the period of conception and development of RCM, and the excesses of its anti-humanism. Second, AM found a further intellectual coordinate in the North American academic political philosophy of its time, both liberal and conservative, characterized by its focus on analytical reasoning, its normative approach and its moral concerns, and best exemplified by John Rawls and Robert Nozick. The marriage of the method of the neoclassical mainstream with that of analytical political philosophy, as well as the interventions of AM in the debate on the theories of justice, resulted in what could be considered the most positive aspect of AM, its attempt to build a normative theory of socialism in opposition to the conservative philosophy of writers like Nozick (Wood, 1989, pp. 44–5).

Having abandoned Marx's method and theory, and reduced the study of class and exploitation ultimately to that of inequality in the distribution of assets, AM proceeded to wage its battle against capitalism on moral grounds, significantly reducing its distance from liberal political thought. Such a prospect was carried out on the basis of the belief that one of the main advantages, with respect to classical Marxism, of an approach rooted in the rational choice paradigm is to highlight the ethical basis of Marxism as well as the ethical assumptions of the Marxian theory of exploitation. Nonetheless, having the effect of dividing the different moments of capital, breaking its totality and ultimately neutralizing 'any conception of capitalism as a *process*, in which these analytically distinct moments are dynamically united', AM's method precludes any explanation of the accumulation of capital as 'ruthless world process' and of its undesirable effects (environmental degradation, alienation, imperialism, crisis and so on.). Its moral battle is thus confined to fighting against the 'academic-intellectual Right' exclusively in normative terms, and with so many less arguments in favour of its moral defence of socialism (Wood, 1989, pp. 75–9).

Restricting its analysis to the sphere of circulation, as typical of mainstream economics, the political philosophies of liberalism, and the ideologies associated with them, AM bases its whole model on premises representing generalizations of 'assumptions specific to capitalism – the assumptions of "freedom", "equality", and market-rationality – and to capitalism only as viewed in a "one-sided" way' (Wood, 1989, p. 58). Reversing the theoretical progress in the understanding of capitalism as a system established by Marx with his critique of political economy, AM's analysis marks a return to pre-Marxist conceptions of political economy, the moral and normative turn having led AM to share many affinities with Utopian socialism. Among these are the separation of the ethical ideal of socialism from the historical conditions of its realization, a theory of exploitation rooted in the sphere of circulation and exchange, a conceptualization of capitalism abstracting from the 'free' character of the exchange between capital and labour from its 'presuppositions'. As a result, AM's analysis implicitly constructs 'a continuum from capitalist to socialist "freedom and equality"'. Missing the coercive character of choice inherent in capitalism's structure of social-property relations, as well as in the compulsions inherent in the market under capitalism, AM conceives of socialist freedom and equality as more of the freedom and equality already present, but fettered, under capitalism, thus posing the difference between capitalism and socialism as one in degree rather than quality. The political point of AM lies exactly in 'the conflation of socialism and capitalism' (Wood, 1989, pp. 84–6).

This conflation has several political implications. First is the marginalization of class politics. If there is no break between capitalism and socialism, and the passage from one to the other will occur smoothly, with socialism growing out of capitalism (a confidence sustained by AM's teleological and technological determinist view of history, and a-historical analysis), then there is no need for class politics. On the other hand, if such conflation is to be understood merely as a rhetorical device, serious doubts arise on its effectiveness as a guide to strategy since 'its moral-rhetorical value depends precisely on ignoring the critical barriers – such as class antagonisms – standing in the way of a smooth transition from one social form to the other', a dismissal sustained by AM's conception of class as income stratification, with no break of continuity nor antagonism or dialectical relation. Second, coupled with the conception of socialism as merely a moral question, the conflation favours the detachment of the socialist ideal from 'any historical foundation in the actual conditions of capitalism'. In the view of AM, socialism grows out of capitalism not in the sense that the latter poses the 'structural and historical conditions' of the first, 'the contradictions which place socialism on the historical agenda, and the agencies capable of carrying out the socialist project', rather in the sense that socialism is the full realization of the ideals of capitalism, that is, socialism as a capitalism that delivers its promises. From these premises follows the political conclusion that, since the transition to socialism will eventually happen in the long term, the task of socialist strategy is to humanize capitalism (Wood, 1989, p. 86).

In defence of AM's methodological stance and of its strategic political usefulness, Carling (1990, p. 107) argues that 'a precedent for such a use of bourgeois theory, which should occur rather quickly to a Marxist', is to be found in Marx himself. Adopting the method of contemporary economics would thus be faithful to the spirit deployed by Marx in *Capital*, that of subverting classical political economy, the mainstream of his day, using it against itself to draw anti-capitalist conclusions. But such a view fails to grasp that, while Marx's subversion of the political economy of his time was based on a harsh and thorough critique of it, together with that of French socialism and German philosophy, AM's use of the method of the mainstream and of analytical philosophy is often uncritical (especially in Roemer). Therefore, adherence to the neoclassical and analytical methods and dismissal of value theory and dialectical reasoning render the critique of AM internal at best, and prevent it from explaining beyond the ideological structures inherent in mainstream social science. Following Wood (1989, p. 59), once AM reduces Marxism to the standards of contemporary social science, 'there is precious little left of historical materialism' since, by returning to a pre-Marxist understanding of exploitation and disassembling the Marxist systemic understanding of capitalism, AM's theory of exploitation overturns all of the central tenets of Marx's political economy. This operation is subject to critique not because of a necessity to defend Marx's political economy and MMPE, rather because it fails to produce 'a paradigm with a superior explanatory power', pointing to a 'pre-Marxist understanding instead of forward beyond Marxism'.

But whither AM today? As the heat has gone out of it, the project lost momentum and ended up being abandoned by its adherents, its leading lights having moved on to different topics in their fields, though consistently with their previous methodology and maintaining their AMist roots. Several reasons can, retrospectively, shed light on both the rise and fall of AM quite apart from its intrinsic limitations. First, AM proved incredibly useful strategically in attacking Marxism from within and helping invigorate a mainstream under attack on many fronts. Indeed, though all AMists claim a legacy of Marx, their work has been in many ways devoted to refuting Marx's theories and results on the basis of neoclassical economics, analytical philosophy and logical positivism as the only possible analytical tools to make Marxism intelligible. A polemical and often dismissive tone against MMPE pervades much of the AM literature as well as continuous attempts to demonstrate internal inconsistency in Marx's work. Ultimately, what AM provided to the discipline of economics was not so much the relevance of its results, rather the plasticity of the mainstream method, thus reaffirming rather than challenging it. But as the ranks of the mainstream grew stronger and those of the heterodox thinner, the strategic relevance of AM to the mainstream dramatically diminished. Second, spelling radicalism in neoclassical language has been an important strategy of academic survival for much US heterodoxy, to avoid eviction from economics departments and make a life within the community of economists easier. At the time of the rise of AM, many established mainstream economists were still prepared and willing to engage with Marxism (Samuelson, for example), and AM allowed its participants to engage with the mainstream community with a shared language. Once this sort of radicalism had grown more secure in its place within the departments and the discipline of economics, AM lost one of its most stringent material pressures. Last but not least, AM eventually found itself with nowhere to go, not least in offering no empirical and historical as opposed to ideal contributions. Caught in a period where Marxism and heterodoxy within economics were relatively strong in the wake of the 1960s but both rapidly in decline under the assault of neoliberalism, its own intrinsic limitations and the declining interest in radicalism prevented AM from proceeding much further with its research programme, being rapidly outflanked by economics imperialism, newer economic history and (new) institutional economics. Today, it tends only to survive in ever more esoteric mathematical models of exploitation, hurling empty gestures of defiance against a stone deaf orthodoxy within both economics and ethics.

4.   Anthropology

Keith Hart

An 'anthropology' is any systematic study of humanity as a whole. The modern academic discipline has its origins in the democratic revolutions and rationalist philosophy of the eighteenth century. The question then was how the arbitrary inequality of the Old Regime might be replaced by an equal society founded on what all people have in common, their human nature. It was thus a revolutionary critique of the premise of inequality and a source of constructive proposals for a more equal future. Such a future was thought to be analogous to the kinship organization that preceded societies based on the state and class division and that could still be observed among contemporary 'savages'. This framework for thinking about social development was retained and elaborated in the nineteenth and twentieth centuries, but it is no longer the leading anthropological paradigm, having been replaced by an ethnographic relativism that is more compatible with a world society fragmented into nation-states.

Marx was a political economist, to be sure; but he also offered a coherent view of the place of capitalism in human history as a whole. For this reason, Karl Marx can be considered to have been the greatest economic anthropologist of all time. Marxism was shaped by a tradition which has been called the 'anthropology of unequal society', and became its most sustained source of development. Rousseau's example inspired Morgan and Engels a century later, while Wolf and Goody have brought the tradition up-to-date. The most influential marriage of Marxism and anthropology has been offered by the French school that flourished in the 1960s and 1970s. This entry reviews the economic anthropology of Karl Marx, the anthropology of unequal society and French structuralist Marxism.

THE ECONOMIC ANTHROPOLOGY OF KARL MARX

According to Marx, the history of precapitalist economies can reveal elements of the basic categories of economic life – value, labour, land, capital and so on – but only modern capitalism makes of them a coherent, objective system of commoditized social relations. Economy now takes on a general subjective dimension that was previously confined to the unsystematic calculations of merchants. Production is both the economy in general, that is, all material activity and, more narrowly, one of four basic economic categories along with distribution, exchange and consumption. Its definition is always coloured by the dominant mode of production. Thus, for us today, productive labour is whatever produces value for capital. The commodity is abstract social labour: its highest form is capital. Only one commodity can add to value and that is labour power, hence the historic significance of the entry of capital into the organization of production. When the market becomes the main means of social reproduction, the combination of money capital and wage labour under conditions of juridical freedom revolutionizes accumulation and productivity.

In the extraordinary passage of *Grundrisse*, known as 'The precapitalist economic formations', Marx lays out a vision of human history in which capitalism is seen as the final dissolvent of those forms of society linking us to an evolutionary past that we share with the animals:

> The original conditions of production cannot initially be themselves produced . . . What requires explanation is not the *unity* of living and active human beings with the natural, inorganic conditions of their metabolism with nature . . . What we must explain is the *separation* of these inorganic conditions of human existence from this active existence, a separation which is only fully completed in the relationship between wage-labor and capital. (*Grundrisse*)

In making that break, capitalism is the enabling force for the emergence of a human society fully emancipated from primitive dependence on nature. It is, of course, not that society itself, but its midwife. Human evolution before capitalism is marked by two processes: the individuation of the original animal herd and the separation of social life from its original matrix, the earth as laboratory.

Marx's ideas about a sequence of modes of production in history are at best sketchy, despite subsequent efforts to generate a formal scheme out of his occasional references to Asiatic (Oriental/Slavonic), ancient, Germanic, feudal and similar precapitalist modes. The economic determination of precapitalist social forms is always indirect. Marx's method was rather to trace out the logic of the tendency of world history, using idealized examples. Indeed he makes it clear in the *Grundrisse* that the historical explanation of particular cases must draw on an ad hoc series of ecological, political and other variables. He never eliminated this tension between philosophical speculation and empirical analysis. Class plays a minor role in his economic anthropology. The *Communist Manifesto* explicitly points to the plurality and confusion of classes, estates and orders in precapitalist societies. Only when commercial logic penetrates the bulk of production does class struggle between the bourgeoisie and the proletariat become predominant. Even then, this is more of a potential dualism, a tendency, rather than historical actuality, since residual classes often play a significant part in the movement of capitalist societies.

Rather than being a case study of Western society, Marx's anthropology is a special theory of industrial capitalism which conceives of the modern epoch as a turning point in world history. Industrial capitalism has set in train a series of events which must bring the rest of the world under its contradictory logic. It is not ethnocentric to deny non-Western societies their autonomous evolution; history has already done that. For Marx then, economic anthropology is a set of analytical constructs of the capitalist mode of production, modified by awareness of the world that preceded it and lies outside capitalism. Some (for example, Lange) consider Marx's greatness to lie in the fine historical sense that he and Engels brought to their study of Victorian capitalism; others (for example, Althusser) see *Capital* as a positive text that escaped from the dialectical historicism and subjectivity of the earlier economic writings. Either way, neither the subsequent Marxist tradition nor academic anthropologists have ever come close to matching Marx's vision of human history as a whole.

THE ANTHROPOLOGY OF UNEQUAL SOCIETY

The most impressive achievement of Marxist synthesis in late twentieth-century anthropology is Eric Wolf's *Europe and the Peoples Without History* (1982). Against the prevailing norm of producing narrowly circumscribed ethnographies as standalone examples, Wolf places a wide range of anthropological knowledge within a comprehensive history of Western capitalist expansion and local response. Rather than adopting the tainted conceptual vocabulary of precapitalist states (Asiatic, feudal and so on), he coins a new term for societies organized by a 'tributary' mode of production. Jack Goody has produced a series of volumes comparing Africa and Eurasia, insisting that claims of Western exceptionalism in respect of Asia are false (Hart, 2006). Goody's vision of world history was drawn from the Marxist prehistorian Gordon Childe's materialist synthesis of the two great turning points – the 'neolithic or agricultural revolution' of 10000 years ago (in which Africa participated) and the 'urban revolution' of 5000 years ago (in which it did not). The industrial revolution marked the third definitive stage in the history of human production and society. Childe derived his basic framework from L.H. Morgan's *Ancient Society* (1877), which some have seen as the origin of modern anthropology. Morgan's achievement was to draw on the contemporary ethnography of groups like the Iroquois to illuminate the ancient Mediterranean origins of Western civilization. At the same time, he identified what are still considered to be the principal stages of social evolution (bands, tribes and states). His work was made more widely accessible by Friedrich Engels in *The Origin of the Family, Private Property and the State*, drawing on Marx's extensive notes on Morgan's book. But all of them got the basic framework from Jean-Jacques Rousseau's *Discourse on the Origins and Foundations of Inequality among Men* (1754 [1984]).

Rousseau's essay deserves to be seen as the first great work of modern anthropology. He was not concerned with individual variations in natural endowments, but with the artificial inequalities of wealth, honour and the capacity to command obedience that came from social convention. In order to construct a model of human equality, he imagined a presocial state of nature, a sort of hominid phase of human evolution in which men were solitary, but healthy, happy and above all free. This freedom was metaphysical, anarchic and personal: original human beings had free will, they were not subject to rules of any kind and they had no superiors. At some point humanity made the transition to what Rousseau calls 'nascent society', a prolonged period whose economic base can be summarized as hunter-gathering with huts. Why leave the state of nature at all? He speculates that disasters and economic shortages must have been involved.

The rot set in with the invention of agriculture or, as Rousseau puts it, with wheat and iron. Cultivation of the land led to incipient property institutions, whose culmination awaited the development of political society. The formation of a civil order (the state) was preceded by a Hobbesian condition, a war of all against all marked by the absence of law. Rousseau believed that this new social contract to abide by the law was probably arrived at by consensus, but it was a fraudulent one in that the rich thereby gained legal sanction for transmitting unequal property rights in perpetuity. From this inauspicious beginning, political society then usually moved, via a series of revolutions, through three stages:

> The establishment of law and the right of property was the first stage, the institution of magistrates the second and the transformation of legitimate into arbitrary power the third and

last stage. Thus the status of rich and poor was authorized by the first epoch, that of strong and weak by the second and by the third that of master and slave, which is the last degree of inequality and the stage to which all the others finally lead, until new revolutions dissolve the government altogether and bring it back to legitimacy. (Rousseau 1754 [1984], p. 131)

One-man-rule closes the circle in that all individuals become equal again because they are now subjects with no law but the will of the master. For Rousseau, the growth of inequality was just one aspect of human alienation in civil society. We need to return from division of labour and dependence on the opinion of others to subjective self-sufficiency. His subversive parable ends with a ringing indictment of economic inequality which could well serve as a warning to our world:

It is manifestly contrary to the law of nature, however defined . . . that a handful of people should gorge themselves with superfluities while the hungry multitude goes in want of necessities. (Rousseau, 1984, p. 136)

Marx and Engels made fertile use of this precedent in their own critique of the state and capitalism, while Morgan's legacy as Rousseau's principal successor in modern anthropology has persisted in the twentieth century. In the postwar period, teams at the universities of Michigan and Columbia, including White, Wolf, Sahlins, Service and Harris, took the economic and political basis for the development of class society as their chief focus. But Claude Lévi-Strauss tried to redo Morgan in a single book, *The Elementary Structures of Kinship* (1949).

The aim of *Elementary Structures* was to revisit Morgan's three-stage theory of social evolution, drawing on a new and impressive canvas, 'the Siberia-Assam axis' and all points southeast to the Australian desert. Lévi-Strauss took as his motor of development the forms of marriage exchange and the logic of exogamy. The 'restricted reciprocity' of egalitarian bands gave way to the unstable hierarchies of 'generalized reciprocity' typical of Burmese tribes. The stratified states of the region turned inwards to the reproduction of class differences through endogamy and the negation of social reciprocity. The argument is bold, but its scope is regional, not global. In any case, its author later abandoned the project in favour of a 'structuralist' approach to studying the human mind through stories.

FRENCH MARXIST ANTHROPOLOGY

French Marxist anthropology enjoyed cult status in the Anglophone world during the 1970s. The crucial text was Althusser and Balibar's (1965) reading of *Capital* that brought Marxist political economy into line with Lévi-Strauss's structuralist methodology and American systems theory. The human subject, dialectical reason and indeed history itself were in effect dropped from their scheme. A deep structure of the ideal mode of production was outlined, having three elements – producers, non-producers and means of production – whose variable combinations were realized as concrete modes of production. Much attention was paid to the relationship between economic, political and ideological levels of the mode of production and to the question of which was dominant and/ or determinant in any given case. Althusser abandoned the ideological notion of 'society' in favour of 'social formations' where, it was recognized, several modes of production were normally combined.

A handful of French anthropologists made substantial contributions to Marxism around this time. Maurice Godelier's *Rationality and Irrationality in Economics* (1966) was the first to cross the Channel. It offers a rather conventional treatment of the formalist-substantivist debate launched by Polanyi, while claiming to synthesize Marx and Lévi-Strauss. Godelier applies the notion of rationality not only to persons but to systems, thereby setting up a contradiction between structure and agency that he cannot resolve. Marxism, says Godelier, can add a specific kind of function to Lévi-Strauss's structures, thereby allowing a complete anthropological analysis of social systems. The result, however, resembles an ecological version of structural-functionalism more than Marxism.

Claude Meillassoux, Emmanuel Terray and Pierre-Philippe Rey all acknowledged their debt to Althusser, while debating ethnographic interpretations of their shared area, West/Central Africa. Meillassoux's *The Economic Anthropology of the Guro of Ivory Coast* (1964) became the main point of common reference. His later synthetic study, *Maidens, Meal and Money* (1981), was an ambitious attempt to compare the main means of accumulation (women, food and capital) in tribal, peasant and capitalist societies. In an essay reinterpreting the Guro ethnography, Terray argued that Marxist analysis is often too crude, labelling all primitive societies in much the same way, leaving non-Marxist ethnographers free to explain their specificity by reference to kinship structures and the like. Instead, emulating the approach of the British structural-functionalists, he laid out a method for classifying the material base of a society in great detail, so that its modes of production may be inferred empirically and concrete particulars incorporated into a materialist analysis. There is little history in this version of historical materialism, even though Terray went on to produce meticulous histories of a West African kingdom. Pierre-Philippe Rey's *Colonialism, Neo-colonialism and the Transition Capitalism* (1971) was an original contribution to the literature on matrilineal kinship, slavery and European penetration of the Congo, in contrast with the prevailing Marxist norm of merely restating what was already known in a new jargon. He outlined here his famous idea of a 'lineage mode of production'. Moreover, he spelled out the 'articulation of modes of production in a structure of dominance', showing concretely how colonial capitalism restructured the lineage and petty commodity modes of production in the interest of accumulation.

We are left with a mystery: how to account for the disproportionate influence of this small band of French Marxists on Anglophone anthropology in the 1970s? It cannot be that they clarified a number of concepts and wrote a few untranslated monographs. Their success may have had something to do with the explicitly synthetic position French structuralism occupied between German philosophy, including Marxism, and Anglo-Saxon scientific empiricism. The modernization of Marx, by incorporating systems theory and dumping the dialectic, produced a version of structural-functionalism at once sufficiently different from the original to persuade English-speakers that they were learning Marxism and similar enough to allow them to retain their customary way of thinking, which had been temporarily discredited by the end of empire.

Meillassoux's Guro book became a mine of parables allowing rival political positions in France around 1968 to be expressed as interpretations of West African ethnography.

Thus one issue was whether elders' disposal of young men's labour should be attributed to control of distribution through marriage exchange (Rey) or rather to the organization of production (Terray). This was in effect a replay of the argument between pro-Soviet and ultra-left factions in Paris. There the question was whether the Soviet Union, in emphasizing state ownership of the means of production, was a genuine instance of socialism or rather a state capitalist society. Whereas the Stalinists held that it was indeed socialist, their opponents such as Bettelheim (1963) claimed that property relations operated only at the level of distribution and a more thoroughgoing Marxist analysis would be based on the organization of production. Seen from the perspective of managerial control of the work process, Russian factories were no different from capitalist firms. It is hardly surprising that these aspects of the debate within French Marxism were missed by their imitators.

French Marxism disappeared by the end of the 1970s, as suddenly as it had burst on the Anglophone scene. It did not survive the great watershed of postwar history, when welfare-state democracy gave way to 'neo-liberalism' and the cultural turn generally known as 'postmodernism'. With its demise went the last vestige of a central focus for debates within economic anthropology. In the period since then, Marxist anthropology has found isolated protagonists, but their voices have not added up to an intellectual movement. One beneficiary of this relative decline has been Karl Polanyi, whose institutionalist critique of liberal economics has risen in prominence of late. In the last three decades, anthropologists have turned for the first time in significant numbers to the ethnographic study of Western capitalism, usually without that critical perspective on world history that Marxism provides. The economic crisis that began in 2008 should change that, by unmasking the pretensions of economic orthodoxy and reinforcing the need to acknowledge our global interdependence. Under these circumstances, a revival of Marxist economic anthropology is desirable and even probable, one that will hopefully pay more attention to Marx's own vision of the economy in human history than was the case the last time around.

5. Capital

Jayati Ghosh

Before Karl Marx – and indeed, after him, in the neoclassical economic tradition – capital (or the means of production) was treated as a resource that is simply a factor of production, analogous to land and labour. This makes it something that exists in all types of economy and over all historical phases, and production occurs by bringing together all the factors of production. In a 'capitalist' or 'market' economy, the various factors of production are seen as being brought together by the market. This view treats all the factors on a par, with each of them getting a return for their contribution to production, so that profits on capital are simply the return to a particular factor, just as labour receives wages and land receives rent.

Marx treated capital very differently, by recognizing that it is much more than a simple resource and expresses more than a purely technical relation of production. The central point about capital for Marx is that it is not a resource in itself, but rather an expression of very specific social relations of production, in particular historical contexts. Thus, all means of production need not be capital. For example, a loom that is required to weave cloth is capital if it is used in a factory by a worker employed to produce cloth to be sold for profit, but it is not capital if it is used in a peasant household to create cloth to be used by the members of the household. What makes the means of production capital are the social relations that underlie the production process.

The particular social form that capital embodies is the relation between employer and worker, which enables capitalist production to take place at all. This requires workers to be 'free' in a double sense. First, they must be 'free' to sell their own labour power, that is, not bound by other socio-economic ties and constraints that could prevent them from working for wages, and not be tied to any particular employer. Second, they must also be 'free' of any ownership of the means of production, so that they have no choice but to make themselves available for paid work for their own survival. This makes labour power also a commodity, sold in the market for a value which is determined by social subsistence norms. The peculiar nature of this commodity is that those who sell it may appear to be and, in some respects are, free, but they live only as long as they find work, and they find work only as long as their labour serves capital.

The concentration of ownership of the means of production in a few hands is effectively what enables capital to play its role in production: 'The existence of a class which possesses nothing but the ability to work is a necessary presupposition of capital' (Marx, 1847, *Wage Labour and Capital* (*WLC*), 'The nature and growth of capital'). This concentration must be based on the expropriation of the means of production from those who previously possessed it, such as peasants and small artisans who could have produced on their own. Marx points out that historically such expropriation (the primitive accumulation of capital) has been a violent process, emphasizing the forcible creation of the 'double freedom' of labour. Capitalist production and capitalist private property 'have for their fundamental condition the annihilation of self-earned private property; in other words, the expropriation of the labourer' (Marx, *Capital I*, ch. 33).

This conception of capital is very different from that which sees it as one among several factors of production that operate on equal terms. Capital is an expression of a class society, in which one class is able to live off the labour of another class or classes, by virtue of control over the means of production. However, it can be contrasted with other class societies such as feudalism, which relies on extra-economic coercion to ensure that one class works to provide surplus for the ruling class, and ensures this not only through force but also a set of religious and political illusions. By contrast, capital operates on a purely contractual economic basis, through voluntary market exchange of goods and commodities. But even to do this, capital also relies on an illusion, what Marx calls 'commodity fetishism'. This can be described as the situation in which relations between people become mediated by relations between things: commodities and money. Commodity fetishism occurs when value is seen as intrinsic to commodities rather than being the result of labour, and the exchange of commodities and market-based interaction are seen as the 'natural' way of dealing with all objects, rather than as a historically specific set of social relations.

CAPITAL IN THE PROCESS OF PRODUCTION

The essence of capital is that it is deployed to produce commodities for profit, not for use-value, or simply to be used. Thus, what is produced must be sold, or exchanged, to generate a profit, and that is the sole purpose of production, rather than to meet existing needs: 'Capital does not consist in the fact that accumulated labour serves living labour as a means for new production. It consists in the fact that living labour serves accumulated labour as the means of preserving and multiplying its exchange value' (Marx, *WLC*, 'The nature and growth of capital').

How is this profit generated? It occurs because production organized by capital generates surplus value, which in turn is based on the distinction between the value created by labour and the value of labour power. According to Marx, only workers can create value, by using the means of production to transform raw materials into finished goods through their labour. When any commodity is produced, the labour that is used in its production does two things: it transfers the value of the raw materials used up in production to the value of the final product, and it adds value over and above what is transferred. This value which is added is necessarily different from, and more than, the value of labour power, which is what the workers receive as wage. This difference, which is the unpaid or surplus labour provided by the worker for the capitalist, forms the basis of profit.

Obviously, in this process, money plays a crucial role. Money capital is a critical part of the circuit of capital. Without it, the transformation of commodities and labour power into something of more value, which forms the basis of the capitalist production process, cannot take place: 'As a matter of history, capital, as opposed to landed property, invariably takes the form at first of money' (Marx, *Capital I*, ch. 4). But money in itself is not capital, it has to be transformed into capital. Thus money as a mean of purchasing consumption goods is not capital; it becomes so only when it is used for the advances made by the capitalist (to purchase inputs for production and the labour power whose use will transform these inputs) to enable production for exchange and profit.

The process of production initiated by capital has the following social results: (1) the product belongs to the capitalist and not the worker; (2) the value of the product includes, in addition to the value of the capital advanced, a surplus value which has been extracted from the workers but which, nonetheless, becomes the legitimate property of the capitalist; and (3) the worker still retains her or his labour power and can sell it again if she or he can find a buyer.

In this process, the distinction between constant and variable capital is essential. This is not the same as the distinction between fixed and circulating capital. Rather, it is based on the argument that capital in itself cannot create value, which is only the result of the application of labour: 'the means of production can never add more value to the product than they themselves possess independently of the process in which they assist' (Marx, *Capital I*, ch. 8). This makes it possible to distinguish between that part of the capital outlay that does not change in value (constant capital) and that part (variable capital, which is the payment for labour power) which does transform in value. Constant capital refers to the outlays on equipment and materials used in production, the value of which is conserved and transferred to the new product but does not change in the production process. However, according to Marx, that part of capital that is represented by labour power does vary over the production process and undergoes a change in value: 'It both reproduces the equivalent of its own value, and also produces an excess, a surplus-value, which may itself vary, may be more or less according to circumstances' (Marx, *Capital I*, ch. 8). The distinction between means of production and labour power is therefore closely related to the distinction between constant and variable capital.

FORMS OF CAPITAL

Industrial capital forms the focus of much of Marx's analysis, and he clearly identified it as the specific form which gives to production its 'capitalist character'. He saw the transformatory power of industrial capital, and noted that to the extent that it assumes control over social production, it revolutionizes not only techniques but also the social organization of the labour process and social, economic, cultural and legal institutions. However, this does not mean that he was unaware of the existence of other forms of capital. Indeed, because capital is clearly identified as a social relation that can take many different forms, Marxian analysis is much more amenable to interpreting different forms of capital through history and in changing circumstances. Marx described usurer's capital and merchant capital as 'antediluvian' forms of capital, which have existed as long as the history of money in many different types of society, but essentially in the form of parasitic relations that did not have the power to transform socio-economic relations. This occurs only when they fuse with industrial capital, when they thereby become integral to the social formation of capitalism.

While Marx did not treat finance capital separately, later Marxists have explored the implications of the emergence of finance capital for the transformation of capitalism itself, through its association with the monopoly phase of capitalism and the strength of the financial oligarchy. While this does not change the fundamental nature of capital, it adds additional dimensions in terms of the effect on the production process and the nature of contradictions that are generated. The more recent theoretical elaboration of other 'forms' of capital – such as social capital, cultural capital and human capital – is of a different order, implying a shift away from the Marxian notion. Since these concepts all tend to treat capital as a pure resource (however it is created), and assume away the underlying social relations, they distort the notion of capital.

DYNAMICS OF CAPITAL

The nature of capital is constantly to transform itself and the society in which it operates: 'The bourgeoisie cannot exist without constantly revolutionising the instruments of production, and thereby the relations of production, and with them the whole relations of society . . . Constant revolutionising of production, uninterrupted disturbance of all social conditions, everlasting uncertainty and agitation distinguish the bourgeois epoch from all earlier ones' (Marx and Engels, *Manifesto of the Communist Party* (*MCP*), ch. 1).

This dynamism of capital has many unprecedented and positive results: a cosmopolitan character of production, which is particularly evident in the current phase of globalization; rapid improvements in technology and the creation of 'colossal' productive forces; immensely facilitated means of communication; the agglomeration of populations into cities; much greater interaction and interdependence of nations not only in economic terms but also in intellectual and creative life. Capital generates new types of production organization and economic institutions: not just the factory system but more recent arrangements, financial institutions and structures, and legal systems. Further, capitalist production has to produce not only commodities and surplus value, but also the capitalist social relation, with the capitalist on one side and the wage worker on the other. This in turn implies the continuing reproduction of a working class that is 'free' from the means of production, through a continuous process of dispossession: 'Capitalist production, therefore, of itself reproduces the separation between labour-power and the means of labour. It thereby reproduces and perpetuates the condition for exploiting the labourer. It incessantly forces him to sell his labour-power in order to live, and enables the capitalist to purchase labour-power in order that he may enrich himself' (Marx, *Capital I*, ch. 23). So capital cannot allow such enrichment of the working class as would lead to workers abandoning the wage labour contract.

An additional aspect of this reproduction of wage labour that was not explicitly developed by Marx but which can be drawn out from his analysis is the need for the social reproduction of the workforce. This is a process that involves and draws in unpaid labour within households, and is typically based on the gender construction within the society, such that women tend to perform most of such work. As this is not paid for by capital, it constitutes part of the surplus labour supporting capitalist production even when it does not directly produce surplus value itself.

At the same time, the accumulation of capital (its 'extended reproduction') can also benefit from the persistence of non-capitalist economies or sectors which may be drawn upon to facilitate the continuous expansion of capital. The household sector is necessarily included within this, but other economies, for example, those under colonial control or peasant-based economies, can also play a similar supporting role, which may be crucial at times. These features do not emerge directly from the 'reproduction schemes' of capital described by Marx, but have been developed by later Marxists and play a central role in Marxian notions of imperialism.

THE CONTRADICTIONS OF CAPITAL

While capital is inherently dynamic and constantly changing, it is also based on many contradictions at different levels. This generates a process whereby capital over time creates the conditions for its own destruction. There are several aspects to this contradictory nature of capital. First of all, like all class societies, the society created by capital is also ridden by conflict. Marx saw class relations between capital and labour as fundamentally antagonistic, even though they are not always expressed openly in these terms. In national income, profit and wage shares always have an inverse relation, and this expresses the fundamentally different interests of the two classes. Thus the dynamics of capital is simultaneously to aggrandise itself and impoverish other classes such as workers and peasants, within and across nations.

Antagonisms are not only between the two classes. The capitalist system also generates intra-class conflict. It pits individual capital against other capitals, as competition is the essence of market relations, and the individual worker against other workers. The system created by capital means that individual capitals are subject to the almost inexorable laws of the system, including a struggle for survival among the capitalists. So individualism, conflict and competition become the driving forces of the system, even when they are implicit and not fully recognized. In addition, there can be contradictions between different forms of capital. At the same time, the system also encourages workers to see themselves not as a group sharing the same fundamental interest vis-à-vis capital, but as rivals in the labour market competing for employment and wages.

Similarly, the accumulation of capital generates higher productivity and transforms systems, but it is also associated with uneven development. A central feature is the centralization of capital, which expresses the inherent antagonism between capitals: 'Accumulation, therefore, presents itself on the one hand as increasing concentration of the means of production, and of the command over labour; on the other, as repulsion of many individual capitals one from another . . . It is concentration of capitals already formed, destruction of their individual independence, expropriation of capitalist by capitalist, transformation of many small into few large capitals . . . Capital grows in one place to a huge mass in a single hand, because it has in another place been lost by many' (Marx, *Capital I*, ch. 25).

The individualism and competition between capitals also create what Marx calls the anarchy of the market and the inevitable tendency towards crises. Overproduction in terms of the market (even when human needs of all the people in the society need not be satisfied) is a characteristic feature simply because of the way individual capitals operate in the drive to generate more profit. The process of accumulation cannot be smooth, but must be uneven and punctuated by crises, and these periodic crises involve the destruction of a significant proportion of existing products and productive forces. Another fundamental contradiction brought about by capital is the loss of control by workers over their own work. This alienation of the workers means that they effectively cease to be autonomous human beings, because they cannot control their workplace, the products they produce, or even the way they relate to each other. Social emancipation is clearly not possible in such a context.

These various contradictions suggest why Marx viewed capitalism as a historically bounded system, which brings about its own demise. Because it is based on competition and conflict rather than co-operation, it leads to continuous and prolonged crises. After a point, it limits the full and free development of the productive forces of society and excludes the possibility of social control and regulation of the forces of nature. This is why crises in capitalist accumulation are also always crises in the perpetuation of the class relations necessary for capitalist production. These also make them opportunities for revolutionary change.

6. Capitalism

Ellen Meiksins Wood

The concept of 'capitalism' is not a Marxist invention. The term 'capital' applied to a stock of wealth goes back at least to the sixteenth century, while 'capitalist' in something like its modern meaning was used in the eighteenth century by the French economist, Turgot, who spoke of 'capitalist' entrepreneurs and a 'capitalist' or entrepreneurial form of organization which characterized, for him, the hitherto most advanced stage of human progress, in which 'capital' was actively employed to generate production for profit. The term 'capitalism' was apparently first used in English by the novelist, Thackeray, in the mid-nineteenth century to denote not an economic system but the ownership of capital.

Nineteenth-century socialists first applied the term capitalism – pejoratively – to describe the economic system they opposed. By that time, the concept was already loaded with the historical baggage of its etymology and assumptions about progress inherited from its predecessors. In particular, 'capitalism' had become more or less synonymous with 'commercial society' as understood by classical political economists like Adam Smith, who regarded it as the last stage of human development. While socialists looked forward to another stage of human progress beyond and superior to capitalism, there was, before Marx, no fundamental challenge to the identification of capitalism with commerce in the manner of classical political economy, and a view of its history as a process of commercialization. The implication seemed to be that capitalism was essentially an extension of age-old commercial practices, which had reached maturity in the modern age with the expansion of cities, markets and trade (Wood, 2002).

Marx himself did not in general use the term capitalism, speaking instead of capitalist production, or the capitalist form of production, or even the capitalist system; and he was less likely to identify the historical moment of the capitalist system as capitalism than as the 'bourgeois' era. The identification of 'capitalist' with 'bourgeois' – in its original meaning denoting a town-dweller – owed much to Enlightenment conceptions of progress and classical political economy, with their assumptions about commercial society. Even the emphasis on capitalist 'production', as distinct from simple exchange, was not by itself enough to distinguish Marx from 'bourgeois' political economy, since others before him, notably David Ricardo, had associated profit with labour in production. The idea that history has been a succession of 'modes of production' also has much in common with ideas already visible in Smith's classical political economy about the sequence of modes of subsistence from, say, hunting-gathering to pastoralism to agricultural and finally commercial society, a process driven by the division of labour, each stage more technologically advanced than the previous one and more capable of creating surpluses.

Yet from the beginning, and long before his mature analysis in *Capital,* there were in Marx's work significant innovations that would transform the conception of capitalism, understood not simply as an extension of age-old commercial practices but as a distinctive social form, with its own specific 'laws of motion', requiring fundamental social transformations to bring it into being. In the *German Ideology*, written with Engels in 1845–46, the stages of development in the division of labour are identified with different forms of ownership: tribal, ancient communal (accompanied by slavery), feudal or 'estate' property, which would eventually give way to 'bourgeois' society, with its own distinctive form of ownership. More particularly, there is, in this early work, an emphasis on the social 'relations' that constitute each historical form. Each stage in the division of labour, each form of ownership, is characterized by specific relations among individuals and 'with reference to the material, instrument, and product of labour'. In 1847, when Marx first wrote his pamphlet, *Wage Labour and Capital*, he elaborated this fundamental principle as it operates specifically in capitalism. Capital, he said, is not, as the economists tell us, simply 'raw materials, instruments of labour, and means of subsistence of all kinds, which are employed in producing new raw materials, new instruments, and new means of subsistence'. Nor is it even just 'accumulated labour that serves as a means to new production'. Capital is also, and above all, a 'social relation'.

Marx's later work would certainly advance far beyond this early pamphlet. When, for example, Engels republished it in 1891, he modified it to take account of a major change that had occurred in Marx's political economy, the distinction between 'labour' and 'labour-power' (see below) that did not appear in the original pamphlet. In his earlier work, Marx also placed more emphasis on the development of productive forces, or technological progress, as the driving mechanism of historical change than he would later in *Capital*. But the fundamental principle that capital is a social relation would be the key to his distinctive conception of capitalism or the capitalist mode of production.

What, then, does it mean to describe capital as a social relation, and what does this tell us about the nature and operating principles of capitalism? Marx constructs his argument on the premise that human beings interact with each other, with nature and with the conditions of labour – the material, instruments and products of labour – to achieve their subsistence and self-reproduction, and that these relations take different forms in different modes of production. In particular, development from one mode of production to another has been a progressive 'separation of free labor from the objective conditions of its realization – from the means and material of labor' (Marx, *Pre-Capitalist Economic Formations (PCEF)*). This also entails developments in modes of exploitation, the specific means by which appropriating classes acquire, and are enriched by, the surplus labour of direct producers.

Before capitalism, direct producers had related to the basic condition of labour – the land – as their property, whether the communal property of one or another form of primitive communalism or the free landed property of the independent small producing household. This meant that appropriating classes could extract surplus labour from direct producers only by what Marx calls 'extra-economic' means, the superior force derived from political, military and judicial status – as, for instance, feudal lords extracted labour services or rent from peasants who remained in possession of land. Capitalism would transform not only the relation of direct producers to the conditions of their labour but also the form in which surplus labour is extracted from them.

Capitalism completely disrupts the 'natural unity of labor with its material prerequisites' (Marx, *PCEF*), and the worker no longer has 'an objective existence independent of labour'. Wage labourers in capitalism have been completely separated from the conditions of their labour. As Marx would explain in *Capital I,* Part VIII, ch. 26:

> The capitalist system presupposes the complete separation of the labourers from all property in the means by which they can realize their labour. As soon as capitalist production is once on its own legs, it not only maintains this separation, but reproduces it on a continually extending scale. The process, therefore, that clears the way for the capitalist system, can be none other than the process which takes away from the labourer the possession of his means of production; a process that transforms, on the one hand, the social means of subsistence and of production into capital, on the other, the immediate producers into wage labourers. The so-called primitive accumulation, therefore, is nothing else than the historical process of divorcing the producer from the means of production. It appears as primitive, because it forms the prehistoric stage of capital and of the mode of production corresponding with it.

The separation of the direct producers from the means of production meant the proletarianization of the labour force, the transformation of direct producers into wage labourers and their exploitation not by 'extra-economic' but by purely 'economic' means. We shall examine this mode of exploitation more closely in a moment. But, first, it is essential to keep in mind that in capitalism, wage labour is employed by capital, and this has fundamental implications for the system's operating principles. Although we can, for purposes of analysis, abstract the idea of capital, and the relation between capital and labour, from the competitive relation among many capitals, it is important to recognize that capitalism operates in the way that it does not simply because the direct producers are wage labourers but because wage labour is employed by capital, and this entails a competitive relation among many capitals.

Wage labour has been employed in non-capitalist societies without producing characteristically capitalist 'laws of motion'. It is true that only in capitalism is wage labour the predominant form of labour, but it remains impossible to explain the specific dynamic of the capitalist system without taking account of competition among capitals. It is significant that while, for certain analytic purposes, Marx does present a conception of capital 'in general' abstracted from relations among many capitals, he reintroduces the competitive relation at precisely the point where he elaborates the specific dynamics of the capitalist system and particularly its tendency to crisis. In short, capitalism as a specific social form, with its own distinctive 'laws of motion', is constituted by these two sets of relations, between capital and labour and among many capitals. It is the relation of labour to capital in the context of relations among many capitals that produces the systemic specificities of capitalism.

We can explore how this dual relation works by beginning with the relation between capital and 'living labour', abstracted for a moment from the relation among capitals. Capitalist exploitation differs from modes of exploitation in which one class with superior power directly appropriates the surplus labour of direct producers by means of extra-economic force. Capitalists do not extract surpluses by means of direct coercion, and workers are compelled to sell their labour-power not by the capitalist's superior force but by purely economic necessity, the propertylessness that obliges them to sell their labour-power to gain access to means of production, the means of labour itself. In fact, capitalist profits are not extracted directly from workers at all. Capitalists pay workers in advance, so to speak, and they have to realize their gains by selling what the workers produce.

Workers seem to be paid for all the work they do: eight hours' pay, for instance, for eight hours' work. This is very different from situations in which peasants produce for their own consumption but are also forced to transfer surplus labour to landlords. There, the nature of the relationship and its exploitative character are transparent. It is obvious that the landlord is exploiting the peasants who forfeit part of their labour to enrich him, whether by paying rent or performing labour services. In capitalism, the transaction between capital and labour is different: the employer pays the worker, not the reverse.

But this appearance is in part misleading, as Marx sets out to demonstrate with his distinction between labour and labour-power: workers are paid for their labour-power for a certain period of time and not for everything their labour produces during that time. Whatever the workers produce belongs to the capitalist, and the capitalist appropriates the difference between what the workers are paid and what their products or services will fetch on the market. Capitalist profit derives from this discrepancy. Just as feudal peasants work partly for their own subsistence and partly for the benefit of their landlord, transferring their surplus labour in the form of rent, workers in capitalism work partly (and, significantly, indirectly) for themselves, and partly for the benefit of the capitalist, who appropriates their surplus labour in the form of surplus value, which is the source of profit.

By itself, however, this mode of surplus extraction cannot account for specifically capitalist 'laws of motion'. It is only in the context of competitive relations among capitals that the relation between capital and labour generates the characteristically capitalist compulsions of continual accumulation, profit maximization and the enhancement of labour productivity required to sustain profitability. That capitalists can make profit only if they succeed in selling their goods and services in a competitive market, and selling them for more than the costs of producing them, means that making profit is uncertain in advance. The social average of productivity that, in any given market, determines success in price competition is beyond the control of individual capitalists. The one thing capitalists can control to a significant extent is their costs. Since their profits depend on a favourable cost/price ratio, they will do everything possible to cut their costs to ensure profit. This means, above all, constant pressure to cut the costs of labour; and this requires constant improvements in labour productivity. Capital must constantly seek the organizational and technical means of extracting as much surplus value as possible from workers within a fixed period of time – the time during which the labour-power of workers belongs to capital.

To keep this process going requires regular investment, the reinvestment of surpluses and continual capital accumulation. This requirement is imposed on capitalists regardless of their own personal needs and wants. Even the most modest and socially responsible capitalist is subject to these pressures and is compelled to accumulate by maximizing surplus value, just to stay in business. The need to adopt such strategies is a basic feature of the system and not just a function of greed. This also means that the object of production is not the provision of social needs but the accumulation of capital. At the same time, the unrelenting need – which is unique to capitalism – constantly to improve the productivity of labour has made the capitalist system exceptionally dynamic. It generates constant improvements in technology and what is conventionally called economic growth, or what Marx preferred to describe as the accumulation of capital. But the same market pressures that make it so dynamic also have contradictory effects. Capitalism is prone to constant fluctuations, not only short-term 'business cycles' but also crisis and a tendency to long-term downturn and stagnation.

Marxist political economy after Marx has not significantly altered his analysis of capitalism as a specific social form, with its own distinctive 'laws of motion'. In the first half of the twentieth century, there were important developments in Marxist theory, but some of the most important were either preoccupied with the contemporary problems of revolutionary movements in countries with relatively undeveloped capitalisms, or concerned the external relations of capitalism, the relations between capitalist powers and a largely non-capitalist world, in the form of imperialism.

One of the most important contributions was Rosa Luxemburg's *The Accumulation of Capital*, which was intended to move beyond, or at least to supplement, Marx's analysis of capitalism as a closed system by considering relations between capitalism and the non-capitalist modes of production, particularly in the form of imperialism. But she did not envisage a time when capital accumulation by means of colonial expansion and oppression would be overtaken by a global capitalist economy no longer dependent on traditional forms of imperialism. Capitalism, she believed, was in its final stages and would be overtaken before its economic imperatives could expand to embrace the globe.

More recently, there have been debates between 'neo-Ricardian' economists and others who have sought to revive and renew Marx's theory of value. Yet some of the most fruitful Marxist work on the nature of capitalism has been done not by political economists but by Marxist historians who have explored its origins and evolution. Marx himself had moved beyond the historical accounts provided by classical political economy and Enlightenment conceptions of progress, especially with his discussion of 'the so-called primitive accumulation' (quoted above) as a process of divorcing producers from the means of production; but, apart from this brief account, he never systematically explored the process of transition from pre-capitalist to capitalist societies. His very sketchy insights into this process would be elaborated by historians, such as Maurice Dobb, and then by Robert Brenner, who completed the move away from the 'commercialization' model of capitalism traceable to classical political economy.

In Brenner's account (Ashton and Philpin, 1985), a new historical dynamic was set in train before the complete expropriation of the direct producers, and as a precondition to it, when tenants in England, although remaining in possession of land, were separated from 'non-market' access to their means of self-reproduction. In what has come to be called 'agrarian capitalism', the conditions of survival and self-reproduction, in particular possession and retention of land, became dependent on the market; and these new social property relations generated the imperatives of competition, the requirements of profit-maximization and the need for constant improvement of the forces of production, which would lead to a historically unprecedented process of self-sustaining growth. In his later work on the contemporary global economy and recent crises, Brenner has built on his insights about the competitive pressures deriving from the market dependence of the main economic actors and on Marx's own account of relations among capitals.

Some Marxist critics (for example, in the 'Symposium on Robert Brenner and world crisis', *Historical Materialism*, vols 4 and 5, 1999) have objected to this emphasis on market dependence in the definition of capitalism, and on the 'horizontal' relation among capitals no less than on the 'vertical' relations between capital and labour. Yet it is hard to see how capitalism as we know it today can be understood in any other way. Capitalism has expanded not only spatially throughout the globe but also into virtually every aspect of life, transforming social needs into commodities, the provision of which is determined not by their use value but by their profitability in a competitive market. The same imperatives of capital accumulation – with all their wasteful destructiveness and short-term requirements of maximum profit – have not only produced recurrent economic crises but have contributed vastly to degrading the environment. None of these features of contemporary capitalism can be explained without reference to both of the system's constitutive relations: the relation between capital and labour *and* the competitive relations among many capitals.

7. Centrally planned economy

Dic Lo and Yu Zhang

The notion of 'centrally planned economy' has been, almost universally, accepted as synonymous with the Soviet-type economic system that had collapsed by the 1990s. Its potential – in terms of desirability and feasibility – has thus been associated with the historical experience of achievements and shortcomings of the Soviet and similar economies. In addition, to a lesser extent and more in popular imagination, (Soviet) central planning has been associated with Marxism or a Marxist regime itself at the expense of its critique of capitalism. And, within Marxist scholarship, central planning has been widely considered to be a necessary condition for the realization of principles of socialism as depicted in Marxist classics, although its realization in practice has always been subject to critique from within Marxism.

Soviet economic development is an ambiguous experience of success and failure. Both its achievements and shortcomings are well known. Its rapid industrialization and trend of catching up with the level of economic development of the advanced capitalist world, prior to and immediately after World War II, was reckoned as a considerable achievement (and, ultimately, allowed for the war to be won). Its stagnation in the two decades prior to its demise is acknowledged to have been catastrophic. The same pattern of development was evident in countries of the Soviet bloc as a whole. The 'Golden Age of Capitalism' was also the Golden Age of the Soviet bloc, which registered a substantial increase in its share of world income. A couple of the member countries of the bloc joined the rank of newly industrializing economies in experiencing rapid economic development in the period 1950–80. The turn to disaster in the 1980s resulted in the collapse both of the countries within the Soviet bloc and the Soviet-type system itself. Meanwhile, throughout its life-span (except in the first decade after the Russian Revolution), the Soviet Union, just like all subsequent members of the bloc, was infused with pervasive bureaucratic control (associated with 'Stalinism', a complex and shifting notion). This both hindered economic development and was detrimental to the realization of the principles of socialism.

A variety of reforms were attempted in the later years of the Soviet bloc of three types. First were Soviet attempts to improve the efficiency of central planning by means of sophisticated methods of data collection and computation, often with the assistance of advanced computers. Second was the Hungarian attempts to supplement the workings of the centrally planned system with market institutions and profit-incentives for the enterprises. And third were the Yugoslav attempts at workers' self-management where major economic decisions were made by market-based autonomous enterprises or local governments with institutionalized workers' participation in management. In the event, all these attempts turned out to be failures in terms of sustaining the bloc's drives of catching up with the income levels of the advanced capitalist world.

It remains unclear in what ways and to what extent these failures were due to intrinsic weaknesses of the reform attempts or, by the late 1980s, whether the failings were sufficient to result in total loss of confidence among the ruling elites (including the intellectuals) in the bloc over the reformability of the Soviet-type system. This, together with the blind faith in the neoliberal notion of the free market system, gave rise to desperate attempts to break with the system precipitously, encouraged and supported by external pressures. This culminated in attempts at systemic transformation known as shock therapy or big-bang reforms.

Outside the Soviet bloc, the Soviet-type system has also been variously experienced. The most important is China. Against the background of a national liberation revolution and a backward ('semi-feudal, semi-colonial' capitalist) economy, China quickly abandoned the central planning system after a brief, albeit tremendously successful try in the first Five Year Plan of the 1950s. This was for both economic and political reasons, associated with 'Maoism'. Economically, the state leadership judged that the top-down approach of central planning was intrinsically unfavourable for resource mobilization, yet this was deemed far more important than 'scientific management' (the claimed distinctive advantage of central planning) for rapid industrialization in a backward economy. Politically, the Chinese leadership gradually came to the judgement that the centrally planned system is intrinsically associated with bureaucratism and antithetical to socialist principles. In the two decades from the late 1950s, therefore, the Chinese economic system was mainly characterized by decentralized planning. This institutional framework largely helped to lay the groundwork for the subsequent, gradualist market-oriented systemic reforms from the late 1970s. The accumulation achieved through the decentralized planning system also paved the way for rapid economic development over the reform era. Nevertheless, as was officially acknowledged, in the periods both of decentralized planning and market-oriented reform, the ideal of Marxist socialism was far from being realized but remained a distant prospect.

CENTRAL PLANNING AND PRINCIPLES OF SOCIALISM

The ideal of socialism can be summarized as the progressive emancipation of labour from alienation. Yet, initially, Marx, in the *Critique of the Gotha Programme*, addresses the realm of distribution. The distinctive characteristic of 'communist society' that has just emerged from capitalism is the principle of equal right in distribution for labour performed. Because of the common ownership of the means of production, 'The right of the producers is *proportional* to the labor they supply; the equality consists in the fact that measurement is made with an *equal standard*, labor.' Marx considered this principle still a bourgeois right, because it takes as given the unequal labour capacity of individuals. He thus argued that, with the continuous increase in affluence and the progressive decrease in the alienation of labour, this principle would gradually give way to the following, truly socialist principle: 'from each according to his ability, to each according to his needs'.

Marx did not analyse whether distribution in proportion to labour would facilitate or block the progressive transition to the realization of the socialist principle. Nor did he explain how common ownership would ensure that principle, apart from stating, in general terms, that 'now, in contrast to capitalist society, individual labour no longer exists in an indirect fashion but directly as a component part of total labour'. The task was left to Engels, who suggests, in the *Anti-Dühring* (Part III, ch. 2) that 'with the seizing of the means of production by society production of commodities is done away with, and, simultaneously, the mastery of the product over the producer. Anarchy in social production is replaced by systematic, definite organisation.' This passage evokes the notion of central planning over society's production.

What is the material base for this new, non-competitive mechanism of co-ordination? Engels's answer is the increasing socialization of production under capitalism. He refers to the expansion of large-scale modern industry through the concentration of capital. The central character of modern industry is 'the division of labour upon a definite plan', that is, conscious planning and organization within individual firms. The increasing predominance of modern industry in the economy, therefore, implies the increasing importance of planning in co-ordinating economic activities – so much so that Engels came out with the notion of 'a society which makes it possible for its productive forces to dovetail harmoniously into each other on the basis of one single vast plan' (Part III, ch. 3).

Lenin, following Engels, attached much importance to the socialization of production as the material base for the construction of socialism, not just in an economic but also in a political sense. For Lenin, in *The State and Revolution,* chapter 3:

> Capitalist culture has created large-scale production, factories, railways, the postal service, telephones, etc., and on this basis the great majority of the functions of the old 'state power' have become so simplified and can be reduced to such exceedingly simple operations of registration, filing, and checking that they can be easily performed by every literate person, can quite easily be performed for ordinary 'workmen's wages', and that these functions can (and must) be stripped of every shadow of privilege, of every semblance of 'official grandeur'.

The socialization of production is thereby seen to pave the way for the withering away of the state as an organ of class power as opposed administration. It provides the foundation for the planned co-ordination and management of production and distribution in the context where 'the whole of society will have become a single office and a single factory' (ch. 5). The crux of the matter, as Lenin repeatedly emphasized, is that the socialization of production has made planning and organizing state functions as well as economic activities simple and easy – they 'have been *simplified* by capitalism to the utmost and reduced to the extraordinarily simple operations' (ch. 5).

But is central planning really that simple? At most, it may be that Lenin's emphasis requires that 'all members of society, or at least the vast majority, have learned to administer the state *themselves*' (ch. 5). The planned co-ordination and management of state functions and economic activities are simple only relative to the capacity of working people. In the meantime, the continuous improvement of the knowledge and skill of working people is also necessary for labour's progressive emancipation from alienation. For Lenin, like Marx and Engels, the separation of politics and economics in capitalism has to be replaced by their reunion in the form of the participation of all members of society in the administration of all major political and economic affairs. It is via this reunion that the division of labour between the management and the managed would tend to diminish and, henceforth, 'the door will be thrown wide open for the transition from the first phase of communist society to its higher phase' (ch. 5).

FEASIBLE SOCIALISM VERSUS CAPITALISM

Feasible socialism needs to be efficient in the broadest terms relative to capitalism to allow for material and social development. This ultimately entails the necessary material conditions that permit continuous improvement in the capacity of working people to allow for the elimination of the division of labour between management and managed. Central is the progressive shortening of the length of alienated labour. In the *Anti-Dühring*, Engels (Part III, ch. 3) made the following point:

> With the present development of the productive forces, the increase in production that will follow from the very fact of the socialisation of the productive forces, coupled with the abolition of the barriers and disturbances, and of the waste of products and means of production, resulting from the capitalist mode of production, will suffice, with everybody doing his share of work, to reduce the time required for labour to a point which, measured by our present conceptions, will be small indeed.

This view follows from the standard Marxian argument concerning the antagonism between the planned production within individual firms and the anarchic co-ordination across the economy as a whole. Emphasizing the contradiction between the socialization of production and private capitalist appropriation has become especially prominent in twentieth-century Marxist political economy, in the wake of the eruption of big business (modern corporations) in advanced capitalist economies. Maurice Dobb (1937), for instance, argues that the distinctive advantage of central planning over the market economy is that *ex ante* planning can overcome the intrinsic uncertainty associated with market-based, atomistic decision-making. And such uncertainties of the capitalist economy, in line with Keynesian understanding, can be of catastrophic consequence.

In contrast, critics argue that central planning has a distinctive disadvantage vis-à-vis the market economy: namely, the central planning authorities would never have the incentive and ability to collect and process the detailed and ever-changing knowledge that is necessary for the efficient allocation of scarce resources. Some arrangements for market co-ordination are necessary to complement central planning, if not to replace it altogether. The idea is that only decentralized individuals have the incentive and ability to generate and utilize the necessary knowledge. These critics, ranging from market-fundamentalist theorists of the (neo-)Austrian School to moderate economists that have sympathy for socialism (for example, Alec Nove), are thus not hesitant to conclude that, with its intrinsic weaknesses, central planning can lead to economic catastrophes.

Does continuously improving the capacity of the working people, in conjunction with the socialization of production, help largely to mitigate the shortcoming of central planning and make it distinctively superior to the market economy? Mandel (1992) attempts to give an affirmative answer to this question from two different directions. First, he contends that the socialization of production, although not necessarily making planning simple in the absolute sense, does imply that the scope for comparatively efficient planning is much larger than is envisaged by market-centred economists. The concentration of capital (especially in the twentieth century) has resulted in the tremendous expansion of big firms. The progressive increase in the number of goods and services that are characterized by inelasticity of demand has further reinforced the case for planning in place of market co-ordination. Second, the jobs of formulating and implementing central planning are not necessarily confined to the state bureaucracy. In terms of ability, the active participation of increasingly educated working people in economic decision-making processes can be at least as efficient as the market-based individualistic activities in the generation and utilization of knowledge. In terms of incentives, the progressive shortening of the length of alienated labour is likely to encourage the expansion of the scope of participation – from matters of immediate interest gradually to society-wide issues. Democratic central planning, in short, is judged to be superior to the market economy.

A crucial question that remains concerns the precise, feasible institutional arrangements through which individual and collective interests can be reconciled. Until this question is adequately answered, it cannot be assumed that the principles of mass participation and democratic control can be achieved as a substitute for bureaucratic control, whilst also resolving the tensions around incentives, abilities and rewards (Sayer, 1995). Consequently, granted that the withering away of the state can only be a long-term process, there is a real likelihood of a divergence of interests between the two main economic agents in the sphere of production: that is, the state and enterprises. And this is in addition to the likely divergence of interests between the state and households in the sphere of distribution. These problems were clearly exposed by the Soviet-type central planning system.

THE SOVIET-TYPE SYSTEM: THE TRANSITION TO/FROM SOCIALISM

First and foremost, from one Marxist perspective, the Soviet-type central planning system is characterized by a contradictory combination of a non-capitalist mode of production and a basically capitalist norm of distribution (Mandel, 1968). The mode of production is deemed non-capitalist because the social surplus product is appropriated by the state, not by private capital. And the purpose or driving force of production is the accumulation of means of production as use values, rather than profit-seeking based on competition for the conquest of markets. Meanwhile, the mode of distribution remains capitalist because it is characterized by exchanges between human labour and the consumer goods produced by this labour – a bourgeois principle of distribution. It can only wither away progressively as the economy becomes capable of ensuring to each human being the satisfaction of basic needs and as, thereby, distribution ceases to have to be based on exchange.

The resolution of these contradictions through the development of the productive forces and the increasingly free distribution of a widening range of basic goods and services presupposes a high degree of consensus in society. It requires mechanisms that ensure active participation by workers in the management of enterprises and of the economy as a whole, the working out of the plan by democratic debate, and close supervision by working people of the (re)formulation, implementation and monitoring of the plan. These all remain very remote from the experiences of central planning: historically, all Soviet-type economies have been infused with pervasive bureaucratic control. The question arises as to whether pervasive bureaucratic control is a contingent product of the specific historical conditions of the Soviet-type economies. Or was it an inevitable product of the system of central planning itself?

This is a question of debate. Economists holding the 'inevitable' view emphasize the complexities of the division of labour in modern societies, and hence, even in a 'pure' Soviet-type system with minimal non-economic hindrance to mass participation, workers would still need to concede considerable power of management to bureaucratic control (Sayer, 1995). Economists that hold the 'contingent' view, in contrast, carry forward to the debate the argument that central planning would become increasingly simple along with the increasing capacity of workers – hence pervasive bureaucratic control is not an inevitable product of central planning (Mandel, 1992). Historically, the reality is that neither of these pure theories has had a chance to be put to the test. The reality is 'one-country (in the transition to) socialism', that is, a relatively backward socialist island surrounded by the ocean of world capitalism. The backwardness deters the active participation of workers in the management of society-wide matters. More urgently, following the famous Preobrazhensky-type argument, backwardness necessitates a development strategy emphasizing heavy industrialization. This strategy carries an intrinsic tendency to preserve the capitalist norms of distribution and control through excessive accumulation and through material incentives for the implementation of the plan. Thus, unless the Soviet-type system is built on the world scale or at least simultaneously in a couple of economically advanced countries, the possibility of eliminating bureaucratic control, and replacing it by mass participation remains no more than an unrealizable dream.

Outside of those with sympathy for socialism, the association of central planning with pervasive bureaucratic control is simply taken as given. The influential theory of the economics of shortage, developed by János Kornai (1980), is representative of such a positivist approach to studying the Soviet-type system. The theory focuses on analysing the implications of the divergence of interests between the state and enterprises, which it takes as the most fundamental determinant of the functioning of the system. The starting point is the notion of the 'soft budget constraint'. This refers to the survival of the enterprise and its access to resources being guaranteed by the state. Behavioural patterns arise out of the enterprise bargaining with the state, rather than in response to performance in competitive markets. At the institutional level, these behavioural patterns are intrinsic to public ownership – any deviation from individualistic property rights would result in a distortion from the discipline relating expenditures to (potential) earnings.

With the soft budget constraint, the enterprise thus has a built-in incentive to expand to gain access to resources. This leads to investment hunger and insatiable demand for inputs. Consequently, at the aggregate level, demand is almost unlimited, leading to pervasive, chronic shortages (demand outstripping supply) as a systemic phenomenon. Production is constrained only by the allocation of physical resources by administrative fiat. Consequently, the enterprise simultaneously experiences shortages of some inputs and excesses in others, and resorts through 'forced substitution' to purchases of whatever goods it can obtain irrespective of production needs and outcomes. The same applies to households, which play a passive role, suffering from shortage in terms of queues, unavailable goods and services, forced substitution and the demeaning relationships between sellers and buyers. Since shortage is a systemic and chronic phenomenon, the policy conclusion is drawn that shortages may be rectified only by changing functioning through fundamental economic reforms. Ultimately, mass privatization is the recommendation (Hare, 1989).

Characteristic of the economics of shortage is its explanation of macro outcomes on the basis of microeconomic theory, focusing on the productive sector. This is considered unsatisfactory by the rival theory of macroeconomic disequilibrium that more fully integrates the household sector into account. Portes (1989) argues that total demand for consumption goods will be affected by the interplay between planners, enterprises and banks which determine wage plan (over)fulfilment. But whether this yields excess demand is another matter. Chronic and sizable imbalances between aggregate demand and supply are impossible. For, with persistent shortage of consumer goods to households, labour supply would be reduced (possibly through reduced work effort) to conform to what goods are available (rather than leading to the accumulation of wages that cannot be spent). Nominal excess demand for goods would be matched by nominal excess supply of labour. But neither has any effect as long as money prices and wages remain fixed. Consequently, the policy recommendation that arises from the theory of macroeconomic disequilibrium is price reform – not necessarily mass privatization – to reduce, and eventually to eliminate, nominal excesses in the supply of labour and demand for goods.

Significantly, each of these approaches, as is also true of Stiglitz (1994), derives entirely from mainstream economic principles developed, however appropriately, for capitalism but extrapolated from capitalism to socialism. Not surprisingly, they do not address the issue of bureaucratic control other than as an obstacle to the market (soft individual budget constraint or systemic consequences of inflexible prices). What they share in common is a failure to consider worker management in place of bureaucratic control. As a result, they can only analyse the transition of the Soviet-type central planning system away from socialism – not the transition to socialism. Yet, these 'bourgeois' theories cannot claim to be superior to Marxist political economy. For, ultimately, what is at stake is the rivalry between two different paradigms in the philosophy of history. The claim of the transition away from socialism hinges on the belief that capitalism will always be superior to any alternative and, thus, will be eternal. The claim of the transition towards socialism, in contrast, is based on the Marxist theory of labour alienation and its progressive emancipation – which implies that the transcendence of capitalism is not only desirable but also feasible.

8.   Class and class struggle

Utsa Patnaik

It is virtually impossible to discuss the concept of class in Marxist theory outside the context of, and without reference to, the concept of mode of production. While pure classes are readily identified with specific modes of production, a problem arises with societies which are transitional from one mode of production to another. The same term, such as 'landlord' for example, will have a very different meaning in a capitalist society than in one which is transitional from a pre-capitalist to a capitalist social formation.

Abstracting from dynamic problems of transition, the Marxist concept of class is based on the relation of groups of persons to the ownership of means of production and the consequent relations of economic exploitation, buttressed by social and political dominance-subordination relations which are generated between these groups. The numerically small groups of persons with property rights over the means of production, whatever the historical origin of such rights might be, constitute the exploiting classes that are able, through their control over these property rights, to extract surplus labour from the much more numerous groups of persons with little or no property rights. The specific forms in which surplus labour is performed by the actual workers engaged in material production, and the forms of appropriation of the economic surplus so produced by the class with property rights, define the character of class relations and, simultaneously, define the specific mode of production. While these concepts are often discussed in the context of capitalist production alone, the analytical power of the concepts of class and mode of production lies in that they represent a sufficiently high level of theoretical abstraction to permit application to a wide variety of historically observed and currently existing social formations. Other than the capitalist mode of production, all other modes are based on direct relations between exploiter and exploited which are sometimes referred to as 'extra-economic coercion', not mediated through the market.

Slave labour, serf labour and wage labour are generally considered to be the main social forms of existence of the labour relation. In a slave labour-based mode of production, the class of slave owners monopolizes not only land and the instruments of production but own the workers themselves in the same manner that they might own cattle. Slavery originates mainly in conquest, and the term slave itself is thought to have derived from 'Slav' much as in South Asia the term '*dasa*', also meaning slave, was originally the name of an ethnic group. Slaves are obliged by the class of slave owners engaged in agricultural and manufacturing production to perform surplus labour and produce output over and above the quantum of labour required to produce their own means of subsistence. This surplus labour is appropriated not as labour directly but as surplus product, which is termed slave rent. In a serf labour-based mode of production characteristic of feudalism, typically a class of overlords comes to exercise property rights over all land, both peasant plots and demesne, but they do not exercise the right of disposal as they wish of the person of the direct producer, the peasant. While the direct producers are not slaves they are not free either. The necessary labour for producing the subsistence requirements of the peasants is performed on the plots of land which they customarily occupy, and till with the instruments and livestock which they possess. However, they are permitted to do so only provided they perform surplus labour to sustain the non-producers. The overlords extract surplus labour from an enserfed peasantry in the form of unpaid labour services which are used to till demesne land or used to produce artisan manufactures. This is the only form of exploitation where surplus labour is separated in both space and time from necessary labour. Hence, it is arguably the most transparent and readily comprehended relation between exploiter and exploited. Other than such direct extraction of unpaid labour, or labour rent, the serfs might also be obliged to pay surplus labour in kind as produce (product rent) or in cash, embodying the value of surplus product (cash rent) or in various combinations of all three. While there might well exist a hierarchy of degrees of unfreedom among serfs, as Moses Finley had pointed out in the context of European feudalism, ranging from personal slaves to virtual freemen, the dominant relation shaping the nature of the production system was serfdom.

Asian forms of feudalism have not been characterized by the extraction of surplus labour directly as unpaid labour services primarily used for production, but have typically involved payment, by an unfree peasantry, of a combined product rent-cum-tax to dual agents, namely, product rent to a class of local overlords and, through these overlords, tax to a centralized feudal state whenever such a state formation came into being. Unpaid labour services of the peasant were mainly used for transporting goods, or for domestic services by the superior property right holders, but not generally for agricultural production. The 'own farms' of the superior landholding classes in Asia, corresponding to demesne lands in European feudalism, were cultivated by hereditary farm servants allowed their subsistence in kind, who were not chattel slaves.

The early descriptions of Asiatic societies by colonial administrators-cum-scholars were somewhat misleading in the light of later research, in that these accounts stressed the existence of the village community of peasants supporting a centralized monarchical state system, but did not note the pervasive existence of a class of local superior landed proprietors extracting product rent from the community of peasants and forwarding a specified part of it as tax to the state (as described in detail by R.S. Sharma, 2005, for ancient India and by I. Habib, 2005, for medieval India).

Hegel had formed his idea of the 'unchanging' nature of Oriental societies on the basis of the early colonial accounts, arguing that the unity of agriculture and manufacture within self-sufficient village communities enabled them to survive through the millennia while ruling dynasties rose and fell. Marx, influenced by Hegel and also with access only to early colonial research, accepted the idea of the internally undifferentiated peasant community paying tax to the state and so conceptualized the 'Asiatic mode of production' as a direct relation between the community and the state. But the historical reality was that payment by the community of peasants was not a pure tax but was rent-cum-tax, collected by local landed proprietors who doubled as the agents of the state. This class of local proprietors continued to exist and extract rent in periods when the centralized state collapsed. The unity of agriculture and manufacture in the Asian village community and its self-sufficiency was no greater than such unity in the nearly self-sufficient great manorial estates in Europe. And, reaching distant lands through powerful merchant guilds and fleets of merchant ships, long-distance trade was certainly far more pervasive in Asia than it was in Europe up to the fifteenth century, before the latter's expansion to the New World. Marxist historians from Asia have therefore preferred to describe Asian economic systems as forms of feudalism which did differ from European feudalism but in inessential respects, and were similar in the essential respect of the existence of a class of landed overlords and monarch, extracting surplus labour in the form of product rent-cum-tax from a subject peasantry.

All pre-capitalist societies, being based on direct relations of domination and subordination between the classes extracting economic surplus and the classes producing it, have institutionalized inequality in the form of complex systems of social and political hierarchy whether as social estates or as castes. In contrast to all forms of pre-capitalist society, the capitalist mode of production in its final form, at least in principle, dispenses with such direct legally unequal and hierarchical relations between classes, the working classes seeking through prolonged struggle to reach a point where the capitalist class is obliged to institutionalize legal and political equality. The class of capitalists and the class of wage workers still face each other as unequal agents in the economic sphere, but at least as legal equals, entering into a contract which does not involve the overt use of force. However, the question arises whether the achievement of 'freedom of the worker under capitalism' in the countries where it first developed was historically contingent on the imposition of 'un-freedom' on workers of other societies (see below).

The early conceptualization by Marx and Engels of the link between classes and mode of production emerges in the frequently quoted passages on the very first pages of the *Manifesto of the Communist Party*, chapter 1:

> The history of all hitherto existing society is the history of class struggles. Freeman and slave, patrician and plebeian, lord and serf, guild-master and journeyman, in a word, oppressor and oppressed, stood in constant opposition to one another, carried on an uninterrupted, now hidden, now open fight, a fight that each time ended, either in a revolutionary reconstitution of society at large, or in the common ruin of the contending classes. In the earlier epochs of history, we find almost everywhere a complicated arrangement of society into various orders, a manifold gradation of social rank.

Marx and Engels go on to point out that:

> Our epoch, the epoch of the bourgeoisie, possesses, however, this distinct feature: it has simplified class antagonisms. Society as a whole is more and more splitting up into two great hostile camps, into two great classes directly facing each other – Bourgeoisie and Proletariat.

There are two main processes which historically acted to complicate the pure antagonism of these two great classes, the bourgeoisie and the proletariat, and ultimately deflected the revolutionary role of the working class in overthrowing capitalism in its heartland, Western Europe. Those who cite the failure of Marx's prediction forget how nearly it came true in France and Germany, and the processes which affected the internal contradictions of capitalist society. The first process had to do with colonialism and imperialism. Unlike all previous modes of production, capitalism from its inception in Europe was associated with rapid external expansion, complete appropriation of the land and natural resources of many pre-existing societies, particularly of the Amerindians, combined with colonial subjugation and forced trade with other more populous and strongly articulated Asian class societies. In Marx's intellectual project, summarized in the very first lines of his Preface to *A Contribution to the Critique of Political Economy*, the last topics of study were to be 'the State, foreign trade and world market':

> I examine the system of bourgeois economy in the following order: *capital, landed property, wage-labour; the State, foreign trade, world market.* The economic conditions of existence of the three great classes into which modern bourgeois society is divided are analysed under the first three headings; the interconnection of the other three headings is self-evident.

The method of abstraction Marx followed was to start with a closed capitalist economy and, although it is clear that his declared intention was to open it up, in practice his entire working life was taken up with the analysis of the first three topics while the last three – 'the State, foreign trade and world market' – were never systematically elaborated. From Marx's articles and news dispatches in the *New York Tribune* we obtain many references to European migration to the New World, Britain's colonial exploitation of India and the drain of resources from the colonially subjugated world to the European industrializing countries. But these phenomena were never formally integrated into his analysis of capitalist accumulation, as they might have been had Marx's working life lasted longer. Marx sharply criticized Ricardo's theory of rent in the *Theories of Surplus Value*, but did not get around to formulating a critique of Ricardo's theory of trade. The dominant Ricardian view of international trade as a process of specialization and benefit to both exchanging parties assumed equal and symmetrical status of countries and, thus, completely ignored the circumstances of colonial trade, which formed a very substantial, and sometimes the major, part of European trade for the two centuries from 1750, accompanying the growth to maturity of industrial production.

The second and related conceptual problem concerns slavery and the class of slaves under capitalism. Slave labour had an important role to play not just in the adolescence but also in the phase of maturity of capitalism, since it was legally abolished as late as 1843 in Britain and effectively ended only a quarter century later in North America with its Civil War. The revival of modern slavery as a major form of class exploitation over a millennium after the slavery of the ancient world was the dubious gift of the rise of the capitalist mode of production. The same eighteenth and nineteenth-century English and French landlords who leased out their land by contract to capitalist tenant farmers at home and obtained capitalist rent also operated plantations based on slave labour in the Caribbean to extract slave rent.

Does it follow that it is incorrect to associate the rise of capitalism with the 'freedom' of the worker? The Marxist analysis of the relation between the growth of free wage labour at one pole of capitalist accumulation and of chattel slavery at the other pole, an analysis which is yet to be undertaken, must take into account the dialectical interaction of these two antithetical forms of exploitation. The capitalist ruling classes imposed unfreedom on many non-European peoples, forcibly removed them from their communities, enslaved and transported millions of persons to the other side of the globe to work plantations for their own benefit, treating slave rent as profit. After the formal abolition of slavery another form of un-freedom continued under the indentured labour system. At the same time, the capitalist ruling classes bowed to the pressure of struggle by wage labour in the home country for political representation and economic improvement through collective bargaining. The bargaining power of wage labour must necessarily have improved through the dual route of out-migration of the unemployed, and the inflow of colonial transfers which boosted domestically generated profits. This question is better discussed under 'class struggle'.

CLASS STRUGGLE

Class struggle may be thought of usefully, first, as a struggle by the exploited classes over what constitutes necessary labour, in which these classes initially demand a reduction of the rate of surplus extraction and, in the process, arrive at a radical questioning of the rationale for the existence of a class of parasitic exploiters monopolizing property. This leads to a political conception of an overthrow of the existing property system and the establishment of an alternative.

The struggle over necessary labour between the peasantry and the landlords in decaying feudal systems contributed to the crisis of these systems and presaged the bourgeois-led democratic revolutions resulting in the overthrow of feudal property and creation of the conditions for the unfettered development of capitalist relations. This class struggle was led by the emerging bourgeoisie in Europe, and the French Revolution in particular also inspired contemporary struggles for the overthrow of slavery (for example, the black Jacobins in Haiti) and against colonial conquerors (Tipu Sultan ordered his subjects to address him as 'citizen', in Karnataka, India). In Asia the process of revolutionary overthrow of feudal property, which came later in the twentieth century, was led primarily by the political parties adhering to Marxism and to working-class ideology, with a commitment to socialize production. The Asian revolutionary movements drew inspiration from the Bolshevik Revolution in Russia, which had inspired a distinctly different strategic vision of revolution, stressing the concept of an alliance of the workers and the peasantry led by the working-class party and informed by proletarian internationalism. This vision had been articulated by Lenin in the context of the existence of a large peasantry in Russia burdened by lack of resources and continuing feudal exactions. The agrarian programme of the Russian Social-Democratic Labour Party had been famously modified from the seizure and nationalization of land to the seizure and distribution of the land to the land-poor peasantry. In the Second Congress of the Comintern, in 1920, a short but significant piece by Lenin titled *Preliminary Draft Theses on the Agrarian Question* discussed the matter of how to distinguish the various classes within the rural population ranging from the landlord to the proletarian. The concept of worker-peasant alliance was developed further in the Chinese revolutionary struggle by Mao Zedong. Taking into account the semi-feudal nature of Chinese society and the specific features of Japanese aggression, Mao Zedong formulated an even broader concept of class alliance in which land reform would treat differentially those landlords who collaborated with the invaders and those who cooperated with the revolutionary forces.

Marx and Engels had initially envisaged the class struggle of the proletariat in advanced countries eventually leading to the overthrow of the capitalist mode of production there, and constituting the first socialist revolutions. That this did not happen has arguably a great deal to do with the success with which the capitalist ruling classes externalized the acute internal contradictions of the capitalist mode of production. The process of primitive accumulation in Western Europe had involved the dispossession of small peasant producers, and resulted in the creation of a large class of labourers 'freed' from their means of production. This exceeded by far the capacity of the industrially transforming domestic economies to absorb this class productively even after allowing for a normal level of unemployment or maintenance of a 'reserve army of labour', because capitalist accumulation entailed labour-displacing mechanization from its very inception.

The peasants expropriated from the land, the workers displaced by mechanization and the famine-stricken Irish population in the mid-nineteenth century could migrate in vast numbers to overseas territories (over 50 million Europeans migrated, mainly to North America, in the nineteenth century alone), relieving the social and political pressures of a swelling reserve army of labour and allowing real wages to rise within the metropolitan centres. Thus, the social and political strains set up by the cycle of dispossession, incomplete productive absorption, unemployment and social strife, were successfully externalized through such massive out-migration to the New World and elsewhere, where the emigrants displaced in turn local indigenous populations from their traditional resources. Further, the growth of metropolitan domestic manufacturing was far higher, and employment growth larger, than would have been the case if wide open, captive colonial markets had not been used to absorb these manufactures. Without this safety valve for the capitalist ruling classes, the nineteenth-century revolutionary workers' movements and uprisings in Western Europe might have developed further, and the direction of struggle might well have taken the political path envisaged by Marx. In the event, the working-class struggles in the advanced capitalist centres increasingly shifted to economic demands. The locus of revolutionary class struggle shifted East to more 'backward' societies, drawing strength from anti-imperialism, decolonization and the striving for a transition to a more egalitarian and democratic society. The new phase of accumulation dominated by finance from the last quarter of the twentieth century has been unleashing new contradictions and has seen a further shift of revolutionary struggles towards Latin America, in which the indigenous peoples comprising the most exploited classes have an increasing role to play.

9. Classical political economy

Hugh Goodacre

'Classical political economy' was Marx's term for the political-economic literature of the bourgeoisie during its rise to power, when it still had an interest in investigating 'the real relations of production in bourgeois society' (*Capital I*, ch. 1, footnote 33), as distinguished from its 'vulgar economics' once it had consolidated its position as the ruling class. The significance for Marx of classical political economy is that its discussions implicitly centre around the 'twofold nature of the labour contained in commodities', which he describes as 'the pivot on which a clear comprehension of political economy turns' (*Capital I*, ch. 1, section 2). Yet Marx claimed that 'I was the first to point out and to examine critically this twofold nature of the labour contained in commodities' (*Capital I*, ch. 1, section 2), for though this was the 'decisive outcome' of the research of these bourgeois writers, they had articulated it in a 'blurred and ambiguous' manner (*A Contribution to the Critique of Political Economy (CCPE)*, ch. 1, Note A) rather than 'expressly and with full consciousness' (*Capital I*, ch. 1, footnote 32).

The literature of classical political economy spans the period 'beginning with William Petty in Britain and Boisguillebert in France, and ending with Ricardo in Britain and Sismondi in France' (*CCPE*, ch. 1, Note A). This entry outlines some of the salient points in Marx's perspective on its achievements and limitations, and concludes with an account of its supersession by, on the one hand, 'vulgar economics' and, on the other, scientific socialism.

A CLASSICAL INQUIRY RESUMED

The beginnings of classical political economy were located by Marx in those writings which reflect the extension of bourgeois activity beyond the sphere of exchange and into the sphere of production. He cites, in this connection, William Petty (1623–1687), who argued that the value of a given quantity of corn is determined by the labour-time required for the production of a quantity of silver of equal value. This formulation clearly represents a substantial step towards the development of an objective theory of value based on the labour embodied in a commodity, but does not yet identify abstract social labour as the form of labour thus embodied, instead singling out 'the particular kind of concrete labour by which gold and silver is extracted' (*CCPE*, ch. 1, Note A). As Marx observes, Petty here reveals that he is still '[c]aught up in the ideas of the Monetary System', that is, the standpoint of the bourgeoisie when its activities had been confined to the sphere of exchange and their preoccupations consequently centred on amassing quantities of precious metals (*CCPE*, ch. 1, Note A).

France was a latecomer to the mercantile phase of capitalist development, and its government attempted to force its pace by protection of manufactures and restraints on agricultural trade. This antagonized the agricultural bourgeoisie, who were leading the introduction of capitalist relations of production. Reflecting their discontent, Pierre Le Pesant Boisguillebert (1640–1714) 'wages a fanatical struggle against money (*CCPE*, ch. 1, Note A). Unlike Petty, who 'acclaims the greed for gold as a vigorous force which spurs a nation to industrial progress and to the conquest of the world market', Boisguillebert associates money with the destructive greed of the French monarchical court, and holds that 'true value' is the value which correctly apportions the labours of producers between different branches of production. For Marx, this standpoint tacitly assumes that value is determined by labour-time, but once again fails to identify abstract general labour as its source, which it regards, instead, as 'the direct physical activity of individuals' (*CCPE*, ch. 1, Note A).

A further step was subsequently made by Benjamin Franklin (1706–1790) in a tract of 1729, in which, like Petty, he equates the labour-time required for the production of corn and silver, but goes on to observe that the money value thus conferred on the corn would need to be recalculated if 'nearer, more easy or plentiful mines' were discovered, whereby less labour-time is required for the extraction of the same amount of precious metal. Franklin was thus the first 'deliberately and clearly' to reduce exchange value to labour-time alone (*CCPE*, ch. 1, Note A; though Marx subsequently cited a passage in a work by Petty which appears to anticipate Franklin's formulation, *Theories of Surplus Value* (*TSV*), ch. IV).

These discussions were renewing an inquiry into the source of exchange value which had been launched two millennia earlier by Aristotle, that 'great thinker who was the first to analyse so many forms, whether of thought, society, or Nature, and amongst them also the form of value' (*Capital I*, ch. 1, section 3). Aristotle realized that the existence of a quantitative relation between two different commodities indicates that they share some kind of qualitative equality, but he was unable to identify the common, and thus commensurable, substance in which that equality lies. Marx's explanation for Aristotle's failure is that this problem cannot be solved 'until the notion of human equality has already acquired the fixity of a popular prejudice' (*Capital I*, ch. 1, section 3). The absence of such a conception of human equality in the slave society of ancient times prevented Aristotle from solving the problem; the initial emergence of such ideas in early modern times explains the progress made in that inquiry by writers such as Petty and Boisguillebert, just as the immature development and limited diffusion of those ideas in the European societies of their time explains the limited nature of their progress; and it is no coincidence that it was from America, with its 'lack of historical tradition', and consequently lighter burden of feudal ideas and institutions as compared with Europe, that Franklin articulated his precocious formulation of what Marx regarded as 'the basic law of modern political economy' (*CCPE*, ch. 1, Note A).

CLASSICAL POLITICAL ECONOMY COMES OF AGE

Writers of the later mercantilist period such as Petty had upheld the particular virtues of manufacture in increasing wealth. The contrasting standpoint of the agricultural bourgeoisie in France, already reflected in the writings of Boisguillebert, was now manifested in definitive form in the writings of the Physiocrats, who famously classified manufacturing as 'sterile' and identified as 'productive' only such labour as was united with the powers of nature. Marx regarded the Physiocrats as 'the true fathers of modern political economy', in that they were the first to establish the forms which capital assumes in circulation – fixed and circulating – as depicted in the *Tableau Économique* of François Quesnay (1694–1774) (*TSV*, ch. II). The weakness of their approach was that they addressed the question of value in a complex form – the circulation of surplus value – before having solved the prior question of the nature of value itself:

> Science, unlike other architects, builds not only castles in the air, but may construct separate habitable storeys of the building before laying the foundation stone. (*CCPE*, ch. 1, Note A)

Marx credits James Steuart (1712–1780) with being the first to identify the category of human labour in the abstract, in his statement that 'Labour . . . which through its alienation creates a universal equivalent, I call *industry*' (cited in *CCPE*, ch. 1, Note A). This formulation is exceptional in that it associates this abstract universal form of labour with a particular social form: his term 'industry' clearly denotes specifically capitalist production. For both in his native Scotland and while in exile in Continental Europe, Steuart had observed societies where the product of labour was still predominantly either consumed by the producer or appropriated as surplus in kind. He thus appreciated that the product was only stamped with the abstract and universal value form in capitalist society – conditions of 'industry'. Steuart realized, in short, that this form is not 'eternally fixed by Nature for every state of society' (*Capital I*, ch. 1, footnote 33).

In this respect, Adam Smith (1723–1790) took a step back from Steuart, representing the determination of exchange value by labour alone as only having pertained in primeval times before the emergence of classes. Once he comes to the analysis of more complex forms – capital, wages, profit, rent – he overlays that theory of value with another which contradicts it. With the development of class society, he argues, value came to be determined through the composition, or aggregation, of the 'natural' revenues of the landlord and the owner of 'stock' as well as the wage of the labourer. Smith continually confuses these two formulations of the source of value, which, as Marx points out, address two distinct issues, the labour embodied in the commodity and the value of labour power, or wage.

The 'immense advance' made by Smith (*CCPE*, 'Appendix 1: Introduction to a contribution to the critique of political economy'), in particular over the Physiocrats, is that he firmly establishes the idea that the value-creating properties of labour are universal to all labour as such, regardless of its sector or concrete purpose. This begs the question of what differentiates this universal property from the particular properties of concrete labour, and Smith 'tries to accomplish the transition' (*CCPE*, ch. 1, Note A) between the two forms by means of the division of labour. While this correctly directs the question into the field of social inquiry, Smith's answer reflects his failure to identify the universal, abstract form of labour as a feature of specifically capitalist production. As Marx comments, division of labour had, after all, been highly developed in other forms of society where commodity production was limited or even absent (*CCPE*, 'Appendix 1: Introduction to a contribution to the critique of political economy, Part I: Production,

consumption, distribution, exchange (circulation), 3. The method of political economy';
Capital I, ch. 1, section 2).

THE 'FINAL SHAPE' OF CLASSICAL POLITICAL ECONOMY

Marx regards Smith as a somewhat naïve thinker, constantly interweaving insights into
the real relations of production with superficial prejudices which flatly contradict them
(*TSV*, ch. III). In contrast, he credits David Ricardo (1772–1823) with a determined
attempt to sustain analytical consistency, founded on an unwavering commitment to the
idea that the mission of political economy is to show the way to the development of the
productive forces. Such consistency was, however, unachievable from within a bourgeois
perspective. With Ricardo, classical political economy 'reached the limits beyond which it
could not pass' (*Capital I*, 1873: Afterword to the Second German Edition).

Ricardo was so utterly 'encompassed by this bourgeois horizon' (*CCPE*, ch. 1, Note
A) that, unlike Smith, he displayed no interest or even awareness of any other socio-
economic system apart from capitalism. For example, whereas Smith had speculated on
the existence of a form of exchange among primitive hunters which differed from that
pertaining once classes emerged, for Ricardo, as Marx wryly observes, it is as though they
'calculate the value of their implements in accordance with the annuity tables used on the
London Stock Exchange in 1817' (CCPE). Ricardo was in this way even more extreme
than Smith in regarding the capitalist system and the form taken under it by exchange
value as 'eternal and natural'. The nature to which Ricardo appeals is, however, very different. For Smith, the existing order is 'natural' in the sense that, by distributing revenues
in their 'natural proportions', it provides all necessary conditions for social harmony and
stability, along with an increasing productivity which allows improvement in the condition of all social classes. For Ricardo, in contrast, the 'natural' condition of society is one
of endemic conflict of interest, in the course of which the proportions in which revenues
are distributed are subject to changes, and these changes threaten destabilization of
economy and society alike, with a universally favourable outcome far from assured.

Ricardo was a leading critic of tariffs on imported corn which, by keeping corn prices
high, were allowing an increasing proportion of the net product to be appropriated
as agricultural rent. He rejected the view that the resulting unproductive consumption of the landlords sustained demand, a view held by his friend Thomas Malthus
(1766–1834), regarded by Marx as a 'shameless sycophant' (*TSV*, ch. IX). For Ricardo,
it was the development of the productive forces which was all-important, and only the
accumulation of capital could ensure this.

The high price of corn – the principal wage good – meant upward pressure on wages,
leaving capital accumulation squeezed by a vicious spiral of rising wages and rent, with the
real prospect of a nightmare scenario, the 'stationary state', a concept which Smith had
contemplated from an Olympian perspective across the broad sweep of more than two millennia of world history, but which Ricardo now specified analytically and raised as an immediate and menacing threat. Nor was this the only element of concern regarding the changing
distributional shares. For now, with the progress of mechanization, issues of productivity
could no longer be subsumed into discussions of the division of labour in manufacture,
as they had been in Smith. Mechanization, argued Ricardo, threatened redundancy and

immiseration of the labouring population generally, a conclusion which he reached only late in life, and which, for Marx, 'bears witness to his *honesty*' (*TSV*, ch. XVIII).

Ricardo's commitment to the development of the productive forces involved relentless opposition to whatever stood in the way of capital accumulation. While sparing no punches in his criticism of the landlords for keeping corn prices high, he agreed with Malthus in opposing poor relief for those upon whom this inflicted hunger, as well as above-subsistence wages; he even endorsed Malthus's notorious attempt to associate the misery of the labouring population with its propensity to over-reproduction. Yet Marx criticizes 'sentimental opponents' of Ricardo, pointing out that he is philanthropic '[i]n so far as it does not involve *sinning* against his science'. Such is his unwavering commitment to the development of the productive forces, regardless of loyalties to persons, parties or classes, including even the bourgeoisie itself; for if the bourgeoisie comes into conflict with this goal, 'he is just as *ruthless* towards it as he is at other times towards the proletariat and the aristocracy' (*TSV*, ch. IX).

Ricardo, in short, 'consciously makes the antagonism of class interests, of wages and profits, of profits and rent, the starting point of his investigations, naïvely taking this antagonism for a social law of Nature' (*Capital I*, 1873: Afterword to the second German edition) – naïvely, because this antagonism could not, in reality, be resolved within the context of 'Nature' as Ricardo saw it, but, on the contrary, could only terminate in the overthrow of the capitalist mode of production itself:

> Classical Political Economy nearly touches the true relation of things, without, however, consciously formulating it. This it cannot, so long as it sticks in its bourgeois skin. (*Capital I*, ch. 19)

Writing in 1873, in the wake of the Paris Commune, Marx commented that Ricardo's unflinching acknowledgement of the instability of class relations under capitalism was only possible in a country such as England, where the class struggle was relatively weak. To raise so directly such probing questions in the more revolutionary conditions pertaining in France and other countries of Continental Europe would have led directly to the questioning of the very viability of the capitalist system itself. Indeed, even before Ricardo's writings had come to the attention of Marx and Engels, aspects of his thought had already been taken by radicals as 'a weapon of attack upon bourgeois economy' (*Capital I*, 1873: Afterword to the Second German Edition).

For such reasons, the entire tradition of English-language political economy was too much for one Continental (Swiss) writer, Jean Charles Sismondi (1773–1842), who, in explicit opposition to Ricardo, denounces large industrial capital. While thus standing in the tradition of the political economy developed in France by Boisguillebert and the Physiocrats, Sismondi at the same time foreshadowed the standpoint of peasant revolutionary movements such as the Narodniks in Russia. Marx acknowledged the value of Sismondi's observations on the ills accompanying industrial advance, but regarded the conclusions he drew from them as tantamount to a rejection of political economy as such, whose entire positive achievement had been, precisely, to bring ever closer to consciousness the true nature – and, with Ricardo, the direction of development – of the forces and relations of production (*CCPE*, 'Appendix 1: Introduction to a contribution to the critique of political economy, Part I: Production, consumption, distribution, exchange (circulation), 3. The method of political economy'; *Capital I*, ch. 16).

THE REPRESENTATION OF CAPITAL FROM CLASSICAL POLITICAL ECONOMY TO VULGAR ECONOMICS

'[T]he first interpreters of the modern world' were, in Marx's view, the proponents of the 'Monetary System', whose response to the growing force in society of capital, in the form of commercial capital, was to identify wealth with precious metals. Though disowned by bourgeois political economy, Marx sees their perspective as a 'historically valid' representation of capital given the sphere to which bourgeois activity was confined in their time (*CCPE*, ch. 2, 4, 'The precious metals', Note C). Indeed, they are 'misunderstood prophets' who prefigure the course of bourgeois political economy as a whole:

> As soon as the modern economists, who sneer at illusions of the Monetary System, deal with the more complex economic categories, such as capital, they display the same illusions. (*CCPE*, ch. 1)

Petty took a step forward in the representation of capital, his observations of society leading him to see the need to account for some kind of revenue-generating power in the hands of the wealthy, lying not only in precious metals but also in all kinds of other material wealth, though he left their revenue-generating power unexplained. With the further development of capitalist relations of production, however, this question could no longer be sidestepped, and Smith correctly narrowed the question down to property in means of production, that is, 'stock'. As the very term indicates, such a representation of capital has an inevitable bias towards 'physicalism', and yet Smith is continually confronted with the need to explore the social mechanisms through which the revenue-generating power associated with 'stock' is circulated and reproduced. This line of inquiry is further developed by Ricardo on the basis of his more dynamic conception of the surplus and its distribution.

This progression in the representation of capital in classical political economy, from the first beginnings of its break with the 'monetary system' to its 'final shape' in Ricardo, reflects what Marx identifies as its scientific aspect, an aspect which is, however, continually undermined and interrupted by attempts to legitimate the capitalist system. Marx referred to this latter aspect as 'apologetics', a term originally used for a branch of early Christian literature defending Christianity against other religions. In the generation following Ricardo, as the bourgeoisie consolidated its rule, the critical, or scientific, function, which its political economy had played in Ricardo's hands, soon began to lose out to its apologetic aspect. For example, John Ramsay McCulloch (1789–1864), commented Marx, adopted some of the language of Ricardo 'to give himself airs', while in effect depleting it of all critical content and making it acceptable to the ruling establishment (*TSV*, ch. XX, 4. McCulloch, b) Distortion of the Concept of Labour Through Its Extension to Processes of Nature. Confusion of Exchange-Value and Use-Value).

There was, however, a limit to the extent to which Ricardo's approach could be trimmed to suit the ideological requirements of an increasingly self-complacent bourgeoisie. Accordingly, from the emasculation of his ideas, bourgeois writers before long moved towards their repudiation and their eventual replacement in the 'marginalist revolution'. With William Stanley Jevons (1835–1882), Ricardo's concept of the determination of rent at the margin of cultivation was abstracted into a means of portraying all kinds of economic advantage as mathematical relations only, thus rendering economic analysis epistemologically incapable of the broader social inquiry into the nature of production relations characteristic of classical political economy. Now capital, no less than any other object of economic analysis, was represented as merely a quantitative, not a social, relation. Such was the nail which Jevons intended to be the final one in the coffin of what he termed the 'mazy and preposterous assumptions of the Ricardian school' (Jevons, 1871 [2001], p. xlv), by which he indicated the entire tradition of classical political economy.

Marx links his epitaph for the 'honesty' of classical political economy with his memorable characterization of the 'vulgar economics' which replaced it:

> [It] deals with appearances only, ruminates without ceasing on the materials long since provided by scientific economy, and there seeks plausible explanations of the most obtrusive phenomena, for bourgeois daily use, but for the rest, confines itself to systematising in a pedantic way, and proclaiming for everlasting truths, the trite ideas held by the self-complacent bourgeoisie with regard to their own world, to them the best of all possible worlds. (*Capital I*, ch. 1, footnote 33)

In short, mainstream economics as we know it today.

FROM CLASSICAL POLITICAL ECONOMY TO SCIENTIFIC SOCIALISM

If a single event may be taken as signalling the stage at which bourgeois political economy accomplished the transition from degeneration to freefall, then the publication of Jevons's *Theory of Political Economy* is surely as good as any, and the date on which he submitted the manuscript to his publisher, 28 March 1871, could not be more symbolic, for this was the very day that the Paris Commune was declared. By the time the book appeared in print, the Commune had been drowned in blood, but Marx could point to it as a harbinger of the coming proletarian revolution that would sweep away the bourgeois dictatorship whose unspeakable horrors he had chronicled in his *Capital*, and replace it with what he termed, characteristically uncompromising in his dialectical mode of expression, the 'dictatorship of the proletariat'.

Divested of its 'bourgeois skin', the scientific aspect of classical political economy could now be placed in the hands of a new readership – no longer the narrow circle of courtiers upon whom Petty 'fawned' and among whom he had circulated his self-serving 'old inferior editions' (*CCPE*, ch. 1, Note A, footnote 2), or the classically educated gentry with the leisure and education to appreciate the elaborate argumentation and florid prose of Smith's *Wealth of Nations*, or the earnest and anxious industrialist tentatively engaging in public life and willing to work through Ricardo's ponderous commercial arithmetic. For now, among the scattered and defeated, though unbowed, revolutionary ranks of communards and their equivalents in Europe and beyond, there arose a new readership identifying with the interests of the proletariat, and, moreover, with the dedication and determination to undertake the demanding task of taking on board the fruits of Marx's labours in *Capital* – a readership of a scale he had sought in vain for his earlier work of 1859, the *Contribution to the Critique of Political Economy*. Taken to its limits and exploding beyond, the scientific aspect of the rising bourgeoisie's classical political economy was now subsumed into a body of thought responding to the ideological requirements of the rising proletariat – scientific socialism.

10. Combined and uneven development

Sam Ashman

The difficulty in Marxist economics of writing about uneven development – as distinct from uneven and combined development, to which we turn shortly – is its omnipresence as a phenomenon. There is the unevenness of development between units of capital in a sector, between sectors, between and within regions of a country, and between and within nations and regions within the world economy as a whole. There is unevenness in profitability, in productivity, in compositions of capital, between departments of production, between circuits and fractions of capital. There is unevenness in the development of the forces and relations of production. Where does one stop? Clearly differential growth, and its connection with the development of the forces of production, within the context of a world economy, is a key component of unevenness within Marxist political economy.

The origins of the creation of systematic uneven development across global capitalism lie in the process of primitive accumulation and the creation of the two poles of the capital relation: the separation of the direct producers from the means of production through extra-economic coercion and the concentration of the means of production in fewer hands. In Marx's analysis, this entails the colonial extraction of wealth and surplus, the sum of which acts as capital, with the role played by the state and by finance central to these processes. Those areas of the world economy from where wealth is extracted are impoverished and less likely to develop their own autonomous accumulation process.

But the original accumulation is not a contingent source of industrial profit. Once Britain had established wage labour and begins capitalist manufacturing, it goes through a long period where absolute surplus value extraction persists with relatively low levels of productivity. The competitive stimulus to change pre-capitalist modes of production is relatively limited as a consequence. Manufacture is a transitional stage to the introduction of machinery. Societies where it develops become subject to new laws of motion and frequent cycles of accumulation – though depending on the weight of capital within any particular state. In Britain's case, not until the Factory Acts is capital forced systematically to pursue relative surplus value extraction, and competition then propels the transition to machinofacture and the real subsumption of labour to capital. This develops within some sectors of capital faster than others but, once established, the fate of pre-capitalist societies is sealed.

The industrialized pull further ahead due to systematic increases in productivity, and the competitive stimulus to change felt through the world market increases. Many societies in 'the periphery' become locked into a global division of labour as primary exporters to the colonial world, with direct producers remaining more closely tied to the land. Technological gaps and shortage of surplus for accumulation provide obstacles to the development of capitalism and to the transition from the formal to the real subsumption of labour to capital. Within industrial capitalism, tendencies towards the concentration and centralization of capital develop as the competitive introduction of new technology is dependent upon a certain level of investment, and increasing labour productivity and wages. The world market connects together commodity producers through competitive accumulation but the latter's global impact, as opposed to plunder, is limited at the origins of capitalism because of reliance on production of absolute surplus value. Industrial capitalism transforms world development further, but the competitive success of some comes at the expense of others, be they capitals, states or regions.

The key argument to be drawn from Marx, then, is that unevenness in levels of development is a systematic, not contingent, aspect of capitalist development. Indeed, the outcome of accumulation is unevenness and not the levelling of development. This is a clear feature of Marx's analysis of capitalism even though the term is not used widely by Marx, nor theorized systematically by him, and his ideas on the subject evolved over time. In later Marxist political economy, uneven development has come to refer to the processes by which capitalism transforms the world but does so through developing the forces of production in some areas but – and as part of the same process – restricting or distorting their development elsewhere. This approach in different theoretical ways has emphasized polarization and not convergence. Such an approach is in sharp contrast to standard neoclassical trade and growth theory which predicts eventual income convergence and perceives uneven development as a more or less temporary departure from 'normal' economic development.

One feature of uneven development is that those outside the heartlands of industrialization develop consciousness of their own backwardness and develop what Gerschenkron (1962) would later call 'ideologies of delayed industrialisations'. Such was the case in Russia at the end of the nineteenth century where there was widespread discussion of uneven development within the socialist movement. It featured in Lenin's analysis of imperialism and of the development of capitalism in Russia. Kautsky pointed to the impact of foreign investment on backward societies, and there were anticipations of the idea of combined and uneven development in Plekhanov, Ryazanov and Tugan-Baranovsky. The term combined and uneven development was coined by Parvus, but is now most closely associated with Trotsky who systematized the theory of permanent revolution and within it the concept of uneven and combined development – a deceptively simple sounding synthesis of a radical departure from the orthodox Marxist thinking of the time. Trotsky's ideas were initially formulated in the years 1904–06, with specific reference to Russia, but were later developed and applied more generally to societies where the transition to capitalism takes place in the context of, and hastened by, the presence of the world capitalist economy.

TROTSKY'S CONTRIBUTION

It is useful to situate Trotsky's contribution in the context of his critique of two alternative conceptions of socio-economic development prevalent in Russia and the political strategies which ensued from them. The first was that of the Narodniks who argued that capitalism could not develop Russia and who argued therefore that Russian peasant communes could form the basis of a socialist economy. The second was that of the

Mensheviks (and the Second International) who argued that Russia must follow the same path of capitalist development as Western Europe and the United States, developing 'fully' capitalist relations of production, before the transition to socialism could be achieved. On this debate Vera Zasulich sought the guidance of Marx, two years before his death, and to whom Marx drafted five replies. Trotsky rejected both of these approaches, arguing that Russia at the start of the twentieth century was simultaneously backward and advanced, combining low productivity peasant production with the most advanced forms of capitalist enterprise. The specific constellation of class forces in Russia meant that the working class was capable both of leading the democratic struggle against Absolutism but also of achieving socialism in a backward country as long as revolution spread internationally. In this way Russian workers would make the revolution 'permanent', an echo of Marx's writings on the 1848 revolution in France.

Trotsky contrasts the development of capitalism in Russia with that of Western Europe. The development of the forces of production in Russia was slow even by the standards set by feudal development, in part because of natural conditions – Russia's geographical situation, its short summer and long winter, the sparse population in vast areas of the country. Nevertheless from the end of the seventeenth century, Peter the Great succeeded in the military modernization of Russia, the forging of an Absolutist state and the establishment of the Russian Empire. This was financed by major increases in taxation which squeezed serfs harder rather than by any reorganization of the countryside. Handicraft production remained tied to agriculture and rurally based, unlike in medieval Europe where craft production developed in urban centres which steadily grew in size. In contrast with Western Europe, Russia's towns were not productive units but centres of military and administrative life, of consumption and not of production. That capitalism in Russia did not develop out of the handicraft system was an important determinant of the class structure and the class nature of both city and countryside. The weakness of the cities meant there was a lack of a counter force to the state which held back a reformation of the church. Whilst there was the same play of social forces, the state was stronger in Russia than in Western Europe relative to the nobility and the clergy, with a strong sense of its own interests.

But Russia's development was not according to its 'inner tendencies' alone (Trotsky, *The Permanent Revolution (PR)*, ch.1). Particularly following the eventual abolition of serfdom in 1861, the Russian state embarked on a rapid modernization programme, and capitalism 'seemed to be an offspring of the State' (Trotsky, *PR*, ch.1). The state accumulated debt in order to provide subsidies and protection for a variety of industries, and so state credit, the currency and industry developed simultaneously. The process was contradictory, with the telegraph and the railways in part introduced for military purposes, and high duties on cotton often driven more by fiscal pressures than by a desire to develop the industry. Nevertheless, the autocracy succeeded in 'transplanting the factory system of production on to Russian soil' (Trotsky, *PR*, ch.1) and 'Europeanization' became the demand of the progressive nobility and aristocratic intelligentsia (Trotsky, (*HRR*), vol. 1, ch.1: *The History of the Russian Revolution* 'Peculiarities of Russia's development'). Landlords who owned factories favoured wage labour and the greater export of Russian grain.

This economic modernization was increasingly forced by what Trotsky called the 'mighty and independent reality which has been created by the international division of labor and the world market', the 'supra-national character of modern productive forces' and the general tendency of capitalist development 'toward a colossal growth of world ties' through foreign trade and capital export (Trotsky, *PR*: Introduction to the German Edition). National capitalisms turn increasingly to the reserves of the world market for development. However this does not erase national differences. Trotsky describes 'national peculiarities' as representing 'an original combination of the basic features of the world process' (Trotsky, *PR*: Introduction to the German Edition). Nonetheless, '[t]he basic criterion of the economic level of a nation is the productivity of labour, which in its turn depends upon the relative weight of the industries in the general economy' (Trotsky, *HRR*, vol.1, ch.1: 'Peculiarities of Russia's development'). Russian industry arises late and does not repeat the pattern of development elsewhere – it adopts the achievements of its forebears, even outstrips them, especially in terms of size of units of production.

European finance plays a central role in Russia's development in two ways. First, in loans made to the state which then lead European financiers, whilst supporting bourgeois democracy in Europe, to support Absolutism's survival as it is the only force in Russia which can guarantee their rate of interest. Second, European capital, in the form of large shareholding companies, provides funding for industry, attracted by Russia's natural resources and its hitherto unorganized labour power. Heavy industry (metal, coal, oil) especially 'was almost wholly under the control of foreign finance capital, which had created for itself an auxiliary and intermediate system of banks in Russia' (Trotsky, *HRR*, vol.1, ch.1: 'Peculiarities of Russia's development'). Light industry was following the same path, and Trotsky argues that about 40 per cent of the stock of capital in Russia was foreign-owned, with that figure higher in leading sectors of industry. English, French and Belgian capital was almost twice that of German. Foreign finance subjected industry to the banks, and to the 'western European money market' (Trotsky, *HRR*, vol.1, ch.1: 'Peculiarities of Russia's development').

The nature of capitalism in Russia is thus a consequence of the interaction of the internal development of production and the state with the external stimulis provided by capital from abroad, both financial and industrial. The peasantry is a reserve army of labour, 'a tributary of the Stock Exchanges of the world' (Trotsky, *PR*, ch. 2), pauperized and proletarianized through heavy taxation as a result of the borrowing by the Absolutist state, the greater part of which was not used for productive investment but sent abroad in the form of interest payments which 'enriched and strengthened the financial aristocracy of Europe' (Trotsky, *PR*, ch. 2). But capital recirculated and returned to Russia in the form of productive investment. So Russian industry arises late, is kick-started by the Absolutist state, but is highly concentrated with a predominance of foreign capital whose investment produces rapid urbanization and large concentrations of workers in cities, transforming Russian towns into centres of commerce and industrial life by the end of the nineteenth century. Russian industry does not compete with urban crafts, only village handicrafts. And large-scale capitalist industry halts the development of town handicrafts, forcing Russia to skip a 'stage' of development previously undergone in Western Europe. At the same time, these external forces are economically dynamic but politically distant, producing a bourgeoisie that is weak, 'half-foreign' and 'without historical traditions' (Trotsky, *PR*, ch. 2), incapable of successfully leading the fight against Absolutist rule.

Trotsky not only draws strategic but also theoretical lessons from his analysis of the specificities of Russia's transition to capitalism. The transition there is very different from

Western Europe because of the backward nature of Russian feudalism but also because of the effect of the pre-existing transitions in Western Europe which speed up the process in Russia but also change its form. Trotsky quotes Marx that '[t]he industrially more developed country shows the less developed only the image of its own future' (Trotsky, *HRR*, p. 1219). But then he takes issue with Marx as methodologically this statement does not start 'from world economy as a whole' (Trotsky, *HRR*, vol. 3, 'Appendix II: Socialism in a separate country') but 'from the single capitalist country as a type' and also because Marx's ('conditional') statement becomes less true as capitalism develops. 'England in her day revealed the future of France, considerably less of Germany, but not in the least of Russia and not of India' (Trotsky, *HRR*, vol. 3, 'Appendix II: Socialism in a separate country'). The possibility of skipping stages is not limitless, but:

> repetition of the forms of development by different nations is ruled out. Although compelled to follow after the advanced countries, a backward country does not take things in the same order. The privilege of historic backwardness – and such a privilege exists – permits, or rather compels, the adoption of whatever is ready in advance of any specified date, skipping a whole series of intermediate stages. Savages throw away their bows and arrows for rifles all at once, without travelling the road which lay between those two weapons in the past. (Trotsky, *HRR*, vol.1, ch.1: 'Peculiarities of Russia's development')

History does not produce a series of exact copy-cat transformations, transitions or catch up but 'a drawing together of the different stages of the journey, a combining of the separate steps, an amalgam of archaic with more contemporary forms' (Trotsky, *HRR*, vol.1, ch.1: 'Peculiarities of Russia's development').

MAJOR DEVELOPMENTS AND APPLICATIONS

Harvard-based economic historian Alexander Gerschenkron is probably the most prominent scholar to have been influenced by Trotsky's approach, though this influence remained unacknowledged. Gerschenkron (1962) stressed 'the advantages of backwardness' in (European) economic development, and the possibility of skipping stages, in his critique of Rostow. Industrialization in Britain posed both an economic and a military threat to both Germany and Russia who both directly adopted the most modern and efficient techniques, utilized large-scale production and emphasized producer goods relative to consumer goods. Different institutional patterns across Europe, particularly with regard to finance, were a consequence of catch-up strategies. In Britain, the accumulated wealth of private capital was a major source of finance, and individual capitalists played a major role in the industrialization process. But British capital did not face major international competition (and there was less emphasis on increasing capital-output ratios during the first industrial revolution). In Germany, 'universal banks' played a major role in financing industrialization and in Russia the state directly mobilized financial resources to create new industries. The different strategies and institutions adopted by latecomers were 'substitutes' for the lack of the 'prerequisites' of development – capital, technology, the necessary financial intermediaries – which forerunners possessed. Gerschenkron argues that a large range of possible substitution patterns exists and also that substitutes may or may not emerge. Backwardness is then defined 'in terms of absence, in a more backward country, of factors which in a more advanced country served as prerequisites of industrial development'. The question to be posed is what 'patterns of substitutions for the lacking factors occurred in the process of industrialisation in conditions of backwardness' (Gerschenkron, 1962, p. 46). To the extent that capital can be imported from abroad, it reduces the necessity for previously accumulated wealth or for original accumulation.

Within Marxism, Ernest Mandel (1970) emphasized 'the laws of uneven development', arguing that combined and uneven development remained relevant in the context of a developed world market because, as exploitation becomes universal, it does not become homogeneous. There is a much neglected application of Trotsky's ideas in Ken Post's 1978 study of Jamaica; the politics of permanent revolution (and surprisingly little about combined and uneven development) are addressed in Löwy (2010); and uneven and combined development has been explained in terms of the articulation of modes of production (Wolpe, 1980). Unsurprisingly, these ideas have not solicited attention within the discipline of economics, though Trotsky's ideas are of particular relevance to the classical debates in development economics. Uneven development has received greater attention in other disciplines such as geography (Harvey, 1996; Smith, 2008), and Trotsky's notion has provoked recent debate in the field of International Relations about the extent to which it assists Marxists to address whether the plurality of states within global capitalism is a necessary or a contingent feature of global development (Anievas, 2010).

The experience of the world economy since the post-war boom has undoubtedly been one of sharp divergence, not convergence, particularly within the developing world. The experience of Africa and much of Asia is in stark contrast with the East Asian newly industrializing countries (NICs) and, more recently, with that of China's historic development – and with it the subordination of hundreds of millions to the logic of global competition. The distribution of unevenness – and the relative power of states – changes with the dynamic growth of capitalism. But neoliberal globalization has produced neither convergence nor catch-up. Developed capitalist economies continue to take over 67 per cent of global flows of foreign direct investment (FDI). China, together with Hong Kong, receives one third of all the inward FDI held by developing countries. The three major global centres of capital accumulation have extended regionally: the United States into Mexico; Europe into Central and Eastern Europe, Turkey and parts of the Maghreb; and Japan into the rest of East Asia and China. This has not only extended production networks but also established larger regional reserve armies of labour. Today's differences in global per capita income are historically unprecedented, with growth accentuating inequality within as well as between countries and regions, and so giving rise to combined and uneven development within nations as well as at the level of the world economy. The division between the developed and the underdeveloped is not fixed or immutable, and the shifting and changing centres of accumulation in the world economy allow for some to develop. But not all can, as the competitive success of a sector or a country comes at the expense of another. And if not all can succeed, convergence is not possible. To explain who does, and who does not, is contingent upon global and national factors but must involve analysis of the role of the state and of finance and the more general balance of class forces and conflict. Combined and uneven development remains, therefore, of relevance for understanding world development, from the early transitions to capitalism to the present day.

11. Commodification and commodity fetishism

Robert Albritton

For Marx, the commodity presents itself in its clearest and most developed form as the product of a factory-like capitalist production process. In this, units of privately owned and controlled capital exploit wage labour to maximize profits. The result is competition with the most profitable units of capital surviving and expanding and the least profitable shrinking and going under. But the commodity is not simply a material input or output of a capitalist production process, it is also a 'social form'. As such, it has a flexibility that enables it to subsume economic relations that cannot be produced as outputs of a capitalist production process. The two most important of these are labour power, which is subsumed to the commodity-form within the labour market, and land (under this category Marx includes all natural resources), which also cannot be capitalistically produced and yet is subsumed in the land market.

COMMODIFICATION

Marx's notion of the 'commodity-form' is crucial in understanding how things that are not capitalistically produced can become commodified by being subsumed under the commodity-form. As a socially constructed form, the commodity lends itself to degrees of institutionalization. Total commodification implies an economy of self-regulating markets, a state of affairs that never exists in history, but which can be constructed in theory. Other social forms such as family forms or political forms lack an internal logic propelling them towards a completion, whereas basic capitalist commodity-economic forms can be thought in their interconnection as a logic that is dynamic and directional. Total commodification implies that all the basic economic variables of capitalism become subsumed to capital's inner commodity-economic logic. This is possible because abstract theory can identify and complete in theory real socio-historical tendencies towards commodification.

Marx never used the term 'commodification', but his entire theory invites its use. The term expresses well the process of something moving towards becoming a commodity by degree, and Marx is acutely aware of the violent struggles behind the creation of private property in land and the production of food as the commodification of the reproduction of life itself proceeds as a precondition for the emergence of capitalism and as its continuing result. Further, while the primary aim of Marx's *Capital* is to trace out the inner logic of capital on the assumption that commodification is complete, he also lets us know that in no actual economy has commodification ever been complete. For example, it is hard to imagine a farm run exactly the same as a capitalist factory (though strong tendencies in this direction now exist with certain types of farms).

Complete commodification would imply a totally laissez-faire state, no trade unions, no oligopoly, and competitive economic sectors throughout. Marx is well aware that no such complete commodification could ever exist, and yet by observing the increasing commodification in history and extending it to completion in theory, we can arrive at an accurate picture of capitalism's inner workings without distortions caused by outside interventions of extra-economic forces.

Marx's theory of capital's deep structural dynamics means that in principle his theory should serve as the basis for all other economic theorizing of capitalism. His abstract theory of complete commodification can be used as a basis for sorting out issues of structure versus agency at more concrete levels of analysis. At more concrete levels, the basic social relations of capital are not fully reified; hence, agency can be theorized in its connection with structure and the value relations of capital can be theorized as they intermingle with relatively autonomous political, ideological and non-capitalist economic practices.

Marx's approach to economic theory invites us to think in these terms, terms that have the potential to develop non-reductionist connections between theory and history and between the economic and non-economic. In this way Marx avoids the extreme formalism, reductionism and market fundamentalism so prevalent in mainstream economic theory. Mainstream economics assumes that actual economies are so close to being totally commodified that abstract theory can be applied directly to them. This economic reductionism is not only fostered by the basic assumptions of mainstream economic theory, but also by the very organization of academic disciplines that tends towards thinking the economic in isolation from other dimensions of social life.

Nearly every mainstream thinker in the history of economic high theory ignores the fact that the commodity form is a social construction – a social form that is often the object of intense struggle. Marx (*Capital I*, ch. 27), for example, discusses the enclosure movement in England that succeeded in converting the enormous amount of land held in common into private property. These enclosures were often met with ferocious resistance on the part of the common people.

Marx demonstrates that some things are more difficult to subsume to the commodity form than others. The reason that in practice a completely commodified labour market is impossible is that as free humans, workers will always organize to resist being reduced to one more commodity input. This empirical fact however, does not prevent us from thinking of labour as totally commodified in theory. It does alert us, however, to be particularly aware of extra-economic supports needed to maintain the degree of commodification that does exist at more concrete levels of analysis.

Throughout the three volumes of *Capital* Marx mentions other economic categories that also pose particular problems for commodification. One of the most important of these is money, because it has never been the case that the international monetary system has been completely regulated by the gold standard (where paper money is always directly convertible into the commodity gold, as we must assume it would be in a fully commodified society). Today not only is the international monetary system intertwined with the international financial system, but also both tend to combine commodity-economic (market) regulation with political regulation. Further, national money supplies tend to be state regulated in response to both domestic and international economic and political pressures. Here again it is important to have the theoretical means to move from fully commodified money at the level of capital's deep structure, to historically specific arrangements with political supports.

Fixed capital, or capital such as machinery that lasts through many circuits of capital, poses special problems for an economy that is striving to be purely governed by self-regulating markets. Often in history capital will forego investing in much more productive new plant and equipment because it is so costly. Thus, for example, because the Japanese steel industry was destroyed in World War II, it made sense for it to retool with the latest most productive technology, while for the most part the USA continued to try to compete with its older less efficient technology. At the level of abstract theory, Marx solves this problem by connecting the replacement of fixed capital with periodic crises, such that the devaluation of capital in the trough of a depression encourages centralization and makes it cheaper to invest in new more productive means of production. Finally, Marx (*Capital II*, ch. 5) refers to a number of specific commodities, which, because of their particular use-values (material, qualitative properties), are difficult to manage purely as commodities. For example, commodities that spoil quickly will be limited to local markets unless technologies of preservation and transportation can expand their range. Typically it takes four days or less for bananas to move from trees located in the tropics to supermarket shelves in North America or Europe. If it took much longer, the market for bananas would be more spatially limited.

Commodities that are extremely costly and that will only return a profit after many years, and hence bear the risk of not returning a profit at all, also present problems. Marx (*Capital II*, ch. 13) mentions the planting of trees to produce lumber as an example. Today, it would include many infrastructural projects such as the tunnel under the English Channel. An even clearer case would be the American space programme, which may never generate profits that exceed costs.

All of the above examples demonstrate the need for economic theory to be able to think clearly about degrees of commodification, often supported by relatively autonomous non-economic practices or non-capitalist economic practices that intervene from the outside into markets and the movement of commodities.

COMMODITY FETISHISM

Lacking a theory of commodification, mainstream economists are likely to fall for the mystifications generated by assuming that complete commodification is simply a natural fact, and it is at this point that commodity fetishism emerges. When this is assumed, social relations, being totally swallowed up by the commodity, magically disappear. In its simplest meaning 'commodity fetishism' refers to a social situation in which people relate socially to each other not directly, but through the mediation of things (money and commodities). A social market connection between commodities and money generates prices, and it is as if prices tell humans what to do in so far as they are economic beings. In other words, ultimately things with price tags order the economic behaviour of humans, even as humans would prefer to think of themselves in charge.

Mainstream economists take complete commodification as given. In sharp contrast, a Marxian economic theory might approach commodification as *the* central problem or question that economic theory needs to deal with. The unquestioning approach of mainstream economists to commodification enables them to think in quantitative terms without any means to theorize the emergence of agency. For them only ad hoc thinking can connect capitalist economic practices to non-capitalist ones, political and ideological practices to economic, or theory to history. In short, they not only ignore the continual historical struggles around the degree of commodification, but also the social life cycles of particular commodities as they are interwoven with social relations in particular historical contexts. This makes it possible for mainstream economists to read a false automaticity into markets, an automaticity that they wrongly believe optimizes economic life.

Marx utilizes the concept 'fetishism of commodities' throughout his economic writings to critique the misunderstandings and mystifications of even the best economic theorists of his day (Smith and Ricardo), whose mistakes stem largely from their failure to understand fully that the commodity is a socio-economic-historical form. Or, in other words, they have no way of thinking about degrees of commodification, or of the capital/labour relation as an historical process that exists to varying degrees and is generally supported or opposed by forms of human agency that are not necessarily purely economic.

Often discussions of Marx's concept 'fetishism of commodities' focuses on *Capital I*, ch. 1, section 4: 'The fetishism of commodities and the secret thereof'. While this section introduces the concept, it is either explicitly utilized or implied throughout Marx's economic writings. The fullest discussion of it occurs at the end of *Capital III* in Part 7, entitled: 'Revenues and their sources'. It is here, at the end of the theory, that the fullest summary of the misconceptions stemming from fetishism are discussed. In the Addenda to Part III of *Theories of Surplus Value*, Marx writes: 'The form of revenue and the sources of revenue are the *most fetishistic* expression of the relations of capitalist production. It is their form of existence as it appears on the surface, divorced from the hidden connections and the intermediate connecting links. Thus the *land* becomes the source of *rent, capital* the source of *profit*, and *labour* the source of *wages*.' On the contrary, Marx makes it clear that wages are a portion of the total value created by labour, and profit and rent are simply portions of surplus value, also created by labour.

Marx goes on to claim that while Smith and Ricardo avoid the most vulgar forms of fetishism, they still remain trapped in some of its basic forms. He writes: 'Ganilh is quite right when he says of Ricardo and most economists that they consider labour without exchange, although their system, like the whole bourgeois system, rests on exchange-value. This however is only due to the fact that to them the *form* of product as commodity seems self-evident, and consequently they examine only the *magnitude of value*' (*Theories of Surplus Value*, Part I, ch. 4).

In order to be as clear as possible about fetishism, it is useful to consider the category 'interest', which Marx considered the most fetishized economic concept. Interest can be schematized by the formula M—M', or, in other words money [M] is lent out for a length of time [—], only to be returned with interest added [M']. According to Marx (*Capital III*, ch. 23), this is the most fetishized form of the commodity because money, which, as pure quantity, already seems divorced from the commodity-form, yet as interest seems to magically enlarge itself over time without reference to any social form whatsoever.

Marx demonstrates that if we peel back the layers of this most superficial and externalized form, we eventually get to total homogenized and commodified labour power creating total commodity value. Interest turns out to be a portion of total profit, total profit turns out to be a transformed form of total surplus value, and total surplus value is the difference between the total value of labour power and the total value created by that labour power. Thus, the inner core of capitalism is a social relationship of exploitation between capital and labour, in which collective homogeneous labour power creates more value than it receives back in the form of the total wage. In contrast, if we remain with the form of interest, we never look beyond quantities that appear in the market, for even profit can be subsumed to interest as simply the interest received by a particular type of capital, industrial capital. If we follow this line of reasoning, all profit springs full-blown from the head of capital (Marx, *Capital III*, ch. 48).

Profit expressed in the most basic form of capital as M—C—M′ (M buys commodity C and sells it for more money M′ or buying cheap and selling dear), at least suggests the possibility of searching for a C that has the power to expand value. For the basic formula, considered in itself, suggests that profits come from some group being in a position to force the rest of society to accept being systematically overcharged. But what Marx is theorizing at this level of analysis is a commodity-economic logic. It follows that the use of extra-economic force in the form of monopoly or state intervention can only be considered at more concrete levels of analysis.

To make sense of this formula, C must be expanded into a labour and production process in which labour power and means of production are combined into a production process that produces a new commodity with greater value than the inputs. According to Marx, 'as the form of profit hides its inner core, capital more and more acquires a material form, is transformed more and more from a relationship into a thing, but a thing which embodies, which has absorbed, the social relationship, a thing which has acquired a fictitious life and independent existence in relation to itself, a natural-supernatural entity' (*Theories of Surplus Value*, Addenda to Part III). A natural-supernatural entity is precisely what a fetish is. Capital appears to be a 'natural' thing, and at the same time it appears to have the 'supernatural' powers of expanding itself while reproducing economic life.

Similarly, it is a mistake to think of a material thing, the earth, as a creator of value. As Marx puts it: 'Land, e.g., takes part as an agent of production in creating a use-value, a material product, wheat. But it has nothing to do with the production of the *value of wheat*. In so far as value is represented by wheat, the latter is merely considered as a definite quantity of materialised social labour, regardless of the particular substance in which this labour is manifested or of the particular use-value of this substance' (*Capital III*, ch. 48). As a part of homogeneous labour utilized by homogeneous capital, agricultural labour will produce, for example, the same amount of value in the same amount of time as any other labour. Once we drop the assumption of homogeneous capital, even the agricultural capital engaged on the most fertile land will tend to yield an average profit, since the surplus profit will be converted into rent pocketed by the landlord. The point is that 'rent' is not simply a quantified thing, but is a social relation in which surplus profit is converted into rent by landlords. Of course, if the connection between the surplus profit and surplus value is ignored, then the social relation between landlords, capitalists and workers can also be ignored. What Marx (*Capital III*, ch. 48) makes clear is that capitalist rent is a specific social relation between capitalists, landlords and workers.

If the wages of labour are viewed as simply the revenue received by a particular factor of production, '[c]apital thus becomes a very mystic being since all of labour's social productive forces appear to be due to capital' (*Capital III*, ch. 48). To cut through this mystification, Marx provides a clear conception of surplus value as the difference between total value created by homogenous labour and the total value of labour power, a conception that grounds class exploitation at the most fundamental level of capital's inner logic.

'Commodity fetishism' helps us keep in mind that when commodification is assumed to be total or complete, the social relations of capitalist production can magically disappear into the commodity-form and what is struggle at the level of history can disappear into the structural concepts of economic theory. In order to combat this we need both a theory of capital's inner logic that can clearly theorize that logic precisely because it assumes totally commodified social relations, and, at the same time, theories that make connections between the theory of capital's inner logic and historical capitalism where there is always specific contention over degrees of commodification. At the level of history but not at the level of abstract theory, both partially commodified social relations and those social relations that act to support the existing degree of commodification need to be fully considered. Since mainstream economists do not see complete commodification as an absorption of social relations, they have no way of thinking the re-emegence of social relations from the commodity-form when commodification is less than complete. Arguably it is this, more than anything else that puts Marx head and shoulders above mainstream economists, and opens the door to exploring mediation between capital's inner logic and history.

12. Competition*

Paresh Chattopadhyay

'Competition of capitals' is one of the areas in Marx's (1972, p. 114) *Critique* which illustrates his '*scientific* attempt towards revolutionising science'. On the basis of his 'completely transformed character of economic science' (Korsch, 1972, p. 93), Marx's analysis of competition was built as a critique of the bourgeois (mainly classical) political economy, against the positions of Smith and Ricardo in particular.

CRITIQUE OF CLASSICAL POLITICAL ECONOMY

Competition of capitals in Marx is very different from competition in bourgeois political economy, which is traditionally associated with the idea that the more the capitals in competition in exchange the more competitive is the economy. For classical political economy, value arose out of natural conditions of production, with competition ensuring greater or lesser conformity of market price to value. Indeed, for classical political economy, 'competition just meant the absence of monopoly and of public pricing' (Schumpeter, 1954, p. 545). Precisely because competition of capitals arose historically in opposition to the monopolies, guilds and regulations associated with pre-capitalist modes of production, the classics conceived of competition purely as a negation to such conditions, as epitomized in the famous Physiocratic slogan 'laissez-faire, laissez-passer'. In this sense, competition between a greater number of producers, consumers and workers ensures more efficient market outcomes, and a more efficient economy more generally. This is, in effect, a 'quantity theory of competition', a phrase coined by Weeks (2010).

Marx rejects the classics' negative approach to competition since it derives from a pre-capitalist historical form, which no longer prevails. More generally, their approach to competition is ahistorical – it has no connection to capital as a historically specific social relation, nor to capitalism as a mode of production – and it is unrelated to Marx's systematic reconstruction of capitalist production relations. In contrast, Marx's analysis of competition of capitals belongs specifically to the capitalist mode of production and not to a generalized, ahistorical notion of competition within generalized market exchange alone. Hence, for Marx (1953, pp. 542–3), competition 'is the free development of the mode of production based on capital'.

Thus, a crucial point in Marx's critique of the classical (quantitative and exchange-related) theory of competition concerns the absence in this theory (with the exception of the Physiocrats) of the idea of capital as a 'social totality' apart from individual capitals (see Marx, 1956, pp. 306–7 on the much admired Quesnay). This idea is absent in Smith

---

* The references in this entry include the author's own translations from the original.

and Ricardo who, under the spell of the '18th century illusion of robinsonade, namely the singular and sigularised hunter and fisher' (Marx, 1953, p. 5), considered society as a collection of individuals undetermined by the social totality. In contrast, Marx emphasizes individual capitals' dependence on social total capital (whose 'fragments' they are) simultaneously with their 'indifference to one another and independence from one another' (Marx, 1953, p. 323). As Rosa Luxemburg (1966, p. 436) wrote, 'Marx, for the first time, has brought out with classic clarity the fundamental distinction between individual capital and social total capital in their movements.'

COMPETITION FOR MARX

Competition of capitals, in Marx's sense, is the interaction of many capitals, or the 'relation of capital to itself as another capital' (Marx, 1953, p. 543). In other words, Marx recognizes that individual capitals can compete on the product market only on the basis of the prior commodification of labour power, and the existence of a 'free' class of wage workers who can, in principle, be employed by any capital. Competition between capitals is predicated upon their ability to recruit workers competing for jobs as a condition of survival. At a more concrete level, the necessity of realizing surplus value in capital's circulation process, after it has been created in production, gives rise to competition in exchange. For Marx, the logical foundation as well as the historical basis for competition between individual capitals in exchange (as fractions, or instances, of capital in general) is the class relation of capitalists as a whole with the 'free' wage workers as a whole (also as a class). Their relationship plays itself out primarily in the sphere of production.

Competition of capitals in exchange is, therefore, the necessary expression of the 'limitless urge of capital to increase surplus value', to create the 'biggest possible surplus of labour time over the time necessary for the reproduction of wage' (Marx, 1976, p. 158). The tendency of capital, as it creates surplus value, to 'go beyond all proportions' and to 'increase productive forces beyond measure' (Marx, 1953, pp. 316, 325) underpins competition, and operates as a constraint on each individual capital in relation to others; it may also give rise to crises.

Capital's essential reality is that it is a social totality based on class relations between capital and labour, from which the nature of competition cannot be legitimately abstracted. Competition of capitals is, then, the 'realisation of the immanent laws of capital, that is, of capitalist production in which each capital appears against the other as bailiff (*Gerichtsvollzieher*)' (Marx, 1980, p. 1630). By the same token, 'free competition imposes on the capitalist the immanent laws of capitalist production as external coercive laws' (Marx, 1987, pp. 273, 314–15). It is 'absurd' to imagine a 'universal capital which would not find itself confronting other capitals to realise exchanges' (Marx, 1953, p. 324). Yet, in the market as presumed sole agent of competition, this foundation escapes our everyday observation. We see only the fractions of this totality – individual capitals competing with one another. As Marx underlines, the 'concrete forms' in which the 'different (individual) capitals confront one another on the surface of society' arise from the 'movements of capital considered as a totality'. Each singular capital forms 'a fragment of the total social capital just as each individual capitalist is only an element of the capitalist class', and the movement of the social capital consists of the totality of movements of all of its autonomous fragments (Marx, 1992, p. 280; 2008, pp. 340, 368).

In competition, individual capitalists appear to face one another not as capitalists but as 'independent commodity producers' in a relation of 'simple exchange' (Marx, 1953, p. 324; 1987, p. 571). Here, capital 'disguises the initial form' in which capital opposes labour (Marx, 1980, p. 1605; 1992, p. 60). In the market, there is only the redistribution of existing values, and the 'source of surplus value is obscured' (Marx, 2008, pp. 9–10). This deception is reinforced when the capitalists sell their products to the workers who buy them as consumers, not as wage labourers. This illusion obscuring the 'inner nature' of capital – capitalist exploitation – disappears when we consider not the individual capitalists and individual labourers but the total social capital represented by the capitalist class confronting the working class (Marx, 1987, p. 524).

Essentially, two separate but closely related points are involved here. The first is that Marx's value theory establishes the origins of surplus value in class relations of production, and the consequences of this for the accumulation of capital, prior to any consideration of competition. Second, though, the processes of competition themselves both conceal such origins and the corresponding nature of competition itself. Confining competition to the sphere of circulation overlooks the 'inner tendency' ('inner nature') of capital to strive for limitless surplus labour through accumulation (Marx, 1953, pp. 316, 450, 638). As Marx underlines, 'the general and necessary tendencies of capital have to be distinguished from its phenomenal forms'. And competition itself is properly analysed 'only when the inner nature of capital is grasped' (Marx, 1987, pp. 314–15; 1965, pp. 853–4). This is because, within exchange, competition to appropriate surplus value depends upon, but is detached from, individual production of that surplus value as the latter is redistributed across capitals from its origins in production (whether through transformation of value into prices of production, or intervention of landed property, finance or more or less temporary market monopolies and unforeseeable market conditions).

It is, therefore, analytically illegitimate to oppose 'monopoly capitalism' to 'competitive capitalism' as two distinct phases of capitalism as some Marxists have done (see, for example, Sweezy, 1970, pp. 265, 268–9), falsely following Lenin's lead to suggest that monopoly eliminates competition. All capitalism is competitive, in the fundamental sense outlined above, of the opposition between capital in general and the working class. What is often called 'monopoly capitalism' is, rather, a phase in the socialization of capital reached through increasing concentration and centralization, and it intensifies rather than eliminates competition. For competition involves the more or less free movement of capitals 'within capital's own conditions', with monopolies 'arising from the capitalist mode of production itself' and considered by Marx as 'natural', falling within the competition of capitals (Marx, 1953, p. 544; 1992, p. 270; 2003, p. 158). None of these aspects of the rule of capital can be grasped through the quantitative approach to competition, focusing narrowly on the number of 'independent' producers on the market.

COMPETITION WITHIN SECTORS

Marx brings out the relationship between individual capital and total social capital at the two levels of competition of capitals: competition within the same sphere of production and competition across different spheres. Here Marx's (1959, p. 119; 1992, p. 257) distinction between 'individually necessary labour' and 'socially necessary labour' is crucial.

For the first level, relating to a single sphere of production, identical products are offered on the market, and must have the same market value. This value of the commodity is determined not by the individual labour time that each individual capitalist requires, but by the social norm of production, which may or may not be equal to the arithmetic average of labour times across the competing producers. Which of the competing groups of producers within the sphere has the decisive effect on the standard of sectoral value depends on the numerical ratio or proportional size of the groups. That is, the value will be determined by the group that predominates over the others by whatever mechanism. This market value, expressed in money, is the market price. But, 'The average of the actual market prices over a period is the market price which represents the market value' (Marx, 1959, p. 197). As Marx argues, the equality of the market price for commodities of the same kind is the way in which the 'social character of value enforces itself on the basis of capitalist production' (Marx, 1992, p. 772). By the same token, the capitals producing more efficiently than the norm reap extra profits (Marx, 1992, p. 254). In the case of agriculture, Marx shows that the monopoly of capitalist farming can artificially inflate the market value as a result of which society in its capacity of consumer overpays for agricultural products: 'What is a minus in the realisation of its labour time in agricultural production, is a plus for a part of society – the landed proprietors', and thus is generated a "false social value"' (Marx, 1992, p. 772; see also Vygodskij, 1976, pp. 101–3).

The competition of capitals within the same sphere of production establishes a unique market value of the commodity by the socially necessary average labour time required to produce the commodity. However, it does not bring about the equalization of profit within the particular sphere: quite the opposite; intra-sectoral competition tends to bring about the dispersion of the profit rates of competing capitals. Here the profits of individual capitalists differ. At this level, too, competition between capitals underpins the production of absolute and relative surplus value, that is, the endless search by each individual capital – as fractions, or instantiations, of the capital relation in general – of alternative ways to extract more surplus value from the working class. These may include, in general terms, the lengthening or intensification of the working day, the reorganization of the production process or the introduction of new technologies. More, or more effective, exploitation becomes a condition of survival for competing capitals, with increasing productivity or surplus value production guaranteeing survival as well as differential access to finance, technology, markets, labour power and so on. All of these processes are thrown together, in greater complexity, in competition at the level of the world economy.

COMPETITION BETWEEN SECTORS

Competition of capitals between the different spheres of production tends to bring about the establishment of the same general rate of profit across different spheres of production, where the profit rates would otherwise differ owing to their different organic compositions of capital and their different turnover periods. The profit corresponding to this general rate of profit on a capital of a given magnitude, irrespective of its organic composition, is the average profit. Consequently, capitalists do not withdraw surplus value or profit produced in their respective firms, or even their respective sectors. They withdraw from the total amount of surplus value or profit produced by the social capital of the combined spheres as much surplus value or profit as falls – on uniform distribution – on each aliquot part of the total capital (Marx, 1992, p. 254).

The fundamental point about the average profit is that capitals of the same magnitude must tend to yield equal amounts of profit over the same period. The capitalists strive, as 'brother-enemies', to 'share among themselves the loot of the labour of others' in the way that one appropriates – on an average – as much unpaid labour as another. Marx calls this 'striving' competition (Marx, 1959, p. 21; 1992, p. 280).

The concept of price of production, which includes the average profit, was not Marx's creation. The same concept existed under various names in classical political economy before Marx. But, as Marx insists, none of these economists had developed the 'distinction between price of production and value'. Price of production is a 'totally external and prima facie *irrational* (*begriffslose*) *form* of the value of commodities as it *appears in competition*' (Marx, 1992, p. 272). As Marx (1992, p. 52) underlines, surplus value and the rate of surplus value are the 'invisible essentials requiring investigation', while the rate of profit and the form of surplus value as profit 'show themselves at the surface of the phenomenon'. Indeed, the whole process of establishing the general rate of profit takes place behind the back of the individual capitalist, thereby completely hiding from the capitalist (as well as the labourer) the nature and origin of profit. To what extent the average profit of the individual capitalist is engendered by the 'global exploitation by total social capital is a complete mystery' to the individual capitalist as well as to the 'political economists who have not yet solved it'. To them the general rate of profit 'appears as given from the exterior'. Marx claims that he has 'revealed this inner connection for the first time' (Marx, 1987, p. 306; 1992, pp. 245–6; 1959, p. 310).

CONCLUSION

Competition of capitals, arising out of the necessity of realizing surplus value after its creation in production, is the necessary mode of manifestation of the limitless urge of capital in general to increase surplus value. The failure of the classics to understand the origin of profit as it appears in competition arose from their incomprehension of capital as a social totality as opposed to individual capitals. There are two levels of competition – within a single sphere and across different spheres of production. The product of each single sphere has the same market value determined not by the individual labour but by the socially necessary average labour. The group which outweighs the other competing groups will have a decisive effect on the average value which, expressed in money, is the market price. Actual market price fluctuates around the market value. Competition across different spheres brings about the general rate of profit out of the originally existing different rates. Profit corresponding to this general rate of profit on a given magnitude of capital is the average profit. The price of production of a commodity is equal to the cost price (in the Marxian sense of constant plus variable capital) plus the average profit. Capitals of the same magnitude must tend to yield equal amounts of profit over the same period.

Marx's critique of Adam Smith and David Ricardo's analyses of the competition of capitals is very sharp. Smith, sharing 'the crude empiricism' of the individual capitalist, 'places himself entirely in the midst of competition and continues to argue sense and nonsense with the *individual capitalist's own logic*' (Marx, 1959, pp. 210–11; 2008, p. 141, emphasis added). Ricardo, in turn, assumes (like the individual capitalist, one could say) the general rate of profit as given instead of analysing how it emerges. Thus Ricardo fails to see that this latter operation already presupposes 'the *partition of the whole social capital between its different spheres of employment* determined by competition' (Marx, 1959, p. 200). Instead of discussing how competition 'transforms values into cost prices' (in the sense of Marx's 'prices of production'), Ricardo, following Smith, analyses how competition reduces actual market prices to cost prices. Ricardo, accepting the Smithian tradition, follows a 'false route' and is preoccupied with only one aspect of competition, 'the most superficial', namely, 'the rotation of actual market prices around cost prices or natural prices . . . the equalisation of market prices in different trades to general cost prices'. Ricardo's 'blunder' comes from the fact that 'knowing the nature of neither profit nor surplus value', he does not separate surplus value from profit, nor does he clearly distinguish between value and 'natural price'. Fundamentally, 'the creation of surplus value can never be understood by the bourgeois economists', because 'it coincides with the appropriation of the labour of others without exchange' (Marx, 1953, pp. 450–51; 1959, pp. 201, 204, 208).

13. Consumerism

Paula Cerni

At the extreme, consumerism is the notion that happiness comes from acquiring and using material possessions. It is an old notion that has gained new supporters and critics with the twentieth-century rise of mass 'consumer society'. When Thorstein Veblen, the founder of American institutional economics, denounced 'conspicuous consumption' in his *Theory of the Leisure Class* (Veblen, 1899), he was chastising an elite that lived through and for consumption; today, consumerism has been linked to 'affluenza', an epidemic gripping millions of 'shopaholics' and infecting society at large. As postmodernist author Jean Baudrillard would have it, consumption has now 'grasped the whole of life'.

Such claims are clearly excessive, but their popularity demands a materialist explanation. This, however, lies deeper than in consumption itself; it flows from the rapid development of commodity production. Compared with all previous historical periods, capitalism has increased the quality and quantity of material wealth at an extraordinary rate. Especially during periods of economic growth, substantial sections of the working population in the developed world have enjoyed daily comforts and occasional luxuries, however defined, in relative safety and security. This kind of consumption represents a 'side of the relation of capital and labour which is an essential civilizing moment, and on which the historic justification, but also the contemporary power of capital rests' (Marx, *Grundrisse*).

The other, uncivilized, side of the relation condemns the majority to exploitation and neglect, politicizing consumerism into a progressive ally in the struggle for higher living standards and consumer rights. Thus, alongside the forces of capitalist production have grown antagonistic consumer movements and campaigns organized by unions, women, governments and groups of concerned citizens. From the struggle of US labour for a living wage, most intense in the aftermath of the 1877 national railroad strike (Glickman, 1997), to recent legislation requiring the listing of ingredients on food packaging, many of these have been of great assistance to working people and to society as a whole. Yet by their very nature they cannot escape the contradictions that create them, and so they are, simultaneously, a civilizing force and a testimony to the power of capital, limited in scope and yet transformed into a larger project if doggedly pursued (Fine, 2005).

Caught in this paradox, Marxists often find themselves pulled toward the extremes, either of a populist and uncritical defence of consumerism or of an elitist and 'puritanical' rejection of consumption and growth. A more balanced response is to acknowledge consumption as an essential humanizing activity, yet one that is inevitably shaped by each particular historical mode of production. The conflicting nature of consumption under capitalism can be attended to by working with consumers to ameliorate everyday conditions while proposing, more radically, a new mode of production to improve quality and raise general levels of consumption to the standards and norms of a twenty-first century global civilization.

CONSUMPTION AND PRODUCTION

Because Marxism's nuanced political critique of consumerism rests on a programme of radical economic change, its theory necessarily brings to the fore the determination of consumption by production. Critics often charge that this represents a theoretical downgrading of consumption, but in so doing they only sever in the mind a connection that practice continually establishes in the world. By contrast, in his writings on consumption Marx starts deliberately from an analysis of this essential connection.

In brief, Marx's argument is that production and consumption are two distinct but related moments within one integrated totality, the cycle of social reproduction. Each moment simultaneously creates itself as the other – production is simultaneously consumption of materials and labour-power, while consumption is simultaneously the production of living beings. But this identity of opposites is not symmetrical, since consumption only happens once the product has been created and in a way dictated by the manner of its production. Eating, for instance, involves different practices and meanings when food is produced on a large-scale industrial basis instead of in small, self-sustaining rural communities. The mode of consumption, therefore, is an aspect of the overall mode of production, while production itself, as a specific phase, is the critical starting point in a process of material change carried out in real time:

> Consumption, as a necessity and as a need, is itself an intrinsic aspect of productive activity; the latter however is the point where the realisation begins and thus also the decisive phase, the action epitomising the entire process. An individual produces an object and by consuming it returns again to the point of departure: he returns however as a productive individual and an individual who reproduces himself. Consumption is thus a phase of production. (Marx, *A Contribution to the Critique of Political Economy* (*CCPE*), Appendix 1)

The cycle transforms the subjective and objective aspects of human experience into each other. In production, the subject materializes his or her own activity, appropriates nature for himself and so creates a subjective object; in consumption, the object returns to the subject, reveals its subjective content and so fulfils its objective capacity to meet the subject's needs. But it is production that creates not only the object but also the subject and the needs:

> When consumption emerges from its original primitive crudeness and immediacy – and its remaining in that state would be due to the fact that production was still primitively crude – then it is itself as a desire brought about by the object. The need felt for the object is induced by the perception of the object. An *objet d'art* creates a public that has artistic taste and is able to enjoy beauty – and the same can be said of any other product. Production accordingly produces not only an object for the subject, but also a subject for the object. (Marx, *CCPE*, Appendix 1)

Consequently, our need and desire for specific objects is never purely natural, but always informed by those objects, which we ourselves produce under specific conditions.

To take a simple example, the need for typewriters existed while society produced type-writers and virtually disappeared with the arrival of affordable printers and personal computers; where it survives, it usually acquires new meanings, for instance, of nostalgia, or as a collector's artefact. The evolution of production, therefore, drives the evolution of needs. This, however, should not be understood in a crudely reductionist fashion. Economic life, especially under capitalism, is a complex unity of diverse moments encompassing production, distribution, exchange and consumption, and touching on other phenomena that are not directly economic. Marx's argument is that, although production predominates, the different moments interact with and determine each other as would be the case with any organic process.

While the need to consume is driven by production, this, under capitalism, is in turn subordinated to capital's imperative to accumulate. Individual consumers experience the weight of an alien need upon their own during the process of exchange. Intense pressure to buy promotes the view, embraced also by some Marxists, that advertising manipulates consumers into acquiring 'false' needs. But if needs are created by objects then advertising induces genuine needs that have already been produced, though the needs, like the objects, are not exclusively the consumers' own. It is therefore production and not marketing that generates a wasteful excess of low-grade materials, poor design and bad taste – altogether, a severe qualitative deficiency of needs irrespective of any reinforcing role played by advertising, pervasive though it may be.

Quantitatively, capitalist production is also caught between tending to produce too much and too little: too much because limited buying power is a potential constraint on sales, and too little relative to the consumptive needs of society given that a profit must be made. When millions of consumers are unable to afford products on the market, individual capitals compete for our attention. They give their wares new charms, as Marx puts it, and dangle in front of our eyes the needs they simultaneously create and deny.

Advertising, therefore, serves the real need of the individual capitalist to sell, to turn goods back into money capital, at the expense not only of the general social need but also of his own resources for accumulation. Here the opposition, inherent to capitalism, between general and particular interests takes the form of a many-sided confrontation – between capitalism as a total mode of production, on the one hand, and individual capitalists and workers, on the other; between producers and sellers; and between sellers and buyers. But this confrontation is already contained in the productive relation of each individual capitalist to his own workforce, as Marx explains:

> Every capitalist knows this about his worker, that he does not relate to him as producer to consumer, and [he therefore] wishes to restrict his consumption, i.e. his ability to exchange, his wage, as much as possible. Of course he would like the workers of *other* capitalists to be the greatest consumers possible of *his own* commodity. But the relation of *every* capitalist to *his own* workers is the *relation as such* of *capital and labour*, the essential relation. But this is just how the illusion arises – true for the individual capitalist as distinct from all the others – that *apart from his* workers the whole remaining working class confronts him as *consumer* and *participant in exchange*, as money-spender, and not as worker. It is forgotten that, as Malthus says, 'the very existence of a profit upon any commodity pre-supposes a *demand exterior to that of the labourer who has produced it*', and hence the *demand of the labourer himself can never be an adequate demand*. (Marx, *Grundrisse*)

AN AGE OF CONSUMER CAPITALISM

In our age of high consumption, this essential relation between capital and labour, this fundamentally uncivilized bond, is easily lost from sight, and the determination of consumption by production appears to be negated by the experience of consuming more and more things made by fewer and fewer people. Consumption, not production, seems to predominate, because in a sense it really does. This experience is novel and confined, since the production of goods – especially agricultural – has been the main economic activity for the majority of the population in most historical societies, and consumption beyond subsistence has usually been restricted to the privileged few.

But in today's advanced Western nations, agricultural employment is minimal and manufacturing employment has also declined dramatically. Here, even domestic and craft goods are increasingly replaced by bought-in manufactures, ready-to-wear fashions, microwavable meals and so on, so that, paradoxically, the further successes of industrial production generate a mass consumer society. As we encounter the world of objects primarily through consumption, so we appear to have freed ourselves from alienating practices of production; yet this freedom results from our own alienation from those practices, and therefore expresses and develops the alienation already contained in them. It is a freedom that is as genuine and rich as it is limiting and shallow.

In the consumption phase of the cycle, objects, subjects and experiences acquire specific traits. The previous industrial age, fixated on the production phase, had viewed each object as a value-laden commodity whose origin, however mystified, was universal human labour; our society sees it mainly as an object of consumption, as a use-value. Whereas value had highlighted each commodity's exchangeability with all others in accordance with a common standard, use-value now highlights the uniqueness of each object and each act of consumption for each particular consumer. And whereas value had united the world of objects into an alien power over society, use-value now fragments the world into a multiplicity of things and society into a disparate assortment of individuals submitting mostly to their own desires (Cerni, 2007).

Consequently, material things now tend to appear not as universal but as particularized entities loaded with personal significance. Even as commodities are further standardized as a result of technological progress and the closer integration of the global economy, we are more likely to perceive the uniqueness of each object because, as consumers, our relation to each object really is unique. For example, although at each given point in time there is only a limited number of mobile phone models on the market, each user deploys the phone in his or her own fashion, becoming more or less attached to or dependent on it, more or less interested in or skilled at using its various features, more or less likely to drop it accidentally and so on. Unsurprisingly, then, a key aspect of mobile phone usage relates to the conscious assertion of this intimate relation between subject and object through personalized accessories, ringtones and so on. Meanwhile largely obscured are the exploitative conditions under which handsets are produced; the monopolization of the market by a handful of firms; any limitations to product development deriving from corporate priorities; and the unnecessarily high charges that still prevent millions from gaining access to this vital technology.

The mobile phone is the kind of economic and cultural object Marxists can pay close attention to through 'vertical' perspectives such as the system of provision approach that reunites consumption with production (Fine, 2002). More generally, if Marx's insights on consumption are to be fully tested against the complex realities of contemporary society, theorists also need to investigate why, seemingly liberated from production yet ultimately driven by it, consumption influences our thoughts and activities far more profoundly than in the past.

Economic theory, for example, has long abandoned the classical approach that rightly emphasized production but, unaware of its historical and conflictive nature, assumed its relation to consumption to be largely trouble-free. With the further development of capitalism and its inherent contradictions, the creation of a rentier or leisure class of capitalists and, finally, the relative deindustrialization of Western societies, consumption has become the paradigmatic activity for most economic theory. Accordingly, concepts such as 'marginal utility', 'marginal propensity to consume', 'revealed preference' and 'rational choice' have highlighted the experiences of purchasers and consumers over those of sellers and producers, calling attention to the commodity's use-value and discarding value as a category of mainstream economic thought. An important task for Marxist economists, therefore, consists in critiquing the different ways such concepts reflect the historical development of capitalism.

In addition to playing a greater role in economics, consumption now also has an enhanced presence in political and cultural life. Political systems were once largely defined by the relation of constituencies – chiefly capital and labour – to the means of production, but today's parties, campaigns and policies tend to conceal these divided interests under appeals to the individuated consumer. Such concealment, however, need not be intentional; it corresponds to changes in class structure brought about by the relative decline of industrial capitalism. The same structural changes have depolarized high and popular culture into a common enterprise that no longer seeks self-consciously to escape from or defiantly to challenge capitalist production. And so consumption, today, appears to foster a truly autonomous and democratic culture based on the free play of desire, meaning-making and choice, a culture that claims to be cool, resistant and at times even subversive, yet glosses over economic inequities and rarely acknowledges the exploitative practices it feeds on. Especially since the 1980s, this culture of consumption has been a key topic for the humanities and social sciences. Another task for Marxist economists, then, in collaboration with colleagues from other disciplines, consists in exploring the relation between the political and cultural aspects of contemporary consumption, on the one hand, and the range of economic practices generated by the existing mode of production, on the other.

Along with these two tasks should go a critical re-examination of twentieth-century Marxist and post-Marxist contributions that, following the wider social and intellectual trend, have paid consumption a great deal of attention yet all too often have decoupled it from its constitutive relation to material production. One effect of such decoupling has been to render consumption a mainly subjective, cultural, symbolic, ideological or psychological phenomenon. Depending on whether the populist or the elitist pull is felt most strongly, this has led either to the postmodernist celebration of the consumer's identity and lifestyle, or, conversely, and building on the work of authors such as Antonio Gramsci and the Frankfurt School theorists, to a bitter condemnation of consumerism as a hegemonic tool. Another, less noticed, effect has been to nudge economic programmes away from a central aim of replacing the current mode of production and toward a narrower concern with reforming, reclaiming or eradicating specific practices of consumption. Notable in this respect are crisis theories that revolve around the concept of under-consumption; perspectives that attempt a convergence with environmentalism around the opposite notion of over-consumption; and feminist Marxist critiques that defend feminized consumption against the alleged male-productivist bias of traditional Marxism.

Whether in economic theory, in politics or in cultural life, consumer capitalism, by its very nature, conceals the production processes that determine its own existence. Yet the tension between the submerged, apparently marginal sphere of production and the brightly lit, seemingly all-encompassing world of consumption cannot be completely suppressed. It resurfaces in different ways at different times, for instance, in the aftermath of tragedies involving adulterated foods and unsafe building construction, or in the concern many consumers and activists have for working conditions in factories and sweatshops. A society that hides from its own truth is at permanent risk of disenchantment. Marxism offers the recovery of a production-based approach as a fully rounded practical alternative to consumerism, and, simultaneously, as a materialist and historical account of how consumerism became one of the most powerful ideas of our time.

14. Contemporary capitalism

Greg Albo

The study of capitalism has entailed both the interrogation of the capitalist mode of production as an abstract-formal object and investigation of the diverse historical forms that capitalism has taken across time and place. From this duality, a distinction in Marxist theory has often been drawn between the examination of the capitalist mode of production as such – the 'pure' theory of capitalism with its distinct 'laws of motion' – and specific historical periods of capitalist development – monopoly capitalism, postwar capitalism, neoliberal capitalism as examples; and particular spatially circumscribed cases – East Asian capitalism, German capitalism or capitalism in New York City. The notion 'contemporary capitalism' has been invoked in Marxist debates as a general term to speak to the historical phasing and evolution of capitalism.

The term contemporary capitalism has, however, no particular bounded conceptual foundation. It is a notion often intertwined with the more sharply delimited theoretical debate within Marxism about the 'periodization' of capitalism. Periodization can, in general terms, be defined as 'the effects of the development of the forces and relations of production on the *form* of social relations within a mode [of production] . . . such a periodisation will reveal itself in the methods of appropriating and controlling surplus value. These methods will assume increasingly socialised forms as the socialisation of production proceeds' (Fine and Harris, 1979, p. 109). The notion of contemporary capitalism has often then been appealed to in suggesting that a new phase of capitalism has succeeded the historical features and class struggles of earlier ones. Historical debates about contemporary capitalism have typically been about transformations in 'patterns of social reproduction' characteristic of different periods of capitalism that require theoretical clarification, and the identification of emerging features, sectors, regions or countries seen as typifying the most 'advanced' features of capitalism.

In terms of the aspect of patterns of social reproduction, it is often claimed that contemporary capitalism has fundamentally altered the economic dynamics of accumulation and the form of the capitalist state. All zones of capitalist society are being compelled to adjust to new organizational and competitive imperatives and, as will be seen, this leads to its being characterized abstractly in a number of ways. For example, the shift from mass production technologies to microelectronic ones has often been interpreted as a transition from Fordism to post-Fordism; and changing forms of macroeconomic intervention as a shift from a Keynesian state to a neoliberal one. Identifying particular ascendant features of capital accumulation is taken to be the essence of contemporary capitalism. These features might be, for example, the organization of the labour process or the internationalization of capital, or the organizational features of a particular state with respect to the forms of coordination and regulation of financial and industrial capital. Debates about contemporary capitalism within Marxian political economy have, therefore, attempted to explain current developments in light of the general laws of the capitalist mode of production; identify new patterns and features of the production, appropriation and distribution of value; and indicate other qualities of social relations and class struggles that appear to be more conjunctural and spatially bounded – a synthesis of economic history and economic theory.

This two-sidedness to the debates about contemporary capitalism reflects the Marxist methodological commitment to the position that capitalism is, in all times and places, a social system driven by the encompassing accumulative imperatives of a world market; yet capitalism is always differentiated by temporally and spatially specific processes of accumulation and stratification and particular class relations necessary for the production of value. Marx made the point that capitalism imposes 'one specific kind of production which predominates over the rest, whose relations thus assign rank and influence to the others. It is a general illumination which bathes all the other colours and modifies their particularity' (*Grundrisse*, Introduction, ch. 1).

This approach distinguishes Marxian political economy from other theoretical frameworks. In neoclassical economics, universal categories of economics and politics mean that debate about contemporary capitalism always pivots around the question of whether the essential human essence to 'truck, barter and exchange' is unfolding as it should with the expansion and intensification of market relations. There exists no methodological precept or theoretical tools in neoclassical economics to distinguish different historical epochs, let alone phases of capitalism, except on such a singular market continuum that identifies social, political and technological factors that allows the market to spread. In contrast, institutional political economy conceives of all historical economies as embedded in more general socio-economic logics, such as forms of rationality, with capitalism dominated by, but not reduced to, profit maximization. In turn, each phase of capitalism is marked by a dominant organizational and technical paradigm determined by its particular forms of organization. The policy challenge is to ensure that the institutions of corporate governance and the administrative form of the state match the socio-technical logics of production. This evolution, for institutional political economy, can be understood by certain universal categories although always with temporal and spatial variations formed as ideal-types.

The essential difference in theorizing contemporary capitalism, and the underlying concern to periodize phases of capitalist development, is located in Marx's fundamental methodological point of departure and his critique of bourgeois political economy in its failure to ask: 'why labour is represented by the value of its product and labour time by the magnitude of that value' (*Capital I*, ch. 1).

CAPITALIST DEVELOPMENT

Development in capitalist societies takes the general form of accumulated money-capital being continually reinvested in expanding means of production and the purchase of labour power for the purpose of increasing the amount of value accumulated as money. The unending search for profits leads to specific tendencies of development, or 'laws of motion' of capitalism. This accumulation implies a continual transformation of the commodities, social relations and class struggles; and thus in the 'social forms' which mediate the tendencies of the capitalist mode of production in concrete history. A number of these tendencies have figured, time and again, in debates about contemporary capitalism.

First, Marxist political economy identifies the labour process as the location for the extraction of surplus value from workers, the organization of production, the changing form of the subsumption of workers, the contestation over work-time and the development of the forces of production. The history of capitalism is defined by transformations internal to the labour process in terms of skills, technology, work organization and conflict over work control. Thus the development of the modern factory system or the implementation of Taylorist work organization and Fordist assembly-line production have often been hailed as the central features defining contemporary capitalism and its dominant mode of capital accumulation. The changes in the labour process from the adoption of new computer technologies in workplaces, for example, is often seen as introducing several new features: the intensification of Taylorism to match the rhythms of new technologies for production and service workers and a multi-skilling for a range of technicians and production support workers; a recomposition of the form in which the conception of work is undertaken by designers and developers and the execution of the work by production workers; a relative decline of individualized piece-work and increase in team-work; and a shift from dedicated machinery to flexible manufacturing systems.

Second, the consumption of labour power in the labour process is premised on the commodity labour power being available for sale. There is a range of factors – skilling, unions, household relations, education – that are necessary to transform workers into a properly constituted supply of labour power available for exploitation. These institutions form the wage relation that underpins the reproduction of workers. Further, the accumulation of capital tends to increase the technical and social divisions of labour as the machines being deployed increase in sophistication and new sectors develop. The demand for labour power is, therefore, continually shifting. A fundamental contradiction exists between the changing labour demand and the need for a stable supply of labour power that is dependent upon the extra-market institutions that produce workers. This contradiction can only be worked out historically in specific places as it is explicitly embedded in class struggles and class formation. It is common to identify the most recent phases of capitalism not with the labour process, but with the conflicts, social compromises and institutions which determine the historical form of the wage relation.

Third, the imperatives of competition lead to the concentration and centralization of capital into ever more complex and larger firms. This entails larger units of capital in terms of the economies of scale forming individual plants, but also more differentiated units of capital and labour processes under the control of any given ownership group. This raises a number of deep-seated problems of control: the process controls over increasingly complex labour processes; the operational controls over spatially dispersed labour processes, particularly of the commodity chains of multinational corporations; the strategic controls necessary to coordinate market strategies across horizontally differentiated units of capital; and the accounting and administrative controls to enforce competitive imperatives on the individual units of capital internal to the firm. Further, the forms that legal ownership of firms take across different shareholder groupings, and the ways that top managers exercise their power to make decisions to invest and fund the expansion of the firm, also take on particular features. The different forms of organizational control has sparked heated debate about contemporary capitalism as being characterized by highly institutionalized distributional relations associated with large bureaucratic firms, or more flexible distributional bargains and 'networked' firms.

Fourth, capital accumulation always occurs within the context of a world market, and individual capitals confront competitive imperatives to internationalize their production. The tendency for the internationalization of capital drives further innovations in communications and transportation in the process of building a new foundation for the world market. The internationalization of commodity, productive and financial capital takes on varied features and relations in different phases of capitalism. The form internationalization takes in different phases also transforms the class alliances of the power bloc between the internal and imperialist fractions of capital in national social formations. This, in turn, carries implications for the specification of the autonomy and sovereignty of the state, the allocation of state functions to international agencies and the coordination of the political-economic relations between the hierarchy of states in the world market. The periodization of the forms of the nation-state and international competition figures prominently in all debates about contemporary capitalism.

Fifth, extra-market institutions and political mediation are always necessary to secure the socio-political conditions that underpin accumulation. States provide both these capacities and the requisite political coercion and legitimation. The tendency toward the increasing socialization of production within capitalism also entails stratification, that is, the increasing role of the state in ensuring the reproduction of capital through infrastructure, support for education and research and development and economic coordination. The social forms of state economic intervention, the technical organization of state apparatuses and the relations between branches of the state vary considerably. For example, during the postwar phase of capitalism, the wage relation was often directly inserted into the state via incomes policies and corporatist institutions such that the nominal reference wage was formed via political mediations as opposed to market mechanisms. But, more recently, state policies helped recompose the reserve army of labour and market disciplines were reasserted in wage formation. The self-expansion logic of capital remains, but the social form of the state and its political mediations become indispensible in locating the most contemporary features of capitalism.

CONTESTING CONTEMPORARY CAPITALISM

While Ernest Mandel (1975, p. 23) claimed that there was 'no satisfactory history as a function of the inner laws of capital . . . and still less a satisfactory explanation of the new stage in the history of capitalism', there have been many signal contributions to the understanding of modern capitalism. The classic text which began to raise the question of emergent features of capitalism shifting the form of capitalist development was Rudolf Hilferding's (1910) *Finance Capital*, itself a response to Eduard Bernstein's revisionist argument that the socialization of capitalism meant that the law of value no longer held and capitalism was simply evolving into socialism. Hilferding presented his book as a diagnosis of the most recent developments in capitalism from the vantage point of Marx's laws. But he extended the theoretical analysis to take into account transformations in money, credit and banking to offer a unique interpretation of modern capitalism as 'finance capital', a fusion of industrial and bank capital into monopolies which were transforming competition and extending it into the international arena. This sparked additional responses from Luxemburg, Bauer, Grossman, Lenin and Bukharin about the features of 'monopoly capitalism' and new tendencies toward economic crisis, nationalization and imperialism. But they all held in common with Hilferding, while arguing within a value-theoretical approach, that a new stage of capitalism had been arrived at, driven by the increasing socialization of production and the monopolistic concentration industry.

The Great Depression and the long boom of 'postwar capitalism' suggested to many that the fundamental dynamics of accumulation had changed as the concentration of economic power altered competition and thus the specific way that the law of value operated. The key statement setting the framework for much modern debate, and certainly for US interpretations of postwar capitalism, came from Paul Sweezy's *Theory of Capitalist Development* (1942). After surveying classical Marxism, Sweezy argued that monopoly pricing power fundamentally altered the pattern of accumulation by forming a tendency for the surplus produced by capitalists to rise, the consumption of workers to be constrained, with military spending, marketing and other factors deployed to counteract permanent stagnation. This interpretation reflected a commonly asked question in radical political economy circles, among them John Strachey and Shigeto Tsuru, with the emergence of the so-called Keynesian welfare state: 'has capitalism changed?'. Theorists for the communist parties in particular took the suspension of competition by monopolization even further and argued that contemporary capitalism had now taken the form of 'state monopoly capitalism'. This concept inferred a particular 'fusion' between the state and the monopolies which, at one and the same time, represented the stabilization of capitalist economies and the possibility of co-existence of two rival systems, and yet the inexorable decay of capitalism as it inevitably gave way to socialism. But other theorists of state monopoly capitalism rejected the notion that the fundamental accumulation dynamics of capitalism had changed, and insisted that the socialization of production had altered the form, magnitude and substance of state intervention into the economy.

Although explicitly rejecting the position that capitalism had fundamentally changed its dynamic, Ernest Mandel (1975) identified a new stage of 'late capitalism'. Mandel insisted that the basic laws of motion still regulated capital accumulation, but what had changed in 'neo-capitalism' was the character of the science and technology deployed, market relations and class struggles that mediate these abstract tendencies in concrete history and that allow for long-term tendencies in the rate of profit and long waves of economic growth. For Mandel, the uniqueness of 'late capitalism' lay in the third technological revolution driving up profit rates, increased military spending, permanent inflation, the increased role of the state and the spread of planning across all organizations.

The economic crisis of world capitalism across the 1970s gave special urgency to re-examining the laws of motion of capitalism in light of current developments. The French regulation school, for example, argued that abstract laws of motion were modified into particular modes of regulation and regimes of accumulation. Thus postwar assembly-line production dominated by semi-skilled workers was governed by the monopolistic regulation of Fordism, while the new flexible production systems have been regulated by a mix of markets and associational governance institutions of post-Fordism. In parallel, the 'social structures of accumulation' approach of American Marxists interpreted contemporary capitalism in terms of a 'capital-labour accord' institutionalized in economic and state structures, while Japanese Marxists developed the 'Unoist' approach to interpret the transition to a new stage of capitalism. Nicos Poulantzas distinctively located contemporary capitalism in the changing form of the state. He linked the new forms of integrated production to transformations in the relations of production and capitalist ownership structures to new alliances in the power bloc and functions in the state. In opposition to prevailing views, Poulantzas (1974, pp. 86, 88) claimed that American hegemony had 'become stronger . . . what is taking place at present, far from signalling as attempt by American capital to "re-establish" its hegemony, is rather an offensive on its part to even undermine the place of a secondary imperialism'.

The most recent assessments of contemporary capitalism have continued many of these themes, particularly about the new forms of the production and the restructuring of the state and classes. But new concerns about the social form of neoliberal globalization have also arisen. One such debate has been in how to characterize neoliberalism itself. For instance, Robert Brenner assesses neoliberal policies as the economic and political response of the capitalist classes' inability to restore profits through creative destruction over the 'long downturn' from the 1970s as firms try to preserve existing investments and government policies block exit, while others have sought to clarify the forms of neoliberalism as a specific phase of capitalism. Another has been centred on financialization, with Gérard Duménil and Dominique Lévy seeing the emergence of a new form of financial capital that also explains both neoliberalism and globalization. Others, following the earlier theses of Sweezy on monopoly capitalism, have contended that financialization represents a further mechanism to cope with capitalist stagnation. Finally, an overarching debate has been how to characterize the contemporary features and competitive form of the internationalization of capital. David Harvey, for example, has defined the new imperialism as a search for a 'spatial fix' to an economic crisis in core countries via 'accumulation by dispossession' in peripheral countries. Still others have registered the new imperialism as, on the one hand, a register of US economic decline as surplus capital accumulates in East Asia in the case of Giovanni Arrighi and, on the other, as a measure of US hegemony as it imposes neoliberal globalization on the world market and reinvigorates its capitalist classes in the process according to Leo Panitch and Sam Gindin.

The changing dynamic and form of capitalism has given rise to numerous attempts to identify and theorize its contemporary features. Mainstream accounts put emphasis on empirical shifts of a 'new economy' without any theoretical content that places these developments within the structures of capitalism. In contrast, institutional political economy has tended to analyse contemporary capitalism within a new set of concepts – post-Fordism or informational capitalism – as an entirely unique development. It has been characteristic of Marxian political economy, however, to anchor its theorization of new developments within abstract concepts – value, exploitation, class, concentration and centralization of capital, state power – necessary to understand capitalist society in general. This allows a focus on underlying determinations, specification of their current forms and theorization of its concrete and complex processes. Following Marx's methodological mandate, this is the study of the form taken by the laws of motion of capitalism in their contemporary phase.

15. Crisis theory

Simon Clarke

The recurrence of economic crises is an undisputed fact of capitalism, yet mainstream economists explain each successive crisis as a singular event, usually attributed to the subjective failings of capitalists and/or of government regulation. For Marxists, by contrast, the tendency to crisis is inherent in capitalist accumulation, an expression of the fundamental contradictions of capitalism. But there is no generally agreed Marxist theory of crisis.

Despite the central role played by the theory of crisis in Marxism, Marx himself never developed a complete theory of crisis. On the one hand, Marx was primarily concerned with analysing the secular tendencies of capitalist development, marked by the concentration and centralization of capital and the polarization of classes that underpinned the progressive development of the working-class movement and would culminate in the inevitable revolution. On the other hand, from a theoretical point of view, the analysis of economic crises presupposes the analysis of competition and credit that Marx never completed. So in his notebooks, Marx regularly postponed a full discussion of economic crises on these grounds. Nevertheless we can outline the key elements of Marx's analysis (Clarke, 1994).

An economic crisis occurs when capitalists are unable to sell their commodities without incurring substantial losses, reverberating through the system in a chain of defaults and curtailing production in a cumulative downward spiral. The theoretical issue is to explain such systemic market failure.

The abstract possibility of crisis is already contained in the separation of purchase and sale. If a significant number of sellers withdraw their money from circulation, rather than using it to buy further commodities, then the latter commodities will remain unsold. For classical political economy such an outcome would be completely irrational since, as Adam Smith put it in Book 4, chapter 8 of the *Wealth of Nations*, 'consumption is the sole end and purpose of all production', so the rationale for selling one commodity would be to buy another. For Marx, by contrast, the 'sole end and purpose' of capitalist production is not consumption but the production and appropriation of surplus value. The sale of commodities represents the reconversion of the capitalist's expanded capital into the form of money with which to renew the process of capital accumulation. The capitalist will devote some of the money realized to own consumption, but the remainder will be reinvested, provided only that there are opportunities for profitable investment. Marx therefore identifies the condition for crisis as the absence of such opportunities. The origins of the crisis lie in the overproduction of commodities in relation to the effective demand at a price that makes it possible to realize the surplus value embodied in those commodities. But what is the source of such overproduction? This is the point where Marx parts company decisively with political economy.

For classical political economy, general overproduction is impossible, so overproduction in one branch can only arise in association with corresponding underproduction in another. The rate of profit in the former branch will be lower and in the latter higher than the average, so capital in the former branch will move to the latter branch to restore equality of profit rates and the proportionality of production. If disproportionality reaches the stage of crisis it can only be because overproduction has been sustained 'unnaturally' by the speculative expansion of credit. For classical political economy, therefore, a crisis is essentially a monetary phenomenon that arises from inappropriately lax regulation by the state authorities.

For Marx, overproduction is not an accidental divergence from the norm of proportional growth, to be eliminated smoothly by competition, but is the essential characteristic of capitalist production. Overproduction is the cause and consequence, the essential form, of capitalist competition. The purpose of capital is not to meet consumer demand but to make profits, and the primary means by which capitalists make profits is not by moving their capital between branches of production in response to marginal differences in the rate of profit, but by introducing new methods of production to reduce their costs. A capitalist who can produce more cheaply than her competitors will produce as much as possible and drive some of these competitors out of the market. Increased production leads to falling prices as supply runs ahead of demand and the more backward capitalists are forced to reduce their costs in turn. If they do not have the resources to introduce new methods of production, they cut their costs by reducing wages, intensifying labour and lengthening the working day. Eventually supply is brought back within the limits of demand as the less profitable capitalists are bankrupted or withdraw from the battle and their workers are thrown into unemployment.

The tendency to overproduction is not an exceptional event, it is the everyday reality of capitalist production, forcing capitalists, on pain of extinction, constantly to expand their markets and cut their costs. The positive side of this contradictory feature of capitalism is that the most advanced capitalists continually create new products and develop new methods of production. However, new products are not developed to meet human needs, nor are new methods of production developed to lessen the burden of labour. Capital accumulation is marked by the continual creation of needs, by the increasing polarization of wealth and poverty, and by the co-existence of overwork and unemployment.

For Marx and Engels, this tendency to overproduction is an inevitable feature of capitalist production, pressing on every capitalist in the form of competition. It also gives rise to periodic, and increasingly severe, general crises which arise when overproduction, spurred on by speculation and sustained by the expansion of credit, affects the leading branches of production. Marx and Engels saw these periodic crises as a recurring phase of the cyclical pattern which is the normal form of capitalist accumulation. Against the classical political economists' presumption that the interaction of supply and demand ensures a constant tendency towards equilibrium as capitalists adjust production to the limits of the market, Marx and Engels insisted that it is only through periodic crises that balance is forcibly, if only temporarily, restored.

The periodic crises of overproduction indicate the objective limits of the capitalist mode of production, but they do not in themselves destroy capitalism. The destruction and devaluation of existing products and previously created productive forces, the conquest of new markets and the more thorough exploitation of old ones, remove the barriers to the further development of the forces of production, paving the way for renewed accumulation only to lead to more extensive and more destructive crises. Nor do these limits determine the inevitability of the demise of capitalism. The tendency to crisis of capitalist accumulation demonstrates in the most striking way the irrationality of capitalism and define the 'weapon' with which the bourgeoisie will 'bring death to itself', but it is the proletariat which will 'wield those weapons' (*Communist Manifesto*).

The development of the proletariat as a political force is determined by the secular tendencies of capitalist development. The cycle of over-accumulation and crisis leads to the concentration and centralization of capital, the separation of productive and commercial capital and the growth of the credit system, which in turn exacerbate successive crises. The secular tendency for the rate of profit to fall, recognized by political economy and reformulated by Marx, further intensifies the concentration and centralization of capital and the intensity of crises, since smaller capitals are more vulnerable and larger capitals are better able to engage in competitive accumulation.

THEORIES OF CRISIS IN THE MARXIST TRADITION

Underconsumptionism

Engels consistently espoused an underconsumptionist theory of crisis, according to which the growth of production tends to run ahead of the growth of consumption, on the grounds that production and consumption are governed by 'quite different laws' (*Anti-Duhring*, Part 3, ch. II). Engels saw this inherent tendency to overproduction as the explanation both for periods of stagnation and for the more dramatic economic crises. However, Marx himself is clear that, far from being governed by 'quite different laws', production and consumption are closely interrelated as two aspects of the reproduction of capital. That capitalism restricts the living standards of the mass of the population and minimizes the number employed does not imply that it will not find a market for its ever-expanding product, corresponding to the ever-expanding mass of surplus value, because the latter can be realized through the purchases of capitalists, either for their own consumption or for the purchase of labour power and means of production to expand their capital further.

The leaders of the German Social Democratic Party (SPD), the first mass Marxist party, adopted Engels's underconsumptionist theory as a theory of the secular tendency of capitalist development to chronic depression. The theory of crisis of the SPD was unsophisticated, crises being seen as a result of the 'anarchy of the market', merely intensifying and reinforcing the secular tendencies of capitalist development and so not having any independent theoretical or political significance. But the dominant view was that the breakdown of capitalism was inevitable and, in the view of many, imminent.

The theory of crisis came to the fore with the challenge to the belief in the inevitability of capitalist breakdown presented by Eduard Bernstein. He insisted that rising incomes and imperialist expansion were reducing the risks of overproduction, while the formation of cartels and the increasingly sophisticated credit system averted the risk of crises. In response to Bernstein, Kautsky reiterated the orthodox underconsumptionist view and denied that Marxism had a catastrophist theory of breakdown.

The most vigorous response to Bernstein came from Rosa Luxemburg, who did espouse a catastrophist theory and insisted that 'the theory of capitalist breakdown . . . is the cornerstone of scientific socialism' (Howard, 1971, p. 123). Against Bernstein, Luxemburg insisted that credit exacerbates the tendency to overproduction and so merely postpones the inevitable crisis at the cost of intensifying it. Rosa Luxemburg sought to set the underconsumption theory on more rigorous foundations in her book, *The Accumulation of Capital* (1913). She distinguished between the periodic crises deriving from the 'anarchy of the market', which regularly interrupted accumulation, and the terminal crisis that would result from the exhaustion of the external market provided by the destruction of pre-capitalist forms of production on a world scale.

Underconsumptionist theories rest on the belief that consumption is the driving force of capitalist production, even though Marx had argued vigorously against this view, insisting that the driving force of capital accumulation is the production and appropriation of surplus value, so that capitalist production expands without regard to the (temporary and expanding) limits of the market. From this perspective, the market is not a limit to accumulation, but merely a barrier to be overcome through the expanded reproduction of capital.

Despite its fundamental theoretical weakness, underconsumptionism consolidated its position as the orthodox Marxist theory of crisis through the first half of the twentieth century, fuelled by the experience of the Depression of the 1930s. In the Soviet Union, 'Varga's Law' asserted that the growth of production was associated with not only a relative but even an absolute decline of consumption. In the West, Paul Sweezy's *Theory of Capitalist Development* (1942 [1968]) sought a synthesis between Luxemburg's underconsumptionism and an analysis of monopoly capitalism to provide a stagnationist theory, according to which capitalism could only be sustained by unproductive expenditure. Sweezy's work anticipated a theoretical convergence between Marxist and Keynesian underconsumptionism that remained dominant until the mid-1960s, especially in the USA where it remains extremely influential among the left.

Falling Rate of Profit Theories

Since the 1970s, the falling rate of profit theory of crisis has established itself as the orthodox Marxist theory of crisis, although the theory had previously only very shallow roots in the Marxist tradition. It has always been recognized that crises are associated with a dramatic fall in the rate of profit, but this has generally been seen as a consequence, not a cause, of the crisis. The secular tendency for the rate of profit to fall was seen as a factor stimulating the concentration and centralization of capital and one that makes crises more likely and more pronounced, but it was not seen as a cause of crises, for both empirical and theoretical reasons. Empirically, the boom that precedes a crisis is generally marked by a rise in the rate of profit. Theoretically, there is no reason for a lower rate of profit in itself to lead to a crisis, since for the capitalist any profit is better than none.

The interpretation of the 'law of the tendency for the rate of profit to fall' as a theory of crisis derives from Paul Mattick's *Marx and Keynes* (1969), which presented the falling rate of profit theory as the revolutionary alternative to underconsumptionist Keynesian reformism. The argument was then elaborated theoretically by David Yaffe and Mario Cogoy. The ensuing debate centred not so much on the means by which a falling rate of profit would result in a crisis, rather than secular stagnation, as on the issue of whether or not the 'counter-tendencies' would be sufficient to check a fall in the rate of profit and so whether the tendency for the rate of profit to fall would be translated into reality.

An alternative form of the theory is the theory of 'over-accumulation with respect to labour power', according to which the proximate cause of the fall in the rate of profit is increasing wages as the demand for labour power runs ahead of its supply. A third interpretation sees the fall in the rate of profit as a result of the militant struggle of organized workers managing to increase their wages and/or resisting the intensification of their exploitation. Neither of these theories remained plausible as real wages stagnated from the 1980s.

The debate around the Marxist theory of crisis in the 1970s generated a great deal of heat but very little light, primarily because none of the contending theorists provided any explanation of why a fall in the rate of profit should provoke a crisis (Shaikh, 1978).

Disproportionality Theories

The principal alternative to underconsumptionism in the first quarter of the twentieth century was not the falling rate of profit theory but the 'disproportionality' theory of crisis, developed most rigorously by Rudolf Hilferding in his *Finance Capital* (1910 [1994]). Marx's argument that the driving force of capitalist production is not consumption but profit implies that the growth of production in each particular branch of production will be determined by the opportunities to make a surplus profit by introducing new methods of production, regardless of the growth of the market. The normal course of capitalist production will, therefore, be one of the disproportional development of the various branches of production. Disproportional growth can be sustained by the expansion of credit and by the ability of capital to open new markets and is countered by the movement of capitals between branches of production, but if overproduction embraces the leading branches of production it can provoke a crisis of general overproduction.

Hilferding developed a disproportionality theory of crisis which was based on a theory of the investment cycle in conditions of imperfect competition. According to Hilferding, a burst of investment in fixed capital increases demand without immediately increasing supply and so boosts the rate of profit, provoking overinvestment. When the increased production capacity eventually comes on stream, the increase in supply leads to a sharp fall in relative prices and in the rate of profit in the newly expanded sectors. This tendency to overinvestment and crisis increases as the turnover time of capital and the proportion of fixed capital increase with capitalist development and is intensified by the emergence of 'finance capital' (cartels of companies employing a large fixed capital organized by their financing banks), which has much reduced the flexibility of capital in response to economic fluctuations and so made modern capitalism much more susceptible to crises.

Hilferding produced a sophisticated analysis of the investment cycle, which influenced both Marxist and bourgeois theories, but the theoretical foundations of this analysis were not specifically Marxist, in that disproportionalities did not arise out of the inherent tendencies of capitalist production, but out of the miscalculations of capitalists, who fail to anticipate the impact on profits of future increases in production. In this context, the rise of finance capital and the intervention of the state should alleviate the tendency to crisis by ensuring that capitalists coordinate their investment plans in anticipation of future market conditions.

A more recent theory of crisis (more precisely, of secular stagnation), similarly based on the barriers to the equalization of the rate of profit erected by fixed capital, has been proposed by Robert Brenner in *The Economics of Global Turbulence* (1998). The significance of fixed capital for Brenner is not that it postpones the appearance of overproduction but that it sustains overproduction by limiting the liquidation of excess capacity by the more backward producers, the persistent over-supply of commodities depressing the rate of profit in manufacturing and so leading to a secular downturn (which Brenner equates with a 'crisis'). Like Hilferding, Brenner essentially offers a theory of the investment cycle (in this case focused on the downswing) which has little Marxist pedigree, but is determined by barriers to competition and the irrational expectations of capitalists (Fine et al., 1999).

CONCLUSION

For Marx the catastrophic crises that periodically disrupt accumulation are only the most superficial if immediate manifestations of the fundamental contradiction of the capitalist mode of production. However, the tendency to crisis is pervasive, since the competitive regulation of capital accumulation is not achieved by the smooth anticipation of market adjustments by omniscient capitalists, but by the process of over-accumulation as the tendency to overproduction runs into the barrier of limited markets. In this sense, Marx's theory of crisis lies at the heart of his critique of political economy, displacing the classical theory of competition, with whose critique Marx and Engels began their explorations in political economy.

Marxist 'theories of crisis' have played more of an ideological than a scientific role in the history of Marxism. While the tendency to crisis might be inherent in capitalism, the determinants and characteristics of any particular crisis are always singular, embedded in the concrete characteristics of capital accumulation at a particular time and place, not reducible to a single abstract determinant, and so the analysis of crisis presupposes a concrete analysis of the contemporary configurations of capital. It was for good reason that Marx devoted far more time and energy to unravelling the complexities of the movements of capital that underlay the crises of his day than he ever did to elaborating a 'theory of crisis' as such.

16. Dependency theory

John Weeks

Dependency theory offers a radical explanation for what is the most striking characteristic of global society: why there are countries at astoundingly different levels of development. When applied at this level of generality, dependency writers use the terms 'centre' ('advanced' or 'core') and 'periphery' to capture the systemic or structural differences between developed and underdeveloped countries.

Dependency theory promotes the view that development and underdevelopment constitute two sides of the same coin, and that the uneven development of countries is based on the systematic extraction of the income and wealth of a large group of peripheral countries by a much smaller group of core countries, primarily through unequal trading, financial and other relations. Consequently, autonomous development in the periphery is contingent upon a socialist alternative. In the abstract, this stance could apply to any two or more countries that are at different levels of development, and between more and less wealthy regions within countries. This generality has prompted critics to accuse it of not adequately relating to capitalism; however, some dependency writers have sought to explain the lack of or the late development of certain regions by reference to the much more specific concept of 'dependent capitalism' (dos Santos, 1978; Cardoso and Faletto, 1979).

FORMS OF DEPENDENCE

In its most common form dependency theory refers to a process that began with the emergence of capitalism in the eighteenth century, though one of the best-known dependency writers dates it from the sixteenth century (Frank, 1967; in later studies Frank pushed the origins of capitalism as far back as 5000 years ago). Since its incorporation into the world system through the expansion of commercial capitalism, the periphery has been subjected to different types of dependence: mercantile during the colonial era, industrial-financial from the late nineteenth century and technological-industrial since the mid-twentieth century. Despite these potential refinements, in practice the most important application of dependency theory has been to the relationship between advanced capitalist countries and less developed countries in the postwar era, most notably between the USA and Latin America. This entry focuses on what most writers consider to lie at the heart of a dependency relationship: surplus extraction.

Dependency authors use various mechanisms to explain the extraction of surplus from the periphery and its transfer to the core. The most analytically important are international transfers associated with the operations of capitalist enterprises (for example, profit remittances and interest payments), systematic bias in the long-term trends in the prices of traded products (following the insights of the Latin American structuralist economists) and unequal exchange through international prices derived from differences in wages among countries (see below). Most, but not all, dependency writers consider the class nature of countries (for example, Marini, 1973; dos Santos, 1978; Cardoso and Faletto, 1979). However, in their analysis class relations (as they were understood by Marx) play only a secondary role as a source of surplus as opposed to relations between core and periphery (usually identified with groups of countries). In its least sophisticated form, dependency analysis considers the wealth of a few countries to be the mirror image of the poverty of many countries, and almost all those living in the former are, one presumes, beneficiaries of the misery inflicted upon almost all those living in the latter. This claim builds upon statements by Engels, Lenin and other early Marxists (but not Marx himself) postulating the existence of a privileged strata of workers in the advanced countries, a so-called labour aristocracy, which indirectly exploits its counterparts in poorer regions of the globe.

It is frequently argued that dependence has created peculiar social structures in the periphery, especially a parasitic *comprador* ruling class, or *lumpenbourgeoisie*. Typically, this class manages the exploitation of the locals on behalf of the centre, exports the products of their labour (and the corresponding surplus) and purchases from abroad goods allowing it to live in luxury amidst the squalor of an otherwise despoiled population. Their high living standards, and the transfers to the centre, are possible only because of the extremely high rates of exploitation in the periphery; as a result, this region lacks both resources and markets for autonomous development. In sum, dependence is based on the coincidence of interests between the elites based in the centre and the peripheral *comprador* class, and it marginalizes and impoverishes the masses.

For Frank and other *dependentistas*, the relations binding the centre and the periphery have generated a process of 'development of underdevelopment': underdevelopment is not a transitional stage through which countries must pass, as in linear theories of transition to capitalism but, rather, a condition that plagues regions involved in the international capitalist economy in which they permanently occupy a subordinate position. For these countries, dependent capitalism is not progressive because it does not lead to the systematic development of labour productivity and the satisfaction of wants in the periphery, while capitalism in the centre is no longer progressive because it is parasitical on the periphery. Therefore, the periphery can develop only after radical political change including, for many *dependentistas*, the elimination of relations of dependence (and the *comprador* class) and the institution of socialism.

The dependentist view that rich countries 'exploit' poor countries has had strong influence in left-wing political discourse, for example, in the anti-colonial movements in the second half of the twentieth century and in the contemporary Global Justice Movement. In the early twenty-first century, it found new life in environmental arguments that the populations of advanced countries collectively owe an indemnity to the populations of underdeveloped countries for the pollution generated to provide higher living standards in the 'North'.

While modern dependency analysis dates from the end of World War II, it flourished in the context of the exhaustion of the postwar boom in the centre, and the crisis of import-substituting industrialization and the decline of Latin American structuralist theory. Nevertheless, dependency views have a much longer lineage that includes some of the most famous figures of nineteenth-century political economy, such as Pierre-Joseph Prouhdon (1809–1865), Jean Charles Léonard de Sismondi (1773–1842) and Russian revolutionary writers known as the Narodniks ('Populists'). These writers pursued the common theme that capitalist exchange resulted in systematic inequality manifested in the class relations between landlord and tenant, merchant and artisan, and capitalist and worker. Marx reversed the causality arguing, instead, that class relations result in systematic inequalities that are reflected in market exchanges (Saad-Filho, 2005).

DEPENDENCE AND DEVELOPMENT

It is obvious that the differences in levels of development across the globe are systematically related to history and region, which gives rise to the crude dichotomy of the 'rich North' and the 'poor South', a geographically suspect distinction at best. The considerable element of descriptive inaccuracy in this dichotomy indicates that an explanation of global inequalities cannot be based on domestic class relations alone. This gives the dependency thesis an apparent analytical advantage over traditional Marxian theory, which would seem to be locked into a purely class explanation.

In the analysis of the Latin American Structuralist school, underdevelopment results from internal power relations exacerbated by the extraction of a surplus from the periphery through a systematic long-term decline in the prices of primary products compared to manufactures. The analytical argument is that primary products are exchanged in competitive markets and their demand is income inelastic, while the producers of manufactures have international market power and the demand for their products is income elastic. Over the business cycle, this combination results in the productivity gains in the production of primary products being transferred to the exporters of manufactures, which are in the advanced industrial countries. This terms of trade prediction resulted in a copious and inconclusive empirical literature lasting a half century. Whatever its empirical validity, the terms of trade argument became less important as many underdeveloped countries emerged as exporters of manufactures, especially in East and Southeast Asia and Latin America, leaving the decline of terms of trade, as it was conceptualized by the structuralists, of potential relevance only in sub-Saharan Africa.

Those dependency theorists who identified themselves as Marxists invoked a different surplus extraction process to explain underdevelopment, inspired by Latin American structuralism (see above) and the US 'monopoly capital' school (and, consequently, by the economic theories of Marx, Keynes, Kalecki and Steindl). This explanation was part of *dependentista* claims that capitalism systematically underdevelops the poor countries. In contrast, the structuralists claim that capitalist development is possible in the periphery through industrialization and comprehensive social reforms. The initial mechanism for the division of the world into developed and underdeveloped countries was the naked violence of colonialism, imperialism and plunder. The usual argument, found in Baran (1957), was that this form of extraction rendered extreme what had previously been relatively narrow differences in development. After the early stage of capitalist development in Europe, when appropriation from backward countries was violent and crude, surplus extraction continued through different and overtly peaceful mechanisms. The visible or exoteric mechanisms included profit remittances, extraction through debt service payments, transfer pricing and capital flight. However, several major authors placed primary emphasis on a concealed or esoteric extraction process, which was partly inspired by the intersectoral value transfers in Marx's transformation of values into prices of production: international 'unequal exchange' (typically, Emmanuel, 1972). The apparent analytical advantage of the international unequal exchange mechanism is that, if valid, it would show a surplus transfer from low to high income countries without relying on the dichotomy between primary products and manufactures, and independent of crude market power. In either case, these transfers depress incomes, welfare standards and investment in the periphery, and produce a distorted growth pattern favouring the production of primary products for export and of luxury goods for domestic consumption.

International unequal exchange presumably arises as follows. If all countries use the same technology and produce the same products (assumptions common with the neoclassical trade theory), and the techniques of production require fixed physical ratios of inputs (including labour), it follows that if each product has a single international price (abstracting from non-production costs), the profit rate will be higher where wages are lower. If capital is mobile internationally, profit rates among countries will tend to equalize for each product and across products. This equalization leads to the transfer of profit from producers in countries with low wages to producers in countries with higher wages. Therefore, competition and the mobility of capital result in systematic and ongoing transfer of surplus value from underdeveloped countries to advanced countries despite what appears to be equal exchange.

However, the unequal exchange mechanism based on national differences in wages is analytically flawed, derived from a Sraffian interpretation of Marx's transformation problem. Assume there are different technologies of production and wage rates in rich and poor countries, but a single profit rate across countries and between industries. There would follow a three-way distributional trade-off between profits and wages in the rich and in the poor countries. For example, if the wage rate in the rich countries is given, there is a trade-off between the profit rate and wages in the poor countries, with 'unequal exchange' (that is, value transfers from the periphery) benefiting capitalists everywhere. Conversely, if the profit rate is given there is a trade-off between wages in the rich and in the poor countries, with value transfers benefiting rich country workers. This model is apparently seductive, but it obliterates the class relations of production within each country. It is as if a 'global' capitalist class and separate 'national' working classes were competing for resources in circulation. This may be satisfactory from a Sraffian perspective, but it is unrelated to Marx's interpretation of (global) capitalism. Second, if there is a single 'global' technology of production and different wages across countries, it is not possible for both the profit rate and the product price to equalize. Either the prices are different and the profit rates equalize requiring trade restrictions, in which case there are no value transfers, or the profit rates vary and the prices equalize across countries. However, in this case all production would migrate to the South, leading to international convergence and the elimination of 'dependence'.

By contrast, a logically consistent mechanism by which international exchange might reinforce global inequalities has been suggested by Shaikh (1979–80), working from a Marxian rather than *dependentista* framework. He argues that trade is determined by absolute, rather than comparative advantage, and absolute costs are determined by the interaction of productivity and wage levels. Under specific and credible assumptions this model generates an underdevelopment mechanism driven by international trade and related changes in monetary variables, because the prices of the same commodities tend to be lower in advanced countries, making them more internationally competitive. As a result, less developed countries tend to run persistent and debilitating balance of payments deficits.

DEPENDENCY AND MARXISM

Though many dependency writers identify themselves as Marxists, their analysis is not entirely compatible with Marxian arguments, as was shown above for unequal exchange. This incompatibility arises because dependency locates surplus extraction at the level of exchanges between countries rather than in the relationship between classes in production, which leads to an emphasis on the subjugation of one country by another, in sharp contrast with Marx's focus on the subjugation of one class by another. Despite their potential advantage of explaining the source of surplus value through exploitation in the process of production, Marxian studies have not examined rigorously how this contributes to understanding global inequality, and Marx's own analysis of the world market remained at the level of intentions. Because Marxian analysis considers capitalism to be technologically dynamic compared to all previous modes of production, it could be taken to imply that underdevelopment is the result of insufficient capitalist development in a country or region. While it is obvious that this implication provides some insight into underdevelopment, it is at best a partial explanation that ignores any 'underdeveloping' tendencies within capitalism, which have been stressed by dependency and non-dependency writers (Weeks, 1981b).

For all its appeal, dependency analysis is plagued by a number of internal inconsistencies that have been the focus of heavy criticism. First, the key problem of identifying the surplus transfer mechanism, examined above, reflects a more general theoretical difficulty that dependency has no explanation for the source and growth of the surplus production of a society. Second, the analysis provides no clear mechanism by which a country passes from dependency to successful capitalist development. During the twentieth century several countries, including Chile, China, Denmark, Ireland, Japan, Norway and South Korea, emerged from the ranks of underdevelopment to approach advanced capitalist development in terms of their income per capita, economic structure or economic and political power. If one important test of a theory is its ability to address the exceptions to its main conclusion, dependency theory would seem to fail. Related to this point, dependency theory seems to suggest that relatively isolated countries, for example, in Latin America and sub-Saharan Africa, would be more likely to grow 'autonomously' than other developing countries which are more closely linked to international trade and financial flows, which is analytically implausible and contradicts historical experience. Third, and derivative from the first two, there is no explanation of the initial division of countries between advanced and dependent; that is, why did Britain colonize India and not the reverse? While Marxian analysis may not have an entirely satisfactory answer to this question, its writers have explicitly addressed the question with a theoretical seriousness that dependency writers have not (for example, Byres, 1996). Fourth, dependency theory is overtly functionalist. It subordinates agency to structure, and assumes that the historical development and the social structure of the periphery can be explained by their functionality with Western capitalism. Development is ultimately impossible under capitalism because there is no scope for independent agency: dependent countries tied to the world market *cannot* develop. However, the claim that capitalist development is impossible in the periphery is insufficient to support the case for revolution. At best, the argument that the periphery is exploited by the centre implicitly makes a case for nationalism. If underdevelopment is due to international integration, the logical solution is not socialism, but a delinked national development strategy. Perception of this limitation in the dependency school is shown by only exceptionally addressing directly the domestic relations of exploitation. In practice, this approach leaves the state as the most important agent of national emancipation, which, again, is incompatible with purported socialist strategic objectives. Whatever the strategic goals of the dependency school, its conclusions are not rendered compatible with the subordination of agency to structure at every stage in the analysis, especially in cruder versions of the theory.

The considerable criticism of dependency analysis for its theoretical inconsistencies and empirical shortcomings does not deny the significance of its concerns, or the extremely large net flows of resources from underdeveloped to advanced countries, especially since the international debt crisis in the 1980s. These flows had a substantially depressing effect on the heavily indebted countries. While not offering direct empirical support for dependency analysis, these flows suggest that neoclassical analysis that views the international economy as harmonious is unsatisfactory, and the Marxian analyses that tend to focus overwhelmingly on class relations remain incomplete.

17. Ecology and the environment

Barbara Harriss-White

At the start of *Capital I* (ch. 1) Marx stated that 'labour is not the only source of material wealth . . . labour is its father and the earth its mother'. But the radio-chemist and energy scientist Frederick Soddy commented that Marx's 'disciples . . . forgot all about the mother' (quoted in Martinez-Alier and Schlupmann, 1990, p. 134). As a result, the development of a Marxist ecological economics was delayed for well over a century (pp. 15–19).

It is widely supposed that Marx ignored the environment, or was hostile to it, or regarded it as a constant, or thought it was inexhaustible despite plunder and exploitation, or had what we now might call ecological insights but did not integrate them into his analysis in *Capital*. Such views have been effectively refuted by, among others, John Bellamy Foster (1999). Marx's environmental analysis is, to be sure, scattered throughout *Capital* as well as his early philosophical works and his keen and voluminous correspondence about the science of the day with Engels and others. It is also a grounded analysis, in which practical theoretical ideas emerge from his treatment of specific environmental problems of his time, which are now compounded by others of today.

At the age of 24 and soon after completing his doctoral thesis, Marx wrote the *Debates on the Law on Thefts of Wood* (1842), in which he recognized private property as theft, the interests embodied in it as antithetical to those represented in customary law and the state as the guardian of private property. Arguably, the seed of his later political economy was germinated by this early analysis of wood theft which he wrote for the *Rheinische Zeitung*.

NATURE

In his writings Marx grappled with the distinctiveness of nature and natural resources in relation to human beings, or Man. 'Man *lives* on nature – means that nature is his body, with which he must remain in continuous interchange if he is not to die . . . man is a part of nature' (*Economic and Philosophical Manuscripts of 1844*, (*EPM*), 'Estranged labour'). This dialogue involves, he says, flows and stocks – not only of materials but also of energy – and their conversion. Engels could explain to Marx that while Man stabilized present solar heat by working, he also squandered past accumulated solar heat through the destruction of forests, depletion of fossil fuels and so on. (Marx and Engels, *Correspondence, Engels to Marx, In Ventnor, December 19, 1882*, in Foster, 1999, p. 385). Energy and materials were not free gifts but can only become valuable through the action of labour. In the system of value under capitalist production relations, however, the full costs of the reproduction of exhaustible resources do not enter the calculation. Nature is therefore 'alienated'.

LABOUR AND METABOLISM

Marx and Engels also grasped the importance of Darwinian theory. They reasoned that while living non-human organisms had through evolution 'accumulated' internal organs or tools ('organ' being derived from the Greek for tool) that made each species uniquely equipped with a 'natural technology', mankind's distinctive evolutionary niche is the capacity to develop and use external tools and technology to modify nature. Labour is thus the 'universal condition' for what Marx called 'metabolic interaction', the process of material exchanges in which nature is appropriated 'for the satisfaction of human needs' (Marx, *Capital I*, pp. 283, 290, in Foster, 1999, p. 80). 'This ecological process of metabolism is regulated from the side of nature by natural laws governing the various physical processes involved, and from the side of society by institutionalised norms governing the division of labour and distribution of wealth etc.' (Foster, 1999, p. 381). Nature and social relations are therefore not independent of each other but co-evolve dialectically: 'the celebrated "unity of man with nature" has always existed in industry . . . just like the "struggle" of man with nature' (Marx and Engels, 1845, *The German Ideology*). Labour is thus a 'natural resource' that is commodified and exploited by capital – a process in which the direct connection between labour and nature is severed (Marx, *Capital I*, ch. 15, section 10). Under commodity production for exchange, matter and energy are continually transformed, labour is alienated from the conditions of production and physical and biological balances are violated (Burkett, 1999).

SOCIAL METABOLISM, THE ECOLOGICAL CRITIQUE OF CAPITAL AND THE 'METABOLIC RIFT'

Although Marx's environmental thought was developed through his analysis of agriculture rather than industrial capitalism, its logic is more widely relevant. He saw in agriculture a kind of activity which can only be commodified by forfeiting the 'entire range of permanent necessities of life required by the chain of successive generations', and which should not be commodified if they are to remain in balance (*Capital III*, ch. 37, Introduction, note 27).

In the context of widely stagnating agricultural yields in the early-mid-nineteenth century, Marx argued that increases in soil fertility were possible, though not inevitable (cited in Foster, 1999, p. 375). '[N]atural (soil) fertility is a limit, a starting point and a basis for increases in the productivity of labour'. Using the work on nutrient cycles by the agro-chemist Justus von Liebig, he criticized both Ricardo and Malthus. Rent, he argued, did not inhere in the quality of the soil. Improvements to land and labour productivity could support growing – and non-agricultural – populations. In 1847 he wrote: soil 'fertility is not so natural a quality as might be thought; it is closely bound up with the social relations of the time' (*The Poverty of Philosophy*, ch. 2, part 4). Later he understood from Liebig's own work on soil nutrients under capitalism that capitalist social relations in agriculture, through the application of chemical fertilizer and by not recycling wastes from consumption, could ruin soil as well as improve it.

Liebig had also developed and applied the concept of '*Stoffwechsel*' (metabolism), which Marx widened to 'social-ecological metabolism' (Foster, 1999, p. 381, note 5). For sure, the productivity of land could be increased by the application of labour and material resources – at that time these were organic nutrients in the shape of guano from Peru, in which Britain had a trade monopoly. But, under the pressure to maximize returns, fertilizer became 'the means of exhausting the soil', since with this intensification of the physical properties of the soil, other nutrients and minerals were wasted – not recycled – 'at heavy expense'.

'Capital' he concluded, gives rise to an 'irreparable break in the coherence of social interchange prescribed by the natural laws of life' (Marx, *Capital III*, ch. 47). 'Capitalist production . . . develops technology, and the combining together of various processes into a social whole, only by sapping the original sources of all wealth – the soil and the labourer' (Marx, *Capital I*, ch. 15, section 10).

TOWN AND COUNTRY

Under capitalist labour relations the archetypical expression of this 'metabolic rift' is an antagonistic relationship between town and country. After the US economist Henry Carey, who also influenced Liebig, Marx called it a robbery system. Here, he describes how towns concentrate the drivers of social progress but also break the nutrient cycle. Minerals and nutrients in food, fibres and agro-industrial raw materials are exported from farms through trade, unequal exchange and plunder, over ever-increasing distances and ever-increasing intensities of energy consumption, making the maintenance of soil fertility ever more difficult. Commodities are consumed in cities but waste resources and animal waste are not returned to the soil. In Marx's day, waste choked the towns and polluted the rivers and sea. Now it is processed (and this too has become a field of capital accumulation) but not returned to the soil, even in organic agriculture. The spatial appropriation and dislocation of metabolic flows has been a key aspect of capitalist accumulation (Burkett, 2006, p. 172).

We can read into the concepts, or metaphors, of 'town' and 'country', the relations between industry and agriculture today, the extreme dislocations between food production and food producers' consumption, and between the reproduction of human society and that of its resource base. Marx saw that nature was not just a 'tap' but also a 'sink' – even if he did not foresee that the global ecological crisis would be driven by constraints in the metabolism of sinks (notably the atmosphere) as well as the exhaustion of taps.

ENTROPY

The understanding of entropy – dissipated energy – is credited to the 1970s thermodynamic economics of Nicolai Georgescu-Roegen; but it is so important conceptually that it needs to be considered here. Marx had focused on materials, and Georgescu-Roegen recognized that the law of entropy applied to materials as well as to energy (Martinez-Alier and Schlupmann, 1990, pp. 1–2; Burkett, 2006). One of the driving forces of industrial capitalism is the replacement of labour by inanimate energy. Under capitalism the physical degradation of energy and materials after production and consumption, and their reconstitution in forms potentially capable of entering into production again, is so completely at variance with the scale of capitalist production cycles that the waste process is 'irreversible': most waste is useless to capital. Depletion due to this irreversibility is accepted because it is not an immediate obstacle to the production of surplus value – but it is an obstacle to sustainable human development.

Liebig had shown that 'rational agriculture is based on the principle of restitution' (cited in Foster, 1999, p. 378). Marx criticized the nineteeth-century sewage system as an example of irrationality: organic recycling would be needed as part of a rational urban-agricultural economy, to complete the metabolic cycle (*Capital III*, ch. 5, section IV). Nowadays it would have to be chemically detoxified prior to any restitution. 'But while upsetting the naturally grown conditions for the maintenance of that circulation of matter, it imperiously calls for its restoration as a system, as a regulating law of social production, and under a form appropriate to the full development of the human race' (Marx, *Capital I*, ch. 15, section 10). Restitution is one precondition for sustained, full and generalized human development. Clearly social relations would have to be transformed for this to be possible. Marx foresaw a dialectical process, impossible under capitalist production relations, involving the systematic application of science to government. 'Freedom in this field can only consist in socialised man, the associated producers, rationally regulating their interchange with Nature, bringing it under their common control, instead of being ruled by it as by the blind forces of Nature; and achieving this with the least expenditure of energy and under conditions most favourable to, and worthy of, their human nature' (Marx, *Capital III*, ch. 48, section III; see also ch. 5, section IV). '[S]ocieties taken together, are not the owners of the globe. They are only its possessors, its usufructuaries, and, like *boni patres familias,* they must hand it down to succeeding generations in *an improved condition*' (*Capital III*, ch. 46, emphasis added). The improvement of the environment, it should be noted, is a stronger requirement than that of modern 'sustainable development' which stresses the maintenance of stocks of material and energy for future generations (Burkett, 2006).

MARX'S LEGACY

Several reasons have been advanced for the long neglect of Marx's environmentalism. Scientific and academic disciplines are confining social constructs: nature does not recognize their boundaries and neither did Marx, whose project was transdisciplinary. Mainstream economics treats the economy as being autonomous from social, political and biological processes, let alone geological, pedological, climatic and oceanic ones; and it deploys restricted conceptions of human motivation. Just as economics substitutes 'the market' and other euphemisms for 'capitalism', the idea of an economy co-evolving with nature is foreign to it. Within economics, Marx's insights have suffered a triple marginalization. First, Marx's contributions were to a grounded theory based on agriculture, whereas agricultural economics today is an ever-more marginalized sub-field of economics (or is rejected outright and reincorporated into 'the new institutional economics').

Second, until the publication of the Stern Review, economics had sectoralized and neglected environmentally informed theory. And third, environmental economics has systematically marginalized Marxian ecological economics, just as neoclassical economics has ignored Marxist economics – along with other heterodox schools which are incapable of being hegemonized.

Attempts have been made to trace two intellectual lines of descent for Marx's legacy on the environment: first, through the 'Russian path' involving Kautsky's *Agrarian Question*, published in 1899, and Lenin's *The Agrarian Question and the 'Critics of Marx'*, from 1901. Each analysed the physical balances between town and country, and Lenin stressed the practical need to conserve the natural environment. It also appears in the use of Marx by early Soviet ecologists and in Bukharin's discussion in the 1920s of metabolic flows and technology in relation to agriculture, in his *Historical Materialism*. Under Stalin's purges of ideas as well as the people who advanced them the conservation of nature was considered 'bourgeois' and concern with it stopped. Bukharin was put paid to. The Soviet disconnection from ecology and its era of 'ecocide' cast a long shadow over Marxist environmentalism in the West where Marxism also fell victim to the rift between natural and social sciences.

The second line of descent is a continuous thread running through the early history of British socialist thought and practice, particularly of the Fabians in their interaction with science in general, and with ecological science in particular. In the 1930s Arthur Tansley developed the modern concept of the ecosystem which applied to the interaction between organisms and their habitats at all scales. He included human beings as exceptionally powerful biotic factors. Both genealogies culminated in a new recognition of Marx's legacy, accompanied by what Martinez-Alier has described as 'surprise if not repudiation', when environmentalism finally entered politics in the 1970s, and it is only recently that a Marxian ecological economics has started to be developed.

CONTROVERSIES AND DEBATES

Because of its somewhat fragmentary nature and long neglect, Marx's ecological thought has inevitably led to debates about its meaning, adequacy and relevance. One strand of these debates concerns the significance of Marx's environmentalism. Having pieced together Marx's environmental thought, Foster (2000) concludes that its neglect by Marxists has been unjustified. For Martinez-Alier and Schlupmann (1990, pp. 219–21), by contrast, Marx failed to develop his analysis of nature-economy-society relationships, in particular the metabolism of energy and thus energy accounts. The concepts of simple and expanded reproduction fail to account for the replacement of used-up means of production in an economy based on exhaustible resources and a regenerative capacity which can be exhausted. Having criticized Ricardo effectively, and because of these analytical inadequacies, Marx's further discussion of natural resources is not through class and intergenerational physical allocations and their waste, instead it is carried out in terms of the implications of rent for the distribution of income, savings and investment and so is more Ricardian and 'metaphysical' than ecological.

A second debate concerns the concept of ecology. The concept was in circulation and known to Marx before he wrote *Capital*. It means the interaction between society, the economy and natural conditions and so might well have been used and developed by him, but was not. Foster suggests that Marx, an ardent supporter of Darwin's theory of evolution but an equally ardent opponent of social-Darwinism, may have been deterred by the fact that Darwin's leading German follower Ernst Haeckel, who coined the term ecology, was a social-Darwinist (Foster, 1999, p. 389, note 7). Whatever the reason, Marx cannot be seen as a precursor of either ecology or ecological economics.

Finally, the relations of humankind to nature involve many different aspects that are necessarily abstracted from Marx's value theory which is based on the labour time of production. Value theory does not preclude the consideration of the impact of accumulation on the natural world. It might even be considered to be an essential starting point in addressing the relationship between capitalism and the environment. But despite the increasing urgency of the issues, the richness of Marx's own account of nature has too often been overlooked by subsequent Marxist value analyses. Nor is the reduction of the environment to the concept of 'externalities' acceptable, as it is to mainstream economics. Ideas such as the sacredness and dignity of nature and human activity also need to be incorporated, and these generate severe problems of incommensurability of values. In ecological economics, but rarely anywhere else, a plurality of incommensurable values has been incorporated. So too is an understanding of the relationship between – and impact of – the meaning and significance of incommensurable values and the material world.

DEVELOPMENTS OF MARX'S THEORY

Contradictions are generated by social relations that are indispensable yet are in opposition, the principal or first one in Marx being between capital and labour. But from the treatments of nature, labour and social metabolism reviewed above it is clear that capitalist production is not just the production of commodities by means of commodities, but requires production conditions that are not produced by commodities at all. James O'Connor has identified three kinds of such conditions. First, nature, before it enters the regulated process of capital, is not itself produced by commodities. Second, the health and capabilities of labour are produced and reproduced outside the circuits of capitalist production (mainly by women). Third, the 'communal general conditions of social production' (communications and other infrastructure) are mainly produced by collective/social action and the state. Through competition and extended commodification, capitalism tends to degrade all three of these non-commodifiable conditions and society resists the exacerbation of the metabolic rift through social movements that O'Connor (1996) argues cannot be subsumed under the first contradiction.

A third contradiction results from the pressure imposed on nature by the need under capitalism not only to produce but also to consume. Costas Panayotakis argues that the two are in contradiction both with each other and with nature. The distributive share (the wage-profit relation) derived from production affects the level of social consumption. But in the competition within capitalist production for returns to increased labour productivity, free time for the consumption of commodities (or for non-consumption and leisure) is a gain to labour. Free time, however, is construed by capital through advertising and planned obsolescence as the search for satisfaction by means of the continual consumption of commodities. Not only does this search fail to create satisfaction, time spent searching and consuming attacks the very notion of free time as social space in which workers can create meaning and could pursue activity other than that which deepens the metabolic rift.

CONTEMPORARY MARXIAN ECOLOGICAL ECONOMICS

Marxist ecological economics examines interactions between environment and political economy as processes of 'natural history'. Paul Burkett (2006) describes this project, developed since the 1990s, as multidisciplinary, theoretically and methodologically pluralist, and receptively oriented to practical politics. The specifically Marxist contribution to it develops the analysis of the materiality and energetics of class relations expressed in economic activity and the creation of exchange value through the appropriation of natural resources. The method, though still in its infancy, is being applied fruitfully at both ends of the town-country rift: to cities, examining the ecological distortions of metabolic stocks and flows (for example, water, biomass, metals, fuels, minerals); and to agrarian social relations and soils, exposing a variety of rifts in nutrient cycles (failures to recycle waste, replacement of organic manure by chemical fertilizer, replacement of animal energy and manure by machines and fossil fuel).

Further to these studies, ecological struggles can take many forms: between capital and labour, or competitive struggles between individual capitals or sectors of the economy, between the state (with or without the complicity of capital) and labour or the state against subsistent peoples, or capital against common property resources, or against non-governmental organizations (NGOs). People also struggle for subsistence and 'sustainability itself' in the face of the deterioration of the environment's capacity to recycle and regenerate sustainably. While all aspects of the process of resource extraction, production, circulation, consumption, social reproduction, waste and natural regeneration are contested, struggles over the control and appropriation of nature's 'taps' (for example, farmland, water, oil and other fossil fuels, metals) are better known and better researched, though not necessarily more important, than those over 'sinks' (for example, waste disposal sites, forest, the atmosphere) (Martinez-Alier, 2007, pp. 286–8).

Marxist eco-feminist economics is as yet a small field examining the impact of the socially divisive economic effects of distinctions and practices based on gender on the environment. Eco-feminist thought develops the concept of the gendered division of labour, studying the ways in which women have a grounded relationship with nature through their socio-biological reproductive activity, compared with the alienated relationship with nature in which men are placed through their distinctive contribution to (environmentally destructive) production. Marxist eco-feminist economists critique the concepts of value involved in the capitalist destruction of nature and develop a class analysis of the material relations of patriarchy expressed in the economy (for example, Johnson 1999, pp. 221–9).

Finally, Marx left it to others to develop quantitative accounts of stocks and flows of energy, minerals and biomass: the task was first taken up in 1920s work on socialization by the political economist Otto Neurath, who was influenced by Marx. The incommensurable values, in which energy and materials have to be accounted for, have been systematized in accounts for the domestic extraction, imports/exports and naturally decomposed and market-recycled wastes of minerals, fossil fuels and biomass. These physical accounts generate measures of net accumulation which differ from those of conventional national accounts statistics. Attempts have been made to make environmental loads measurable and thus comparable through weight or energy equivalents. Initial results show unequal materials and energy exchanges between developing and advanced capitalist economies. But while such physical accounts have been established for many Organization for Economic Cooperation and Development (OECD) countries they have yet to be systematically developed worldwide. And their analysis in terms of their implications for different social classes is a project for the future (EUROSTAT in Martinez-Alier, 2007, pp. 280, 290–1, note 20, p. 292, note 29).

THE ECOLOGICAL QUESTION: CAN CAPITALISM SURVIVE?

The capitalist commercialization of the earth's resources and sinks (land and forests, oceans, the air), and the environmental depredations of Soviet and Chinese industrialization and 'heavy agriculture', have damaged biodiversity, natural recycling processes and ecological resilience to the point where there is now a crisis threatening the existence of not only global capitalism but human society itself. The ecological question is the biggest of our time. Will capitalism survive and prevail at whatever cost to humanity? Underpinning the view that it will, the logic of capitalism depends on the production relations of commodified labour, not on fossil fuels. Resource scarcities increase prices, which induce technical change and new physical and social arrangements; so does capitalist competition in its search to reduce the costs of labour. Since capitalism requires non-commodified conditions to reproduce, it will continually de-commodify and re-commodify the private and public spheres as it de-materializes. The resulting planet may be unattractive and may not even support human life on today's scale, but capitalism will be humans' final mode of production on earth.

Certainly a 'new' or 'green capitalism' is being created and promoted by Al Gore and others. Taking the logic and economic inequalities of capitalism as unchallengeable, this view envisages a combination of energy- and materials-efficient technologies (including nuclear energy, biofuels, genetically modified organisms and geo-engineering together with a politically directed commodification of carbon emissions [Carbon Cap and Trade schemes and the Clean Development Mechanism]). Along with some eco-socialists and green parties but for different reasons, some capitalists call on the state to secure the efficient use of energy and develop renewable energy, since market forces are doing neither sufficiently fast (Altvater, 1993).

But such proponents of a 'new capitalism' neglect capital's logic of expanded reproduction and the historical relations between materials, energy and labour under capital – the metabolic rift. The range of untried, risky and even as yet impracticable measures envisaged by the 'new' or 'green' capital' school ignores the principle of precaution which should govern any rational social response to the known risks and unknown uncertainties involved. Altvater (1993), by contrast, does not think capitalism can survive. Among his several lines of argument two stand out as relevant here. First, capitalist (and communist) industrialization was only possible using energy from fossil fuels, which is why it is such a prime object of competitive military security worldwide. The high 'energy density' of fossil fuel has allowed the development of physical and social infrastructure (pipe-lines, tankers, motorways) whose working life stretches 40–50 years into the future. It is incompatible with the lower density of renewable energy (wind farms, solar-photovoltaic energy). Second, the domination of finance capital over manufacturing capital requires material growth to generate returns exceeding the interest on loans. To date, the logic of accumulation and the necessity of growth have overwhelmed gains in materials and energy efficiency per unit of output. A 'new capitalism' would have to be of a kind for which nothing presently indicates that it is capable of emerging from capitalism as we now know it (Sarkar, 1999; Panitch and Leys, 2007).

The 'de-materialization' of capitalism which appears necessary for the globe to survive under its continued hegemony also faces massive obstacles in the shape of the undemo-cratic politics through which the process of capitalist commodification itself proceeds. It is clear that nothing less than a global mobilization of labour and 'mankind', demanding its de-materialization, is needed to initiate and legitimate the process and finally, in order to govern its metabolism sustainably in the interests of human development for all, to transcend capitalism itself.

18. Economic reproduction and the circuits of capital

Ben Fine

In *Capital I*, Marx is primarily concerned to identify the sources of surplus value in the process of production and the evolving manner in which the working class is exploited as accumulation of capital proceeds. He also identifies the consequences of capitalist production for other economic and social phenomena, such as unemployment, uneven development and so on. In *Capital II*, Marx focuses upon how such capitalist production is integrated into the sphere of exchange, in the more general movement of commodities and money through the market. This is both a shift of emphasis as well as the working up of value relations into more concrete forms.

CIRCUITS OF CAPITAL

The key organizing concept for Volume 2 is the industrial circuit of capital, $M-C...P...C'-M'$. Here, money capital M is advanced to purchase means of production, C (comprised of raw materials or constant capital, c, and labour power or variable capital, v); this is then deployed in the production process, where surplus value, s, is added to give rise to newly formed commodity capital, C'; these commodities are then sold on the market to realize that surplus value (and the additional advance of M) in the form of money $M' = M + m$, say. The whole process is then open to being repeated although, to be taken up later, there is the extra money, m, now available which can either be hoarded, spent on consumption, added to the existing circuit or initiate (some part of) a new one.

Marx emphasizes that the industrial circuit of capital involves a continuous motion through its various phases, not least as exchange gives way to production and back again but also in the processes within each phase as the activities involved require production itself or buying and selling. For this reason, it is useful to represent the circuit as such in Figure 18.1 (Fine, 1975).

This also has the advantage of highlighting other aspects of the circuit. First, there is a clear structural demarcation between the spheres of production and exchange (the latter sometimes ambiguously referred to as the sphere of circulation as opposed to this applying to the circuit as a whole). Second, it is arbitrary to begin (and end) the circuit with M (or M'). Marx also identifies the commodity, $C'-C'$, and productive, $P-P$, circuits of capital (but not $C-C$ as this does not always begin exclusively with capitalist agents as workers simply sell labour power to gain money to purchase means of subsistence). Third, whilst each and every element of the circuit is essential for its functioning, for Marx, the key determining aspect is the production of surplus value in the sphere of

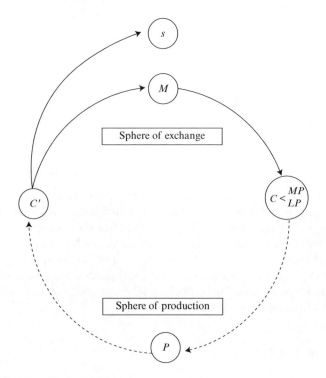

Figure 18.1   The circuit of capital

production. This does not prevent other approaches from seeing things differently by reference to the other circuits. From the perspective of the commodity circuit, C′-C′, it is as if the buying and selling of commodities is the crucial aspect of the capitalist economy, and for M-M′, it is the mobilization and allocation of money. And for each of these, the productive circuit, or production itself, is incidental or at most an inconvenient interruption in the processes of buying and selling or making of money.

So, for Marx, production of surplus value drives the circuit but it is dependent upon circulation as a whole. And, of course, a circuit of industrial capital does not exist in isolation from other circuits, being dependent upon them both to furnish constant capital and to realize commodity capital. Consequently, the circulation of capital as a whole requires the interaction of any number of individual circuits. This, at the most elementary level, is represented by specifying two distinct circuits – one to produce means of production, c, and denoted by sector I, and the other to produce means of consumption, and denoted by sector II. This disaggregation of the circuits into these two sectors is not arbitrary but highlights, as will be seen, the separate circulation and location of constant and variable capital. The total circulation of capital is, in addition, the total circulation of value, incorporating some non-capitalist as well as capitalist exchanges (with workers use of wages for consumption). Once again, it is useful to represent the total circulation of capital in diagrammatic form as shown Figure 18.2.

Here, sector II has been turned upside down in order that its money capital, M_{II}, and that of sector I, M_{I}, can flow in and out of the pool of money, M. Apart from this

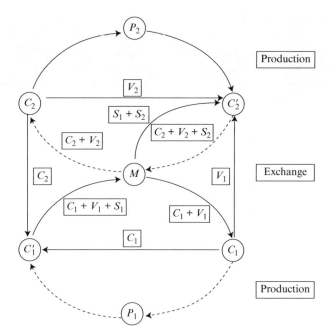

Figure 18.2   Economic reproduction

connection between the two individual circuits, some further connections can also be drawn, from C_{II} to C_I', from C_I to C_I', from C_I to C_{II}', from C_{II} to C_{II}', and, somewhat differently from the others, from the pool of money, M to C_{II}'. These indicate, respectively, the use of constant capital in sector II to purchase commodity capital from sector 1, the use of constant capital in sector I to purchase commodity capital from within the sector, the use of variable capital in sector I to purchase commodity capital from sector II (by workers), the use of variable capital in sector II to purchase commodity capital from sector II (ditto), and the use of all surplus money to purchase consumption goods from sector II (for simple reproduction, see below). In addition to the direction of flows of values and of money, and the intervention of production, these are also indicated in quantitative terms as appropriate.

Leaving aside production, the coordination required in exchange alone is apparent in terms of value magnitudes. Taking any of the points, C_I, C_I', C_{II}, C_{II}' M, it is possible to establish balance between value magnitudes by equating money and value flows, in and out. Using lower case letters for individual sectors and taking C_I, for example, it follows that $c_I + c_{II}$, the total value of constant capital purchased, must equal $c_I + v_I + s_I$, the total of constant capital produced. Consequently, $c_{II} = v_I + s_I$. Similarly, at C_{II}, total purchases are $v_I + v_{II} + s_I + s_{II}$ (workers and capitalists consumption), and this must equal total output of consumption goods, $c_{II} + v_{II} + s_{II}$. Exactly the same value balance results as before.

SIMPLE REPRODUCTION

This condition for simple reproduction (in which the economy is without accumulation) has been perceived by many commentators, especially but not exclusively orthodox, as Marx's anticipation of conditions necessary for equilibrium in the simple form taken by his 'model' (see, for example, Morishima, 1973, for a leading mainstream economist sympathetic to Marx and appreciative of his potential contribution to, and anticipation of, much orthodoxy). There are compelling reasons to reject this interpretation of Marx, even though intended as *ex post* praise. First, at a general level, Marx is deeply hostile to any notion of equilibrium since he understands an economy, and society, as always evolving in response to underlying tensions rather than these being the source of unchanging outcomes as they are balanced against one another. Second, the balance is itself expressed in terms of the highly complex notion of value. This does itself comprise three separate elements, each of which have to be in balance – magnitudes of money, of use values and of labour time. Third, there is no presumption that these magnitudes remain at rest, or in fixed proportions to one another, from one period to the next, although this is logically possible, nor that the balance is itself established at something approaching what might be thought of as full employment. Fourth, then, Marx's reproduction scheme is best seen as an *ex post* account of what must have occurred for the circulation of capital to have been realized or, to put it another way, the production of surplus value requires such balances to be established in exchange in order that the surplus value can be successfully realized.

As indicated, this is all independent of the overall scale at which production and circulation take place. As a result, Marx is able to draw two important conclusions. One is that capitalism is able to reproduce itself from one period to the next, that it can generate sufficient demand to absorb the surplus value and corresponding commodities that it has generated. This is despite subsequent underconsumptionist views within the Marxist tradition, most notably associated with Rosa Luxemburg (1913), to the effect that capitalism can only do this by depending upon non-capitalist sources for market demand that are themselves undermined by being transformed into capitalism. And capitalism is not necessarily plagued by disproportionality crises in which production of means of production outruns production of means of consumption as suggested by Tugan-Baranovsky in the early 1900s (see Grossman, *The Law of Accumulation and Collapse of the Capitalist System*, 1929, for a contemporary critique of this and Luxemburg for mechanical and erroneous use of Marx's method in general and his reproduction schema in particular). Second, though, the scheme generates an understanding of the possibility of crises inherent within the capitalist system (and Marx is able to reject Say's Law since a general glut of commodities is possible for it can correspond to hoarding of, or insufficient, money in circulation as acknowledged by Keynesianism). For any break in circulation or reduction in the value magnitudes involved will have corresponding knock-on implications for the circulation of capital as a whole.

In a sense, this allows non-Marxist theories of crisis to be situated in relation to Marx's scheme. The Keynesian liquidity trap, for example, could be interpreted as the retention of money within the pool, M, insufficient investment deriving from too low a level of $c_I + c_{II}$, and insufficient aggregate demand from deficient expenditure $v_I + v_{II} + s_I + s_{II}$ on consumption with multiplier effects to investment, confidence and so on. Significantly, all of these explanations (as well as those resting on disproportion – too much or too little of means of consumption relative to means of production) are drawn to focus upon the sphere of exchange alone, the central area of our diagram, with the production of surplus value marginalized at the periphery. But, for Marx, the production of surplus value is what drives the system of exchange and not vice versa, even though exchange does enjoy an independent life of its own to some degree both allowing crises to originate there and appear as if they do so even if the capacity to produce and accumulate surplus value is what is at stake for the system as a whole.

EXPANDED REPRODUCTION

This is an appropriate point at which to introduce reproduction on an extended or expanded scale. In this case, capitalists do not consume the surplus $s_I + s_{II}$, but invest a portion of it. For this to be so, output $C_I' c_I + v_I + s_I$, must exceed current level of constant capital, $c_I + c_{II}$, so that $v_I + s_I > c_{II}$ (or, equivalently, total expenditure of workers and capitalists $v_I + v_{II} + s_I + s_{II}$ should exceed total output of consumption goods, $c_{II} + v_{II} + s_{II}$). Necessarily, the same considerations around balance apply as for simple reproduction – for accumulation to proceed at whatever level, there must be simultaneous balance across use value, monetary and labour balances.

But, whilst it is and proven irresistible to interpret such balances in terms of equilibrium, they are conceptually opposite to any notion of an economy at rest (especially as in orthodox theory that may even interpret Marx as a forerunner of general equilibrium theorizing across the economy as a whole). For reference to accumulation signals that the reproduction schemes, simple or expanded, are based upon 'given' value relations. Yet, as already elaborated in *Capital I*, accumulation is associated with rising productivity and reduced values, especially with the production of relative surplus value. This means that simple reproduction of existing values is always in tension with expanded reproduction of transformed values, reinforcing the point that the reproduction schemes are not about equilibrium. On the contrary, they lay out the structures and processes involved in the production and circulation of (surplus) value even as values themselves are changing. These issues are then taken up in *Capital III*, not least in Marx's treatment of the so-called transformation problem and the law of the tendency of the rate of profit to fall.

ECONOMIC AND SOCIAL REPRODUCTION

Marx's reproduction schemes provide the framework for pursuing, or locating, a number of other topics, some of which are addressed by himself within *Capital II*. One of these is his treatment of unproductive labour. This is defined in relation to the industrial circuit of capital as any wage labour that does not produce surplus value. This can be for one of two reasons. Either wage labour is not employed by capital at all as in the hiring of workers for the provision of personal or other services, such as servants or state officials, without this leading either to the production of commodities or, necessarily, surplus value. Or wage labour can be employed by capital within the sphere of exchange for the purposes of handling trade or for dealing in finance. Such unproductive labour is taken up in *Capital III*, where Marx develops his theories of merchant and banking capital.

Marx also addresses the role of fixed capital in *Capital II*. This is defined by its lasting for more than one circulation period in the circuit of capital, and it is presumed to pass on its value piecemeal over its lifetime. This does itself sharply reveal the contradictory nature of reproduction across use value, exchange value and value. For the use value of fixed capital is the productive services that it provides and, with constant capital in the form of repair and maintenance, these could last more or less indefinitely. This would mean that the value passed on as constant capital by fixed capital from one production period to the next would be small. And, if the life of the machinery, say, could be extended beyond what is normal, some extra profit can be appropriated.

There is, then, pressure for the lifetime of fixed capital to be as long as possible. On the other hand, fixed capital is open not so much to physical as to economic and technological obsolescence, and for two different reasons. Given machinery will tend to be produced more cheaply, and its value reduced, as production of relative surplus value is realized in machinery-producing industries. And, in addition, more powerful and proficient machinery will also tend to displace the old. This all means that capitalists have an incentive to shorten the life of their machinery in the sense of retrieving the value it passes on in as few a number of circulation periods as possible. The result is that the reproduction of fixed capital is subject to competing tensions across its turnover and renewal (see Weeks, 1981a, for a uniquely insightful discussion).

The industrial circuits of capital, and corresponding economic reproduction, also defines or frames, without determining, the position of economic and social activity that does not fall entirely within its orbit. Here, again, two examples are illustrative. The social reproduction of the workforce is reduced to a narrow economic reproduction within the schemes simply by virtue of the payment of the value of labour power, v_I and v_{II}, to the workers, and their corresponding purchase of consumption goods out of $c_{II} + v_{II} + s_{II}$. It follows that the reproduction of labour power otherwise takes place outside the schemes and, as such, must be analysed separately. Within Marxism, this has given rise to the domestic labour debate which has served to highlight the extent to which the (household) labour of social reproduction falls disproportionately upon women who are, thereby, exploited in terms of contributing surplus labour even if not directly under the control of capital as wage labourers.

There are a number of issues here. One is whether wives, for example, are exploited by their husbands – if, within the household itself, one works more than the other and receives less by way of consumption, although this is compatible with male workers being both exploited by capital and overall despite 'subsidy' as it were from a wife. The problem here is that exploitation is primarily being reduced to a matter of differential distribution of consumption, a significant issue in its own right but of limited analytical purchase in specifying relations of production as opposed to those of distribution (for consumption) narrowly interpreted as how much to each person. For Marxism, capitalist exploitation is about individual and systemic relations of control within production as well as the consequences for distribution and consumption. Whilst these cannot be extrapolated to those that prevail within the household or elsewhere, they do have a major influence upon them (not least as consumption goods tend to be derived by commodity purchase however much they are worked by domestic labour as well).

Another issue is whether capitalists exploit women without employing them as wage labourers because they are contributing to a cheaper value of labour power (the exploitation is presumed to be passed on through the male's lower wage) – an interesting parallel is to be found in the cheap labour power hypothesis pioneered by Wolpe (1972) which suggested bantustans reduced its value for the apartheid labour force in manufacture and agriculture. And a third is whether domestic labour produces value or not (since it reproduces labour power as a commodity) and, hence, is productive.

The latter two questions have generated more heat than light in part because they have also been part and parcel of a political debate over whether there should be a demand for wages for housework (see Fine, 1992a, for an overview). This has meant that designating domestic labour as exploited (by capital) or not and as producing value or not have taken on polemical significance. In relation to the value of labour power, the role of domestic labour has to be situated in a complex and multifaceted analysis of the determinants of different elements in the standard of living and how they are distributed across the working class (Fine, 2002). And, by reference to value production, domestic labour is non-productive (neither wage labour nor a source of surplus value for capital) even though it may be exploited (contribute surplus labour) and contributes to the reproduction of that very special commodity labour power. For Marx, though, productive labour is located in a circuit of industrial capital, geared towards the production of commodity for a profit.

The domestic labour debate is just one prominent example of the practice of treating all surplus labour under capitalism, even if not under capital, as if it were, or could be treated as similar to, labour productive of surplus value as defined by the industrial circuit. The same approach has been used in the context of education and the creation of skills, as this creates more valuable labour power. But, once again, as with domestic labour, even though teachers and other workers in the state education system may be exploited in contributing more labour time than is represented by their pay or consumption, they do not labour directly under capitalist relations of production as defined by an industrial circuit of capital. So, to treat them as if they do is both to flatten our understanding of productive labour and to extend it to other types of labour which have their own forms of organization, with the tendency to treat all types of surplus labour as if they are mutually equivalent (Fine and Harris, 1979).

In short, to focus upon economic reproduction in terms of the circuits of capital is both to highlight central aspects of capitalism and to acknowledge the limits of such an analysis as far as economic and social reproduction more generally is concerned. Capitalism does have a tendency to incorporate more and more activity under its umbrella of productive labour. But this is not and cannot be absolute, in part for structural reasons (wage labour in the sphere of exchange, and other labour involved in social reproduction of the workforce) and also because of countertendencies including that of the state to take on the role of social reproduction unproductively and the capacity of unproductive labour to prosper because of extremes of wealth and unemployment (creating a market for personal services). In addition, the cheapening of commodities both undermines domestic production (as in cheap and convenient foods, for example) and reinforces it, with domestic appliances (most notably in the entertainment industries, for example).

19. Exploitation and surplus value

Ben Fine

Marx's value theory comprises an evolving dialogue between a number of elements. These include: the critical reconstruction of classical political economy; the specification of capitalism as a historically specific mode of production with its own structures, processes, agencies and laws or tendencies of development; and the logical reconstruction of the categories of capitalism as they historically present themselves. Both as starting point for exposition and as a conclusion of ongoing analysis, Marx deploys his own version of the labour theory of value as a key concept. For him, value is defined by the labour time of production but its analytical validity derives from the material relations of capitalist commodity production itself. For these bring different concrete labours into equivalence with one another as abstract labour in the fetishized form of exchange values through the market and as expressed in money form (Saad-Filho, 2002; Fine and Saad-Filho, 2010).

COMMODITY EXCHANGES AND THE PRODUCTION OF SURPLUS VALUE

As such the labour theory of value might just as well be confined to pre-capitalist commodity exchange. And, for some, such as Adam Smith, that is where it should be confined given the complexities attached to price theory once profits and rents become a component part of price. But, for Marx, the challenge is to explain how it is that value relations are able to underpin exploitation under capitalism especially, as compared with exploitation under other modes of production, exchange is freely engaged by market participants. For Ricardian socialism, for example, that the wage does not fully exhaust net output is evidence enough of exploitation, that wages are too low, and profits are accordingly an appropriation of value at the 'distributional' expense of workers. Such an explanation is inadequate for Marx, with profits simply being taken at the expense of wages just as feudal dues are taken at the expense of peasants. How does this exploitation materialize in practice under capitalism as no direct appropriation and coercive compulsion seems to be involved?

Significantly, commenting on *Capital* himself, Marx (*Marx-Engels Correspondence 1867*, 'Marx to Engels in Manchester') indicates how important his contribution is in this respect:

> The best points in my book are: 1. (this is fundamental to all understanding of the *facts*) the *two-fold character of labour* according to whether it is expressed in use-value or exchange-value . . . 2. the treatment of *surplus-value regardless of its particular* forms as profit, interest, ground rent, etc.

What is meant by these points and why are they so important? Marx begins with simply commodity exchange in which all commodities exchange at their values and denotes this by C-M-C, with the first commodity C being exchanged for the second C through monetary exchange. The two commodities are of different use values but of the same value (and so is the money also). By contrast, the formula for capital begins with money which purchases commodities and, subsequently, sells for a higher value, M-C- M′, with M′ bigger than M to allow for profit. But if commodities exchange at their values, how is it possible that M should have become M′? The answer is that somewhere along the way, there must have been some addition of value. As labour time in production is the only source of value, production must intervene between M and M′, M . . . P . . . M′. On this basis, if only in *Capital II*, Marx expands the formula for capital to M-C . . . P . . . C′- M′, the industrial circuit of capital. It indicates that the original advance of money capital, M, is used to purchase means of production, C, which are then deployed in the production process, P, yielding commodities, C′, which have contained within them the extra value that will make for the difference between M′ and M.

LABOUR AND EXPLOITATION

This still leaves unanswered how the extra value has been obtained in the passage from C to C′. C can now be divided down into two components, the raw materials that go into making up the final production. Marx refers to this as constant capital, c, because it simply passes on the value that it already has within it to the newly produced commodities, C′. In addition, C includes the purchase of a very special commodity, what Marx terms labour power, the discovery of the double character of which he perceives as one of his claims to originality. Note, first, though that it is not the labourer that is purchased as this would be slavery. Nor, despite the almost universal use to the contrary, is it labour that is purchased. For Marx, it is not possible to purchase labour as this is activity, work, undertaken after the commodity labour power has been purchased. Whilst there may be some obligation to work in light of the exchange, what, how much and how effectively, have yet to be settled as the exchange M-C takes place prior to work in the production process, . . .P . . ., itself.

In light of this, Marx understands the labour power that has been purchased within M-C to be the capacity to labour. For convenience, this is seen as the hire of the labourer for the day, although wage contracts can take on many different forms. What then is the use value of the commodity labour power? In general, labour power, whether commodity or not, has the capacity to create use values although it is not unique in this respect as use values can also be created naturally without the intervention of labour, not least a sunny day as a source of warmth, or rain as a source of water. However, under a commodity producing society, labour power has the unique socially and historically specific capacity of creating commodities themselves, not only use values but also (exchange) value. In other words, unlike any other commodity, labour power has the use value of creating value and, knowingly, or otherwise, that is why it is purchased by capitalists.

But what of the (exchange) value of labour power itself. The crucial point here is that this need bear no relation at all to the amount of labour that is, subsequently, performed any more than the rental for a car places a limit on how far and how long it is driven (within the limits of the hire contract and the car's physical capacities). In short, the amount of value produced by labour power out of its unique use value as creator of value bears no relationship as such to its own value as a commodity.

So the capitalist, in advancing M is able to purchase a commodity, labour power, that has the capacity to produce more value than it costs. Just how much more value is not predetermined but is a matter of conflict between capital and labour in the process of production itself. What is essential for successful capitalist production, however that conflict is resolved, is that the amount of value, or living labour, contributed by labour power should exceed its own value. Otherwise, M' would not exceed M. Now Marx terms as variable capital, v, that portion of M that is advanced to purchase labour power. This is to contrast it with constant capital, c, whose value is merely preserved in the production process. It is not simply, however, that v will lead to more value but that the extra amount itself contributed is variable in the sense of being uncertain as dependent upon how long and intensively the worker adds value in the production process. In addition, whilst M and C are made up of a value magnitude of $c + v$, C' and M' incorporate the value contributed over and above $c + v$, and Marx denotes this by surplus value, s. As a result, living labour, l say, is made up of $s + v$, and the value of each commodity can be broken down into its constituent components, $c + v + s$.

By pinpointing the double character of labour power, Marx discovers the origins of surplus value. Whilst motivated by the search for profit on the part of the capitalist, a much more general and deeper result has been obtained. This is that profit depends upon surplus value but that the latter can also serve as the basis, within capitalism, for other sources of exploitative revenue such as rent and interest. Having first identified their common origins in surplus value, much of the two later volumes of *Capital* and *Theories of Surplus Value* is concerned with how this surplus value is circulated and distributed through exchange as profit, interest and rent. Prices of production (and the transformation problem), profit from commercial as opposed to productive activity, and the role of banking and landed property can all be addressed both as contradictory forms of surplus value and as attached to specific material processes across production and exchange. But, before this can be undertaken, a large proportion of *Capital I* is devoted to examining how surplus value is itself produced, both in the grand sense of what makes it possible and in the narrower sense of what goes on in capitalist production in detail at workplaces themselves in terms of technologies, discipline and so on.

As already indicated, the labour, or value, contributed during the working day is divided into two components, $l = s + v$. These can be measured in money once realized through sale of the commodities produced. But the value represented by v is advanced prior to production (or, irrespective of when workers are paid, they must be hired in advance of production). By contrast, surplus value accrues as a result of, and is only realized together with, recompense for wages paid, after the production process has been completed. Within Marx's approach, this means that there is not a simple distributional division of net output between capital and labour other than as an *ex post* accounting identity, as suggested by Ricardo and his Sraffian followers. Rather, as indicated, advance of v is a precondition of production, and s is its consequence. The relationship between v and s is not a fixed sum distribution but depends upon how much s is extracted out of the production process – how hard and long labour can be made to work.

But why should labourers allow such exploitation rather than working on their own account and enjoying the full fruits of their labour? There are two aspects to an answer. First, workers have no choice. They are unable to work on their own account in general because the only way in which they can gain access to the means of production other than their own labour is through their selling labour power. This is indicative of the class relations peculiar to capitalism – the separation of workers from possession of means of production, their monopoly ownership by a class of capitalists, and yet the formal freedom of workers from feudal or other obligations to work. Second, then, capitalism veils its particular form of exploitation, the class appropriation of surplus labour, through the formal equality that individuals have before the market even if all are free to buy and sell or not from positions of great inequality from which the compulsion to work, or wage-slavery, derives.

This inequality of position does prevail, however, outside the market as such, in the domain of capitalist production. Here, prior to the transformation through the production process of v into l (or v plus s), capital's imperative is to extend s as far as possible for a given v, and this involves conflict and the attempted exercise of authority in the production process. For the use value of labour power becomes one of producing not only use values and values but, first and foremost, it is to produce as much surplus value as can be achieved. How is this done? Marx discusses this both in broad theoretical terms and also in great empirical detail.

ABSOLUTE AND RELATIVE SURPLUS VALUE

Theoretically, he offers the distinction between the production of 'absolute' and 'relative' surplus value. For absolute surplus value (ASV), the surplus value produced is expanded by the simple expedient of lengthening the amount of time for which a worker is required to work for a given value of labour power, v. The most elementary form of ASV is extension of the working day, from eight to ten hours, for example. But value contributed in return for a given value of labour power can be increased by other methods as well. These include increasing the intensity of work – filling out the amount of time during which labour is done during the working day by eliminating breaks, by making work continuous and by multitasking – and by extending work to women and children. Interestingly, the latter indicates that Marx considers the value of labour power not simply as the wage that is paid to the individual worker but one part of the relationship by which the working class is reproduced – and how much work is performed by the working-class family to be able to gain access to common standards of consumption through purchased commodities. In the context of ASV, Marx also details the conflicts between capital and labour over the length of the working day during the course of the nineteenth century, and the more general attempts to gain and implement legislation restricting the length of the working day and offering protection to working-class women and children.

What characterizes ASV, then, is the production of more (surplus) value but without modification of production processes and productivity (other than in imposing discipline to work longer and harder). By contrast, production of relative surplus value (RSV) does not depend upon the production of more value but the redivision of a given working day in favour of surplus value. Formally, this is achieved through reducing the value of labour power by increasing productivity either directly in the wage goods industries themselves or in the sectors that produce raw materials for use in consumption goods. For a given set of wage goods, productivity increase will mean a lower value of labour power (to the extent that this is not offset by an increase in the level of wages).

Marx's theory of RSV, though, goes far beyond a simple definition in a number of respects. For he puts forward a theory of productivity increase specific to capitalism. He observes that it involves the working up of ever more raw materials into final products – so much wood and nails and so on, into chairs and tables. This is not simply more output out of the same inputs (as with neoclassical economics and its shift of a production function). Nor is it to deny that productivity increase can come from the invention and use of new products and technological processes, and the more economical use of inputs. Indeed, Marx emphasizes how much more than other modes of production capitalism deploys science and technology in the service of capitalist production. This cannot, however, be the subject of a general theory of productivity increase because it is liable to be product and process specific. In contrast, capitalism does systematically proceed by the working up of more raw materials by workers in a given time.

And Marx traces out how this is achieved. He begins with manufacture, literally production by hand. The hand, though, can be displaced by a specialized tool, and the arm by a central source of power. The division of labour into specialized tasks can then be recombined in the form of machinery. In this way, Marx perceives capitalism as tending to displace workers from the process of production and locating them as minders of machines. Such a transformation of the methods of production (compared to reliance upon those inherited from pre-capitalism) leads Marx to refer to the specifically capitalist method of production as machinofacture or the factory system, and he sees this as the real subordination in production of the worker to capital (as opposed to the formal subordination associated with ASV).

In addition, production of RSV is associated with an increase in the mass of raw materials used per worker, as more use values are worked up into final products. This itself also depends upon more fixed capital per worker. For Marx, the production of RSV gives rise to an increasing technical composition of capital, and this is a major factor underpinning his understanding of many economic and social aspects of the capitalist mode of production. These include the process of competition under capitalism, by which larger capitals are more productive and eliminate the smaller. Such competition does itself depend upon competitive access to finance, which increasingly underpins the accumulation of capital and a much more general restructuring of capitals into larger units. Similarly, capitalist production tends to expand in some localities and to decline in others, giving rise to combined and uneven development (not least between town and country as well as between nations). And the displacement of workers from the production process and the need for them in ever larger numbers in ever larger factories both creates and draws upon a reserve army of labour or unemployed. Accumulation both throws workers out of work and draws them back in again.

Significantly, though, the importance of the production of ASV and RSV is not confined to the economy alone however broadly conceived. Explicitly for later Marxists, especially in Lenin's *Imperialism*, the two main ways of producing surplus value are understood in terms of sequential periods of stages of capitalism. Production of ASV marks the period immediately following upon the transition to capitalism. In contrast, the specifically capitalist methods of production attached to the production of RSV mark a more advanced, monopoly stage of capitalism, more dependent upon productivity increase than crude exploitation of the working class.

Indeed, such a stage of capitalism is only fully established once legislation has been implemented to constrain such exploitation. For, paradoxically, the more absolute surplus value is extracted, the higher tends to be the value of labour power socially. Overwork and low living standards mean shorter lives and less surplus value per worker over a shorter working life. Legislation to protect workers, and welfare measures on their behalf, impart an impetus to the production of RSV whether gained through working-class struggle itself for such measures or the enlightened self-interest of large-scale capital in competition with and to eliminate cruder forms of exploitation. Either way, crises tend to intensify the pressure to revert to production of ASV and to erode welfare gains, as capitalists engage in the struggle for competitive survival and to shift the burden of the crisis to the working class. At a grander level, the production of RSV reveals both the contradictions of capitalism – how the growing capacity to produce creates crises, unemployment and misery – and the potential for such capacity to be used for socialist alternatives.

THE VALUE OF LABOUR POWER

Exploitation and the rate of surplus value are clearly closely linked to the value of labour power. The higher this is, the lower is exploitation and vice versa. So how is the value of labour power determined? Marx himself referred to moral and historical elements, by which is generally understood what is customary. Within the Marxist literature, especially where it is deductively inclined as with Sraffianism, this has given rise to dual definitions of the value of labour power. One is as a bundle of use values, what the working class on average gets to consume. The other is as a quantum of value. For a static economy, one without any productivity change, the two coincide with one another. But, otherwise, productivity increase would lead to a lower value of labour power by the first definition and to a larger bundle of moral and historical elements by the second definition.

What, then, is the value of labour power – a bundle of goods or a quantum of value? Within Marx's own writings, he appears to switch between the two. For the production of relative surplus, for example, a fixed bundle seems to prevail as productivity increase reduces the value of labour power. But, for the law of the tendency of the rate of profit to fall, based on productivity increase, the rate of surplus value is taken as given for the law (but allowed to increase as a countertendency). This raises the question of how is productivity increase distributed between capital and labour, thereby redefining the value of labour power in physical and value terms. For some, such as Lebowitz (2010), the answer lies in the strength of organization and class struggle derived from the working class at the point of production, as measured by what he terms the degree of separation (the more workers are united, the more they gain from accumulation). For him, Marx and his followers have been unduly concerned with the objective power of capital without taking due account of the power of resistance from labour.

Fine (1998, 2002, 2008) takes a different view, arguing that such resistance is not overlooked within Marx and Marxism, especially in detailed studies of struggles within and around labour markets and for the moral and historical elements in determining the value of labour power – with Engels's study of the housing conditions of the English working class being a classic. But such struggles need to be appropriately located at a more concrete level of analysis that distinguishes between and within different labour markets and different items of consumption. The moral and historical element in the value of labour power should not be understood as an average across all workers. Rather it reflects differentially determined and differentially distributed norms of consumption and labour market conditions, across both monetary remuneration and the levels and composition of use value consumption. This is reflected in different food, health, pension, housing and transport systems and so on, each deeply and uniquely rooted in different ways and to a different extent in capitalist production and exploitation. And labour markets are also differentially organized and rewarded according to the ways in which the labour process within and across different workplaces have been integrated into economic and social reproduction. This is not to deny the significance of class struggle and organization at the point of production (and elsewhere) nor the validity of the value of labour power as a concept. Rather, it is to locate and reconstruct such concepts at more concrete levels in conformity to the more complex material functioning of capital itself.

20. Feminist economics

Radhika Balakrishnan and Savitri Bisnath

This entry focuses on four themes: (1) class, sex and gender relations as categories of analysis; (2) linkages between production, reproduction and cooperative conflict within the household; (3) the relationship between paid and unpaid work; and (4) the flexibilization of labour.

BEYOND CLASS AS A CATEGORY OF ANALYSIS

Early feminist economists criticized Marxist analyses of labour by arguing that they universalized the male worker in industrialized economies as representative of all workers; thereby foreclosing a more complex, gendered analysis – one that is grounded in the lived realities of women and men, and of uneven power relations within the labour market, the household and the economy. Feminist analysis moved beyond situating the economic man as the norm in definitions of economics to considerations of humans in relation to the world (Nelson, 1993).

They built on the Marxist category of class to bring in sex and gender relations in order to better understand women's and men's positions, roles and responsibilities in the labour market and society as a whole. In particular, feminists argue that power in economic relations is erased by standard theories and models that de-emphasize difference as constraints or differences in natural endowments, while erasing variables such as distinct capabilities and access to resources between and among women and men. This focus also enables analyses of those commodities and processes that are necessary for capital accumulation, including the reproduction of the labour force.

Resulting from these critiques early feminist interventions expanded the Marxist notion of production to highlight and discuss reproduction as a critical contributing factor to the production process. Reproductive work is done within the household and is typically conducted by women. Such work includes the caring of children and the cooking of meals for family members. It is often unpaid and supports social reproduction and human development. So-called reproductive work helps sustain one of the critical components of the production process – labour (Elson, 1993). Feminist analyses, grounded in both the material realities of women as workers in the waged labour market and the role of reproduction to the production process, served to usher in a field of economics that placed the material realities of women to the fore:

> [A] significant part of economic life takes place in an area of production largely ignored
> in standard economic analysis, namely household production of non-marketed goods and
> services, which are vital for social reproduction and human development. There is a dynamic

interaction between this production and that of the market economy, as household members, especially women, must allocate their time between the two. (Floro, 1995, p. 1913)

HOUSEHOLD, REPRODUCTION AND PRODUCTION LINKAGES

Feminist economists, building on the Marxian contributions to the domestic labour debate of the 1970s, attempted to engender economic analyses through prioritizing and analysing reproductive work and power relations within the household. Highlighting the process of reproduction as well as its linkages with the production process, feminist economists prioritized the household as a critical site from which to understand the ways in which gendered power relations in part affect the positions of women as paid and unpaid workers. Women play dual roles in the economy, as workers in the production of commodities and as unpaid caregivers within households. As such women and gender relations are integral to the capitalist mode of production.

In the earlier decades of feminist analysis, informed by feminist scholarship on development, feminist economists also illuminated the connection between labour market segmentation and sex segregation, highlighting the ways in which sex segregation is linked to the reproduction of the labour force. For example, in her article 'Reproduction, production and the sexual division of labour', Beneria (1979, p. 204) argued that:

> women's participation in production, the nature of their work, and the division of labour between the sexes [can be] viewed as the result of women's reproductive activities.

An analysis of women's role in reproduction is essential to understanding both the extent and nature of their participation in productive activities, including their role as a flexible reserve of labour. Under a wage labour system they are often the source of cheap labour for capitalist enterprises. However, their contributions are for the most part unrecognized and remain unaccounted for, specifically reproductive work within the household. This erasure has in turn facilitated the formulations of allocative and distributive policies and actions that are gendered, in that they disproportionately favour men, for example, calculations of social security benefits that are often based on paid work. This analysis then shifted to an understanding of the role that women play in the care economy (Folbre, 1995).

Feminist theorists also expanded the analysis of women's issues to emphasize gender relations. The shift from 'women' and 'sex' to 'gender' and 'gender relations' brought power relations between women and men into the picture. The sole reliance on sex as the analytical category for addressing inequalities faced by women and men failed to deal adequately with those relationships and institutions through which inequalities are perpetuated. This theoretical framework for understanding women's positioning as well as their roles and responsibilities in developing countries did not question the rules, procedures and practices of the key institutions, such as trade rules, labour market policies and development planning, through which development and economic policies are formulated and implemented. This is clearly seen in development planning with the shift in planning approaches from women in development to gender and development.

Women's choices and preferences are informed by their positions in society. Thus, uneven development between countries and asymmetrical power relations within global institutions constitute situations where nation-states and women and men do not enter into, or participate in, international trade and the global economy on equal terms (see below). Feminists from developing countries in particular argue for feminist attention to be paid to issues relating to race, caste and the location of countries within the global economic order.

This theoretical framework, coupled with the prioritization of gender relations *and* sex as categories of analyses, enabled feminists to understand better that women's structural positionings vary depending on their race, class, age and their country's structural position in the international economic and political orders, and are partially (re)constituted through their relations with economic, political and socio-cultural institutions and processes. In addition there emerged a recognition that, though constrained, women's participation in productive activities has the potential to reconstitute reproductive roles.

CONTRADICTORY EFFECTS OF LABOUR MARKET PARTICIPATION

The Marxist tradition has focused on class conflict with the assumption that the household is undifferentiated and family relations are harmonious and egalitarian. Feminists introduced the realities of uneven power relations and conflict within the family. In the 1980s and 1990s, they argued for a model of the household as an economic unit (Sen, 1983, Elson, 1998) by pointing to both cooperative and conflicting elements in family relations (Sen, 1983).

They also introduced the notion of bargaining among family members by arguing that the distribution of resources and work within the household are in part informed by power relations among different individuals within the family. For example, adult male family members tend to be better placed to bargain because of their position in the labour market. It is important to note that women's and men's locations in the labour market are in part linked to access to employment opportunities, productive assets, education as well as sex discrimination in the labour market. The relationship between reproduction and production raised a critical point of investigation: how is relative bargaining power affected by the production process?

Agarwal (1997) argues that gender relations impact on economic outcomes in multiple and contradictory ways. This is in part because of the differing capabilities between women and men, access to, and control of, resources and their resulting positions in formal and informal labour markets. She also notes that gender relations interact with other structures that promote socio-economic hierarchies based on class, caste and race, and serve to reinforce inequalities within the labour market, communities and the larger economy.

For example, within the neoliberal framework, labour is assumed to be mobile. However, this assumption erases the facts that skilled tends to be more mobile than unskilled labour, and that citizenship matters. Further, it fails to differentiate between the ability and cultural acceptability of female and male workers to move from one type of job to another, or to move from one spatial location to another in the pursuit of a job. In addition, and to varying degrees, women have been forbidden by legislation from working night shifts, principally 'for their protection' and, in some contexts, because of the impropriety of women being in public spaces at night. At first glance this can be interpreted as a feminist action. However, this type of 'protective' labour legislation has the paradoxical result of protecting men's jobs (Bisnath and Elson, 1999). In other words, the economic is never prior to the social but always constitutive of it.

Research conducted in the Americas and Asia enabled feminist scholars to document the contradictory nature of employment on women and their families. For example, at the same time as participation in the export processing zones exploited stereotypical notions of women as submissive and docile (particularly in the Asian context), thereby enabling managers to insist on repetitive and monotonous work for long hours, women's bargaining positions within the household shifted when they became wage earners.

Feminists have also brought attention to the multiple roles that women often play. As a result they have the double burden of participating in both paid and unpaid work. This dual role and responsibility have the effect of undermining their position and negotiating power in the paid labour market.

ECONOMIC RESTRUCTURING AND LABOUR MARKET FLEXIBILIZATION

Over the last 30 years the flexibilization of production has increasingly disintegrated production processes at the national and international levels. This is most obvious in the case of the services and manufacturing sectors where activities performed abroad are now combined with activities performed more cheaply at home. This shift in international trade patterns makes it more profitable increasingly to outsource parts of the production process, further breaking up the production chain across countries and regions. From this restructuring emerged the need to examine cycles and trends in the relationship between the global distribution of labour and skill sets and the disintegration of the production chain. Given that social benefits are typically linked to participation in full-time employment, the insecure labour market also makes it more difficult for women to establish those rights and entitlements that are often critical to their well-being, specifically at the end of their lives.

Men and women participate in, and are affected by, international trade in multiple ways: as producers, consumers, traders and caregivers. As noted above, increases in international trade have improved the demand for female labour in specific sectors of, and areas in, the world economy. For example, a critical factor in the location of foreign factories is the availability of a suitable labour force that increases profit by increasing the output to cost ratio. In the 1960s, developing countries, with their low wages and perceived low skilled female workforce, became attractive to foreign capital. This ushered in a new type of wage employment for women, particularly in the manufacturing sector where women were selected for their 'nimble fingers' in what was referred to as the global assembly line.

As markets expand, an increasing number of women are employed in the labour-intensive and low-wage textile and garment industries, specifically in South east Asia and Bangladesh, as well as in electronics and pharmaceuticals companies. As world trade in services has increased and multinationals expand their outsourcing activities, women's employment in the services sector has also grown. An increasing number of women are employed in professional services such as accounting, banking and information technology, including offshore airline booking, mail order, credit cards, word-processing and tourism-related occupations. World trade in services also favours labour migration of women, specifically as domestic workers, for example, women from the Philippines.

However, increased access to jobs, while positive, is not sufficient to increase women's well-being. The gain in the demand for female labour must also be compared to the rise or decline in the proportion of jobs that have security of employment, protection against unfair dismissal, as well as rights for pension, health insurance and parental leave. Historically, women workers in many sectors of the economy have rarely enjoyed the wide spectrum of social and economic rights specified in national and international legislation, including the right to social protection and to form and/or join trade unions. The processes of trade liberalization, privatization and decentralization also often result in an increase in both employment instability and unemployment. Because Free Trade Zones resulted in the geographical dispersion of production, the bargaining power of workers and unions was undermined, as workers were forced to compete across borders. In addition there was little transfer of technology, knowledge and profits to host countries.

Generally speaking, high-wage countries tend to have a more highly skilled labour force than low-wage countries. In addition, women are generally relegated to lower skilled jobs in comparison to men. This is in part linked to access to education and perceived future employment opportunities. In addition, shifts in demand have the potential either to increase or decrease employment, with women often being the first to be let go when there is shrinking demand. Because women typically possess low skill sets they often remain in sectors that are low skilled and vulnerable. Research on subcontracted employment reveals that women are often in the most precarious jobs, with no benefits, and are easily expendable: hired and fired with the changing tide of the market.

Within the concrete context of women's and men's experiences in the production process, feminists call for an expanded traditional analysis of international trade, the global economy and the process of economic globalization. They argue for an approach that documents, analyses and theorizes about the ways in which women's and men's positions in production and reproduction, within specific spatial and temporal contexts, inform market structures and trade, and is in turn impacted by them. In addition, they underline the importance of a theoretical framework and analysis that link women's and men's participation in the labour market with relevant institutions and cultural processes that inform their lived realities as women and men as these elements are intimately connected with the gendered outcomes of production.

CONCLUSION

In this entry we trace the contributions of feminist theorists to economics. We highlight the shift from the model of the rational economic man to a framework that uses sex (fe/male) and gender relations as essential categories of analysis in discussions of the production process and the labour market. We also underline the functional linkages between women and men as both workers and reproducers of the labour force, thereby positioning the household as a critical site for a better understanding of the processes of production and reproduction, while highlighting the ways in which productive and reproductive work can serve to both increase opportunities as well as erode them. This entry provides compelling reasons for engendering analyses of the production process in order to better understand and address gender inequalities and discrimination.

21. Feudalism

George C. Comninel

The idea of feudalism is enormously contested among historians and theorists of all stripes. With some notable exceptions, non-Marxist British historians have generally conceived 'feudalism' as a formal hierarchy of lords and fiefs – a 'technical' conception identified with F.L. Ganshof (Comninel, 2000a). Recently, whether feudalism in those terms ever even existed has been challenged (Reynolds, 1996). Marxists – and other socially oriented medievalists like Georges Duby (1968) – have instead followed Marc Bloch in focusing on 'feudal society', comprising peasants as well as lords (Comninel, 2000a). While often posed as alternatives, these views are compatible (to whatever extent a formal feudal hierarchy actually existed). Marxists concerned with feudalism as a system of class relations cannot, in any case, dismiss relations among lords as irrelevant.

Marxists, however, generally differ from non-Marxists in conceiving feudalism as one of a sequence of 'modes of production' or forms of class society. Usually grounded in a brief account of such modes by Marx, Marxist approaches must confront three basic sets of questions: (1) how, when and why was there a transition from ancient society – usually understood in terms of a 'slave mode of production' – to feudal society; (2) how should the class relations of feudalism be conceived; and (3) how, when and why was there a subsequent transition from feudalism to capitalism.

A further issue has been how, if at all, historical developments elsewhere relate to European feudalism. Focusing on any domination of peasants by landowners, some accounts have multiplied feudal and 'semi-feudal' societies across the globe. The debates over feudalism, therefore, remain too numerous and complex to detail in any short survey. Certain lines of enquiry, however, have been influential.

One crucial contribution was the 'Transition Debate' launched by Paul Sweezy and Maurice Dobb (1978). In retrospect, this mostly exposed the weakness of Marxist accounts of feudalism and the transition to capitalism down through the 1960s. Presuppositions about modes of production and historical processes bedevilled the debate, revealing how little agreement there was over Marx's ideas and methods, and how to apply them. The core disagreement was over Sweezy's contention that feudalism was fundamentally defined by the absence of market relations, lordly 'income' taking the form of compulsory labour by serfs, challenging Dobb's broader conception of feudalism as the appropriation of peasant surpluses through rent, whether in labour, kind or money. Ultimately, neither conception is adequate.

Despite its limitations, the debate importantly focused attention on the discussion of feudal rent in *Capital III*, chapter 47. Marx argued that, because peasants in the first instance produce to meet immediate household needs, 'surplus-labour for the nominal owner of the land can only be extorted from them by other than economic pressure, whatever the form assumed may be'. Indeed:

> all forms in which the direct labourer remains the 'possessor' of the means of production and labour conditions necessary for the production of his own means of subsistence, the property relationship must simultaneously appear as a direct relation of lordship and servitude, so that the direct producer is not free; a lack of freedom which may be reduced from serfdom with enforced labour to a mere tributary relationship.

In this context Marx uttered a striking statement of historical materialist method:

> The specific economic form, in which unpaid surplus-labour is pumped out of direct producers, determines the relationship of rulers and ruled, as it grows directly out of production itself and, in turn, reacts upon it as a determining element. Upon this, however, is founded the entire formation of the economic community which grows up out of the production relations themselves, thereby simultaneously its specific political form. It is always the direct relationship of the owners of the conditions of production to the direct producers . . . which reveals the innermost secret, the hidden basis of the entire social structure and with it the political form of the relation of sovereignty and dependence, in short, the corresponding specific form of the state.

Applying equally to capitalist and pre-capitalist societies, this statement dramatically underlines a crucial distinction between them. In the capitalist mode of production, surplus is appropriated through seemingly purely economic relations, formally distinct from relations of political power; in pre-capitalist modes of production no comparable separation of the political from the economic can exist. Instead, pre-capitalist surplus appropriation depends on 'extra-economic coercive force' (whether manifest or implicit). This recognition of the fundamentally extra-economic character of pre-capitalist class relations marked a significant theoretical advance.

When the Transition Debate began, Marx's *Grundrisse* was almost unknown. A small part concerning pre-capitalist economic formations was subsequently published in which Eric Hobsbawm confronted problems with mode of production analyses (1965); the whole appeared in 1973. This previously obscure work had considerable impact upon those attending to the Transition Debate. Perry Anderson, particularly, drew together elements from these sources in a highly original and influential account of the arc of Western European history from antiquity to capitalism (1974a, 1974b).

Anderson's work transformed the way feudalism was conceived by Marxists and non-Marxists alike by identifying 'parcellized sovereignty' as its specific form of pre-capitalist extra-economic coercion. He also rejected outright the idea that the feudal mode of production existed outside Europe, making the novel (often overlooked) argument that non-European societies must be investigated without preconceptions, looking for historically specific class relations and modes of production, rather than attempting to fit them into a European model. It is ironic, therefore, that his own analysis of European history is undercut precisely by its limitation to the usual few modes of production.

Anderson begins with an ancient world characterized by a slave mode of production. He argues this was self-limiting in its dependence on an external supply of slaves, causing a transition to feudalism during the later Roman Empire. Feudalism then characterized the entire Middle Ages, remaining dominant well into the modern era. The capitalist mode of production, however, developed in medieval urban interstices where Roman legacies persisted, igniting economic take-off and eventually producing 'bourgeois revo-lutions' that established contemporary societies. This account has been challenged on several key points, from the existence of a slave mode of production to the idea of bour-geois revolution (Comninel, 1987; Wood, 1988). When taken as a whole, however, it also reveals how difficult it is to make sense of Western European history with just these three modes of production.

On the one hand, it is hard to comprehend the complex histories of ancient societies – from the early Athenian polis and early Roman republic, through the rise of Hellenistic monarchies and growth of Roman imperial power, the heyday of the *Pax Romana*, and ultimately the later Empire's huge *latifundia* and stifling bureaucratism – based on the single idea of a slave mode of production. On the other hand, Anderson takes feudal society to have developed from the third through to the ninth centuries; then undergoing profound crisis and population collapse from the mid-fourteenth through fifteenth centu-ries; only to survive in revised and transitional form as the 'Absolutist State' through the eighteenth century. Little of the ancient world seems to fit the slave mode of production attributed to it, and of 1500 years of the feudal mode of production, 1100 are spent in transition or crisis!

Setting aside the overall account, it is striking that, although Anderson does more than simply acknowledge extra-economic coercion in conceiving feudalism, identifying its specific form to be 'parcellized sovereignty', he offers little more of substance in build-ing on this. Instead, the largely unexamined possession of coercive power by holders of estates seems to develop into parcellized sovereignty merely through a long-term decline of central state power. The essential elements of transition from slave to feudal modes of production, then, are a replacement of household and barracks slaves by dependent peasant tenants (of various statuses), accompanied by an accelerating recession of public authority in Rome and its successor kingdoms. It is in these terms that the transition is conceived to unfold between the third and ninth centuries.

While this analysis asserts continuity at the level of the estate (indeed, it becomes hard to distinguish between Roman *latifundium* and medieval manor), it poorly accords with the substantial political and legal continuity at the level of the state that is now generally recog-nized in the early Middle Ages. In large part, this is because there is no place in Anderson's account for the survival of large numbers of free persons not living as dependent tenants on lordly estates, for which the evidence is incontrovertible into the tenth century. Among historians who continue to think in terms of 'feudal society', there is, indeed, widespread recognition that it came into existence very rapidly between the later decades of the tenth century and the early eleventh century – centring on the year 1000 – through a 'trans-formation', or even 'revolution', based precisely on a parcellization of sovereign royal power, in the first instance among regional magnates, from whom it increasingly devolved, eventually reaching the level of individual *seigneuries* (Comninel, 2000a).

THE FEUDAL TRANSFORMATION AND FEUDAL MODE OF PRODUCTION

This sudden transformation of much of Western Europe, through the fragmentation of previously royal power in the empire established by Charlemagne, had enormous consequences, marking a rupture far more profound than the 'fall' of Rome. To begin with, regional magnates erected fortifications and, as castellans, arrogated the fundamental royal powers of the *ban*: taxation, command and the provision of 'justice' in courts. Public courts that had continued to serve free men into the mid-tenth century thus became appurtenances of the estates of lords, whose primary relationship with peasants now took the form of territorial jurisdiction. As a result, villages of free peasants, previously independent of lords and manors, were suddenly subject to the arbitrary authority of a lord – through judgements in his courts, obligations to build and maintain fortifications and roads and, especially, unrestrained taxation. Almost immediately, the sovereign powers of jurisdiction became by far the most lucrative element of lordly property. Lordship was itself transformed, from an informal status of men with many dependents on their estates – the 'magnates' – into a formal Order in society. In this new social conception, the lordly second Order was vested with secular rule, although the Order of the Church had formal precedence.

Within the labouring third Order, any distinction between free and unfree disappeared entirely, outside the cities. Virtually all rural producers became subject to immediate lordly rule, and were made to pay dearly for it. Most taxes, dues and fines took the form of money payments, and a rapid re-monetarization followed. Indeed, minting became a lucrative right of sovereignty enjoyed by lords possessing sufficient jurisdiction.

During the heyday of feudal society, the population of Western Europe roughly tripled, mostly between 1100 and 1250. Forests were cleared, wetlands drained, and wastes generally reduced and transformed through varieties of production. Trade revived, generating dramatic urban growth in northern Italy, where cities acquired republican self-government in conjunction with a take-off both in manufacture of luxury goods (for example, Florentine woollens) and imports from the East, satisfying growing demand from newly rich feudal lords in northwest Europe. Towns also grew in the feudal heartland, and great gothic cathedrals were built. Western European lords increasingly organized the conquest and colonization of Eastern Europe. Culture was transformed by chivalry, and a new pre-eminence of the Church at the apex of society. And, of course, the Crusades were launched. In short, feudal society quickly and fundamentally transformed Europe, in ways that most Marxist historians and theorists have completely overlooked because of preconceived ideas about the nature, number and timing of pre-capitalist modes of production, and the transitions between them.

Still, Marx's assertion that the specific form of surplus appropriation is the key to both the political and economic organization of society is readily revealed to be sound for parcellized sovereignty in the feudal mode of production. Not only was parcellized sovereignty the immediate means for extra-economic appropriation of surplus, and foundation for the relations between lords and peasant producers, but it figured centrally in the organization of feudal production. Pre-capitalist agrarian production has in most times and places depended on self-reproducing peasant households (agrarian production by barracks slaves was common only in parts of Rome's West, between the second century BCE and the third century CE, and never dominant even then). Outside of areas of irrigation and water-course management, formal intrusion into largely autarkic household production was limited, and even then individual households remained largely self-managing beyond the particulars of water supply.

The feudal mode of production, however, was dramatically different, its open-field systems of collective crop and livestock management directly dependent upon the court of the lord. Rotation of crops was known prior to the feudal transformation, and sometimes practised on the lord's fields in manors. Only after the establishment of parcellized sovereignty, however, were lordly manors integrated with the fields of peasant villages and all fields subdivided into narrow strips, each possessed by separate individuals (including the lord), widely scattered but equally divided among two, three or – rarely – four fields of systematic crop rotation (Verhulst, 2002). The court of the lord was essential in regulating this system – as is evident in the continued role of the 'court leet' in the village of Laxton, Nottinghamshire, the only place where open-field farming is still practised. The more productive the soil, and the greater its maximum potential population, the more important was the court's role in coordination and regulation. In subdivided fields, livestock must be kept away from crops, and crops grown in sequence for collective harvests and the use of stubble for herds pastured in common. With open-field agriculture, virtually every aspect of production is directly subject to legal regulation – more intrusive, even, than practices of irrigation.

Such collectively regulated, labour-intensive production tends to maximize the population supported by pre-capitalist peasant production, varying in form, details and degree of intensity with geography and quality of the land. This generalized non-capitalist intensification of production – not grounded in innovation, but in upholding custom as law through effective local jurisdiction – was responsible for the demographic upsurge of feudal Europe. For lords, demographic growth translated into more residents subject to fines, dues and per capita taxes, with increases over time not only in the extent of land in production, but in output per hectare. For peasants, it increased resources both in households and in the village as a whole, expanded total production and potentially also the standard of living (if greater lordly impositions could be resisted).

The implications of such patterns have been extensively analysed by demographically inclined historians (Aston and Philpin, 1985). What they have failed to recognize, however, is that such patterns are not general to pre-capitalist societies, even within Western Europe, but follow directly from the transformation of early medieval manors and independent villages into feudal *seigneuries,* ruled through parcellized sovereignty in wholly novel ways, and with unprecedented consequences. While it is true that the crisis of feudal society in the mid-fourteenth century was caused by over-population of the land relative to its productive capacity, this was no 'natural' phenomenon, but the consequence of a specific system of class relationships operating over time.

The historical details of feudal societies are sufficiently well-established for this brief overview to provide an adequate means of entry and analysis. Once the specific social form that emerged from the parcellization of sovereignty around the year 1000 is clearly distinguished from the sort of manorial society that preceded it, much of the errors and confusion in prior accounts can be sorted out. What remains especially to be noted, however, is that this feudal transformation grew out of, and was centred upon, the monarchy constructed and repeatedly extended by the Franks. The heartland of feudalism was the most completely developed areas of Frankish rule, primarily northern France and western Germany, from which it spread. The subsequent imposition of feudalism in Eastern Europe, southern Italy and the Crusader states is notable, but by far the most significant extension of the feudal mode of production was through the Norman Conquest of England.

ENGLISH 'FEUDALISM' AND THE TRANSITION TO CAPITALISM

Prior to the Norman Conquest, Anglo-Saxon England had developed a strong central state, in striking contrast to contemporary Continental developments. As Duby observed, feudal society in England was, therefore, unique:

> Inside the 'manor', authority over men and over land, domestic lordship and land lordship, coincided. On the other hand the autonomous *seigneurie banale*, the independent territorial lordship, did not, properly speaking, exist at all. William the Conqueror held all the castles. (1968, p. 194)

Through the Conquest, William made good a real claim to the throne, not only acquiring, but strengthening its central power. His retention of a system of effective royal courts had the most profound historical consequences.

William carved out some 10000 manors in England, conveying most to his followers. Through this largely new social framework, virtually the whole of feudal social relations of production, and virtually the whole range of feudal exactions, were introduced into England. Open-field agriculture, with its subdivided fields and manorial courts, was imposed, along with its usual geographic variations. The manorial courts exercised nearly complete jurisdiction over roughly three-quarters of the peasantry, whom royal jurists determined to be unfree based on the burden of their obligations. The courts also possessed jurisdiction over production in the open-fields, regulating free and unfree alike.

In France, all peasants equally were subject to arbitrary lordly jurisdiction, except as villages eventually purchased charters of freedom to fix their obligations. In England, however, although most peasants were unfree, and conceived as chattels of the manor, roughly one-quarter were taken to be free (having less onerous obligations) and, thus, entitled to justice in the King's courts. In these, a Common Law of property rights developed – limited, however, to the free peasants and lords having 'freehold' tenures. Initially, royal justices counterbalanced the local power of lords, issuing writs holding them to account for abuse of free peasant property (Comninel, 2000a). These royal writs were so effective in preserving property rights, however, that lords themselves soon turned to them to protect infants and other vulnerable heirs, for which feudal law was wholly unreliable.

The specific form of extra-economic surplus appropriation in England, therefore, differed crucially in relation to the state, compared to France, and with this difference a double legal system developed during the feudal era. English manors partook in the general historical patterns of the feudal mode of production, through the open-field production regulated in their manorial courts. Royal courts, however, evolved to provide elaborate instruments protecting freehold – but not customary – property rights. The Common Law established truly effective abstract property rights, which underlay the day-to-day regulation of customary tenurial succession and open-field production in the manorial courts.

As Robert Brenner first demonstrated (Aston and Philpin, 1985), the final crisis of feudal society brought radically different results in England and France. Through unique historical processes that enclosed the open-fields and eliminated customary law, Common Law property rights emerged as the foundation for agrarian capitalism in

England, eventually leading to fully capitalist society through the Industrial Revolution (Comninel, 2000a). In France, by contrast, specifically feudal forms of politically constituted property increasingly were transformed into state offices within the 'Absolutist State' – no longer truly feudal, but still entirely non-capitalist (Comninel, 1987). Only after the Napoleonic Wars did industrial capitalist social relations of production begin to transform the various non-capitalist Continental societies that had developed through historically specific paths following the crisis of feudalism.

22. Finance, finance capital and financialization

Thomas Marois

Today, few topics dominate problems of the economy, politics and development more than finance. Indeed, money, the credit system and finance are integral to the reproduction and expansion of capital accumulation processes. Yet what we inherit from Marx comes in part as a set of disorganized notes and references to others' work on finance, these then reorganized by Engels into *Capital III*. Foundational as his ideas are, the dynamics of finance have become more developed and complex than in Marx's time. Unlike many other aspects of Marxism, there have been relatively few elaborations of the theory of finance from a Marxist perspective, and these have failed to keep up with material developments themselves. The most promising work has been around the concepts of finance capital and, more recently, financialization which, a century apart, have grappled with Marx's ideas in a way consistent with his initial propositions on credit and finance.

For Marx, the importance of credit and the financing of capitalist development derives from the historical importance of money capital in capitalist production. In particular, credit emerges from exchange relations in general but between different fractions of capital in particular. Money is required to pay wages and buy means of production and, in this way, money serves as capital. The source of money capital in the productive circuit of capital may come in the form of a loan to a productive capitalist. It is not simply the act of borrowing but the intended use of the money capital to generate profit of enterprise that is important. Money that describes this form of circulation becomes capital and is already capital in itself by its very destination (Marx, *Capital III*, ch. 4). The process of financing accumulation constitutes a relationship between money capitalists, who earn interest, lending to productive capitalists, who earn profit, in a way that enables the expansion and reproduction of capitalist social relations of production.

Marx refers to this form of money capital as interest-bearing capital, that is, money lent out for a price (interest) for which the lender relinquishes control of the original sum lent. Interest represents a claim on the surplus value created in the prospective productive process. Because money capitalists can decide whether to finance an industrial firm or not (that is, exercise allocative control), they are an especially powerful fraction of the capitalist class. Yet the supply of interest-bearing capital is in part reliant on recurrent access to the idle money savings (hoards) of all capitalists (and, as seen later, also those of all other individuals and collectives). In the form of a developed credit system, financial institutions pool all idle savings and transform them into concentrated money capital resources available to a few productive capitalists. Larger pools of available money capital enable more aggressive accumulation. As Marx writes, the credit system emerges as 'a new and terrible weapon in the battle of competition' and is transformed into an 'enormous social mechanism for the centralisation of capitals' (*Capital I*, ch. 25). At the same time, the circuit of money capital, or making more money from money, appears progressively divorced from production and the exploitation of labour, and is therefore seen as the most fetishized form of capital.

FINANCE CAPITAL

The first and most impressive systematic attempt to develop Marx's ideas on finance came from Rudolf Hilferding's *Finance Capital*. Published in German in 1910, *Finance Capital* received great praise from his Marxist contemporaries such as Kautsky, Bukharin and Bauer. Yet it is Lenin's work on imperialism (*Imperialism, the Highest Stage of Capitalism*, 1916) that owes a great analytical debt to Hilferding, but also an apology for eclipsing his insights on finance. *Finance Capital* elaborates on Marx by looking at what was occurring in Germany and Austria to interpret the great historical transformations in the relations between money, credit, banks and industrial capital. Hilferding remains theoretically consistent with Marx by seeing capitalist profit as originating in production and realized in circulation (ch. 9). Likewise, his core understanding of finance sees the credit system socializing many people's money for use by a few in order to overcome the barriers individual private property poses for capitalist production (ch. 10). The result is that Hilferding sees modern capitalism as defined by processes of concentration, which tend to eliminate 'free competition' through the formation of cartels and trusts in a way that brings bank and industrial capital closer together as 'finance capital'. As a whole, *Finance Capital* is a brilliant but uneven elaboration. The parts dealing with money have limited strengths, but the analysis of the joint-stock company (JSC), share capital, the stock exchange, fictitious capital, promoter's profit, banks and concentration take us well beyond the notes left by Marx.

Hilferding's understanding of the JSC is based on a distinction between individual ownership and corporate shareholder ownership (ch. 7, section 1). Under a JSC form of ownership, the barriers to raising capital for expansion can be overcome by issuing shares and raising equity on the stock exchange. Shares are claims to profit or titles to income from future production whose return is not fixed in advance. Anyone can advance their money savings as share capital in a JSC. For Hilferding, stock exchange activity takes on a speculative dimension, which he likens to a game of chance, because of the price changes seen in shares (ch. 8, section 1). While unproductive, this speculation is essential to the stock exchange's function of enabling the conversion of money capital into fictitious share capital and then back into money capital at will. In other words, the JSC, share capital and the stock exchange enable the circulation of fixed capital in money form.

Because individuals can convert their shares into money in the stock exchange as they wish, Hilferding sees shareholding capital as money capital, itself a potential form of fictitious capital. The concept of fictitious capital comes from Marx's understanding of interest-bearing capital and the financing of productive activity by means of credit. Hilferding analyses fictitious capital as different forms of borrowed capital and the significance of the market value of these financial titles. At base, fictitious capital form capitalized claims to profit convertible into money capital (ch. 7, section 4). Shares, as a claim on future profit, are a form of fictitious capital because they do not comprise existing productive capital but a share of future revenue (ch. 7, section 1). Similarly, state bonds are forms of fictitious capital insofar as the bonds do not represent existing capital but a share in the annual tax yield.

The JSC shares are valued in the stock exchange according to the profit they potentially bring (ch. 11), and profits are divided according to one's shareholdings. However, control of a JSC is more complicated. Hilferding emphasizes that shareholders need not own all the JSC shares (that is, the whole company as with individual ownership) (ch. 7, section 2). Rather, large shareholders can dominate a JSC and exert effective control without necessarily even owning 50 per cent of the JSC. For small shareholders falling under the influence of large ones, share ownership does not confer any ownership of the JSC means of production in any real sense. Hilferding thus poses the problem of the separation of ownership from economic control under share ownership (ch. 7, section 3).

The separation of ownership from control alongside the buying and selling of shares through the stock exchange opens opportunities for banks to bring firms under their control by purchasing shares (ch. 7, section 3). However, Hilferding innovatively points to another important way banks begin to acquire and exercise control over JSCs. This is through 'promoter's profit', which arises whenever a JSC is formed through the transformation of productive profit-yielding capital into fictitious interest-yielding capital (ch. 7, section 2). The promoter or issuing bank creates the corporate shares to be sold and, as the issuing bank, drops out of the process after the initial sale of shares (ch. 7, section 1). According to Hilferding, promoter's profit, 'or the profit from issuing shares, is neither a profit, in the strict sense, nor interest, but capitalized entrepreneurial revenue. It presupposes the conversion of industrial into fictitious capital' (ch. 10). Furthermore, banks as promoters can retain possession of part of the shares issued, which allows banks to begin to exercise majority control (ch. 7, section 2).

Hilferding pointed to the advantages of the JSC over privately owned companies. For one, available money capital is no longer a barrier to expansion because a wider pool of credit is accessible to JSCs, no longer being dependent on the concentration of individual property (ch. 7, section 3). At the same time, JSCs are more resilient because, even if an individual shareholder may lose out if the price of their shares fall, another person will purchase the shares at a cheaper price betting on the restructuring and recovery of the JSC. Through this, the JSC can remain intact. Yet Hilferding sees that in this process there is a tendency towards the concentration of enterprises with banks progressively assuming a greater position of power in relation to industrial capital. Be it through the initial share promotions, the granting of finance, or by using the bank's capital to purchase existing shares, banks are able to gain access to JSC management and boards of directors. The banks' functionaries earn bonuses in addition to the benefit of exerting influence over the JSC operations. In these ways, banks hold an enduring interest in many JSCs and acquire a decisive voice over JSC operations (ch. 7, section 2, ch. 8, section 3).

Hilferding thus establishes a logic to how investment credit pulls banks and industry into ever-tighter association. Because banks have an initial interest in a JSC, they must monitor such enterprises and can do so by establishing bank directors on their boards. Little by little, banks establish themselves in a position of power over the JSC. Furthermore, such developments within banking and industry reinforce and mutually impact upon one another. Overcoming barriers to financing leads to concentration in industry that in turn leads to concentration in banking. More and larger banks increase available productive credits, while JSC formation shares increase promoter's profit increasing the banks' capital base. In turn, banks increase their claim over industrial profits and increase their role in financing enterprises, furthering concentration (ch. 11). This creates a situation where banks have an interest in eliminating competition between industries due to their spreading participations within and across them. In consequence, there is a growing tendency to restrict competition between banks leading to the formation of cartels and trusts in a way that minimizes competition.

In this way is formed 'finance capital', the coming together of banks and industry with the former assuming a dominant position. Capital becomes finance capital as its supreme and most abstract expression. Yet finance capital is also given a real social and political force insofar as it organizes around protective policies at home and for expansion internationally. Finance capital as such is linked to the state and imperialism, insofar as the state seeks to enhance power by exporting not only commodities but also capital. The political response to this situation, then, involves progressive forces taking over the state and the banks. This political aspect of Hilferding influenced Lenin and his analysis of imperialism the most, insofar as Lenin emphasized the aggressive and expansionary tendencies of finance capital, leading to imperialist wars, thus relegating Hilferding's more analytical study to a degree of obscurity.

The analytical treatment of finance and finance capital tailed off after Lenin, with the first English translation of *Finance Capital* only appearing in 1981. The reasons are partly conjunctural. In the postwar period of more state-led industrialization, attention turned to analyses of monopoly capitalism (see Baran and Sweezy, 1966). The idea of finance capital was criticized as constituting a far more transitional phase than Hilferding had suggested and pointed instead to the rise of large, management-controlled and self-financed monopoly corporations. Time would also reveal that *Finance Capital* had further deficiencies. Today the dismissal of market-based finance for a thesis suggesting convergence towards a German bank-based model is untenable, even though such differences persist among countries. In this, 'finance capital' has proven too static a concept, and too reliant on the empirical circumstances that inspired it for a general account of capitalism. This is not, though, to dismiss Hilferding's substantial contribution to a Marxist understanding of finance, based on the articulation of finance with productive capital, which has subsequently been taken forward in a number of directions.

David Harvey's (1999) *Limits to Capital* offers a notable synthesis of Marx and Hilferding by placing them on a more general footing in light of postwar developments and the changes in finance since the 1970s. Harvey's contribution is substantial, and only some of his specific innovations can be highlighted. First, while seeing that the credit system functions to mobilize money as capital, Harvey (1999, p. 262) emphasizes the greater complexity today insofar as many more people, including workers, are drawn into the financial system through interest on savings, home mortgages, personal pensions and share options. Second, Harvey understands the functioning and development of the credit system as linked to competitive pressures to reduce barriers to the flow of capital but in a way not restricted to banks and 'finance capital' (1999, p. 263). Moreover, Harvey sees developed credit systems as far more crisis-prone than finance capital allows, which requires that state and private sector financial managers must become increasingly capable of managing financial risks. Third, Harvey maintains that the credit system enables the circulation of fixed capital in anticipation of future productive profits or state revenue (1999, p. 264). Harvey adds to this the individual consumption of expensive durable goods, such as cars and homes, whose interest payments are also linked to future wages as a counter-value. Fourth, Harvey likewise sees the credit system as enabling the creation of fictitious capital, defined as a 'flow of money capital not backed by any commodity transaction' (1999, pp. 265–6), emphasizing the expanded opportunities, debt imperatives and complications this raises for capitalists and states alike (1999, pp. 265–8). Finally, in contrast to a synthesis of industrial and bank capital tending to eliminate competition, Harvey highlights the potential for intra-class conflict as capital-in-general is converted into 'the common capital of a class of money capitalists', whose particular interests may not correspond to the general interests of capital (1999, p. 271). In these ways, Harvey brought Marxist understandings of finance in line with the historical transition to neoliberal capitalism.

There have been relatively fewer attempts to update 'finance capital' as such. Carroll (1989) provides an emblematic example, whose updating of finance capital focuses on the growing international mobility of money capital, the mounting disciplinary power of finance capitalists over integrated circuits of capital and their political organization in the New Right. In contrast to Hilferding, Carroll focuses on the combined and uneven processes of financial expansion, or how the internationalization of money capital and its financial imperatives are differentiated by domestic institutions and accumulation patterns. Uniquely, he highlights how finance capital can have a family-based holding systems variation that allows for the centralization of strategic control such that any tendency towards market-based finance is weakened. Finally, Carroll stresses Hilferding's point that financial power is closely tied to the ownership of blocks of shares in corporations, but in a modern way not restricted to banks. Major shareholders exert strategic power over senior corporate managers, and financial institutions exert allocative power over non-financial firms. This has been a major issue in Marxist accounts of finance insofar as joint-stock ownership is now the dominant form of ownership in firms (Itoh and Lapavitsas, 1999, p.107, Duménil and Lévy, 2004c).

Recently, there has been general agreement that capitalist development has been transformed with the growth in global financial processes since the mid-1970s in both flows and the institutions mediating and supporting these. According to Duménil and Lévy (2004b, p. 660), the current period of neoliberalism, since the 1980s, is an expression of the reasserted power of finance, defined as the upper fraction of capitalist owners and their financial institutions. Only recently, however, have these quantitative changes in finance given rise to a new body of Marxist theorizations on finance.

FINANCIALIZATION

For theorists of the 'Monthly Review' school, like Sweezy, it was not clear until the late 1970s that advanced capitalism required large pools of loanable capital to smooth the realization of value. However, by the late 1990s, Sweezy (1997) had pinpointed three important historical trends since the mid-1970s: '(1) the slowing down of the overall rate of [economic] growth, (2) the worldwide proliferation of monopolistic (or oligopolistic) multinational corporations, and (3) what may be called the financialisation of the capital accumulation process' – three interrelated trends characteristic of the transition to late (monopoly) capitalism. Subsequently, Foster's (2008) elaboration posits financialization as creating larger and more frequent financial bubbles that become increasingly destructive. Still, for this school there is no imminent reason for a breakdown derived from financialization insofar as stagnation in the productive sector can coexist with inflation in the financial sector indefinitely. What Foster does see, however, is the emergence of a new hybrid phase of the monopoly stage of capitalism, that of 'monopoly-finance capital'.

Another account of financialization comes from Lapavitsas (2009) and dos Santos (2009) who build on Marx and Hilferding, as well as earlier work by Itoh and Lapavitsas (1999). They explore key trends in financial incomes within the advanced capitalist states, and argue that the current crisis is a result of financialization, which has arisen primarily in the USA since the 1970s. More specifically, financialization is due to large industrial and commercial firms abandoning banks as a source of credit, opting instead to raise financial resources in open markets or through self-finance by relying more on retained earnings. Consequently, banks have had to find new sources of revenue by offering new financial services to individual workers. Banks have become more dependent on lending to individuals, a process affected by reduced public provision of housing, education, pensions and so on. At the same time, commercial banks have turned towards dealing more in open financial markets through bonds, equities and derivatives. Within this framework, Lapavitsas re-emphasizes how the control of finance trumps the ownership of capital alongside problems of imperialism (for example, the holding of international reserves in the periphery). However, vital to the problem of financialization today is the exploitative role of financial expropriation, seen as foundational to the current crisis. Financial expropriation is defined as the extraction of financial profits directly out of individual personal income (for example, from earning fees and commissions). Financialization in this sense involves both appropriating individual wages as a source of profit in combination with more financial market operations.

In contrast, Ben Fine (2010) has advanced an argument that financialization is central to the nature and persistence of neoliberalism, and in this way seeks to locate financialization on broader footings. His account similarly stresses the quantitative expansion of forms of capital in exchange and how the logic and imperatives of interest-bearing capital have extended across all economic activity. However, Fine is critical of Lapavitsas's and dos Santos's work on financialization as being too focused on the expropriation of working-class income, which he rejects as a systematic aspect defining contemporary capitalism. Instead, Fine looks at how economic and social reproduction in general is more and more articulated through the financial system, and this being constitutive of financialization.

After decades of relative theoretical and empirical neglect, the work now being done on financialization signifies a fruitful opening for Marxist theories of finance. Part of this renewal involves reconsidering and testing concepts and categories posed by Marx and elaborated by Hilferding. The debates underway today are welcome, and contribute enormously to our understandings and periodization of contemporary capitalism. Indeed, 'financialization' is the most exciting of openings for Marxist political economy.

23. Friedrich Engels

Paresh Chattopadhyay

Famous as the co-founder (with Marx) of the materialist conception of history, and Marx's closest associate and comrade in arms, Friedrich Engels (1820–1895) contributed most to the diffusion of Marx's ideas and popularized them particularly amongst the working class. Engels first met Marx in 1842, but their lifelong friendship began from 1844 in Paris. Subsequently, Engels produced a series of works on politics, political economy, history and philosophy in close collaboration with Marx, and he devoted his final years to the editing of Marx's *Capital II* and *III*, together with the third and fourth editions of *Capital I*. Engels left unfinished his own work on the natural sciences, posthumously published as *Dialectics of Nature*.

Engels's best-known works are *Anti-Dühring* (1878), *Socialism, Utopian and Scientific* (1880), based on three chapters of *Anti-Dühring* and whose worldwide diffusion was second only to that of the *Communist Manifesto*, the *Origin of the Family, Private Property and the State* (1884) and *Ludwig Feuerbach* (1888). *Anti-Dühring* became a compendium on which generations of Marxists have been brought up. David Riazanov (*Karl Marx and Friedrich Engels*, ch. 9) wrote: 'For the dissemination of Marxism as a special method and a special system, no book except *Capital* itself, has done as much as *Anti-Dühring*'. To place Engels's work in proper perspective, it is helpful to keep in mind that: 'As a consequence of the division of labour that existed between Marx and myself, it fell to me to present our opinions in the periodical press, that is to say, particularly in the fight against opposing views, in order that Marx should have time for the elaboration of his great basic work. Thus it became my task to present our views, for the most part in a polemical form, in opposition to other kinds of views' (Engels, *The Housing Question*, Preface). The rest of this entry is concerned almost exclusively with Engels's work on economics, and the controversies it has generated in and of itself and as interpreter of Marx.

EARLY WRITINGS

Engels's economic work spreads over pre-Marxian (1842–45) and Marxian (1845–95) phases. Communist before Marx, Engels started his critique of capitalism with his reports from Manchester to the *Rhenish Newspaper* (1842), focusing on the embrace of Chartism by the English working class as the expression of their collective consciousness. Engels describes here what will be taken over in the *Communist Manifesto* six years later as the spontaneous formation of the proletariat as class and party (Rubel, 1982, p. cxi). Two outstanding works by Engels came out of this phase: *Outlines of a Critique of Political Economy* (1844) and the *Condition of the Working Class in England* (1845), both of which were highly praised by Marx who called the first a work of genius and added, regarding the second, that it showed '[h]ow completely Engels understood the nature of the capitalist mode of production' (*Capital I*, ch. 10, section 2, note 15). Marx cited both of them several times in *Capital*.

The *Outlines* starts by asserting that economic science is the science of enrichment, a 'developed system of licensed fraud'. No classical economist ever questioned private property, from which arises competition and the war of all against all: behind the philanthropy of liberal economics there is the hidden slavery which is no less inhumane and cruel than its ancient form. While reviewing the principal concepts of political economy – value, price, cost of production and labour – Engels shows that, while determining the value of a product as the relation between the cost of production and utility, the 'liberal [political] economist' does not define the subjective factor of this relationship, that is, how utility depends on hazard, and the mood or fancy of the rich. In other words, the so-called equivalence between value and price, or between capital and labour, masks the decisive phenomenon of modern society: the division of humankind between capitalists and labourers. For Engels, the law of competition is that there is always a gap between demand and supply, whence the continuous volatility of the market. Commercial crises thereby repeat regularly like the epidemics of the earlier times. A natural law, this is founded on the ignorance of those affected. With conscious production all this disappears.

While the *Outlines* is a critique of political economy at a theoretical level, the *Condition* is applied analysis, studying the condition of the English workers empirically. Engels points out that the changes wrought by the industrial revolution in England had the same significance as the political revolution in France, and whose 'mightiest result . . . is the English proletariat' (Introduction). Small industry created the middle class (bourgeoisie), large-scale industry created the proletariat and raised the 'elect of the middle-class to the throne, but only to overthrow them' ('The industrial proletariat'). Engels notes the tendency towards the centralization of ownership in industry ruining the small bourgeoisie. In this society, there is 'war of each against all' ('The great towns'). Under the prevailing conditions of unregulated production and distribution of the means of life, the whole process could collapse at any moment as part of a more general economic cycle every five years or so. The factory owner faces volatile market prices, oversupplying and precipitating a crisis once prices start to fall. Once improvement sets in, demand and prices increase. Speculation begins to operate with 'fictitious capital' expanding until a situation arises where the commodities can no longer be readily sold. The downturn begins. Panic sets in. Bankruptcies follow. 'So it goes on perpetually, – prosperity, crisis, prosperity, crisis . . . this perennial round in which English industry moves' which, consequently, must have an 'unemployed reserve army of workers . . . able to produce the masses of goods required by the market in the liveliest months . . . This reserve army . . . is the "surplus population" of England' ('Competition').

LATER WORKS AND THE CRITICS

With these two texts ended Engels's pre-Marxian, independent works on the critique of political economy. Henceforward he would either write jointly with Marx – such as the

Holy Family (1845), the *German Ideology* (1845–46), the *Communist Manifesto* (1848) – or, on his own, handling the exposition and diffusion of Marx's work. In this regard, notable are his many reviews; for example, of *A Contribution to the Critique of Political Economy* (1859) and of *Capital I*, his unfinished 'conspectus' on *Capital* (1868), *Anti-Dühring* (1878) – except for one chapter composed by Marx – 'Prefaces' to his edition of *Capital II* (1885) and *III* (1894) and his 'Supplement and Addendum' to Volume 3. Given Engels's polemical point of departure arising from the original 'division of labour' between Marx and himself, his important economic ideas are best seen when placed in the context of his opponents' arguments against his interpretation of Marx.

Engels has been criticized for his editorial work on *Capital II* and *III*, and for his positions on commodity production and the method of political economy. These criticisms received a fresh lease of life after the publication of Marx's so-called 'principal manuscript' for *Capital III*. To have a proper perspective about the first question let us see how Engels himself viewed his editorial task of bringing out in print the work left by Marx in an incomplete, fragmentary state, often in several variants. We are here concerned only with Engels's edition of *Capital III* and not his edition of *Capital II*. Engels underlined that his aim was to make a 'readable copy' of the manuscript producing a text 'as faithful as possible', and to intervene only where it was absolutely unavoidable (*Capital III*, Preface). However, it has been alleged that, instead of exactly reproducing Marx's text, Engels took liberties with it and made a number of changes of his own in the body of the text. Instead of going through the space-consuming detailed comparison of the two texts, we may refer here to the critique of Maximilien Rubel, arguably the most knowledgeable Marx scholar after David Riazanov.

Rubel had himself, several decades earlier, translated and published (in French) his own editions of Marx's work, calling them, significantly, not '*Capital*' II and III, but 'Materials for *Capital*, Books II and III'. Rubel faulted Engels basically for publishing the manuscripts as a *finished* work, whereas they were 'only drafts, often fragmentary and on the whole incomplete'. On Engels's editorial work as a whole, Rubel observed that Engels showed 'remarkable scruples in his work. The homage that one can pay him is to follow his path, to work like he did on the original composition and its formless materials' (Rubel, 1968, p., cxxiii). Rubel returned to the same theme about three decades later, when the controversy over Engels's editorship erupted. Maintaining his earlier critique of Engels's edition as falsely giving the impression of *Capital II* and *III* as finished work, he nevertheless offered high praise for Engels's 'honesty, modesty, scruples and faithfulness towards his friend's legacy' and questioned the claim of the new editors regarding the discrepancies between Marx's original manuscripts for *Capital III* and edited text by Engels. Rubel added: 'This is not the case. To be convinced about this it is sufficient to compare numerous places from the "original" with the corresponding places in the Engels edition. One gets the same Marx as that what Engels mostly copied and what the new Exegesis offered' (Rubel, 1995, p. 524). Finally, we learn from a contemporary scholar, Hubmann (2005), that the 'editor Engels' followed the rather common nineteenth-century 'conception' – 'totally different from ours' – of editors publishing the works left unfinished by writers like Hegel and Nietzsche aiming to make their texts readable and comprehensible.

The second criticism against Engels concerns his position on the status of commodity production in Marx's work as expressed by him in his edition of *Capital III*. Here he allegedly 'historicized' commodity production and the law of value: 'the Marxian law of value holds generally, as far as economic laws are valid at all, for the whole period of simple commodity production' that is, 'from five to seven thousand years' (*Capital III*, Supplement by Frederick Engels, 'The law of value and rate of profit'). This position gave rise to the so-called historical transformation problem; with 'simple commodity production' under pre-capitalism where commodities are exchanged at their values but which are then exchanged at their prices of production under capitalism. This, according to Engels was 'not only. . . a purely logical process, but . . . a historical process'. He further asserted that Marx's point of departure in *Capital I* was 'simple commodity' and not 'capitalistically modified commodity' (*Capital III*, Preface). Engels has been criticized for *introducing* the concept of simple commodity production and for holding that simple commodity is the starting point of *Capital*. The critics appear to be right on the second point. Marx explicitly states that '[t]he wealth of those societies in which the capitalist mode of production prevails, presents itself as "an immense accumulation of commodities"' (*Capital I*, ch. 1). In contrast, Engels's first statement seems to be directly derived from Marx's own statement (*Capital III*, Supplement by Frederick Engels, 'The law of value and rate of profit'):

> The exchange of commodities at their values . . . requires a *much lower stage* than their exchange at their prices of production, which requires a definite level of capitalist development . . . it is quite appropriate to regard the values of commodities as not only *theoretically* but also *historically* antecedent (prius) to the prices of production.

This text is an embarrassment to some of Engels's critics who have dismissed it as incidental or as due to the unfinished state of Marx's manuscript. However, this is not a unique statement from Marx. In his 1861–63 notebooks we also find the same idea. Similarly, the concept of 'simple commodity (production)' is not Engels's invention. With Marx this concept (*einfache* or *blosse Waare*) refers to a commodity which is not the product of capital. As he says, '[i]n the simple commodity, particular kinds of purposeful labour, spinning, weaving, etc., are incorporated, objectified, in the spun yarn, the woven cloth'. But '[t]he product of the capitalist production process is neither a mere *product* (a use value) nor is it a mere *commodity*' (Marx, *The Direct Process of Production of Capital*). Engels's expression 'whole period of simple commodity production' is, however, not unambiguous. If it means a period when simple commodity production prevailed in society, then, besides remaining undemonstrated, the phrase would also contradict Marx's well-known position that commodity production in pre-capitalist societies was on the whole only partial, mostly involving a surplus over immediate consumption. It is only under capital(ism) that commodity production predominates in society. There is no pre-capitalist commodity *society*. Interestingly this is also Engels's own position in his 'Conspectus' on Marx's *Capital* and in the *Anti-Dühring*.

The criticism of Engels's 'historicism' is a part of the generalized criticism of Engels's pairing of 'historical/logical' as the supposed method of Marx's economic work, first presented in his review of Marx's *Contribution to the Critique of Political Economy* and later carried over in his 'Supplement' to *Capital III*. In general, the critics faulted Engels for misunderstanding Marx's method. Let us underline that, at different places, Marx himself uses logical/historical as his method. In the above passage from which Engels derived his methodological approach, we read that 'it is quite appropriate to regard the values of commodities as not only *theoretically* but also *historically* antecedent (prius) to the prices of production'. Similarly, Marx (*Capital I*, ch. 13) wrote that a multitude of workers labouring simultaneously in the same space or field of activity on the same kind of commodity under the same capitalist 'constitutes, both historically and logically, the starting-point of capitalist production'. In fact, Marx himself has been criticized for historicizing the economic categories while reducing the role of the dialectic in his journey from *Grundrisse* to *Capital*. However, it will not do to speak simply of 'dialectic' in Marx without further specification. Marx's 'dialectical method' is the 'direct opposite' to Hegel's in having a 'materialistic basis' (*Capital I*, Afterword to the second German edition). Indeed, to conceive of the materialist conception of history without history is simply absurd: 'the economic categories . . . bear the stamp of history' (*Capital I*, ch. 6). Referring to the 'bourgeois economists who regard capital as an eternal and *natural* (not historical) form of production', Marx (*Grundrisse*) underlines that 'our method indicates the points where historical investigation must enter in, or where bourgeois economy as a merely historical form of the production process points beyond itself to earlier historical modes of production'.

Despite his unquestionable merits, Engels's methodological approach is not without problems. His contention that the movement of thought must be the mirror image of the historical course (in Marx, 1859 [1980], p. 253) directly contradicts what Marx wrote in 1857 (Engels was seemingly unaware of this text): the '[h]uman anatomy contains a key to the anatomy of the ape'. Marx also distinguishes between the 'method of inquiry' and the 'method of presentation' (*Capital I*, Afterword to the second German edition). The first inquires into the 'forms of development' of the matter, only after which can the second presents the matter's 'real movement' adequately. A similar approach had been used by Marx previously. When referring to capitalism, he distinguished between two kinds of conditions: those of its historical genesis and those that are produced by capitalism itself. He observed that 'to develop the laws of bourgeois economy, therefore, it is not necessary to write the *real history of the relations of production*' (*Grundrisse*).

Beyond these controversies, Engels also reflected on the new forms of organization of capitalism in his day, leading to capital's increasing concentration and centralization. He underlined the change in the form of capital ownership through the joint-stock company – already signalled earlier by Marx – which transformed individual ownership of capital into its collective ownership. Correspondingly, new forms of organization of production like trusts emerged through which free competition was changing into monopoly. However, these new forms proved inadequate for an unhindered accumulation of capital, necessitating increasing intervention by the state in the economy – including the state's partial ownership of capital. Thereby '[t]he capitalist relation is not done away with. It is, rather, brought to a head' (Engels, *Socialism: Utopian and Scientific*, Part III). Engels also noted important developments in the stock exchange since Marx wrote about it in 1865. He underlined the gradual conversion of different branches of industry as well as banking, trade and agriculture into joint-stock companies, which extended to the colonies and underpinned the process of colonization.

Finally, like Marx, and taking capitalism as a historical rather than a natural or eternal mode of production, Engels also envisaged a society beyond capital based on the free 'association of producers', that is, socialism.

24. Geography

Erik Swyngedouw

Capitalism is an extraordinary and revolutionary geographical project. Marx was acutely aware of both the spatial constitution and the geographical dynamics of capitalist social relations. Later Marxist theories of political-economic change and of imperialism have further elaborated and explored how the geographies of accumulation are both space-forming and space-dependent: eighteenth- and nineteenth-century colonialism, twentieth-century imperialism and contemporary globalization each confirmed the inherently spatial constellations and geographical contradictions of capitalism. The spatial choreographies of class struggle, the contradictions of the capitalist urbanization process (already exquisitely analysed by Engels in *The Condition of the Working Class in England*) and the devastating capitalist transformations of the environment dovetail with the combined and uneven geographical development of capitalism to signal the relevance of geography for Marxist political economy. Consider, for example, how speculative urban redevelopment and the production of fictitious land capital in association with a particular configuration of financial markets triggered the global crisis of capitalism starting in 2007. As always, capitalist crisis is, at least partially, always geographically constituted.

It is surprising, therefore, that it took over a century for geographical thought and Marxist political economy to come together. Notwithstanding the legacy of late nineteenth-century radical geographers like Elisée Reclus and Peter Kropotkin, or the spatially and environmentally sensitive twentieth-century Marxist thought pioneered by Karl Wittfogel, Antonio Gramsci, Walter Benjamin, Henri Lefebvre, George Lukács and Guy Debord, the 'spatial turn' of Marxism really emerged with the seminal works, in the 1970s, of Manuel Castells, David Harvey, Neil Smith and Doreen Massey, among many others (see Peet, 1977; Merrifield, 2002). In particular, David Harvey's work, arguing for a historical-geographical materialist perspective, shows how geographical configurations are not just a consequence of capitalist development but, instead, an integral part of capitalist transformations. This entry charts the main tenets and contributions of geographical thought to the Marxist critique of political economy.

FROM HISTORICAL MATERIALISM TO HISTORICAL-GEOGRAPHICAL MATERIALISM

Historical-geographical materialism mobilizes a dialectical perspective to understand the production of nature and space and to propose possible emancipatory geographical transformations. Merrifield (1993, p. 521) summarizes a dialectical perspective on place and space as follows:

> Social space must be posited as material *process*. This process represents the rootless, fluid reality of material flows of commodities, money, capital and information which can be transferred and shifted across the globe . . . From this standpoint, social space . . . represents simultaneously a network of exchange and a flow of commodities, communication, energy and resources.

Similarly, space-as-a-thing acquires meaning, significance and a particular geographical form in and through the relations with which it is infused and through which it becomes produced. For example, the making of the urban built environment or the cutting down of the Amazon rainforest operates through socio-spatial processes of appropriation of nature and its socio-metabolic transformation through the capital accumulation process. Capital is, consequently, both space-dependent and space-forming and class and other social struggles are inscribed in space, while mobilizing geographical tactics in the process (see below). In addition, emancipatory (socialist) politics implies the transformation of socio-physical space and the production of new, freer and more egalitarian, geographies. It has been the staple of Marxist geography to disentangle the socio-spatial processes through which socio-spatial configurations are produced and transformed under capitalism, in their ecological, economic, political, socio-cultural and ideological instances. Places or concrete geographies are considered to be key elements for theorizing the dialectical dynamics of socio-spatial processes.

For Marxist geography, production, broadly defined as the socio-physical metabolism of nature, is the starting point. The dynamics of the particular social relations under which this takes place in a capitalist market economy are associated with a particular temporal and spatial organization of society. This territorial structure of capitalism is contradictory and the socio-spatial dynamics of capitalism are inherently unstable. The produced territorial configurations or coherences (like cities, regions, environments, landscapes of production and consumption) are highly differentiated and give the geographical landscape its sweeping diversity, heterogeneity and difference. Concrete socio-physical geographies are historically produced and their historical-geographical dynamics are shaped by continuous and diverse social struggles, in which the class struggle for control over, ownership and distribution of (produced) nature is central. These struggles are always infused by a myriad of non-class based cleavages and conflicts such as ethnic, gender or territorial conflicts, or by conflicts outside the realm of production, and they too take distinct geographical forms.

Marx and Engels's writings are peppered with implicit and explicit references to the spatiality of capitalism and spatial strategies of resistance (see Smith, 1984; Harvey, 2006). Harvey's academic project, in particular, not only systematized the Marxist understanding of the temporal-spatial ordering of capitalism and of how space as a socially produced 'thing' enters into the perpetual transformation of capitalism, but pushed the theory further and filled in some of the gaps that Marx had left open or incomplete (Harvey, 1999).

Unsurprisingly, urbanization, uneven development and growing environmental problems are the central processes examined by Marxist geographers. Not only are the geographies of uneven development, the deepening environmental crisis, and the tumultuous reorderings that characterize the contemporary city arenas around which many social and political movements crystallize, they also exemplify the central loci where the dialectics and contradictions of capitalism and its associated social struggles are most acutely expressed. The socio-spatial relations embodied in the geographical conditions through which capitalism operates reveal systematic differences in positions of power which, given their socio-spatial constitution, result in an uneven geography of change at all spatial scales. Whether at the scale of the human body itself, the city, the region, the nation or, indeed, worldwide, the dialectics of socio-spatial power geometries show a distinct, but interlinked, heterogeneity and differentiation, and produce a socio-spatial unevenness that is characterized by systematic mechanisms of empowerment/disempowerment, oppression/subordination and appropriation/exploitation. The excavation of these dynamics is an integral and necessary ingredient for formulating and developing alternative, more humane, historical-geographical trajectories.

THE GEOGRAPHICAL CONSTITUTION OF CAPITALISM

'Labour is, in the first place, a process in which both man and Nature participate, and in which man of his own accord starts, regulates, and controls the material re-actions between himself and Nature . . . By thus acting on the external world and changing it, he at the same time changes his own nature' (Marx, *Capital II*, ch. 7).

In recent years, there has been a resurgence of Marxist geographical thought on the environment. Despite the fact that much of twentieth-century Marxism has been largely oblivious to questions of the environment, the very foundation of historical-geographical materialism resides in the ontological principle that living organisms, including humans, need to transform (metabolize) 'nature' and, through that, both humans and 'nature' are changed. Marx hastens to add that this metabolic transformation of nature (and thus environmental change) is always a social and, thus, historical process. While we cannot eat thoughts and ideas, the latter are nevertheless equally deeply implicated in this process. In other words, both nature and humans are profoundly social and historical from the very beginning (Smith, 1984; Castree, 1995).

Although early Marxist geography tended to focus on questions of distribution and power among and between humans, the very materiality of this social process in terms of the inevitable physical transformation of nature and the production of new 'natures' (both materially and socially) remained as a presupposition. For example, consider how the ecological footprint of the urbanization process transforms socio-environmental conditions both nearby and far away (Heynen et al., 2005). The political ecology of capitalism suggests how the social appropriation and transformation of nature produces historically specific social and physical natures that are infused by a myriad of social power relationships (Swyngedouw, 2004). The environmental problem has become one of the central questions in geographical Marxism. Health, resource depletion, access to environmental amenities, the production of new genetic materials, environmental degradation and their socio-ecological formation are directly materially and socio-culturally connected to the particular social relations through which nature is metabolized. While capitalism necessarily widens and deepens the ecological footprint of its operations in socio-ecologically deeply disturbing manners, a historical-geographical-materialist perspective insists on the possibility of a social mastering and 'production' of nature that resembles more the tender loving relationship expressed by masters of the violin or the piano rather than that enacted by the bulldozers and master-managers of capitalist exploitation.

GEOGRAPHICAL POLITICAL ECONOMY

The starting point of geographical political economy is the socio-physical metabolism of nature. The dynamics of the particular social relations under which this takes place in a capitalist market economy are associated with a particular temporal and spatial organization of society. This territorial structure of capitalism is contradictory (that is, full of tensions and conflict), and the socio-spatial dynamics of capitalism are inherently unstable (for a detailed analysis see Harvey, 1999, 2010). It will suffice in this context to summarize them briefly (see also Swyngedouw, 2000).

First, capitalist society is based on the spatial circulation of capital, organized as a geographically interlinked network of production, exchange and consumption processes with the socially accepted goal of profit-making as its driving force. Accumulation of capital, which also takes concrete geographical forms manifested spatially primarily in the capitalist urbanization process, is the correlative of this circulation process. Such circulation of capital is predicated upon the organization in space and the movement through space of money, commodities and labour. In the process, distinct but uneven geographies (of production, consumption and communication) are actively constructed.

Second, the above suggests that a capitalist economy is necessarily expansionary or growth-oriented, and predicated upon an expanding inclusion of nature (in all its human and non-human forms) into capitalist social relations of production. A deepening and accelerating transformation of environments is an inevitable part of successful accumulation.

Third, as the expansion of capitalism is based on the mobilization of living labour, geographically highly diverse and uneven patterns of labour emerge. These inscribe the social division of labour within increasingly complex, variegated and uneven spatial divisions of labour and mobilities of capital and labour.

Fourth, as surplus value is generated by living labour, but appropriated by the owner of capital in the form of profit (or transferred to the state in the form of taxation, to land and resource owners in the form of rent, or to financial institutions in the form of interest), the above condition suggests that accumulation is not only based on an exploitative relationship, but the schemes of appropriation and distribution of surplus also take specific and concrete geographical forms, choreographed by the dynamics of class and other social struggle and the tactics and strategies of the state.

Fifth, given the territorial organization of the capital circulation process, these conflicts too are inscribed in, and unfold over, space. Social struggles of a variety of kinds alter existing geographical configurations. This struggle in and over space can be exemplified by conflicts over land use, housing, or geographical and environmental amenities, or over the distribution, allocation and appropriation of natural or socially produced resources, infrastructures and geographical arrangements.

Sixth, individual capitalists operate in a competitive context in which they engage in a struggle with each other over the socio-spatial conditions of surplus value production, appropriation and transfer. Consequently, all manner of intra-class conflicts unfold over the control of spaces of production or consumption and the flows of commodities, labour and capital. These conditions of inter- and intra-class struggle render the capitalist economy inherently technologically and organizationally (and hence spatially) dynamic. The competitive character of capitalism induces the need for continuous productivity increases, an expanding resource base, diminishing turnover times (the annihilation of space by time and accelerating time-space compression), lowering costs and expanding markets. They demand continuous changes in the geography of production, consumption and exchange and, hence, produce new and restless geographical landscapes.

Seventh, this instability of the circulation process erupts from time to time in problems of over-accumulation or over-production, a situation in which capital in all its forms (commodities, money, productive equipment, built environment) and labour lie idle side-by-side. Dramatic examples of this include the Great Depression of the 1930s, the stagflation (economic stagnation combined with high inflation) of the 1970s and most recently the financial crisis starting in 2007. These conditions of over-accumulation can take the form of high inflation, high unemployment, low or negative economic growth, idle equipment, under-utilized infrastructure and over-capacity in certain sectors. It is the moment when the perversions of capitalism are shown in their most brutal form. While capital desperately seeks new ways to maintain profitability and ransacks the world's spaces in search of accumulation potential, unemployment increases and some forms of capital are devalued (particularly those stuck in place – like the built environment). Such crises become etched into the geographical landscape. Over-accumulated forms of capital are devalorized, and sometimes even physically destroyed. Forms of chronic or instantaneous devaluations of capital are inflation (devalorization of the money-form of capital), debt defaulting and writing-off of debt, unemployment, stock market crashes, real estate depreciation, physical destruction of productive, consumptive and circulating capital, stockpiling of unsold commodities, volatile currency exchange rates and deindustrialization. Such devalorizations of (forms of) capital are always place-specific and affect different social groups in different ways, but can easily ripple over space and erupt in general regional, national, continental or global crises.

Eighth, the perpetual threat of crisis is contained by means of a continuous restructuring of the capital circulation process. This takes the form of technological, socio-environmental and organizational change (with all the related socio-spatial changes in the organization, requirements, qualifications and the like of the labour force, companies and government regulations), profound geographical change and relocation (in the form of direct investment, new resource use, relocation, and the search for new markets or the migration of the labour force – what Harvey calls a spatial 'fix' to conditions of over-accumulation). While older socio-economic and organizational forms of capital are devalued or become obsolete, others are created anew to reinvigorate the capital accumulation process. This can take the form of, for example, the radical transformation of devalorized city centres (gentrification, large-scale urban redevelopment), the exploration of new resources (like uranium in the atomic age), long-term investment in new infrastructure (a temporal 'fix') or the mushrooming of new spaces of production (for example, in certain regions of China or India). The dialectic of accumulation/devalorization produces a perpetually shifting mosaic of uneven geographical development (Storper and Walker, 1989).

Ninth, the above socio-economic geographical dynamics are always inscribed in a historically produced institutional, political, ecological, ethnic and cultural landscape. This produces territorial configurations or coherences that are highly differentiated and geographical landscapes of extraordinary diversity. In addition, the search for the 'new' and for the production of new spaces of production and consumption finds on its way all sorts of already existing communities, ecologies and geographies which are transformed, often destroyed and/or incorporated. Of course, this process meets with all manner of conflict, resistance and, occasionally, revolts.

SOCIALISM/COMMUNISM AS A GEOGRAPHICAL PROJECT

Marxist geography, from its early formulations to later more sophisticated perspectives, has always sought to see and address possibilities for radical-socialist transformation, even in the smallest of places or events. The search for possible different futures, for a social economy embedded in a truly humanizing geography of everyday life at the scale of the body, the urban, the region or the globe has been the leitmotiv of much of Marxist geographical work (Harvey, 2000). The forging of strategic political alliances with those who struggle for freedom from repression and for emancipation from domination is where Marxist geography and geographers continue to make an important contribution. This contribution lies not only in a permanent critique of the geographical conditions and dynamics of capitalism, but also in pushing the frontiers of imagining geographical political-economic trajectories in which difference, heterogeneity and the unrepressed expression of desire coincide with an egalitarian socio-economic and inclusive political order (see Castree et al., 2010). Transformative politics too are inscribed in space. Geographical political economy has shown that an a-spatial theoretical analysis cannot fully explain or account for the particular dynamics of capitalism. Most importantly, socialist political struggles have to be sensitive to the geographical constitution of the social, on the one hand, and engage with the thorny issue of how to produce emancipatory and egalitarian geographies of everyday life, on the other.

25. Global commodity chains and global value chains

Susan Newman

Over the last two decades a number of approaches to the study of commodity supply have emanated from across the social sciences (for example, supply chains, global commodity chains, global value chains, the French filière approach and food systems). Various approaches differ in their origins and dynamics and draw from widely different and eclectic theoretical frameworks, such as regulation theory and transaction costs economics, on the one hand, and convention, performative and actor-network theory, on the other. What these approaches have in common is that each emphasizes attention to the chain of activities connecting production to consumption and proceed with detailed case studies of individual chains.

The broader collection of work that deals with the chain of activities from production to consumption of a commodity has been referred to by Bernstein and Campling (2006a) as 'commodity studies'. As they point out, commodity studies 'has no common purpose, object of analysis, theoretical framework or methodological approach' (Bernstein and Campling, 2006a, p. 240), and any review will necessarily be partial and selective. This entry concentrates on what has been termed the Global Commodity Chain/Global Value Chain (GCC/GVC) literature, which is itself far from coherent in terms of objects of analyses or theoretical framework. GCC/GVC is chosen owing to the prominence that it has gained since the late 1990s in policy and academic circles. Indeed, despite its origins in Marxist world systems theory, GVC analysis has even been promoted in the research of the World Bank, various United Nations (UN) agencies including the Food and Agriculture Organization (FAO), International Labour Organization (ILO) and the United Nations Industrial Development Organization (UNIDO), the Asian Development Bank, the UK's Department for International Development (DfID), United States Agency for International Development (USAID) and Germany's Deutsch Gesellschaft für Technische Zusammenarbeit (GTZ), amongst others, in particular in the areas of agricultural supply chains and small enterprise development. Moreover, the development and application of the GCC/GVC approach can be seen as a collective project of its proponents most visibly in the Global Value Chain Research Network based at the Institute of Development Studies (IDS) at the University of Sussex boasting over 400 members (see http://www.globalvaluechains. org).

This entry draws out some of the key features of GCC/GVC analyses and other closely related approaches, not only to appraise them critically in and of themselves but also by way of pointing to their contribution to the understanding of contemporary capitalism and its political economy.

ORIGIN OF THE COMMODITY CHAIN CONCEPT

The commodity chain concept has its roots in the World Systems Approach (WSA) where it was conceived of as a network of labour and production processes whose end result is a finished commodity. The approach is deployed as an intermediate unit of analysis, where the totality of all commodity chains makes up the world system (more specifically, the global production system) (Hopkins and Wallerstein, 1982).

The WSA has its roots in dependency theory and accepts the stratified and hierarchical structure of the global economy and society as a longstanding and central feature of global capitalism. The WSA approach sought to understand the dynamics of social change and accumulation on a world scale by focusing on global systems (world systems) rather than single societies (or nation states). In this way the concept of the commodity chain is just one way of getting to the notion of a 'world-scale social economy' (Hopkins and Wallerstein, 1982, p. 36):

> What is decisive is neither transport of goods nor exchange of 'values' [between serially related production processes], but instead whether the trade in question is or is not an integral segment of a larger complex of interrelated production processes. (Hopkins and Wallerstein, 1982, p. 36)

As part of a conceptual schema of interrelated concepts applied to constructing the notion of the modern world system, the commodity chain within the WSA is explicitly understood as a heuristic tool:

> [A] conceptual schema, and the relations among the concepts which we used to gain our new vantage point must then be reworked in the light of the increments to our understanding which our newly acquired angle if vision affords us. (Hopkins and Wallerstein, 1982, p. 37)

GLOBAL COMMODITY CHAINS

While the commodity chain concept emerged over the course of the 1980s in world-systems research it does not appear as a distinct analytical approach until 1994, with the publication of the first manuscript length treatment of commodity chains edited by Gereffi and Korzeniewicz (1994). The chapter by Gereffi in this volume laid out a framework for the study of what he called global commodity chains. This launches the concept of the commodity chain itself as 'global' and an object of analysis in and of itself. The central organizing ideas within Gereffi's framework have persisted in a substantial body of subsequent work under the aegis of GCC/GVC research.

For Gereffi and his followers, the 'global' concept of the commodity chain was not simply a heuristic device applied to the study of capitalism but a distinct phenomenon in contemporary capitalism exemplified by what much of the globalization literature sees as a significant shift in industrialization on a world scale in the 1980s and 1990s:

> Economic globalisation has been accompanied by flexible specialization, or the appearance of new, technologically dynamic forms of organization . . . Capitalism today thus entails the detailed disaggregation of stages of production and consumption across national boundaries, under the organizational structure of densely networked firms or enterprises. (Gereffi and Koreniewicz, 1994, p.1)

According to Gereffi, a GCC has three key dimensions: (a) a physical input-output structure; (b) a territoriality; and (c) a governance structure which describes the overall coordination and relative coherence of a chain. In principle, GCC/GVC research entails the identification of the full set of actors involved in the production and distribution of a particular good or service and mapping out the relationships that exist among them with the aim of finding out where and how value addition takes place, the division of labour and the distribution of rewards along the chain.

GCC/GVC research has, in practice, focused almost exclusively on chain governance as a central concept. Closely related to governance is the notion of 'drivenness' which describes the extent to which certain firms in certain positions in the chain – so-called lead firms – are able to steer its functioning to their own benefit. In the original version of the GCC framework, Gereffi posits two ideal types of governance structures based on drivenness. Retailers and branded marketers act as lead firms in buyer-driven commodity chains (BDCCs), specializing in design, branding, marketing and financial services. Production itself is contracted out to a network of independent firms that obtain necessary inputs and organize supply to hegemonic retailers. BDCCs tend to be found in labour-intensive consumer goods industries. By contrast, producer-driven commodity chains (PDCCs) are usually found in capital- and technology-intensive industries, where heavy transnational corporate activity is usual in the coordination of production through a vast network of subsidiaries, suppliers and subcontractors.

Development of the GCC/GVC analytical framework has taken the form of constructing ever more complex categories and typologies describing chain governance and drivenness to fit with the growing number of diverse case studies. Along with governance, the concept of upgrading has featured prominently in GCC/GVC analyses. In effect, upgrading describes the process by which actors/firms operating at lower value added segments can move towards higher value added activities within a given chain or diversify into higher value added activities across chains. Gereffi viewed the period from the 1980s as a distinct phase of global capitalism, with upgrading in the GCC/GVC analysis being shaped by the literature on post-Fordism. Accordingly, the increasing competitiveness associated with the post-Fordist context of global production and competition has meant that firms' face an imperative to upgrade as a condition of survival.

In the context of developing countries, from its initial roots in critique of the world system, GCC/GVC analysis has been influential in guiding policy relevant research framed in terms of understanding the governance structure of individual value chains and in identifying opportunities and challenges for developing country firms to upgrade:

> One of our hopes is that the theory of global value chain governance that we develop here will be useful for the crafting of effective policy tools related to industrial upgrading, economic development, employment creation, and poverty alleviation. (Gereffi et al., 2005, p. 79)

Indeed, such posture is seen as most significant for the pursuit of 'sustainable development' in the global economy which no longer seems, as in world-system theory, to constrain if not deny the achievement of such goals:

> While the search for paths of sustainable development in the global economy is an inherently difficult and elusive objective, our task is greatly facilitated by having a clearer sense of the

various ways in which global value chains are governed, and the key determinants that shape these outcomes. (Gereffi et al., 2005, pp. 99–100)

FROM GCC TO GVC

How did this shift occur? As mentioned, GCC is one of several chain or network approaches to the study of production, trade and globalization which include global production networks, global production systems and filières. The shift in terminology from global commodity chains to value chains or global value chains was the outcome of a deliberate attempt to incorporate scholars studying production networks in the global economy from a variety of approaches into the global value chain research network. The adoption of global value chain analysis was agreed upon at the formation of the research network at a meeting held in Bellagio, Italy in September 2000, and announced in a special issue of the *IDS Bulletin*.

Rather than a simple shift in nomenclature, Bair (2005) argues that the transition from GCC to GVC represents a marked shift in theoretical foundations of Gereffi's earlier framework and the adoption of narrow economic concepts such as transaction costs and value added while discarding broader (political economy) concepts such as the international division of labour, core and periphery and unequal exchange (and world-systems theory more generally). In this light, criticisms of the GCC/GVC framework can be roughly divided into two categories. The first has largely been raised and dealt with from within the GVC literature itself. These concern: the rigid determinism in relating the industrial organization of chains, governance and upgrading; the lack of analytical rigour and the overly descriptive nature of chain studies; and chain typologies that do not sufficiently account for the diversity of empirical case studies. Ever more complex chain typologies, ideal type governance structures and upgrading mechanisms have been included in the development of GVC analysis in response to these criticisms, with analytical concepts and categories borrowed in an ad hoc fashion from the fields of international business, industrial organization and trade theory.

The second broader category of criticism emerges as a result of the divorce of GCC/GVC analysis from its intellectual lineage in world-systems theory in particular and critical political economy more generally. The firm constitutes the main analytical building block in Gereffi's framework and subsequent developments by Gereffi, Humphrey, Kaplinsky and Sturgeon. Governance structures are characterized by the relative size and influence of firms within a chain, with lead firms occupying a uniquely powerful position in terms of their ability to shape outcomes along a chain and the distribution of value added. Upgrading takes place at the level of the firm. In this way, labour and other social categories have been almost entirely absented from GCC/GVC analysis both as actors within the chain (how the labour process contributes to the creation of value) and the extent to which workers play a role in chain reorganization (in the form of upgrading or otherwise) as well as their affect on workers. This is in stark contrast to the concept of the commodity chain within world-systems theory where the importance of labour is recognized.

GCC/GVC analyses have been almost exclusively preoccupied by the vertical nature of the chain and, in so doing, have focused on endogenous explanations for changes in the structure of chains, to the neglect of inter-chain interactions and the relationship between chains and their wider social, historical, political and economic context. One stark omission from the GCC/GVC literature (with a few recent exceptions) has been the neglect of finance, both as an object of analysis (as in financial value chains) and financialization and its affects across chains. For example, the rise of equity finance and commodity derivatives markets brings into question the functioning of chains as well as their definition (resulting changes in social relations along chains as well as the processes of accumulation) quite apart from the role of (futures) commodity markets in speculative movement in prices and redistribution of value added.

There has been recognition by some practitioners of GCC/GVC analysis of these limitations. Bair (2005, pp. 167–8) has called for a 'second generation of GCC research' that will study 'how chains are articulated within and through the larger social, cultural and political-economic environments in which they operate'. Examples of the so-called 'second generation of GCC research' have been published in the *Economy and Society* special issue of 2008 edited by Gibbon, Bair and Ponte, with contributions that emphasize the social embeddedness of chains. But such omissions of problems of coherent conceptualization and analytical embeddedness go hand-in-hand with the longer standing analytical opportunism within the GCC/GVC that evolves by casual incorporation of new theoretical strands and select empirical determinants. This is most notable recently in the shift to global networks, most closely associated with collaboration around the work of Sturgeon.

A MULTITUDE OF THEORIES AND CONCEPTS

The theoretical content of GCC/GVC analyses is increasingly both diverse and eclectic with little coherence across the multitude of case studies. This diversity reflects the method of GCC/GVC based on detailed empirical analyses on a chain-by-chain basis. There has been a tendency for the theoretical content of GCC/GVC analyses to shift according to fashions across the social sciences. This is evident from Gereffi's departure from world-systems theory to embrace post-Fordism informed by the French filière approach and its application of regulation theory, as well as the continuing appeal to broader concepts including the international division of labour, core-periphery and unequal exchange alongside industrial structure, governance based on the power of lead firms, organizational learning and industrial upgrading. More economistic strands of GCC/GVC analyses have been increasingly drawn to adopting concepts such as value addition and transaction costs taking it further away from its roots in radical economic sociology.

Further, the openness of the GCC/GVC approach has allowed for the superficial incorporation of almost any social theory on an instrumental basis resulting in the eclecticism of theory across studies that reflect the distinct character of individual contributors as well as rapidly changing fashions across social theory. For example, in their attempt to tackle the rigidity of governance typologies and the determinism of the GCC/GVC approach and the apparent lack of theorization of governance and upgrading from within the GCC/GVC framework, Gibbon and Ponte (2005) adopt conventions theory (CT) in order to deal with normative aspects of chain governance resulting from intangible aspects of 'value' created through branding, advertising and labelling, for example. In their paper published within the special issue of *Economy and Society*, CT is dropped in favour of Callon's theory of 'performativity' which has come to the fore in recent years in the work of Donald McKenzie.

GCC/GVC, GLOBAL CAPITALISM AND ITS POLITICAL ECONOMY

The detailed case study approach of GCC/GVC analyses has yielded a large and diverse body of rich empirical work that has been extremely informative on the diverse forms that contemporary capitalism takes. As noted by Bernstein and Campling (2006b, p. 443), GCC/GVC analyses have made a significant contribution to political economy:

> not least in appreciating the scale and sophistication of typically intense competition in the *circulation of commodities* as a key dynamic of today's capitalism wherever sufficient purchasing power is present or anticipated.

However, as already remarked, the shift from commodity chains as a heuristic device to an object of analysis, via the divorce of the chain from its broader theoretical framework aimed at studying the political economy of capitalism, has led to a tendency for studies to be preoccupied with the vertical nature of the chain without paying due attention to horizontal factors that contextualize and determine chain outcomes. Taking the chain in isolation has also limited the extent to which GVC analysis can be applied to systemic understanding of both historical and contemporary capitalism. This problem is evocatively and succinctly put by Bernstein in the following metaphor:

> [T]he advantages of the filière approach in cutting a particular 'slice' from larger economic organisms to examine under the analytical microscope, may have corresponding disadvantages if we lose sight of the entities from which the 'slice' is extracted, how and where it fits into, and is shaped by, other elements of those entities. (Bernstein, 1996, p.128, in Bernstein and Campling, 2006a, p. 262).

For Bernstein and Campling (2006a, 2006b) the challenge for various commodity chain approaches is:

> how to reinsert the 'slices' identified by commodity studies – whether defined by, and to varying degrees combining, particular commodities, regions, forms of capital, corporate organization and strategy, systems of regulation, and so on – in the larger entities from which they are extracted. (Bernstein and Campling, 2006b, p. 444)

The relationship between GCC/GVC analysis and Marxist political economy can be explored both by way of criticism of GCC/GVC, via reference, for example, to commodity fetishism (see Bernstein and Campling, 2006a) or to the limitations of transactions costs as applied to economic organization and governance as defined by non-market forms of coordination precluding 'capital' and 'class' from the analysis, and in exploring the way in which commodity chains might be reinserted into a broader political economy framework.

The systems of provisions (SOP) approach has been developed quite separately from GCC/GVC as an alternative chain construct (Fine and Leopold, 1993). The SOP approach adopts an explicitly historical materialist methodology and rejects ideal types to specify chains in favour of understating individual SOPs as contingent upon the socially and historically specific forms taken by the accumulation of capital on which they are based. The dynamic and definition of a SOP is thus given by both interactions internal to a specific chain as part of a SOP as well as the broader dynamics and shifting accumulation processes under capitalism.

The SOP approach retains Marxist value theory and its theory of production. In this way, SOPs and the chain forms that appear are products of the structuring of accumulation in production and through consumption in practice. Thus, chains are reinserted into their broader political economy, albeit in a different way from that conceptualized by Hopkins and Wallerstein.

26. Globalization and imperialism

Ray Kiely

In many respects, the concepts of imperialism and globalization can be regarded as opposites, representing particular political points of view, the former, Marxist, and the latter, liberal. Similarly, globalization can be regarded as an idea that had some influence in the 1990s, but with the 'return of geo-politics' after 2001, theories of imperialism were increasingly revived, rendering notions of globalization redundant. Despite this, Marx can be regarded as one of the foremost prophets of capitalist globalization and his work also provides suggestive comments for the development of a theory of imperialism. And Marxists have also attempted to develop theories of contemporary globalization which move beyond the debates derived from classical Marxist theories of imperialism.

As a theorist of capitalist globalization Marx recognized that, in contrast to previous modes of production, capitalism was uniquely dynamic in its capacity to develop the productive forces. This sometimes led him to suggest that there would be a relatively straightforward diffusion of capitalism throughout the globe. This kind of approach informed some Marxist debates in the 1970s, and debates over globalization from the 1990s onwards, the latter of which suggested that liberal policies would promote global integration and a convergence between rich and poor countries. Nevertheless, Marx also contended that the expansion of capitalism led to a hierarchical international division of labour in which some countries were placed in a subordinate position, and so the 'exploitation' of countries was rooted in the uneven development of capitalism and thus the exploitation of one class by another. This latter view laid the basis for later theories of imperialism, which focused on the impact of capitalist expansion into the 'peripheral' areas of the world economy.

However, the principal concern of classical Marxist theories of imperialism was to explore the geo-political relationship between core capitalist powers. These theories developed in the wake of increasingly hostile relations between imperialist powers (culminating in the First World War), and a new wave of colonial expansion from the 1880s onwards. Imperialism was associated with a new period of capitalism based on the growing concentration and centralization of capital and the increased integration between financial and industrial capitalism, leading to a new era of finance capital, and an increase in the export of capital. Non-Marxist theories such as Hobson's argued that this capital export was a result of the lack of demand among lower income groups in the metropolitan countries, which could be resolved by a redistribution of income within these countries. Lenin, on the other hand, argued that redistribution was unlikely to take place in the context of capitalism and so argued that imperialism through the export of capital was inevitable. Classical theories of imperialism did point to some important manifestations of a new era of capitalism, above all rivalries between developed capitalist states (Bukharin and Lenin). Also significant was the centralization and concentration of capital (Bukharin, Hilferding and Lenin), a strategic coincidence between domestic protectionism and exclusive trading policies between colonizer and colonized (Hilferding) and, in some places, closer ties between industry and finance (Hilferding). But there were many weaknesses too: capital export tended to go to already developed countries more than the colonies and semi-colonies; the developmental impact of capital that went to the periphery and semi-periphery was under-theorized, with a tendency to suggest some form of catch-up with the imperialist powers, alongside reference to the parasitic and stagnant nature of this new phase of capitalist development; and a tendency to exaggerate the similarities between imperialist powers – for instance, the close ties between financial and industrial capital applied to Germany but not to Britain (Barratt-Brown, 1970).

The precise connection between imperialism and inter-imperialist rivalries was also under-theorized. The uneven development of national blocs of capital was a process that was ridden with conflict at the time, but it was less clear why this made imperialist war inevitable. One dissenting voice in the debate was Kautsky, who argued that war was just one possibility among others, and who foresaw that imperialist powers may in the future cooperate in a new era of ultra-imperialism. Rather than seeing inter-imperialist rivalry as an ongoing feature of international capitalism, this period was characterized by conflict between an established capitalist power, Britain, which attempted to maintain its dominance through free trade imperialism, against rivals who were attempting to catch up the dominant capitalist power through protectionist policies at home and colonial policies overseas. This, of course, did not explain the specificities of the alliances and conflicts between the imperialist powers, but the wider point was that this more open account of imperialism was not trying to use a general theory to substitute for particular events such as the First World War.

These issues became all the more relevant in the context of the post-war, liberal international order promoted by the USA. This order was characterized by increased cooperation between developed capitalist powers. While this cooperation was partly a product of a non-capitalist enemy, the Soviet Union, it also reflected a gradual move to a more open international order, characterized by more open borders, for capital at least. Some significant protectionist compromises were made to allow for post-war reconstruction in Europe and Japan, and 'development' in the former colonies, but these were regarded as temporary measures, part of a period of transition to a more liberal order. This order was thus closer to what Kautsky had envisaged, albeit under US leadership. Global integration through more open trade and foreign direct investment encouraged all domestic ruling classes to cooperate. This did not mean that conflict – economic or geo-political – had ended between the capitalist powers, but most of it reflected pressure on the US state to exercise greater responsibility in managing international capitalism. Moreover, the increased internationalization of productive capital eroded any straightforward identification of the link between territorial states and national capitals, such as that associated with Bukharin's argument concerning national blocs of capital. Where British hegemony had failed, the USA was successful.

However, by the 1970s, US hegemony was under threat as Germany and Japan revived, leading some to identify the possibility of a return to inter-imperialist rivalries. This was reinforced by threats to the dollar as the international reserve currency, stagflation and economic crisis, and social and political unrest. However, rather than a new era of competing blocs and protectionist pressures, the crisis of the 1970s was resolved by neoliberal restructuring in the 1980s. This was particularly associated with US Federal Reserve Chair Paul Volcker's decision to increase interest rates from 1979, which paved the way for a global restructuring of capitalism, in which confidence in the dollar as the main reserve currency was restored. The liberal international order was thus consolidated and expanded in this era.

Much of the current debate echoes earlier divisions concerning the reality of geo-political competition as against increased cooperation between core capitalist states. Some Marxists have suggested that the cooperation of the post-1945 order has ended. This is due to the collapse of the Soviet Union, which has undermined the need for cooperation between capitalist states; the unilateralist US response to the terrorist attacks of September 2001; and, from 2007, the most serious economic downturn for 60 years. Despite these developments, unilateral moments have been ongoing features of US foreign policy and have existed alongside more multilateral means for promoting US hegemony. Moreover, capital and capitalist states have been increasingly internationalized, which has served to undermine any simplistic revival of classical theories of imperialism (Panitch and Gindin, 2004). This is one reason why some writers questioned the utility of a Marxist theory of imperialism, and even focused on a post-imperialist order that some called globalization. Some have therefore concluded that geo-political competition has ended in a new era of 'Empire' (Hardt and Negri, 2000), based on transnational capitalist hegemony (Robinson, 2004), rather than the hegemony of any one particular capitalist state.

Much of the mainstream literature on globalization correctly recognizes increased integration, reflected in increased flows of productive and especially financial capital, and the growth of state cooperation in and through international institutions. But much of this transformationalist approach conflates description and explanation and, ultimately, tends towards the tautology that specific manifestations of 'globalization' can be explained by a theory called 'globalization'. Such approaches also underestimate the way in which states, and some states in particular, have promoted globalization. A second problem is that these theories tend to downplay the largely neoliberal character of globalization. These two issues are central in addressing the nature of contemporary imperialism. In particular, there is a need to understand the imperialist nature of the US state (and its relations with other states, including so-called hegemonic challengers), and the relationship between 'core' and 'periphery' in the neoliberal international order.

The post-war period had seen the development of theories of imperialism that focused on the effects of the expansion of capitalism into the periphery. This gave rise to a number of debates, and the divide was essentially between those that emphasized the progressive diffusion of capitalism versus those that stressed the development of underdevelopment. Soviet views suggested that imperialism hindered capitalist development in the Third World, but argued that an anti-imperialist national bourgeoisie could play the role of developing the productive forces along capitalist lines. Underdevelopment theory also emphasized stagnation, but argued that national bourgeoisies were complicit in this because they had close ties to imperialist interests overseas and agrarian interests at home (Frank, 1967). The mechanisms that sustained this underdevelopment were not always made clear, but appeared to include the repatriation of profits from Third to First World and unequal relations of exchange.

The problem with these views is that they assumed that the Third World would remain stagnant so long as it remained part of the Western-dominated world economy. However, some countries in the periphery experienced high rates of growth, not only in East Asia. Attempts to explain this away by stressing the dependent nature of late capitalist development did not always convince, not least because this tended to set up a Eurocentric dichotomy between normal capitalist development in the core and abnormal development in the periphery. This led some writers to resurrect Marx's diffusionist views and that, therefore, imperialism was the pioneer of capitalism (Warren, 1980). But this view was equally problematic – while dependency theorists constructed a norm to show how later developers deviated from it, diffusionists used it to claim that late developers were converging around it.

An alternative approach was to accept that capitalist development was occurring, but this did not automatically mean that catch-up with the core countries was taking place. Late developers faced certain disadvantages as international capital tended to concentrate in established locations, drawing on advantages generated by previous rounds of accumulation. These agglomeration tendencies included economies of scale, technological capacity (and research and development), skills, infrastructure, tacit knowledge and credit. Global uneven development also had specific local manifestations, based on state formation, class struggles and resistance, and this meant that significant changes occurred over time, but equally this did not mean convergence in the world economy, because even mature capitalist development was uneven and unequal.

These debates retain a great deal of relevance in the current era. Some Marxist theorists have suggested that the globalization of manufacturing production has promoted certain forms of global convergence, and eroded core-periphery divisions. But globalization of manufacturing has taken a particularly uneven and unequal form. Since 1980, while the core countries' share of manufacturing exports has fallen, its share of manufacturing value added has increased while, for the developing world outside of Asia, the reverse holds (UNCTAD, 2002). Thus, in many cases, participation in global production networks is negatively correlated with manufacturing value added, while some countries with substantial manufacturing production but low rates of participation in global production networks have higher rates of manufacturing value added.

Core countries still tend to dominate in high value sectors, with high barriers to entry, high start-up and running costs, and significant skill requirements. In the periphery, there are large amounts of surplus labour, and barriers to entry, skills and wages are low. While this gives such countries specific competitive advantages, at the same time the low entry barriers mean that competition is particularly intense and largely determined by cost competition through downward pressures on wages. Apologists argue that such production is a starting point, allowing countries to upgrade as more developed countries shift to higher value production. But this assumes that upgrading is more or less inevitable when, in practice, upgrading has taken place through states deliberately protecting themselves from import competition from established producers via a process of import-substituting industrialization and export-oriented incentives. In the context of neoliberalism discipline through free trade, upgrading is far from inevitable and, indeed, in face of competition from established overseas producers, is unlikely to occur.

These points also have implications for the argument that US hegemony is in decline. While the USA has massively increased its trade deficit since 1982, this has not necessarily been at the expense of productive capacity. It has increased its exports and its share of world output as against its competitors in Europe since the early 1980s. At the same time, capital has increasingly internationalized, part of which has involved the subcontracting of lower value, labour-intensive production to the developing world. China has been most successful in attracting production of this kind. It has used this to develop national champions through import-substituting policies, but to date, its success has been limited. Nonetheless, it does have a large trade surplus with the USA based on its concentration on labour-intensive exports. But China chooses to finance US deficits through the purchase of US Treasury Securities, thus locking it into a US Treasury-Wall Street dollar led international regime. China could shift its priorities, and echoing Hobson's proposals for ending imperialism in 1902, restrict the export of capital and stimulate domestic demand at home. Despite some rhetoric, the Chinese Communist Party (CCP) so far appears to be content to remain part of this order. The world economic crisis may change things, but again the nature of imperialism today shows how drastically things have changed since the days of Lenin and Bukharin. The global crisis had its origins in the USA but this quickly spread throughout the globe, not least to China where falling demand led to many factory closures. While the CCP expressed concern about the falling value of the dollar (and thus the value of their own dollar denominated assets), there has not been a massive shift away from that currency, not least because the Chinese want to preserve the value of their investments. Furthermore, it makes little sense to characterize the crisis as one between different states representing national blocs of capital, not least because the correspondence between national territories and national capitals is so much lower now than in the pre-1914 period, including (and especially) in China. This global integration of capital does not erode the nation state, or even necessarily end geo-political competition, but it does mean that imperialism has changed its character enormously from the time when the classics were written.

Finally, this alternative account of imperialism has implications for understanding the most visible manifestation of US imperialism today, that of military intervention. Some accounts see such interventions as necessary for continued accumulation or representing the interests of specific capitals – such as those arguments associated with the idea of wars for oil. However, the opening up of the international order in recent times, while violent, has largely not been through official military action. Furthermore, an intervention in one specific country (such as Iraq) is unlikely to give the invading country any strategic advantage over others, as the international oil industry is too open to trade and investment from a number of countries for one particular one to have absolute control.

More interesting for understanding contemporary military intervention are those liberal arguments for humanitarian imperialism, in which intervention takes place to save countries from 'non-integrating' rogue or failed states, and integrate such territories into the liberal zone of peace. But this is deeply problematic. The case for liberal imperialism too often relies on the separation of intention from action, with the result that undesirable actions are excused by liberal good intentions – including torture, collateral damage and many 'small massacres'. However, actions can never be excused by intentions, and this is the last line of defence for the liberal imperialist scoundrel. But there is a second point too, related to the political economy of neoliberal imperialism, which is that the aims of military action are doomed to failure. This is because the idea of integrating the so-called non-integrating gap is counterproductive. It is envisaged by contemporary liberal imperialists that military action will be followed by neoliberal policies and aid designed to integrate countries into the global economy. In this sense, we can see contemporary 'military humanitarianism' as a form of structural adjustment. The problem however, as the analysis above makes clear, is that for later developers, neoliberalism subordinates or even marginalizes 'non-integrators', rather than integrating them (Kiely, 2010).

This analysis takes us a long way from the concerns of the classical theories of imperialism, but it gets to grips with contemporary international realities. This is not to say that nothing can be learned from older historical accounts, but perhaps the most useful parallels today can be made with the mid-nineteenth century of British hegemony, free trade and the liberal imperialism of John Stuart Mill, and the problems associated with this political project, rather more than the analysis of the classical Marxists just prior to 1914.

27. International political economy

Alejandro Colás

International Political Economy (IPE) constitutes both an academic field of study and a concrete domain of social relations. In the Anglophone world, IPE – or as it is sometimes rendered, Global Political Economy (GPE) – is generally taught and researched as a sub-discipline of International Relations (IR) or Political Science. It is nonetheless a self-standing scholarly domain emerging in the course of the 1970s, with its own seminal texts, canonical figures and specialized journals, most notably the *Review of International Political Economy* and *International Organization*. In essence, it is a field of inquiry concerned with the interaction on a global scale between states and markets (Gilpin, 1987; Strange, 1988).

As such, IPE also refers to a range of social phenomena that emerge from the powerful integration at the international level of political institutions and economic processes. It constitutes a sphere of socio-economic and political interaction broadly coterminous with the world market, or the global economy – including production, trade, credit and consumption. Phenomena ranging from international migration to the global regulation of money flows to the global governance of intellectual property rights to the administration of overseas development assistance, all fall within the purview of IPE. Above all, IPE seeks to bridge the three keywords of its title. Against the mainstream approaches to IR, it emphasizes the economic underpinnings of geopolitical or diplomatic power; in contrast to orthodox economics, it underlines the political dimensions inherent within market transactions; as opposed to conventional political science, IPE underscores the global context of political decision-making and institutional design.

From a Marxist perspective, little of this intent is controversial. The complex interaction between politics and economics is axiomatic to the Marxist tradition, as is the global scale of this relationship (a book exclusively dedicated to 'the world market' was after all identified by Marx as the sixth volume of his incomplete 'critique of political economy'). Unsurprisingly, therefore, much of contemporary IPE is inspired by, and works within or against the Marxist explanatory framework that, accordingly, attracts an unavoidable presence within the literature. Yet, at the same time, the field of IPE also throws up a number of challenging questions for Marxists and non-Marxists alike, four of which will be broached below.

The first of these broad themes revolves around the origins and dynamics of the world market itself. Some mainstream IPE is entirely ahistorical and simply takes capitalist markets as given. Other liberal views see the emergence of a global economy in the course of the 'long' sixteenth century (1450–1650) essentially as the cumulative result of the Smithian tendency to 'truck, barter, and exchange'. Humans, so the argument runs, have always engaged in long-distance trade and the European discovery of the

Americas, coupled with the technological and socio-political (chiefly naval and monetary) innovations of that period simply accelerated the economic integration of existing regional trade networks into a world market. This conception of the IPE thus claims that comparative advantage, free trade, a specialized division of labour and open competition are fundamentally responsible for integrating the global economy and encouraging worldwide growth and prosperity during the modern era.

Marx dismissed such narratives as 'Robinsonades' which, like the notion of original sin in theology, seek to explain the original or 'primitive' accumulation of capital as a result of a mythical division between 'two sorts of people' (or nations, one might add): 'one, the diligent, intelligent, and, above all, frugal elite; the other, lazy rascals, spending their substance, and more, in riotous living' (*Capital I*, ch. 26)). In contrast to such 'insipid childishness', Marx posits an alternative, materialist account of the birth of the capitalist market: one where 'conquest, enslavement, robbery, murder, briefly force, play the great part' (*Capital I*, ch. 26) be it through the 'discovery of gold and silver in America, the extirpation, enslavement and entombment in mines of the aboriginal population, the beginning of the conquest and looting of the East Indies, the turning of Africa into a warren for the commercial hunting of black-skins' (*Capital I*, ch. 31) or the forced 'process of divorcing the producer from the means of production' in England and, later, continental Europe (*Capital I*, ch. 26).

Marxist approaches to IPE thus assume that capitalism has been an international mode of production from the outset, and emphasize the role of political force (that is, violence, plunder, dispossession and enslavement) in its emergence, against the liberal conceptions of the world market as a natural and essentially peaceful outgrowth of commercial exchange. Such Marxist approaches tend, however, to diverge on the exact role that international structures play in the global reproduction of capitalism. At one end of the spectrum, the work of Immanuel Wallerstein and his followers (inspired more by the materialist geographer Fernand Braudel than by Marx) conceive of capitalism as a world system characterized by unequal exchange relations between core, semi-peripheral and peripheral regions of the globe (Wallerstein, 1974a). From the 'long' sixteenth century onwards, world-systems theorists argue, successive European hegemons have structured global production and exchange in ways that favour the capitalist development of the core at the expense of the underdevelopment of the periphery. As the peripheral economies of Latin America, Asia and Africa supplied primary materials extracted through slavery, tribute and plunder to the European core, the latter processed, sold and accumulated these commodities to create capitalist wealth. At play here is an understanding of the global political economy principally as a system of exchange, ordered through a rigid geographical structure enforced by mercantile empires.

At the opposite end of the spectrum is the so-called 'political Marxism' of Robert Brenner and his collaborators, who understand capitalism mainly as a historically unique set of social property relations that emerged first in the English countryside and thereafter expanded across the globe. The emphasis in this case is upon a very specific transition from feudalism to agrarian capitalism in sixteenth-century England, characterized by the expropriation of direct producers from their means of subsistence and the accompanying creation of a competitive market for labour, land and agrarian produce. England emerged from this fraught and complex transformation as the leading capitalist power by the end of the seventeenth century and, in the course of its subsequent overseas expansion, sought to impose such capitalist social property relations on other parts of the world. The success of these attempts at exporting capitalist social relations were highly uneven, to say the least, as slavery persisted in the British Caribbean until the mid-nineteenth century and the British East India Company ran the Raj like a tributary state until 1857. But the point Brenner and his colleagues make is that it was distinctively capitalist impera- tives that drove the creation of a modern world market. In this account, production is emphasized over circulation as the distinctive feature of global capitalism. 'Vertical' class antagonisms tend to trump 'horizontal' geographical power struggles as agents of change in the world economy. Consequently, the tight spatial hierarchies favoured by world- systems theorists are rejected in favour of more dynamic conceptions of the capitalist global political economy as a set of competing centres of capitalist accumulation.

A number of other Anglophone critical scholars – Giovanni Arrighi, Eric Wolf, David Harvey among them – subsequently presented their own accounts of the birth and devel- opment of the world economy that fall in between these polar extremes. Yet these debates are not merely about the periodization of the world market, they are also of considerable conceptual significance in our understanding of other dimensions of IPE.

One area where these conceptual debates play themselves out – offering the second challenge for Marxist IPE – is the place of the national state in the global capitalist system. If the world market has generated a universal space of economic interdepend- ence mediated through capitalist exchange, why is it fragmented into almost two hundred nominally independent territorial jurisdictions with sovereignty? Put more succinctly, why is the world politically divided when it appears economically integrated?

There are, predictably, multiple answers to these critical questions within IPE. So- called 'mercantilist' or 'statist' approaches to the discipline emphasize the role of eco- nomic statecraft in forging a world market. On this account – sometimes identified with Realism in IR – the world's most powerful states stack the workings of the global market to their advantage through political, juridical and military means. That is, they use their political power to enforce unequal economic relations (Krasner, 1978). On this reading, the world market is understood not as an independent, self-regulating sphere as liberals tend to view it, but rather as a domain that is subordinated to and instrumentalized by powerful states. National states 'precede', and to a great extent 'create' the modern world economy. Realist-Mercantilist IPE starts from the premise that IR are always anarchical and that states constantly compete for power in a zero-sum game. The world economy is simply another field of play in that game.

Some Marxist conceptions of imperialism, as will be seen shortly, share with Realism- Mercantilism the view that economic rivalry among the most powerful states sooner or later leads to violent conflict, war and the forceful acquisition of land and resources at the expense of competing states and colonized populations. This is essentially how Lenin described imperialism, for him the monopoly stage of capitalism, which led to World War I. This sort of argument has also been presented by Peter Gowan in a more sophisticated and comprehensive form for the contemporary international political economy. In *The Global Gamble*, he illustrates how American policy-makers used the end of the Cold War, and the 'unipolar' moment that accompanied it, to refashion the global political economy in the USA's national interest (Gowan, 1999). Central to this account is what he labels the 'Dollar-Wall Street Regime' – a political-economic dispensation of global power forged through President Nixon's decision to 'float' the US dollar, that combined the public, political authority of the US Treasury with the private, economic power of Wall Street banks. The Realist-mercantilist inspiration to such a regime was, for Gowan, transparent: 'The United States government has done its constitutional duty. It has put America first. The whole point of the Nixon moves to destroy the Bretton Woods system and set up the Dollar-Wall Street Regime *was to put America first*' (Gowan, 1999, p. 31). Although Gowan shares the Realist assumption that, in an international system, states compete for power, influence and prestige, he simultaneously emphasizes the domestic class power underpinning the foreign policy of states and the consequent hierarchical structuring of inter-state relations through the combination of political, military and economic instruments of rule and domination.

The complex relationship between the modern states system and the capitalist world economy – their respective emergence, co-constitution and the place of the national state in the reproduction of the global market – remains an unresolved arena of dispute, discussion and research in IPE. Marxist approaches to the question agree that the capitalist state in one form or another represents a 'political moment' in the cycle of global capitalist accumulation – generally defending and advocating the interests of the elite within any given country. But this in itself does not explain why there is no world state corresponding to the world economy; nor, at least, why the experiments at creating supranational political entities like the European Union have not been generalized across the world.

The notion of 'hegemony' has gone some way into addressing these thorny issues and represents the third broad problematic of IPE. Like the world market or political economy, hegemony is a category used by mainstream and critical IPE scholars alike, albeit in radically different ways. The term derives from the Greek for 'leadership' and is deployed in IPE and IR to describe and analyse the coordinating role played by a leading state in sustaining world order under conditions of international anarchy. Orthodox conceptions of hegemony underline the centrality of the leading state in stabilizing the global economy. On this reading, global hegemons (Britain in the nineteenth century, the USA after 1945) supply the rest of the capitalist world with a range of global 'public goods' like a universal currency, an open, rule-governed and predictable trade regime, and institutions of global governance, such as the World Bank and the International Monetary Fund, that minimize transaction costs and maximize the reliability of global exchange to the benefit of the world capitalist economy as a whole. The anarchical condition of the international system is thus mitigated through the stabilizing mechanisms and institutions coordinated by the leading or hegemonic state.

There exist two broad types of Marxist responses to the question of world order. The first draws on the classical theories of imperialism pioneered by Hobson, Lenin and Bukharin, emphasizing the continuing role of war, violent conflict and geopolitical and economic domination in upholding the capitalist world order. Here, order is not equated with stability (especially for the bulk of the planet's population): British and, subsequently, US hegemony produce world orders characterized by recurrent socio-economic crisis, sharp geographical inequalities, constant geopolitical upheaval and persistent environmental destruction. By this account, the alleged 'public goods' provided by the self-appointed hegemons support the continuing domination of the rest of the globe by a handful of powerful Northern economies which, in turn, deliver benefits only to a tiny minority of the world's elite. This centrality of domination over consent and coordination defines imperialism.

The other Marxist understanding of world order takes its inspiration from writings of the Sardinian communist Antonio Gramsci. Pioneered by Robert W. Cox, it conceives of global hegemony as 'a form of dominance of a particular kind where the dominant state creates an order based ideologically on a broad measure of consent, functioning according to general principles that in fact ensure the continuing supremacy of the leading state or states and leading social classes but at the same time offer some measure or prospect of satisfaction to the less powerful' (Cox, 1987, p. 7). Cox and his fellow neo-Gramscian IPE scholars rooted this peculiar combination of coercion and consent firmly in capitalist social relations of production. Against mainstream conceptions of hegemonic world order, neo-Gramscians give social classes and their attendant institutions – think-tanks, trade unions, political movements and business organizations – a central role in the legitimation of such hierarchical orders. Hegemony on this reading is exercised by the most powerful, for the most powerful. Moreover, it cuts across states to include relations of exploitation in the various transnational realms of production. Yet, like liberal conceptions of hegemony, neo-Gramscians also emphasize the substantive benefits derived by formally subordinated states and classes through the hegemonic arrangement of world order. In contrast to Leninist theories of imperialism, neo-Gramscians underline the role of multilateral cooperation and consent in the management of a capitalist world order and, therefore, also contemplate a significant role for subaltern states and social forces in the reproduction of such orders. A good example is the way in which western European social-democratic forces actively supported integration into the US sphere of influence after 1945 for fear of communist takeover.

Once again, the contrast between Leninist and neo-Gramscian understandings of world order is not absolute. Many other critical and Marxist IPE theorists – Kees van der Pijl, Stephen Gill, Craig Murphy and William I. Robinson – have delivered insightful studies on the nature and workings of the IPE, which straddle the ground between, or develop more comprehensively aspects of, each of these approaches. Such diversity of Marxist-inspired conceptions of world order and hegemony indicates the continuing salience of that tradition in analysing and explaining IPE today.

Much the same is true of the final key concern of contemporary IPE, namely, 'globalization'. It has been said without excessive irony that Marx and Engels's 1848 *Communist Manifesto* is one of the first dissections of capitalist globalization. This is not simply because, as Hirst and Thomspon have so forcefully demonstrated, many of the characteristics of contemporary globalization are recognizable in the internationalism of the nineteenth-century *belle époque*. More substantially, it is also because Marx and Engels's key categories – value, modes of production, class exploitation, primitive accumulation and so forth – continue to be central to the understanding of IPE today.

For the past four decades, both mainstream and critical IPE have developed concepts and theories – interdependence, hegemonic stability, international regimes, historical blocs, embedded liberalism, the competition state – that are indispensable to a critical understanding of our 'globalized' world. IPE scholars of various ideological and methodological persuasions have, moreover, produced important studies on subjects ranging from regional integration, financial crises, offshore money markets and the role of patriarchy in the reproduction of global capitalism. These all indicate the vibrancy of IPE as a realm of study, and the centrality of political economy to the workings of globalization.

Yet their explanatory adequacy cannot be settled on the purely empirical criteria of whether and how well such categories describe contemporary capitalism. Ultimately, questions remain over whether (and how) the global economy has become more inter-dependent; has the function of the state shifted from providing welfare to competing for international investment? has the erstwhile Third World now become a pole of capitalist accumulation? These, and other issues, hinge on the prior conception of the nature of, and relationships between, territorial states and capitalist markets, and their dialectical and systemic attachment to the global or world economy. Marxist analyses, as this con-tribution has aimed to show, diverge on many of these questions, and certainly do not always have ready-made, settled or persuasive answers. But the materialist conception of history offers a distinctive and comprehensive set of categories and propositions that place the peculiar origins and dynamics of modern states and markets at the heart of our understanding of the global political economy.

28. Karl Marx

Lucia Pradella

Karl Marx was born on 5 May 1818 in Trier, a city that had been under French administration from 1794 until 1814 and where the memory of the 1789 revolution remained strong. The years in which Marx lived were, for all of Europe, revolutionary: production was in a process of endless transformation, first in Britain and then on the continent; together with the scale of modern industry, the number and organization of workers continued to grow. In France, the bourgeois revolution, breaking the last remnants of feudalism, summoned the 'fourth estate' into the battlefield. And the latter, for its part, began to unite and become self-conscious, struggling to conduct the revolution to its radical end, beyond the formal rights of equality and liberty. These historical dynamics were reflected in Marx's own experience and in his trajectory, from radical-democratic ideals to communism.

He came from a moderately well-heeled family; his father, a Jewish lawyer, converted to Protestantism, was a cultivated man, educated to Enlightenment rationalism. After completing the 'Gymnasium', Marx first went to university in Bonn, where he dedicated himself to juridical studies. But in Berlin, the cultural centre of Germany, he studied philosophy and history, entering the circle of Young Hegelians. In 1842, in collaboration with Bruno Bauer, Marx founded, and subsequently directed, the *Rheinische Zeitung*, a democratic newspaper based in Cologne. His articles on the social conditions of the Mosel peasantry provoked government censorship, forcing Marx to leave the newspaper, itself suppressed in the following months. His activity as a journalist pushed Marx towards questioning the social conditions of the working class, forcing him to 'to discuss what is known as material interests' (*A Contribution to the Critique of Political Economy* (*CCPE*), Preface) and to deepen his knowledge of political economy. This became his main occupation in Paris, 'the capital of the new world', where he was forced to move with his young bride, Jenny von Westphalen, in 1843, to continue the social and political propaganda that had become impossible in Germany. There he had the opportunity to establish a dialogue with various socialist and revolutionary organizations, while he engaged in studies of political economy, the French Revolution, the conditions of the working class, and socialist and communist thought.

The intellectual impulse that moved Marx to study political economy was also due to his reading of the *Outlines of a Critique of Political Economy* by Friedrich Engels, who was then working in Manchester, one of the main centres of the industrial revolution. Both England and France were privileged vantage points from which to observe modern bourgeois society, being much more advanced than Germany, where extreme political fragmentation was an obstacle to capitalist development. Engels's *Outlines* was published in the only edited volume of the *German-French Annals,* alongside the introduction to the *Contribution to the Critique of Hegel's Philosophy of Law* and an essay *On The Jewish Question,* both by Marx, who was the editor of the journal *German–French Annals* together with Arnold Ruge. In the *Critique*, Marx argued that Hegel's attempt to overcome the separation between the state and civil society was both false and illusory; only the practical critique by the proletariat could abolish the social relations that underpinned that division. Subsequently, the *Economic-Philosophical Manuscripts of 1844* represent Marx's first systematic confrontation with classical political economy through use of philosophical categories developed from a critical reading of Hegel and Feuerbach. The alienation of labour, its reduction to the status of a commodity, is identified as the origin of the fundamental divisions in modern capitalist societies, that is, the estrangement of workers from the product of their labour and from their very activity, nature and other human beings. In the *Manuscripts*, Marx argues that the transformation of current social relations depends on the abolition of private property by the proletariat, the only force capable of creating a new social form, organized rationally according to the needs of the human species, and in which labour could become a source of individual realization as well as sociality. This totalizing and revolutionary character of the Marxian critique of capitalism continued to pervade all his writings, although they eventually broke free of their philosophical foundations and found a new point of departure in the immanent critique of political economy.

In September 1844 Marx and Engels spent ten days together and, having ascertained their broad political and intellectual accord, began their lifelong collaboration. Their first work was *The Holy Family*, a polemic against Bruno Bauer and his separation of philosophical critique from political praxis. In 1845, following pressures from the Prussian government, Marx was expelled from Paris and moved to Brussels. There he was joined by Engels, who had earlier that year published the *Condition of the Working Class in England,* the result of extensive studies based on documents and direct observation of the living and working conditions of the workers. Aware of the importance of concrete experience of English reality, Marx journeyed to Manchester with his friend in the summer. There, they studied political economy and English socialism, and established contacts with leaders of the working-class movement. This was an important stage in the elaboration of a 'new conception of history' – according to which '[t]he mode of production of material life conditions the general process of social, political and intellectual life' (*CCPE*, Preface) – and of the programme of revolutionary socialism. These were developed through critique of idealist doctrines and petty bourgeois and utopian positions, and these found expression first in the *German Ideology* (written in 1845 but unpublished until 1932) and then in *The Poverty of Philosophy*, Marx's 1847 polemical work against Proudhon. From his notebooks of the period it emerges that Marx studied economic history from a global perspective, the only approach compatible with the international character of capitalist production and trade. The unity between theory and praxis, argued for in the *Theses on Feuerbach*, did not remain on paper. In Brussels, Marx dedicated himself to organizational work, founding the Communist Correspondence Committee, establishing international connections and holding lectures on matters of interest to the working class, including those later published in *Wage Labour and Capital* and *On Free Trade*. In these pamphlets, criticizing the naturalistic representations of classical political economy, Marx argues that capital is a historically determined and transitory social relation of production founded on exploitation both within and between nations.

These efforts culminated in the foundation of the International Communist League, described by Engels as 'the first international movement of the working class', which united the members of the League of the Just, the Communist Correspondence Committee, English Chartists and German refugees dispersed across Europe. The First Congress, on 9 June 1847, was attended by Engels, who convinced the League to change its motto from the League of the Just's – 'All men are brothers' – to 'Working men of all countries, unite!' The Second Congress, held at the end of that year, gave Marx and Engels the task of writing the political and theoretical programme of the League, *The Communist Manifesto.* Although both capitalist production and the working-class movement were still limited, *The Manifesto* already provided a global account of the development of capitalism and expressed for the first time the worldview and the political aims of communists: the theory of class struggle and the revolutionary role of the proletariat, whose victorious revolution in Europe would lead to the end of all antagonisms between nations.

Shortly after the publication of *The Manifesto*, the 1848 revolution spread throughout Europe, setting ablaze the political order established at the Congress of Vienna. Banished from Belgium, Marx (to whom the central committee of the League had attributed full powers) moved to Paris, and then to Cologne. There he founded the *Neue Rheinische Zeitung – Organ der Demokratie*, a newspaper supporting the unification of Germany and providing a focal point for the German workers' societies in the unfolding revolutionary struggle. However, the repression in the wake of the June insurrection signalled the advance of the counter-revolutionary forces that rapidly extended their action, with the help of Czarist Russia, beyond Prussia and the Austro-Hungarian Empire, finally culminating in the *coup d'état* of Louis Bonaparte in France. The social revolution was halted, and the communist groups were systematically repressed. In Cologne, the 1852 trial against members of the central committee of the International Communist League led them to disband it. Marx and Engels ceased direct political involvement. They reconstructed the history of the failed revolution in *The Class Struggle in France, The Eighteenth Brumaire of Louis Bonaparte, Revelations Concerning the Communist Trial in Cologne* and articles in *Revolution and Counter-Revolution in Germany*.

Expelled from both Germany and France, Marx settled in London in the summer of 1849, where he remained for the rest of his life. As many other refugees, his family suffered extreme poverty in the first years of exile leading to the death of three of his children between 1850 and 1855: Edmund, Franziska and Edgar. Under pressure, Engels reluctantly decided to return to his 'accursed commerce'. He started managing the English branch of his father's firm and, as a result, he could support Marx financially. London, the metropolis of capitalism and the centre of an expanding empire, was 'a convenient vantage point for the observation of bourgeois society', where Marx decided 'to start again from the very beginning and to work carefully through the new material' available at the British Museum (*CCPE*, Preface). He wanted to understand how the crisis of 1848 had been overcome by a new cycle of prosperity, which seemed to postpone indefinitely the outbreak of European revolution. The 'London Notebooks' (1850–53) denote a period of intense study of theories of money, wage and rent, and scrupulous research on the Asiatic mode of production and the relationship between capitalism and colonialism. Marx's research was also influenced by his collaboration with the influential *New York Daily Tribune*. For over ten years, beginning in 1851, Marx wrote articles on current events, including financial policy, economic crisis and colonialism in Asia (his author-ship of the whole of this material was recognized only in the first half of the twentieth Century). He also followed the Crimean war, the Spanish revolution and the American civil war, without ceasing to publicize the living conditions and political struggles of the working class in several countries. Through these analyses, he gathered fundamental elements for the development of his critique of political economy.

If the enormous expansion of commerce and of the empire had been among the major factors pulling Britain out of the crisis, it also amplified the scope and risk of new crises. Under the impulse of vast anti-colonial movements throughout Asia, Marx traced a relationship between anti-colonial struggles and the working-class movement in Europe, modifying substantially the conception of international revolution he had initially conceived in the *Manifesto*. His analysis was soon validated, if without the pre-dicted revolutionary outcomes. The Indian uprising was one of the pivotal causes of the 1857 economic crisis that enveloped the world market. Marx was enthusiastic about the crisis, even though it did further destabilize his own financial circumstances, because of the reduction in his commissions from the *New York Daily Tribune*. Hoping for an immi-nent revolutionary outcome, Marx returned to his work on the *Outlines of the Critique of Political Economy ('Grundrisse')* (published in Moscow, in 1939). These manuscripts represent his first attempt to expose systematically the theory of capital on the basis of a plan modified in 1861–63 and again in 1863–65. In June 1859 Marx published only one part of his original project as *A Contribution to the Critique of Political Economy*. There, he develops his analysis of the dual nature of labour embodied in the commod-ity, which he defines as 'the pivot on which a clear comprehension of political economy turns' (*Capital I*, ch. 1). In contrast, the classical political economists, although tracing value back to labour, could not distinguish clearly between abstract and concrete labour, naturalizing value-creating labour and eternalizing the system founded on wage labour.

The 1857 crisis gave impulse to a number of social movements: in Russia for the sup-pression of servitude; in the United States for the abolition of slavery; and, in Europe the workers began to mobilize again at syndicalist and political levels. Communications began to be established between workers' committees in different countries. In July 1864, an international meeting in solidarity with the Polish insurrection against Russian domination took place in London. English trade unionists and French workers agreed to found an association aimed at the coordination of the political activities of the working class in different countries. The International Workingmen's Association was founded on 28 September. The meeting was also attended by Italian followers of Mazzini, French socialists and Blanquists, Polish revolutionaries and members of the former 'Communist League', including Marx. His activity in the Association was central, aimed at reinforcing international solidarity which, according to Marx's Inaugural Address, was the condi-tion for the conquest of political power and the emancipation of the proletariat. Unlike the Communist League, the First International was not a predominantly political and propagandistic organization; it was also syndicalist. The International grew vigorously in its first years of activity, partly as a consequence of the strike movements following the upswing of 1868. It gained new members and spread to new countries, including England, France, Belgium, Switzerland, Italy, Spain, Portugal, Germany, the United States, Denmark, Holland and Austria-Hungary. In the same period, the political standing of Marx and Engels increased sharply. They affirmed the necessity of political struggle and to sustain the fight for the unification of the German and the Italian nations. The latter would lead to significant progress for the working-class movement in these two countries and, therefore, internationally. In turn, the intensification of the struggle for Irish independence in the late 1860s raised the colonial question. Marx and Engels affirmed the right of the Irish workers to have an independent organization within the International, and pushed the English workers to sustain the Irish struggle as a necessary condition for their own emancipation.

In 1868 the International's Brussels Congress passed a resolution recommending workers to read the first volume of *Capital*, published in 1867. There, Marx explained systematically the laws shaping the antagonisms of bourgeois society, and identified the kernel of these antagonisms in the conflict between wage labour and capital, whose origin is founded in the exploitation of labour. He demonstrates that capitalist accumulation extends and increases the exploitation of the workers on a global scale, although with important national differences: 'in proportion as capital accumulates, the lot of the labourer, be his payment high or low, must grow worse' (*Capital I*, ch. 25). The impoverishment of the workers is, therefore, not limited to declining wages, but it affects all dimensions of their lives. Accumulation is founded on, and at the same time reinforces, the cooperation of labour, which is the objective condition for the conscious union of the workers. *Capital* intends to provide the theoretical underpinnings for this union, in order 'to set free the elements of the new society with which old collapsing bourgeois society itself is pregnant' (*The Civil War in France*, The Paris Commune). Therefore, *Capital* offers not only a descriptive analysis of capitalism, but it also aims to contribute to the revolutionary overcoming of bourgeois society.

The Paris Commune of 1871 demonstrated the capacity of the working class to organize itself and conquer political power. The armed workers held the French capital for two months, giving birth to 'a government of the working class' which, for Marx, was 'the political form at last discovered under which to work out the economical emancipation of labor' (*The Civil War in France*, The Paris Commune). In *The Civil War in France,* Marx argues that the repression of the Commune was possible only because of the lack of international solidarity. The International was left fundamentally weakened in its aftermath, because it rapidly lost most of its forces membership not only in England – where the leaders of the trade unions, apprehensive of its communist tendencies, resigned – but also in the two pivotal countries of continental Europe, France and Germany, where the suppression of the Commune had disintegrating effects. At the Hague Congress in 1872, the anarchist faction, which was against direct participation in the political struggle, was expelled. Marx and Engels proposed to move the General Council to New York to 'defend it from disaggregating elements', and because the United States had become, through mass immigration, 'the world of labour at its highest', and the nation where the party could finally become truly international.

Marx subsequently abandoned direct involvement in the Association but continued to follow its activity as well as the evolution of the working-class movements and the formation of mass political parties in Western Europe. In 1875 he intervened critically, although not publicly, against the programme of the *Sozialistischen Arbeiterpartei Deutschlands* through his *Critique of the Gotha Programme* and, in 1880, he collaborated in the formulation of the programme of the *Parti Ouvrier* in France. He also followed the evolution of the Russian revolutionary movement, Russian being the first language into which *Capital* was translated. Despite his deteriorating health, Marx was now able to devote time to the French translation of the first volume of *Capital*, which re-elaborated entire sections of the book, and he worked on the manuscripts of the second and third volumes of *Capital* (published for the first time in the MEGA II, Marx and Engels, 2003; Marx, 2008). Although Marx published only sporadically in the last years of his life, his notebooks show the extent to which he continued to research across all fields of knowledge, including mathematics and the natural sciences but, especially, those directly related to *Capital*. In the 1870s, his studies became more focused on global history: he deepened his research on pre-capitalist societies and colonialism; reflected on the historical developments of agricultural production, traced the evolution of different forms of communal landed property; and he expected to rewrite the section on ground-rent in the third volume of *Capital*, in which Russia would occupy a central role as a historical model. Marx also studied recent developments in archaeology, ethnology and anthropology, according great importance to these new disciplines and focusing in particular on evolutionist authors. Engels's book *The Origin of The Family, Private Property and the State* was based on these notebooks. Marx wrote with Engels, in the preface to the second Russian edition of the *Communist Manifesto* (1882), that, if a peasant revolution in Russia sparked the signal for proletarian revolution in Europe, and if both could complement one another, the rural commune could offer the basis for the transition to communism. He therefore denied any gradualist, positivist or deterministic vision of the revolutionary process, contrary to those who affirm that the universalization of the capitalist mode of production is both inevitable and a precondition that must be fatalistically imposed upon all peoples of the world prior to the realization of socialism.

After Marx's death, on 14 March 1883, Engels took upon himself the task of publishing the second and third volumes of *Capital* and following up the developments of the international movement of the working class.

29. Knowledge economy

Heesang Jeon

In this entry, we attempt to incorporate the role of knowledge into value theory. Whilst this is self-sufficient in itself, it is part of a broader initiative to reconstruct the 'knowledge economy' from a Marxist perspective, in light of the deficiencies and flaws of prevailing theories of the knowledge economy and cognitive capitalism. Incorporating knowledge into value theory is the first step and the basis upon which more concrete and complex theories of the capitalist economy, and what are taken to be its novel contemporary features, can be developed. More narrowly, the case of information commodities is instrumental in that it helps to identify the role of 'knowledge labour' in relation to commodity-producing labour, albeit in extreme form: in brief, knowledge labour is essential for commodity production, and it takes part in value production through the process of 'virtual intensification' of commodity-producing labour.

KNOWLEDGE ECONOMY AND COGNITIVE CAPITALISM

The knowledge economy has become increasingly popular in policy and public discourses since the late 1990s. This is an outcome of a number of distinct but interrelated developments in contemporary capitalism: the rapid emergence, evolution and spread of information and communication technologies; the diffusion of intellectual property rights regimes; the expansion of markets for technology and commoditization of knowledge. However, the concept of the knowledge economy has often not gone much beyond gathering these loosely related developments under the same arbitrarily defined umbrella. More specifically, prevailing theories of the knowledge economy tend not to question its historical specificity, nor attempt to analyse its conditions of existence. This is not surprising considering that the knowledge economy is often analysed on the basis of current ahistorical (economic) theories – as in notions of compressing time and space. For example, in orthodox economic theory, knowledge is considered as a type of economic 'good', albeit with a distinctive cost structure due to its allegedly peculiar (ahistorical) nature of being non-rivalrous and (partially) excludable. This underpins a general justification of intellectual property rights, because these allow for knowledge as an economic good to be traded whilst acknowledging the potential presence of market imperfections.

Knowledge has also drawn much attention from leftist writers, not least those in the tradition of Autonomist Marxism. For these writers (Hardt and Negri, 2000, 2004; Corsani et al., 2001; Vercellone, 2007), as opposed to knowledge economy theories, knowledge is qualitatively distinct from economic goods. It is so particularly in its role in class struggle in which knowledge is considered as the source of class power. Contemporary capitalism is argued to be in transition to cognitive capitalism in which workers appropriate the role of knowledge production from capitalists, and the hegemonic form of labour is immaterial or 'cognitive labour'. The class struggle between capitalists and workers around the appropriation of surplus under the new circumstances is considered as an underlying force shaping contemporary 'cognitive capitalism'. This leads to the bold statement that the labour theory of value is no longer valid under cognitive capitalism. Whilst labour remains the source of wealth for cognitive capitalism, it does so because labour produces immaterial products such as knowledge and communication. In contrast, commodity-producing labour is seen to play no important role in the production of value as can be seen in the case of information commodities, which is an epitome of this transition to cognitive capitalism (see below). In this view, knowledge is not only distinguished from, but even opposed to economic goods (or commodities). Whilst the knowledge economy (or cognitive capitalism) is considered to be historically specific, knowledge (or knowledge labour) is privileged at the expense of commodities (or commodity-producing labour) (see Jeon, 2010 for a more detailed critique of cognitive capitalism theory).

These claims are debatable at three levels, with the defence of value theory against the cognitive capitalism theory remaining, as yet, limited within the literature (as opposed to the bolder claims of cognitive capitalism as capturing the essence of the contemporary world). First, whilst knowledge has always been important, it should be theorized in a way that incorporates it into existing theories of the capitalist economy, with value theory in particular to the fore. For this, the relationship between knowledge (or knowledge labour) and commodities (or commodity-producing labour) needs to be clarified without privileging one at the expense of the other. Second, the knowledge economy should be understood and reproduced in theory as concrete and complex forms of the abstract relation between knowledge and commodities, developed under specific historical circumstances. This should be done by way of infusing knowledge into the processes, structures and relations of capitalism, marking distinctions across the variegated presence and role of knowledge in all value processes. Thus, the knowledge economy should not be theorized as a 'stage' of capitalism in which – presumably – knowledge somehow supersedes commodities, as argued by cognitive capitalism theory. Third, this raises the need to reinterpret and revitalize the labour process debate. If we understand deskilling as a tendency, it is necessary to identify counteracting tendencies, not least those related to the class struggle around knowledge at the workplace. This can contribute to developing alternatives to the Foucauldian critique of the deskilling thesis which emphasizes subjectivity at the expense of value analysis. Thus value and labour process theory need to be extended to analyse the nature and transformation of knowledge labour in capitalism, especially in its relation to commodity-producing labour, with special reference to the nature of contemporary capitalism. The remaining sections will focus on showing how the role of knowledge can be incorporated into value theory consistently by taking the case of information commodities as an example.

KOREAN DEBATES ABOUT THE VALUE OF INFORMATION COMMODITIES

Software and information goods such as digital music and video, as members of the world of commodities, are part of our daily lives. They are produced by capitalists seeking to make a profit. Hence, despite the open source movements and widespread digital piracy, information is and has, to a greater or lesser degree, always been commodified under capitalism. In this sense, they do not seem different from other physically based commodities. How should they, then, be differentially addressed and are there qualitative differences for the current period of cognitive, knowledge economy, capitalism?

As commodities, information goods are use-values and values. Just like other commodities, the value of information commodities is determined by the socially necessary labour time to produce them. The difficulty is that, whereas a significant amount of labour time is required for the first unit, it is (close to) zero for the rest. How does the labour time expended or required to produce the first unit affect the value of the others? To answer this question, first of all, we need to distinguish labour that creates something original, for example, music, painting, design, software specifications, source code and better production methods, from labour that creates commodities based on the product of the former, in the form of mass production. Let us call the former knowledge labour and the latter commodity-producing labour. With this distinction introduced, it is obvious that, whereas the labour for the first unit includes both knowledge and commodity-producing labour, the labour for the second only includes the commodity-producing labour independent of this prior knowledge labour. Then the question can be reformulated as follows: how does knowledge labour creating source code affect the determination of the value of information commodities? Whilst focusing on the specific example of software, this is both of significance in its own right and a purer form of other examples of knowledge work.

The issue of the nature of value in such circumstances has been subject to a close Korean debate on the value and price of information commodities (Kang et al., 2007; Jeon, 2011, for example), with two different answers offered at opposite extremes. One group has argued that the value of information commodities is determined by the socially necessary labour time to (re)produce them. Once knowledge in the form of source code has been produced, knowledge labour is no longer necessary for the (re)production of information commodities because of the costless reusability of the knowledge. This means that labour time for knowledge production neither is added to nor affects the value of information commodities. Hence, the value of information commodities in general borders on zero because production simply requires the replication of compiled binaries, for example, in case of software. But the price of such commodities is a monopoly price and, as such, bears no systematic relationship to (more or less zero) commodity value. The other group has proposed a shared cost approach, in which the presumption is that value has been contributed by knowledge labour that is shared across the individual information commodities produced. Knowledge is considered to be identical to fixed constant capital which, correspondingly, transfers value to the final product in a piecemeal fashion.

There are flaws in both views. In the case of the former, knowledge labour is seen to have nothing to do with the production of value, even if knowledge labour is indispensable for the production of information commodities. How could we buy a digital file of the song *Yesterday* if the Beatles had not composed and recorded this song? There is no question that knowledge labour determines the use-value of information commodities. This suggests that knowledge labour should affect the value of the commodities as well. Although the latter, that is, the shared cost approach, outlined above, attempts to incorporate the role of knowledge labour for the production of the commodity and its value, it is flawed in that it assimilates knowledge and fixed capital. Fixed capital transfers value to final output because production results in its 'wear and tear' (Marx, *Capital I*, ch. 8) or 'daily loss of use-value'. In contrast, knowledge, whose existence is independent of information commodities, does not change, or deteriorate, with its subsequent use in production of information commodities; therefore, no value is transferred to information commodities from knowledge. In addition, according to this view, the value of commodities depends upon the quantity produced; therefore, it is determined *ex post*, since the value contributed by knowledge labour decreases as the quantity produced increases.

THE ROLE OF KNOWLEDGE IN VALUE THEORY

Knowledge, for example, music, design, recipe and software source code, can be used an unlimited number of times and, in this respect, it is qualitatively different from information commodities like music CDs, digital music files and iPhone apps that are prominent at the time of writing. As a corollary, knowledge labour is distinguished from commodity-producing labour even though both are needed for the production of commodities. Significantly, this distinction is not limited to the production of information commodities. Take the example of automobile production. A new model requires initial design, building of a prototype, testing and fixing of defects, as well as market research and so on. Only after this can mass production begin. The labour expended in these activities taking place before mass production comprises knowledge labour. In other words, knowledge labour is necessary prior to commodity-producing labour at least for every new commodity, and some conception afresh is generally required for renewal of production of continuing commodity production.

Despite the significance of knowledge production in this respect, analysis has traditionally been focused on commodity-producing labour instead, especially in labour process theory. Whilst the distinction between conception (= knowledge labour) and execution (= commodity-producing labour) is often drawn, the main theme of labour process theory in the Braverman tradition has been to debate the deskilling and degradation of work. In other words, the role of knowledge, and of knowledge labour, has been primarily addressed through the prism of polarization of conception and execution, with conception tending to be stripped from the deskilled worker, or not. Whilst labour process theory acknowledges that conception is necessary, its role in the production of value is neglected if not completely ignored.

Developing a Marxist account of knowledge requires a heuristic use of some concepts Marx deploys in *Capital I*, such as intensification of labour, collective labour, complex labour and individual value. It is necessary first of all to point out that the distinction between knowledge labour and commodity-producing labour is present in Marx. As 'purposeful activity', knowledge production or conception precedes commodity-producing labour. Marx says, 'the architect raises his structure in imagination before he erects it in reality', and 'at the end of every labour-process, we get a result that already existed in the imagination of the labourer at its commencement'. In addition, knowledge signals an 'exclusively human' characteristic (*Capital I*, ch. 7). Humanity is distinguished from other species in that there is need for knowledge labour (of conception) before labour of immediate production itself. At this abstract level, the distinction between conception and execution has the following characteristics. First, this distinction is ontological. Despite feedback mechanisms such as learning-by-doing, conception always precedes execution but, in turn, it can only be realized through execution. Second, the distinction as such, drawn at the most abstract level of analysis, is ahistorical, excluding any determinations specific to capitalism. A key question is how this distinction is developed and reproduced specifically under capitalism.

Marx's analysis of the capitalist forms of cooperation shows that this distinction takes the form of a tendency for separation between conception and execution at the workplace. For Marx, cooperation is 'the fundamental form of the capitalist mode of production' (*Capital I*, ch. 13). And, in addition, cooperation is associated with the formation of the level of collectivity in general and collective or combined labour in particular. Thus, when different individual workers collaborate, they work together to achieve common goals. Under cooperation, individual workers not only perform individual labours but the productivity of collective labour exceeds the sum of individual contributions both quantitatively (how much) and qualitatively (what can be achieved). Further, in its simplest form, cooperation, can take place by gathering workers together but, in most cases, cooperation involves coordinating and organizing the production process. And, as labour becomes collective, so the knowledge and goals of labour also become collective. This gives rise to a group of workers that are more or less dedicated to the realization of these goals and the design, coordination and adjustment of the production processes. Marx mentions the emergence of overseers in this context but knowledge labour as such is not identified. However, skill consists of knowledge at the collective level as well as drawing on the skills of individual workers. Collective skill or knowledge cannot be reduced to a set of individual skills as it includes knowledge that exists irrespective of individual workers, not least as embodied in fixed capital. Finally, the separation between conception and execution 'is completed in modern industry, which makes science a productive force distinct from labour and presses it into the service of capital' (Marx, *Capital I*, ch. 14). Science is incorporated into the labour process 'as an independent power' (*Capital I*, ch. 25), which is reflected in Marx's distinction between 'universal labour' and 'co-operative labour' (*Capital III*, ch. 5): 'Universal labour is all scientific labour, all discovery and all invention . . . Co-operative labour, on the other hand, is the direct co-operation of individuals'. Whilst Marx implies that the products of universal labour or knowledge labour are freely available, which is true only exceptionally in contemporary capitalism, he at least acknowledges that this distinction is necessary and says, '[b]oth kinds play their role in the process of production'. Put differently, the tendency for separation between conception and execution goes beyond individual firms and is further developed at more complex levels when the social division of labour is introduced.

If we go back to the division of labour within firms, both conception (or knowledge labour) and execution (or commodity-producing labour) are inherently collective. For example, we can consider many different and diverse types of knowledge required for automobile production, simply as knowledge for automobile production. Likewise, different concrete labours such as coating, painting, assembling and final testing are forms of collective automobile-producing labour. Then how does knowledge around automobile production affect the value of automobiles?

Consider this in light of intra- and inter-sectoral use of knowledge labour. For the first, if an individual capitalist makes more productive use of knowledge than the sectoral norm, the commodities produced by the capitalist will have a lower individual value and the capitalist will be able to accrue extra surplus value over the norm in the form of higher profit. The comparison between (collective) labours in terms of productivity is possible in principle only when they produce the same commodity. In this case, if one has a higher labour productivity than another, this might be because of different use of collective knowledge or because of differences in skills of individuals. Accordingly, knowledge labour makes commodity-producing labour 'exceptionally productive' and act as 'intensified labour' (Marx, *Capital I*, ch. 12). Second, though, the sectoral average level of knowledge might be higher than the social average. For example, the level of knowledge for automobile production might be higher than for paper production. In this case, the commodity-producing labour of all the individual capitals in the automobile sector is underpinned by higher levels of knowledge on average and so serves as intensified labour. In other words, the average labour of such a sector serves as complex labour and comprises 'intensified, or rather, . . . multiplied simple labour' (*Capital I*, ch. 1), even if the concept of complex labour is introduced by Marx at a more abstract level of analysis before we consider collectivity. For example, labour of jewellers is complex and produces more value in a given time than the labour of spinners. Complex labour produces more value precisely because it requires significant efforts in education and training, incorporating more knowledge than other simple labours. And, like values as socially necessary (abstract) labour time across commodities more generally (produced by different concrete labours of different skills for whatever reasons and of whatever origin), such differences in labour complexity and intensity are brought into equivalence with one another through exchange relations. And, as seen earlier, labour in capitalism is collective. In addition, collective skill or knowledge is formed out of cooperation. Even if machinery dominates individual workers, workers use machinery as instruments of production at the collective level. Knowledge produced in its own (non-value) generation process serves, in the labour process, as the knowledge of the value-producing collective worker. Even if individual workers perform simple labour, collective knowledge can intensify that labour and raise value contributed at the sectoral level.

In sum, and put differently, knowledge labour neither creates value directly nor transfers value indirectly during the production process. But it allows for virtual intensification of commodity-producing labour. Intensity of labour, which is not explicitly defined by Marx, is the degree of expenditure of labour power during a given period of time and is related with the pace of work. Thus, more intense work has the same effect as extension of the working day. With given conditions of labour, intensity of labour generally remains unchanged, but introduction of better production methods usually leads to increased intensity of labour because the transformation of the labour process often involves more effective utilization of workers, removing any kind of unnecessary breaks during work time. In contrast, virtual intensification refers to a social process by which the same amount of labour time produces more value without any changes to intensity of labour, and hence through increase of (collective) productivity and/or complexity. However, virtual intensification is counteracted as competitors within and across sectors catch up. As a result of these mutually contradictory processes, sectoral norms of knowledge, and thus the level of the aggregate social knowledge, increase. This can be considered as a law of capitalist accumulation.

Where does this leave the value of information commodities? As mentioned earlier, in this case, commodity-producing labour is minimal if not non-existent. Consider the example of digital music. Once an original recorded song is encoded into a digital format and placed on a server, production of a copy does not require human labour at all. When the user pays for the song, the server generates a copy based on the predetermined algorithm, possibly encrypting it or adding a watermark to prevent piracy, and transmits it to the user through the internet. Monitoring operation status and resolving technical issues do require human intervention whose frequency is proportionate to the number of transactions. Ironically, only this labour comprises commodity-producing labour. On the contrary, to enable this automatic production of digital music, composition and recording of music, development and deployment of the server-side music catalogue, search, purchase and download applications are required. All the various concrete labours expended to produce these comprise knowledge labour. However, even if the commodity-producing labour time expended for each digital copy of the song is approximately zero, the value of each copy is higher than zero due to the process of virtual intensification. The digital content industry is a knowledge-intensive sector, and inevitably the sectoral knowledge level is higher than the social average.

CONCLUSION

The incorporation of the role of knowledge attempted here is confined to the production of value, and thus is partial. But it can serve as the starting point for the more complex and concrete theorization of the role of knowledge in the capitalist economy. For example, knowledge is required for all kinds of labour, productive and unproductive. Intellectual property rights need to be analysed in terms of commoditization of knowledge as well as their influences on the determination of value. A new category may or may not be needed to capture the role of intellectual property rights analytically. The role of knowledge in financialization, neoliberalism and globalization needs to be analysed. Through the course of these analyses, the complex and concrete forms of knowledge and its expanded role should not be simply assumed, but should be situated and explained in relation to class and other relations that persist in their basic structures and processes.

In sum, as we successively move towards more complex and concrete issues, value theory must guide the analysis. Considering that theories of the knowledge economy and cognitive capitalism exert ever more influence, value theory and Marxist political economy in general are on the defensive again. Whilst this is unfortunate, we have no choice in defence of value theory but to develop a more positive account both of knowledge and contemporary capitalism. Here, we have shown, albeit at abstract levels, that value theory is strong enough to accommodate the role of knowledge. It is neither outdated nor inflexible. Complex and concrete phenomena which seem to contradict value theory are the very reason why we need value theory. But the power of value theory should be proven by developing better accounts of contemporary capitalism than the theories of the knowledge economy and cognitive capitalism.

30. Labour, labour power and the division of labour

Bruno Tinel

Marx's discussion of the labour process under capitalism is complex and sophisticated, involving a range of concepts that draw upon, refine and develop his value theory. His analysis cuts across observations on the nature of production in general, through to its specifically capitalist features, incorporating both empirical and theoretical content. Despite the fact that *Capital I* is subtitled 'The Process of Production of Capital', Marx's analysis of the labour process remained unfinished, and much of it unknown until the appearance of the so-called 'missing appendix' to Chapter 6. Its publication inspired a labour process literature that remains one of the most fertile areas of Marxist research.

LABOUR AND LABOUR POWER

The relationship between labour and labour power offers a crucial distinction between Marxist and non-Marxist political economy, especially mainstream economics. It lies at the heart of Marx's explanation of exploitation under capitalism, and heavily informs his vision of the capitalist mode of production itself. Marx calls labour power the capacity to work, and (the performance of) labour is its use value. The capitalist does not buy an agreed amount of labour but labour power, in order to use the labour of the worker over an agreed if contested period of time.

Through primitive accumulation, the capitalist mode of production transforms labour power into a commodity by putting working people in a situation that requires the sale of their labour power for a money wage, as the only means of accessing consumption. Marx identifies two conditions for this: first, the owner of labour power sells it only for a limited period (no slavery is involved); and, second, social survival depends upon this sale. This entails the treatment of labour power as a simple use value but it cannot be detached from the human subject that owns it and to which it is returned before being sold again. As subjects, humans are not commodities but, from the point of view of the buyer, the labour force should be deployed as such, available for passive use like an object like other productive inputs (for Marx, the terms 'subject' and 'subjective' refer to humans and the terms 'object and 'objective' refer to things). Outside of capitalism (and even within it if subordinate to other motives and the motives of others), work is not simply a means to obtain consumer goods but also an end in itself as a source of achievement and gratification as can also occur within limits within capitalist employment too. The situation for the capitalist as purchaser of labour power is different, although motives other than pure pursuit of profitability can arise, again within limits. Labourers, waged or otherwise, will then be liable to try and escape from situations that do not satisfy their own goals, however much these may be consciously defined and determined.

As labour power is the sole commodity with the use value of creating value, the capitalist tries to extract as much surplus value as possible by consuming it. It is necessary for work to be for longer than the social labour time necessary to (re)produce the value of the labourer's means of subsistence. But these relations are not specified in the contract between the buyer and the seller. They are not apparent in the sphere of circulation, but reside in what Marx called the hidden abode of production.

LABOUR PROCESS

Value is created by a labour process. By labouring, humans transform their material environment and also their own nature. Animals, like spiders or bees for instance, also act upon the material world in ways in part similar to a weaver or an architect. But the specificity of human labour is that 'at the end of every labour-process, we get a result that already existed in the imagination of the labourer at its commencement' (*Capital I*, ch. 7). Human production is oriented towards a purpose to which the labourer more or less consciously subordinates other purposes for a period of time. Whatever its social form, the labour process consists in transforming objects, whether prepared by previous labour or not, through the use of instruments of labour 'which the labourer interposes between himself and the subject of his labour, and which serves as the conductor of his activity'. Resorting to instruments is one of the hallmarks of human labour.

In the capitalist labour process, 'the labourer works for the capitalist instead of for himself'. Hence, labour power is consumed to produce use values embodying surplus value. The technology of production and the instruments of labour that already exist in the pre-capitalist era are not initially modified by the capitalist who is obliged to use the labour 'as he finds it'. The subordination of labour to capital will lead to changes in the organization and the methods of production only at a later period (see below).

SIMPLE COOPERATION

Simple cooperation is not specific to the capitalist mode of production, and survives within capitalism itself outside the realm of formal work in the home or with friends combining in a common endeavour. It certainly existed in various pre-capitalist civilizations at different levels of development. When a large number of people are simultaneously working together for the same common purpose, they are able to realize a more than proportionate addition to production or even to allow for products that would otherwise be impossible. The combination of their closely related actions creates a specific social productive power, or collective labour. The more numerous the labourers working together, the more it is necessary to organize the sequencing of their actions, otherwise disorder could limit the productive effect of the collective.

Whereas 'Egyptian kings' and 'Etruscan theocrats' resorted to this specific power of the collective labourer to build pyramids or temples, capitalists use it systematically. In contrast to its scattered, weak and infrequent pre-capitalist forms, cooperation is considered by Marx as the 'fundamental form of the capitalist mode of production' (*Capital I*, ch. 13). Gathering many wage labourers under the direction of a single capitalist presupposes that the concentration of important means of production in a few hands has occurred previously. Then, the primitive capitalist division of labour can develop. Initially, the employer, turned from a small master into a capitalist, takes on enough labourers to be relieved from manual, or execution, work and specializes in direction, conception and trading. Later, once the business has grown enough, the supervisory function can be delegated to specialized functionaries, possibly wage labourers themselves.

THE DOUBLE NATURE OF COMMAND

As with the production process, capitalist command is double-sided. On the one hand, the social aspect of cooperation makes it necessary to coordinate individual actions to set collective labour in motion. The systematic use of cooperation in capitalist production gives the illusion of the 'eternal necessity' of the capital of command, as an element of entrepreneurship, not least because the capitalist both rewards each worker individually and appropriates the benefits of collective labour. It is as if profit derives from such coordination, especially as it is entangled with other functions of the business such as marketing.

On the other hand, the capitalist requires labour power to yield surplus value during its time of hire, which entangles a different function of direction, disconnected from cooperation as such. This necessarily confers an authoritarian form to command since the labour has to be exploited, creating 'the unavoidable antagonism between the exploiter and the living and labouring raw material he exploits' (*Capital I*, ch. 13). Despotism changes form with the development of cooperation, as it obviously creates a resistance among workers who not only try to preserve themselves from overexploitation but also try to extend their freedom of movement, or achieve a degree of independence at work. Resistance constantly obliges capital to renew the technology and the organization of the labour process to circumvent any loss of control, and not simply to increase productivity. Indeed, the cooperating labourers' resistance can increase with their number, and the struggle between labour and capital induces a continuing evolution of the means of control implemented by capital to overcome the workers' resistance to its domination.

Does the capitalist command because of specialized knowledge of how to run industrial production? For Marx, the reverse holds: capitalists decide how to rule the labour process not because they do it well, but because they have the power to do so through their command over the means of production.

THE BABBAGE ARGUMENT

For Marx, the social and manufacturing divisions of labour are distinct but neither is purely technological and both derive from the relations of production. A social division of labour exists in all societies; it corresponds to the distribution of work, including crafts and specialities, for all production throughout society – who does what and how (as well as what is defined as 'work' itself as has been emphasized by the feminist critique of the downgrading of women's work in general and 'domestic' labour in particular). The manufacturing division of labour corresponds to the subdivision of work into its constituent elements and the allocation of these to specific types of workers for the creation of specific final products. It becomes generalized only under capitalism, before which workers would tend to create final products on their own account. Marx borrows from Charles Babbage the idea that a minute division of labour and specialization, that is, the capitalist division of labour, has only a few temporary effects on productivity which weakens the appeal of Adam Smith's argument based on dexterity, drawn from the example of a pin factory. Babbage reasons on the basis of monetary prices. He shows that dividing labour is mainly a means to reduce wage costs because it enables the manufacturer to select skill levels accurately and more cheaply. As dividing and specializing labour reduces the time and cost of apprenticeship, the master has an incentive to divide up the labour process: by requiring less and more readily acquired skills, minute specialization induces a reduction in wages and increases the supply of workers available to do any job.

For Babbage, manufacturers introduce minute specialization not primarily for productivity reasons but for profitability. And simplifying tasks through the division of labour also prepares the way for the replacement of human labour by machines. The rise of constant capital per labourer and technological enhancement are the decisive factors in productivity improvement. Marx closely follows and deepens Babbage's argument by reference to the notion of a 'trade'.

THE SUBJECTIVE STAGE OF THE DIVISION OF LABOUR

A trade is made up of a set of specialist skills and techniques. It rests upon the dexterity associated with several more or less specific and sophisticated tools, and craftsmen both conceive and carry out their own work. There is no separation between conception and execution, since the trade enables the worker to control the labour process of an entire commodity. Craftsmen who possess their own means of production can control the product and sell it on the market and, thereby, be independent. As will be seen, Marx explains, first, how the labourer is dispossessed of the control on the product, through the 'formal subordination' of labour to capital, and then of the control of the labour process, through the 'real subordination' where capital destroys trades and takes possession of professional knowledge and technology.

In the first stage of capitalist development the small master becomes capitalist, ceasing to take part in the labour process as such. Wage labourers engage in simple cooperation: they are still in control of the labour process, with the capitalist having authority over the craftsmen as opposed to their work itself. The subordination of labour to capital is purely 'formal' (Marx, *The Process of Production of Capital, Draft Chapter 6 of Capital, Results of the Direct Production Process*, 1864, ch. 6): the capacity of the capitalist to constrain the workers rests only on their economic dependency. The threat of lay-off is historically and logically the primitive moment of labour's subordination to capital.

This formal coercion is a decisive stepping-stone to the 'real' appropriation of the production process by capital. It is sufficient to enable capitalists to implement the first stage of the minute division of labour and specialization. This phase corresponds to the 'subjective' division of labour. It consists in breaking trade up and destroying individual control over the production process by specializing workers on a limited range of tasks. The whole production process is recomposed on the basis of the tasks comprising it. This division of labour is considered as subjective in the sense that task separation and specialization do not rest upon a material process but on a convention, or an obligation, imposed on workers by the employer. After simple cooperation and before the rise of machinery, a new specialization limiting individual skill takes place around the methods attached to trades. By increasing demand and the concentration of capital, the intensification of production leads each operation to be subdivided in turn, including the tasks of conception and management. Compared to handicraft, the labour force becomes either specialized into a few tasks or not specialized at all if it is 'general' labour.

The essence of the minute division and specialization for Marx is that, by transforming the complex labour of craftsmen into the simple labour of unskilled workers, it reduces the necessary labour time for the reproduction of the workers, which amounts to a reduction in the value of labour power. This split of handicraft into a set of simple tasks shifts distribution in favour of capital, not so much because of productivity increase as because of the reduction in variable capital. Indirectly, the division of labour increases competition amongst the workers at each level of the skill hierarchy because each job, being simplified and easier to perform, can now be fulfilled by a greater number of workers. Minute specialization makes each individual worker more dispensable and more easily replaced. For Marx, following Babbage, the main economic effect pursued by capitalists with the division of labour is to reduce the bargaining power of workers.

But, in addition, the command of handicraft knowledge is progressively appropriated by (the representatives of) capital. Increasingly, capital dominates all knowledge useful for production; by substantially separating conception from execution, the minute division of labour subjects workers to production, and increases their dependency. From that moment on, the labour process is not primarily shaped by the producer (as a craftworker) but by capital for the production of surplus value. The worker is not only constrained by virtue of the threat of dismissal, but also by the division of labour within production itself. The labourer is both 'formally' dependent and placed in 'real' subordination to capital by the remoulding of the production process.

REAL SUBORDINATION THROUGH THE OBJECTIVE DIVISION OF LABOUR

On the basis of the distinction between formal and real subordination of labour, Marx offers, in *Capital I*, extensive theoretical analyses (for example, about absolute and relative surplus value) and empirical studies (especially illustrations from English industry) of how one gives way to the other in the evolution of the capitalist labour process. This process essentially involves the development of machinery within the factory system, what has been clumsily termed machinofacture. With real subordination, the division of labour becomes objective; it is embodied in machinery designed by capital for its specific purpose. For, once the subdivision of tasks has taken place in workshops, individual and collective workers can be replaced by specialized tools, combined through common energy sources and incorporated into machines. Whilst machinery needs to be taken care of by unskilled labour, more skilled labour is also necessary to conceive and maintain it.

The diffusion of machinery tends to render specialized labour redundant as unskilled labour prevails. But as machinery production and use themselves require crafts and specialisms, these too are progressively transformed, with use of machinery itself increasingly becoming subject to factory production. With the generalization of machinery, machines substitute themselves for others through technical change. Machinofacture, then, underpins the segmentation of the labour force. Specialized workers are replaced by a relatively undifferentiated labour force, whilst a labour force specialized in production, maintaining and monitoring of machinery (and of workers) is required by capital. It forms a superior class of workers which Marx considers as liable to be numerically insignificant. But such segmentation is never fixed and involves an ongoing process which evolves as accumulation proceeds. Marx offers the hypothesis that the share of unskilled labour tends to rise, but labour force segmentation is complex, diverse and differentiated by its own internal organization and characteristics as well as subject to factors external to the economy (access to skills and gendering, for example) (Fine, 1998).

Accordingly, the postulate that skilled labour becomes residual is unconvincing as an empirical trend as opposed to a contradictory tendency. For the labour-capital struggle in the production sphere is a struggle over the control of the labour process and equally over skills. Nothing in Marx's analysis can support the idea that capital has already won this struggle forever, and Marx himself considers that, at the beginning, new branches of production require skilled labour as do new technologies. Moreover, workers specialized in conception will tend to increase with capital accumulation in requiring more machine building and technological knowledge. As Duménil and Lévy (2004b) show, capital requires increasing levels of skilled labour to fulfil management jobs; the functions of direction are themselves increasingly subject to a division of 'labour'.

Finally, for Marx, technology is not given exogenously or by the imperatives of production narrowly conceived. Rather, embedded in (surplus) value production with its relations of command and control, it is also mobilized by capital to appropriate workers' knowledge and to render the labour force dependent and subordinate.

FROM MARX TO MARXISM

Contrary to technological determinist approaches, Marx does not consider modern society 'as issuing directly from smokestacks, machine tools, and computers' (Braverman, 1974, pp. 12–16). During the 1970s, authors like Coriat (1979), Friedman (1977) and Marglin (1974) deployed this insight in different ways to address the history of the early capitalism, old and new management strategies, forms of worker resistance and so on. But the most fruitful and pioneering contribution belongs to Braverman. He shows how the principles of Taylor, though presented as 'scientific', are nothing more than techniques of labour control or, for Taylor, 'asserted as an *absolute necessity for adequate management the dictation to the worker of the precise manner in which work is to be performed*' (Braverman, 1974, p. 62). Three principles can be identified: first, the labour process is dissociated from the skills of the workers; second, execution is separated from conception as far as possible; third, management uses its monopoly over knowledge by a 'systematic pre-planning and pre-calculation of all elements of the labour process' (p. 81), 'to control each step of the labour process and its mode of execution' (p. 82).

Braverman shows through many documented examples how the orderly application of those principles to industry and then to clerical labour throughout the twentieth century leads to a massive deskilling of workers and to their gradual displacement by machinery ensuing from a scientific-technological revolution that feeds the reserve army of labour. After Braverman, the so-called 'labour process debate' gravitated around two different poles, one led by progressively inclined empirical sociologists and the other by Foucaldian approaches, with each focusing upon contingent factors in the role of workers' resistance and their individual subjectivities. Those contributions increasingly distanced themselves from Braverman and from Marxist concepts more generally, ultimately leading to 'the neglect of objective relations [that] betrays acceptance of capitalism, and in turn, an acknowledgement of defeat in the struggle to free labour from the despotic rule of capital' (Spencer, 2000, p. 240).

Turned against itself, labour process analysis is even used by management studies to formulate more effective strategies of control through the acknowledgement, and incorporation, of labour's subjectivity. But a new generation of Marxists has begun to rejuvenate the radicalism of Marx's addressing different topics (job quality, subcontracting, class structure and so on), and seeking to finesse the complexities of surplus value production as both a material (production) and a social (relations) process with both objective and subjective content.

31. Labour theory of value

Ben Fine

The labour theory of value (LTV) has long had appeal in economic analysis for three entirely different reasons. One is that the labourer is an essential source of products; another is that only labour warrants credit for production as opposed to natural sources of wealth; and the third is that labour quantitatively explains price in some sense. Significantly, with the partial exception of the last, these motivations for the LTV are ahistorical and asocial. By contrast, Marx's LTV, which is the critical culmination of previous contributions, relates the LTV to (capitalist) commodity production alone. This gives it its distinctive character, without which it is open to serious misinterpretation and, as such, subject correctly if misguidedly to rejection. In other words, it is important to recognize that there is no such thing as *the* LTV as the nature of value and how it is understood and justified is controversial. This has not always been recognized for reasons that will be explained subsequently.

Initially, though, consider the definition of value based on labour time of production as popularly conceived. As such, this is what might be termed a physicalist understanding of value as labour time. How much labour has gone into a product, just as how much energy or cotton. Such an approach is popular with neoclassical and technicist interpretations of the LTV, drawing primarily upon deductive methods. But it has also been more informally deployed by classical political economy (especially Ricardo) and Sraffianism/neo-Ricardianism, generally leading to the rejection of the LTV. In this approach, any product requires some contribution of what is called living or direct labour, the time spent collecting berries or on the production line of a car factory. This can hardly make up the total labour time of production since, for example, work may have gone into cultivating the berry patch prior to the picking or in manufacturing component parts (or constructing the factory and machinery itself) in case of car making. These component parts in the process of production have themselves been produced by living labour in the past which is now termed dead or indirect labour. Of course, this dead labour, when living, may have itself depended upon the dead labour of previous products. Just as the seeds of today are the consequence of seeds of the past, so is the labour that has gone into producing them, apparently locating the labour that has gone into production in a potentially infinite regress. Despite this, value is defined as the sum of direct and indirect labour time that has gone into producing the product (with an averaged sharing of the dead labour, such as machinery, that is used across a number of products).

Even at this elementary level of defining value by the labour time of production, a number of problems present themselves. First, what will count as labour? Feeding of cows will clearly take some time in producing milk, but what about the (domestic and, therefore, mostly unpaid) labouring that goes into producing the labourer? Even more extreme, the labourer's sleep takes time and is essential for production to take place but surely does not count as labour? Second, even if what counts as labour is resolved, which of that labour counts towards value itself? Should it be everything that is designated as labour or should the latter be handled selectively, some of which counts as value and some of which does not and, if so, how is this demarcation to be made? The sleep might not be counted as labour, whilst making the bed might and yet still not count as part of value (as opposed to labour gone into making the bed, sheets and blankets). Third, even if we now know what is to count as labour, and what labour is to count as value, how do we add up across different labours to compile value of products? Bear in mind that this issue prevails across differences in both dead and living labours since the labours that have gone into a product both directly and indirectly derive from different labourers doing different tasks at different times. Fourth, both in the present and at any time in the past, different labours will have been exercised with different levels of productivity. So how are labours that count as value, but of different productivities, to be added up with one another? Are some labours to count as contributing more value than others or do we simply average across the different labours?

For most treatments of the LTV, these are merely tedious issues that are not so much addressed as wished away and unrecognized. It is simply presumed that it is obvious which labour should count as value, by how much it should count, and all labour should be treated as equal irrespective of its type, skill and timing. There are two, generally unconscious, reasons underpinning this casual disregard of what would otherwise be fundamental issues. One is that (capitalist) commodity production is unwittingly taken as the standard. Labour counts as value only if it contributes to the production of a commodity (and is liable to be attached to a wage labourer). This means that we do have a strict criterion for what counts as labour. On the other hand, it tends to be presumed, erroneously, that such a standard can be carried over to non-commodity production and allows possibly non-wage labours to be identified and added up to make for the value of products where commodities are not involved. As it were, conditions of commodity producing society are universalized as if they applied to all societies and circumstances.

Note, though, that this still leaves unresolved how to count labours of different skills, types, productivities and time. It is simply presumed that these add up with one another (like adding across different fruits, for example, as opposed to a single fruit, which might itself be of various sizes and other qualities). A second reason for dismissing this problem is that it has become second nature to do so within economics irrespective of whether the LTV is under consideration or not. This is notable in neoclassical economics with its presumption of a production function in which the labour input is taken as a single aggregate for a country as a whole, for example.

In these treatments of the LTV there is a paradox in that a far from well-grounded understanding of capitalism as the basis on which to define value, with some continuing fudges around different types of labour, is extrapolated to a universal definition of value for non-capitalist societies. For Marx, this gave rise to a paradox in that he strongly praised classical political economy (and Ricardo in particular) for using the LTV as an analytical tool for understanding capitalism but, equally, Marx was harshly critical for not having grounded the LTV in its social and historical preconditions and forms of existence in capitalist commodity society. This is perfectly illustrated by Adam Smith's approach to the LTV (Milonakis and Fine, 2009). He argues that it does hold as an explanation of price in what he terms the rude or primitive society where there is no property in either capital or land and so no profits or rents so that labour can command all that is produced. But, by the same token, he suggests that the LTV breaks down outside the rude society where capital and land stake a claim on output. What is striking here, irrespective of the merits of the argument, is that the LTV is being extrapolated to a (rude) society in which there is no exchange and so no prices. There is no need for a value theory other than in a make-belief rude society in which we ask at what prices products would exchange if they were exchanged and as if in a commercial society without property.

Smith's error reflects his use of the LTV as an 'instrumental' theory of value (Pilling, 1980, shows how great promoters of Marxism, such as Maurice Dobb, Ronald Meek and Paul Sweezy were inclined towards instrumentalism): how well does it allow us to explain prices, and the same is true of Ricardo's instrumentalism taken to extreme in his LTV. Ricardo defines value as labour time of production without regard to the problems previously raised and then asks, does value explain price. Whilst correctly dismissing Smith's argument that the presence of profits and rents necessarily invalidate the LTV in this respect, he does conclude, however reluctantly, that price will depend not only upon labour time of production but also upon how slowly capital is turned over and the level of capital composition of production (the ratio of dead to living labour), with each of these increasing price relative to value in order to allow for equalized profitability on capital advanced.

Subsequently, instrumental approaches to the LTV, especially but not exclusively as a theory of price (falling profitability is also involved), have focused on varieties of solutions to the transformation problem, Sraffian and otherwise, some claiming to reject (Marx's) LTV, others to rescue it (Fine, 1986). So, on the face of it, the LTV as traditionally conceived, both before and after Marx, raises a number of issues of purpose, definition and scope of application. Some of these issues have been overlooked, some have been highlighted (for rejection purposes), but they are only resolved through close specification of the peculiar and more subtle approach adopted by Marx himself.

MARX'S VALUE THEORY

This has been laid out on numerous occasions – that value should be seen as a social relation between producers and of exploitation, admittedly with a quantitative element but not one that can be reduced to a physicalist and instrumental content (Elson, 1979a; Fine and Saad-Filho, 2010). Marx's LTV is often associated with that of Ricardo and *the* LTV, but it is both different and differently motivated, not least for being socially and historically grounded. This is best understood by detaching Marx from an instrumental theory of value and seeing him as implicitly asking the question of under what circumstances does value exist in society itself. This is part and parcel of his materialist method in which concepts deployed should not be sheer inventions with instrumental purposes (for example, a theory of price) but be seen to correspond to how society itself is organized. More specifically, for Marx, for the LTV to be valid, there must be some social mechanism (not some mental exercise other than as its reflection) by which different labours are specified to be counted as value and by which they are added together. The answer is to be found only in a commodity producing society.

Why is this so? First and foremost, for commodity production, the social and histori-cally specific property that commodities have in common is that they are the product of different types of labour (what Marx calls the concrete labours corresponding to different jobs) that are brought into equivalence with one another through the market, or via their exchange values. When we say that one table is equivalent to three chairs, say, we (or, more exactly, markets) are expressing the relative values of two products in terms of their use values. But, through this mechanism, the different types of labour that have gone into producing the commodities are also being brought into equivalence with one another even if indirectly and through the medium of the market.

This is the basis of Marx's theory of money and also his theory of commodity fetish-ism since these represent the form and the consequence, respectively, of the way in which concrete labours are brought into equivalence and count as value. But what of the conun-drums previously raised around what counts as labour, what counts as value and how can these be added together? The crucial point here is that these issues cannot invalidate Marx's value theory. For this is based upon the insight that the processes of production, and corresponding labours, associated with commodity production are routinely and necessarily brought into equivalence with one another. The question is not whether the multiplicity of processes and determinants along the route from production to exchange invalidate the LTV or not, but how these take place and how they are to be reproduced in theory, something that cannot be proved by definition of labour value, but only by following the processes from production to exchange.

Second, Marx acknowledges the problems involved by drawing the distinction between concrete labour, associated with a particular production process and production of a par-ticular use value, and abstract labour. The latter is the form taken by labour in general in a commodity producing society. Once concrete labours are brought into equivalence with one another, they count as abstract labour much the same as apples, pears and cherries can count as fruits by conventional classification once some equivalence is established between them by which they can be measured (number, weight or volume, for example). In contrast to both concrete labour and fruits, abstract labour is a social property, a consequence of the equivalences established between commodities through the market (or not in case of production that is not of commodities and so which do not count as abstract even if concrete labour). Making a bed is definitely concrete labour but it is not abstract labour unless it is brought into equivalence with other concrete labours through the market system.

Third, in this light, Marx's political economy should not be understood as the axiomatic deduction of properties from the LTV but the more concrete development and refine-ment of that value theory. It requires a closer specification of the relationship between concrete and abstract labour. This has been captured by Saad-Filho (2002) in terms of the normalization, synchronization and homogenization of labour. Normalization involves the equivalence between the living labours producing a given commodity at any one time, each of these labours potentially involved in different aspects of the process of production and of different skill, intensity and productivity. Synchronization concerns the equivalence between different, dead and living, labours that create a given commod-ity over time since each commodity will incorporate concrete labours that have been expended in the past to provide for the constant capital deployed. And homogenization addresses the equivalence established between different labours engaged across different commodities as relative prices are formed (sometimes, somewhat inappropriately, associated with the so-called transformation problem). For each of these processes, it is inappropriate to approach them as simply seeking to work out how much an individual's labour should count abstractly. Rather, it is a matter of exploring the social processes by which the equivalences are established, not least, for example, as production processes evolve with the accumulation of capital, with deskilling and reskilling, the formation of the collective and cooperative worker, and the processes of competition between capitals.

Fourth, by defining the LTV as specific to commodity producing society, it is not only society itself that brings different types of labour into equivalence through the market as abstract labour, this also determines what labour counts as value and what does not. On a first cut, value is only produced by labour that is directly geared towards the production of commodities. This would count out domestic labour, for example, or (wage) labour that is hired for the provision of personal services. It would also count out state officials and so on. Significantly, much of this depends upon distinguishing between productive and unproductive labour. But, as with other categories of analysis in Marx's political economy, the distinction between labour that does and labour that does not produce value is subject to further refinement. In relatively advanced production processes, many only produce commodities cooperatively and only indirectly as cogs in a wheel along a production line. But such workers are under the command of capital, subject to the imperative of profitability, as opposed to production within the household or otherwise not for commodity production. And wage labour for profit, within the sphere of exchange (dealing in commodities or finance), is also deemed within Marx's value theory not to produce value because it is involved in its circulation rather than its creation.

CONTINUING VALUE CONTROVERSY

In short, Marx's value theory is both a starting point for unravelling the capitalist economy (the most advanced form in which value exists) and a point of return for refining the notion of value in light of logical and historical analysis. As such, the LTV has remained extremely controversial, even with sympathizers to Marxism, and the LTV's more general propositions concerning class and exploitation, rejecting it as inadequate and erroneous. This all begins with Ricardo's dilemma of extreme commitment to an instrumental LTV but finding that it needs modification if value were to be able to explain price. This has its modern counterpart in neo-Ricardianism, with the rejection of Marx's value theory other than as at most a sociology of exploitation, or its complete abandonment in light of the so-called transformation problem. Value cannot explain price, so it is suggested, so value must go.

This longstanding antipathy to Marx's LTV is, as explained, a consequence of instrumentalism and the axiomatic deductivism associated with mainstream economics. But it goes much further than the presumed deficiencies in Marxist value theory as a price theory. As observed in Fine (2001) and Fine et al. (2010), the very same developments within capitalism, such as divergence of value and price, that lead some to reject value theory, are understood by its proponents to make it essential. For the critics, it is not just differing compositions of capital that render value theory invalid. Rather, it is more or less anything taken from the panoply of factors that might influence the nature and course of the capitalist economy, with renewal of rejection as new factors come to the fore. In the past, it has been the presence of differing compositions of capital, monopoly and of insufficient demand. More recently, it has been the role of labour in economic and social reproduction (in the household or through the state, as with education), and most recently the knowledge economy has been presumed to invalidate Marx's LTV.

These issues certainly present challenges to Marx's value theory but they are challenges that can and must be met. Of course, as indicated, value analysis of such phenomena cannot simply be deduced from an abstract theory of value alone. Whether it be monopoly or knowledge, realization of commodities or domestic labour, the material relations involved have to be located in relation to the continuing accumulation of, and exploitation by, capital. Indeed, Marx seems to have anticipated much of these points in a letter to Ludwig Kugelmann of 11 July 1868:

> The chatter about the need to prove the concept of value arises only from complete ignorance both of the subject under discussion and of the method of science. Every child knows that any nation that stopped working, not for a year, but let us say, just for a few weeks, would perish. And every child knows, too, that the amounts of products corresponding to the differing amounts of needs demand differing and quantitatively determined amounts of society's aggregate labour . . . Where science comes in is to show *how* the law of value asserts itself. So, if one wanted to 'explain' from the outset all phenomena that apparently contradict the law, one would have to provide the science *before* the science.

In short, to return to our three opening themes, the social, ethical and material roles of labour in the capitalist economy are themselves part and parcel of the value relations out of which that economy, and society, are constituted. In this vein, Marxists often refer to capitalism as dominated by the law of value (and question whether the law of value prevails across the globe including exertion of its influence on non-capitalist production and economic and social affairs more generally). Although this can be mistakenly interpreted to mean that Marxism implies the economy is subject to iron laws, in extreme requiring that commodities exchange at their values, it is more appropriate to understand the law of value as a mode of investigating how labour is globally organized and reorganized under the influence of a world economy dominated by capitalism.

32. Market socialism

Makoto Itoh

Market socialism explicitly incorporates the market into the socialist economic order in contrast to a model of a totally planned socialist economy which seeks to eliminate the market. This notion has historically attracted broad attention on two occasions: firstly, in the period when the Soviet-type of centrally planned economy was being formed in the 1920s and 1930s, after the Russian revolution and, secondly, half a century later, when the Soviet-type economy stagnated and eventually collapsed. The Chinese experiment can be conceived as a practical model of market socialism, though it does not officially present its theoretical basis.

MARKET SOCIALISM AND THE SOCIALIST ECONOMIC CALCULATION DEBATE

In the first two decades after the Russian revolution, the argument for market socialism was presented in the so-called socialist economic calculation debate. The idea was to defend socialism against the theoretical critiques offered mainly by von Mises and Hayek in the Austrian tradition (Hayek, 1935). At this point, their critique was still based upon a theoretical view close to neoclassical static price theory, though Hayek's position eventually changed. According to them, rational economic calculation under socialism, in order to determine the most efficient combination of means of production among technically available options, and the social allocation of resources, was impossible with the means of production publicly owned and allocated by collective economic planning.

If the labour time necessary to produce goods and services is calculable, including the labour time consumed in the form of means of production, von Mises and Hayek accepted it might serve as a common unit for rational economic calculation. But, following Böhm-Bawerk's critique of Marx's labour theory of value on the grounds of the theoretical difficulty of reducing complex labour to simple labour, for example, they argued that the neoclassical notion of prices balancing demand and supply in the market on the basis of the private ownership of goods and services would be indispensible for rational economic calculation.

Several socialist economists defended the rational feasibility of the socialist economy based upon the public ownership of means of production. They sought to show how prices of publicly owned means of production could be decided by the central planning board to satisfy consumers' needs and secure the full employment of available resources. Dickinson (1933), for example, replied to von Mises showing that the Supreme Economic Council (SEC) can calculate rational prices to achieve full employment in accordance with consumer demand. A demand curve for each type of consumption good can be derived by observing reactions in the market, in which selling agencies raise prices when stocks fall short and lower prices when stocks accumulate. Similarly, a demand curve for the ultimate factors of production (such as land, mineral resources and certain numbers of workers registered as willing to do specific jobs) can also be obtained. When the quantities of these ultimate factors of production are known, the SEC can fix their prices according to demand and supply functions to ensure full employment. The problem could be resolved into a set of simultaneous equations as in general equilibrium theory.

Hayek accepted this solution in theory. However, he insisted on its being academic for two reasons. Firstly, all minutely detailed knowledge and information on changes in technologies, the possibilities for economizing means of production and the shift in consumers' tastes, could not be collected by the central planning authority to incorporate them into their calculation of prices. Secondly, even if this difficulty was somehow overcome, the number of different products entering into the system of simultaneous equations would be hundreds of thousands, and too large for practical annual solution.

Lange (1936, 1937) responded to Hayek's polemics, formulating a classic model of market socialism where the time-consuming process of calculation is omitted. In this model, a socialist society includes public ownership of means of production, but it allows freedom of market choice in consumption and jobs. The preferences of consumers, as expressed by their demand prices, are assumed to serve as guiding criteria in the production and allocation of resources. The income of consumers is composed of two different portions. One is the receipt for labour services. The other is the individual's share in the income derived from the capital and natural resources owned by society. This social dividend could be distributed in many different ways, for example, equally per head, or according to age, or size of family. The Central Planning Board (CPB) strategically determines the rate of accumulation before distributing the social dividend.

Two rules are imposed on the managers of public firms. Firstly, the factors of production must be combined in order to minimize the average cost of production, so that the marginal productivity of factors is equalized. Secondly, the scale of output should be determined at the level where marginal cost equalizes the price of the product. Prices of services of labour and consumer goods are determined on the market, and managers operate according to these rules. The prices of means of production are initially put forward by the CPB as parametric indicators by which alternatives are quantitatively compared. Given such prices, the quantities of means of production demanded and supplied would also be determined. If the prices failed to make demand and supply meet, the error would appear as a surplus or deficit of the goods or resources in question. The CPB must raise the price of a commodity if demand exceeds supply and lower it if the reverse is the case.

Thus, a set of equilibrium prices can be determined through a process of trial and error, much like a competitive market. In this model, as Lange points out, the CPB need not compile complete lists of demand and supply functions, nor does it need to solve hundreds of thousands (as Hayek estimated) or millions (as Robbins suggested) of equations. The trial and error procedure would work better and more swiftly to identify the equilibrium prices in a socialist economy than in a competitive capitalist market, for the CPB has much wider knowledge of what is going on in the entire economic system.

Lange's model of market socialism effectively counters the assertion by von Mises and

Hayek that, in a socialist economy, the rational prices of means of production under public ownership could not be determined, at least as far as static economic conditions are assumed – they could do as well, if not better, than in (a model of) the capitalist economy. This is surely the substantive content of the model, turning on its head the neoclassical arguments for the superiority of private capitalism, even if the practical consequences were limited. Thereafter, Hayek shifted the emphasis of his critique of the collectivist socialist economy to the comparative advantage of a real market economy in generating innovation, drawing upon the role of localized knowledge.

Dobb (1937) and Sweezy (1949) observed that Lange's model of market socialism gave a complete answer to the question initially raised by von Mises and Hayek. They thought, however, that the model did not yet fully demonstrate the advantages of a socialist economy over a competitive market economy in a model of general equilibrium of prices, stressing the ability of a socialist economy to set up long-term and progressive investment strategies with more egalitarian goals, thus avoiding problems due to the short-sighted and narrow-minded rationale for investment in a capitalist economy. Ecological considerations might have also figured, had this debate taken place today.

The Soviet-type economy grew steadily through five-year plans, in contrast with the disastrous Great Depression of the 1930s in the capitalist economies. It also managed to endure the debilitating impact of World War II, spawning follower countries, while continuing to grow faster than most capitalist countries. With the defeat of anti-socialist critiques in the theoretical debate on one side, and the apparent success of the economy through Soviet planning on the other, the socialist economic calculation debate ceased to attract attention for several decades.

MODELS OF MARKET SOCIALISM FOR THE ECONOMIC REFORMS OF SOCIALIST COUNTRIES

The debate re-emerged as the demand for the reform of Soviet-type societies intensified across Eastern Europe. Models of market socialism were regarded as desirable alternatives to the Soviet model of centrally planned and undemocratic socialism. The need for reform of the Soviet system strengthened with the progressive deterioration of its economic growth from the mid-1970s. Favourable factors such as easily mobilizable labour and natural resources for the construction of heavy industries, which facilitated economic growth through the Soviet-type central planning, were being exhausted and economic reform became essential.

Hayek's critique of the irrationality of the centrally planned economy was recalled by Lavoie (1985), among other neo-Austrians, with special attention to Hayek's view of the limited capacity of the capitalist market economy to promote innovation through the use of locally dispersed knowledge. The socialist economic calculation debate was rekindled on a broader terrain, encompassing a wider variety of models and considerations. Is it possible to build a spontaneous motivation for economic dynamism under the conditions of socialist ownership of the means of production? Can socialist economies rapidly generate and deploy new technologies? How can socio-economic decision-making be democratized by reforming the excessively centralized state bureaucracy?

Brus (1973), who had cooperated with Lange in Poland, reformulated his model into a more functional model of market socialism, by classifying economic decisions into three categories: (1) Basic macroeconomic decisions, such as those concerning the growth rate, the division between communal and private consumption and regional industrial structure. These must be more actively addressed by the CPB than is the case in Lange's model. (2) The choice of private consumption goods as well as occupation should be undertaken in a free market, as with Lange. (3) Operational decisions concerning the size and the composition of inputs and outputs, the methods of production, the selection of the suppliers and purchasers, as well as the detailed determination of remunerations, should be undertaken by individual enterprises or industrial sectors. In this respect, the model was a more decentralized version of market socialism, weakening centralized bureaucratic power and broadening opportunities for democratic participation of workers. It served as a guide for the social reform movements beginning within Eastern Europe.

A British economist, Alec Nove (1983), sought to sketch a model of 'feasible' socialism, achievable within 50 years, drawing upon his examination of the historical experiences of the Soviet Union, Eastern Europe and China. The political system is assumed to be a multi-party democracy. There can be many different types of production unit, to encourage citizen initiatives, including socialized enterprises with workers' self-management, cooperative enterprises and individual agents such as craftsmen. There would be no large-scale private ownership of the means of production. The functions of central planning would be the determination of major investments, the monitoring of decentralized investment to avoid duplication, the administration of infrastructure such as electricity production and railway services, and some regulation of foreign trade. Democratic voting would determine the boundary between consumer goods and services to be provided free and those to be purchased on the market.

Roemer (1994) formulated a new model of market socialism drawing upon Analytical Marxism. It incorporates a system of joint-stock companies as the most important economic unit for producing goods and services. Both the public ownership of companies and the basis of egalitarian economic life among people are to be realized by distributing equal amounts of vouchers for purchasing shares to all the citizens when they become adults. If a person manages to purchase shares of an efficiently managed firm, she or he can earn higher dividends and make capital gains through the increase in share prices. As long as all the shares held by individual citizens are returned to the state upon death, the fundamental nature of public ownership of shares and, therefore, also of joint-stock companies is sustained. The choice of investments by individuals and institutions (such as banks, pension funds and mutual funds) in the stock market would monitor and induce managers of companies to maximize profits and pursue innovation. However, a problem remains of how to monitor and discipline the managers of firms in accordance with the interest of general citizens.

PRACTICAL AND THEORETICAL SIGNIFICANCE

It is striking how the models of market socialism had no lasting impact on social reform movements in Eastern Europe and in the Soviet Union. Instead, 'a shock therapy' for rapid and complete transition to a capitalist market economy was adopted. By contrast, in the systemic change in China since 1978, the market has been introduced more gradually under the continuing Communist Party (CCP) leadership. This model has delivered high economic growth, while the CCP has declared a socialist market economy in the Constitutional Law of 1993. Whether theories of market socialism have influenced the Chinese road is debatable. The Chinese economic reforms have been implemented through continuous experimentation, rather than being led by theoretical models. Indeed, the Chinese socio-economic system now contains various forms of enterprise, economic units, management and ownership of means of production that are much more complex than in the models of market socialism.

Thus, these models have lagged behind the variety and complexity of our historical experience. There are issues of political forms, collective ownership other than through the state, distinctions between different types of goods and services whether produced through the market or not. Consideration must also be given to how to ensure democratic workers' self-management in the workplace. Therefore, models of market socialism may remain flexible, and they can be selected according to the social and historical conditions, and may not easily converge towards a single 'correct' model.

We need further to consider how the models of market socialism can be understood on the basis of Marxian theory. To a large extent, the discussion of market socialism so far has not been grounded on Marxist theory. In extreme form, this is characteristic of the first market socialism debate, which was conducted within the confines of neoclassical theory. Although Marx himself did not draw a blueprint for a future socialist economy, unlike the earlier utopian socialists, his conception of a future society was based on 'a community of free individuals' (*Capital I*, ch. 1). However, we do not need to narrow down the alternatives beyond capitalism just to a democratically planned economy, as Mandel (*In Defence of Socialist Planning*), for example, argued against Nove. Moreover, there is certainly room to utilize Marx's basic economic theories in order to understand theoretical possibilities for market socialism. Two points are illustrative.

Firstly, in neoclassical economics, as well as in classical political economy, the market is conceived as a natural economic order of liberty, originating from the natural human propensity to exchange and better oneself. This is a naturalistic view of the market economy, without objective understanding of the real origin and the roles of the market economy throughout history. In the same vein, the market economy is always conceived to be fully developed (to form a natural order of liberty) and indistinguishable from the capitalist market economy. Within such a frame of reference, the systemic change in the Soviet bloc countries towards a market economy tends to be conceptualized only as a transition to a fully capitalist economy, since market socialism must continue to leave more or less significant 'unnatural' planned economic aspects within society.

In contrast, Marx clearly recognized that commodity exchange originated before capitalism, as external trade between communal societies, separate from communal intra-social orders of pre-capitalist societies. Accordingly, forms of the market economy, such as commodity, money and some kinds of capital, coexisted with various communal social orders. Only when human labour power is commodified on a social scale could the market economy develop fully into a capitalist economy. By the same token, the market economy can also exist in post-capitalist forms of societies as market socialism, in combination with associational public ownership of major means of production. This can be regarded as a preparatory stage for socialism, prior to full communism where the market is fully subordinated or eliminated as in Marx's own idea for a future society. But, as long as the labour market persists, a fundamental issue remains about how to overcome the alienated, commodified form of the labour power of the wage workers. Lange already suggested an avenue for the solution in his model, at least as far as the choice of jobs and goods on the market is concerned.

Secondly, most models of market socialism have been based upon the neoclassical theory of price, bypassing Marxian value theory. Nor has Marx's idea to use labour time as the unit of account in an associational economic plan been put to use in Soviet-type planning, with its calculations based more on Sraffian-type physical input-output analysis. Although Stalin (*Economic Problems of Socialism in the USSR*) once asserted that economic laws, such as the law of value, must be utilized for the construction of socialism, he confused the law of value specific to the market economy with a natural law, far from discussing market socialism or how to apply Marx's value theory to Soviet planning. After de-Stalinization, Liberman ([1962] 1966) suggested introducing a more prominent role for profit in the USSR in order to promote productivity growth. His argument remained, however, within the framework of the Soviet system of public prices, and was not linked with theories of market socialism, nor with Marx's idea of using labour time as an accounting unit. Marx's law of value based upon labour time has thus not easily been applied or used in models of either planned economy or market socialism.

Can we really apply labour time as an accounting unit in a practical model of market socialism? One solution is a full socialist wage model of market socialism (Itoh, 1995). In this, all the social income (value added) annually produced is distributed to the workers according to their labour time, without leaving a social surplus or profit to the enterprises. The social funds necessary for communal consumption and accumulation are collected *ex post*, as a tax on wage income. Since the education and training costs for socially necessary skilled or complex workers are covered by the social funds, these costs need not be retrieved by individual workers or families. Everybody is thus basically paid the same. As a social foundation of economic democracy with socialist egalitarianism, labour time expended by any worker, including complex labour, is thus to be counted equally as physical time for purposes of remuneration. Equilibrium prices can be achieved by trial and error, and would tend to be in direct proportion to labour time crystallized in goods and services. This model would render the social relations among workers, both towards their labour and the products of their labour, transparent as a true basis of associational democracy, as was proposed by Marx. But the later Hayek problem of how to ensure incentives for innovation would need to be addressed as an additional consideration within this basic model.

33. Marx and underdevelopment

Mauro Di Meglio and Pietro Masina

In Marx (and Engels) the systematic critique of political economy is indistinguishable from the political and ethical commitment towards the overturning of the capitalist system and the making of a more egalitarian world. Given this thrust, Marx's repeated assertions of a progressive role played by the bourgeoisie and capitalism has bewildered some of his readers. For example, it is often claimed that Marx was unable to grasp the historical impact of British colonialism and free trade policies on the economic development of the so-called backward countries. These critics claim that Marx optimistically (and naively) believed that British expansion would promote industrialization and, therefore, capitalist development, ignoring the 'development of underdevelopment' implications of European domination, which was, later, emphasized by the 'neo-Marxist' dependency theories (Owen and Sutcliffe, 1972; Kiernan, 1974). At a more general level, Marx has been criticized for his supposed Eurocentrism and evolutionism, that is, for privileging the history of Europe as the conceptual framework for understanding the rest of the world, considering pre-capitalist European history in terms of a set of necessary and inevitable stages, and using these stages as a way of conceptualizing non-European history.

In other words, Marx and most Marxist thinkers reproduced rather than challenged their predecessors' biased interpretation of non-European history. This was, presumably, due to Marx's inability to overcome historicism, or the theory of development underpinning liberal philosophies of history. This conception of history sees it as the narrative of the development of modern subjects and cultures, originating in Europe and then spreading outside it, according to a 'first in Europe, then elsewhere' structure of global historical time (Chakrabarty, 2000).

Marx's progressivist view of capitalism is typically condensed by Avineri (1969, p. 3): 'It is true that capitalism is the most brutalizing and dehumanizing economic system history has ever known . . . Yet to Marx, capitalism is still a necessary step toward final salvation, since only capitalism can create the economic and technological infrastructure that will enable society to allow for the free development of every member according to his capacities.' Evidence in support of this interpretation can be found in some of Marx and Engels's writings; for example, the *Communist Manifesto* (1848), the writings on India (1853) published in the *New York Daily Tribune* and numerous passages of the *Grundrisse*, written in 1857–58.

Indisputably, the notion of 'progress' runs throughout Marx's work, reflecting the influence of British political economy, classical German philosophy and French proto-socialism (Melotti, 1977, p. 2). Nevertheless, this interpretation is problematic in several ways. For example, it takes Marx's thought as monolithic, whereas his views on the 'progress' wrought by capitalism changed significantly over time, and the traditional interpretation tends to downplay the shifts in Marx's thinking between the 1840s–50s and the 1860s–70s. Furthermore, one should not forget that Marx 'was caught up in the basic epistemological tension of any and all attempts to analyze large-scale, long-term processes of social change' (Wallerstein, 1985 [1991], p. 151): that is, to work simultaneously at a very abstract level, describing the basic principles of the capitalist system, and at a very concrete and historical level, analysing the capitalist development process in specific contexts. Since this tension could not be eliminated, Marx resorted to alternating emphases in his writings, depending on the specific purposes that those writings were addressing. This 'epistemological tension' makes it particularly difficult to reconstruct Marx's thinking on colonialism and underdevelopment: these issues were mostly discussed in newspaper articles and letters, that is, in texts that did not have the same theoretical coherence and depth of his major works. It is therefore not surprising that Marx's writings in this context have generated heated debates in which different and even contrasting views have emerged in the attempt to reconstruct Marx's 'true' thinking.

THE PROGRESSIVE ROLE OF THE BOURGEOISIE AND COLONIALISM

In considering the future of the countries subjected to European colonial domination in the nineteenth century, Marx and Engels acknowledged the progressive implications of capitalist modernization, looking at the bourgeoisie as an effective economic and political force able to transform the world, destroying non-capitalist societies through its global expansion and planting the seeds of progress in 'lower' civilizations. This progressive role of the bourgeoisie is particularly evident in the *Communist Manifesto*. Since the bourgeoisie 'cannot exist without constantly revolutionising the instruments of production' (ch. 1), and it is in need of constantly expanding markets, it increasingly operates on a world scale, transforming the economic and social structures of the so-called backward nations:

> [It] draws all, even the most barbarian, nations into civilisation. The cheap prices of commodities are the heavy artillery with which it batters down all Chinese walls, with which it forces the barbarians' intensely obstinate hatred of foreigners to capitulate. It compels all nations, on pain of extinction, to adopt the bourgeois mode of production; it compels them to introduce what it calls civilisation into their midst, i.e., to become bourgeois themselves. In one word, it creates a world after its own image. (Marx and Engels, *The Communist Manifesto*, ch. 1)

Traditional societies – both the European feudal system and pre-capitalist systems in other regions – were not idyllic, built as they were upon pervasive forms of exploitation. The diffusion of capitalism implied the replacement of traditional forms of exploitation 'veiled by religious and political illusions' with 'naked, shameless, direct, brutal exploitation' (Marx and Engels, *The Communist Manifesto*, ch. 1). Marx and Engels were, therefore, well aware that capitalism meant bringing exploitation to a higher level, and that the destruction of pre-capitalist formations could imply more miserable living conditions for the proletariat and for the populations subjected to colonial domination. However, at least until the 1850s, the prevailing theme for Marx (and Engels) was the progressive historical mission of the bourgeoisie: liberation could only occur after the establishment of modern (capitalist) forms of production. And, outside Europe, the transition to capitalism depended on the extension of colonialism and imperialism.

Marx's views on colonialism are expressed in a number of articles on India published as part of his journalistic collaboration with the *New York Daily Tribune*. In these writings, England is seen as responsible for a double mission in India: 'one destructive, the other regenerating the annihilation of old Asiatic society, and the laying the material foundations of Western society in Asia' (Marx, *The Future Results of British Rule in India*, 22 July 1853). There is no complacency here in describing this ruthless historical process, but the prevailing argument supported by Marx in the 1853 articles was that the transformation of the underdeveloped areas stemming from the inner logic of the capitalist mode of production had a progressive nature. That is, 'regardless of the darker sides of the destruction of the pre-capitalist modes of production in the colonies, [the bourgeoisie] plays a progressive role due to its superior ability to create the material preconditions for development' (Vujačić, 1988, p. 474). In Marx's own words, 'whatever may have been the crimes of England she was the unconscious tool of history in bringing about [a] revolution [in the social state of Asia]' (Marx, *The British Rule in India*, 10 June 1853).

A similarly critical appraisal of the worldwide expansion of the capitalist mode of production is expressed by Marx in his speech *On the Question of Free Trade* (1848), where he denounces the myth of free trade leading to a sort of international brotherhood in which each country would specialize on production in harmony with natural advantage. Rather, free trade is a form of 'cosmopolitan exploitation' reproducing on a larger scale the same destructions that capitalist development unleashes within a single nation: 'All the destructive phenomena which unlimited competition gives rise to within one country are reproduced in more gigantic proportions on the world market.' Although he acknowledges the importance of protectionism for establishing large-scale industry in any given country, he also warns that protectionism would not prevent dependence upon global markets dominated by free trade. Marx's support for free trade is, therefore, motivated by the need to hasten the development of the capitalist system and accelerating the process of its demise.

UNDERDEVELOPMENT AND THE EXTRACTION OF SURPLUS VALUE

Despite some degree of ambivalence, until the end of the 1850s, Marx emphasized the progressive role of the colonial expansion of British capitalism, and he conditionally supported free trade policies. However, Marx's views changed significantly in the 1860s, when he explicitly disavowed his earlier thesis about the 'double mission' of British industrial capital. Critical remarks had been formulated in the *New York Daily Tribune* in the 1850s, where Marx talked of a transfer of surplus value from India to Britain because of the colonial arrangement, and made careful calculations of this drain (see Patnaik, 2005, pp. 70–71). In the same period, Marx also expressed his support for Chinese resistance during the Second Opium War (Anderson, 2010). Despite these earlier doubts, a real change of perspective only occurred with his involvement in the Irish Question and his studies of Russia and the Russian revolutionary movement.

As many commentators have pointed out (Davis, 1967; Mohri, 1979; Shanin, 1983), the theoretical position towards which Marx moved from the 1860s was that the destruction of the old society would not necessarily create the conditions for a new and more advanced one. On the one hand, he showed a growing awareness that capitalist development in the metropolis was supported by an incessant extraction of huge amounts of surplus from the colonies and semi-colonies (Patnaik, 2005, p. 71). On the other hand, Marx recognized that the destruction of old societies through colonial domination, rather than creating the basis for regeneration, often prevented the autonomous development of a modern economy in those colonies. Colonial rule not only impeded the development of industry through coercion, but also used the forcible integration into the world market to strengthen the dependence of colonies on the metropolis. In this sense, British free trade deprived pre-capitalist societies of the conditions for the autonomous development of their productive forces and the creation of an independent national economy. This change of attitude in Marx's analysis went along with a shift from a unilinear to a multilinear philosophy of history (Anderson, 2010).

The evolution in the analysis of the relations between metropolis and colonies allows not only a better understanding of the creation of dependency for the colonies but also a reassessment of the importance of the extraction of surplus value for the metropolis. Marx seems to recognize that the so-called 'primitive accumulation' should not be considered as confined to the (European) genesis of capitalism, but as a continuing process, a point subsequently made by Rosa Luxemburg and by dependency theory and world-systems analysis.

This change of perspective seems evident in his writings on the Irish Question (1867), where Marx talks of a regime that 'since 1846, though less barbarian in form, is in effect destructive, leaving no alternative but Ireland's voluntary emancipation by England or life-and-death struggle', and where he argues that '[e]very time Ireland was about to develop industrially, she was crushed and reconverted into a purely agricultural land' (Marx, *Outline of a Report on the Irish Question*, 16 December 1867). What the Irish need is '[s]elf-government and independence from England', 'an agrarian revolution', which the English cannot accomplish, and, in open opposition to his views of the 1850s, 'protective tariffs against England' (Marx, *Letter from Marx to Engels In Manchester*, London, 30 November 1867). Thus, Marx is moving away from nineteenth-century 'modernization theories' towards an understanding of what later generations would call 'dependent development'.

Similar remarks on the connections between different areas of the world capitalist system can be found in *Capital I*, especially in section 7, ch. 15, where Marx stated that 'A new and international division of labour, a division suited to the requirements of the chief centres of modern industry springs up, and converts one part of the globe into a chiefly agricultural field of production, for supplying the other part which remains a chiefly industrial field.'

The influence of the Russian populists on Marx's views on the effects of capitalism also played a role in the change of his theoretical stance. The populists assumed the possibility and desirability for Russia to bypass the stage of capitalism, and promoted a non-capitalist strategy of industrialization relying on the 'advantages of backwardness', supported and controlled by the state, based on the Russian peasant community (*Obshchina*).

While in subsequent years Lenin criticized the Russian populists as a 'petit bourgeois' and conservative version of European romantic thought, Marx was apparently aware that they gave voice not only to the problems of small producers against large-scale capitalist production, but also to the specific problems of a 'backward' agrarian country against highly developed capitalist economies. The search for such a strategy was bolstered by the awareness of the difficulties stemming from their coexistence with the capitalist countries of Western Europe, whose competition was considered an insurmountable obstacle to capitalist development in Russia. The idea of 'uneven development', first formulated by Pyotr Chaadayev, according to which Russia was turning into a proletarian against the bourgeois nations of the West, provided the theoretical core of the populists' political analysis, and their 'world-historical' perspective allowed them to raise the issue of the problems faced by a peripheral country in the development of its productive forces within a hierarchical world system. In this sense, Russian populism can be considered not only as a petty producers' ideology, but also as the first ideological expression of the specific features of the economic and social development of 'late coming' countries (Walicki, 1969; Shanin, 1983).

Marx's involvement in the issues raised by the Russian populists spurred his interest into a new set of problems, which were peculiar to countries engaged in the search for a non-capitalistic way to overcome economic and social backwardness. In the drafts of his letter to Vera Zasulich (March, 1881), where he expressed his optimism about the perspectives and revolutionary potential of the Russian rural communities, Marx focuses his attention on problems such as unequal development, the advantages of backwardness, the possibility of technology imports accelerating industrial development, the role of cultural contact and, more generally, the problem of the global interdependence of societal transformations.

In his reflections on the Russian revolutionary perspectives, Marx came to a new understanding of 'uneven development'. In a famous passage in the Preface to the First German Edition of *Capital* (1867), Marx had suggested that the nation 'more developed industrially' would show, 'to the less developed, the image of its own future'. While in that context he was clearly referring to England and Germany, a subsequent Marxist tradition used that notion to define a general rule of capitalist development. This deterministic vision was noticeably confuted by the 'late' Marx, for whom the prevailing forces in the international trading system would prevent the autonomous industrial development of the backward countries. As it has been suggested by Shanin (1983, pp. 17–18), although the idea of 'dependent development' was not explicitly formulated, its foundation was laid.

MARXIST TRADITIONS ON DEVELOPMENT AND UNDERDEVELOPMENT

In parallel with the gradual change in Marx's views of the role of capitalism and the relationship between development and underdevelopment, the history of Marxist thought on these issues during the twentieth century also showed two phases. Simplifying, the first phase, until the early 1960s, exhibits the optimistic evolution of the 'first' Marx; the second gained significance since the 1960s, emphasizing the global scope and the uneven consequences of global capitalism as a world system.

The Second International (1889–1914) promoted a version of Marxism that was far more positive than the 'first' Marx himself was on the progressive role of capitalism. A deterministic reading of capitalist development prevailed, according to which capitalism would develop the productive forces and then eventually break down through its own contradictions, paving the way for a socialist revolution. Such a view was further reinforced by Bolshevism which, after 1917, became the most influential interpretation of Marxism in the world. This approach deeply influenced the analysis of the so-called 'colonial question', which occupied an important space in the debates within the Communist Party of the Soviet Union (CPSU) and the Comintern (the Third International, 1919–43).

During the 1920s, the debate within the CPSU on the modes of 'socialist accumulation' and on the 'national question' saw the Stalinist line prevail. This emphasized the priority of building 'socialism in one country', and implied a strategy of isolation to overcome the constraints imposed by capitalist encirclement. This strategy for the communist movement was based on an evolutionist interpretation of Marxism, which postulated that each country should go through successive stages of development in order to reach socialism. These stages had to be reached in each country in which socialist revolutions had succeeded.

This version of Marxist thinking became dominant during the 1930s and continued to prevail until the mid-1960s. This evolutionist version of Marxism was symmetric to contemporary liberal thinking, only differing for the country identified as the most advanced – the Soviet Union against Great Britain and the United States.

The liberal view that underdevelopment was the result of persisting feudal economic relations exerted a strong and protracted influence over the Latin American communist parties, that is, the same region which eventually gave birth to the main alternative view on these issues. In the Marxist literature, the bourgeois-democratic revolution was, therefore, defined as a revolution against the old relations of production, and considered a prerequisite for backward societies to achieve autonomous development. This revolution should overthrow the old political system and liberate the country from imperialist dependence, making possible a new economic expansion. This bourgeois-democratic revolution required an alliance between the progressive sectors of the bourgeoisie and the proletariat against the traditional rural oligarchies, and it should promote the development of capitalist industrial sectors against the pre-capitalist monopolies and privileges. Imperialism and colonialism had prevented social and economic progress, and the bourgeois-democratic revolution would bring not only political emancipation but also economic development.

Since the 1960s, this evolutionist Marxist interpretation (along with the parallel liberal narrative of the modernization perspective) was eventually rejected by the so-called dependency theories and, later, by world-systems analysis. The historical significance of these critical approaches, beyond their inadequate understanding of specific historical circumstances, was their challenge to orthodox Marxist analyses on development and underdevelopment, which colluded with liberal thought. This was, in turn, part and parcel of a geopolitical collusion between the United States and the Soviet Union on the world scene (Frank, 1967; Wallerstein, 1974b). Although not unchallenged, and even charged with not being Marxist (Warren, 1973; Brenner, 1977), this 'neo-Marxism', with its emphasis on the 'development of underdevelopment' and core-periphery capitalist relations in the *longue durée* seems consistent with, and inspired by, the views that Marx expressed since the 1860s, and it is especially valuable in the understanding of past and present inequalities.

34. Marxism and history

George C. Comninel

Only a broad and selective account of Marx, Marxism and historiography can be offered here, neglecting much that is profoundly important. The historical works and ideas Marx had to confront were thoroughly Eurocentric, notwithstanding his own interests in Asia and the Americas. At the same time, Marxism has had a tremendous impact on non-European historiography, and the relationship between European and other histories is enduring. Even in English, there is the work of C.L.R. James and Eric Williams on the Caribbean, to say nothing of the historiography of India. While the omission here of much of the history of the world (as well as race and gender) is unavoidable, it is regretted. This account should be taken as a starting point for further enquiry.

Marx was born in the Francophile Rhenish city of Trier only three years after it was taken over by reactionary Prussia following the defeat of Bonaparte. Across Europe, the French Revolution posed the issues of the day, and its meaning and place in history were matters of great political import. In innumerable ways, the Revolution cast a long shadow through ideas and movements during the next two centuries, and not only in Europe. The impact that the French Revolution had on historiography is so intertwined with the ideas of Marx and the development of Marxism that it requires special attention, but with a critical eye as to what was specific to Marx (see below).

HISTORY AND THEORY

The connections between Marxism and the study of history are enormously complex and the subject of intense debate among Marxists and their critics. The influences Marx and Marxism have had on historical conceptions and research do not necessarily reflect the nature and meaning of either Marx's own ideas or those of subsequent Marxists. Many would argue that for the most part these influences have been based on misinterpretations of Marx's work, not least by those considering themselves to be Marxists. The ideas that have been most influential include: that '[m]en make their own history, but they do not make it as they please' (*The Eighteenth Brumaire of Louis Bonaparte*, ch. I); that history has been determined by a succession of forms of class exploitation, generally conceived in terms of 'modes of production'; and that economic forces and relations, and their contradictions, have been the primary determinants of history within the forms of class society and between them. These ideas, however, have frequently been understood in terms of historical determinism; economic and/or technological determinism; the historical necessity of specific stages and processes of transition; the subordination of politics to economics, with class fundamentally being an economic category; and the limited role of human agency.

Running through the debates over the relationship between Marxism and historiography is the question – too often obscured – of whether what is at stake are issues of theory and method, or issues of research practice and interpretation. In the structuralist Marxism of Louis Althusser, this question is meaningless and inherently anti-Marxist: theory is taken to be the foundation of all scientific knowledge; the theory required for history is understood to have been established once and for all by Karl Marx; 'historicism' – history unshaped by Marxist theory – is a most profound error (Thompson, 1978; Comninel, 1987, pp. 82–102). In polar opposition to this view stand both genuine empiricists, denying that theory has a role in the acquisition of knowledge, and post-structuralists and others who instead push the social construction of knowledge towards the point that all accounts – especially in history – are conceived to be equally valid.

Even among those inclined to adopt such positions, however, it is rare to find scholars – again, especially historians – who do not in practice give attention to both the terms of analysis and the implications of evidence. Certainly, all historians work with a given framework of concepts and at least a broad sense of an overarching 'story' to history, even if only absorbed from general culture and pre-specialist education. At the same time, whatever one's theoretical approach, one must be able to reconcile it with evidence however constructed and selected. If these sets of issues broadly constitute, respectively, the terrains of 'historical social theory' and 'historiographical research', it is clear not only that there is a relationship between the two, but that the line between them is blurred. The huge literature on Marxism as historical social theory cannot really be discussed here, but one cannot consider Marx's impact on historiography without some attention to theory.

The centrality of historical social theory is immediately evident in Marx's work. *The Manifesto of the Communist Party* asserts at the outset that 'The history of all hitherto existing society is the history of class struggles', a conception framing Marx's entire revolutionary political project. It is fundamental to his thought that the history of class societies culminates in the self-emancipation of the working class, not merely ending the capitalist form of class society, but engendering the emancipation of all humanity from oppression and exploitation. Throughout the critique of political economy that formed the greatest part of his work, Marx took pains to locate the specifically capitalist forms of social relations of production within history, challenging those claims of classical political economy (repeated in different form in neoclassical theory) that the fundamentals of economics are timeless and universal. The historical specificity of his critique is especially clear in the theoretical ground-clearing of the Introduction to the *Grundrisse*. His analogy of learning about the anatomy of the ape from the anatomy of humans depends precisely on that they are different.

Marx wanted not simply to interpret the world, but to change it (this goal itself being an aid to understanding). He never approached history merely as an academic scholar, but drew upon it to inform his political analysis and critique of capitalism. The terms of his analysis, for both the nature of capitalist society and the political objective of the working class, are grounded precisely in that overview of history developing through processes of exploitation and struggle articulated in the *Manifesto*. Yet, while his own conception of history focused on class oppression and struggles against it, he consciously drew upon historical accounts of class that were prominent in the historiography of his time. Marx wrote to Joseph Weydemeyer in 1852 that:

Now as for myself, I do not claim to have discovered either the existence of classes in modern society or the struggle between them. Long before me, bourgeois historians had described the historical development of this struggle between the classes, as had bourgeois economists their economic anatomy. (5 March 1852, Marx to Joseph Weydemeyer in New York)

Although Marx's own ideas must be understood in relation to the dominant liberal ideas of his time, this and other references make it clear that, in contrast to the liberal economic thought that he so systematically subjected to criticism, he never undertook a comparable critique of liberal historical conceptions. Any appreciation of Marxism's contribution to the study of history therefore must take into account not only the impact of earlier historical social theory on Marx's own ideas, but the continuing influence of liberal historical conceptions within Marxism as well as without.

During the seventeenth and eighteenth centuries, a materialist and economistic conception of historical progress emerged in association with liberal political and economic ideas. In 1748, the future political economists Adam Smith and A.-R.J. Turgot independently conceived human society to have developed through four stages characterized by distinct 'modes of subsistence': hunting and gathering, pastoralism, agriculture and commerce. Within a decade this concept had been applied to the history of law, asserting that the characteristic forms of property of each mode of subsistence provided a corresponding legal foundation. Historical development through the stages of these modes was conceived in relation to economic and social improvement, constituting the underlying substance of humanity's 'progress'. In many and varied forms – whether emphasizing climate, population growth, technology, trade, division of labour, rationality or some other source of change – this stagist conception of history as unilinear progress has figured prominently in social theory ever since (Comninel, 1987, pp. 53–74).

THE IDEA OF BOURGEOIS REVOLUTION

During the French Revolution, this idea of progress through stages was adapted to defend the struggle of the non-noble bourgeoisie against the aristocracy as historically necessary, ending an outmoded form of rule in favour of one promoting modern commerce. In reality, less than 10 per cent of the bourgeoisie were merchants or engaged in industry and, when successful, they almost invariably purchased ennobling offices and joined the aristocracy. That nobles were formally barred from engaging in commerce, however, lent plausibility to the claim that the struggle of the bourgeoisie to establish political equality – and access to higher offices – was tied to the rise of trade, and so marked a decisive transition between historical epochs. The moderate revolutionary leader, Antoine Barnave, wrote the first such account of 'bourgeois revolution' while awaiting execution in 1793, and works written from this perspective were widespread during the first half of the nineteenth century, as liberal progressivist social theory informed historiography, political economy and philosophy (Mellon, 1958). Marx's historical ideas were fundamentally shaped by this pervasive liberal perspective.

The July Revolution of 1830 gave France a moderate liberal constitutional monarchy, and it is telling that its leading politician was François Guizot, a historian long renowned for his view that progress in civilization was driven by a rising bourgeoisie, culminating in bourgeois revolution. In most of Europe, however, reactionary states held sway, and even the most anaemic liberalism remained subversive and revolutionary. Yet opposition was widespread. Many concurred at least that the liberal Revolution of 1789 had been necessary. Others looked beyond the Revolution's early days to embrace radical Jacobin republicanism, the egalitarian direct democracy of the *sans-culottes*, or even the socialism of Gracchus Babeuf's 'Conspiracy of Equals'. Certainly, there was no shortage of adherents to the reactionary party of order; but everywhere there were liberals, republicans, democrats and socialists, all of whom measured historical progress in relation to the high water mark of the French Revolution. This was the context in which Marx and Engels composed the *Manifesto* (Comninel, 2000b).

There was nothing novel about the account of the French Revolution in the *Manifesto*; what was new was the call for proletarian class revolution. As the 1848 Revolution in France seemed to repeat the course of 1789 – but, as he famously observed, the second time as farce – Marx had occasion in *The Eighteenth Brumaire of Louis Bonaparte* to engage in more specifically historical analysis than usual. What is striking is the extent to which this analysis corresponds to historical evidence rather than to the idea of bourgeois revolution. Despite the claim in the *Manifesto* that industrial capitalism had already developed to the point that the working class was ready to be its gravedigger, putting an end forever to class rule by the capitalists, Marx here makes clear that the industrialists were far from dominant even within the bourgeoisie, having to contend with 'aristocracy of finance', 'the large landowners', and the 'high dignitaries of the army, the university, the church, the bar, the academy, and the press' in addition to the 'republican faction' that initially came to power in 1848 (Marx, *The Eighteenth Brumaire of Louis Bonaparte*, ch. II). His account stresses the continual growth of state offices from the old regime, through all the phases of the Revolution, and each successive regime down to 1851, when half a million civil officials were matched by another half million in the army (ch. VII). It is not easy to reconcile these historical details and the political processes to which they speak – the roles of state finance and state offices looming large in the structure of dominant class interests – with the classic conception of bourgeois class revolution. That Marx put complicated historical analysis ahead of a simple reaffirmation of the account offered in his call to arms gives insight into his priorities.

Marx's extension of progress to proletarian class revolution would have been anathema even to the most liberal bourgeoisie; but his ideas remained little known outside radical circles prior to the Paris Commune of 1871. Thereafter, with the establishment of the Third Republic, political polarization within France intensified, throwing republicans into an enduring but uncomfortable alliance with the radical Left. Most famously in the Dreyfus Affair, but throughout the Third Republic, authoritarian political movements and figures associated with the military and the Church constituted a real threat. Against the anti-republican and anti-democratic reactionaries among the clergy and social elites, even conservative republicans found it necessary to defend not only the liberalism but the radicalism of the Revolution, accepting that these formed 'a bloc', in Clemenceau's words.

This defence of historically necessary bourgeois revolution as the true foundation for republican France was carried into the increasingly professional halls of academe when Alphonse Aulard became in 1885 the first Chair in the History of the Revolution at the Sorbonne. Aulard embraced democratic Jacobinism, but neither as a socialist nor a defender of Robespierre. The leading French historians of the Revolution that followed

Aulard not only embraced the republican mission of the bourgeoisie, but did so openly as socialists, and increasingly as Marxists: from Jean Jaurès, leader of the socialist Section française de l'internationale onvrière (SFIO), the French section of the workers' International, through Albert Mathiez and Georges Lefebvre, to Albert Soboul, a member of the Parti communiste français (PCF), the French Communist Party. Outside of France, meanwhile, it was not unusual for mainstream historians to shun the overtly class analysis of 'bourgeois revolution', yet often they just substituted a diluted version of the liberal progressivist original (such as a 'democratic' or 'Atlantic' revolution).

The defeat of France by Nazi Germany in 1940 brought reactionary forces to power behind the actively collaborationist Marshal Pétain, strongly supported by the Church. Following the Liberation, the revived (Fourth) Republic continued to suffer from a broad lack of credibility, worsened by the Cold War and anti-colonial struggles in Vietnam and Algeria. After Charles de Gaulle (a devoutly Catholic general) established the politically stable, moderately liberal, yet fundamentally conservative Fifth Republic – further undercutting the old Right, tainted by Vichy – the unity of republican defence lost its urgency. By the late 1960s, challenges raised abroad to the idea of bourgeois revolution finally had impact within France, and the previously unacceptable view that the originally liberal Revolution of 1789 became radical by 'skidding off course' rapidly gained favour. In the wake of 1968, a profound reaction took root not only against Marxist historiography, but Marxism in general. At the same time, ironically, genuine problems of reconciling the classic account of the Revolution with historical evidence were being recognized even by Marxists like Régine Robin (Comninel, 1987).

Following 1917, the idea of 'bourgeois revolution' had become increasingly important not only in France, but within Marxist theory generally. Its widespread acceptance was taken to vindicate Marx's ideas, and it was incorporated into the historical analysis of many national contexts. Given not only its once-vaunted pre-eminence, but its political significance within some forms of Marxist theory, it is not surprising that many Marxists have been disinclined to abandon the concept, despite its liberal origins. Notwithstanding the great body of evidence that the French bourgeoisie of the old regime had not been capitalist – and that capitalist social relations of production existed in neither industry nor agriculture – most Marxist historians of the Revolution continue to offer accounts that seek to reconcile history with this theory rather than consider other explanations of the role of class relations (Comninel, 1987, pp. 180–205; Heller, 2006). This allegiance to the idea of bourgeois revolution has opened a gulf between Marxist and mainstream historiography precisely where once they coincided.

HISTORY, ECONOMY AND SOCIETY

Besides the idea of bourgeois revolution, there have been other points of connection between liberal social theory and Marxism. Max Weber's contributions to social thought were in important ways reactions against Marx and Marxism. Weber conceived himself to be an economist rather than a sociologist, going so far as to characterize marginal utility theory as a primary tool for understanding social action, especially in modern capitalist society. His terms of analysis often gave different meanings to those used by Marx, marshalling them against Marxism. While he incorporated the idea of class, he reduced it to a purely economic category, indeed, merely a 'market position' (Wood, 1995).

At the same time, his work has been noted for stressing the roles of institutions, the state and status within a broad historical framework emphasizing the growth of rationality. Many theorists and historical sociologists have therefore taken Weber's ideas to be an alternative or supplement to what – ironically – they have understood as Marx's purely economic conception of class. Still others have sought to develop original approaches informed by both Marx and Weber. Barrington Moore Jr, Charles Tilly and Michael Mann, among others, have made use of the ideas of class and class conflict in important works of non-Marxist historical sociology that have verged on historiography, and influenced many historians. Among Marxists specifically writing in relation to historical social theory, the work of Perry Anderson and Ellen Meiksins Wood have had particular impact (Comninel, 2003), though Marxist historians in general have engaged issues of theory to a greater extent than non-Marxists (see below).

While Marx's work has often (mistakenly) been criticized for being economistic, the focus on economic factors attributed to him has contributed to the development of economic history. Far from being inherently Marxist, much economic history has been anything but, as may be seen from the work and influence of the German, English and French 'Historical Schools' of economics. Aside from economic history as such, however, significant currents of 'social' historical research have emerged from the study of broadly economic issues in history.

In France, Marc Bloch and Lucien Febvre founded the *Annales d'Histoire Économique et Sociale*, from which the '*Annales* school' of social history developed into a major force. This school set itself against Marxist approaches from the start, and has grown increasingly far from its original emphasis on the connection between the economic, social and cultural in the formation of *mentalités* (Hunt, 1986). Nonetheless, its contribution to viewing history over the *longue durée* – as in the work of Fernand Braudel – clearly must be taken in light of Marxist perspectives. Bloch's work on feudalism and French rural history also opened the way for the study of social history in the ancient and medieval eras, in which Marxists like Guy Bois have figured importantly.

The existence of formal institutions of unfreedom, and other social, political and cultural differences highlighted by the classic liberal idea of historical progress leading to modernity, have on the face of it given credence to conceiving ancient and medieval societies in terms of class. In Britain, however, such a pointedly 'social' interpretation of history continued to face entrenched conservative opposition within historiography not only into the second half of the twentieth century, but into the twenty-first. Still, inspired by the wrenching dislocation of rural society by early modern enclosures, and the devastating effects of the Industrial Revolution on workers, significant contributions to social history were made by non-Marxist but socialist or left-liberal historians in the first half of the twentieth century, notably R.H. Tawney, G.D.H. Cole and John and Barbara Hammond (Wilson, 1993).

Following the Second World War, the Communist Party Historians Group formed in Britain, including some of the most significant historians of the twentieth century: Maurice Dobb, Christopher Hill, Rodney Hilton, Eric Hobsbawm, George Rudé, Raphael Samuel and E.P. Thompson, among others. What is especially striking is the way in which members of the Historians Group played pivotal roles in both transforming the practice of history, and advancing historical social theory. They did so in the first place through conscious commitment to making historical experience available and relevant to ordinary working people. Not only did they write in clear, plain English, but they focused particularly on the historical struggles of labouring people and the oppressed against the powerful. In the perspective from which they wrote, and their emphasis on struggles, this work went beyond 'social' history to establish a new historiography of 'history from below' (Kaye, 1984).

This dedication required unearthing and restoring evidence previously ignored by historians, such as police records, reinforcing their commitment to the labour of historical research. As Marxists, they continued to work with well-defined theoretical concepts, but as historians they followed the evidence. Where Christopher Hill wrote an unalloyed account of the English Civil War as bourgeois revolution in 1948, he came instead to embrace a far more nuanced conception of that conflict, without abandoning the ideas or centrality of class and class struggle (Kaye, 1984; Comninel, 2003, pp. 49–50).

Inspired by broad unity among anti-Fascists before and during the War, a small group within the Historians Group founded, on their own initiative, the journal *Past and Present* in 1952, in the depths of the Cold War and rampant American McCarthyism (see Hill et al. 1983). It was conceived from the start as an independent journal of social history, with non-Marxists on the editorial board (initially bolstered by a veto over Marxist pieces, never used) as well as among its contributors. Launched with explicit commitment to the tradition of Bloch and Febvre, it has maintained greater continuity in this regard than the *Annales*. Its enduring attention to the relationship between social theory and the practice of historiography is evident not only in periodic contributions on the subject, but in the notable debates that have appeared in its pages.

HISTORY AND DEBATE

A series of debates – comprising both exchanges among Marxists, and between Marxists and non-Marxists – have been central to the continuing influence of Marxism within historiography. Setting aside debates over the legitimacy of Marxist thought as such (and the issue of bourgeois revolution discussed above), these have clustered around concepts of analysis – particularly regarding historical periodization and transitions – the relationship between theory and practice, and the validity of the premises underpinning historical social theory. There have been too many issues of debate even to summarize here, but several have had especially broad implications.

One important debate has been over the transition between feudalism and capitalism, sparked by the historical analysis of Maurice Dobb, which engaged Marxists from many countries during the 1950s, 1960s and 1970s. E.P. Thompson's work went significantly beyond the enormous contribution he made to the study of history from below, advancing theoretical ideas that had an important impact, and also generated considerable controversy. As Harvey Kaye and Ellen Meiksins Wood have emphasized, Thompson's key theoretical contribution was his conception of class as a relationship, not a 'thing'; one formed through historical processes, not through the 'articulation' of an abstract, ahistorical structure (Thompson, 1968, pp. 9–10). This conception has been the subject of much contention because it has been taken to reduce class to 'class consciousness', whereas Thompson conceived 'class' to exist prior to its realization in fully formed classes, and even in its seeming absence (Kaye, 1984, pp. 193–207; Meiksins Wood, 1995, pp. 67–84). This conception of class as a relationship – grounded in oppression and existing and/or developing exploitation, and entailing collective forms of struggle as well as common experiences – focuses on historical processes of social and cultural class 'formation', in contrast to conceptions of class as either a social or economic position, or a form of consciousness. Beyond this particular contention over the meaning of class, Thompson engaged in a lengthy and far broader debate with Perry Anderson over the latter's structuralist Marxist conception of English history, as well as an even more polemical critique of Althusser (Thompson, 1978).

Thompson's approach to the processes of class in history – sketched in theoretical terms, but more fully realized in his historiography – played a crucial role in the development of what has been described as 'political Marxism'. The work of Robert Brenner built upon Thompson's ideas, and was pivotal to the 'political Marxist' re-grounding of historical materialism in historically concrete processes of class struggle and social change (Aston and Philpin, 1985). Brenner argued in a seminal article in *Past and Present* that, on the basis of specific differences in the nature and outcome of class struggles during the later Middle Ages and the early modern era, the processes of historical development within class societies took profoundly divergent paths not only between Eastern and Western Europe, but also between England and France.

Brenner's article gave rise to a celebrated debate comprising a number of prominent non-Marxist scholars and the Marxist Guy Bois (who coined the term 'political Marxism' as criticism, though, as often happens, it has since been accepted by proponents). As Brenner further established through his reply to critics, and has since been supported by a growing body of research and analysis drawing upon his and Meiksins Wood's contributions, the evidence does not support the idea that England and France shared a common history of progress through fundamentally identical social, economic and political forms down to the era of the French Revolution. On the contrary, these two societies differed profoundly in their legal and political forms of social property relations from early in the Middle Ages, leading to vastly different forms of class society.

As Brenner, Meiksins Wood and other 'political Marxists' have emphasized, this broad challenge to what has largely been 'presumed' within historical social theory since the eighteenth century does not at all constitute a challenge to Marx's essential conception of history as the history of class struggles. Capitalism did not emerge through the ahistorical articulation of a mode of production, but through concrete processes of class relations; and did not emerge everywhere, but uniquely in England, and far later than is usually conceived. This, as Brenner and Meiksins Wood have argued, is a very serious challenge to 'liberal' social thought, while implying an analysis of contemporary capitalism that returns to Marx's most basic ideas. When Marx's historical materialism is taken seriously as an invitation to explore the oppression and exploitation revealed by historical evidence, as well as the processes of struggle by producers and other oppressed people, it can only strengthen the validity of his insights, and lend credence to his political project of human emancipation.

35. Method of political economy

Branwen Gruffydd Jones

Marx's major contributions to political economy include both the substantive content of his theoretical and historical analysis of capitalism, and the distinct method of historical materialism. To a significant extent, the developments in method enabled Marx to produce his profound theoretical analyses of the workings of capitalism. The method of historical materialism as developed and practised by Marx and Engels has been subject to rival interpretations. Engels, and later Lenin, characterized Marx's approach as having been informed by German idealist philosophy, French socialism and English political economy. In considering these three components, it is possible to illustrate how Marx's method differs from that of classical political economy, since it was in part through his critical engagement with it that he developed and distinguished his own approach. The method of historical materialism can also be considered in relation to the vexed question of science and explanation, drawing upon the work of Derek Sayer, Bertell Ollman and Roy Bhaskar, who underline the non-positivist features which define Marx's method. Finally, it is also worthwhile examining in some detail another methodological concern which has arisen since the time of Marx: the question of eurocentrism.

MARX AND PHILOSOPHY

Marx's early works (such as the *Paris Manuscripts* of 1844) were influenced by Hegel, and through his critique of Hegel's thought Marx arrived at insights which became central to the development of his own thought and, especially, his method of inquiry. Hegel proposed an analysis of human history, historical change, development and progress in terms of the development of ideas and consciousness. The historical movement propelling development was located in the dialectic. Briefly, the dialectic entails a notion of tension between antagonistic elements, and development through the resolution of such tensions in a manner whereby aspects of both are retained in the new form. Historical movement is not arbitrary or predetermined, but emerges through the development and resolution of conflicts, tensions and antagonisms. Marx greatly admired Hegel's presentation of the dialectic, but rejected the idealist basis of Hegel's thought. Marx therefore incorporated some of Hegel's insights into a totally different, materialist conception of history. Historical change is not rooted in or characterized by the development of ideas, as Hegel proposed; rather, Marx argued, ideas and consciousness – as well as culture, norms, institutions and so on – are shaped by material conditions and practical experience. Marx and Engels developed their approach in the *German Ideology*, emphasizing in contrast to Hegel and subsequent German idealists that 'Consciousness does not determine life, but life determines consciousness'. Marx placed the activities of productive labour at the centre of his analysis, understanding production and labour in a broad sense, in order to highlight that individuals can reproduce themselves only in the context of society on the basis of shared, social activity, and that individual and societal reproduction entails practical interaction with and transformation of material nature. The ways in which production is organized and practised differs enormously between societies and epochs. However, in most societies there is an uneven distribution of resources, with some groups maintaining themselves by means of appropriating the labour of others. This constitutes the root of differing and conflicting interests between groups or classes in society, distinguished according to their differing position in relation to the distribution of resources and organization of production. Marx located the struggles between classes as the basic source of dynamism and historical change.

Having 'settled accounts' with German idealist philosophy, Marx devoted the bulk of his life's work to developing an analysis of capitalism. His critique of capitalist society shared much with the French socialists such as Proudhon, Fourier and Saint-Simon, especially their identification of private property as the heart of the alienation and impoverishment of workers in capitalist society. However, Marx was critical of French socialism for various reasons. He argued that socialists must start by examining current conditions and contradictions, rather than try to design solutions for the future. He criticized their proposals for change – which, for example, sought to realize equality of wages, or advocated a return to agricultural labour in order to move beyond capitalism – as not being based on an adequate understanding and analysis of the operation of capitalism, and the real relations between private property, money, accumulation, exploitation and immiseration. Marx and Engels thus referred to their own approach as scientific socialism in order to distinguish it from the utopian socialism of their French counterparts.

MARX AND CLASSICAL POLITICAL ECONOMY

Marx wished to analyse capitalism in its 'purest' and most developed form (the reasons for which are discussed below). He identified England as the *locus classicus* of the capitalist mode of production, and London the best place to observe bourgeois society, and hence focused his empirical analysis primarily on England. He likewise identified the major works of political economy as naturally arising in England and Scotland, in response to the developments taking place there. This primarily included the works of Adam Smith and David Ricardo but also others such as Thomas Malthus, Richard Jones, James Mill and John Stuart Mill. Marx's main criticism of bourgeois political economy – the reason why he termed it 'bourgeois' – was that it saw the relations of capitalism as being eternal and natural, rather than historically specific, demanding of explanation and potentially transitory.

Marx respected and praised the work of the major political economists, and built on their insights in his own analysis of capitalist accumulation. William Petty had recognized labour as the source of material wealth; Adam Smith had pointed to the importance of the division of labour, and that value arises somehow from labour. David Ricardo, whose analysis of value Marx considered to be 'by far the best', distinguished between use-value and exchange-value, and saw that prices reflect the cost of production, rather than simply supply and demand. Thus they had advanced far beyond earlier economists who saw value as the property of things, and riches the property of men. Marx identifies in Ricardo's work the beginnings of analysis of contradictions – the antagonism of class interests, of wages and profits, of profits and rent – but sees Ricardo's contribution as taking the bourgeois science of economics as far as it could go.

However, Marx's crucial insight and criticism was that the classical political economists did not see these economic forms as historically specific, as the product of a particular historical development of a unique system of social relations of production, and therefore demanding of historical explanation. This is because they failed to distinguish between the historically specific, and transhistorical, aspects of social phenomena. Instead they analysed the economic and social forms of bourgeois society, and assumed these to be valid for the whole of humankind throughout all history. For example, Marx criticizes the bourgeois political economists' notion of the free isolated producing individual. He argues that the classical political economists take as their starting point the individual of bourgeois society – a society of free competition – who, at least within the market, appears to be free from the bonds of society. They do not see beyond this apparent condition to the real social relations through which these 'free' isolated individuals are dependent upon each other, in a state of unfreedom. This dependence is not manifest in personal relations of domination, as with tenant and landlord, but in the impersonal relations manifest only in the exchange of things. They fail to see the historical specificity of this situation, and so assume the isolated individual to be common to all societies throughout history, rather than the particular product of a specific historically produced form of society.

Marx accuses the political economists of starting at the end point, assuming as given precisely the historically produced social and economic forms which require explanation. In contrast, Marx is conscious of transhistorical features of all societies: human beings produce the means of their own subsistence; this is necessarily a social process involving cooperation, and consisting of interaction with and transformation of nature, by means of tools and knowledge, which are themselves the products of past human labour. These and other features, including some form of division of labour, are common to all societies – indeed are part of what is definitive in being human. But Marx recognizes that this in itself does not enable a sophisticated understanding of any specific society; in order to arrive at such an understanding it is necessary to distinguish the particular ways in which such common features appear in different forms in different societies, focusing not on what human societies have in common, but on what differentiates them.

In contrast to the classical political economists, Marx's approach enables him to identify the social relations which generate the empirical or experienced forms specific to capitalism, and to reveal what he calls the fetishism attached to capitalist economic forms. The opening chapter of *Capital I* analyses the commodity, the 'basic cell-form' of capitalist production. This analysis not only forms a crucial core to Marx's political economy, but also reveals some of the key features of his method and how it differs from that of the classical political economists. Marx's analysis of the commodity distinguishes the transhistorical and historically specific aspects of production and social organization presupposed by the commodity form. Marx claimed that, for all their insight into value, the classical political economists failed to unravel the mysteries of bourgeois economy because they did not distinguish between value and the form of value. After identifying a key aspect of capitalist production – commodity exchange – they stopped, assuming this feature to be eternal, and inherent in human society as such. Marx's recognition of the historically unique differentiation between concrete and abstract labour in commodity exchange enabled him to unravel the form of value (exchange-value), in addition to the substance (labour) and magnitude (labour time) already identified by the political economists.

Adam Smith identified the general proposition that labour as such is generative of value, and in this respect Marx noted that Adam Smith made a great advance. However, Smith failed to see this as definitive of a particular social formation or mode of production. Marx argues in contrast that it was precisely the particular nature of relations of production under capitalism that led to the historical reality, and therefore the concept, of labour-in-general, as identified by Adam Smith. As with the isolated individual, so with 'labour as such': the classical political economists assumed unproblematic and natural what required theoretical and historical explanation. Marx's recognition that social labour is expressed in value, and that value is measured in money, revealed the social relations contained within the material body of the commodity. Thus he identified the fetishism of the most basic element of capitalist production: the relations between people manifest as relations between things. Marx credited the achievements of the classical political economists, but showed them to be blind to the historical specificity of the features of bourgeois society that they had so carefully analysed, because they 'obliterate all historical differences and . . . see in all social phenomena only bourgeois phenomena' (Marx, *A Contribution to the Critique of Political Economy (CCPE)*, Appendix 1).

HISTORICAL MATERIALISM, SCIENCE AND ABSTRACTION

This brief look at Marx's critical engagement with the classical political economists highlights a defining feature of his method: the need to distinguish carefully between the transhistorical and historically specific, and to acknowledge the historical specificity of all social phenomena. This capacity to 'denaturalize' the social world by underlining the historically produced and potentially transient or changeable, rather than natural and eternal, features of the present (above all the capitalist present) is of tremendous political import, but carries further demands in terms of method. How does historical materialist political economy make sense of specific features of capitalist or other societies? How are social conditions and processes explained? What is the relationship between historical analysis and theoretical development? These questions of method rest in part on underlying assumptions of ontology and epistemology – the theory of how the world is made up, and to what extent and how it can be known.

There remains considerable debate over what are the principles of method and, more specifically, of ontology and epistemology, informing Marx's work. This is in part because Marx's explicit treatment of method and philosophy of science is confined to relatively few brief statements and remarks scattered throughout his works. Some important discussions of method are provided in the *German Ideology* and in *Grundrisse*, but the argument of scholars such as Derek Sayer (1987) derives as much from attending to Marx's practice, as evident in his many substantive works of theory and historical analysis, as from specific statements of method. Marx never completed a fully elaborated argument and justification of his own method and the ontological and epistemological principles upon which it rests. After elaborating his critique of Hegelian idealism, largely for purposes of 'self-clarification', he did not present a detailed elaboration of his own position but went on to the more pressing task of addressing substantive problems of political economy and political struggle.

Marx and Engels frequently insisted, however, that theirs was a scientific method, in contrast to that of bourgeois political economy as well as others on the left – idealists and utopian socialists. Both the weight of the influence of positivism in social inquiry in the twentieth century and the strength of the critique of positivism has resulted today in the widespread conflation of any mention of 'science' with a positivist understanding. But, while an adherent of the values of the Enlightenment, the principles of method informing Marx's work and his understanding of science were not positivist or empiricist. The model of social ontology underpinning Marx's approach consists of social relations which structure the interaction of agents, roles and practices – in Marx's formulation, 'society does not consist of individuals, but expresses the sum of interrelations, the relations within which these individuals stand' (Marx, *Grundrisse*). Marx based his claim that his approach had the status of science by offering a theoretically adequate analysis of the necessary causal properties, tendencies and powers of the historically specific social relations of capitalism.

This brings us to the role of abstraction in Marx's method, and the relationship between abstract and concrete analysis. Marx employed forms of abstraction in order to separate analytically the essential and necessary qualities of social phenomena from the effects of contingent or 'extraneous' processes, circumstances and interactions, to be able to develop a theoretical understanding of social relations as they operate in their 'pure' form. As mentioned above, this is evident in that in order to understand capitalism Marx focused mainly on the context of England, where, in the nineteenth century, capitalist social relations had developed to a greater and fuller extent than elsewhere. In trying to understand theoretically the relationships between certain dynamics of capital, Marx at times deliberately chose to ignore or hold to one side other intervening processes – such as foreign trade. This is only ever a form of abstraction employed for the purpose of theoretical development regarding one particular aspect of capital, however, and in abstracting in thought from complicating circumstances Marx was not suggesting that such circumstances did not prevail in any specific context. The theoretical knowledge gained through analytical abstraction does not map directly onto existing circumstances and processes, precisely because of the greater complexity of concrete reality. This aspect of his method is important in all sorts of areas. For example, in emphasizing theoretically the two main classes of capitalist society, the bourgeoisie and proletariat, Marx was well aware that, in practice, class relations are manifest in many complex and varied forms. In returning to concrete analysis, therefore, theoretical understanding must always be combined with careful and detailed examination of the specificity of historical context, contingency and circumstance in order to explain prevailing conditions, processes, events and outcomes.

In discussing Marx's method it is also necessary, if only briefly, to distance the principles and practice of Marx's political economy from the myths and stereotypes which persist in offering a distorted caricature of historical materialism. First, Marx's political economy is not characterized by economic determinism, as implied by dwelling solely on the poorly understood formulation of a determining relationship between 'economic base' and 'superstructure'. The principles of historical materialism entail that the significance of 'the economy' in any particular society or era is in itself historically specific, depending on the particular configuration of social relations and material conditions in and through which social life is organized. As Derek Sayer has elaborated, when Marx discussed 'the economy' and 'relations of production' he used these terms not as precise and finite empirical referents but as multidimensional and relational abstractions, which encompassed political, cultural, material and ideational dimensions. Second, a historical materialist analysis of capitalist development does not entail subscribing to a teleological or evolutionary view of historical change or 'progress' involving a linear and necessary transition through various 'stages' of development. Marx did distinguish different forms of economy or modes of production in the long history of European societies, and moreover did suggest an understanding of historical development in the sense of non-accidental or non-trivial processes of historical change. But Marx explicitly did not see such stages as necessary or inevitable, nor as making up *the* sole path of historical change that all societies were destined to follow, sooner or later.

HISTORICAL MATERIALISM AND EUROCENTRISM

Stereotypes and caricatures aside, there are other problems and challenges which merit serious consideration. Limitations of space permit brief consideration of only one, eurocentrism. Was Marx's analysis of capitalism and its global expansion limited by a tendency to view the properties of European or Western culture as superior to other societies and, therefore, to judge Europe's domination of them as essentially progressive, and to overlook the violence inherent in European capitalist expansion through colonialism and imperialism?

If approached in terms of the content of Marx's work, evidence can be marshalled both to support and reject this view. Marx was a severe critic of the dispossession of non-European societies, acknowledging the 'notorious fact that conquest, enslavement, robbery, murder, briefly force, play the great part . . . the methods of primitive accumulation are anything but idyllic' – methods of 'undisguised looting, enslavement, and murder' (*Capital I*, ch. 26, ch. 31). He abhorred '[t]he profound hypocrisy and inherent barbarism of bourgeois civilization' which 'lies unveiled before our eyes, turning from its home, where it assumes respectable forms, to the colonies, where it goes naked' (Marx, *The Future Results of British Rule in India (FRBRI)*). Marx also highlighted – though did not elaborate in depth – the central role of transatlantic slavery in the origin and development of capitalism. On the other hand, writing in Europe in the nineteenth century and largely reliant on the work of others for his knowledge of non-European societies, Marx could hardly but have reproduced some of the prejudices of the age which postcolonial scholarship has rightly subject to profound critique. The method of historical materialism is by its nature not eurocentric, however, but *anti*-eurocentric. The method of historical materialism demands that the specificity of all societies and contexts be apprehended on their own terms. This is wholly contrary to the dominant tendency of Western scholarship to approach non-Western societies through, at best, a comparative, and more usually a teleological and hierarchical lens, comparing and judging non-Western forms against the

European norm or ideal. In this sense of method, a proper historical materialist analysis of the political economy of colonialism, for example, would necessarily emphasize the irreducible significance of racial ideology. Therefore, analyses such as those of Fanon and Cabral are in part consistent with the method of historical materialism, which would precisely require, as Fanon put it, that Marxist analysis 'be slightly stretched every time we have to do with the colonial problem' (Fanon, 1967, p. 31).

36. Mode of production

Jairus Banaji

Marx's own sense of history was best encapsulated in the view that societies historically had assumed distinct economic forms, and that much of the history of Europe at least revolved around the differences between such forms or 'modes of production', as he called them. In a broad historical perspective, the history of Europe was defined by an exuberance of economic forms, compared to what Marx saw as the monotony and stagnation of 'Asiatic' development (or non-development). Here 'Asiatic' included Russia and embraced the most diverse cultural formations from the Islamic regions of the Near East to China. It was clearly a 'residual' category, a sort of 'non-Europe' which Marx believed (or half-believed) embodied a common economic structure where the ruling class, *if* one could speak of one, was subsumed in the state and the mainspring of the economy lay in the tenacity of unchanging village communities. This model is usually called the 'Asiatic mode of production' and was a sort of default category, the most sense Marx and Engels could make of societies whose history was largely inaccessible to them.

The two most general senses in which Marx used the term 'mode of production' are as (1) an 'epoch of production' (Marx, *Grundrisse*, cf. Marx, *Capital II*, ch. 7, section 1) or 'economic formation of society' (Marx, *Capital I*, ch. 10, section 2, ch. 31), of which the best example is capitalism itself, and as (2) a 'mode of labour', 'labour process' or 'form of production', that is, an organization of labour based on the requirements of a given type of industry or branch of production, for example, agriculture. These are different senses of the term, one more historical than the other and broader in scope. The second, less historical, sense is used repeatedly by Marx in *Results of the Direct Process of Production* (the only surviving part of the manuscript of the very first version of *Capital I*) when discussing the formal subsumption of labour under capital, and it is this subordinate sense that Marx retains when he refers to the 'specifically' capitalist mode of production, meaning by this the 'real' subsumption of labour into capital, that is, the restructuring of labour processes to generate relative surplus value, the form best adapted to the nature of capital. This sense is exemplified in passages of the following type: 'The subordination of the labour process to capital does not at first change the real mode of production in any way, and its only practical effect is as follows: the worker comes under the command, the direction, and the overall supervision of the capitalist.' Under formal subsumption, '[a]s yet there is no difference in the mode of production itself. The *labour process,* seen from the *technological point of view,* continues exactly as it did before.' By contrast, 'With the real subsumption of labour under capital there takes place a complete [and a constant, continuous, and repeated] revolution in the mode of production itself.' It is in this more technological sense that Marx refers to the 'mode of production of the guild', or to agriculture as a mode of production ('Agriculture forms a mode of production *sui generis*' (Marx, *Grundrisse*)) or to the 'mode of production' of small-holding peasants which 'isolates them from one another' (Marx, *The Eighteenth Brumaire of Louis Bonaparte*, ch. 7).

It is the first, more purely historical meaning that is celebrated as encapsulating Marx's view of the way we should visualize the general evolution of Europe from Antiquity to the modern world. References dispersed across Marx's writings have generated a canonical genealogy which sees Europe's past (more precisely, the past of Western Europe) moving from slavery to feudalism to capitalism in a sort of inflexible succession spanning whole centuries. Yet Marx himself had to emphasize the contingency of that process when he referred to his description as a 'historical sketch of the genesis of capitalism in Western Europe', not 'the *marche generale* [general path] imposed by fate upon every people' (Marx, letter from Marx to editor of the *Otecestvenniye Zapisky*). Marx paid scant attention to 'pre-capitalist' modes of production, and much of the subsequent literature on these reflects the uncertainties and formalism this engendered. How were modes of production to be understood? How much complexity should we attribute to them? Could one simply read them off some register of forms of exploitation of labour? Did the feudal mode of production mean much more than the prevalence of serfdom? How widespread was it historically? Which modes of production could best account for the evolution of societies outside Western Europe? And, most crucially, because of its political implications, should Marxists see transitions to capitalism simply replicating some universal model or fixed sequence such as that implied in the metanarrative of Europe's development? On the last issue Marx's own response was emphatically negative.

MARX AND SLAVERY

Marx thought that much of *pre*-capitalist history could be mapped out in terms of just three basic modes of production: the slave mode, the feudal mode and the tributary (or 'Asiatic') mode (O'Leary, 1989; Haldon, 1993). The Asiatic mode has been called the 'Loch Ness monster of historical materialism' because of the huge amount of controversy it generated, but the slave mode of production is no less problematic, unless all one means by it is any form of production based on the use of slave labour (an ahistorical usage). In fact, Marx avoided the term, preferring alternatives like 'slave system', 'slave economy' and so on. At the very least, a slave 'mode of production' would have to imply a concentration of slave labour in enterprises other than households, for example, in the mass production workshops that turned out highly standardized products for the ceramic and building industries of southern Italy in the last two centuries of the Roman Republic or, even more obviously, plantation slavery. But the idea that the whole of the ancient economy was characterized by these forms of production is no longer accepted today. Moreover, as Wendy Davies points out, 'Since it is axiomatic [within traditional Marxism] that the slave mode gave way to the feudal mode, Marxists have to deal with the gap between the end of classical Antiquity (and ancient slavery) and the fully fledged serfdom which characterised the feudal model of the late Middle Ages, *a gap of some six or seven hundred years*' (Davies, 1996, p. 231, emphasis added).

It scarcely makes sense to see a transition between modes having a longer shelf life than the mode it supersedes! In fact, closer attention to the way Marx himself handled slave production shows a more sophisticated grasp of the nature of Roman slavery. In *Capital III*, chapter 20, he writes: 'In the ancient world the effect of commerce and the development of merchant's capital always resulted in a slave economy; depending on the point of departure, only in the transformation of [a] patriarchal slave system devoted to the production of immediate means of subsistence into one devoted to the production of surplus-value.'

It may seem odd to find the idea of 'surplus value' coupled with the slave system but Marx repeatedly reasoned in terms of the analogy with capitalism itself. In *Capital III*, chapter 47, section 1, he described the agrarian economies of Carthage and Rome as showing the 'greatest analogy to capitalist agriculture'. He repeatedly suggests that the investment in slave labour was a form of 'fixed capital', for example, 'In the slave system, the money-capital invested in the purchase of labour-power plays the role of the money-form of the fixed capital, which is but gradually replaced as the active period of the slave's life expires' (*Capital II*, ch. 20, part 4, section 12), or, more concisely, '[t]he slave-owner buys his labourer as he buys his horse. If he loses his slave, he loses capital' (Marx, *Capital I*, ch. 10, section 5). When Marx deals with modern (plantation) slavery, this aspect is even more pronounced. In the plantations, where 'production is intended for the world market, the capitalist mode of production exists, although only in a formal sense . . . the business in which slaves are used is conducted by *capitalists*' (Marx, *Theories of Surplus Value*). Again, 'The fact that we now not only call the plantation owners in America capitalists, but that they *are* capitalists' (Marx, *Grundrisse*). Or finally, 'Where the capitalist outlook prevails, as on the American plantations' (Marx, *Capital III*, ch. 47, section 5). However one characterizes classical or Roman slavery, modern plantation slavery was certainly a form of capitalism, and one implication of this is that modes of production are more complex sorts of entities than the labour relations on which they are founded. Relations of production are not reducible to given forms of exploitation of labour.

MARXISTS AND FEUDALISM

A major theme to emerge from recent historiography is the persistence of slavery through Late Antiquity and the early Middle Ages down to about the ninth century. If the use or even widespread presence of slave labour were sufficient to justify talk of a slave mode of production, this would mean having to posit the existence or survival of such a mode until fairly late into the Middle Ages, an option favoured by Bonnassie, who links the extinction of slavery to the agrarian expansion of the tenth century (Bonnassie, 1991, pp. 151–2). This strand of history sees feudalism emerging from a violent and dramatic rupture around the 'year 1000'. The general model has been extensively debated and heavily critiqued, but the least it establishes is that the degradation of peasant status which we call serfdom was a 'late' phenomenon; in Catalonia, which inspired the thesis of the 'feudal mutation', not much earlier than the thirteenth century.

For Marx serfdom was a central feature of the feudal mode and peculiar to that form of society (Engels had different views), so the problem raised by a belated serfdom is how we characterize the late Roman Empire and the early Middle Ages. In some general sense, there clearly was a transition from slavery to feudalism, but how or at what level do we grasp that? The kind of bondage that defined serfdom evolved only gradually and much later, so that the *mancipia* of the post-Roman world were not serfs in the strict (medieval) sense but a conglomeration of slaves and freed people of whom the majority were provided with service holdings and more like farm workers than peasants. The manor, in contrast, was a purely Frankish innovation, a model actively propagated by the ruling classes of Frankish society and bound up with the creation of peasant tenures. Ros Faith's (1997) monograph on the Anglo-Saxon 'inland' is a model of how a newer Marxist historiography can tackle some of these issues, while Wickham's book offers a wide-ranging basis for discussing them, even if his own theorizations are scarcely convincing, especially the view that we should identify the feudal mode with 'coercive rent-taking' or that the feudal mode was the 'normal economic system of the ancient and medieval periods' (Wickham, 2005, p. 535).

PERIODIZING CAPITALISM

Marx refers in the *Grundrisse* to the 'Mercantile system' as an 'epoch where industrial capital and hence wage labour arose in manufactures . . . Industrial capital has value for them [the Mercantilists] . . . because it creates mercantile capital.' When exactly was that? In *Capital I*, chapter 26, the sixteenth century is the watershed that inaugurates the 'capitalist era'. 'In the 16th, and partially still in the 17th century, the sudden expansion of commerce and emergence of a new world-market overwhelmingly contributed to the fall of the old mode of production and the rise of capitalist production' (Marx, *Capital III*, ch. 20). Yet Marx was willing to allow for a sporadic capitalism in the Middle Ages. The clearest reference is *Capital I*, chapter 26: 'we come across the first beginnings of capitalist production as early as the 14th or 15th century, sporadically, in certain towns of the Mediterranean'.

Indeed, the distinction implied in these passages can be theorized more than it has been. Marx himself argued: 'In the preliminary stages of bourgeois society, trade dominates industry' (*Grundrisse*). But what *were* the 'preliminary stages'? Maxime Rodinson grappled with the problem in *Islam and Capitalism* (1997), suggesting that the Muslim world of the Middle Ages had a highly developed 'capitalistic sector', meaning one largely dominated by merchant and 'financial' capital. Because a specifically Marxist historiography of capitalist origins is so mesmerisingly Anglocentric and focused on developments from the sixteenth century onwards, there has been no systematic attempt (by Marxists anyway) to map the origins of capitalism on a wider Mediterranean canvas, using the hints given by Marx. Commercial partnerships, bills of exchange, transfer banking, the widespread availability of money, the growing power of the merchants' guilds and the evolution of business firms were all signs of the emergence of a substantial business economy (Sombart's term) by the thirteenth century, which it seems strange not to characterize as capitalist. But of course this was a form of capitalism dominated by moneyed capitalists (merchants and bankers above all) and drawing on traditions inherited in part from the Islamic world, where the partnership was a highly developed institution with a strong legal tradition.

The *Annales* historian Frédéric Mauro suggested that the period between the Renaissance and the French Revolution should be seen as the 'era of commercial capitalism'. However, the origins of this epoch go much further back, even if, like all origins, they are impossible to pin down with any precision. What can be argued with some plausibility is that the 'preliminary stages' that Marx referred to straddled a long history from at least the twelfth century to the late eighteenth. The powerful rivalries of the age of 'Company capitalism' were completely different in character from the banking and commercial capitalism of the thirteenth and fourteenth centuries. Portuguese expansion, driven by the commercial bourgeoisie and backed by the monarchy, marks off the fifteenth century as the true watershed. It was this phase that ended in the decline of Dutch commercial supremacy and the subordination of commercial to industrial capital, as Marx put it (*Capital III*). Commercial capitalism spawned the slavery of the Americas. The plantations were 'capitalist creations *par excellence*' (Braudel, 2002, pp. 272ff.). The Dutch merchant capitalism which Marx saw dominating the seventeenth century (Marx, *Capital I*, ch. 31) was a capitalism founded, in large measure, on sugar. But long before that and indeed throughout the era of commercial capitalism, capital extended its sway over whole sectors of production (in iron-work, textiles, shipbuilding and the cottage industries) through the *Verlagssystem* (Braudel, 2002, pp. 316ff.).

In short, the theoretical distinction we need here is one between capitalism in this more general sense, a sense which allows for the commercial capitalism of the twelfth to the eighteenth centuries, and what Marx himself called the 'capitalist mode of production'. The latter is only a historically developed form of capitalism in the more general sense which in this way acquires a wider purchase and helps resolve problems that continue to mystify Marxists. The model here is one of 'combined' development rather than the linear succession between modes of production familiar from the 'transition' debates (Banaji, 2010). The 'preliminary stages', as Marx called them, threw up distinct configurations of capitalism, from the foundries of northern Kiangsu in the eleventh century (Hartwell, 1966, pp. 44ff.) or the capitalist groups who dominated the economy of Venice in the thirteenth (Cracco, 1967) to the 'massive syndicates' that controlled the Glasgow tobacco trade in the eighteenth century (Devine, 1975). The slave plantations of the seventeenth century and later were one configuration within this general landscape, 'capitalist' enterprises but not quite of the form that Marx would see as typical of the 'specifically' capitalist mode of production, that is, industrial capitalism.

ARTICULATION?

Whatever one thinks of the distinction just proposed, there is the separate issue of how capitalist production can integrate diverse forms of exploitation and ways of organizing labour in its drive to produce surplus value. This is particularly clear in agriculture where it often accounts for an integration of household labour into capitalism. The use of sharecropping and labour-tenancy on capitalist farms in the late nineteenth/early twentieth centuries is a striking example of a capitalism based on family labour systems. The literature on agrarian capitalism displays an impressive variegation of labour systems and general ways of controlling and exploiting living labour that capitalist landowners deployed according to the special requirements of different crops, landscapes and labour processes.

Indeed, agrarian studies is one area where Marxists or Marx-influenced scholars have turned out superlative work, which includes the rich South African debate to which Tim Keegan and Helen Bradford were major contributors. The upshot of much of this work is that relations of production are not 'reducible' to forms of exploitation of labour, since capitalist relations of production are compatible with a wide variety of forms of labour, from chattel slavery, sharecropping or the domination of casual labour markets, to the coerced wage-labour peculiar to colonial regimes and of course 'free' wage-labour. Indeed, the widespread use, under fascism, of forced labour in large industrial concerns like Daimler-Benz (Hopmann et al., 1994) shows how simplistic it is to read relations of production off some imagined register of labour types. To construe the ways labour is exploited and controlled as distinct relations (and therefore modes) of production is to end with a model that sees the 'capitalist' world economy as structured by an articulation of different modes of production (usually 'feudalism'). But historical materialism needs to move beyond this motionless paradigm to a construction of the more complex ways capitalism works. The huge commercial expansion of the nineteenth century very largely involved an integration of peasant agriculture into industrial capitalism, which in turn spurred the expansion of more local systems of commercial capitalism and a widespread dispossession of the peasantry.

Thus what the world economy of the nineteenth century threw up was an articulation of 'forms of capitalism' more than a combination of modes of production, in other words, economic changes driven by the gigantic expansion of industry and the rapid growth in demand for cotton, tobacco, silk, indigo and so on. The gravitational pull of European and American industry wrought changes in the distant countrysides they drew on through local trajectories of accumulation and dispossession. The pre-histories of a more fully developed capitalism and the struggles bound up with primitive accumulation were only ways in which 'capitalist world commerce', in Marx's expression, 'destroys all forms of commodity production which are based either on the self-employment of the producers, or merely on the sale of the excess product as commodities', 'revolutionis[ing] . . . the entire structure of society in a manner eclipsing all former epochs' the world over (*Capital II*, ch. 1, section 2).

37. Money

Paulo L. dos Santos

Marx's contribution to political economy contains at its most fundamental level a distinctive and robust monetary theory, which underpins his understanding of the commodity form, value as the regulator of economic and social intercourse, the sustainability of capitalist accumulation, crises, and of the forms taken by the social relations of capital.

The three volumes of *Capital* and the *Grundrisse* lay out a comprehensive theory of commodity money. This contribution resolved the problems of monetary theory facing political economy in the mid- to late-nineteenth century. It identified all functions of money in capitalist economies, grounding its ability to perform them on its embodiment and command of value. It offered an endogenous, logical account of the emergence of the money-form of value from the contradictions posed by systematic commodity exchange. It provided a definitive refutation of the quantity theory of money as well as of Say's Law. And it provided the foundations for the analysis of capitalist credit systems, credit money, and their relationship to the accumulation of capital.

While founded on the existence of a commodity money that embodies value, Marxist monetary theory provides solid analytical bases for tackling contemporary monetary systems, in which money has lost all direct connections with bullion. Specifically, Marx's identification of the value of money as the basis for the performance of all monetary functions, and his corollary endogenous theory of money, provide unique tools for tackling contemporary money.

MONEY IN EXCHANGE

Marx's theory of money is an integral part of his analysis of commodity production and exchange, offering two distinctive and innovative insights over classical political economy. First, Marx grounds money's most immediately evident function as a means of exchange on its ability to measure capitalist value relations. Second, Marx sketched out the logical foundations for the endogenous emergence of money in commodity production.

Money's most fundamental function is to offer commodities a measure of value. Commodities contain the dialectical unity of use value and exchange value. They come into existence as specific physical/material usefulness is imparted into them by concrete labour during production. They are also consumed on the same basis. But their sale requires the negation of specific use values, as commodities interact with each other in markets in accordance to their exchange values. Money helps resolve the contradiction posed by the process of sale, during which commodities need to act simultaneously as particular, physical/material use values and as general, socially determined exchange values.

By offering a measure of exchange value, money allows commodities to be use values as themselves and exchange values as definite quantities of another, money commodity.

While the exchange of products and the use of money are antediluvian practices, these did not constitute the core of social reproduction until the development of industrial capitalism. Systematic market exchange, generalized competition among capitalist producers and the development of the wage-labour relation established socially necessary labour time or abstract labour as the substance of value. Under such conditions the money commodity itself contains value. As with all commodities, this value is conditioned at the most abstract level by the socially necessary labour required in its production, and more concretely by the equalization of risk-adjusted profits across capitalist enterprises. At this level of analysis, because commodity money embodies value it can provide a measure of value and function as a means of exchange. The value of commodities is anchored on the technical and social conditions, and relative profitability, of their production and sale. The money commodity expresses those values as prices, based on its own value.

VALUE FORMS AND THE 'RIDDLE OF MONEY'

Marx tackled the 'riddle of money', offering an original logical account of the endogenous emergence of money as the monopolist of direct exchangeability with all other commodities. His account centred on the distinction between the substance and forms of value in commodity exchange:

> Here, however, a task is set us, the performance of which has never yet even been attempted by *bourgeois* economy, the task of tracing the genesis of this money-form, of developing the expression of value implied in the value relation of commodities, from its simplest, almost imperceptible outline, to the dazzling money-form. By doing this we shall, at the same time, solve the riddle presented by money. (Marx, *Capital I*, ch. 1, section 3)

Analysis begins with the most basic form of value, which arises in simple, isolated or accidental exchange. Here a commodity seeking sale (the relative commodity) expresses its exchange value in the material form of a given quantity of another (equivalent) commodity. This expression does not assure exchange, as the owner of the equivalent commodity may or may not agree to the proposed terms. But it does bestow upon the equivalent commodity a limited degree of moneyness, as it may now provide a measure of the value of the relative commodity and a means of exchange if its owner accepts the seller's offer (Sekine, 1997).

The generalization and spread of the commodity form of social reproduction is predicated on systematic and repeated exchanges between commodity producers. The second value form discussed by Marx, the 'total' or 'expanded' form, points towards such repeated interactions. Here the relative commodity expresses its exchange value in the material form of given quantities of all other commodities. As before, the expanded expression of value bestows on all equivalent commodities a limited degree of moneyness or ability to buy. But the existence of equivalent expressions of a commodity's value in the bodies of all other commodities already points to the existence of a common, socially determined substance of value, which 'shows itself in its true light as a congelation of undifferentiated human labour. For the labour that creates it now stands expressly revealed as labour that ranks equally with every other sort of human labour' (Marx, *Capital I*, ch. 1, section 3, B. Total or Expanded Form of value, 1. The Expanded Relative form of value).

However, the expanded form of value suffers from important limitations:

> In the first place, the relative expression of value is incomplete because the series representing it is interminable. The chain . . . is liable at any moment to be lengthened by each new kind of commodity that comes into existence . . . In the second place, it is a many-coloured mosaic of disparate and independent expressions of value. (Marx, *Capital I*, ch. 1, section 3, B. Total or Expanded Form of value, 3. Defects of the Total or Expanded form of value)

In addition, each commodity possesses its own expanded form of value. There is no reason to expect all expanded forms to be mutually compatible, nor can any of them provide the basis for the universal expression of commodity values.

These limitations are overcome in the general form of value. Here all commodities express their value in the form of particular quantities of the same equivalent commodity. It develops as a particular commodity is regularly chosen to act as the equivalent for all other commodities, acquiring an additional use value because it is directly exchangeable for all other commodities. Here the value of each commodity is not only distinct from its own particular physical/material use value, but from that of all other commodities. Value appears as exchange value, common to all commodities, in the body of the general equivalent. The general form of value is the fundamental form of money for Marx.

Marx motivates the emergence of the general form of value by reversing the equivalent form. But such a simple reversal does not provide a logical foundation for understanding the choice of a particular commodity as the universal equivalent, or the 'social action . . . of all other commodities [that] sets apart the particular commodity in which they all represent their values' (Marx, *Capital I*, ch. 2). Two types of properties of commodities may help account for the choice of a particular commodity money. First, their particular physical/material qualities. Durability, homogeneity, divisibility and ease of transport render commodities like precious metals particularly good candidates. This is also true of commodities whose physical/material use value can be most easily attenuated, facilitating the development of their exchange value as additional, social use values (Sekine, 1997). More significantly, Marx also points to the specific origins of commodity exchange in trade between societies as conditioners of the selection of particular commodities as universal social equivalents:

> The particular kind of commodity to which [universal equivalence] sticks is at first a matter of accident . . . The money-form attaches itself either to the most important articles of exchange from outside, and these in fact are primitive and natural forms in which the exchange-value of home products finds expression; or else it attaches itself to the object of utility that forms, like cattle, the chief portion of indigenous alienable wealth. (Marx, *Capital I*, ch. 2)

This ability to buy confers it a new use value, making it more likely to receive further requests for sale. As a result, the social norms established in the first instance in external exchange will tend to spread into internal exchanges, helping isolate particular commodities as universal equivalents (Lapavitsas, 2005).

Once a commodity is fixed as the universal equivalent the money-form of value emerges, in which all commodities express their exchange value on the body of the money commodity. The standard of price is set on this basis as institutions, typically states, determine the conventional subdivisions of the money commodity. In this specified form, money performs a distinctive additional function as the standard of price.

MONEY AS MONEY

Marx also identified important functions performed by money apart from its functions in exchange. These were termed money as money, and include its capacity to function as a means of hoarding, means of payment or settlement, and as 'world money'. Money can perform these functions because it offers the most general embodiment, and thus command, of value. They may be understood as the foundation for Marx's rejection of Ricardo's Quantity Theory and Say's Law. Together with money's functions as capital, not discussed here, they also underpin the Marxist approach to credit systems.

As the most independent and general embodiment of value, money offers a means to store value in the form of hoards and has the ability to settle obligations entered into when exchange is mediated by a promise of payment in the future. These functions facilitate the withdrawal, injection, creation and destruction of means of exchange in the economy, conditioning the endogenous determination of the quantity of money actively circulating in commodity exchange.

Money has the ability to serve as a store of value because 'it is the universal representative of material wealth, because it is directly convertible into any other commodity' (Marx, *Capital I*, ch. 3, section 3, A. Hoarding). Hoards of money concentrate the ability to buy and bestow social power on their holders. Marx well understood the subjective motivations for money hoarding, noting the sisyphean character of seeking to use quantitatively finite money to satisfy the insatiable desire to hoard wealth. Marx, however, did not found his analysis of hoarding and its role in accumulation on such subjective motivations, preferences or on factors bearing upon them, such as interest rates.

In *Capital II*, Marx considers a range of structural reasons why money hoards emerge spontaneously in the course of social reproduction. The movement of value through the circuit of capital poses inevitable delays giving rise to stagnant pools of money (and commodities). The accrual of sales revenues is lumpy. The pace of their flow back to accumulation via reinvestment hinges on the existence of prospects for profitable investments. Fixed investment is also lumpy, and commodity inputs are purchased gradually. Finally, precautionary hoards of money are formed as capitalists attempt to ensure the continuity of the circuit and prepare for possible input price fluctuations (Itoh and Lapavitsas, 1999). The resulting money hoards form the systemic basis in capitalist social reproduction for the advance of loanable money capital, the creation and circulation of credit money and the development of the credit system.

Marx also identified money's function as a means of payment. Money can settle obligations entered into when a commodity is sold against a future promise of payment. Consequently, money also provides the foundation for the circulation of such promises of payment, which economize on the need for money to mediate exchange. When promises to pay mediate exchange, 'money functions only ideally as money of account, as a measure of value' (Marx, *Capital I*, ch. 3, section 3, B. Means of Payment). This development is spontaneous and gives rise to financial intermediaries, who specialize in the acceptance, issuance, transformation and clearing of the resulting credit money.

There are of course limits to the diffusion of commercial credit. Imbalances in obligations due at the same time force net debtors to settle with money proper. More significantly, while during booms capitalists may increasingly rely on credit substitutes (and other instruments) for money, the inevitable subsequent credit or monetary crises see the spread of doubts about debtors' capacity to make timely payments on those substitutes, sparking a desperate and destructive dash for cash.

Finally, money settles imbalances arising in trade between national capitalist economies. This may only be generally accomplished by a money-form devoid of national peculiarities; an internationally acknowledged measure of value. For Marx, gold was the most appropriate form of such a world money. As a result, involvement in international trade required national economies to maintain precautionary hoards of the world money. The later development of international credit and settlement systems, and the rise of particular capitalist states with unquestioned political and military pre-eminence over others, have facilitated the use of particular national currencies as effective substitutes for such a world money.

THE QUANTITY THEORY AND SAY'S LAW

Hoarding and the creation and destruction of credit money regulate the quantity of means of exchange in circulation. This regulation is anchored on the needs of commodity circulation, in which money mediates exchange and expresses commodity prices on the basis of its own value. Sufficiently large departures by money prices from the underlying realities of commodity values create, in contemporary terms, arbitrage opportunities involving the withdrawal or insertion of means of exchange into circulation. At the same time, this regulation takes place through financial mediations that introduce distinctive contradictions to the process. The consequent endogenous and potentially problematic determination of the quantity of means of exchange in circulation provided the foundation for Marx's rejection of both the Quantity Theory of Money and Jean-Baptiste Say's 'law of markets'.

Marx understood and made use of the equation of exchange, which describes, for a given period of time, the relationship between the quantity of commodities traded, Q, their price, P, the quantity of money in circulation, M, and its velocity, V, given by $PQ = MV$:

> The total quantity of money functioning during a given period as the circulating medium, is determined, on the one hand, by the sum of the prices of the circulating commodities, and on the other hand, by the rapidity with which the antithetical phases of the metamorphoses follow one another. On this rapidity depends what proportion of the sum of the prices can, on the average, be realised by each single coin. But the sum of the prices of the circulating commodities depends on the quantity, as well as on the prices, of the commodities. (Marx, *Capital I*, ch. 3, section 2, B. The currency of money)

Since the value of commodities and money are determined prior to their entry into exchange, stability in money velocity requires the quantity of money in circulation to vary in order to accommodate the needs of exchange successfully. In the first instance, these variations take the form of adjustments in money hoards and the spontaneous creation and destruction of credit money. The management of bank reserves relative to outstanding credit-money claims on banks subsequently generalizes these processes. Marx here clearly turns the quantity theory on its head, rejecting the notion that the quantity of money in circulation determines prices in favour of a theory of endogenous money.

Adjustments in the volume of money in circulation can ensure the circulation of commodities. But they are governed by financial decisions made on the basis of individual profitability and confidence among competing capitalists, ensuring recurrent credit and monetary crises. Further, the very intervention of money into the exchange process means that, unlike barter, not every sale needs to be followed by an equivalent commodity purchase by the seller. If such purchase proves counter to the seller's profitability, the proceeds of the sale will lay temporarily idle, laying the basis for disruptions in commodity circulation. Here Marx's views run counter to Say's Law, according to which every sale lays the basis for an equivalent purchase, ensuring no demand shortages disrupt commodity market equilibrium.

THE CONTEMPORARY RELEVANCE OF MARX'S MONETARY THEORY

Contemporary monetary systems pose a significant challenge to the letter of Marx's monetary theory. Founded on inconvertible state liabilities possessing no intrinsic value, they would also appear to validate the notion that commodity prices follow from the quantity of money in circulation. Yet Marx's value-theoretic approach to economic and monetary relations lays the basis for fruitful and distinctive analyses of contemporary monetary systems, and for robust refutations of latter-day, monetarist restatements of the Quantity Theory.

All forms of money freely convertible into commodity money will generally command value in proportion to the latter's embodiment of value. This is not the case with inconvertible money, whose command of value may be understood to emerge as the result of more complex and concrete determinations. The timely realization of commodity values and surplus-value as prices (of production) and profits is conditioned by the economy's state of demand. Under weak demand conditions realization may be time consuming or incomplete, possibly lowering prices; exceedingly strong demand may trigger inflationary increases of prices. In both cases, the value commanded by money, as established in prices, is linked to the dynamics of production and accumulation, as well as to the cycles of booms and crisis endemic to capitalist economies (Foley, 1983).

Without the regulating forces provided by convertibility into a money commodity, conscious interventions by capitalist states into the functioning of monetary and credit systems have acquired an augmented role in such processes. By stipulating the terms upon which it supplies its own monetary liabilities to private, profit-maximizing credit-system institutions, and regulating various aspects of their operations, capitalist states influence the pace of credit extension and the circulation of credit money, conditioning aggregate demand. Through these and other complex mediations, they thus influence the pace of profit realization and the value commanded by their own monetary liabilities.

Under this light, the currently widespread inflation targeting regimes in monetary policy can be interpreted as unwitting attempts to manage an inconvertible money by influencing the evolution of the value it commands. The greater monetary, credit and economic stability of such regimes compared to earlier attempts to base monetary policy on target quantities of monetary aggregates is a testament to the primacy of money's value – and not its quantity – in conditioning the performance of its functions.

Finally, the Marxian emphasis on the social relations defined by monetary phenomena affords distinctive insights into the international realities of contemporary money. The US dollar currently serves as a problematic form of world money: it is the chief currency of international trade, settlements of international balances and of international reserves held by national monetary authorities to support the international price of their own currencies. Yet it has been officially inconvertible for almost four decades, and effectively for much longer. The reasons for this peculiar role for liabilities of the US state must ultimately be sought in its overwhelming political and military dominance.

The consequent use of the US dollar as a reserve currency significantly enhances international demand for dollar-denominated assets. This in turn enhances scope for US monetary policy and eases costs of borrowing within the dollar zone, with corresponding opposite effects in weaker, smaller or less developed economies. The resulting effective transfers of wealth in favour of the US economy constitute a peculiar tribute paid to the internationally dominant capitalist power that may be distinctively conceptualized by Marxist political economy as an integral, monetary moment of contemporary imperialism.

38. Neoliberalism

Gérard Duménil and Dominique Lévy

At the end of the 1970s, capitalism entered into a new phase, neoliberalism (Duménil and Lévy, 2001, 2004a; Harvey, 2005; Saad-Filho and Johnston, 2005). Neoliberalism is a class phenomenon whose basic economic and political mechanisms, both nationally and internationally, are tightly intertwined. In this analysis, a historical perspective is essential.

A PHASE OF CAPITALISM

There are various ways of periodizing capitalism. Alternative criteria are the movements of the profit rate (upward or downward trends), the forms of competition (the alleged 'atomistic' competition or monopolistic competition) and the configurations of the class structure (the rise of the 'middle classes'). The definition of neoliberalism as a phase of capitalism refers to a distinct set of phenomena, the succession of 'social orders'. Involved are the hierarchies and compromises among classes or fractions of classes. Which classes dominate and through which mechanisms? Which social alliances prevail?

The interpretation of a new period would be vain if the features of the previous period(s) were not made explicit. Consider first the emergence of new forms of capital ownership (the corporate revolution) and the rise of the modern financial sector between the late nineteenth and early twentieth centuries, following the major crisis in the 1890s. Capitalism underwent another three structural crises in the following decades: the Great Depression in the 1930s, the crisis of the 1970s and the crisis at the beginning of the twenty first century. 'Structural crises' are meant here to refer to periods of lasting perturbations concerning accumulation, growth and employment, as well as macroeconomic and financial stability. The crises of the 1890s and 1970s followed episodes of declining profit rates and, as such, can be denoted as 'profitability crises'. The Great Depression and the crisis of the 2000s were the combined outcomes of underlying trends in the real economy (as the disequilibria of the US economy in the case of the crisis of the 2000s) and waves of financialization.

These four crises marked the beginnings and ends of three distinct phases of capitalism. While the first and third periods can be characterized by the comparatively unchecked domination of financial interests and upper income strata in general, the first post-war decades were a period of social compromise.

The first decades of the twentieth century saw the dominance of the bourgeois class, in a new social setting, at a distance from corporations, whose ownership of the means of production was expressed in the holding of securities (shares and bonds). Simultaneously, managers were performing the tasks of what Marx had denoted as the 'active capitalist'.

This first phase can be called a 'first financial hegemony'. The leading social actors during this period can be broadly defined as the upper fractions of the capitalist classes and the top of the pyramid of wage-earners, with a significant overlap between these two groups. Financial institutions played a crucial role in the establishment and in the exercise of this power. Capitalist classes and financial institutions can be jointly denoted as 'finance' in a broad sense.

The Great Depression and World War II destabilized this social arrangement. The engine for the establishment of a new social order was the pressure of the workers' movement, that is, class struggle worldwide. A first characteristic feature was a form of 'containment' of the interests of capitalist classes. Corporate governance was targeted to growth and technical change, and the primary objectives of policies were sustained economic growth and full employment. The other facet of this social order was an alliance between the popular classes of production workers and clerical personnel, on the one hand, and managerial personnel, on the other, including higher ranking government officials. The term 'compromise' refers to this relationship between popular classes and the upper fractions of wage-earners under the leadership of the latter. This post-war compromise can be called 'social democratic' in reference to diminishing inequality, social protection (welfare), education and so on, as in most European countries but also in the United States. An alternative denomination is 'Keynesian compromise' when the emphasis is on monetary and fiscal policies and large-scale state intervention in the economy. The two aspects were combined in practice.

As the Great Depression and World War II had destabilized the first financial hegemony, the structural crisis of the 1970s created the conditions for the establishment of another social order, in which the power and income of capitalist classes, in alliance with the managerial classes, were restored. This was the second financial hegemony in the history of modern capitalism, known as neoliberalism.

Although the periodization above can be applied to the history of most major capitalist countries, there was a broad diversity of features and trajectories. For example, the containment of financial interests after World War II was more severe in Europe and Japan than in the United States, with stronger intervention by governments and more sophisticated welfare systems. Parts of the economy were nationalized, and the financial sector worked in favour of accumulation within the non-financial sector.

Neoliberalism itself underwent successive phases that correspond, more or less closely, to the three decades of its history to the end of the 2000s. The 1980s were a phase of implementation, often difficult, with the crisis of banks and savings and loans associations in the United States and the debt crisis in the periphery. The 1990s were the heyday of neoliberalism in the centre, notably the United States (Kotz, 2003). During this decade, neoliberalism was imposed across Latin America and Asia, at the cost of major crises. The 2000s can be seen as a period of dramatic expansion, leading to the crisis of neoliberalism in the later years of the decade.

THE SECOND FINANCIAL HEGEMONY

Within the term 'neoliberalism', the component 'liberalism' suggests a reference to a free-market economy, and this is certainly an appropriate characterization of what neoliberalism is about. It should be emphasized, though, that this market is 'capitalist'. Liberalism refers here to the freedom to act on the part of economic agents. In any capitalist economy, this freedom is that of capitalist owners to hire and fire, while salaried workers sell their labour power if they can. But, here, there is also a matter of degree.

Neoliberalism gradually lifted regulations limiting the initiative of enterprises. One specific field of deregulation was the financial mechanisms. The regulatory framework imposed in the wake of the Great Depression, such as the separation between commercial and investment banking or the regulation of interest rates, was suppressed. After World War II, borders between countries typically placed limits on the exercise of this freedom, in particular on the deployment of transnational corporations. One well-known achievement of neoliberalism was to lift such barriers as much as possible. Most restrictions to foreign trade and to the international mobility of capital have been removed. Despite this, the neoliberal states have remained strong actors when this is required by neoliberal objectives.

This first feature is far from defining all facets of neoliberalism. In each country, the new social order imposed a new discipline on workers, notably more demanding labour conditions, stagnating purchasing power and restrictions on social protection. In the United States, the purchasing power of the great mass of wage-earners has not risen since the 1970s, in sharp contrast with the first post-war decades. A stricter discipline was also imposed on management. However, managers became active protagonists in the neoliberal endeavour, notably financial managers. The primary objective of high management is the creation of shareholder value, the central pillar of the new corporate governance regime. To this, one must add the dramatic transformation of policies and regulations in which government officials are directly involved. Neoliberal macroeconomic policies, especially monetary and exchange rate policies, focus on ensuring price stability rather than full employment, as had been much more the case under the previous (Keynesian) period.

All of these well-known aspects of neoliberalism point to a social order whose objective was a restoration of the power and income of the upper classes. This class objective of neoliberalism is apparent in the transformation of income distribution in the United States. The share of the total income of US households received by the 1 per cent with highest incomes fell from 17 per cent prior to World War II to 8 per cent during the 1970s. It subsequently soared to about 18 per cent during the neoliberal decades, signalling a new concentration of income distribution to the benefit of the top of the social pyramid.

A first mechanism of concentration of income was the increased profitability of the corporations. The main factors underpinning higher profitability were the stagnant purchasing power of the bulk of the wage-earners (for example, through the increasing use of subcontracting to increase labour flexibility and reduce costs), investment in countries where labour costs are low, the use of new production and management technologies (such as information technologies) and so on. Furthermore, in 1979 the Federal Reserve suddenly increased interest rates (the '1979 coup'), generating large flows of interest to lenders. While long-term annual real interest rates to the strongest US enterprises fluctuated around 2.1 per cent in the 1960s and 1970s, they reached a plateau of 5.9 per cent during the second half of the 1980s and 1990s, after a few years in which even higher rates had prevailed. The sharp rise of the debts of households and the government was the source of large flows of interest to the benefit of the lenders. The transformation of corporate governance also led to the distribution of large flows of dividends, and stock market indices began to rise consistently. Setting the value of the New York Stock Exchange (NYSE) index corrected for the rise of the US GDP deflator at 1 in the first quarter of 1980, the index grew to 5.47 in the third quarter of 2000. Taking advantage of deregulation, both nationally and internationally, the financial sector entered into new and very risky innovative procedures in search of high returns. Very large flows of high income were generated within the sector, to the benefit of capital income and high 'wages' (including bonuses and realized stock options).

NEOLIBERALISM – NEOIMPERIALISM

Neoliberalism is often abusively reduced to 'globalization'. The global aspect of neoliberalism is certainly important; for example, under neoliberalism several traditional components of globalization that reached unprecedented levels. Free trade, the international movements of capital and the corresponding investment worldwide, global financial mechanisms (with the rise of international banking and tax havens) and currency exchanges are all involved. The crucial role of the dollar, used as international currency, was not created by neoliberal globalization, but it strengthened in the context of dramatically increased international transactions.

'Neoliberal globalization' is another name for imperialism in the age of neoliberalism. It refers to the set of practices and processes that supports the extraction of a 'surplus' from less economically advanced countries, always with the collaboration of local elites – whether this surplus can be interpreted as a form of surplus-value or not is a moot point beyond the limits of the present analysis. This surplus may result from direct or any other type of investment, or imports of raw materials, energy or consumption goods at low cost. That countries of the periphery may 'want' foreign investment does not alter the nature of this relationship, just as workers are eager to be exploited in selling their labour power. New forms of informal domination have been substituted for the traditional empires of the past, but the political instruments of imperialism remain corruption, subversion and war.

During the 1990s, the flows of corporate profits from US direct investment abroad, whose two components are profits retained abroad within the affiliates of transnational corporations and interest and dividends paid out by these affiliates to the US parent corporation, rose from 1.4 per cent of US GDP at the beginning of the decade to 2.0 per cent at the end, with a sharp acceleration during the 2000s (3.8 per cent in 2008). Concerning the income from other investments (mostly interest), a sudden increase occurred in the early 1980s following the 1979 rise in US interest rates (from an average of 0.6 per cent of US GDP in the 1970s to 1.6 per cent in the 1980s).

In the case of the United States, there is an asymmetrical aspect to the exports of capital, since the country is financed by the rest of the world. Due to its foreign trade deficit, the main imperialist country in the world is not a net exporter of capital, but a major net importer. By the late 2000s, the US economy was receiving financial investments (amounts outstanding) from the rest of the world at twice the rate of US investment overseas. However, a more detailed analysis reveals that the rates of return realized on US capital exports are about twice as high as the rates obtained by non-residents investing in the United States. This is largely due to the composition of the investments, the United States being the leader of direct investment abroad in the world rather than standard portfolio investment on which returns are lower.

A BROAD VARIETY OF TRAJECTORIES

The emphasis in the previous sections is on the United States, Europe and Japan; in contrast, other regions of the world went through significantly distinct trajectories. The main victims of neoliberalism were Latin America and Africa, while a number of Asian countries, of which China is emblematic, took advantage of neoliberal globalization. The case of Russia is also distinctive.

Neoliberalism placed all workers in the world in a situation of competition. This was the effect of the simultaneous reduction of trade barriers and the increased mobility of capital. China belongs to the group of countries in which labour is cheap, that offers guarantees to domestic and foreign investors and that benefited from the new global order. A growing share of the total global commodity production is realized in these territories; simultaneously, the workers in the developed countries were forced to accept deteriorating labour conditions and stagnating or declining purchasing power and social protection. But the availability of cheap labour is only one among the factors that allowed for the prevalence of strong growth trajectories in these countries. Countries like China or Russia are engaged in a process of primitive capital accumulation, a transition to capitalism from their earlier Soviet-style model. In the case of China, a strong government and political stability were crucial elements. The country entered the international division of labour but protected itself against the ravages of neoliberalism with strong state intervention and control of capital flows and the exchange rate.

Latin America switched from the post-war import-substitution models to neoliberalism, sometimes with extreme consequences as in Argentina during the 1990s. After several decades of progress after World War II, the purchasing power of wage-earners in these countries was comparatively high. Major cuts were realized, especially in Argentina. These countries were the target of international investment but their earlier growth trajectories were dramatically broken. Neoliberalism caused major crises in this region, as it did in Asia.

THE CRISIS OF NEOLIBERALISM

When assessed from its own class objectives, up to the mid-2000s, neoliberalism could be judged a success. The income and wealth of the wealthiest fraction of the population rose tremendously, in absolute terms and in comparison to the rest of the population. The crisis of the end of the 2000s highlights, however, the contradictions inherent in this bold class endeavour (Duménil and Lévy, 2011).

A first category of determinants of the crisis can be broadly classified under the general heading of 'financialization'. Financial mechanisms developed tremendously during the neoliberal decades, both in size and content (financial innovation). During the first decades, large financial institutions grew rapidly, for example, pension funds. These financial mechanisms were crucial instruments in the imposition of the new discipline of capital (as in the role of asset managers) and allowed for tremendous returns to the benefit of the most advanced segments of capitalist classes. Most of the ingredients of the years after 2000 were already present, notably securitization, derivatives markets and the cutting-edge financial institutions such as hedge funds. This was true worldwide, but the United States was leading in most respects and opening new paths. There was a sharp acceleration of financialization in the 2000s. Major financial variables reveal steep upward trends during the decade, especially since 2004. The crisis at the decade's end demonstrated the fragile architecture of the new financial edifice.

The second set of factors is typically rooted in the United States. It is the trajectory of external disequilibria of the country. Its main components are the US trade deficit, its financing by the rest of the world and the growing indebtedness of US households. Both neoliberal corporate governance targeted to stock market performance and the high propensity to import of the US economy imposed the rise of household debt to support demand and the continuing production in the national territory. But, in the 2000s, the costs of this arrangement included the mortgage wave, notably its subprime component, securitization, credit default swaps and so on. When this fragile chain was broken, around 2006, the effect was that of a seismic wave and the entire financial edifice was unsettled.

By the late 'noughties', the issue is whether neoliberalism can survive the contemporary crisis. If it does, it will be with serious adjustment. The transition to a new social order would not necessarily mean a straightforward return to a social compromise as during the post-war years or, even less, a more radical transformation. Other variants of 'regulated capitalism' might prevail. A new social arrangement can certainly be found between the components of upper classes. Only the pressure of a powerful popular movement can impose a more progressive outcome from the viewpoint of popular classes. Distinct paths could be followed in various regions of the world.

39. Neoclassical economics

Dimitris Milonakis

Neoclassical economics denotes the body of economic theory that has its roots in the so-called 'marginalist revolution' and has come to dominate modern economic science, especially since the Second World War. It is also variously called orthodox or mainstream economics, although the meanings of these three terms are not identical and vary over time. Neoclassical economics represents the main modern expression of what Marx called 'vulgar economics', with which I start this entry.

FROM CLASSICAL POLITICAL ECONOMY TO VULGAR ECONOMICS

Marx made the distinction between classical political economy (CPE) and vulgar economics. The difference lies in their scientific content. By CPE Marx meant 'that economy which, since the time of W. Petty, has investigated the real relations of production in bourgeois society' (*Capital I*, ch. 1, footnote 33). Its greatest representatives were Adam Smith and David Ricardo. Although CPE represented the interests of the bourgeoisie, it did so at a time when this class was on the ascendancy, the class struggle with the proletariat was as yet undeveloped. CPE had true scientific content because it tried to investigate, however incompletely, the essence of bourgeois relations of production. David Ricardo was its last great representative who made the antagonism of class interests central to his inquiry. With him 'the science of bourgeois economy had reached the limits beyond which it could not pass' (*Capital I*, Afterword to the Second German Edition).

After Ricardo, bourgeois economics ceases its investigation into the true nature of bourgeois relations and becomes a class weapon in the hands of the bourgeoisie. The decade between 1820–30 was a period of rapid developments in political economy, '[i]t was the time as well of the vulgarising and extending of Ricardo's theory' (*Capital I*, Afterword to the Second German Edition). The chief characteristic of vulgar economics, after Ricardo, is that it stays at the level of appearances, showing no interest in penetrating behind them in search of deeper truth. In doing so, it serves the interests of the bourgeoisie sharing with them their notion of the capitalist mode of production as 'the best of all possible worlds' (*Capital I*, ch. 1, footnote 33). As Marx (1867, p. 175) puts it, 'vulgar economy . . . ruminates without ceasing on the materials long since provided by scientific economy, and there seeks plausible explanations of the most obtrusive phenomena, for bourgeois daily use' (*Capital I*, ch. 1, footnote 33). Thus political economy loses its scientific credentials and becomes pure apologetics.

The roots of vulgar economics lie in some of the elements to be found in the political economy of both Smith and Ricardo, alongside its scientific content, which Marx expounded in the three volumes of his *Theories of Surplus Value*. The most decisive factor in the vulgarization of political economy, however, according to Marx, was the maturation of class struggle which took place during that decade, with the year 1830 being of vital importance. 'In France and in England the bourgeoisie had conquered political power. Thenceforth, the class struggle, practically as well as theoretically, took on more and more outspoken and threatening forms. It sounded the knell of scientific bourgeois economy. It was thenceforth no longer a question, whether this theorem or that was true, but whether it was useful to capital or harmful, expedient or inexpedient, politically dangerous or not. In place of disinterested inquirers, there were hired prize fighters; in place of genuine scientific research, the bad conscience and the evil intent of apologetic' (*Capital I*, Afterword to the Second German Edition). For Marx (*Capital I*, Afterword to the Second German Edition) 'the most superficial and therefore the most adequate representative of the apologetic of vulgar economy' was Bastiat. Say was another representative of this group, who took the vulgar aspects of Smith's political economy and developed them into a distinct theoretical system. But, after Ricardo, another trend of post-Ricardian, but less superficial, vulgar economics was developed which tried to reconcile the interests of the bourgeoisie with those of the rising proletariat. John Stuart Mill was the best representative of this group. Such an attempt, however, to reconcile the irreconcilable, was, according to Marx, bound to fail.

THE MARGINALIST REVOLUTION

The period between 1830 and 1870 was one of crisis of CPE and of Ricardian economics in particular. John Stuart Mill attempted a synthesis of Ricardian economics with utilitarian principles and was the main representative of CPE in this transitional period. At this time, CPE came under attack from three main quarters: Karl Marx, the German historical school and utilitarianism. The culminating point of this transitional period was the 1870s. In the early years of this decade, three economists, the Englishman Stanley Jevons, the Frenchman Leon Walras and the Austrian Carl Menger, writing independently of one another, put forward novel principles for building a new political economy. Their contribution gave rise to what is now called the 'marginalist revolution' and became the basis of what was later called neoclassical economics. The latter took shape in Alfred Marshall's *Principles of Economics* (1890 [1959]), with its author subsequently considered the founder of neoclassical economics. With him, the transition from (classical) political economy to (neoclassical) economics is complete. Neoclassical economics then becomes the main form of vulgar economics, although it took some time until it became perfected and dominant.

So what are the principles that the marginalist revolution established and, related to this, what is this thing called 'neoclassical economics'? The two basic pillars on which the marginalist revolution was erected were the deductive method adopted from David Ricardo and utilitarianism inherited from the English philosopher Jeremy Bentham. The former refers to the method of developing a theory by starting with given assumptions and premises and, through syllogism and the use of the rules of axiomatic logic, moving to what are effectively conclusions predetermined by the starting points. 'The main concern of the economist', says Walras (1874 [1954], p. 52), 'is to pursue and master pure scientific truths.' To do this, economic science should get rid of 'prescientific vestiges and survivals' (Winch, 1973, p. 60), such as the social, historical, philosophical, political and ethical elements. Unlike classical political economy, it must become a value-free science in pursuit of pure truth and devoid of normative questions about what ought to be done. In this way, Walras identifies economics with natural science. To achieve this, the focus of attention should move away from the processes of growth and distribution, as with CPE, to the process of exchange and the determination of prices. Not only that: since value in exchange is a magnitude that is measurable, and the object of mathematics is to study magnitudes, it follows naturally that '[the] pure science of economics is a science which resembles the physico-mathematical sciences in every respect' (Walras, 1874 [1954], pp. 71–2).

With marginalism, the macro-dynamic view of the economy espoused by most (but not all) classical economists gives way to static equilibrium analysis, by analogy with static mechanics. The basic vehicle of this transformation is the concept of marginal utility. One of the chief implications of the adoption of this concept is that the subject matter of economic science shifts from the investigation of the causes of wealth and its distribution, to the interrogation of the economic behaviour of individuals, especially in the form of (utility) maximization. 'I have attempted to treat the Economy as a Calculus of Pleasure and Pain', says Jevons (1871 [2001], Preface, p. vi), in typical Benthamite, utilitarian fashion. In this way the objective theory of value of CPE (which took the form of the labour or cost of production theory of value) gives way to a subjective theory based on individual utility. The concept of marginal utility, being a mathematical concept, was also instrumental in giving a great impetus to the mathematization of economics. At the same time concern with economic aggregates such as classes or the national economy gives way to what Menger called atomism, or what later, following Schumpeter, came to be known as methodological individualism. The latter refers to the method of explanation whereby the whole is explained in terms of the properties of its individual parts (members) (Milonakis and Fine, 2009, ch. 6).

NEOCLASSICAL ECONOMICS

The term 'neoclassical economics' was coined by the old (American) institutionalist Thornstein Veblen to depict the economics of Alfred Marshall (Aspromourgos, 1986). Before the publication of Marshall's *Principles of Economics* in 1890, marginalism, although on the ascendancy, had not yet become the dominant school. Until 1890 John Stuart Mill's *Principles of Political Economy* was still the basic textbook. It was left to Marshall to make the marginalist principles more widely acceptable. This is why Marshall is considered the founder of neoclassical economics. For one thing, Marshall's book was more tractable and simple than Walras's highly technical analysis. He was also the first to provide a 'complete' theory of price based on the marginalist principles. Building upon the work of the early marginalists, Jevons, Walras and Menger, but also on the second generation marginalists Böhm-Bawerk and Wieser, one of Marshall's basic contributions was the bringing together of the two sides of an exchange, demand and supply, as the basic determinants of price. The demand curve is derived from the consumer preferences through the law of diminishing marginal utility, whereas the supply curve derives from the law of diminishing marginal productivity. The equilibrium price in a given market is established, *ceteris paribus*, where the demand and supply curves of the product intersect. This is Marshall's method of partial equilibrium as opposed to Walras's general equilibrium model incorporating simultaneous interaction of all markets. We also owe to Marshall the distinction between short run and long run, the concepts of consumer surplus, increasing returns, external economies and elasticity.

The final turn in this marginalist transformation of economic science was given by Lionel Robbins in the 1930s. With him the subject matter of economic science was no longer the quest to uncover the laws that govern production, distribution and consumption of wealth, as with the classicals, not even to understand the business of everyday life as with Marshall, but 'the science which studies human behaviour as a relationship between ends and scarce means which have alternative uses' (Robbins, 1935 [2008], p. 75). Hence economics becomes the science of choice. Generally the basic principles that make up neoclassical theory are methodological individualism coupled with the rationality assumption in the form the maximizing individual agent (homo-economicus), the abstract/deductive method, the equilibrium theory of price coupled with the subjectivist theory of value and the marginalist principles. Substitution at the margin becomes the basis through which both production and consumption are analysed. The distribution of income and wealth is also based on the marginal productivity of the factors of production. Hence profit is equal to the marginal productivity of capital and the wage to the marginal productivity of labour. In this way the unequal distribution of income, rather than being the result of the exploitation of one class by another, is justified as being equivalent to each factor's contribution to production itself.

With Marshall and Robbins then, the move from 'political economy' to 'economics' becomes firmly established with all the substantive and methodological changes this terminological switch symbolizes. This transformation brought with it a triple reductionism. First is the reductionism to the individual as the key analytical building block. The economy thus becomes treated as the mere aggregation of its individual parts. Second is an asocial reductionism, where the economy is reduced to market relations and treated in isolation from its broader social context. Third is anti-historicist reductionism through which economic science is divorced from history. Historical specificity is lost and the theory becomes universal in application. Hence, specifically capitalist categories such as profits and wages become factor rewards characteristic of any society, irrespective of the social relations of production underpinning rewards and the forms in which they accrue.

NEOCLASSICAL ECONOMICS AFTER THE SECOND WORLD WAR

The rise of neoclassical economics to dominance was a long drawn-out process with Alfred Marshall playing a pivotal role not only substantively but also institutionally. Indeed, he was the main force behind the institutionalization of economics as a distinct field of study. Until the Second World War, however, neoclassical economics in its Marshallian form, although on the ascendency, had not yet achieved the nearly complete dominance in the Anglo-Saxon academic world which it came to enjoy after the war. The whole period between the marginalist revolution and the Second World War was a period of pluralism in economic science, with intense debates between the different schools of thought that were flourishing in different parts of the world at roughly the same time, be it in the form of marginalism in Great Britain and other parts of Europe, the Historical School in Germany and the American (or old) institutionalism on the other side of the Atlantic.

This picture changes dramatically after the Second World War. Following the publication of Keynes's *General Theory of Employment, Interest and Money* (Keynes, 1936 [1973]), the distinction between microeconomics and macroeconomics becomes firmly established. The former deals with the behaviour of economic agents such as households and firms, all treated as maximizing individuals, while the latter deals with economic aggregates such as national product, unemployment, inflation and so on. At the same time the process of mathematization also sets in. As seen already, the seeds for the mathematization of economic science were sewn early on with the emergence of marginalism but did not become dominant until the Second World War when it was given a new impetus by the works of Hicks's *Value and Capital* (1939) and Samuelson's *Foundations of Economic Analysis* (1947), culminating in the mathematical proof of the existence of equilibrium in a Walrasian general equilibrium model by Arrow and Debreu in 1954. Since then, the Samuelsonian tool of constrained optimization borrowed from thermodynamics became the symbol of the new formalist era, accompanied by Americanization and standardization of the discipline. This process, which has been dubbed the 'formalist revolution' in economics, reached a climax approaching near total dominance by the 1970s. The basic attribute of the formalist phase of neoclassical economics is the fetishism of the deductive (mathematical) model building method. Following the formalist revolution, anything that is not modelled is simply not considered as 'rigorous', 'scientific' economics and is left aside. Keynes's economics could be thought of as the first major victim of the formalist revolution. Only those aspects of Keynes's thought that could be modelled survived, while all novel and radical aspects of his thought were either more or less left out altogether or else were reformulated in mathematical or diagrammatical form, more or less beyond recognition. Macroeconomics thus becomes more and more subsumed under microeconomics with the principle of methodological individualism reigning supreme. And, although new tools such as game theory have been introduced, they remain tied to these two pervasive principles: methodological individualism and abstract deductive model building.

This process culminates in the micro-foundations of the macroeconomics project, which signifies the almost total eclipse of macroeconomics as a field of study distinct from microeconomics. This is coupled with Milton Friedman's monetarist and, later on, Robert Lucas's new classical counter-revolution in macroeconomics, propelled by the stagflation crisis of the 1970s. This is the economics of the early neoliberal era of Reagan and Thatcher, based on the twin assumptions of rational expectations and the efficient-market hypothesis. It signifies a return to the virtual world of the economist's imagination, inhabited by perfectly rational and egotistical human beings, forming rational expectations about the future and exchanging their products in perfectly competitive and efficient markets. This has led within macroeconomics to the overt elimination of Keynes's economics and its transformation into a new diluted form of Keynesianism based on the notion of microeconomic market imperfections, with Stiglitz as one of its leading representatives. This literature is known as New Keynesian Economics or New Information Economics based on market failures arising from imperfect and costly information.

The characteristic features of the formalist age have witnessed the near total dominance of the neoclassical paradigm, with its representatives enjoying an institutional monopoly over the positions in top universities and academic journals, attracting the lion's share of funding, occupying central public positions and being awarded 90 per cent of Nobel Prizes in economics. This dominance has brought with it a total indifference and an intellectually frightening treatment of the history of economic thought and of methodology both of which have been dropped from most undergraduate and postgraduate courses in economics. This is accompanied by an unprecedented intransigence and intolerance towards alternatives and an indifference towards any criticism, even internal criticisms that derive from within its own ranks. At the same time, following the (re)definition of economics as the science of choice, the scope of its application has expanded enormously. Despite dependence on a narrow set of questionable principles, in the last half century economists have applied their 'economic' tools to issues well beyond what traditionally has been thought of as the subject matter of economic science, such as marriage, drug addiction, politics and so on. This process of colonization of the subject matter of other social sciences by economics has been called 'economics imperialism' (Fine and Milonakis, 2009).

What has not changed is its vulgar character and its apologetic nature which, if anything, has become more and more pronounced. This is evident following the recent global economic crisis which has brought into question virtually every aspect of mainstream economics but does not seem to have led to self-reflection on the part of its practitioners on anything other than a minor scale. To the apologetic nature of mainstream economics should be added the direct vested interests of many academics, especially in the financial sector, a feature that was exacerbated during the financialization era. Neoliberalism, and the growing power and influence of the financial sector this has brought about, has played an important role in the latest developments in economic science. Deep down, however, it is the very nature of the system and the ideological need for its justification that lies behind this type of theory.

40. Neo-Ricardianism

Sungur Savran

Neo-Ricardianism is the name given to a school in economic theory that was highly influential among the left intelligentsia internationally in the 1970s and 1980s. The school owes its theoretical achievements to the seminal work of Piero Sraffa, an Italian economist and a friend in his younger days of Antonio Gramsci. Sraffa spent his later years in Cambridge, UK. His *magnum opus* is *Production of Commodities by Means of Commodities*, published in 1960 simultaneously in Italian and English. The neo-Ricardian school used the highly original theoretical framework developed by Sraffa to attack, at a first stage, neoclassicism, the dominant school of thought in economics in the world then and now. After achieving a resounding, albeit ephemeral, success in its battle against neoclassical economics, neo-Ricardianism turned its arrows on the Marxist critique of political economy. An international controversy then broke out between neo-Ricardianism and Marxism in the sphere of value theory, consuming the better part of the energy of leftist economists in many countries, and drawing contributions from the English-speaking world, Italy, India, France and other countries. This controversy subsided in the early 1990s.

SRAFFA, RICARDO AND NEOCLASSICAL ECONOMICS

Sraffa's *Production of Commodities* is a dense treatise of merely one hundred pages bearing the subtitle *Prelude to a Critique of Economic Theory* (Sraffa, 1960). In this book, Sraffa investigates the relationship between price formation and the distribution of the product between wages and profits under very strict assumptions resulting in the isolation of the question at hand from all other important factors, above all from changes in the methods (technology) of production.

The theoretical framework Sraffa offers for the investigation of the relationship between prices and distribution was meant to resuscitate the approach to the study of the capitalist economy developed by one of the giants of Classical Political Economy, David Ricardo, in his *Principles of Political Economy and Taxation*, first published in 1817 (Sraffa, 1951). Sraffa wished to provide a corrective to the difficulties of Ricardo's labour theory of value, which ran into trouble in its effort to explain the effect of distribution on values. Ricardo assumed values to be determined in some 'fundamental' sense by the labour embodied in each commodity. Not being able to separate the determination of values by labour embodied from the impact of distribution on the values (or prices) of goods, Ricardo in his later years desperately searched for a so-called 'invariable measure of value' that would serve this purpose, especially in his underestimated posthumously published essay, *Absolute Value and Exchangeable Value*, composed in 1823, immediately before his death.

Sraffa sought a solution to this Ricardian problem through the devising of an ingenious measure of value, which he called the 'Standard Commodity'. This was an 'average' mix of commodities whose total value would in some sense remain invariant to changing distribution between wages and profits (in a static economy without productivity change). The standard commodity is a composite, if otherwise arbitrary, mix of goods which can be used to show the distribution between profits and wages along a single dimension as if the prices of individual goods within it were irrelevant (even though each of these prices changes with the change in distribution). On this basis, Sraffa claimed to have solved the Ricardian problem. Of course, the practical significance of the standard commodity is limited in view of the assumptions on which it is constructed, in particular the fact that it is invariably modified by the slightest change in the production conditions of any commodity.

This necessarily brief summary of Sraffa's theoretical project should make it clear why his followers came to be known as 'neo-Ricardians'. Despite this effort to revive Ricardian economics, Sraffa's followers were not defenders of the labour theory of value, itself considered by them to be an indefensible and hopelessly contradictory theoretical framework in both its Ricardian and Marxist versions.

Sraffa and his followers used this theoretical framework to stage an all-out attack on neoclassical economics, which resulted in the so-called 'Cambridge controversy', a name that reflects the fact that the major protagonists worked and lived in Cambridge, Massachusetts, USA, for the neoclassicists, and Cambridge, UK, for the Sraffians.

In a nutshell, the neo-Ricardian critique of neoclassicism is based on the assertion of the impossibility of measuring the value or magnitude of capital prior to and independent of the rate of profit, thus demolishing the basis of the fundamental neoclassical concept of the 'production function' and of the explanation of distribution as an outcome of the 'marginal productivity' of capital as a 'factor of production' (see, for instance, Bharadwaj and Schefold, 1990, Kurz and Salvadori, 2003). The whole edifice built around the notion of 'production function' now turns out to hold true exclusively for a single-sector economy. This result is reinforced by the possibility of 'reswitching', a singular result of Sraffa's study of the relationship between distribution and prices. According to this, in contradistinction to the received wisdom of neoclassical theory, which posits an inverse relationship between capital intensity and the rate of profit, once we leave a world with a single good, a more capital-intensive technique can cede its place to a more labour-intensive technique as the rate of profit rises, but may again become more profitable at even higher rates of profit. This phenomenon of capital reversing severs qualitatively, let alone quantitatively, the canonical tie established between the marginal productivity of capital and the rate of profit. The attack by Sraffians on neoclassical theory was so powerful that even the doyen of neoclassical economics, Paul Samuelson, felt compelled to enunciate famously the verdict that 'We are all Sraffians now'. However, the resilience of neoclassical economics is proven not only by its continuing domination over the academic curriculum around the world, but also by the continued use of the neoclassical one-sector production function across the discipline.

THE NEO-RICARDIAN CRITIQUE OF MARX'S VALUE THEORY

The prominence given to the work of Sraffa by the Cambridge controversy created the urge to examine the implications of his theory for Marxist political economy. It should be noted that many neo-Ricardians, including Sraffa himself, have a Marxist background. The neo-Ricardian interest in Marxist value theory went through two stages. During the first stage, lasting throughout a good part of the 1970s, neo-Ricardians alleged that there were serious deficiencies in the theoretical corpus of the Marxist critique of political economy, but that these could be overcome, and the Marxist project salvaged, through the contribution of the insights of Sraffian theory. The publication of Ian Steedman's highly influential *Marx After Sraffa* (Steedman, 1977) was a watershed signalling the transition to a second stage in the controversy, since it baldly asserted that much of what had so far passed as Marxist economics had to be discarded for the sake of logical consistency and replaced – rather than buttressed as had been argued in the earlier stage – by Sraffianism. The names emblematic of the first stage were Maurice Dobb and Ronald Meek, two veteran Marxist economists from Britain, while among the economists conducting the all-out assault of the second stage, in addition to Steedman himself, were John Eatwell and Geoff Hodgson, from Britain, and Alessandro Roncaglia, from Italy. Economists such as Joan Robinson, from Britain, and Pierangelo Garegnani and Luigi Pasinetti, from Italy, who were extremely influential in the spread of the Sraffian analysis in general, played an inconspicuous part in the debate with the Marxists.

In the controversy that pitted neo-Ricardians against Marxists, the argumentation put forth by the neo-Ricardians can be broken down into three major propositions:

1. A 'critical proposition', which alleges that Marx's labour theory of value is inappropriate as a theoretical framework for the analysis of capitalism. This proposition is based on claims that Marx's theory is (a) fraught with logical inconsistencies and/or (b) redundant (and, therefore, superfluous).
2. An 'affirmative proposition', which states that what the neo-Ricardians consider the most fundamental questions relevant to the analysis of capitalism can be treated satisfactorily and in a logically consistent manner using Sraffa's framework.
3. A 'theoretical proposition', which claims that a materialist theory of capitalism can be erected on the basis of the Sraffian theory, independently of and without having recourse to the basic structure of Marx's theory of value.

These propositions will now be examined one by one, summarizing the neo-Ricardian arguments and briefly reviewing the Marxist responses.

THE 'TRANSFORMATION PROBLEM' AND NEGATIVE VALUES

The 'critical proposition' is the aspect of the overall controversy to which most attention was devoted. The notorious issue of the transformation of values into prices of production, allegedly a cul-de-sac for the Marxist theory of value, was the major testing ground for this proposition. The neo-Ricardians buttressed their argument about the transformation problem with two distinct claims. First, they charged Marx's transformation algorithm with logical inconsistency: Marx assumes that the rate of profit is equal to total surplus value divided by total social capital but, in the so-called price system, the profit rate diverges from this assumed 'value' rate of profit. This inconsistency, it is held, is independent of the transformation of the input values into prices of production. Second, the neo-Ricardians claimed that, irrespective of this inconsistency the value system is redundant and, hence, superfluous, for the correct price system can be obtained through the use of the Sraffian system based on the physical quantities of inputs and the exogenous determination of one of the variables of distribution (either the wage rate or the rate of profit – usually the former, but the latter for Sraffa himself, through its association with the rate of interest formed in money markets).

According to the neo-Ricardians, the so-called transformation problem found its definitive solution in Sraffa's theory. This works in two steps. First, the neo-Ricardians referred to the solution Sraffa is supposed to have brought to Ricardo's problem of the invariable measure of value, through the standard commodity. From their proposition that Marx's transformation problem was simply a modified version of Ricardo's search for an invariable measure of value, it followed that Sraffa's framework was also a 'solution' to the equally unresolved transformation problem of Marx.

The response of the Marxists to this line of reasoning can be summed up in several arguments. First, although the Marxists diverged among themselves on the issue of the transformation of values into prices of production, all concurred that the allegation that Marx's algorithm is internally inconsistent does not hold. Moreover, the divergence of the rate of profit between the so-called value and price systems is not independent of the assumption one makes as to whether input values should be transformed or not. Quite the contrary: Marx's idea that the rate of profit is equal to total surplus value divided by total capital is a logical consequence of his choice of not transforming the input values. This is corroborated by the fact that if input prices are not transformed, the rate of profit in the so-called price system does not diverge from the value rate of profit. Second, the allegation of superfluity is a simple misunderstanding of the theoretical status of the Marxist theory of value on the part of the Sraffians. This theory fulfils many different functions in the analysis of capitalism (see below), and would not be superfluous even if it were redundant in the determination of prices and the rate of profit (see, for instance, the debate in Steedman et al., 1981, Mandel and Freeman, 1985, Freeman and Carchedi, 1996).

As for the argument suggesting that Sraffa's framework is a solution to the transformation problem, this suffers from three misconceptions. The first has been relatively neglected in the literature. Sraffa's standard commodity is, contrary to received opinion, not relevant to the problem Ricardo faced and tried to solve through the invariable measure of value. The problem Ricardo was grappling with was to distinguish the impact on values of a change in production conditions ('absolute value') from the impact of a change in the distribution of the product between the classes ('exchangeable value'). Sraffa assumed the first impact away through his intentionally restrictive framework, which holds production conditions constant. Therefore, the standard commodity does not, in the general case, provide a clue as to whether the change in the value (price) of a commodity derives from a change in production conditions or from a change in distribution. Since every production matrix has its unique standard commodity, Sraffa's ingenious device simply cannot serve to reflect in isolation the change in value as a result of the change in production conditions.

Second, even if it were true that Sraffa's standard commodity is the right answer to Ricardo's problem, it would not follow that it would equally be a modern solution to Marx's transformation procedure. The reason is that Marx's transformation of values into prices is itself a solution, within the framework of the labour theory of value, to the unresolved problem faced by Ricardo, that of separating two concepts of value, 'absolute value' and 'exchangeable value' in Ricardian terminology. By establishing two different levels of abstraction, Marx distinguished these concepts clearly. Value (or exchange value) was treated at the level of abstraction of capital in general, where it was only a question of taking up the relationship between capital and wage labour (in *Capital I*), while price of production was located at a more concrete level, taking the influence of competition, and hence distribution, into account (in *Capital III*). Once this distinction is established, it is possible to determine separately the impact of a change in production conditions (value) and the impact of a change in distribution (price of production). The need for an invariable measure of value vanishes.

Finally, a common sense issue is overlooked. Sraffa's framework involves only a set of prices. In contrast, the transformation is between values and prices. Adopting the Sraffian framework does away with values, removing the very necessity of transformation. So, whatever may be made of Sraffa's theory, it certainly is not a solution to the 'transformation problem'.

The allegation of inconsistency in Marx's value theory also depends on the generation of anomalous arithmetic results, for example, negative values, when what is held to be the Marxist concept of value is applied to joint production (a situation where more than one commodity is produced through the same production process) and to the value of fixed capital (a special case of joint production since it involves both output itself and older machinery). Since no commodity can reasonably be expected to have been produced through the expenditure of a negative amount of labour, the existence of negative values is adduced as proof that Marx's value theory is logically inconsistent.

The argument regarding negative values has been shown to be false. Negative values are obtained on the basis of an equation system that is supposed to faithfully represent the determination of values according to Marx's labour theory of value. Upon closer inspection, however, it turns out that this system disregards the distinction Marx explicitly makes, in *Capital III*, between 'individual' values and 'social' value when different techniques are used to produce the same commodity. When more than one production techniques exist for a single commodity, Marx's method is to arrive at a social value that is different from the distinct individual values the different techniques would have yielded. But the equation system used to generate negative values assumes an 'identity', rather than difference, between the individual values that result from the different techniques and between these and the final social value. Hence, it is not Marx's value theory but a disfigured concept of value that generates negative values. So the contradictions that ensue cannot be attributed to Marx's theory (Mandel and Freeman, 1985, pp. 211–19).

SRAFFA AS A SOLUTION TO MARX'S PROBLEMS?

The 'affirmative proposition' postulated that, as opposed to Marx's theory, Sraffa's theoretical framework was logically consistent. The Marxist side of the controversy questioned this postulate by pointing out that the exogenous determination of distribution led inevitably to contradictions in the Sraffian framework. As has been pointed out above, exogenous determination of distribution can come about as a result of the setting of either the wage rate or the rate of profit outside and independent of the system of equations. It turns out, however, that whichever variable is chosen for independent determination, there is no guarantee that the resulting real wage will be sufficient even for the bare survival of the workers. Since this survival is a presupposition of the equation system set up by Sraffa, the system simply does not respond to its own requirements (Savran, 1979).

Finally, the 'theoretical proposition' held that a materialist theory of capitalism could be constructed on the basis of Sraffian economics. This is tantamount to saying that Marx's project of deciphering the codes of the capitalist mode of production can be preserved while jettisoning the theory of value. The neo-Ricardians located the sole importance of value theory in the exposition of the phenomenon of exploitation, for which they proposed a theoretical explanation that did not refer to value theory.

This proposition is a consequence of the neo-Ricardian misreading of the purpose that Marx wished to serve in writing *Capital*, and the role and function of value theory in the edifice of his work. First, even if it were true that prices and distribution can be established without recourse to values, that is, Marx's value theory is redundant in this sense, discarding value theory eliminates the possibility of discovering the historical specificity of capitalist social relations. It is thanks to his analysis of the value form that Marx reaches the concept commodity fetishism which shows that, in the domain of the real relations of production under capitalism, and not only in the world of ideology, relations between people appear as relations between things. Further, and most tellingly from the point of view of the transformation 'problem', the transformation of values into prices and of surplus value into profit is not a nuisance for Marx's theoretical edifice, but is a source of superiority over competing theories, because it shows that, under capitalist conditions, the form of appearance of the social relations diverges from their essence, even concealing it.

Second, exploitation in Marx's sense cannot be demonstrated except through the labour theory of value. The reason is that exploitation here means the appropriation of part of the labour of the worker (surplus labour) by the capitalist. Unless it can be proven that profit, interest, commercial profit and so on have their source in this surplus labour, no amount of effort to prove that these are not simply the counterpart to the 'productivity of capital' will suffice. And once the labour theory of value is jettisoned, this becomes impossible.

Third, Marx's aim in *Capital* is not only to decipher capitalist relations of production but, more importantly, to explain the laws of motion of capital. This can only be done at a level of abstraction that isolates the relationship between capital and labour from all other intruding factors, including competition. It is thanks to this level of abstraction, in *Capital I*, where values are logically embedded, that Marx can analyse capitalism as a mode of production rather than a mode of distribution, explain the dynamics of the production and reproduction of the relation between capital and wage labour in addition to the production of commodities, and develop the seminal concept of the (formal and real) subsumption of labour under capital.

CONCLUSION

The critical assault waged on the Marxist theoretical edifice by the neo-Ricardians proved to be a passing storm in the horizon of the Marxist analysis of the capitalist mode of production. All the allegations of the neo-Ricardians were rebutted effectively. The most substantial benefit of the controversy that raged in the 1970s and the 1980s was that it spurred Marxists to sharpen their tools and elaborate their concepts in more refined terms, which is no small gain. The theoretical framework provided in *Capital* still remains the indispensable basis upon which a correct understanding of capitalism can be reached.

The question of what has remained of Sraffa and neo-Ricardianism may also be asked on this fiftieth anniversary of the publication of Sraffa's *opus magnum*. Not much, one is tempted to answer, since the Sraffa-based critique of neoclassicism has been relegated to the domain of memory and that of Marxism has turned out to be unfounded. However, one should not neglect the present-day alliance between neo-Ricardianism and post-Keynesianism. The latter school rejects the neoclassical bases of what Joan Robinson once called 'bastard Keynesianism', that is, the so-called 'grand synthesis' in the post-war period between Keynesian macroeconomics and neoclassical microeconomics. In this, post-Keynesianism is surely comforted by the existence of an alternative value theory whose lineage can be traced back to Sraffa. It is no small irony to see that Keynes, who, in his own *opus magnum*, *The General Theory*, set out to demolish Ricardianism, should finally come to owe the independence of his theory from neoclassicism to neo-Ricardianism.

41. New technology and the 'new economy'

Tony Smith

First-time readers are often surprised by the depth of Marx's appreciation of capitalism's technological dynamism:

> The bourgeoisie, during its rule of scarce one hundred years, has created more massive and more colossal productive forces than have all preceding generations together. Subjection of Nature's forces to man, machinery, application of chemistry to industry and agriculture, steam-navigation, railways, electric telegraphs, clearing of whole continents for cultivation, canalisation of rivers, whole populations conjured out of the ground – what earlier century had even a presentiment that such productive forces slumbered in the lap of social labour? (*Manifesto of the Communist Party* (*MCP*), ch. 1)

But Marx also insisted that this same system alienated working men and women from the things they produced, from their own activities and from each other. In his view this alienation could only be overcome by overcoming capitalism.

For many decades, defenders of capitalism dismissed Marx's criticisms. Beginning in the 1980s and 1990s, however, a growing number conceded that alienation had indeed pervaded economic life. In sharp contrast to Marx, however, they insisted that the fault did not lie with capitalism, but with the technologies and forms of social organization of the old 'industrial economy'.

FROM THE INDUSTRIAL ECONOMY TO THE 'NEW ECONOMY'

Mainstream critics of the 'old economy' base their account on the paradigmatic technologies of the industrial period of Marx's day and beyond. These were large-scale, single-purpose machines, requiring massive investment in fixed capital. Shifting from one product line to another required scrapping old machinery and installing new equipment, which units of capital did not want to do before obtaining a satisfactory return on their investment. Satisfactory returns on this investment required extended product runs ('economies of scale'). Numerous mainstream theorists now grant that extensive consumer alienation was the inevitable result, due to the limited extent a single product could meet the unique wants and needs of diverse consumers. They also concede that similarly serious problems afflicted work relations. Mass production condemned most workers, in offices as well as factories, to a lifetime of repetitive and alienating work as mere cogs in a vast apparatus.

Fortunately, these writers proclaim, a new 'information age' is emerging, with different paradigmatic technologies and novel forms of economic organization (Tapscott, 1997).

This 'new economy' transcends the flaws of the industrial period, making Marx's criticisms of capitalism hopelessly outdated.

Information technologies are now embodied in 'general purpose' machines (computer numerically controlled machine tools, robots and so on). These machines do not have to be replaced every time a new product is required. They can simply be reprogrammed, enabling shorter runs of more diverse product lines ('economies of scope'). For an increasing range of goods, electronic networks also allow individual consumers to communicate to producers instantaneously and almost costlessly the specific features of a product they desire. These technologies thereby allow many categories of commodities to be efficiently produced on a mass scale according to specifications meeting the unique wants and needs of individual customers. For 'new economy' theorists, this 'mass customization' transcends the consumer alienation of the industrial age.

Defenders of the 'new economy' also insist that workplace alienation of the industrial age can now be overcome. A flexible production system of short product runs, adjusting rapidly in response to shifts in consumer demand, requires a flexible ('multiskilled') and empowered workforce. Firms must now mobilize the tacit and explicit knowledge of their workforce throughout the organization if they hope to be successful. But workers will share ideas about improving productivity and product design only if they are treated as partners, rather than as mere costs to be minimized. And so, these authors assert, it is in the interest of employers to provide extensive training, delegate authority to autonomous work teams, offer compensation schemes rewarding entrepreneurial activity within the firm and so on.

The contrast between the hopes of 'new economy' theorists and the brutal realities of contemporary global capitalism could hardly be starker. Mass customization has spread, and product runs have significantly shortened. But stratospheric levels of consumer debt mock the promise of a consumer utopia. And the rhetoric of 'empowered knowledge workers' appears equally ludicrous in the face of involuntary unemployment on a massive scale and stagnant real wages.

Nonetheless, theoretical defences of the 'new economy' continue unabated. Problems are explained away as the fault of incompetent politicians, greedy financial speculators and labour unions stuck in the past. A dynamic 'knowledge economy' in which human flourishing is furthered to the greatest feasible extent remains within reach across the globe. All that is required is the right sort of political will.

Marx would have been very sceptical of the 'new economy' perspective. For one thing, 'every degree of the development of the social forces of production, of intercourse, of knowledge etc. appears to [capital] only as a barrier which it strives to overpower' (*Grundrisse*). In other words, capitalism continually generates 'new economies'. From a Marxian viewpoint, however, the main problem lies elsewhere: as long as the essential determinations defining capitalism remain in place, no 'new economy' can overcome the social antagonisms rooted in these determinations.

MARX'S CRITIQUE OF CAPITAL AND CAPITALIST TECHNOLOGY

Perhaps the most fundamental feature of capitalism is that '[u]se-values must therefore never be looked upon as the real aim of the capitalist . . . The restless never-ending process of profit-making alone is what he aims at . . . [t]he never-ending augmentation of exchange-value' (*Capital I*, ch. 4). The aim, in other words, is the appropriation of surplus-value, formed by the difference between the money capital invested in the production and distribution of commodities and the money received from their sale. It follows that, in capitalism, technologies are never simply means to further human ends. They are first and foremost means to further the end of capital, the 'never-ending augmentation of exchange-value'.

In any society subjected to this 'valorization imperative' there will be a strong bias in the direction of technological change. Research addressing the wants and needs of those who lack significant purchasing power will be systematically neglected. And research likely to have commercializable applications in the short term will be systematically favoured over investigations of the long-term health and environmental effects of those applications (*Capital I*, ch. 15, section 10).

Marx thought that the pernicious effects of the valorization imperative are most apparent in the capital/wage labour relation. Wage labourers are required to perform surplus labour beyond that producing an amount of value equivalent to their wages. Insofar as technologies in the workplace reduce the latter period of time, they extend the former:

> Like every other increase in the productiveness of labour, machinery is intended to cheapen commodities, and, by shortening that portion of the working-day, in which the labourer works for himself, to lengthen the other portion that he gives, without an equivalent, to the capitalist. In short, it is a means for producing surplus-value. (*Capital I*, ch. 15)

Not surprisingly, the scientific-technological knowledge embodied in machinery is experienced by individual workers as an 'alien force':

> In no way does the machine appear as the individual worker's means of labour . . . [T]he machine which possesses skill and strength in place of the worker, is itself the virtuoso . . . [S]cience which compels the inanimate limbs of the machinery, by their construction, to act purposefully, as an automaton, does not exist in the worker's consciousness, but rather acts upon him through the machine as an alien power, as the power of the machine itself. (*Grundrisse*)

Collective organization can overcome an individual worker's sense of powerlessness. But collective organization may be undermined by divisions within the workforce, and technological change fosters such divisions in a variety of ways. Technologically induced unemployment can set those desperate for work against those desperate to retain their jobs (*Capital I*, ch. 25). Technologies may also make the threat of shifting investment from one group of workers to another more effective. Technologies that deskill those enjoying relatively high levels of remuneration and control over their labour process also shift the balance of power between capital and labour in favour of the former (*Capital I*, ch. 15, section 4). Technologies that undercut the effectiveness of strikes warrant mention as well:

> [M]achinery not only acts as a competitor who gets the better of the workman, and is constantly on the point of making him superfluous. It is also a power inimical to him . . . It is the most powerful weapon for repressing strikes, those periodical revolts of the working-class against the autocracy of capital . . . It would be possible to write quite a history of the inventions, made since 1830, for the sole purpose of supplying capital with weapons against the revolts of the working-class. (*Capital I*, ch. 15)

It is important to stress that the social consequences of technological innovation are indeterminate in any particular case. Labour history shows that the very technologies introduced to divide the workforce, deskill certain categories of workers or break strikes may in certain contexts contribute to worker unity, enhance the skills of other workers and help labour struggles succeed. Nonetheless, ownership and control of capital grants its holders the power to initiate and direct the innovation process in the workplace. As long as this power is in place, Marx thought, technological change will tend to reinforce the structural coercion and exploitation at the heart of the capital/wage labour relation.

Marx also argued that technological change is a major factor generating uneven development in the capitalist world market. Technology is a major weapon in inter-capital competition (*MCP*, ch. 1). Units of capital with access to advanced research and development (R&D) are best positioned to establish a virtuous circle in which increasing returns provide the funds necessary to operate at or near the scientific-technical frontier in the future, making it more likely they can successfully introduce the next generation of innovations and appropriate the next generation of increasing returns. In contrast, units of capital without access to advanced R&D necessarily tend to be trapped in a vicious circle. Their inability to introduce significant innovations prevents them from enjoying above average returns, restricting their ability to participate in advanced R&D in the succeeding period. This in turn limits future innovations and future profit opportunities.

Finally, Marx held that the very investments in technological change introduced to further capital accumulation tend to undercut the accumulation process. From their individual standpoint, it is rational for firms to invest in capital-intensive technologies in pursuit of short-term profitability. But, as they do so, a collectively irrational result necessarily tends to arise: an overaccumulation of fixed capital, manifested in excess capacity and declining rates of profit.

THE 'NEW ECONOMY': A CRITICAL PERSPECTIVE

As 'new economy' theorists correctly assert, information technologies have significantly transformed the social world in recent decades. But these developments have hardly made Marx's critique of capital irrelevant. The valorization imperative remains in place in today's so-called 'new economy' no less than in previous variants of capitalism (Smith, 2000).

As a direct result, some forms of knowledge continue to count far more than others in the so-called 'knowledge economy'. For example, less than 5 per cent of privately funded medical research focuses on diseases common in poor countries. And investigation of the long-term health and environmental effects of biotechnologies, nanotechnologies and other new innovations continues to be severely underfunded in comparison to research directed to commercializing those innovations in the short term.

Wage labour remains the dominant social form of living labour in the global economy. The introduction of advanced information technologies in capitalist workplaces has been correlated with an intensification and extension of the workday for some, and unemployment for others, even though gains in productivity could be used to reduce labour time with no loss of livelihood or living standards. Workers' role in determining the design and use of machinery in the labour process continues to be radically restricted, despite all the rhetoric of worker 'empowerment'. Information technologies have enabled cross-border production chains to proliferate, making it much easier for workers in different regions of the globe to be played off against one another. And the process of objectifying workers' skills in machinery has accelerated with information technologies, as has the use of these technologies to continue operations during strikes. The electronic monitoring of the workforce on a massive scale, and the extreme work process fragmentation that mathematical modelling of labour processes and employees allows, are other features of the 'new economy' corroborating the continued relevance of Marx's account of technological change in the capitalist workplace. In the 'new economy', as in the old, workplace machinery remains 'a means for producing surplus-value'.

Uneven development in the world market also continues to be a defining feature of the so-called 'new economy'. Extensive national innovation systems have been put in place in prosperous regions of the globe to speed the development of commodifiable innovations. More than 95 per cent of all R&D is undertaken in these regions. Units of capital in the global North derive tremendous competitive advantages from this. The growth of scientific-technological knowledge is not the solution to severe poverty and inequality in the capitalist world market, as 'new economy' theorists blithely assert. It is a major contributing cause, as Marx understood.

Finally, key sectors of the 'new economy' (computers, communication equipment, semi-conductors and so on) have proven to be as susceptible to overaccumulation difficulties as core sectors of the 'old economy' were previously. Indeed, the tendency to overaccumulation crises has been strengthened by the spread of effective national innovation systems. The moment a new cluster of innovations with significant commercial potential emerges, research expenditures, tax breaks, credit allocations, and a multitude of other direct and indirect subsidies are mobilized in a number of regions more or less simultaneously. In use-value terms, the technological dynamism of the 'new economy' is thereby furthered. In value terms, however, things are more complicated. The more national innovation systems are in place across the globe, the sooner overaccumulation difficulties tend to arise in emerging industries and sectors, and the more the period in which high profits can be won from a competitive technological advantage is compressed.

As overaccumulation difficulties persist in the world market, the pressure to increase profits through the heightened exploitation of wage labour intensifies. Speculation in financial markets also necessarily tends to increase, since financial bubbles generally offer greater opportunities for profit than additional investment in sectors suffering from overcapacity. It should not be overlooked that, in the so-called 'new economy', the largest private-sector investment in information technologies, the greatest concentration of knowledge workers and the fastest rate of product innovation have all been found in the financial sector, with predictably disastrous results. Predatory activities in vulnerable communities become more attractive to capital as well, as Marx noted and contemporary experience tragically confirms (*Capital I*, ch. 25, section 5, D).

A NEW 'NEW ECONOMY?

The disturbing features of the 'new economy' discussed in the previous section are rooted in the social forms of capital, such as the commodity form and the wage form. In recent years, a new generation of 'new economy' theorists has emerged who believe that, with the proper political support, these forms will gradually cede central place to the acutely different social forms of 'commons-based peer production' (Benkler, 2006). This 'new economy' variant is based upon cooperative knowledge work undertaken within information networks outside the capital/wage labour relation. Its products ('knowledge goods') are then freely distributed within these networks, outside the commodity form.

The contemporary significance of commons-based peer production should not be underestimated:

> Ideas like free Web-based e-mail, hosting services for personal Web pages, instant messenger software, social networking sites, and well-designed search engines emerged more from individuals or small groups of people wanting to solve their own problems or try something neat than from firms realizing there were profits to be gleaned. (Zittrain, 2008, p. 85)

Encryption software, peer-to-peer file-sharing software, sound and image editors and many other examples can be added to this list. 'Indeed, it is difficult to find software *not* initiated by amateurs' (Zittrain, 2008, p. 89). Individuals cooperating outside capitalist firms have also collectively produced encyclopedias that have proven useful to millions, entirely new genres of music, unprecedented access to diverse sources of information and commentary about events across the globe and so on.

The potential of this form of production to further human flourishing is incalculable. The realization of this potential, however, will be severely restricted as long as capital reigns.

Capital, of course, is happy to appropriate the results of commons-based peer production as a 'free gift'. The use of open source software has been estimated to save IBM US$ 400 million a year. Nonetheless, the 'ceaseless augmentation of value' requires the sale of commodities produced by wage labourers. As long as capitalism continues the resources invested in the production of free knowledge goods will be dwarfed by those devoted to the production (and appropriation) of proprietary knowledge and proprietary products.

Finally, the time and energy social agents have available to participate in commons-based peer production will also be severely limited by the coercive pressure most face to sell their labour power and perform extensive surplus labour for capitalist firms. Marx wrote, 'Since all *free time* is time for free development, the capitalist usurps the *free time* created by the workers for society' (*Grundrisse*). The relatively limited time available for the free development of commons-based peer production is a striking illustration of this thesis.

Fulfilling the immense promise of commons-based peer production (and other potentially progressive aspects of the 'new economy') will require more than electing one set of political elites instead of another. It will require a fundamental transformation of production relations, democratizing control of investment and production in all major sectors. Only then will talk of a truly 'new' economy be justified.

42. Political science

Alison J. Ayers

Relations between political science and Marxism constitute a case of mutual neglect. The enduring debates between Marxists and non-Marxists which have exercised other disciplines are largely absent within political science. This entry outlines the origins and contours of such antipathy and highlights key Marxist critiques in terms of five myths that govern political science. It also details post-war and more recent Marxist contributions to understanding the 'political' in capitalism, focusing on the relationship between the 'political' and the 'economic'.

A CASE OF MUTUAL NEGLECT

The mutual neglect of political science and Marxism, as Bertell Ollman (1978) has argued, is rooted in the historical peculiarities of both Marxism and political science. Marx's explicitly 'political writings' include *The Communist Manifesto*, *The Class Struggles in France*, *The Eighteenth Brumaire of Louis Bonaparte*, *The Civil War in France* and *The Critique of the Gotha Programme*. However, the focus on critique of the capitalist 'economy' expounded in *Capital* led many of Marx's followers to attribute a significance to the different social spheres in proportion to the consideration accorded them in his then published writings.

This error was facilitated by the commonplace interpretation of the relationship between the economic 'base' and the socio-political-cultural 'superstructure', and the tendency towards economic determinism within orthodox Marxism. While such readings of base and superstructure have been widely discredited, for many Marxists the view prevailed that the character and development of 'extra-economic' spheres could be largely ignored or, alternatively, determined from the economic sphere. Accordingly, given the minor role attributed to the state within orthodox Marxism, 'it is little wonder that academics who chose to study politics were not attracted to this theory' (Ollman, 1978, p. 101).

However, the history of the discipline of political science has also contributed to this mutual neglect. Prior to the late nineteenth century, the study of politics was subsumed within philosophy, political economy, history or law. Since its inception as a formal discipline (with the establishment of a political science department at Columbia University in 1880), political science has focused overwhelmingly on the political process abstracted from wider social processes and relations.

In contrast to other disciplines which began as attempts to understand the social whole, the origins of political science lie in jurisprudence and statecraft, and the discipline has continued to be exercised primarily by concerns to make existing political institutions more efficient: From Machiavelli to Kissinger, Huntington and Fukuyama, 'political science has been the domain of those who – believing they understood the realities of power – have sought their reforms and advancement within the system' (Ollman, 1978, p. 101).

This principal concern with forms and properties of political institutions (and the criteria to evaluate them) is traced to historical antecedents in Greek, Roman and Judeo-Christian systems of political thought, continuing through Renaissance and Enlightenment political philosophy. Formal governing institutions and treatises also dominated the largely ahistorical constitutional and legal studies which occupied political studies in most Western countries (with the exception of the USA) through the nineteenth century to at least the World War II period.

But concern with political practice and the 'real' world is most evident in the highly empiricist 'behaviouralism' that has dominated political science in the post-war era. Advanced predominantly in the USA under the aegis of systems theory, the 'behavioural revolution' eschewed the analysis of state and power for study of the political system and decision-making. Behaviouralism became closely associated with pluralist theory which, linking European political theory with US political science, avers that decision-making is the outcome of conflict and bargaining between different interest groups in a purported condition of 'dispersed inequalities' (Barrow, 2008).

FIVE MYTHS OF POLITICAL SCIENCE

Self-congratulatory accounts notwithstanding (cf. the introduction in Robert Goodin and Hans-Dieter Klingemann's *A New Handbook of Political Science*, 1996), the discipline is mired in a protracted crisis. Numerous commentaries have alluded to 'the tragedy' of political science, 'the crisis' of political science or 'the flight from reality in political science' (Barrow, 2008). Indeed, noting that 'Whoever it was who called economics the "dismal science" should have another look at political science', Ollman (2000, p. 561) details five myths that govern the discipline: the claims to study 'politics' and to be scientific, the separability of the political, the purported neutrality of the state and the extent to which the discipline advances the cause of democracy. This section outlines Marxist critiques of these myths in terms of methodological inadequacies, the sociology of knowledge and the striking absence of capitalism within mainstream political science analyses. The following section examines post-war and more recent Marxist analyses of the 'political' in capitalism.

For all the talk of 'politics', political science has never established precisely what it should study. A fixation with methods and techniques has displaced interrogation of the objects of study, such that many minor and superficial matters receive inordinate attention whilst fundamental issues and relations are largely ignored, or not even perceived (Ollman, 2000; Barrow, 2008). Behaviouralism narrowed the field of study through its focus on (quantifiable) political behaviour, abstracted from the embodiment of history, economy and sociology in political institutions. More recently, rational choice approaches have taken 'the miniaturization of political science one step further by dismissing what people actually do politically and concentrating on their decisions to do it, on the calculations involved . . . in making choices' (Ollman, 2000, p. 555). Far from benign neglect, Marxist critics recognize an ideological function within this myopic intellectual-cum-political agenda, highlighting the significance of the study of 'such trivia' for what 'it hides, disguises and rejects' (p. 560).

Political science's method-driven approach has been heralded in terms of the claim to be 'scientific'. Behaviouralism sought (ostensibly) to extend the methods of the natural sciences to a science of politics. More recently, rational choice–methodological individualism has sought to import formal, deductive, mathematical models predominantly from economics. Despite some differences, both approaches subscribe to a cumulative, neutral or value-free political 'science'. Yet, as Marx's critique of empiricism laid bare, the naive objectivism underwriting such approaches belies any scientific or objective pretensions. Rather, political science, in common with vulgar economics, 'everywhere sticks to appearances in opposition to the law which regulates and explains them' (*Capital I*, ch. 11). Relatedly, scientism disguises the relation between mainstream political science and established politico-economic power, masking a partisan defence of the status quo (Barrow, 2008).

The privileging of 'real appearances' is starkly evident in disciplinary adherence to the bourgeois conceptual separation of 'political' and 'economic' domains. Accordingly, political science claims to understand politics and the state (to the limited extent it concerns itself with the state) whilst wholly disregarding the capitalist context that provides a fundamental part of the explanation for both. Lost in such falsification are the essential relations and exchanges that enable us to understand how the whole works, and how the 'political' works as a part of that. But also forfeited is 'the potential inherent in the whole . . . for becoming something other than it is'. That is to say, by obscuring capitalism, political science also succeeds in obscuring socialism – both the possibility of socialism, as well as the contours of a socialism emergent from the radical critique of capitalism (Ollman, 2000, p. 560).

The analytical exclusion of capitalism is also the condition of possibility for treating societies as 'democratic'. Rejecting the examination of political ideas (such as democracy) as free-floating abstractions, Marxists argue for the importance of historical contextualization. Accordingly, as Ellen Meiksins Wood has detailed: '"Formal" democracy and the identification of democracy with *liberalism* would have been impossible in practice and literally unthinkable in theory in any other context but the very specific social relations of capitalism' (1995, p.14). It was only with the apparent separation of the economic and the political, intrinsic to capitalism, that there emerged a separate 'economic' sphere constituted by its own power relations not dependent on juridical or political privilege.

The treatises of liberal democracy which dominate political science leave untouched this 'whole new sphere of domination and coercion created by capitalism, its relocation of substantial powers from the state to civil society, to private property and the compulsions of the market' (Wood, 1995, p. 234). Liberal democracy, whether in its institutional or ideational form, was never intended to extend its reach into the 'economic' realm. Rather, protecting the invulnerability of the economic sphere to democratic power has become an essential condition of democracy (Wood, 1995). Political science has been highly instrumental in furthering such ideological practices, legitimating 'formal' democracy 'within' the narrowly circumscribed limits of capitalist rule. Indeed, Ollman argues that the principal task of political science has been to 'avoid' capitalism. With capitalism absented, political science can then present the state as neutral – that is, comprised of a 'set of institutions independent of the capitalist class, and therefore more or less available to any group that organizes itself effectively to use it' (Ollman, 2000, p. 561).

Given the omnipresence of capitalism, its interrogation remains crucial in making our research genuinely scientific, that is, capable of exposing how the state and politics work, and how, with the democratization of undemocratic capitalist social relations, they might yet be made to work for everyone (Ollman, 2000). Marxists within (and without) the discipline have made important, although not unproblematic, contributions to such understanding.

MARXISTS ON THE 'POLITICAL' IN CAPITALISM

Characterization of Marx's writings as 'economic' or 'political' is misleading. Even in his most technical 'economic' writings, Marx portrayed the world in its political aspect. Exposing the historical and political embodiment of 'the economy' and the impossibility of abstracting the 'economic' was, after all, a key aspect of Marx's critique of bourgeois political economy. As such, Marx's critique differs radically from bourgeois political economy in that it does not create rigid discontinuities between economic and political spheres. Marx is able to trace the continuities because he treats both the economy and the political sphere, not as networks of disembodied forces, but rather sets of social relations (Wood, 1995).

Many variants of Marxism have since abandoned Marx's subversive critique, perpetuating instead – in different forms and to varying degrees – the bourgeois conceptual separation of the 'political' and the 'economic' (Wood, 1995; Bonefeld, 2003). This apparent separation is obviously not merely a theoretical problem, but rather has a very immediate practical embodiment in the separation of economic and political struggles that has characterized modern working-class movements (Wood, 1995), undermining the possibilities for revolutionary socialist practice.

The conceptual separation of the 'political' and the 'economic' was starkly evident in the base-superstructure metaphor which dominated Stalinist orthodoxy, but is also the case in many of the post-war attempts to analyse the 'political' and its relation to the 'economic'. These theories have generally sought to address the 'reductionism' of the base-superstructure metaphor:

> both its denial of human agency and its failure to accord a proper place to 'superstructural' factors, to consciousness as embodied in ideology, culture or politics. Corrections to this reductionism have commonly taken the form of a so-called Marxist 'humanism', or else an emphasis on the relative autonomy of the 'levels' of society, their mutual interaction, and a deferral of determination by the 'economic' in the last instance. (Wood, 1995, pp. 51–2)

Several of these theories and debates have been particularly influential. Ralph Miliband's *The State in Capitalist Society* (2009) critiqued the pluralism of behavioural political science through historical and empirical analysis of the state in capitalist society. Detailing the means through which capital attained and reproduced its dominance over the British state, Miliband argued that capital monopolized both political and economic power conferring direct and indirect control over the state apparatus, the economy and the means of legitimating its rule. In the ensuing Miliband-Poulantzas debate, Miliband's account was critiqued for advancing an 'instrumentalist' theory of the state (whereby the state was conceived as an instrument of the capitalist class) and a 'voluntarist' theory of class struggle (which saw the only limits to the articulation of state power as residing in popular resistance). Missing from such accounts was a theory of the 'structural' relationship between civil society and the state. Accordingly, for Miliband, the class character of the state was not inherent in its form but rather was the contingent outcome of class struggles (Clarke, 1991).

Conversely, informed by the structural Marxism of Louis Althusser, Nicos Poulantzas's theory of the state emphasized the autonomy and specificity of the state in relation to both the economy and class actors (Clarke, 1991). Althusserian Marxism conceptualized the social structure in terms of relatively autonomous, discrete and externally related 'regions' or 'instances' (the political, economic and ideological) with economic determination postponed to a distant 'last instance'. As such, Poulantzas's studies of the political in capitalist society focused on the notion of 'autonomy', seeking to construct the 'political instance' of the capitalist mode of production and establish the 'type' of state which structurally facilitated this mode of production (Wood, 1995). Underpinning such an approach was the attempt to construct a Marxist political theory assuming erroneously that Marx's work amounted to a Marxist 'economic-science' (Bonefeld, 2003).

The so-called state-derivation debate of the 1970s rejected such approaches, examining the 'internal relation' between capitalism and the state. Despite notable differences within this debate, theorists such as Elmar Alvater sought to 'derive' the categories of the political from analysis of the economy: 'This was not a "derivation" of categories from human social relations – but a derivation of the political from the economic; the economic was presupposed and the political appeared as a mere derivative of economic categories' (Bonefeld, 2003).

Since the 1980s, various forms of 'poststructuralist' Marxism have perpetuated the structural distinction of the economic, political and ideological 'instances' through attempts to integrate them as levels of a complex totality, whilst emphasizing the relative autonomy of the superstructures (Lacher, 2008). This was evident in the various 'regulation theories', most notably the Parisian regulation theory of Michael Aglietta and Alain Lipietz, which advanced the 'functionalist' argument that a regime of accumulation required a corresponding mode of regulation in the interests of stable accumulation. The mode of regulation was construed therefore as a functional requirement of the regime of accumulation – reproducing the separation of the economic and the political in the analytical distinction between regime of accumulation and mode of regulation (Lacher, 2008).

Drawing on Poulantzas and the Parisian regulationists, state theorists such as Bob Jessop and Joachim Hirsch sought to establish the relationship between the 'relatively autonomous' instances of the economic and political through the 'reformulation' of state theory. Examining the question of social reproduction more broadly, such theorists argued that crises of governance were themselves constitutive of capitalist crisis, not simply the secondary effects of the exhaustion of a regime of accumulation. The notion of a structural correspondence between the levels of a complex totality depended upon the hegemony of a particular class fraction, which could secure structural coherence and systemic reproduction. At any conjuncture, different 'hegemonic projects' existed corresponding to multiple possible regimes of accumulation. Which accumulation strategy emerged depended on the specific hegemonic bloc of social forces. However, within such accounts, the focus was confined largely to clashes between different fractions of the ruling class, rather than the struggle between capital and labour (Lacher, 2008).

Also influential within the poststructuralist Marxist turn of the 1980s was the neo-Gramscian school in International Political Economy, particularly the historical-structural approach of Robert Cox. Coxian analysis sought to overcome economistic and structuralist Marxisms, through a Gramscian-inspired historicism and humanism. Apart from the controversies regarding such readings of Gramsci, Cox's account was constrained by the analytic and conceptual framework he deployed, particularly its Althusserian-Poulantzian heritage. Eliding structural determination by inflating conjunctures into structures, 'Cox has simply replaced the *grand structuralism* of the capitalist mode of production by a *structuralism en miniature* of the "historic bloc", without satisfactorily accounting for the process of transition between structures'. As such, in common with other poststructuralist Marxist approaches, Coxian analysis can understand social change only 'within' the reproduction of capitalism (Lacher, 2008, pp. 62–3).

Underwriting these various accounts remains the conceptual separation of the 'political' and the 'economic'. Indeed, what unites these disparate approaches is precisely their differing attempts at reworking this foundational conceptual proposition (Lacher, 2008). The argument is not therefore against any particular (re)formulation of the relationship between the political and the economic (although some accounts are certainly more illuminating than others), but rather, against the a priori categorical separation of the 'political' and the 'economic' itself. Such theorizing, which recurs time and again, rests on thoroughly bourgeois foundations. Marx's destructive critique is thereby effectively abandoned for a 'rhetorically radicalised bourgeois research project' (Bonefeld, 2003).

By contrast, Open Marxism and so-called 'political Marxism' have been influential in rejecting the conceptual separation of the political and the economic. Open Marxism emerged, in large part, as a response to the 'closed' Marxism of the 1980s. As such, 'openness' referred not only to the programme of empirical research but, more significantly, to the openness of Marxist categories themselves: 'it is the openness of theory which construes itself as the critical self-understanding of a contradictory world'. The theory of the state is identified as 'arguably *the* site where the difference between structuralist and dialectical/critical (that is 'open') Marxism emerges most clearly' (Bonefeld et al., 1992, pp. xii, xv). Despite its insightful theoretical analysis, Open Marxism's own methodological position has been sharply critiqued – in particular the highly circumscribed 'openness' of its categories.

The designation 'political Marxism' was coined – pejoratively – by a Marxist critic who claimed that such accounts inverted the primacy of the political over the economic. Associated with scholars such as Robert Brenner and Ellen Meiksins Wood, 'political Marxism' was engaged in a much more radical critique than the claim of 'politicism' implies: it did not seek to simply invert the supposed order of priorities, but rather was based on a prior denial of the very existence of the 'economic' and 'political' as separable entities. Thus, as Wood (1995, p. 25) argues: '"Political Marxism" . . . is no less convinced of the primacy of production than are the "economistic tendencies" of Marxism. It does not define production out of existence or extend its boundaries to embrace indiscriminately all social activities. It simply takes seriously the principle that a mode of production is a social phenomenon.'

Seeking to overcome the debilitating dualism between structure and history introduced through Althusser's structuralism, political Marxism draws heavily on the work of E.P. Thompson, including his assertion that, in seeking to study social processes as a totality, historical materialism must reject the reified concepts of the 'economic' and 'political'. Influenced by Thompson's own historical writings, political Marxists have provided insightful historical analysis, notably on the transition from feudalism to capitalism, although Brenner's accounts, in particular, have been widely criticized for a latent Eurocentrism.

CONCLUSION

As is well known, Marx initiated a very wide-ranging critique of bourgeois sociality as a whole, which went significantly beyond the more evident concerns of *Grundrisse* and *Capital*. It included an understanding of the development of capitalism as 'intimately bound up with wider social changes, in politics, law, culture, morality' and 'exhibited an eminently *historical* grasp of these interlinked changes' (Sayer, 1985, p. 221). Marx had planned a series of works critiquing law, ethics, politics and so on, with the stated aim to present these as a 'connected whole'. These works were not completed:

> The omission has had incalculable effects . . . our perceptions of Marx's legacy have been skewed by the sheer weight and majesty of *Das Kapital*. It towers over interpretation, insistently (it seems) beckoning us to 'the economic' as the alpha and omega of proper historical materialist concern. (Sayer, 1985, p. 224)

However it is crucial to recall that Marx envisaged what became *Capital* as part of a much broader critique of bourgeois sociality that would also embrace law, ethics, politics and so on (Sayer, 1985). Now more than ever, this wide-ranging critique of bourgeois civilization as a whole continues to be necessary – including the place of the 'political' within it. But such critique is not to be developed on the fetishized foundations of bourgeois thought: it 'must take as its starting point the unity of human experience, not the fragmentation of that experience in the alienated forms of "ideology", "politics" and "economics" which capital seeks to impose on it' (Clarke, 1991, p. 38).

43. Population and migration

Deborah Johnston

Writings by Marx on population cannot fail to afford some entertainment to the reader. His enmity towards the work of that principal of population theory, Thomas Robert Malthus, was expressed in highly emotive language, with Marx describing him variously as 'a shameless sycophant of the ruling classes', a 'plagiarist', a 'wretch' and a 'baboon'.

Marx's disagreements with Malthus were two-fold – whether or not a law of population existed; and whether there was a positive or negative relationship between fertility and poverty for the English working class. On the former, Malthus had argued that there existed a natural law such that the labouring classes would have children until the point that population growth was checked by famine and disease. Higher incomes for the poor would simply lead to higher population growth rates as it would take longer for poor households to suffer the consequence of large family sizes. Underlying this was Malthus's assertion that food supply could not grow as fast as population. Although he did not explicitly analyse the fertility decisions of the poor, Malthus suggested that they resulted from a lax moral stance, which he contrasted to the moral restraint exhibited in the late marriage of the wealthy.

For Marx (*Capital I*, ch. 25), however, there was no such law of population and he envisaged instead that 'every special historic mode of production has its own special laws of population, historically valid within its limits and only in so far as man has not interfered with them'. Fertility decisions were the by-product of the situation of a particular class within the mode of production. Rather than high fertility leading to poverty, Marx argued that, in a context in which children were economically active, poverty forced the English working classes to have higher fertility rates. Furthermore, Marx argued that population pressure was necessary for capitalism. Overpopulation, relative to the needs of capital, kept wages low and workers docile. Given that relative overpopulation, or relative surplus population, was a result of the workings of the capitalist system, it was the nature of labour demand rather than growth in labour supply that led to poverty and starvation.

As Eric B. Ross (1998, pp. 3–5) has noted, Malthus's writings acted as a defence of the economic system, with explicit support for private property rights and limited government intervention to relieve the conditions of the poor. Transfers from the rich would not solve a problem rooted in the individual attitudes of the poor. Malthus suggested that, in response to welfare handouts, the poor would simply have more children, while the wellbeing of the morally superior rich would be diminished. Ross (1998, p. 7) and other writers from a political economy perspective have argued that the enduring attractiveness of Malthusianism has resulted from this ability to obscure the systematic production of poverty and instead ascribe it to the natural behaviour of individuals.

More recently, neo-Malthusians have expanded Malthus's focus to consider the impact of population growth more widely. This new focus has considered, inter alia, the impact on government expenditure, 'human capital' and, importantly, environmental conditions. However, a key fault line exists between those neo-Malthusians who look at local relationships and those who have a global outlook. A leading writer among the former, the biologist Garret Hardin theorized that population growth in a context of open-use of agricultural resources would lead to local economic and environmental disaster – a 'Tragedy of the Commons'. The corollary of Hardin's model is that private property rights are essential. In contrast, a new institutionalist perspective, such as that of the 2009 Nobel Prize winner, Elinor Ostrom, would suggest that, in certain conditions, effective and sustainable self-government of common property can emerge. Political economy writers have also criticized Hardin for his overly simplistic view of common ownership, which is rarely open-use. However, they have been concerned about the failure to consider resource rights and fertility decisions in historical context (Ross, 1998, p. 201). This can be seen most clearly if we consider the work of another leading neo-Malthusian, Jean-Philippe Platteau. His work on Africa sees population growth leading to the local degradation of natural resources and, in extreme cases, social conflict. For Platteau, the problem is that African social systems do not adapt either their technology or their institutions to larger populations. The victims are blamed for their own situation, and again there is no mention of the historical roots of resource depletion nor of the current economic pressures on African populations.

A systematic challenge to neo-Malthusian writing on Africa comes from writers who use both historical investigation and detailed anthropological case studies to reassess the logic of indigenous technology and institutions in agriculture. This approach seeks to show that indigenous people develop technology in harmony with environmental conditions. Rather than a single law of population and environmental degradation, writers such as Melissa Leach argue that environmental problems take different forms in different places. Detailed anthropological studies and revisions to the historical record have been generated (using, for example, aerial photography and satellite images to chart the change over time in vegetative cover in West Africa). For example, Leach has challenged standard accounts of long-term reduction in forest cover in parts of West Africa, showing instead that, in some areas, human activity has increased forest cover.

However, there are important weaknesses in Leach's work, and other work like it. Most important is the absence of any role for commodification or of its effects on social structures and resource use. Bernstein and Woodhouse (2001, pp. 295–8) have argued that, by attaching difference to locale (that is, to consideration of different relations between the population and environment in different places), this approach ignores social inequality and social differentiation (that is, the consideration of the different relations between people and the environment in the same location). Using a study of four areas of environmental fragility in sub-Saharan Africa as an illustration, they argue that the interaction of people with their environment 'is permeated and shaped by specific dynamics and patterns of commoditization, and the specific (and variant) forms of social differentiation they generate' (p. 319). In contrast, both neo-Malthusianism and the counter-narrative of historicized social anthropology focus on the incentives and knowledge of farmers within an undifferentiated and 'pristine' community, which (improbably) exists in isolation from the wider market or the state.

Other neo-Malthusian writing considers the impact of population in global, rather than local, terms. A leading exponent, the demographer Paul Ehrlich, has argued that growth in the world's population (predominantly from poor countries) has led to resource depletion and will end in catastrophe. For Ehrlich, each additional person contributes more to environmental degradation than the last, as areas of plenty are exhausted and people switch to the use of more fragile resources. However, writers using Marxist political economy have argued that it is vital to consider how consumption and production occur. Ross (1998, p. 208) argues that in Ehrlich's work, '[i]nstead of any critical assessment of the unsustainability of a market economy, at least in regard to large-scale environmental problems such as global warming, it is the poor whose lifestyles and habits are meant to change'. For Philip McMichael (2009) the expansion of the current agricultural system will lead to ecological crisis, but this is not driven in a simplistic way by population growth. Instead it is the nature of consumption and production in the current capitalist world system. He argues that corporate food regimes have normalized the 'meatification' of diets, with significant environmental implications due to meat's substantial 'ecological hoofprint' (pp. 240–1). At the same time, industrial agribusiness is dependent on 'chemical fertilizers, pesticides and herbicides, mechanization and food transport' (p. 242). His conclusion is not that population growth among the poor should be curbed, but that there must be a change in the diets of the rich and in agricultural production systems.

MIGRATION: AN EQUILIBRATING FLOW?

In much neo-Malthusian writing, it is assumed that increasing demographic pressure in poor countries will lead either to intra-country or transnational migration. However, rather than consider such underlying causes, the standard neoclassical theory of migration focuses on the proximate decision to migrate. The seminal neoclassical work by John Harris and Michael P. Todaro, first published in 1970, suggests that the (intra-country) migration decision is based on expected income differentials between rural and urban areas. Even if there is urban unemployment, there will be migration to urban areas if the expected urban income (that is, the expected urban wage adjusted for the urban unemployment rate) exceeds expected rural income. The assumptions are that the wage in urban areas is higher than the wage in rural areas and that the urban labour market does not clear (due to the actions of unions or government regulation), while the rural labour market is perfectly competitive. A similar approach was developed by Robert E.B. Lucas and applied to transnational migration in Southern Africa.

In the 1980s, a challenge to the standard neoclassical model was developed by Oded Stark and others using the New Economics of Labour Migration (NELM). NELM was a response to two weaknesses in the standard neoclassical model: the focus on the individual and the assumption of perfect information. In contrast NELM considers migration as a household risk-reduction strategy. Individuals within the household will migrate to minimize overall household risk provided that migration income is not positively correlated with other household income. In NELM, individuals may also migrate to mitigate household liquidity constraints, if they find the pattern of remittances superior to the pattern of other household income. Migration then acts as a way to deal with incomplete markets, for example, hedging the risk of crop failure or with credit market failures that prevent households borrowing.

Whether in the standard neoclassical approach or in NELM, migration is an equilibrating flow, where individuals move from lower- to higher-paid activities or from higher- to lower-risk activities. That these differentials correlate with different political territories (in the case of Lucas) or different geographic areas (for Harris-Todaro or Stark) is merely incidental, in the sense that there is no theory about why earning or risk differentials prevail. Thus, the variables that really matter are determined outside the mainstream models. A set of complementary theories has been developed more recently to explain how (international) migration is perpetuated over time. These focus on the way that migrant networks spread, institutions supporting transnational movement develop and the social meaning of work changes in receiving societies (so that certain jobs are labelled as 'immigrant jobs') (Massey et al., 1993, pp. 448–50). These theories certainly assist in explaining how migration flows are perpetuated, but still do not tackle the fundamental issue of why migration occurs in the first place.

In contrast, writers from a political economy perspective have been concerned to illustrate how migration patterns, particularly transnational, are structured by particular conjunctions of economic opportunities, political rights and class and other social relations. Political economy writers have also eschewed notions of migration as an equilibrating force, explaining it instead by a particular pattern of 'uneven' (and combined) economic development, which favours certain classes, races and regions while disadvantaging others. There have been two broad approaches: one that considers the way that migrants are used in receiving countries; and the other that considers the factors driving migration in the first place. In the former category, Marios Nikolinakos (1975) has looked at the role migrants play in the labour requirements of advanced capitalist societies. For him, migration swells the relative surplus population (the reserve army of labour), thereby keeping labour costs low and creating obstacles to labour organization. The advantages of migrant labour are further elucidated in theories of dual or segmented labour markets. Michael Piore suggests that the labour markets of advanced capitalist economies are characterized by dualism, with 'primary' sector jobs existing alongside 'secondary' sector jobs. Primary sector jobs exhibit high wages, good working conditions, employment stability, chances of advancement and due process in work rules. Jobs in the secondary market, in contrast, tend to have low wages and fringe benefits, poor working conditions, high labour turnover, little chance of advancement and often arbitrary supervision. Piore, therefore, rejects the notion that all workers are deskilled and homogenized in advanced capitalism, seeing instead dualism as skilled workers in capital-intensive industries perform 'strategic' tasks and so become more valuable than other workers. Capitalists 'are forced to invest in these workers by providing specialized training and education' (Massey et al., 1993, p. 442). These skilled workers are able to earn higher wages and secure better working conditions.

Importantly, the allocation of primary and secondary sector jobs reflects specific worker characteristics. Secondary sector workers may face discrimination in the primary market (for example, women or minorities), may lack education or may not have the social networks that can link them to primary jobs. All of these disadvantages may be experienced by migrants, who in addition may face legal restrictions on primary sector employment. As a result, migrant workers may be particularly concentrated in the secondary sector, with few obtaining primary sector jobs. Conversely, Piore has argued that migrant workers are essential for the maintenance of profit rates in the secondary sector in advanced capitalist economies, where domestic sources of such workers, especially women and youth, have been exhausted. Consequently, a constant stream of migrant workers is needed to sustain the rate of profit in the secondary sector.

The conditions that will produce this stream of transnational migrant workers have been the focus of a separate group of political economy writers, who focus on the conditions within migrant-sending countries. Again a clear contrast with the neoclassical approach is evident. While the mainstream sees migration as a result of limited market development (resulting in wages lower than elsewhere or markets that are less complete), political economy theorists argue migration has been spurred precisely by the market penetration that has occurred. The penetration of capitalist economic relations into poor countries is seen as destroying traditional systems of land tenure and traditional forms of social and economic organization, creating a population prone to migrate. Elizabeth M. Petras uses a world-systems approach to argue that migration from the periphery to the core is a secular feature of the modern world-economy. Robin Cohen (1987, pp. 94–110) also links international migration to the penetration of capitalist relations in poor countries, giving as an example the way in which surrounding countries were transformed into labour reserves for South Africa as a direct consequence of the forces that enriched its neighbour. Cohen's work (1987, pp. 145–78) also reminds us that the state has a role to play in regulating or controlling migrant flows, given the importance of migration to capitalist development. However, tensions exist and states will have to 'match their immigration policies and practises to the racism of their electorates and the labour-power needs of their industrial and service sectors' (p. 156).

CONCLUSION

Writers from a political economy perspective have not only helped us understand the fundamental causes of migration, they have also illustrated the limitations of the neoclassical choice-theoretic approach. It is clear that whether migrating to construction sites in Dubai or to peri-urban townships in South Africa, migrants are often 'choice-disabled', in the sense that they face a limited set of opportunities in the face of overwhelming pressures to maintain survival, either for themselves or for their families. The reason for this restriction of opportunities has been at the heart of much political economy work on migration.

Political economy work on migration has also shown that the impact of migration depends on the character of labour demand and the structure of labour markets. A similar conclusion is reached in work on population growth. The fundamental argument is that there is no universal law relating population growth to poverty or degradation, and that instead the impact of population growth will depend on the nature of production relations in each and every mode of production. While this does not have the sound-bite simplicity of neo-Malthusian writing, understanding this is crucial in denying the argument that the poor are to blame for their own poverty.

44. Productive and unproductive labour

Simon Mohun

Productive labour is labour that creates value and surplus value; unproductive labour does not. The definition is simple, but deceptively so, for whether to make the distinction, and if so how, are among the most controversial issues in Marxist economics. Partly this is because, as with so much else, Marx both built on and transformed the categories of productive and unproductive labour that he had inherited from his predecessors (primarily Adam Smith). Partly it is because Marx never developed a systematic treatment in his own work, so that the category has to be recovered and interpreted from widely scattered sources among writings put together for publication after his death by Engels (*Capital*, Volumes II and III) and Kautsky (*Theories of Surplus Value*). And partly it is because capitalist economies have changed since Marx's day, so that what is unproductive has a historical specificity that writings in the late nineteenth century could not anticipate.

PRODUCTIVE AND UNPRODUCTIVE LABOUR ACCORDING TO ADAM SMITH

The second half of the eighteenth century witnessed the beginnings of substantial economic transformation as factories in towns began to supersede rural cottage industry. These new places of work could exploit new sources of energy, and were characterized by closer control over the production process, which enabled further extension of the division of labour. Substantial economies of scale were thereby achieved. At the same time, the enclosures of common land coupled with increasing economic differentiation in the countryside provided the labour for the new factories as the rural poor were increasingly forced to seek their subsistence through the market by selling their labour power.

In the late eighteenth century, Adam Smith at least partially recognized the novelty and the scale of these developments. He saw capitalism as an emergent system with positive feedback, governed by an 'invisible hand': the extension of the division of labour increased productivity and incomes (and, after a lag, population), that, in turn, created the demand which enabled further extension of the division of labour and specialization. But he was then faced with the problem that not all labour contributed to this process. Investment in factory labour did; but outlays on personal servants, while they might marginally contribute to increases in demand, otherwise did not, for their outputs (the personal services) were directly consumed by their employer. If no output is produced for sale, there are no proceeds to cover costs and finance investment. Hence expenditures on personal servants consumed rather than produced wealth, and their labour was 'unproductive'. Smith then substantially muddled matters by contrasting the labour that produced physical goods with the labour that produced services; the former was productive, the latter unproductive. In an economy in which most services were directly consumed and very few were marketed, the inconsistencies generated by the two different definitions, one based on the contribution to wealth creation, and one based on the materiality of the product, were not especially apparent. But as capitalism developed, the two approaches were correspondingly increasingly incompatible.

THE MARXIST ACCOUNT OF PRODUCTIVE AND UNPRODUCTIVE LABOUR

Nearly a century later, Marx took Smith's first definition and reworked it in a different framework. Instead of focusing on wealth (the sum of produced and non-produced use values), Marx focused on value. His general perspective was that what differentiated class societies was the form in which the surplus product was extracted from those who produced it. In commodity-producing societies, this took the form of a sum of money (profit) which, according to the labour theory of value, was the form in which surplus value was realized. Consequently labour was productive if and only if it produced surplus value. The distinction between the labour that produced a physical output as a commodity and the labour that produced a service as a commodity was, therefore, irrelevant.

The focus on the production of value rather than the production of use value has an unfortunate implication, concerned with the simple issue of nomenclature. 'Productive' seems to entail that work is done and something is produced. Cooking a meal for oneself is certainly an act of labouring activity and, as long as the meal is edible, produces a use value. But such labour is not a purchased input in a capitalist production process. Of course, people must eat to survive, but the issue is not whether the labour is necessary; it is whether it produces surplus value. For the latter to obtain, labour power must be a commodity. Only when labour power is a commodity is there a wage; wage labour produces commodities for sale, and only when commodities are sold is surplus value realized. In this sense, only commodity-producing wage labour counts. All other (non-wage) labouring activity, no matter whether essential or trivial, fulfilling or destructive, is neither productive nor unproductive. Much of such labouring activity is of course crucial to social reproduction (consider the care of small children, for example), but the question of what is surplus value producing is considerably narrower in scope.

In general, the distinction between productive and unproductive labour is not apparent in *Capital I*. For Marx here dealt with two major themes, each illustrated with copious historical detail. First, he analysed how capital produced surplus value and, second, he analysed how surplus value produced capital. In each of these themes, he explicitly assumed 'equal exchange' or 'exchange of equivalents'. This was because Marx wanted to show that, even on the extreme assumption that the seller is always paid the full value of the commodity she sells, he could explain how surplus value (and hence profit) arises, and how its magnitude is determined. Thus the worker, free to sell her labour power to any purchaser, and free of any means of production that might enable non-market access to the means of subsistence, sells her labour power at its value. The purchaser, now the owner of the labour power, then consumes the commodity purchased. This means putting the worker to work for a specified period of time; the outcome is that an output is produced that can be sold for more than the cost of the labour time that the capitalist purchased. That is, the use value of labour power to the purchaser is the subsequent work done, which produces greater value than the value of labour power. This value difference is unpaid surplus labour, or surplus value, accruing to the owner of the commodity labour power. But this argument can only be made precise if value-equivalents are exchanged, which in turn implies that all the labour concerned is productive labour. If the use value of labour power is the ability to create new value that is greater than the value of labour power, that labour power must be an attribute of a productive worker. For unproductive workers do not create value. Hence in *Capital I*, apart from occasional asides, there is nothing substantive about unproductive labour.

If productive labour produces surplus value, what does unproductive labour do? First, if surplus value is to be produced in money form, output must be sold. If wage labour is engaged in a production process that produces no marketed output, then value and surplus value are not being produced. While of little consequence in Marx's day, all capitalist economies have witnessed substantial growth in wage labour that produces no marketed output. This is labour that works for 'general government', producing output for direct consumption (either individually or collectively), and financed by taxation and the sale of debt. The state has always been responsible for the management of inter-capitalist rivalries (through its diplomatic corps and its armed services, for example), the policing of internal class conflicts through the protection of private property (police and judiciary) and general executive administration. But the state has also increasingly taken responsibility for the infrastructure for the reproduction of labour power (health, education, social security, housing and care for the elderly), as well as a fluctuating number of economic functions (subsidies to industry, physical infrastructure such as bridges and roads and direct economic interventions). This involves employing large numbers of people in general government, but all such labour is unproductive.

The best way to approach the classification of wage labour that does produce a marketed output is through consideration of the circuit of capital. Consider a capitalist with a sum of money to invest, hence with capital in money form. The process of investment means engaging in a set of activities to purchase labour power and non-labour inputs; capital is thereby transformed from money form to productive form. Then a second set of activities ensues whereby the inputs are transformed into outputs (of higher value); capital is thereby transformed from productive to commodity form, awaiting sale. Finally, a third set of activities occurs, which transforms capital from commodity to money form, so that the whole process can repeat. As capital moves round the circuit, it exists successively as a stock and a flow. Starting from a stock of money capital, capital flows through a set of processes to finish as a stock of productive capital; call this the Phase 1 flow. From a stock of productive capital, capital flows through a production process to finish as a stock of commodity capital; call this the Phase 2 flow. And from a stock of commodity capital, capital flows through a set of processes to finish as a stock of money capital; call this the Phase 3 flow. Consider then the labour employed in these three flows:

Phase 1: These are a set of transactions in the market whereby inputs are purchased. While such transactions can be simple, frequently they are not, because non-labour inputs of fixed capital are expensive because of their 'lumpiness'. Hence credit is frequently involved in their purchase. This in turn entails a set of functions in financial markets both to spread risk and to consolidate a large number of small sums of money into the larger sums needed. When debt is sold by financial agencies, the typical payment is a rate of interest. But while the transaction has a commodity form, no commodity is produced, so that there is no immediate value-equivalent to match the payment of interest. The interest payments are a claim on the surplus value yet to be produced (in Phase 2) and realized (in Phase 3), and because of this precommitment to an uncertain future, there is always an element of speculation involved. Financial instruments can be very complicated, particularly when the sale of debt creates flows of interest that can be securitized into new financial instruments to be bought and sold. Moreover, the transfer of title involved, as money capital is transformed into commodity capital, can also be complex, involving commercial law firms, accountancy firms and so forth. The multitude of non-equivalent exchanges of value involved are all sales of services in exchange for claims on future surplus value. Despite the complexity of these transactions, their function is simply to transform money capital into productive capital, a stock of money into a stock of inputs ready for production. They do not change the total value of the capital; they merely change its form. Thus the labour that transforms money capital into productive capital is unproductive.

Phase 2: In the production process, the capitalist consumes the use value of the purchased labour power by setting the labour to work with non-labour inputs (the means of production). The consumption of labour power is the production of new value and a transfer of (a portion of) the value of the means of production to the final product. If value is to expand, the new value, or value added, must be greater than the value of labour power, and that extra value is surplus value. The whole process is a transformation of productive capital into commodity capital of higher value, both a change of form (like Phase 1) and a change of magnitude (unlike Phase 1). Consequently, the labour that effects this transformation is productive labour. Further, the greater the extent of the division of labour, the more the process of production requires planning and coordination. Such labour too is productive. Yet the way in which technology is developed under capitalist relations of production is not a class-independent process. A capitalist division of labour involves processes of deskilling, hierarchies of supervision and a general policing of an authoritarian organization of production based on the giving and receiving of orders. The labour involved in such policing acts as surrogate for capital, and is therefore unproductive. In capitalist production processes, it is impossible in general, both conceptually and empirically, to separate the productive labour that plans and coordinates from the unproductive labour that supervises and polices. Unproductive labour, here, is financed directly out of the surplus value produced by the labour it supervises.

Phase 3: In order for surplus value to be realized as a sum of money, commodity capital has to be transformed into money capital, which requires that the produced commodities be sold. Conceptually the simplest phase, in this transformation of capital's form, no new value is created, and so the labour that effects the transformation is unproductive. As well as the labour directly involved in the sale of outputs, labour generating advertising services aimed at boosting sales is unproductive, as is the labour that is devoted to recording flows of transactions (bookkeeping and accountancy). Labour involved in promoting the war of competition, fought through market share is similarly unproductive. Unproductive labour in Phase 3 is financed out of the revenues derived from sales. For example, advertising agencies charge a fee for their services, and that fee has to be found from the revenues accruing to the firm purchasing advertising services. Advertising revenues originate in the unpaid labour that produced the commodities whose sale the advertising firm is promoting; and similarly for bookkeeping and accountancy services, and all other services designed to facilitate the transformation of commodity capital into money capital. This transformation is again one of form and not one of magnitude. But, although the labour performed in this transformation creates no new value, those who do not supervise are nonetheless exploited in the same manner as non-supervisory labour in Phase 1, in the sense that revenues accrue that are greater then the cost of the labour time employed in generating such revenues. But the value flows that finance these revenues are produced elsewhere.

In sum, Phases 1 and 3 together comprise the sphere of circulation, a set of C-M-C circuits. These circulation circuits change the form of capital, and not its magnitude. Only labour without supervisory responsibilities in Phase 2 is purely productive, changing both the form of capital and its magnitude.

To get some idea of orders of magnitude of productive and unproductive labour, consider the US economy in 2007, in which total private sector employment amounted to 115.4 million. More than six million (5.3 per cent) were employed in finance and insurance (Phase 1). About 21.5 million (18.7 per cent) were employed in wholesale and retail trade (Phase 3). About 6.2 million (5.4 per cent) were employed in areas related to purchase and sale: advertising and related services, accountancy and bookkeeping services, management consultancy services (which also relate to production), offices of bank and other holding companies and of corporate, subsidiary and regional managing offices, and real estate, rental and leasing services (Phases 1 and 3). Some 13.1 million in value-producing sectors (about 17.8 per cent of the total in those sectors) had some supervisory responsibility (Phase 2). And both transfers of property rights and production activities require a framework of legal services, and, occasionally, investigative and security services (almost two million, or 1.7 per cent). In addition, some eight million (7 per cent) were employed in administrative and support services, whose location in the circuit of capital is often ambiguous, and whose productive and unproductive characteristics are therefore difficult to disentangle. Even ignoring this latter category, certainly well over 40 per cent of US private sector employment in 2007 was unproductive. Finally, outside of the private sector, almost 18.5 million (around one in seven of all full-time equivalent employees) were employed by general government.

USES OF THE CONCEPT

The method that Marx adopted in establishing his categories of analysis was one whereby the further development of the category required the supersession of the assumption that generated it. This is a delicate procedure, since it is easy to criticize it for producing a contradictory analysis, results that are inconsistent with assumptions. One example of this methodology is the way in which Marx used the assumption that commodities exchange at money prices proportional to their labour values to show that such exchange cannot in fact be the case, for it contradicts the empirical analysis of competition and its tendency for capital flows to equalize the rate of profit. This latter requires exchange at prices of production, which will in general differ from the prices proportional to labour values because of differing compositions of capital. This entails that unequal or non-equivalent exchange is the norm.

At the level of the individual capital, an assumption of equal exchange in order to identify the value-creating process, and hence also productive and unproductive labour, is therefore inappropriate except at the most abstract level. Unequal or non-equivalent exchange is the norm, and the only difference between the output of a purely productive capital and a purely unproductive capital is that the former produces a money value that is different from the labour value of its output, whereas the latter produces no value at all. But this difference is invisible to the observer: both employ inputs to produce outputs in order to maximize their profit, and it is not possible to say how much value is produced by any individual firm. Indeed, what is productive and what is unproductive is not a sensible question to ask of an individual capital.

Because, in an unequal exchange, what one party gains the other must lose, in the aggregate all such gains and losses must cancel out. Total value added (whether in money or in labour) is invariant to the vicissitudes of exchange. Hence in the aggregate, payments to unproductive labour are financed out of aggregate surplus value, so that, in the aggregate, productive labour finances unproductive labour. The amount of productive labour and the degree of its exploitation are together an index of the total profits that are potentially available to an economy. But since unproductive labour is ultimately paid out of surplus value (no matter how complicated the processes by which this occurs), the amount of unproductive labour in an economy determines how much profit is actually available. However, unproductive labour is not necessarily thereby a deadweight loss, for its consumption of surplus value might raise overall profitability (as in the 'managerial revolution' in the early twentieth century). While any empirical analysis will, therefore, find a clear association between a rising rate of surplus value and a rising ratio of unproductive to productive labour, what is required is to analyse just how the 'technologies' of production and circulation interact to produce such a relationship. Because most work on productive and unproductive labour has tended to remain at the level of the elaboration and contestation of theoretical categories, such detailed empirical work to date remains undeveloped.

45. Race

Alfred Zack-Williams

Race is a nebulous and indeed a muddled term with at least two basic meanings: first, it defines a group of people who share genetically determined features considered by members of society to be socially significant. The second refers to a set of beliefs and attitudes about human differences and not the differences themselves. Both definitions are premised on the knowledge that 'race' is not intrinsically linked with biological or genetic differentiations among human beings. Thus as Audrey Smedley (1999) has observed: '"race" as a biological concept cannot be supported by the facts that we have learned about human biological variation and their genetic basis' (p. 4). These beliefs, attitudes and practices are products of human interaction under given material and cultural circumstances; as such race is a social construct and not a biological fact. Whilst some writers have rejected the notion of race as an analytical concept (Miles, 1994), people are often classified according to physical characteristics, such as skin colour, hair texture, body and nose shapes; all features which superficially belie that all humanity stems from a single biological heritage. Indeed, the obsession with racial taxonomy and hierarchy led nineteenth-century writers, such as Joseph Arthur Count de Gobineau to develop classificatory categories such as: Negroid, Mongoloid, Caucasoid and Australoid. Such categories soon formed the basis of race science and the racialization of the world with Caucasian at the top of the racial pyramid, and those further away from Europe spatially and contemporaneously being relegated to the bottom of the hierarchy. In the human sciences, 'race' refers to a group connected by common origin; in this case it is often used intermittently with 'ethnicity', though the latter refers to groups or people sharing a common history and culture.

MARXISM AND RACE

The phenomenon of race remains on the margins of historical materialism, and many commentators have observed that classical Marxism, because of its preoccupation with the concept of class, failed to provide a systematic analysis of the dynamics of race and class (Cashmore, 1988; Belkhir, 2001), though there are references to race strewn throughout the works of Marx and Engels. Furthermore, race and ethnicity were not treated in their own right, but were seen as a product of false consciousness, which would disappear along with 'all the muck of ages and become fitted to found society anew' (*German Ideology*). For example, whilst reference was made to race as an economic factor in slavery in the United States (Cashmore, 1988), it was left to later Marxists such as W.E.B. Du Bois, Eric Williams, Oliver Cox, Stuart Hall, Robert Miles and Paul Gilroy to present a systematic analysis of the relationships between slavery and racism, between capitalism and slavery, and the continuing alienation of racial groups. Much attention was concentrated on what was seen as the immediate or pressing concerns: class, the national question and division within the working class. Nonetheless, it is important to note that in the last three decades there has been a series of neo-Marxist analyses of social differentiation based on 'race' and 'ethnicity' as well as class. Miles has attributed this tendency to the work of the black British Marxist and activist, A. Sivanandan, whom he accused of using the idea of race 'to refer to distinct, biologically defined groups of people . . . race is as much a reality as class, both concepts referring to some quality that all people possess' (Miles, 1994, p. 38). In this sense, Miles argues that Sivanandan treats race as a reality *sui generis*, and a reality, which at once both parallels and mediates class.

The migration of former colonial subjects to the cities and towns of the former colonial powers of northern Europe created the context for further deepening of the Marxist theory of race and racism. The crisis of late capitalism in the 1970s, triggered by cost-push inflation and information communication and technology, impelled structural transformation, accompanied by widespread unemployment, and attacks on working-class living conditions, which in turn had the effect of dividing the working class along racial lines. Thus Powellism, which sought to impose neoliberal solutions on the working class even before the emergence of Thatcherism and Reaganomics, became the rallying point for the white working class as xenophobia and racism divided the working classes. As a consequence, Marxist analysts turned their attention to addressing the issue of racism within a wider framework of the political economy of migration (Castles and Kosack, 1973; Miles, 1994) and, in particular, whether racism is simply an ideology. Writers such as Michael Banton (1991) drew attention to the influence of colonialism on racist ideology. Others such as Miles and Goldberg cautioned against explanations based solely on the colonial experience, by suggesting that the roots of racism can equally be traced back to pre-capitalist social relations within European societies and that its reproduction is determined no less than by the rise of the nation state; and that its origins can be traced back through the European Enlightenment and to the Reformation in particular.

The divide within Marxism on the issue of race continues, with some writers (Gilroy, 1987) defending the utilization of the concept of race on the grounds of praxis, arguing that the concept is utilized by victims of racism in aiding political mobilization in anti-racist struggle. However, these terms are also contested as witnessed by the emergence of alternative nomenclatures such as Asian, African-Caribbean, as well as the generic Blacks and Ethnic Minorities.

RACISM AND CAPITALISM

An early attempt at analysing how American capitalism impacted on its black population and transformed it into caste-like segregation was the aim of the work of W.E.B. Du Bois. In order to effect change in African-American conditioning, Du Bois in his early writings embarked upon the approach of 'positivistic sociology', in the quest for objectivity by marshalling empirical data. However, whilst urging sociologists to direct their attention to contemporary problems, for him the vexed issue remained how scientific knowledge could help to liberate his people, and he soon became convinced that empirical data alone could not convince white Americans to undo the workings of prejudice and racial discrimination in order to alleviate the conditions of blacks. He abandoned the scientific method of empirical research embodied in his *The Philadelphia Negro* in favour of the 'soulful voice' (of his *The Souls of Black Folk*), including subjectivity, autobiographical and historical sociological approaches (Appelrouth and Edles, 2008). This approach has been described as a precursor to the interpretive shift that began to emerge in sociology in the 1980s. Du Bois introduced the concept of the 'colour line', with important subjective or non-rational dimensions, which became instrumental as a heuristic tool in explicating how the colonization and exploitation of Africa and Africans became central to world history:

> Africa's poverty is inexorably linked to colonisation and imperial domination; the wealth of the colonial empires of England, France, Germany, and the United States 'comes directly from the darker races of the world'. (Appelrouth and Edles, 2008, p. 289)

Du Bois characterized African-Americans as having a 'double consciousness', as Americans (or insiders), yet remaining on the fringes of American society, unable to escape the burden of colour. Rejecting the notion of black inferiority contrary to the Social Darwinism of the late nineteenth century, which he put down to white prejudice, thus foreshadowing the work of Swedish sociologist Gunnar Myrdal (1944), Du Bois criticized the small number of successful African-Americans whom he saw as being too eager to seek favour with whites, as they severed ties with blacks still needing their support. In this respect Du Bois's argument corresponds to Marx's analysis of alienation as this relates the subjective experience of the alienated or estranged worker to the mode of production or their position within the capitalist class structure.

The work of another African-American, Oliver C. Cox, much more than Du Bois, sought to locate the analysis of the African-American predicament within a Marxist analytical framework. He set out to construct a Marxist theory of race relations, by pointing out that these were fundamentally different from caste relations, as was claimed by most of his contemporaries. Cox's work, which is situated within the perspective of historical sociology, tried to argue that the racism or race prejudice against African-Americans can be traced to the European expansion from the fifteenth century onwards, which also paralleled the development of the capitalist system. For Cox racism was an ideology articulated by the ruling class in order to justify the exploitation of non-European labour. Thus Cox (1970, p. 393) noted that racism is 'a social attitude propagated among the public by the exploiting class for the purpose of stigmatising some group as inferior so that the exploitation of either the group itself or its resources may be justified'. Furthermore, and like later writers such as Castles and Kosack, Cox argued that racism/race prejudice served the additional purpose of dividing the working class, thus reducing the chances of challenges to the ruling class.

Satnam Virdee (2010, p. 136) has argued that, despite the magnitude of the contributions of Cox and Du Bois, their work has been 'ostracised and marginalised by the predominantly white sociological community of the 1950s and early 1960s'. In the case of Cox, Virdee argued that this is the product of the McCarthyism of the post-war years. Miles has argued that the marginalization of Cox's work stems from there no longer being any interest in his central theme, that is, the comparison between caste and race relations. Miles who is very critical of Cox's work has described it as functionalist and economistic, and that his analysis of race prejudice is not consistent with the concept of capitalism as a mode of production.

The work of 'western Marxists' (Anderson, 1976) on race continued its path with major contributions from Robert Miles, Paul Gilroy, Stuart Hall and the Centre for Contemporary Cultural Studies (CCCS) at the University of Birmingham. There are clear differences in emphasis between these contributions, but what unites them is that their work is grounded on the materialist conception of history as it relates to the groups they are studying. However, collectively they have been criticized by Virdee for their 'relative detachment from any form of emancipatory political project'. He observed:

> From the miserable Marxism of the Frankfurt School's Theodor Adorno and his claims of working class incorporation through the culture industry to the structural Marxism of Louis Althusser and his termination of the emancipatory subject via the ideological state apparatus, this body of work has expressed a deep pessimism about the possibility of progressive social change in late capitalism. In this sense, it contrasts sharply the classical Marxism or praxis philosophy of Luxemburg, Gramsci, and Marx himself, who conceived the materialist method as not only providing the means of understanding history, but also of making it through political interventions. (Virdee, 2010, pp. 138–9)

The major concern of these writers has been the need to explicate labour market segmentation whereby some workers (for example, African-Americans) were mainly employed as strike-breakers, while others (such as migrant workers in Western Europe) were relegated to the least desirable jobs. Not only does this strategy create a dual labour market but, by pitching white against black workers, this helps the reproduction of capitalist hegemony (Virdee, 2010), and the major beneficiary of this strategy is the ruling capitalist class whose income is augmented. And the major losers are the victims of the racist labour market (Reich, 1978). Reich argued that racism did not bring material gains for the white working class; furthermore, Virdee pointed out that there is evidence to confirm that when black and white workers cooperate, the incomes of both groups tend to rise significantly. Reich's argument that the white working class did not benefit from racism has been questioned by Virdee, who observed that such a position creates a caricature of this class as cultural dopes, suffering from false consciousness or denuded from the quality of homo economicus. Bonacich (1980) too has questioned Reich's conclusion by pointing out that for the working class to remain the primary perpetrators of racism, they must *ipso facto* have a material interest in reproducing racism.

STUART HALL AND THE CCCS SCHOOL

Virdee (2010, p. 142) has noted that Hall's (1980) article 'moved the epicentre of the race/class debate firmly across the Atlantic to Britain', by privileging political economy and, thereby, focusing the debate on the role of the state, politics, ideology and culture. For Hall what was needed in this debate on the heuristic role of historical materialism in capturing the nature of racialized relations in different societies was an engagement with the Structuralist-Marxism of Louis Althusser and Antonio Gramsci, both prominent at the time. Such a project must be non-dogmatic and be able to address the interface between the superstructure and the economic infrastructure. Thus, borrowing the concepts of articulation from Althusser and hegemony from Gramsci, and by drawing attention to the complexity of modern society, Hall was able to focus on the economy, politics, ideology and culture, which constitute the economic base and the superstructure, respectively, each with 'relative autonomy' from the other, though linked in contradictory ways. This approach is not dissimilar to the neo-Marxism of the French Marxist anthropologists (Claude Meillassoux, Pierre-Philippe Rey, Maurice Godelier and Emmanuel Terray) who, utilizing Marxist concepts such as 'articulation of modes of production', 'surplus product' and 'exploitation', were able to locate instances not just of exploitation, but also how one mode of production (capitalism) can stifle the progression of the pre-capitalist modes, in order to serve its (capitalist) interests and accumulation needs. According to Virdee, the structuralist approach of Hall and his collaborators at the CCCS set off a genuine paradigm shift in addressing racism, drawing attention in particular to racism as far from an epiphenomenon, relatively autonomous within its own reality, and in need of an additional layer of explanation to incorporate the concept of hegemony.

In his work on hegemony, in the context of 'Thatcherism' and defined as a 'state of total social authority', Hall concentrated his analysis on the political and ideological (superstructure) spheres of the social formation, to establish how ruling classes secure their rights to rule over all of society through manufacturing consent. Though Virdee accepted that Hall has presented us with a productive and non-reductionist method of unravelling the gridlock in the debate of race versus class, which dogged both Marxist and Weberian analysis, he has criticized Hall's attempt 'to renew Marxism as a non-dogmatic method of analysis and action' à la Althusser, thus banishing the idea of human subjectivity in what Virdee called 'Marxism without guarantees'. For Hall, at the level of politics and ideology, there is a dialectical rapport: race operates through class, thus it is appropriate to talk of the 'racialisation of class and the classification of race' (Virdee, 2010, p. 144). The attempt by Hall to restore the (racial and class) subjects into history via Gramsci's concepts of ideology and hegemony is doomed to failure if attempted through the lens of Structuralist-Marxists. For the latter precludes notions of interpellation, whereby individuals are constituted by their own active ideologies, with self-propelling identities, and otherwise restricting any transition to a higher level of consciousness. Virdee (2010, p. 146) observed that any notion of working-class interpellation challenges the established Marxist theory of working-class self-emancipation, enshrined in the work of both Marx and Gramsci. Thus, he observed that:

> The outcome is that despite his well-intentioned attempt at rethinking Marxism, Hall ends up offering a portraiture of the white working class that, like the Utopian Socialists before him . . . reduces this class to a mere victim of the degradations inflicted by the capitalist system, a class with little capacity to resist the power of ideology in fragmenting and dissipating resistance to elite rule.

The theme of race and nation was also a major concern of Paul Gilroy, one of Hall's lieutenants at the CCCS, but who later broke from his mentor by rejecting the materialist conception of history (Miles, 1994; Virdee, 2010). Looking at the cultural politics of race and nation, Gilroy drew attention to how nationalism in post-war Britain became intertwined with racism, to the extent that the white working-class attachment to racist nationalism superseded class solidarity with those now burdened by racism. Gilroy explored the possibility of reversing this trend to ensure working-class solidarity, in order to further socialist politics. To achieve this goal, Gilroy argued that it is imperative for black autonomous struggles to be reconstituted as class struggles and *ipso facto* contributing to the process of class formation by synchronizing both race and class consciousness. Whilst some of his burgeoning ideas emerged from his contribution to *The Empire Strikes Back*, it was in his *There Ain't No Black in the Union Jack* that saw his attempt to split race from class. According to Virdee the theory of class was replaced by the theory of social movements, including feminism, ecology and youth movements.

46. Radical political economy in the USA

Al Campbell

The rise and fall of radical political economy (RPE) in the USA (see Lee, 2009) is rooted in the rise and fall of the social radicalization there of the 1960s and 1970s. This radicalization was ideologically dominated by a (vague) New Left (NL) social critique of (US) capitalism, notwithstanding that many radicals rejected such critiques as inadequate.

US RADICAL POLITICAL ECONOMY AND THE NEW LEFT

Since the term NL was created to refer to everyone with a radical critique of the system other than the 'Old Left' (OL), it included many different strands of political thought and ideologies. In addition, in the early years of the NL in the mid-1960s, many prominent members and groups pointedly declared themselves 'anti-ideological', asserting that pure activism would replace ideology. Most currents in the NL fairly quickly came to realize that they had an ideology whether they acknowledged it or not, and so turned to its conscious development. In practice this resulted in approaching one or another of the orientations that existed in the (small) US left, above all Stalinism, Social Democracy, Anarchism, (US) Radical Populism or Marxism. The various NL individuals and currents typically eclectically mixed these and, in addition, continually made major changes to their theories and ideologies over relatively short periods of time. All of these points together indicate the need for caution when referring to 'a NL ideology'. For a compact treatment of a significant number of the threads in the US NL ideological tapestry, see Young (1977). I will simply refer to 'the vague NL ideology'. It was largely a product of the specific history of that US radicalization. Above all, it was defined by things in the existing society that it was against. Critically absent was an alternative based on a radical social theory – by implication, the alternative was just to eliminate the problems.

Two central issues divided the NL from the OL. The first was the issue of class. The OL had always recognized the need to fight against all forms of oppression. For example, many though far from all of the leaders of the fight against racism both after and before World War II were part of the OL or strongly influenced by it. But the OL at the same time argued that class oppression played a special role in the maintenance and reproduction of capitalism. Capitalism's goal was the accumulation of capital which required and rested on class oppression and exploitation. Other forms of oppression could be just as individually damaging as class oppression, but they did not play the same role in the continual reproduction of capitalist social relations. The NL, to the contrary, argued strongly for the absolute theoretical symmetry of all forms of oppression as sources of exploitation, leading to the political idea of 'multi-vanguardism'. One of the founding documents of the premier NL RPE group in the USA (discussed further below) reflected this concept: 'The organization opposes all exploitation on the basis of class, race, gender, ethnicity, sexual orientation and other social/economic/cultural constructs' (URPE, 1968). As the NL went on to develop its ideologies, it drew on (among other sources) C. Wright Mills's (1956) model of elites based on power, and consciously opposed this to the Marxist concept of class based at its deepest level on economic exploitation. Mills's concept was particularly suited to a view of multiple, conceptually equivalent, exploitations.

The other central issue for the NL presented itself Janus-like with two related but conceptually very different faces. Negatively (in several senses of that word), the NL exuded a politically primitive anti-authoritarianism. This was an important endogenous contribution to the NL's general inability to create sustainable institutions. Positively, the NL championed the concept of Participatory Democracy against both the OL and bourgeois democracy. Long after the NL disappeared, this latter idea has remained as a permanent contribution (or 'rediscovery', as the idea existed before the NL), and is still being debated and developed by many (proto) social movements in the USA that continue to fight against capitalism.

THE DECLINE OF US RADICAL POLITICAL ECONOMY

Five considerations concerning the decline of RPE in the USA follow. Two are exogenous (to RPE) causes, one is an endogenous cause and two are measures of its decline.

The first and fundamental cause for the decline of RPE in the USA was the end of the social radicalization and the rise of social conservatism. Second, the field of economics in which RPE largely operated shifted from 'Bastard Keynesianism' (or 'neoclassical Keynesianism', or 'the neoclassical synthesis') to neoliberalism. Both in politics and in economics what used to be conservative became liberal (in the US sense of the term), and what used to be small far-right positions became standard conservative, which in turn became politically and especially ideologically dominant. Symbolically, for example, in many dimensions the economic, and even a number of social, policies of Clinton and Obama are more conservative than those of Nixon. Endogenously, the NL's general anti-authoritarian nature hamstrung its ability to form large and powerful organizations that could both protect its members operating in hostile job situations, and at a deeper level, carry out an ideological battle, with voices large enough to not be ignored, against the new dominant ideology in society and economics.

The first measure of the decline of RPE is conceptually straightforward. By and large, most of the RPE currents that formed organizations, including in particular those that published journals, did not disappear, and this entry will discuss a number of these below. However, the memberships in these organizations, and the number of RPE economists outside these groups, declined sharply.

The second measure of the decline was more subtle but more important in a number of ways, RPE's 'qualitative decline'. Some individuals and currents (not all) in RPE adopted (or shifted partially toward adopting) important parts of the core ideological presuppositions of neoclassical economics, and incorporated them into their work. The most important of these are the related axioms of methodological individualism, human nature as 'homo oeconomicus' and market fundamentalism.

As a first illustration of this, consider the large amount of work done by radical economists showing that there exist strategies that give cooperative solutions to repeated non-cooperative games such as the Prisoners' Dilemma. All this work rests on methodological individualism and homo oeconomicus. This includes in particular the unrealistic restriction that 'players' are not allowed the discursive interaction and meaningful bargaining that is pervasive in all social structures, and which gives rise to changes of intended behaviour. As a second illustration, consider the degree to which markets have been accepted as efficient, and, as an additional step beyond that, as therefore economically necessary. This contrasts sharply with the dominant assumption of RPE in the 1960s and 1970s that markets and their logic, including the shaping of non-market social institutions in accord with the needs of markets, were the central cause of the prevailing economic problems, and beyond that, of stunted human development. The solution then was either to have 'markets' that were so regulated that they no longer operated according to market logic but rather according to the democratically determined will of society, or to replace markets altogether by non-market democratically planned production and distribution. By the 1990s the majority in RPE of even those committed to socialism had adopted, specifically in the name of efficiency, some vision of 'market socialism'.

RADICAL POLITICAL ECONOMY IN THE USA TODAY

Despite the decline just indicated, US RPE was never more than a small current in US economics, but nor has it entirely disappeared today. The following is a very brief sketch of a number of the major groups or currents in today's diminished US RPE.

The Union for Radical Political Economics (URPE) was the premier NL RPE organization in several senses: it was founded at the height of the NL; its founders were New Leftists; its programme was thoroughly NL; and it reached out immediately to NL-oriented economists (while being open from its birth to other currents, as discussed below). URPE's stated goals at its birth reflect the ideology of NL RPE: 'First, to promote a new interdisciplinary approach to political economy which includes also relevant themes from political science, sociology and social psychology. Secondly, to develop new courses and research areas which reflect the urgencies of the day and a new value premise. Such areas include the economics of the ghetto, poverty, imperialism, interest groups, and the military-industry complex. And thirdly, political economics should be sensitive to the needs of the social movements of our day, and have more group research, with an approach that links all issues to a broad framework of analysis' (URPE, n.d.).

Two institutional characteristics of URPE were key to its survival. First, URPE created a respected RPE journal, *The Review of Radical Political Economics*. Second, URPE fought for and won from the American Economic Association the right to organize a significant number of its own panels at the yearly national economics convention. In line with its goal of promoting a broad approach to political economy, URPE from the beginning was open not only to economists from a NL perspective, but to any others who promoted a political alternative to the mainstream. These include in particular Marxists, non-Marxist Socialists, Sraffians, Post Keynesians, Radical Institutionalists, Feminists, Social Economists and many who did not adhere to any particular single current of thought but attacked mainstream economics for being economically unrealistic.

Three significant groups and a current in today's RPE in the USA were founded by URPE members (on their own initiative, not as URPE projects). They are particularly worth mentioning for indicating that the NL RPE's often simplistic anti-authoritarianism prevented it from developing a clear and consistent 'line' and promoting it. Those who wanted to do this had to set up an organization outside of URPE, even though they generally remained members of URPE. The Association for Economic and Social Analysis was founded in the late 1970s and is best known for its journal *Rethinking Marxism*, launched in 1988. The group promotes a (broadly defined) line of postmodern Marxism (see, for example, Gibson-Graham et al., 2001), and the journal focuses on debates in Marxist theory largely among academics. *Dollars and Sense* was founded in 1974 to provide clear economic explanations to readers not economically trained. Their publications are also widely used for teaching by RPE academics. The Institute for Women's Policy Research was founded to provide research-based results for intervention into both public policy debates and academic debates on the socio-economic situation of women.

While there are always different self-understandings by different practitioners of any paradigm, this has been particularly true for the Social Structures of Accumulation (SSA) current of RPE. Some present it as a mix between Marxism and American Institutionalism (and some of those use it specifically to disassociate themselves from the label of Marxism). Others present it as consistent with Marxism as a 'mid-level theory' between Marx's overall abstract theory of capitalism and the concrete institutional analyses that Marx carried out and which Marxism requires. As SSA never established a journal nor supporting organization and remained a current, its nature is often understood to be defined by two books, Gordon et al. (1982) and Kotz et al. (1994). But hundreds of papers that self-identify as lying within the SSA paradigm have been published or presented over the last three decades, and so the interpretation and use of the paradigm is more widespread and diffuse than that. Its central concept is that in some periods capitalism's institutions are coherent, and this has allowed rapid capital accumulation, while between these periods incoherence has erupted giving rise to crises until new coherent capitalist institutions are established. In the last decade a major shift to the foundations of the paradigm has been introduced by some adherents. They view the former formulation as confounding the issue of the rate of capital accumulation with the issue of the sustainability of the circuits of capital. They argue instead that there are basically two medium-term sustainable capitalist institutional structures, each with a different primary crisis tendency. The post-World War II type gives more rapid capital accumulation, while the neoliberal type has slower accumulation but nevertheless institutional coherence and hence medium-term sustainability (Kotz et al., 2010).

The largest OL group in US RPE is the 'Monthly Review school', named for their journal which was first published in 1949, although the school's defining theory was not developed and presented until 1966 (Baran and Sweezy, 1966). Also called the 'Monopoly Capital school', its core tenet is that capitalism has restructured itself since the time of Marx and Engels to a position where monopolies are the 'dominant element' in the economy. Further, Monopoly Capitalism produces greater surplus (see Baran and Sweezy, 1966, p. 10 for their explanation of their switch from Marx's concept of surplus value to 'surplus') than the prior competitive capitalism, and this has caused the primary contradiction within capitalism to have changed from Marx's time to being the absorption of the surplus. Much Marxist political economy rejected this version of underconsumptionism as inconsistent with Marx's value theory. The current editor of *Monthly Review* has given the most sophisticated defence of the school's basic position in Foster (1986), but it remains disputed.

Monthly Review and later *Monthly Review Books* have played an important role in supporting US Marxist RPE during its decline. A combination of energy, principled radicalism and a policy of promoting a non-academic accessible writing style whilst publishing many Marxist points of view other than their own (and devoting only a small part of their total publishing to the question of the theory of Monopoly Capitalism) have given them a readership much larger than merely the supporters of Monopoly Capital theory. They have consistently opposed the drift of many former NL currents ever further away from Marxism and, in particular, have given attention and space to the issue of class (as one of many issues addressed), which almost, though not quite, disappeared from large parts of RPE over its decline.

Science and Society is the next most influential RPE journal coming out of the OL. Published since 1936, it was loosely associated with the Communist Party of the USA during the rise and early decline of US RPE. It now describes itself as a journal of Marxist scholarship that does not adhere to any particular school of contemporary Marxist discussion.

Founded in 1941, the Association for Social Economics (ASE) is an RPE organization whose mandate is to seek to explore the ethical foundations and implications of economic analysis, along with the individual and social dimensions of economic problems, and to help shape economic policy that is consistent with the integral values of the person and a humane community. Given that this is consistent with RPE in general, the ASE publishes articles by, and has a membership that includes, people from all currents in US RPE. Among all the perspectives that appear in the articles in its two journals or are presented in its conferences, various interpretations of American Institutionalism have some degree of predominance, though nothing even beginning to approach hegemony. While as noted above American Institutionalism has permeated to one degree or another all US RPE, the ASE is the largest RPE group that could be broadly called Institutionalist.

Founded in 1979, the Association for Institutionalist Thought is much smaller than the ASE, more specifically and consciously Institutionalist and radical, and has no journal. Its members draw most heavily on the work of Veblen, but also on Dewey, Ayres, Commons, Mitchell and others 'as a basis for their investigation of social problems'. Some members have been more influenced by and are sympathetic to (some of) the views of Marx, while others more by NL-inspired RPE. Dugger (1989) presents a discussion by a collection of authors of the issues of concern to, and the general framework of, Radical Institutionalist.

A final current of relative weight in heterodox economics in the USA today is Post Keynesian economics. It is debated by both its practitioners and those in other radical currents whether this should be thought of as radical. Noting that the origin of the word 'radical' is from the Latin word for 'roots', it is argued that the near exclusive Post Keynesian focus on money and finance precludes it from analysing the real roots of capitalism's problems which lie in its particular form of social production and distribution. On a more applied level, almost all Post Keynesians advocate reforms that could be carried out within the frame of capitalism, and a large number of Post Keynesians consciously advocate a reformed 'more humane capitalism'. On the other hand, particularly those Post Keynesian who describe themselves as radical see their reforms as part of a process, as transitional or 'revolutionary reforms'. They argue that social change does not come about as a 'big bang' result of perfect policy prescriptions (including post-capitalist prescriptions), but rather from a back and forth process of the change of existing institutions and social consciousness. Capitalism will not be replaced by a more humane system unless people fight to change it and, given that most people in the First World support capitalism despite their discontent with many of its consequences, they will not begin to learn to fight for a better world around a call to overthrow capitalism.

The *Journal of Post Keynesian Economics*, founded in 1978, is the leading US journal publishing Post Keynesian research, though such research is also published by many other journals in the USA, including several of the radical political economy journals mentioned above. The Levy Institute and the Political Economy Research Institute (PERI) are two broadly Post Keynesian institutions important to RPE in the USA today. The latter is more representative of the current of 'radical Post Keynesians' that was referred to above although, as always, neither is the work at PERI hegemonically dominated by a radical Post Keynesian orientation, nor is that orientation entirely absent from some Post Keynesian works from other institutions. And, once again, it is important to stress the degree of mixing of ideological currents in US RPE; PERI, for example, has significant NL and Marxist elements (varying from author to author) mixed in with its Post Keynesianism.

In a context for the discipline of economics as a whole in which the mainstream, pure neoliberal or otherwise, exerts an extraordinary stranglehold, the fate of US RPE is itself of great significance, not least because of the extent to which orthodoxy's disciplinary monopoly derives from the Americanization of economics. This comment must not be understood to imply that the global prospects for Marxist political economy and RPE mechanically depend upon the attempt to roll back the near hegemony of the mainstream in the USA and to promote its RPE as an alternative. What is important to understand is the relation between radical alternatives to the status quo and progressive ones, for it is this that makes the state of this small current so important even in the short run. It exerts an undue influence, for good or for bad, as opposition to the US orthodoxy or, at times, complicit with it both in analytical content and focus of subject matter (according to the extent of US centricity). The decline of, and directions taken by, US RPE have been major problems not only for the more coherent but smaller current of Marxist political economy, but also for the broader and larger group of progressive economists, in just the same way that the decline of US radicalism more generally has been a cause as well as an effect of the decline in global progressive outcomes.

47. The rate of profit

Simon Mohun

The rate of profit per year is defined as profits (an annual flow) divided by capital advanced (a cumulated stock of past investments). While the definition seems precise, there is a great deal of ambiguity over what to include. The numerator, profits, can conceptually be considered as anything between all net output that is not wages to a narrow accounting definition of what remains after all obligations have been met. As regards the denominator, Marx included wages, because wages were payment for labour power which was subsequently consumed in the labour process as actual labour performed. In reality, wages are typically paid in arrears as workers are compelled to extend credit to capitalists, and (along with circulating means of production) are small relative to the stock of fixed capital. So the denominator, capital advanced, is conventionally a measure of money tied up in fixed assets and inventories. What definition is appropriate is ultimately dependent on the purpose of the analysis for which it is required.

As a measure of the return to capital advanced, the rate of profit is a crucial statistic for a mode of production based on profitability. Competition will tend to equalize all rates of profit through capital flows from less to more profitable activities but, at any point in time there will be a range of individual profit rates dispersed around such a notional equalized rate. In contrast, the aggregate or macroeconomic rate of profit for the economy as a whole is a weighted average of individual rates of profit (the weights being the proportions of capital advanced by each individual firm to the total capital advanced in the economy, both evaluated at the prevailing prices). It is most easily measured as the proportion of net output not returned as wages to the aggregate fixed capital stock. Since this macroeconomic rate of profit is a measure at any point in time of how profitable all firms are relative to the total fixed capital stock, it can be considered as a measure of the profitability of 'capital in general', and this rate of profit is generally used in empirical work.

LTRPF IN HISTORICAL CONTEXT

Marx's law of the tendency of the rate of profit to fall (henceforth LTRPF) is one of the most celebrated and controversial aspects of his work. It touches on what is meant by a tendential law, it presumes a particular approach to technical change and it is closely related to his theory of crisis. Curiously, it took some time for this to be established. Crisis (whether of profitability or underconsumption or disproportionality) was originally interpreted as an expression of the contradictions of capitalism, realized through the anarchy of the market as a break or interruption in the circuits of capital. But by the end of the twentieth century, the LTRPF as the generator of crises was one of the defining features of 'orthodox' Marxism. And it was interpreted as a matter of necessity: the accumulation of capital was necessarily punctuated by crises because the LTRPF was necessarily produced by that same accumulation. Without an argument for necessity, the way was considered open for reforms of capitalism that could manage accumulation and avoid crises. So intertwined with the argument for necessity are subtexts concerning orthodoxy, fidelity to Marx, revisionism and reformism, but space precludes further consideration of these.

However, the argument for 'necessity' is complex. Rather than a logical deduction from a priori axioms, the Hegelian tradition interprets 'necessity' as something that is 'real'. That is, a tendential law explains real patterns of capital accumulation as rational, as theoretically comprehensible, but it does not say anything about what other patterns of accumulation might be possible. A major difficulty in the arguments about the LTRPF is a lack of clarity in the distinction between necessity in this Hegelian sense, and necessity as a logical deduction, and this lack of clarity is a recurrent theme in what follows.

The idea of a falling rate of profit was not specific to Marx. It was commonplace in the political economy of the first half of the nineteenth century, deriving from the work of Smith and Ricardo. For Ricardo, the rate of profit would fall because of diminishing returns to land and an unchanging technology of production. As cultivation spread to land of inferior quality, landlords of better quality land could extract more rent; with wages given by subsistence requirements, profits would therefore be squeezed until the incentive for accumulation disappeared entirely, and the economy entered a stationary state. Marx replaced the 'natural' determinants of rent (diminishing returns), wages (biological subsistence) and profits (a residual) with social determinants (including organizations of labour processes in industrial production that generated productivity increase). In so doing, he replaced the Ricardian vision of falling profitability and long-run stagnation with a different vision of profitability that depended not on stagnationist tendencies but on the dynamism and technical progressivity of capital accumulation.

LTRPF: THE ISSUES

Expositions of the LTRPF occur in a number of different frameworks, but there are two positions that between them embrace most of the arguments. What they have in common is an interpretation that Marx considered that the rate of profit would indeed actually fall (but see Reuten, 2004). What divides them is their assessment of the cogency of what they see as his argument.

One position (sometimes dubbed 'fundamentalist') argues that the LTRPF is an empirical law generated by technical change; the rate of profit is 'really' falling, and should the empirical evidence show the contrary, then either there is something wrong with the measurement of what is shown or this contrary evidence is but a temporary deviation from the long-run trend. The opposite extreme (sometimes dubbed 'Sraffian' or neo-Ricardian) argues on the basis of the individual behaviour of profit-maximizing capitalists that Marx was wrong in his argument that the rate of profit would fall. If it falls, it cannot do so for the technical change reasons that Marx gave, but only in response to wages rising more than in proportion to productivity. So, in the extreme case of a constant real wage rate, the fundamentalist position is that the rate of profit must fall because of technical change, and the Sraffian position is that the rate of profit cannot fall in the presence of technical change.

These two positions frame much of the debate, but they are both misleading. The approach taken here will emerge out of consideration of five issues:

1. The nature of technical change: individual capitalists innovate in order to outcompete their rivals. Innovations increase labour productivity through reorganizations of the labour process that increase the means of production per worker. The innovating capitalist will therefore be able to sell at a lower value and take extra market share. What is the adequacy of this description of innovation?
2. Innovation and the rate of profit: how does innovation impact on the rate of profit? How should the fundamentalist and the Sraffian arguments be assessed?
3. Profitability and crisis: does a falling rate of profit lead to crisis?
4. Measurement: how should the variables in the argument be measured (in labour values or in prices, and if the latter, then which)?
5. Empirical analyses: what is the empirical time-path of the rate of profit?

THE NATURE OF TECHNICAL CHANGE

Why does technical change have to involve the substitution of non-labour for labour inputs? Profit-maximizing capitalists are interested in any viable cost reductions, so that it is hard to see why labour costs should be privileged over non-labour costs. But putting the matter like this rests on a confusion between the two senses of 'necessity' mentioned earlier. As a matter of logic, no costs are privileged. Yet historical development has indeed seen a fall in the proportion of production labour costs to total costs, and this historical development has to be theoretically comprehended.

Were other types of technical change to occur in a historically significant manner, they too would have to be theoretically comprehended. This immediately raises the challenge of how to understand contemporary technical change in the service sector, in which many outputs are inseparable from the labouring activity that produces them. This strongly suggests that there is a historical specificity to Marx's own explanation, in which the cotton industry was particularly important, and that later developments in capitalism require his method rather than his specific answers.

INNOVATION AND THE RATE OF PROFIT

A common ('fundamentalist') argument runs as follows. Competition will force the generalization of an innovation across all capitalists, so that in the aggregate, the value of capital advanced rises. Since constant capital (in the denominator) can in principle rise without limit, but surplus value (in the numerator) is bounded (absolute surplus value by the length of the working day, and relative surplus value because the value of labour power cannot go to zero), then the rate of profit must necessarily fall.

There are a number of difficulties with this. First, there are counteracting tendencies to the LTRPF. Marx identified five: raising the rate of exploitation, cheapening the elements of constant capital, depressing wages below the value of labour power, relative overpopulation and foreign trade. The last three are somewhat eclectic, and the list could be added to with little difficulty. The problem rather lies with the first two, for it is not obvious why they are 'counteracting', since they are intrinsic to the processes that produce the LTRPF. This in turn raises the more general question of what is a tendency and what is a counteracting tendency.

One way this can be understood is to focus on the circuit of capital as an organizing category. The process of production converts productive capital into commodity capital of greater value. Value is added to the value of productive capital, that is, the pre-production process values. Only when post-production process outputs are sold are new values realized. So changes in values (falls in the value of labour power raising the rate of surplus value, and/or cheapening the elements of constant capital) are counteracting because they require the impact of circulation for their establishment. What is fundamental is the change in labour productivity, a process that is prior to the consequent changes in values. This locates the LTRPF, not as an empirical fact, but as a tendency of the production process considered abstractly, before the effects of circulation are considered. It identifies the LTRPF and its counteracting tendencies as a way of organizing thinking about how the rate of profit is formed in reality through the structures and processes of capital accumulation. An analogy sometimes used is the law of gravity: everything tends to fall to the ground. There are counteracting tendencies such that, for example, people and buildings stay upright, but the processes that give rise to these cannot be understood except on the prior basis of the law of gravity.

This same approach explains movements in the compositions of capital. For Marx, it was definitionally true that the only way to gain a productivity increase in the production of a commodity was to increase the mass of means of production per worker. He called this ratio the 'technical composition of capital' (TCC), and, given his definition of innovation, the TCC must rise over time. But in value terms matters are more complicated, because the translation of a rise in a ratio theoretically denominated in use values to one denominated in values depends on how the patterns of (productivity enhancing) innovation reduce unit values. This clearly affects the conversion of the TCC into a value ratio. One way to proceed is to abstract from the effects of productivity increases on values. Then the TCC becomes, in Marx's terminology, the 'organic composition of capital' (OCC), a ratio of constant to variable capital at pre-production process values, and if the TCC rises, the OCC must necessarily rise. Allowing feedback effects of the fall in values resulting from productivity increases converts the OCC into the 'value composition of capital' (VCC). Marx successfully formulated the difference between the OCC and the VCC, but asserted that as the OCC rose, the VCC would also necessarily rise, if not by as much. The pattern of productivity increases and the consequent falls in unit values are contingent, so that movements in the VCC can diverge from movements in the OCC. In general, one would expect the two to move together. But empirical actuality and logical necessity are not the same, and the interpretation of Marx's assertion depends on which sense of 'necessity' is used.

The OCC is measured in pre-production values, and hence is the index that pertains to the process of production itself. The VCC allows for the feedback of circulation and the establishment of new values. Hence the OCC is relevant to the LTRPF and the VCC to the counteracting tendencies. Overall then, the issue is not one of the simultaneous consideration of a multiplicity of different factors that impinge on the quantitative determination of the rate of profit. It rather concerns the sequential order of determinations at successively lower levels of abstraction to make sense of a complex yet determined concrete reality (Fine, 1992b).

A further difficulty with the effect of innovation upon profitability is commonly encountered in the Sraffian literature. Suppose the real wage is constant. Why would innovation take place at all, if it results in lower profits after the innovation is generalized? One appealing response is to say that competition forces the issue; each individual capitalist innovates to obtain a temporary advantage, but the actions of all, taken together, produce a fall in the rate of profit, behind the backs, as it were, of each individual capital. This argument is, however appealing, logically incorrect. The Okishio theorem shows that, provided the real wage is constant, the overall outcome after the innovation is generalized cannot lower the rate of profit (Roemer, 1981). This result depends upon the specification of a linear technology, a particular notion of competition, and an equilibrium methodology establishing prices of production that support an equalized rate of profit. Then whatever are the new equilibrium prices consequent upon a technical change, the (equalized) rate of profit can be no lower than the (equalized) rate of profit that obtained prior to the innovation, as long as the real wage is constant. In this approach, the only way to guarantee a fall in the rate of profit is through a rising real wage rate; then labour-saving technical change might be considered a counteracting tendency (Himmelweit, 1974).

As an exercise in the comparative statics of equilibrium prices, the Okishio theorem is well established. But its relevance to the LTRPF is controversial for three reasons. First, methodologically, its simultaneous equation approach is different from Marx's sequential successive determinations approach, and this requires some caution in identifying causality. Second, as a matter of logic, to assume a constant real wage (an unchanging basket of use values) is quite different from assuming a constant value of labour power (an unchanging amount of social labour time represented by what workers receive for the sale of their labour power). Third, and empirically, the theorem fails accurately to reflect historical patterns of both competition and capital accumulation. The typical historical pattern of accumulation and technical change exhibits rising labour productivity, rising compositions of capital, falls in the value of labour power, rises in the rate of exploitation and rises in the real wage. Assuming a constant real wage means that all the gains of technical change accrue to capital, and historically this is just not true.

PROFITABILITY AND CRISIS

It is not obvious why a falling rate of profit should in and of itself lead to crisis. Forward-looking competing capitals will try to do the best they can whatever the prevailing conditions of general profitability. If the general rate of profit falls to 5 per cent from 10 per cent, say, then nothing is implied, other than that less money can be made today than yesterday. For this to result in an interruption in the circuit of capital (through, for example, cash-flow problems creating difficulties in meeting obligations such as servicing past debt), more information is required on how firms have financed their past and current activities. And different methods of financing are historically contingent: sometimes they will lead to crisis and sometimes they will not. Hence falling profitability alone will not result in crisis; greater specificity and more detail (at lower levels of abstraction) are required in order to show whether and how crisis occurs.

MEASUREMENT

In Marx's theory of value, at the level of capital in general, commodities are denominated in money, formed out of the ratio of the value of the commodity in question to the value of money. Marx generally took the latter to be gold with an assumed value of unity, so that the value of a commodity was the same numerically whether measured in units of socially necessary labour time or in units of money. Prices thus formed ('direct' prices or 'simple' prices) are incompatible with the formation of a general rate of profit through flows of capital in competition. So the notion of a value rate of profit (as the ratio of surplus value to constant capital, both measured in units of socially necessary labour time) is not logically coherent, unless two conditions hold. First, profits are equal to surplus value divided by the value of money, and second, the sum of the money invested in non-labour inputs is equal to the sum of those non-labour inputs measured in units of socially necessary labour time divided by the value of money. In general, these two conditions cannot both hold. This problematizes the significance of the value rate of profit.

One response is to assert the irrelevance of value analysis to economic analysis and to propose an analysis based entirely on prices. In the Sraffian approach, labour values are indeed unnecessary, and arguments such as the Okishio theorem proceed as expositions of the implications of price of production equilibria. What is lost from this excision of the labour theory of value is any notion that total value added represents total labour time expended. The labour theory of value is thereby mis-identified with a theory of equal exchange. A second response is to argue that the rate of profit in terms of prices is a more concrete expression of the value rate of profit. Retaining the notion of profit as unpaid labour time then requires some account of the unequal exchange that quantitatively transforms constant capital from value terms (for some value of money) to price terms, and a precise and convincing account of this quantitative transformation has not thus far been forthcoming. A third response is to argue that this second response is misconceived. The labour theory of value requires both that aggregate value added exactly represents total social labour time expended, and that the value of labour power is the money wage multiplied by the value of money. Then aggregate profit exactly represents unpaid labour time. This framework applies to any set of prices, not only the equal exchange prices necessary for the meaningfulness of the value rate of profit, and not only the unequal exchange equilibrium prices of production necessary for the Okishio theorem. With generalized unequal exchange, unlike in the other responses, the labour theory of value retains its explanatory power in the empirical analysis of aggregate relations of production for any prices whatsoever. The higher order determinations and abstractions thereby retain their encompassing explanatory power (Foley, 1986; Mohun, 1994).

EMPIRICAL ANALYSES

The art and science of empirical work are not easy. Research must show how theory can comprehend the data. But at the same time, great care must be taken to identify any anomalies that appear to contradict the fundamental determinations of the theory. Adding immunizing ad hoc explanations in the face of anomalies renders theory tautological and thereby discredits it as a theory. But neither is theory merely description of empirical reality. It is a self-determined articulation of concepts which can explain significant features of the historical processes of capital accumulation and technical change. Successful explanation is then confirmatory of the theory, but anomalies must always be interrogated to understand whether they can ultimately be understood by the theory or whether they undermine the theory.

There has been considerable empirical work on the rate of profit through the last quarter of the twentieth century, mostly focused on the US economy because of the long runs of data that exist for the USA (for example, Weisskopf, 1979; Moseley, 1991; Duménil and Lévy, 1993, 2004a; Mohun, 2006, 2009). The first issue concerns the reliability of that data. For the US economy, productive and unproductive labour can only plausibly be estimated from 1964, and the distinction relies upon combining rather different data sets using annual data. If the distinction is ignored, then quarterly data are available from 1948, and annual data from 1929. Prior to 1929, the data have to be drawn from a variety of sources. While aggregate annual net output and wage data are reasonable back to around 1890, the fixed capital stock data prior to 1925 are much less reliable.

Different studies are rarely directly comparable, sometimes because the time periods are different, but more generally because the data are very sensitive to different assumptions made. These include whether analysis should consider the whole economy, the corporate sector or just the manufacturing sector; whether the focus should be on the pre-tax or the post-tax rate of profit; how general government (supplying goods and services financed by taxes and debt) should be treated, and how the self-employed should be treated; whether (all, some or none of) the imputations in national accounts data should be eliminated; whether the housing stock should be included in the stock of fixed capital; and what sort of data should be used (labour values derived from input-output tables or national accounts data, and if the latter whether at historical or replacement cost prices). Further, different studies have different aims, ranging from whether the data support some interpretation of Marx to how a Marxist approach can understand what has happened. Choices made are not arbitrary, but depend upon theoretical presuppositions, and upon what the analysis is designed to show.

A second (but not independent) set of issues concerns the decomposition of the rate of profit. To consider the rate of profit as the ratio of the rate of surplus value to the VCC (essentially following Marx) raises the issues of how, if at all, to account for the distinction between productive and unproductive labour, and whether it makes conceptual sense to think of a Marxian rate of profit (the outcome of considering productive labour alone, and, perhaps, the OCC rather than the VCC) as behaving differently from the actual rate of profit. Of course, the same issues arise with an alternative decomposition of the rate of profit into the product of 'profit share' (the ratio of profits to net output) and 'capital productivity' (the ratio of net output to the fixed capital stock), but this decomposition is in many ways easier to use. The profit share depends on the ratio between real net output

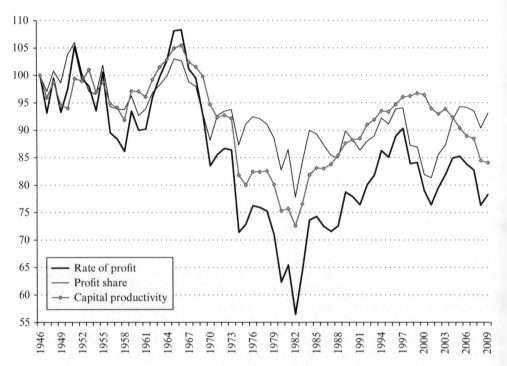

Figure 47.1   The US rate of profit and its decomposition, 1946–2009 (1946 = 100)

per hour, or labour productivity, and the real wage rate per hour, rising (falling) when the former increases faster (slower) than the latter. Capital productivity depends upon the ratio of labour productivity to real fixed capital per hour (a proxy for the TCC), rising (falling) when labour productivity increases faster (slower) than the TCC proxy. (It also depends upon a price term, neglected for simplicity.) The advantage of this decomposition is now transparent, for it focuses directly on the relationship between labour productivity and the TCC, and labour productivity and the real wage. The classical Marxian decomposition is less transparent in this regard.

Figure 47.1 extends the data presented in Mohun (2006) to cover the period 1946 to 2009. In terms of the major choices that have to be made, the data are pre-tax, at current prices, for the whole US economy; General Government and Private Households are excluded entirely, as are all imputations except employer contributions for health and life insurance; and the income of the self-employed is divided into a wage and a profit component. Profits are defined as net domestic product less wages, and the fixed capital stock includes tenant-occupied residential structures and inventories.

Several features are of interest. First, there is no simple long-run tendency for the actual macroeconomic rate of profit to fall. Rather, the post-war period was characterized by a sustained downswing (1966–82), and a sustained upswing (1982–97). Second, a focus on secular rather than cyclical movements throws a sharp light on capital productivity. There were periods when it was broadly flat (1946–53) so that there was little change in the increase in the TCC required to elicit a given productivity increase. There were periods when it fell (1953–58, 1966–82, and 1999–2009), so that given increases in labour productivity required the TCC to rise more rapidly (the classical Marx case). And there were periods when it rose (1958–66 and 1982–99) when labour productivity rose faster than the rise in the TCC. Moreover, while the profit share and capital productivity tend to move together, this is not true for the years 2000–09. Third, there have been just two significant crises since 1946. One of these, culminating in 1982, was a classic falling rate of profit crisis. The other, beginning in 2007, was more ambiguous.

CONCLUSION

Arguments concerning the LTRPF and its counteracting tendencies require some care, both logically and methodologically. The method of determination through greater concretization is a difficult one, because the successive abstractions are both ordered and defined each in relation to all the others. Further, greater concretization can produce effects that appear to contradict higher order abstractions. But those effects still derive their meaning through the higher order abstractions and their determination (that buildings stay up does not negate the law of gravity). Further, this self-reflexivity of the whole nexus of abstractions and their development does not mean that the articulation of concepts cannot be investigated for logical coherence; neither does it mean that their articulation is arbitrary. The ultimate test is whether that articulation comprehends and illuminates actual concrete historical development. Neither the fundamentalist nor the Sraffian approaches pass that test.

The LTRPF is an essential part of the theoretical framework with which to comprehend the world. But it is only a part, and it should not be interpreted as some sort of mechanistic empirical law of a falling profitability. Empirical reality, just like the theory that has to comprehend it, is both richer and more complex than that presupposed by any mechanistic interpretation of the LTRPF as an empirical law. The LTRPF and its counteracting tendencies provide a framework, but no more than that. The challenge then is to explain the historical reality of significant periods both of falling and of rising profitability.

48. The regulation approach

Stavros D. Mavroudeas

The regulation approach was pioneered in France in the 1970s by political economists including Michel Aglietta (1979), Alain Lipietz (1985) and Robert Boyer (1990), investigating capitalism's long-term dynamics of change and stability. It enjoyed considerable international impact until the 1990s when its influence receded. However, it continues to command considerable influence in certain areas of Radical Political Economy. Moreover, concepts coined by the regulation approach, such as Fordism and post-Fordism, have acquired a life of their own and are being employed in several fields (for example, regional development, consumption and labour process theory).

Regulation's popularity stemmed from its purported ability to provide an intermediate analysis which would gear abstract Marxist Political Economy to analyse concrete historical processes. In addition, it promised to resolve the structure-agency riddle and unify the analyses of economics and politics under capitalism. These expectations were not fulfilled, and the current state of demise of the regulation approach is testimony to this.

Regulation's declared aim is the analysis of the crisis-ridden process of capitalist development. It is argued that crises, far from leading to the collapse of capitalism, generate structural transformations that facilitate its survival and longevity. Systemic contradictions aggravate social antagonisms and produce economic failures, which dictate significant reconfigurations of the system's modus operandi in order to secure its existence. The key to this survival is the support to capitalist economic relations by appropriate institutional frameworks. Underneath this assumption lies the belief that capitalism's purely economic mechanisms are unable to secure its reproduction (Jessop, 2001, p. 5). However, for regulation, these institutional supports are not generated by a general mechanism but are always conjunctural historical products.

Regulation's starting point, then, places heavy emphasis on historical specificities and institutions, while historical accidents play a far more important role than in classical Marxism. Institution-building is, ultimately, considered as the prolonged but impermanent solution to systemic contradictions but, despite their importance, the regulation approach lacks an explicit theory of institutions. Finally, its emphasis on the bumpy, but ultimately successful, reproduction of the system mars regulation as a functionalist approach.

THEORY AND CONCEPTS

In order to study this crisis-cum-transformation process regulation constructs its fundamental conceptual pair:

(a) The 'Regime of Accumulation' (RoA) reflects the way surplus is distributed between capital and labour in each period so that production is coordinated with demand. It encompasses the essential economic conditions (technology, the labour process and the combination between the departments of production) for the operation of the system and is posited at the level of given economic structures.
(b) The 'Mode of Regulation' (MoR) designates the institutional forms and social compromises that are necessary for the reproduction of the RoA. The MoR is less determinate than the RoA, since it relies on historically specific factors. It encompasses the modalities of wage determination, the forms of competition and coordination of economic activity, the structure of the international system, the state management of money and the cultures of consumption.

Each RoA is compatible with several potential MoRs, and which one will prevail in practice is an open historical question. Despite this potential flexibility, each MoR is especially compatible with a particular RoA, because the coupling of a RoA with an inappropriate MoR leads to a dysfunctional socio-economic architecture requiring a systemic transformation. The regulation approach recognizes two specific types of RoA:

(a) In 'extensive accumulation' pre-capitalist production processes were incorporated into capitalism's framework without major changes: the traditional forms of production and consumption were not radically recomposed. The coordinated development of the departments producing means of production and means of consumption was achieved with difficulty, and the pace of accumulation encountered recurrent obstacles.
(b) In 'intensive accumulation', which followed, the production process was reorganized radically along capitalist lines, and the workers' way of life was restructured. The two departments of production were integrated, and the pace of accumulation became more stable.

Similarly, two historical MoRs are recognized:

(a) In the 'competitive MoR', more appropriate for extensive accumulation, pure market mechanisms predominate. Thus, output adjusts to price which, in turn, responds to changes in demand. In particular, wages are very flexible and adjust to price movements, so that real wages are either stable or rise slowly.
(b) In the subsequent 'monopolist MoR', more appropriate for intensive accumulation, market mechanisms are modified radically via state intervention. Pure market relations play only a minor role in adjusting social demand and production. These adjustments are exercised mainly through a complex set of institutions, conventions and rules which constantly aim to develop effective demand at the same rate of growth of production capacity. Wages are set according to social compromises between capital and labour (for example, wage changes can follow inflation and productivity growth).

These canons of regulationist analysis have not remained stable. Rather, the regulation approach is infamous for the easy transformations of its theoretical architecture.

It began by slowly distancing itself from Althusserianism and, subsequently, moving towards post-structuralism and post-modernism (see Mavroudeas, 1999). The notion of 'regulation' – inspired from cybernetics (Lipietz, 1997) – itself facilitated the relaxation of Althusserian structuralism. The latter's concept of 'reproduction' argued that structures condition the behaviour of agents in order to ensure their reproduction. The regulation approach introduced degrees of indeterminacy and feedback relations. The MoR encompasses all those relations that motivate the social agents towards fulfilling the roles which the structures attribute to them. However, neither the structures' ability to motivate nor the agents' conformity to them are guaranteed. The agents' actions can diverge from the requirements of social reproduction, and these divergences are resolved by the MoR – unless they accumulate to the point of setting off a major crisis. In the meantime, minor crises help to change the structures until a major crisis breaks out. Additionally, the MoR encompasses relations that are primarily economic but also institutionally organized; thus politics enters the scene.

Aglietta's first definition of regulation's conceptual pair, in his 1974 PhD thesis and its 1979 published version, bore heavy Marxist and structuralist overtones. As Aglietta (1979, p. 380) admitted, these concepts were elaborated as means through which Marx's general theory of capitalism could analyse historically concrete social situations. Hence, he superimposed the law of capital accumulation upon the RoA and the MoR.

Following regulationist works significantly modified this theoretical configuration. The CEPREMAP-CORDES (1977) collective paper discarded the superimposition of the law of capital accumulation and relaxed the one-to-one correspondence between the RoA and the MoR. But even CEPREMAP's definition of the MoR (as the institutional support of the RoA) was later considered too functionalist. Therefore, in later versions it acquired even greater autonomy from the concept of the RoA; for example, the MoR may or may not secure the reproduction of the given RoA. Thus, the MoR became almost equally important and co-determining with the RoA. This became the orthodox regulationist version.

In later works the correspondence between the RoA and the MoR was relativized even further (see Mavroudeas, 1999), with political relations assuming equal importance with the economic, while discursive and ideological elements acquired an increasing status. In Aglietta's initial formulation, the MoR was the economic-cum-institutional meso-periodic basis of social hegemony. In contrast to the RoA, it also covered ideological and political factors. Subsequently, their correspondence became dynamic, since historical contingency could lead to several MoRs being associated with a given RoA. Hence, their relationship was founded simultaneously on the (economic plus institutional) structural level, and on the individual or subjective level (habits, individual actions of the agents and so on). In even later formulations, the MoR was posited almost exclusively within the realm of politics. Thus, it became even more historically concrete and almost totally autonomized from the RoA. Some newer regulationist formulations slid openly towards methodological individualism (for example, Lipietz, 1997), with individual agents becoming the main subjects of the MoR. Social classes disappear almost completely, and are substituted by trans-class social groups of short-term duration. The creation of these groups basically depends upon the individuals' subjective motivation. This change of scope is even more pronounced in other works (for example, Aglietta and Orléan, 1982; Aglietta and Brender, 1984) where class analysis is openly discarded. These conceptual changes have weakened the regulation approach. The definitional obscurity and the equalization of economy and polity have led to the confusion or the conflation of regulation's fundamental concepts of MoR and MoA, as recognized by many regulationists (for example, Boyer, 1989). It is no longer obvious that the RoA is the fundamental and determining aspect in periodizing, with the MoR as its more flexible, institutionally supportive outcome. Because many of the institutional regularities formulated under the concept of the MoR are economic, and because the RoA is also increasingly defined in terms of (contingent) struggle, the two notions tend to be conflated. So there is confusion over levels of abstraction and determination, as well as in fitting the whole scheme to the continuing evolution of capitalism itself.

PERIODIZATION AND STYLIZED FACTS

The regulation approach periodizes capitalism on the basis of the historically contingent correspondence between RoAs and MoAs. From the mid-nineteenth century until World War I, extensive accumulation predominated accompanied by competitive regulation. Mass production was limited as output was produced mainly on numerous small-scale enterprises. In turn, mass consumption was non-existent since workers did not purchase capitalist consumption goods but covered their needs through non-capitalist products (marketable or not). During this period the extraction of absolute surplus value predominated and the subjugation of labour to capital was only formal. The intra-war period is considered as an unstable transitional phase characterized by the emergence of intensive accumulation (Taylorism and mass production), but without mass consumption. The real subjugation of labour to capital was introduced and, with it, the predominance of relative surplus value. The 1929 crisis – perceived as an underconsumption crisis – marks the beginning of this period. Fordism, introduced after World War II, is considered the 'golden era' of contemporary capitalism because it coupled the intensive RoA with its functional counterpart, the monopolistic MoR. Capitalist mass production found its outlets in the workers' mass consumption of capitalist products.

Finally, the regulation approach maintains that, in the 1970s, Fordism enters a crisis and post-Fordism emerges as its successor. This period is characterized by the introduction of new information technologies, small-scale production processes, the relaxation of standardized production tasks, the growing significance of the service sector and new lifestyles as stimuli of consumption. However, neither the crisis of Fordism nor the characteristics of post-Fordism are defined sufficiently clearly. For example, the exhaustion of Fordism is attributed at times to the demand-side (the end of mass consumption and the emergence of fragmented tastes and market niches) and, at other times, to a vaguely explained exhaustion of Fordist modalities of exploitation of the workers. Moreover, nearly thirty years after its purported emergence a coherent definition of post-Fordism has yet to be offered.

The regulationist periodization of capitalism hinges upon highly debatable stylized facts or empirical generalizations. Two of these are critical for the regulationist edifice. First is that mass production (which is being equated with Taylorism) only became dominant in the interwar era. However, Marx himself had correctly posited the real subjugation of labour to capital as simultaneous with the predominance of the extraction of relative surplus value long before the twentieth century, which has been confirmed by later studies (see Brenner and Glick, 1991).

Second is the belief that capitalist products dominated workers' consumption only after World War II. This hypothesis is also unsustainable, since the (capitalist) commodification of the workers' consumption is necessary for the formation of a class of wage labourers and, therefore, for the establishment of capitalism. Indeed, workers' consumption provided a mass market for capitalist products long before the Fordist era, and this mass market was created without an institutionally secured wage. Last but not least, the post-war 'social contract' between capital and labour has been heavily disputed (Mavroudeas, 2003).

If these two crucial stylized accounts do not hold then the importance placed by the regulation approach on both the interwar and the post-war periods becomes difficult to justify. Regulation considers the first period as the harbinger of Fordism, and the second as Fordism per se. Setting aside the unclear historical and analytical case for post-Fordism, Fordism itself represents the main object of study of the regulation approach, and the historical era whose putative specificities have dictated the very form of regulationist theory. Duménil and Lévy (1988) have offered a meticulous examination of these stylized accounts, by comparing the pre-war, interwar and post-war eras for the USA and France and their results, especially for the USA (which was Aglietta's model case) do not support key regulationist claims.

Despite their neatness, the regulationist stylized facts do not stand up to historical scrutiny, which is a grave problem for a theory whose main focus and attraction lies in historical specificity.

A MIDDLE-RANGE THEORY

Regulation is a middle-range theory (Mavroudeas, 1999) which, in contrast to grand theory, either rejects abstract general principles or remains agnostic towards them. A middle-range theory is based on intermediate concepts with a more immediate identification with concrete phenomena. Because of close identification with concrete historical reality, middle-range theories tends to evolve flexibly in response to more or less shifting empirical evidence. However, their explanatory power remains limited by virtue of their selective use of historical evidence and the loss of a general picture of social transformations. These shortcomings pose grave limitations to the analysis of periods of socio-economic change, when relations and processes that were previously significant are downgraded or even disappear altogether.

Regulation belongs to the set of middle-range theories springing out of the crisis of radical theory after the high-point of activism in the 1960s, and which also include flexible specialization and social structures of accumulation. Characteristically, the regulation approach departed from Marxism by maintaining that it needed historical specificity. Attention focused on the post-war period by presuming that major transformations took place which radically changed the modus operandi of capitalism. There was recourse to the concrete, and an attempt to discover within it the appropriately refined theoretical tools. Initially, these drew upon abstract general laws and, later, in conformity to the more general fashion for relativism, eschewing 'essentialism' or its scapegoat – usually economism – deploying intermediate concepts based on a multi-causal framework including the economy, politics, ideology, culture and so on.

In this vein, most regulationist intermediate concepts focused on institutional forms for two reasons. Firstly, institutions offered to disillusioned left intellectuals a suitable explanation for the supposed structural incorporation of the working class within capitalism. Secondly, institutions provide the most appropriate material for the construction of intermediate concepts. They are immediately observable and variegated, and encompass a wide variety of factors (economic, political, cultural, ideological, legal and so on) which can be incorporated at will.

Regulation's historicism and institutionalism were underpinned by the philosophical trends of the times. These trends began with a relativized structuralism and, eventually, evolved towards post-structuralism and post-modernism. In retrospect, the regulation approach failed in its most important aims, as is reflected in its meteoric rise and fall. Instead of unifying economics and politics, it ended up juxtaposing them, and instead of resolving the structure-agency riddle, it degenerated into methodological individualism. Drawing on its middle-range nature, it has incorporated selectively the theoretical fashions of successive periods. Hence, it prioritized economics and structure during its first phase, and politics and subjectivity in its later phases, especially as its postulation of a post-Fordist regime proved theoretically ill-founded and empirically grounded in, at most, a small number of marginal phenomena.

49. Rent and landed property

Erik Swyngedouw

The Marxist analysis of land rent is one of the most intricate, contested and debated themes in the history of Marxist intellectual thought, not least because Marx never completed a full analysis of rent. The third volume of *Capital* and *Theories of Surplus Value* offer the most systematic accounts of Marx's theorization on rent. The contours of the problematic are nevertheless clearly drawn. As Haila (1990) puts it, the main theoretical questions related to the vexed problem of rent are (1) how does (the substance of) rent emerge, that is, why does land have a price, expressed in the form of rent; why and how does land rent vary over space and in time, (2) who or what are its agents, what are their behavioural patterns and mutual social relations, and (3) what is the economic role of rent in the process of capital accumulation and coordination?

The theoretical difficulty resides not only in explaining why land has an exchange value but apparently no value (defined as socially necessary labour time), but also in accounting for its apparent anomalous character in the process of capital accumulation. While land rent constitutes a potentially major source of income for landowners, the private and exclusive ownership of (and therefore monopoly over) land also obstructs the accumulation of capital for which the payment of land rent constitutes a major drain on profits (as both capitalists and workers need access to land for production and reproduction). Competition for and the mobilization of land of different absolute, relative or relational qualities plays a pivotal role both in allocating capital flows as well as in generating extraordinary profits (as, for example, the real estate bubble during the period 2000–07 testifies).

Marx's theory of rent, developed primarily with an eye towards agricultural land and other (natural) resources, but which was subsequently extended to include urban or locational land rent, draws on, but radically reformulates, Ricardo's classical theory of the origin of and differences between agricultural land rents (Fine, 1979). For Ricardo, who takes an embryonic marginalist position, the origin and the level of rent are determined by the differential fertility (naturally given and/or socio-physically improved through capital investment) of agricultural land. Farmers will keep cultivating new lands until the point that the least fertile land will not yield profit. This 'marginal' land, for Ricardo, generates no rent. The difference of yield between the more and the least fertile land constitutes for him both the origin and magnitude of land rent. That difference accrues to the landowner in the form of rent. In other words, for Ricardo, the origin of rent resides fundamentally in the intrinsic, albeit possibly humanly transformed, characteristics of the soil (its fertility). In his analysis, Ricardo necessarily abstracts away from the historically constituted process of the formation of private landownership. His theory was later extended by Johann Heinrich von Thünen, who spatialized rent by including location in the analysis. For von Thünen, land rent is not only determined by the natural character-istics (given or produced) of the soil, but also by the cost of location or, rather, the cost of overcoming the distance and other obstacles (like topography) between the farm or market and the particular plot of land. In the twentieth century, William Alonso would bring this perspective to the theorization of urban land prices and use.

These classical theories of rent were radically revised and reformulated by Marx. For Marx, value does not arise from the 'natural' characteristics of things. These character-istics are a 'free' gift of nature. Value, in contrast, arises from the socially necessary labour time required to produce a given commodity under capitalist social relations of produc-tion. The starting point for Marx is that land – like interest on capital for the owner of money-capital – is an entitlement to the landowner in return for surrendering the use of that land to someone else. The fundamental relationship through which rents arises is a social one, that is, between landowners, on the one hand, and those who wish to make use of the land, on the other (Ball, 1977, 1985). As Marx put it: '[l]anded property is based on the monopoly by certain persons over definite portions of the globe' (*Capital III*, ch. 37).

FORMS OF RENT

The owner of the land will not surrender ownership without proper recompense. However, this understanding of the foundation of rent does not reveal anything about the magnitude of land rent, the origin of landed property or the role of rent in capital accumulation and coordination. Obviously, different pieces of land (whether natural, agricultural or urban) have different and often competing uses, different prices and play, depending on the social relations and struggles that are articulated around them, different roles in different places and at different times.

Determining the magnitude of rent, however, remains theoretically complex and empirically intractable. Marx basically distinguishes between four forms of rent: mon-opoly, absolute, differential rent I (DRI), and differential rent II (DRII) (Harvey, 1999). These different, but interrelated, forms of rent, taken together, determine the magni-tude of land rent. However, each form plays a different role and has a different origin, although all are appropriated by the capitalist landowner. Monopoly rent, as the word suggests, relates to the specific and unique characteristics of a particular piece of land. Consider, for example, how the ownership of a waterfall (under historical-geographical conditions in which hydro-power is an important means of production), a plot of land in the officially designated Champagne region in France or an ice-cream stall near a summer tourist attraction generate surplus profit for the owner by virtue of the unique character of the land or location. Monopoly rents are basically redistributions of surplus value between different forms of capital.

Absolute rent, in contrast, derives from the imperfect mobility of capital as a result of fragmented and dispersed landownership. The latter leads to a situation – in contrast to an otherwise unobstructed equalization of rates of profit across sectors – whereby the organic composition of capital is lower in agriculture because rent takes a part of the surplus value that would otherwise result from greater accumulation, a higher organic composition and productivity increase. The classic example is agriculture where, histori-cally speaking, the organic composition of capital (and hence productivity) was or still is lower than in other sectors. This lower value composition results in a situation whereby agricultural products tend to trade above their price of production and, therefore, yield absolute rent. Here again, absolute rent derives from the distribution of surplus value from sectors with a higher to a lower organic composition of capital as a result of the manner of equalization of rates of profit in a context of dispersed land ownership and monopoly control over land, and the payment of rent as a condition of access to land (Fine, 1979, 1980a).

Until the 1960s, most Marxist thought on rent focused on these two forms of rent. The political implications of this were significant. Most Marxists, like Ricardo, considered landownership as a historically archaic feudal remnant that, although transformed by and incorporated into capitalism, constituted a drain on capital accumulation. It also pitted landowners against both industrial capitalists and tenanted farmers. Landowners were both parasitic on capital accumulation elsewhere and a formidable barrier to the proper functioning of the law of value. Both absolute and monopoly rent expressed the relative political-economic power positions and struggles between landowners and non-owners over the appropriation of the surplus value produced.

This approach has changed since the late 1970s, when greater attention began to be paid to the other two forms of rent that Marx identified. This was also a period during which the theoretical and political attention shifted from a focus on agriculture to urban land rent production and distribution (Scott, 1976). Indeed, the levels of DRI and DRII derive from an entirely different process. These forms of rent refer to the way in which the mobilization of a particular piece of land affects the value of the commodities produced in or through it. In other words, DRI and DRII are strictly parallel to the role of techno-logical and organizational change in determining value as socially necessary labour time (and play similarly important roles in inter-capitalist competition). While it is still the landowner who is entitled to these rents, the origins of these parts of the total land rent are very different. DRI is related to the absolute, relative or relational qualities of land as a means of production: it refers to the 'different qualities' of land with 'equal amounts of capital' invested in it. These differing qualities are the result of given, but usually histori-cally produced, socio-natural differences between different plots of land with respect to their ability to sustain the production of value when mobilized in a specific capital circu-lation process. Indeed, agricultural, resource or urban land of different qualities requires different mobilizations of living labour to produce a given commodity with a given mag-nitude of capital investment. Consider, for example, how oil wells differ in terms of ease of oil extraction depending on, among others, geological conditions. The difference in the average labour time it takes to produce a given quantity of, say, oil or wheat as a result of differential quality of the land (ease of access or fertility) defines the level of DRI. As such, Marx combines Ricardo's theory of rent with his own theory of value as socially necessary labour time. Rent here modifies or represents the mechanism through which the law of value operates, even in a context of dispersed and private monopoly ownership of land that obstructs the equalization of productivities over time through competition and the capital accumulation process. The difference in DRI between two pieces of agri-cultural land resides in the extra surplus value that is generated by cultivating the more fertile (or better located) land.

DRII also derives from different qualities of land. However, in contrast to the dif-ferences underpinning DRI (which assumes a given level of capital investment), DRII derives from 'differential capital investments' in pieces of land of 'equal quality'. In other words, the fertility of agricultural land can be enhanced (and over time greatly so) by capital investment (fertilization, soil engineering, new crops and so on); similarly, the productive capacity of urban land can be improved by new investments in the built environment. This form of investment is strictly speaking identical to other forms of capital investment in the form of technological or organizational improvements in the production process. To the extent that capital investment in the labour process reduces the socially necessary labour time, extra surplus value is generated. Marx defines this surplus, made possible by the sinking of capital into land, as DRII.

In sum, while rent accrues to the landowner by virtue of the monopoly ownership of land, the magnitude of land rent (and hence the price of land) is composed of four distinct components: monopoly and absolute rent, and DRI and DRII. It is empirically extraordinarily difficult to disentangle these four parts in the actual determination and movement of land prices (and controversy over their exact role and status keeps raging), but, analytically speaking, they are both clearly distinct and of fundamental importance in understanding land rent and its role in the capital accumulation process.

It is now also possible to extend the above analysis to locational rent. Urban land rents (those related to the built environment) are forms of locational rent par excellence. The existence of urban rent (that accrues to the owners of houses, factories, infrastructure and the like) too is rooted in a specific social relationship, that is, the private ownership of land. While absolute rent and DRII are identical to the examples above, concerning agricultural land, DRI takes a slightly different form. While DRI as defined above derives from the socio-natural differences of plots of land, DRI in the case of urban rent relates primarily to 'locational' differences. The latter refer to the position of a particular plot of land in relation to all other possible positions and/or to its position within a larger geographical configuration (Swyngedouw, 1992). This locational rent in the case of production, that is, the superior qualities of a particular place to engage a labour process that requires a lower socially necessary labour time than another location and so generates surplus profit, is exactly the source of surplus profit that Marx defines as DRI. What is intriguing here is that 'superior location' does not derive from 'naturally' given conditions but, entirely, from historically and socio-spatially produced conditions. The historically-geographically produced conditions place a specific location in a distinctive (advantageous or disadvantageous) position vis-à-vis other places. Consider, for example, the difference in rent (or land price) between a central Manhattan location, on the one hand, and a rival location on the outskirts of, say, Cairo, on the other. In sum, urban DRI derives from the accrued advantages that have been produced over time as the collective outcome of many successive rounds of capital investments in space and its associated uneven development. These collectively or socially produced 'locational' effects have a great (and, over time, an increasing) effect on land rents, something that can be cashed in 'freely' by the landowner, irrespective of his or her own capital investment in the land.

It follows that all manner of individual investments, collective interventions or state policies directly affect the magnitude of DRI. In addition, this opens up a vast terrain of possible trade-offs or choices for capitalists. For example, they can decide either to invest in superior technologies or to relocate to cheaper locations (or do both simultaneously). Much of the changing geographies of capital accumulation and its associated dynamic mosaic of uneven geographical development derive exactly from the space/technology trade-offs that capitalists make on a daily basis (Harvey, 1999).

RENT AND CAPITAL ACCUMULATION

Now that we have summarized Marx's theory of the origins and magnitude of land rent and some of its applications, we are in a position to explore the vital but highly contradictory roles that land rent plays in the capital accumulation process. Land rent constitutes a drain on capital accumulation in the sense that, while value is generated through the labour process, rent is appropriated by the landowner purely by virtue of ownership of the land. From this vantage point, landownership is fundamentally parasitic. Moreover, it pits landed capital against productive capital, often resulting in frenzied inter-capitalist struggles between landowners and other capitalists. However, this parasitic function is complemented by a series of vitally important functions of landownership.

First, landownership serves a decidedly ideological function as it helps to legitimize the commodification and private ownership of everything as the basis of and for social organization. Although landownership constitutes a barrier for capital accumulation (productive capital would be more profitable if it did not have to surrender some of its profits to landowners), ownership of land (in the form of resources, farmland, housing and the like) is one of the pillars of a system of generalized commodification and private ownership of means of production and reproduction. Second, land rent also plays powerful economic and regulatory roles in capital accumulation. The rent relation orders the uses of land and organizes the spatial division of labour through its influence in allocating different moments, activities and socio-technical forms of production to different places and, as such, land rent organizes and regulates the landscapes of production and consumption. Third, through this allocation mechanism, land rent helps to coordinate capital investment by assigning different forms of capital to distinct locations and activities, producing an unequal and uneven spatial division of labour. Finally, rent mediates and helps to regulate the distribution of investment across interest-bearing, productive and landed capital.

All this turns land rent into one of the most powerful and contradictory aspects of the political economy of capitalism. Not only does it pit landed capital against productive and interest-bearing capital (and its associated intra-class conflicts) but it also shapes the conflicts between land for reproductive use (in housing or subsistence agriculture), land for resource exploitation (or ecological reserve), land as a form of capital investment (for landowners), land as a productive asset (comparable to other means of production) and land as a form of fictitious capital that circulates as a purely financial asset (for financial capital).

This complex set of contradictions points to the need for the state (or another extra-economic configuration) to regulate and coordinate the uses of land so that, of all the diverse means of production and reproduction, land is among the most tightly regulated and intensely contested. Not only is landownership (that is, what one can do with one's land) often strictly regulated by the state through zoning, building codes, planning and so on, the state is itself an active agent in land markets (particularly through zoning, infrastructure planning and construction, public investment in urban development, appropriation laws and the like). Needless to say, an intense social struggle unfolds over land use, land rights and access to land. Small changes in the rules governing land can have an extraordinary impact on the level of rent and, consequently, on profits generated through landownership.

RENT, FINANCE AND FICTITIOUS CAPITAL

In recent years, attention has moved to the increasing role of land rent (as claims on future value) and the role of land as a financialized asset. As David Harvey (1974, 1978) argues, titles to land are functioning increasingly as forms of fictitious capital, comparable (albeit not identical) to other financial assets. Rent has become one of the possible forms of generating future claims on value, and land titles have become integral parts of financial capital investment portfolios. Land markets increasingly function as markets in (paper) titles to future returns and they have become an integral part of, often speculative, fictitious capital circulation and accumulation. Arguably, this is the fully developed capitalist form of the mobilization of land. While ultimately still grounded in the formation of absolute, monopoly, DRI and DRII forms of rent, there is a complex and dynamic relation at work under capitalism that combines the continuous production and transformation of locational rents (for example, through speculative real estate urban redevelopment), the production of temporary monopoly rents (cashing in on design, climate, amenities, 'cultural capital' and the like), the involvement of the state in producing geographical configurations that enhance DRI for specific locations and so on. The financial crisis starting in 2007 undoubtedly arose out of the extraordinary speculative carousel of increasing rents while turning these promises into fictitious capital assets through complex derivative financial instruments. As with all forms of fictitious capital formation, these speculative carousels are sustained as long as the promises for securing future value entitlements are maintained. The recent history of global capitalism conclusively shows how land and land rent play a pivotal role in capital accumulation while intensifying the very contradictions that are the signature hallmark of mature capitalism.

50. The Social Structures of Accumulation approach

Stavros D. Mavroudeas

The Social Structures of Accumulation (SSA) approach is a current of contemporary US radical political economy. The latter emerged out of the student militancy and other social movements of the 1960s. These, particularly in the USA, were fomented by the 1973 economic crisis and the Vietnam War. The expansion of radical political economy led to formidable disputes with mainstream economics. This was coupled with the rediscovery of older radical theories, especially those inspired by the Marxian tradition. Remarkably, this new radicalism attempted to renovate these older theories by producing new 'synthetic' versions. Student radicalism slowly trickled into academia and spawned vibrant and influential currents of radical political economy, which flourished until the conservative onslaught of the 1980s. The creation of the Union of Radical Political Economics (URPE) provided an organizational umbrella for these initiatives.

The emergence of radical political economy was a global phenomenon in the late 1960s. For example, at the same time and with very similar aims, influences and assumptions, the Regulation Approach (RA) was proposed in France. As the term suggests, radical political economy was not simply a continuation of the old political economy traditions (mainly Classical, Marxist and institutionalist) but a new breed which combined different versions and theories. One of its main features was a new appetite for the historically concrete as opposed to the abstractness and generality of older traditions. Hence, most of the emerging approaches to radical political economy attempted either to marry contemporary features (and reinterpret those of the past) with grand traditional theory (especially in starting out) or to supersede the traditional (at later stages). This appetite for historical concreteness was expressed in radical political economy's quest for 'intermediate theories' that would bridge the abstract general analyses of the old political economy traditions with everyday reality. The vehicle for these intermediate theories was usually the adoption of a middle-range methodology. Intermediate concepts directly established links between abstract and the most concrete phenomena, often focusing on the relationship between the economy and the social and political institutions prevailing in specific historical periods. Indeed, the re-emergence of Institutionalism was one of the main aspects of radical political economy. In this way, radical middle-range theories were born, and RA and SSA represent the two most popular versions.

SSA's founding hypothesis is that the reproduction of the capitalist system is not based solely on capital accumulation but also requires appropriate institutional structures. This was first tentatively proposed in an essay by David Gordon, and it was followed by a series of books co-authored by Gordon, Edwards, Reich and Bowles (see McDonough et al., 2010 for an account of the evolution of SSA). The main aim of these works was to offer 'an intermediate level of analysis, focusing on the logic of long swings and stages of capitalism' (Gordon et al., 1994, p. 13). The central question was how to explain the fluctuations over capitalism's long-term evolution and, in particular, the emergence of acute economic and social crises. From this stemmed the SSA's emphasis on long-run dynamics and long waves. However, traditional long wave theory (either Marxist or mainstream) was considered too economistic and mechanistic, paying insufficient attention to social aspects and the impact of class struggle. Thus, long waves were replaced by 'long swings' and Institutionalism – borrowing from the traditional Veblenian school but also bordering on the 'new neoclassical institutionalism' (Kotz et al., 1994, pp. 3–5). Although a demand-side perspective was rejected as inadequate on its own, Keynesian influences came through the emphasis on the uncertainty affecting investment decisions: a functional SSA should create security and predictability and, thus, facilitate investment.

Unlike RA, which spread from France all over the world, the SSA remained a predominantly US approach with limited influence elsewhere (see Kotz et al., 2010). Overall, it followed the same trajectory as other radical middle-range theories. After an inauguration followed by high expectations, it experienced a period of consolidation and expansion both in content and appeal. Similar to RA, SSA has expanded to other branches of the social sciences, particularly sociology and regional theory, while withdrawing to a significant extent from economic analysis per se. In contrast with RA, SSA has strengthened its attachment to Marxism and avoided falling under the sway of postmodernism (for more detailed comparisons of SSA and RA see Kotz, 1994b; Mavroudeas, 2006).

As the post-1968 era passed, many of its associated empirical beliefs proved unfounded or fleeting. This has prompted a crisis in almost every radical middle-range theory, because of their close identification with particular empirical foundations. Thus, RA has been unable to define post-Fordism (the supposedly 'new' regime of accumulation) securely and, in the same vein, SSA theorists cannot agree on whether the current period represents a new SSA and, if so, what are its main features (McDonough, 2008). More recent analyses – though not unanimously accepted – argue that there is a new SSA, constructed around neoliberalism, globalization and financialization, one not necessarily promoting rapid economic growth as previously asserted for other newly emerging SSAs (Kotz et al., 2010).

THEORY, CONCEPTS AND PERIODIZATION

SSA's main intermediate concept is the economic, social and political institutions that constitute the environment within which the capital accumulation process operates. These institutions are posited as external to the decisions of individual capitals but they are internal to the macrodynamics of capitalist economies. A period of vigorous accumulation requires the existence of an appropriate SSA. However, every long expansion contains the seeds of its own destruction and, ultimately, both the SSA and capital accumulation collapse, ushering in a possibly long period of stagnation. This is surpassed only when a new SSA emerges. It is posited that the main function of a SSA is to stabilize capital-labour class struggle, intra-capitalist competition and international relations in directions that are functional to the historically specific pattern of capital accumulation. In particular, the construction of different regimes of labour control constitutes the main basis of the SSA approach.

An SSA includes two boundaries:

(a) The 'inner boundary' separates the capital accumulation process itself (the profit-making activities of individual capitals) from their institutional (social, political, legal, cultural and market) framework.
(b) The 'outer boundary' is more fluid since different elements fall within or outside it. It separates the structures and processes that directly and obviously impinge upon the accumulation process (most obviously the economic) from those that affect it only tangentially or occasionally (the non-economic as such).

On the basis of this historically contingent relationship between capital accumulation and its institutional framework, SSA theory distinguishes periods and stages in the evolution of capitalism. In contrast with RA, SSA theory does not propose a universal periodization of capitalism but simply a general toolbox facilitating an appropriate periodization for each country.

The model example was proposed for the USA, with three SSAs. The first extends from the end of the Civil War to the turn of the twentieth century. The second (or monopoly SSA) runs from the beginning of the twentieth century until World War II. The third covers the postwar era. As mentioned previously, there is a debate over whether the neo-conservative wave of the 1980s onwards led to a new SSA and, if so, what are its defining features. Similar to other such radical middle-range theories, the main benchmark – against which other periods are defined – is the postwar era. This SSA, in the case of the USA, is described by three institutional elements affecting the power of capital vis-à-vis labour, foreign countries and US citizens: the 'capital-labour accord', which assured management control and labour peace in exchange for rising wages and job security; 'Pax Americana', which established an international system favourable to US capital; and the 'capital-citizen accord', which protected capitalists' pursuit of profits while covering some basic citizen needs through public sector provision and demand management.

Accordingly, SSA theory constructs elaborate macroeconomic models geared towards empirical testing. In a typical case, Weisskopf (1994) offers two such models: a neo-Marxian model focused on class struggle as decisive for the profit rate, which determines (with a time lag) the rate of accumulation; and a neo-Keynesian model focused on social conditions affecting investors' expectations (through past experience) and, thus, determining demand growth. In these respects, the SSA tends to pick an ambiguous path around emphasizing class struggle between capital and labour as dysfunctional (or not) and class compromise as functional (or not) with, as exemplary illustration, the wage settlement as too high at the expense of profits or too low as the expense of (Keynesian) demand, although other institutionalized factors addressing such dualisms in class relations can be incorporated (over productivity and employment, for example).

SSA AND MIDDLE-RANGE THEORY

SSA theory suffers from the general deficiencies of radical middle-range theories. Its close identification with particular rightly or wrongly emphasized empirical beliefs and the corresponding eclecticism severely curtail its explanatory power. Moreover, its attachment to theory drawn from empirical beliefs associated with particular epochs weakens its analytical power when these epochs pass. With such transformations, intermediate middle-range concepts become notoriously unable to meet their purpose – explaining historical reality – unless the more abstract concepts are amended as history proceeds. As such, the middle-range analytical toolbox tends to become at best a theoretically informed empirical taxonomy. Together with a tendency to theoretical eclecticism – around Keynesianism, Marxism and varieties of Institutionalism – there is a corresponding flexibility in accommodating national and chronological differences and details across national SSAs themselves. Both theoretical and empirical elements tend to be chosen to fit whatever is focused upon as appropriate national characteristics, with the features of US capitalism to the fore.

The SSA approach also suffers from a series of other problems. Its conceptual toolbox is far from elaborate and cannot explain precisely – despite copious attempts (for example, Kotz, 1994a; Reich, 1994) – how an SSA supports accumulation and why expansion and stagnation phases last long and why they end. The gist of its answer is to appeal to the indeterminacy of class struggle, which ends up functioning as a 'black box'. The same holds for the crucial transitions from one regime of labour control to another, for which decisive factors from the labour process through trade unionism to political and institutional forms require close examination of corresponding systemic developments in the rhythms and patterns of accumulation.

In this light, another problem with SSA is the questionable prioritization of the relationship between the capital accumulation process and the institutional framework as the main locus of intermediate analysis. The institutional framework and social, political and ideological relations are a derivative of economic relations. But if stages change when economic are disarticulated from institutional relations then the two are equated. In practice this results in focusing on institutional changes and thus embracing Institutionalism, which relativizes even more the whole analytical toolbox and jeopardizes its explanatory power. After all, given the great flexibility of institutional forms, it can always be argued that whatever course capital accumulation takes it has been institutionally sustained or, as necessary, impeded in case of crisis. This is more a phenomenology than an explanation.

And crisis theory poses another problem. In general, the SSA approach does not ascribe to a particular general theory of crisis (for example, underconsumptionism, disproportionality, falling rate of profit) but argues that economic crisis can take any of these forms depending upon specific historical circumstances that can be tracked empirically. However there is a marked sympathy towards the profit-squeeze theory, with low wage underconsumptionism not far behind, with one or other of these taken as the inevitable consequence of successful accumulation. This is evident in the explanations of the 1973 crisis and its aftermath (for example, Gordon et al., 1998, p. 254) but also in the late nineteenth-century US slowdown (Reich, 1994, p. 43). The profit-squeeze theory of crisis has been proposed by Glyn and Sutcliffe (1972) and, similar to the SSA approach, overemphasizes the role of class struggle. But such theories of crisis have themselves been shown to be inadequate both theoretically and in their scope of factors considered (see Chapter 48).

Finally, there are also problems with several of the SSA's empirical postures. The most controversial is the post-World War II capital-labour accord. It suggests that the postwar 'golden age' was founded on social peace in the shop floor which was itself based on a compromise between capital and labour. Labour dropped revolutionary and political aspirations in favour of wage increases conceded by capital. The SSA approach adopted this argument from an influential USA liberal thesis proposed by Commons and Perlman with particular reference to the USA as an 'American exceptionalism' (McIntyre and Hillard, 2008). SSA fielded a more moderate but also more general version. The accord was 'limited' and did not imply a total cease of class struggle. Further, the accord was not unique to the USA but a global phenomenon in advanced capitalist countries after World War II. It is supposed to have lasted from the early 1950s until the early 1970s. However, this stance has been criticized on both analytical and empirical grounds. Analytically, it has been disputed whether there can be such a long-term truce in class struggle. And the empirical validity of the accord thesis has been disputed even by those sympathetic to the SSA approach. Fairris (1994, pp. 206–7) accepts that (a) the accord was wishful thinking more than a reality and (b) workers' shop floor power actually decreased over the postwar period. McIntyre and Hillard (2008) offer a devastating critique by surveying the labour relations literature and concluding that there was no accord but simply a short-lived truce.

Overall, the SSA approach has offered significant insights into the functioning of modern capitalism. Its focus on historical specificity and its use of empirical evidence has contributed by invigorating contemporary political economy. On the other hand, its middle-range perspective and many of its associated empirical beliefs have limited its contribution. In particular, its general project of constructing an intermediate analysis as a way of understanding both the long-run transformations of the capitalist system and its everyday life – similar to the aims of other radical middle-range theories – has proven to be a dead end.

51. Socialism, communism and revolution

Al Campbell

From the development of his version of historical materialism in the 1840s to his death, Marx consistently referred to the society that would arise from the resolution of the contradictions of capitalism as communism. This can be understood in terms of the use of the terms communism and socialism in Europe in the 1840s. Even as Marx closely mirrored Feuerbach in his materialist rejection of Hegel's idealism, he sharply, and crucially for his theory of history, went on to reject Feuerbach's materialism (and all other previous materialisms) because 'the thing, reality, sensuousness, is conceived only in the form of the *object or of contemplation*, but not as *sensuous human activity, practice*, not subjectively' (*Theses on Feuerbach*). It was from his interaction with the French communist secret societies (and their German émigré reflection, the League of the Just) that Marx discovered the concept of worker self-emancipation, and with that the broader philosophy of praxis that is such an essential element of Marxism. Engels emphasized this in 1890 when explaining why they had called their 1847 work the *Manifesto of the Communist Party*:

> Socialism in 1847 signified a bourgeois movement, communism a working-class movement
> . . . And since we were very decidedly of the opinion as early as then that 'the emancipation
> of the workers must be the task of the working class itself,' [from the *General Rules of the
> International*] we could have no hesitation as to which of the two names we should choose.
> (*Manifesto of the Communist Party* (*MCP*), Preface, 1890 edition)

By the 1870s the usage of these terms by Marxists changed, but they continued to be concerned with the same issue Marx expressed 30 years earlier in his famous comment to Ruge: 'we do not dogmatically anticipate the world, but only want to find the new world through criticism of the old one'. Socialism whose 'historical action' was to come from the ideas of some advocate was referred to as 'utopian', while socialism whose historical action was to arise from the struggles of the working class in its own self-interest was referred to as 'scientific'. Marxists at the time used the terms scientific socialism and communism as synonyms and, while Marx himself generally described the system likely to arise out of capitalism as communism, he too occasionally used the term scientific socialism as a full synonym.

For Marx and his co-thinkers, not only were all social structures in a constant state of change but, in particular, the change from one mode of production to another had to be understood as a transformation that could only occur over time. In his *Critique of the Gotha Programme*, Marx (1875, ch. 1) referred to two phases in the development of a post-capitalist communist society. Concerning the first phase, he wrote: 'What we have to deal with here is a communist society, not as it has *developed* on its own foundations, but, on the contrary, just as it *emerges* from capitalist society; which is thus in every respect, economically, morally, and intellectually, still stamped with the birthmarks of the old society from whose womb it emerges'. In this first phase of a 'co-operative society based on common ownership of the means of production' the key characteristic for Marx was that 'individual labor no longer exists in an indirect fashion but directly as a component part of total labor' under a conscious collective plan. Then 'the individual producer receives back from society – after the deductions have been made – exactly what he gives to it . . . The same amount of labor which he has given to society in one form, he receives back in another.' Marx argued that this 'defect' of the dependence of the organization of work on the exchange of equivalents, a bourgeois principle of right, is 'inevitable in the first phase of communist society'. And it was only by transcending this with a principle of distribution according to need that one could establish a communist society that rested on its own foundations, a communist mode of production, a second and higher phase of communism. 'In a higher phase of communist society . . . only then can the narrow horizon of bourgeois right be crossed in its entirety and society inscribe on its banners: From each according to his ability, to each according to his needs!'

While the final transformation of the usage of the words socialism and communism to that used by most (not all) Marxists today is often ascribed to Lenin, this change was widespread among Marxists and non-Marxist Social Democrats at the beginning of the twentieth century. Lenin went to great lengths to point out that Marx himself did not use the terms that way, but that this was nevertheless their current usage. Socialism became identified with Marx's first phase of communism, and 'full communism' or simply communism with his higher phase of communism.

For Marx, socialism as a phase in the process of the transition from capitalism to full communism would be characterized by the elimination of many of the negative characteristics of capitalism. That capitalist production decisions are made by individual capitals, are directed toward capital accumulation and are coordinated by markets results in two particularly important restrictions on human development. The first is a socially inefficient application of human labour to the transformation of nature. The second is the restriction of workers to being objects of the social process instead of its subjects. And this economic system is enforced through the political rule of the capitalist class. Hence, as seen above, Marx considered as one negation of capitalism that with socialism the means of production would be owned collectively by the producers themselves, thus ending the capitalist system of production decisions and labour allocation. These would now occur according to a plan of conscious cooperation generated by the entire society, acting as a single entity serving its own collective interests. Politically this socialist economic system would be enforced though the democratic rule of the majority, the working class.

Similarly, full communism would be characterized again by a 'criticism of the old', the elimination of further barriers to authentic human development that still existed under socialism. Above all this would involve a change in both the nature of the work by which humans reproduce their conditions of existence, and how they understand their collective and individual need for work. Work time would be further cut as the forces of production increased and 'all the springs of co-operative wealth flow more abundantly'. Work would no longer stunt human development through the 'subordination of the individual to the division of labor, and . . . also the antithesis between mental and physical labor'. Note that this does not mean an end to the division of labour. Most crucially, work would no longer be 'external forced labour'. But for Marx to complete the change in the nature of work to 'really free work' required more than the negative removal of external imposition, it required that work assume a character that could develop the worker's individual and species human potential, and thereby become something that 'has become not only a means of life but life's prime want'.

REVOLUTION

'Between capitalist and communist society there lies the period of the revolutionary transformation of the one into the other' (*Critique of the Gotha Program*, ch. 4). Marx's theory of revolution concerns the how and why of that transformation. The Marxist theory of revolution can be formulated in two ways, as the resolution of the conflict between forces and relations of production, and as the pursuit of human development. The two formulations are not incompatible, and both are repeatedly presented in Marx's work. Either by itself, however, through its emphasis on one aspect of the nature of revolution, is subject to being interpreted in a partial and one-sided way that would be incorrect. For Marx the two formulations are two different aspects of a single theory of revolution.

Revolution as Resolution of the Conflict Between Forces and Relations of Production

Already in 1847 Marx and Engels wrote of how both the conflict between the constantly more powerful forces of production and the relations of production had led to the bourgeois revolution that overthrew feudalism, and the same type of conflict was then unfolding which would lead to the revolutionary overthrow of capitalism:

> At a certain stage in the development of these means of production and of exchange, the conditions under which feudal society produced and exchanged, the feudal organisation of agriculture and manufacturing industry, in one word, the feudal relations of property became no longer compatible with the already developed productive forces; they became so many fetters. They had to be burst asunder; they were burst asunder . . . A similar movement is going on before our own eyes . . . For many a decade past the history of industry and commerce is but the history of the revolt of modern productive forces against modern conditions of production, against the property relations that are the conditions for the existence of the bourgeois and of its rule . . . The productive forces at the disposal of society no longer tend to further the development of the conditions of bourgeois property; on the contrary, they have become too powerful for these conditions, by which they are fettered, and so soon as they overcome these fetters, they bring disorder into the whole of bourgeois society, endanger the existence of bourgeois property . . . [T]he bourgeoisie [has] forged the weapons that bring death to itself. (*MCP*, ch. 1)

The importance of this formulation lies in its emphasis on the contradictions in the current economic, political and social order as the root cause of the revolution and the new future that it engenders. This gives rise to Marx's position indicated above that we can see the general shape of the future (but not the details, due to the importance of historical contingency) by studying the present conflicts and considering likely forms of their resolution. It is also the source of Marx's many famous 'laws of motion of society', again understood as tendential and not mechanically determined outcomes. This position is presented in opposition to the approach of the 'utopian socialists', that a better future will come from the desirable ideas from the minds of social reformers.

The weakness of this formulation, when taken by itself, is its openness to a one-sided interpretation that ignores or greatly underemphasizes the role of humans (in particular, the working class) as the necessary active agents to resolve these contradictions. We saw above that this was at the heart of Marx's break with (or transcendence of) Feuerbach's philosophy. Here care must be taken not to settle for attacking a straw man, in order to understand the depth of what this involved for Marx's theory of revolution. Feuerbach of course knew that social contradictions do not resolve themselves without human agency. But for him the proletariat would exercise a 'passive practice', directed by (German) philosophy. By 1845 Marx and Engels (for example, *Theses on Feuerbach* and *The German Ideology*) moved to replace this weaker idea of human agency in the revolution with the concept of a much more 'active practice' and stronger agency, that of 'self-activity' or 'revolutionary praxis'.

Revolution as Pursuit of Human Development

From their earliest writings Marx and Engels saw socialism/communism, and hence the revolutionary process that would give rise to it, as the result of the human vocation for self-development. Most often this was stated negatively, in terms of the limitations that capitalist society and its relations of production placed on authentic human development. Marx wrote extensively on this, especially in terms of alienation, well before he immersed himself in his detailed studies of how capitalism functioned. Both Marx and Engels maintained this view throughout their lives. Occasionally they stated so positively and directly. Consider the following two from among the many references to this formulation of socialism/communism as the removal of capitalism's barriers to 'the development of all human powers' or 'what is truly human'. From Marx's early work:

> If man draws all his knowledge, sensation, etc., from the world of the senses and the experience gained in it, then what has to be done is to arrange the empirical world in such a way that man experiences and becomes accustomed to what is truly human in it and that he becomes aware of himself as a man. If correctly understood interest is the principal of all morality, man's private interest must be made to coincide with the interest of humanity. (*The Holy Family*)

And from Marx's later work:

> In fact, however, when the limited bourgeois form is stripped away, what is wealth other than the universality of individual needs, capacities, pleasures, productive forces etc. . . . The absolute working-out of his creative potentialities, with no presupposition other than the previous historic development, which makes this totality of development, i.e. *the development of all human powers as such the end in itself.* (*Grundrisse*, Notebook IV, emphasis added)

This presentation of Marx's theory of revolution, less common than the former presentation during the twentieth century, has attracted growing attention today as a complement to that position, particularly as a current in the discussion of 'Socialism of the 21st

Century'. Two works that present this formulation of Marx's theory of revolution at greater length are Draper (1977) and Löwy (2005).

The importance of this formulation lies in its addressing Marx's concern with Feuerbach by placing human self-activity at the centre of his theory of revolution, as Marx held was necessary. It makes clear an aspect of Marx's revolutionary worldview too often downplayed or ignored by some advocates of scientific socialism, what Fromm (1961, p. vi) referred to as Marx's 'faith in man, in his capacity to liberate himself, and to realize his potentialities'. If this latter is not possible, then the Marxist political project itself becomes utopian. When understood as a complement to Marx's theory of revolution as the resolution of the conflict between the forces and relations of production, it precludes a politically sterile theory of revolution that counterposes a focus on the laws of motion of capitalism to a focus on the human actors who must effect all changes.

The weakness of this formulation, when taken by itself, is its openness to voluntarism, an incorrect understanding of the potential for (revolutionary) change that downplays or ignores the objective limitations imposed (again not mechanistically determined) by the environment that the protagonists are operating in. Attempts to effect revolutionary transformations that are inconsistent with the existing state of the contradictions in a particular capitalist formation can be much worse than ineffective. Such voluntarism can give rise to actions that retard the movement to remove the capitalist barriers in beginning the process of building a socialist/communist society.

CONCLUSION

Socialism/communism for Marx arose from, and was defined by, a resolution of the conflicts in capitalism, contradictions that limited the realization (and further development) of humanity's potential. This was understood to be a historically contingent and not mechanistically determined process. Among other negations of capitalism, socialism as the first phase of this process would be characterized by two essential transformations. The first is the economic liberation from the capitalist market system through its replacement by an economy run according to a democratically determined collective plan. The second is the political liberation from the rule of the capitalist class through the institution of working-class or popular democracy. Among other negations of socialism, full communism as the second phase of this process would be characterized by three essential transformations. The first is the reduction and humanization of work, including an end to the subordination of the individual to the divisions of labour (which does not mean an end to the division of labour) and with that the antithesis of manual and mental labour. The second is an accompanying change in the understanding of work from something negative that is externally imposed and which is merely necessary for physical survival, to something that develops humans as individuals and as a species. The third is the replacement of the old principal of right, the exchange of equivalents, by a new principal of right that yields distribution 'to each according to his needs'.

Marx's theory of revolution then concerns the how and why of the transformation from capitalism to this socialism/communism. Marx presented his theory of revolution in two complementary ways. On the one hand, this revolutionary transformation is the working out of the conflicts of the forces and relations of production in capitalism. On the other hand, this revolutionary transformation results from the vocation of humans as individuals and as a species to achieve their potential. The former formulation stresses the objective basis for the revolutionary transformation and guards against a revolutionary voluntarism that could arise from the second formulation by itself. The second formulation stresses the necessary central role of self-activating humans in creating a better world, and guards against a mechanistic determinism that could arise from the first formulation by itself. Both of these presentations appear throughout Marx's work, and one can only understand Marx's theory of revolution as the simultaneous presentation of them both.

52. Sociology

Alberto Toscano

Among all the academic disciplines, sociology is today alone in according more or less canonical status to Marx. The presence of Marx among the 'founding fathers', and the absorption of a number of Marxian concepts into sociological common sense, have nevertheless been accompanied by an abiding suspicion of the supposedly reductive assumptions of Marxism, perceived as a tradition of thought that subsumes the social to the economic. As the political and ideological underpinnings of the contrast between sociology and Marxist political economy have become less urgent, however, greater possibilities for constructive critical dialogue have opened up. At the same time, much contemporary social theory – from actor-network theory to postcolonial studies – is predicated on the repudiation of what are regarded as foundational tenets of Marxism, above all the assumption of totalizable entities like history, capitalism and the social. Widespread emphasis on constructivism, historical difference and multiplicity poses interesting challenges to Marxist political economy, which differ in many respects from the criticisms levied at Marxism by mainstream sociology in the twentieth century.

Marx's own intellectual development overlapped with the disciplinary prehistory of sociology. Though Marx took a dim view of the positivist system-building of Auguste Comte, who had coined the neologism 'sociology' in 1838, Comte's own erstwhile mentor Saint-Simon, alongside Charles Fourier and Robert Owen, was presented by him and Engels as a utopian forerunner of a modern, scientific socialism. Writing in the aftermath of the French revolution, the utopian socialists registered the class antagonisms and economic tensions characterizing an emergent industrial society. But the immature character of the class struggle, as well as their hostility toward revolution, meant that their transformative vision, devoid of a real historical subject, could only devolve into sterile and fantastic plans, or ameliorative projects of reform. Ironically, the formation of a 'new social science', searching after 'new social laws' – as Marx and Engels write in the *Manifesto* – appears as a result of the inability to discern the real historical conditions of class struggle and capitalist development. The gradualist, evolutionist and anti-political nature of these utopian doctrines, seeking harmonious progress rather than disruptive revolution, can also be fruitfully linked to the class perspective of their advocates, who present the struggle as one between the industrious and the idle, rather than the exploiters and the exploited. Whatever its accuracy, the analysis of utopian socialism marks an important dimension of Marxism's contribution to sociology, to wit the study of the historical, political and economic context for the emergence of particular views of society. This social science of social science may be viewed as a precursor of various sorts of reflexive sociology, for instance, in the work of Pierre Bourdieu.

Marx's historical and theoretical explanation of the uniqueness of capitalism or 'modern bourgeois society' is at the heart of his contribution and challenge to sociology. Many of the social phenomena identified by Marx in *Capital* and other writings – from the increasingly abstract character of social relations under capitalism to the deskilling of labour, from the dynamic of technological innovation to the destructive impact of capitalism on traditional modes of life and production – became the stock in trade of sociological narratives of industrial modernity. Yet, as Marx himself repeatedly noted, his primary contribution lay not in the depiction of the effects of capitalism, nor even in the identification of class struggle, but in the understanding of the logical structure and historical tendencies of modern bourgeois society. Here, Marx's critical insight that the legal, political and ideological facets of social life were to be grounded in what Enlightenment thinkers and Hegel called 'civil society', and that the 'anatomy' of civil society was to be located in political economy is crucial.

Classical sociology tended to view the individualization of society as a problem to be countered by corporatism, as a vehicle of freedom or as a kind of inexorable fate. Marx's turn to political economy permitted him to evade the moral antinomy of individualism and collectivism for a systematic investigation of capitalist society which accounted for the simultaneous reality of atomization (through an ever-intensified division of labour, the dissolution of communal bonds by commodity exchange and the rise of the political ideology of the citizen) and socialization (in the increasing significance of cooperation for production, the coagulation of social knowledge in science as a force of production, the increasing interdependence of society and, through the formation of a world market, of humanity as a whole). This dialectic was entirely missed by the Parsonian view of Marx as a utilitarian. Though Marx had argued philosophically in his early writings for a view of human individuals as fundamentally social beings, he did not juxtapose a normative view of the social to the realities of capitalism. Rather, he sought to identify the manner in which capitalism both fostered and brutally denied the potential for the development of polyvalent social individuals. Instead of playing social interests off against individual interests, as the likes of Durkheim would later do, Marx's immanent critique of political economy sought both to show the weakness of the liberal faith in the benevolence of the market mechanism and to outline the possibilities for emancipation borne by modern bourgeois society.

The very idea of contradiction can be regarded as a powerful way of thinking about the relationships between systemic tendencies, political-economic constraints and social potentials. Thus, the dynamic of technological development harbours a promise to escape the realm of social necessity, at the same time as the imperatives of capitalist accumulation result in the continued exploitation of otherwise superfluous work and the reproduction of an immiserated reserve army of labour. An understanding of the restless dynamism of capitalism, but also of the several limits that capital accumulation throws up to its own perpetuation (from overaccumulation to underconsumption, from disproportionality to ecological destruction, without forgetting class struggle itself) sets the Marxian tradition apart from those sociologies which perceive the problems of order, stability or cohesion as ones that could be addressed without transforming or indeed abolishing the class relation. Like early variants of utopian socialism, contemporary calls for revitalizing social capital, rebuilding communities or establishing a harmonious society – which often find their way into the normative or prescriptive dimension of much academic sociological writing – neglect the underlying necessity in capitalist society of the production of social inequality and instability. Is this to say that the accusations of economism and determinism are on the mark?

Like many sociologists after him, Marx presents modern society as a complex system of compulsions and constraints, in which the free will of the individual may be a legal and political postulate, but cannot lie at the basis of social explanation. The agency of capitalists, for instance, is that of 'personifications' of the accumulation process, which in some of his pages appears as an 'automatic subject'. Though their individual actions may be the object of denunciation and disgust, as they often are in Marx, they are the 'bearers' of a historical logic they do not master. But as his early preoccupations with alienation and estrangement suggest, Marx never forgets the source of this seemingly autonomous system of abstract domination in labour power. Though the effect of capitalist imperatives on the organization of production and society may be similar to a Weberian 'rationalization', or to other narratives of modernity as an increasingly depersonalized, mechanized and nihilistic time, the contradictory reliance of capitalism on living labour, and the formation of this living labour into a class, means that, even in brands of Marxism which have let go of any teleological perspectives on the inevitability of socialist revolution, the possibility of collective agency can never be excised.

Despite Marx's own protestations, the analysis of classes remains at the core of the contribution of Marxist political economy to sociological research. While not denying the realities of the antagonism between labour and capital, classical sociology had already questioned the idea of a class structure deriving principally from placement in the production process – presenting class identity in terms of relations to the market, life-chances and emphasizing the co-determinant role of status. The past three decades, beginning with diagnoses of the qualitative and quantitative marginalization of the industrial working class in advanced capitalist economies, have witnessed an increasing attack on the centrality of class analysis, which has been taxed for its essentialism and inability to register the complexities of identity-formation and power in contemporary societies. Thus, approaches that had at one point appeared as complementary or corrective to Marxian class analysis – from the study of the powers and knowledges that discipline the individual bodies of docile workers to the feminist emphasis on the role of housework in the reproduction of labour power, and of patriarchy in the perpetuation of class domination – have grown estranged from the materialist investigation of relations of production and relations in production (to borrow Burawoy and Wright's useful distinction). Faced with the persistence or exacerbation of inequality, much sociology has bypassed a systematic account of the economic bases for its production, resorting instead to a vocabulary of exclusion, whose moral impetus is rarely matched by analytical acumen.

Strands of contemporary social theory that still retain an orienting reference to Marxism – for instance, the 'post-workerist' tradition whose most prominent figure is Antonio Negri – maintain a view of capitalist exploitation as the basic fact of contemporary life but, perceiving this exploitation as increasingly directed at society as a whole (hence their reliance on Foucault's notion of biopolitics), they present the exploited not as a class but as a 'multitude'. Relying on remarks in the *Grundrisse* about the increasing insignificance of individual labour-time (though downplaying the centrality of organic composition to Marx's argument), they underscore the contradiction between increasingly 'cognitive' productive forces grounded on immediately social cooperation and the individualizing relations of production based on imposing the wage-form and property rights (for example, through patenting digital goods produced in non-commodified peer-to-peer networks). In this case, we can see that denials of some of the fundamental tenets of Marxist political economy (the law of value) can be accompanied by reinstatements of some of its most orthodox schemas (the potentially revolutionary contradiction between forces and relations of production).

Aided in this by politically expedient forms of Marxist dogmatism, it can be said that much contemporary social thought has latched onto the changing appearance of class phenomena to dismiss their reality. The lost centrality of the paradigmatic male industrial worker, and of the 'working class' as a social identity, together with the apparent ubiquity of cultural, cognitive and affective work, has produced a kind of disciplinary blindness to the persistence, or even intensification, of many of the class dynamics analysed by Marxist political economy. The continual commodification of social relations, the effective increase in working hours (both waged and effective), and the often pitiless Taylorization of 'cognitive' labour (in call centres, but also in educational and cultural sectors) are opaque phenomena unless we maintain a Marxist focus on class as exploitation, and a continued engagement with the contradictory reproduction of class relations in the institutions and ideologies of capitalist society. Rather than treating variations in the forms of state power, economic institutions and modes of subjectivity as objects of a purely descriptive or empiricist social science, Marxist political economy can allow sociology to delve into the mechanisms that make it so that capitalism can only reproduce itself by continually transforming its institutional and ideological environment, by justifying class exploitation in novel ways and by eliciting cultural forms in keeping with its regime of accumulation. Attention to the dynamics of capitalist reproduction, and the resistance to it, can allow a rich political-economic contextualization of a number of prominent themes in recent social theorizing, from the emergence of the network as an organizational form to the Foucauldian concern with the politics of life and populations, from the preoccupation with materiality and the body to debates on the aesthetics of postmodernism. Some fruitful dialogue between Marxist political economy and sociology can already be seen in recent depictions of neoliberalism as a utopian ideology, a form of 'governmentality', or a project aiming at the restoration of class power.

Teleological formulations which Marxism inherited from a certain nineteenth-century ideology of progress have also led many Marxists and sociologists to ignore the capacity of Marxist political economy to account for the centralizing and homogenizing tendencies of capitalism, together with its abiding reliance on differentiation and division. As Marxist geographers have perspicuously indicated, the unique indifference of capitalism to specific use-values and concrete-labours is a source of the kind of production of sameness descried by critics of modernity, but it also underlies a fundamental opportunism, today exacerbated by the predatory mobility of financial capital, for which (technological, cultural, economic, geographical) difference appears as an asset. The 'return' of varieties of formal subsumption of labour (putting-out systems), the reliance in certain sectors on absolute rather than relative surplus-value, the persistence of primitive accumulation (or accumulation by dispossession) to compensate for the limits of expanded reproduction, the creation of artificial rents in intellectual property, or indeed the persistent resort to cheap manual labour where investment in automation is not lucrative – all of these are phenomena that a non-teleological political economy with roots in Marx's analysis of capitalism is well equipped to account for, while in mainstream sociological thought they are often treated either as manifestations of 'globalization' or as arguments against any underlying logic of social change.

Though polemics against Marxism have waned, contemporary sociology still remains in many ways determined by its attempt to demarcate itself from the critique of political economy. Turns to difference, complexity, culture and materiality can be made intelligible in part through their negative reference to an essentialist, deterministic and economist Marxism. But a broad move from explanation to description, from totality to multiplicity, and from macro- to micro-sociological perspectives has also entailed the abandonment or attenuation of many preoccupations of classical sociology. Thus, rather than providing a different form of class analysis, class has been sidelined as a preoccupation. And, whilst departing from sociology's traditional concern with the uniqueness of modern industrial capitalism, post-structuralist and postcolonial perspectives have questioned the very existence of 'capitalism' as a unified system or category. Ironically, much of this anti-essentialist attack has taken place not so much against Marxism as against the understanding of economic behaviour in neoclassical economics, mainstream development theory and neoliberalism. Economic sociology and economic anthropology have thus been enlisted to demonstrate the precariousness and constructed character of markets, moneys and the economy – in many ways breaking with the implicit reliance on marginalism and neoclassical economics of earlier mainstream social research. Much of this research has generated important insights into the technological, relational and cultural embeddedness of social relations of production, consumption and distribution, as well as pointing to the kinds of symbolic and material force necessary to reproduce the conditions for accumulation.

But, aside from references to the substantivist vision of livelihood in Karl Polanyi, the sociological exploration of the socio-technical devices that make the fiction of homo oeconomicus possible has generally refrained from combining its empirical inquiries with a broader critical explanation of the dynamics of capitalism as a whole. Recent sociological inquiries provide rich descriptions of the underpinnings of economic behaviour. However, they have a hard time accounting for the broader systemic compulsions which set the (contradictory) parameters for the strategies and operations of individuals, firms and states. This is largely because of their neglect of the specificity of capitalism as a society in which the social form of labour is dictated by the value-form, and in which concrete-labours and human differences are subsumed by the commensurability of abstract labour and the general equivalence of money. Thus, inquiries into the role of mathematical theories in 'performing' the economy, or attention to the ubiquity of technical devices that make market transactions possible, often ignore the potent contribution of Marx's theory to account for the real (that is, non-mental, determinate) abstractions that dominate a society uniquely driven by an accumulation indifferent to its content, just as they forget that non-human agency takes specific forms in a world of commodity-fetishism where social relations between individuals really appear as social relations between things. The Marxist critique of political economy should not be presented as a reified, nostalgic description of nineteenth-century industrial capitalism. It is, instead, a method for understanding a society dominated by the value-form, founded on exploitation and reproduced through historically mutable institutional and ideological arrangements. Seen in this light, it becomes possible to envisage ways in which detailed sociological ethnographies of economic life can be brought into dialogue with Marxist method, understood as a method that ascends from the simple abstractions it extracts from the critique of political economy to their complex, concrete and conjuncturally specific existence in different domains of accumulation and production.

Throughout its history, Marxism has been alternatively viewed as precursor, a component or a rival of sociology. A constitutive resistance to academic disciplinarity, and a principled objection to treating the social as a distinct sphere of human life, means that – despite Bukharin's attempt in the 1920s – Marxism could never truly present itself as a 'system of sociology'. This has not precluded the production of important sociological research founded on Marxian methods, from the writings of Kautsky and Mehring at the end of the nineteenth-century, to the studies of fascism in the 1930s and 1940s by associates of the Frankfurt School, to inquiries into the labour process and class reproduction in the 1970s and 1980s. Burawoy and Wright have even proposed 'sociological Marxism' as a platform from which to build a non-teleological Marxism and a project of socialist emancipation after the collapse of communist orthodoxy. The recent return of economic preoccupations to the forefront of sociological research, and the widespread delegitimation of neoliberalism, can provide a rich context for a reflexive, critical Marxism once again to affect the shape and trajectory of sociological research.

53. The state

Bob Jessop

This entry is primarily concerned with the contributions of Marx and Engels to the critical analysis of the state in capitalist societies, the richness and strengths of which are often overlooked due to exaggerated concern with the more propagandistic and relatively early text of the *Communist Manifesto* and/or with the more abstract and more directly economic analyses of works such as *Capital*. Here more attention is given to the full range of the work of these figures. The entry then turns to the theoretical and political analyses of the social democratic and communist movements and also examines the contributions of the Frankfurt School, Antonio Gramsci and successive generations of postwar Marxist theorists.

MARX AND ENGELS

Marx and Engels engaged in several sorts of analyses of the state – critiques of political theory analogous to Marx's critique of economic categories in classical and vulgar political economy, historical analyses of the development, changing architecture and class character of specific states; conjunctural analyses of particular political periods and/or significant events; analyses of the form of the capitalist type of state – albeit primarily from the viewpoint of its fit with the logic of capital accumulation; historical analyses of the state (or its equivalent forms) in pre-capitalist modes of production and in contemporary societies outside of Europe and the United States; and more strategic, politically motivated accounts that were intended to influence the course of political debates within the labour movement.

In his *Critique of Hegel's Philosophy of Right* (1844) and his *Introduction to the Critique of Hegel's Philosophy of Right* (1843), Marx argued that the emerging bourgeois social formation was characterized by the institutional separation of (a) the 'public sphere', with the state at its centre, in which politics is oriented to the collective interest; and (b) 'civil society', in which private property and individual self-interest are dominant. Against Hegel's claim that the modern state could and would represent the real common or organic interests of all members of society, Marx argued that it could represent only an 'illusory' community of interest beneath which would lie the continuing antagonisms, crass materialism and egoistic conflicts of a society based on private property ownership and waged labour. Thus he concluded that Hegel had failed to recognize that the real world itself was contradictory and undermined attempts to secure political unification and that true emancipation and a true community of interests required the abolition of private property.

THE STATE IN HISTORICAL MATERIALISM

The specific economic form, in which unpaid surplus-labour is pumped out of direct producers, determines the relationship of rulers and ruled, as it grows directly out of production itself and, in turn, reacts upon it as a determining element. Upon this, however, is founded the entire formation of the economic community which grows up out of the production relations themselves, thereby simultaneously its specific political form. It is always the direct relationship of the owners of the conditions of production to the direct producers . . . which reveals the innermost secret, the hidden basis of the entire social structure and with it the political form of the relation of sovereignty and dependence, in short, the corresponding specific form of the state. (Marx, *Capital III*, ch. 47)

This implies that the social relations of production (not the forces of production) shape the social relations of domination and servitude. It does not mean that specific state policies can be read off directly from the current economic conditions. Rather Marx argues that the 'form of political organization' corresponds to the 'form of economic organization'. Thus an economic order based on private property, the wage relation and profit-oriented, market-mediated exchange naturally 'fits' or 'corresponds' with a political order based on the rule of law, equality before the law and a unified sovereign state. This highlights the 'formal adequacy' of bourgeois democracy to a consolidated, profit-oriented, market-mediated capitalist mode of production. In this context, economic struggle will normally occur within the logic of the market (that is, over wages, hours, working conditions, prices) and political struggle will normally occur within the logic of the representative state based on the rule of law (that is, over defining the national interest, reconciling the particular interests of citizens and property owners within an 'illusory' general interest). This means that class is absent as an explicit organizing principle of the capitalist type of state – there is no legal monopoly, no exclusivity of political power for the dominant class – it must compete on formally equal terms with members of subordinate classes for power.

This leads Marx to write in *The Class Struggles in France, 1848–1850*, that there is a basic contradiction at the heart of a democratic constitution. For, whereas it gives universal suffrage to the proletariat, peasantry and petty bourgeoisie, whose social slavery the constitution is to perpetuate, it sustains the social power of the bourgeoisie by guaranteeing private property rights: 'From the first group it demands that they should not go forward from political to social emancipation; from the others that they should not go back from social to political restoration.' This contradiction explains why Marx rarely resorts to directly economic arguments in explaining the development of specific political regimes or the content of specific state policies – for this depends on a specific dynamic of political struggles rather than on immediate economic circumstances. He therefore pays careful attention to state forms, political regimes, political discourses, the balance of political forces and so on, as well as to changing economic circumstances, economic crises, underlying contradictions and so on.

Marx's historical materialist approach highlights the 'formal' analysis of the relation of sovereignty and dependency in the capitalist mode of production. A formal analysis is not superficial: it focuses on 'social forms' and their material effects – form does make a difference! But his approach also considers, when appropriate, the historical dimension, that is, state-building. An adequate state form must be constructed; it does not emerge automatically along with bourgeois relations of production. As the *Communist Manifesto*

(1848) notes, it took many centuries of political class struggle before the bourgeoisie – aided by the establishment of large-scale industry and the world market – finally gained exclusive political control through the modern representative state. This and other analyses highlight the zigs-and-zags, leads-and-lags in the rise of the modern representative state – if it does, indeed, emerge. Moreover, given its inherently contradictory nature, it is also vulnerable to destabilization if the compromise between subordinate and dominant classes around their political and social power respectively breaks down.

CAPITAL, NATION AND THE STATE

Marx considered capitalism to be a political as well as economic phenomenon. This is clear from his many discussions of the state's role in promoting primitive and routine accumulation and in securing the conditions for social order in class-divided social formations. An important point that would merit further development is his observation that '[t]axes are the existence of the state expressed in economic terms' (*Moralising Criticism and Critical Morality*, 1847). But he never wrote the 'missing book on the state' (one of six books once anticipated to comprise *Das Kapital*) with the result that he focused more on the economic than the political dynamic of accumulation and, indeed, given the absence of the proposed book on labour, on the viewpoint of capital more than the working class.

Some key points nonetheless emerge. First, individual capitals are prevented from using direct coercion in the labour process and in their competition with other capitals but the state protects private property and the sanctity of contracts on behalf of capital as a whole. This enables capital to insist on its right to manage the labour process, to appropriate surplus labour and to enforce contracts with other capitals. Second, capitalism requires free wage labour and the state creates this through its role in ending feudal privileges, promoting the enclosure of the commons, punishing vagabonds, imposing the obligation to enter the labour market – but the state also enables workers to exercise ownership of their own labour power freely, secures conditions for the reproduction of wage labour, imposes factory laws, responds to the housing question, secures cheap food and so on. Third, the modern representative state does not itself engage in profitable economic activities – capital prefers to provide them itself and to get the state to undertake economically and socially necessary activities that are unprofitable. The nature of these latter activities changes across social formations and over time. Fourth, the modern state finances its own activities from taxation – this is a necessary burden on capital (an unfortunate cost of doing business to be displaced elsewhere if possible); and/or from public debt – which limits the state's freedom of manoeuvre under threat of a 'capital strike' and/or 'capital flight'. Thus the modern state's activities depend on a healthy, growing economy – which ties political programmes to economic imperatives.

Marx and Engels often note that, while capitalism tends to develop the world market, there are many states. In their time, the uneven development of capitalism even in Europe and the weakness of many small states prompted the emergence of national states to organize large internal markets and compete with other economies and their national capitals. Most states also adopted protectionist policies, whether national or imperial in organization. Further, when Marx and Engels wrote, individual citizenship and democracy could be better organized around national states and/or nation-states, which could provide the basis for an illusory community of interests. Accordingly, Marx and Engels generally backed the development of national states on the grounds that they facilitated the organization of democratic struggles, initially for an ascendant bourgeoisie, later for the working-class movement. Their views on nationalism, however, were mixed. On the one hand, they recognized that, historically, some nations are oppressed and deserved political freedom; on the other hand, they believed that not all nations could build states and exercise self-determination (some of their reasons were patently xenophobic and racist) and that nationalism also divides the working class (remember that the *Communist Manifesto* ends with the cry, Workers of all countries, unite!).

Marx analysed legislation on the length of the working day and the employment of women and children as instances of the need for state intervention in the organization of labour markets and working conditions in the interests of capital itself as well as working-class families. Competition between capitals (in a period when absolute rather than relative surplus value was the dominant axis of competition) prevented any individual capitalist from being the first to cut hours, reduce female and child labour and improve working conditions. Yet cut-throat competition produced growing infant and adult mortality, demographic decline and declining productivity – all of this reported by factory inspectors and other state officials. Trade unions, 'bourgeois socialists' (see the *Communist Manifesto*), philanthropists and progressive capitalists (who could make profits through relative surplus value) allied to press the state to pass legislation against the will of many individual capitalists. This is an example of what Engels would later call the role of the state as the 'ideal collective capitalist' (see below).

Marx was also strongly interested in what the French Revolution and the subsequent development of the French state suggested about the contribution of the bourgeois democratic regime to capitalist economic and political development. *The Eighteenth Brumaire of Louis Bonaparte* (1852) is justifiably the most famous of his writings on France. It is a study in the 'specificity of political struggles' on the terrain of the modern state – there is no class that is directly and unambiguously represented as such on the political scene and Marx takes great pains to decipher the 'class bases' and/or 'class relevance' of different political forces, for example, political factions, political parties, the army, paramilitary forces, political mobs, intellectuals, journalists and so on. Marx did not regard these linkages as transparent or straightforward but as deeply problematic and highly mediated. He thereby shows that 'the state' is not a simple 'committee for managing the common affairs of the whole bourgeoisie' and/or 'the executive committee of the ruling class' (as Marx and Engels suggest for propagandistic reasons in the *Manifesto*). Different regimes have different effects on class struggle, privileging different interests and making it easier or harder to build economic stability, political order and social cohesion. Bonaparte's *coup d'état* was an opportunistic effort to seize power that was accepted because of a growing 'political' crisis (only loosely rooted in economic crisis) and widespread fears about the collapse of social order in a period when the dominated classes were politically paralysed and/or inclined to support a strong leader. Yet the very autonomy of the Bonapartist dictatorship as 'the consolidated dictatorship of the whole bourgeoisie' also threatened the economic interests of the dominant classes. Within a short period, however, state power was once more tied to capitalist interests through the growth of state debt and the Bonapartist state's role in promoting economic expansion, the expropriation of the peasantry and overseas economic adventures.

This text also studied the organizational problems facing subordinate classes in moving from being classes 'against capital' to classes 'for themselves', that is, from resisting to abolishing capital. Two famous examples are (a) the small-holding conservative peasantry, which, because of their rural isolation, relations of production and dependence on usurious capital and local political figures, form a class like 'potatoes in a sack form a sack of potatoes' and therefore need to be represented by others rather than doing this themselves – Louis Bonaparte performed this task rhetorically but not in practice; and (b) the *Lumpenproletariat*, declassed elements, that are inherently disorganized, side opportunistically with one camp or another, and hence prove unreliable allies. More generally Marx developed a rich vocabulary for analysing political class relations, for example, class in charge of state, supporting classes, literary representatives, political parties, the class relevance of political discourses and so on. This vocabulary is politically specific and not reducible to issues of economic class relations.

Engels discovered the class state in action in Manchester when Marx was still critiquing Hegel's idealist theory of the state. In *The Condition of the Working Class in England* (1845) Engels explored the class nature of the local and national state in promoting industrialization and suppressing working-class organization. He was an expert on military affairs and warfare and wrote much, as did Marx, on specific political conjunctures and particular aspects of state policy. In later life, he attempted to develop a general theory to explain the origins of the state and its contribution to economic development. He also elaborated significant arguments on the autonomy of the legal system in capitalist societies and the importance of legal ideology; these insights cast important light on the autonomy of the modern state. In other work he studied the specificity of the capitalist state, which he described occasionally as 'the ideal collective capitalist'. This denotes the state's role in articulating and promoting the 'collective' interests of capital against those of particular capitals – a task it could perform precisely because it was not a real capitalist but a political force standing over and against civil society and hence capable of acting on behalf of all capitals (hence its 'ideal' character).

LATER MARXIST VIEWS

This entry cannot provide a comprehensive historical and thematic survey of subsequent Marxist theories. Instead it identifies some broad trends and notes some major lines of analysis. The Second International (broadly social democratic) and the Comintern (Marxist-Leninist) inclined to one-sided accounts of the state. These were closely linked to political practice, that is, they served party-political and trade union purposes, rather than more 'academic' interests. Both movements tended to see the state either as an instrument of particular capitalist interests or the wider ruling class(es) in specific national or imperialist contexts and/or as having changing forms and functions that largely reflected the underlying economic base. Whereas the Second International tended to believe that a parliamentary road to socialism might be possible, the Comintern followed Marx and, more importantly, Lenin in arguing that even the bourgeois democratic republic was essentially capitalist and should be replaced with a new state form based on direct democracy – an aspiration that conflicted with the eventual development of party dictatorships. These theories were modified in light of continuing changes in capitalism, imperialism, militarism, the clash between the capitalist and socialist blocs, and, likewise, as more crisis-prone periods alternated with more stable periods (for example, the Great Depression versus the postwar boom). But these modifications left the basically instrumentalist and/or reductionist nature of the overall approach untouched.

The interwar period saw two significant developments in Marxist theorization. First, early Critical Theorists debated contemporary trends towards a strong, bureaucratic state – whether authoritarian or totalitarian. This allegedly matched the development of 'organized' or 'state capitalism' to an enhanced role for the mass media in securing the ideological power of the dominant class(es), and to efforts to incorporate or else brutally repress the trade union movement. These ideas are still influential. And, second, albeit largely unnoticed at the time outside Italy, Antonio Gramsci, a leading figure in the Italian Communist Party who was imprisoned by the fascist government, developed a radically new approach in his prison notebooks to the state and state power. This approach has been very important since his work was published in the 1960s and 1970s.

Gramsci rejected instrumentalism and class reductionism and aimed to develop an autonomous Marxist science of politics as it operated in capitalist societies as well as to establish the most likely conditions and suitable strategies for revolution in the 'West' (Western Europe, North America) as opposed to the 'East' (that is, Tsarist Russia). He argued that a Leninist vanguard party and revolutionary *coup d'état* were inappropriate for the 'West' and he advocated a mass movement that would establish its national-popular hegemony before an eventual politico-military resolution. Gramsci defined the state as: 'the entire complex of practical and theoretical activities with which the ruling class not only justifies and maintains its dominance but manages to win the active consent of those over whom it rules' (Gramsci, 1971, p. 244). He focused on 'the state in its inclusive sense' (or 'integral state'), suggesting that the 'State = political society + civil society' and that state power in the West is best analysed in terms of 'hegemony armoured by coercion'. He identified two modes of class domination: 'force' (the use of a coercive apparatus to bring the mass of people into conformity and compliance with the requirements of a specific mode of production) and 'hegemony' (the successful mobilization and reproduction of the 'active consent' of dominated groups by the ruling class through their exercise of intellectual, moral and political leadership oriented to a 'collective will' or 'national-popular' consensus). Force was not exclusively identified with the state (for example, fascist paramilitary terror squads) nor hegemony with civil society (the state also has ethico-political functions). In this context, Gramsci focused on the relative weight in different societies of coercion, fraud-corruption, passive revolution and active consent.

Three of his arguments are especially noteworthy. First, he argued that ethico-political ideas were important elements in the reciprocal shaping of the economic base, the juridico-political superstructure, and the moral and intellectual field. He used the notion of 'historical bloc' to refer to the resulting structural unity of a social formation. Second, he proposed the concept of 'hegemonic bloc' to refer to a durable alliance of class forces organized by a class (or class fraction) that has proved capable of exercising political, intellectual and moral leadership over the dominant classes and the popular masses. Gramsci gave a key role here to 'organic intellectuals', that is, intellectuals with an organic link to either the ruling or revolutionary classes, able to articulate hegemonic projects that express their own long-term class interests in 'national-popular' terms. Third, he emphasized the need for a decisive economic nucleus as the basis for long-term hegemony and criticized efforts to construct an 'arbitrary, rationalistic, and willed' hegemony that ignored economic realities.

Marxist interest in the state, going well beyond the main prewar approaches and arguments, revived in the late 1960s and 1970s. Efforts were made to show that states in advanced capitalist economies could not abolish capital's contradictions and crisis-tendencies through measures such as Keynesianism, planning and the welfare state. Such work also sought initially to derive the necessary form and functions of the capitalist state from the basic categories of Marx's critique of political economy and to prove that contemporary states could not escape the basic constraints of the capital relation. This literature rapidly became more abstract and inward-looking and most of it is now forgotten. But several of the better analysts did formulate two key insights that remain highly relevant.

First, in turning from functional analysis to form analysis, Marxist state theorists discovered that form 'threatens' function rather than 'following' from function. Thus this generation of Marxist scholars explored how the institutional separation of the state from the market economy, a separation which was regarded as a necessary and defining feature of capitalist societies, results in the dominance of different (and potentially contradictory) institutional logics and modes of calculation in the state and the economy (for a survey, see Jessop, 1982). There is no guarantee that political outcomes will serve the needs of capital – even if (and, indeed, precisely because) the state is operationally autonomous. This conclusion fuelled work on the structural contradictions, strategic dilemmas and path-dependent (that is, historically conditioned) development of specific state forms. Similar conclusions were reached, of course, by Marx and Engels in their theoretical and political studies.

Second, gradually abandoning views of the state apparatus as a simple thing or a unitary class subject, Marxist theorists analysed state power as a complex social relation (Draper, 1977; Holloway and Picciotto, 1982). They studied the biases inscribed in different forms of state and political regime and the factors that shaped their strategic capacities. They showed that the state as an ensemble of institutions had a specific, differential impact on the ability of various political forces to pursue particular interests and strategies in and through access to and control over given state capacities – themselves always dependent for their effects on links to forces and powers beyond the state (Poulantzas, 1978; Jessop, 1982, 2002). More attention was also paid to the variability of these capacities, their organization and exercise. This prompted greater emphasis on the relational nature of state power and on states' capacities to project their power into social realms well beyond their own institutional boundaries. And, as with the first set of insights, it also led to more complex studies of struggles, institutions and political capacities. These views were also anticipated in the work of Marx and Engels, especially in their historical analyses and their overall emphasis on the nature of state power as a social relation, and, equally importantly, especially for postwar scholarship, in the work of Antonio Gramsci.

CONCLUSION

It is surprising in many respects how much recent scholarship has recovered some key (but often unrecognized insights) of Marx and Engels. They argued that capitalism requires a clear separation between the economy within the capitalist mode of production and the juridico-political system within this same mode of production. Each system had its own logic – profit-oriented, market-mediated exchange versus orientation to the 'national interest' (which was not reducible to crude class interests) that offered some prospects of reconciling competing individual interests. While the bourgeois democratic republic was the best means to achieve this 'formally', it does not follow that: (i) all capitalist states will be democratic; (ii) once democratic regimes are established, they cannot be overturned; or (iii) the specific policies pursued by bourgeois democratic states, let alone by all states in capitalist society, will be 'substantively adequate' to capital accumulation or the overall reproduction of capitalist relations of production. Indeed, it would be a great mistake to treat every state in a capitalist society as possessing the features of the capitalist type of state as analysed in more abstract terms in Marxist work. There is no obvious, one-to-one correlation between economic class interests and the forms of political representation and the organization of political forces. In particular, one must recognize tendencies towards state failure (and 'failed states') and the distinctive features of political and state crises. It is therefore necessary to explore the specificities of political class struggle through a conjunctural analysis of the horizons of action of various political forces, their class relevance, if any, and their implications for the reproduction of economic, political and ideological class domination over different time periods. But it is also important to relate these specificities to the overall critique of political economy – without which one risks falling into one-sided political analyses and misses the connection to the overall logic or dynamic of capital accumulation.

54. 'Transformation problem'

Alfredo Saad-Filho

The transformation of values into prices of production (TVPP) is one of several shifts in the form of value examined in *Capital*. These shifts are introduced sequentially, as Marx gradually reconstructs the processes of capitalist reproduction and accumulation across increasingly complex levels of analysis. Briefly, in *Capital I* Marx reviews the process of production of (surplus) value, including the determination of commodity values through the competition between capitals producing identical use values (intra-sectoral competition). *Capital II* examines the conditions of social and economic reproduction through the circulation of the (surplus) value produced across the economy. Finally, *Capital III* addresses two aspects of the distribution of (surplus) value. First is distribution across competing industrial capitals in different sectors, which concerns the possibility of capital migration and, consequently, the allocation of labour across the economy and the composition of the output. Second are the relationships between industrial, commercial and financial capital and the landowning class, showing how part of the surplus value is captured in exchange as commercial profit, interest and rent.

   The Anglo-Saxon literature has tended to see these processes in isolation from one another (unrelated stages in the analysis and, correspondingly, separate theories of price, profit, interest and rent), with treatment of the TVPP focused narrowly on the quantitative relationship between vectors of equilibrium values and prices, and the corresponding redistribution of surplus value and profit. This analytical separation is incorrect, because these processes are integrally related to one another, and to the logic both of capital accumulation, and of Marx's *Capital*. Nevertheless, this separation is, largely, due to the fact that this literature perceives the TVPP, uniquely, to articulate the intangible domain of values with the visible realm of prices. Other contributory factors include the flirting engagement of mainstream economists, who saw in the TVPP an opening to attack the logical consistency of Marxism, and the wish of Sraffian economists to sideline their most significant rival amongst the heterodoxy (for a review, see Elson, 1979b; Fine, 1986). At another level, the TVPP has often provided the canvas for contrasting rival interpretations of Marx's theory of value (MTV), and the pretext for shunning it altogether.

THE 'PROBLEM'

Capital III opens with Marx's conceptual distinction between surplus value and profit. This is followed by the examination of the impact on the rate of profit of changes in turnover time, the rate of surplus value, and in the quantity, quality and value of inputs. In chapter 8, Marx points out that these factors, which govern changes in the general profit rate abstracting from competition, may also explain differences amongst profit rates of capitals competing across distinct sectors of the economy. This observation introduces the concept of inter-sectoral competition, marking a shift in the level of analysis. However, instead of immediately exploring this development, Marx turns to the differences between the technical, organic and value compositions of capital (TCC, OCC and VCC). He addresses the TVPP only in the following chapter.

In chapter 9, Marx contrasts five capitals equal to 100 but with different proportions of c and v, illustrating that capitals produce distinct use values with varying combinations of living labour, raw materials and machinery. Marx points out that these capitals will produce different amounts of surplus value because of their distinct OCCs, defined as c/v. For example, using only two sectors instead of Marx's five, one unit of capital invested in the steel industry typically employs less workers – and, therefore, directly produces less surplus value – than one unit of capital in the textile industry. Using Marx's notation, these capitals might be represented as, say, $80c + 20v$ and $20c + 80v$. Supposing the rate of surplus value is 100 per cent ($s/v = 1$), the output values will be $80c + 20v + 20s = 120$ in the steel industry, and $20c + 80v + 80s = 180$ in the textile industry. Therefore, their profit rates, $r = s/(c + v)$ are, respectively, 20 per cent and 80 per cent.

Classical Political Economy recognized that this difference is incompatible with inter-sectoral competition, which creates a tendency towards the equalization of profit rates. For Ricardo, a more sophisticated analysis was required, which he unsuccessfully endeavoured to provide (and for which Sraffa is presumed to have found a solution albeit at the expense of MTV; see Milonakis and Fine, 2009). In contrast, for Marx, while the abstraction that commodities exchange at their values permits the explanation of the production of (surplus) value, this level of analysis is insufficiently developed to account for inter-sectoral competition and, therefore, the composition of output and the distribution of labour. Their explanation requires a more complex form of value, which Marx called prices of production.

This shift, or transformation, in the form of value does not simply 'erase and replace' the previous abstraction (commodity values determined by socially necessary labour time) as if it were wrong or merely a special case (of equal OCCs). Nor is Marx confronting a purely logical (neoclassical) problem of finding a price vector that satisfies arbitrary static equilibrium conditions. Finally, Marx was fully aware that the input values had not been transformed in his presentation in *Capital*. Rather, in Marx's presentation the abstract content of value is being reproduced in a more complex and concrete form as prices of production, preserving the prior analysis and addressing additional (more concrete) aspects of capitalism on this basis. Unfortunately, Marx's presentation of the transformation is hampered by the unfinished status of *Capital III*. This has contributed to overlapping disagreements about what Marx really said, what he would have said if he had been able to finish this volume, and what he should have said in order to be 'right' according to differing interpretations.

In *Capital III*, Marx calculates the average of the profit rates of the five capitals in his example, and derives the prices of production of the output as $p_i = (c_i + v_i) (1 + r)$, where i represents the capital ($i = 1, \ldots, 5$) and the average profit rate is $r = S/(C + V)$, where S, C and V are the total surplus value and constant and variable capital. Therefore, while commodity values include the surplus value produced by each capital, the prices of production distribute the surplus value produced to equalize the profit rates across different sectors. In the numerical example provided above, the values of the output are 120 and 180, the average profit rate is 50 per cent ($r = 100/200$), and the prices of production of the output are 150 and 150.

The distribution of surplus value to equalize profit rates amongst competing capitals gives rise to 'profit' as a form of surplus value: this conceptual difference mirrors the difference between the 'production' of surplus value, and its 'appropriation' as industrial profit (at this level of analysis, other forms of profit, as well as interest and rent, are not present yet). Marx claims that the sum of prices is equal to the sum of values (in our case, $120 + 180 = 150 + 150$), and that the sum of surplus values is equal to the sum of profits ($20 + 80 = 50 + 50$). These aggregate equalities illustrate Marx's claims that prices of production are transformed values, and that profit is transformed surplus value. In other words, each capitalist shares in the surplus value produced according to their share in capital advanced, as if receiving a dividend on an equity share in the economy's social or total capital as a whole.

Marx's transformation procedure has been criticized primarily because of a supposed logical inconsistency: he calculates the price of production of the output (steel and textiles) on the basis of 'untransformed' values of the inputs – whereas capitalists will have bought their inputs (including steel and textiles) at prices of production, not values. However, these commodities cannot be purchased as inputs at one set of prices (120 and 180) and sold at 'different' prices (150 and 150) as outputs, because every sale is also a purchase for one or other capitalist. Further, this implies that the 'value rate of profit', as calculated by Marx as $S/(C+V)$, is also not the monetary rate of profit at all since both numerator and denominator need to be recalculated at their prices of production as opposed to their values. In other words, Marx gets the rate of profit wrong and, even if he did not, he still gets prices wrong!

ALTERNATIVE INTERPRETATIONS

The charge of inconsistency was issued soon after the publication of *Capital III*, and it was brought into prominence in the Anglo-Saxon literature by Paul Sweezy (1942). The subsequent debate has focused on the algebraic difficulties of transferring monetary quantities across sectors in an economy in static equilibrium, starting from direct (untransformed) prices, a single value of labour power and equal rates of exploitation, and arriving at an identical material equilibrium with a single wage rate and an equalized profit rate, while, at the same time, validating Marx's aggregate equalities between total price and total value, and total surplus value and total profit. These controversies became especially prominent with the emergence of radical political economy in the late 1960s, and even attracted the attention of leading mainstream economists, especially Paul Samuelson, Michio Morishima and William Baumol. Alternative solutions to the 'transformation problem' proliferated, depending on the structure of value theory envisaged by competing authors and their choice of starting conditions, constraints and desired outcomes including, almost invariably, which aggregate equality should be sacrificed in order to 'preserve' the other. These transformation procedures were deemed to be significant because they would either 'validate' or 'deny' selected aspects of Marx's theory of value – or, even, the entire logical core of Marx's theory.

(A)   NEOCLASSICAL AND SRAFFIAN

The neoclassical and Sraffian critiques of Marx are essentially identical if differently motivated and rooted. They postulate two equilibrium exchange value systems, one in values (defined as quantities of embodied labour) and the other in equilibrium prices. The value system is described by $\lambda = \lambda A + l = l(I - A)^{-1}$, where λ is the $(1 \times n)$ vector of commodity values, A is the $(n \times n)$ technical matrix and l is the $(1 \times n)$ vector of direct labour. Given the same technical matrix, the price system is described by $p = (pA + wl)$ $(1 + r)$, where p is the $(1 \times n)$ price vector, w is the wage rate and r is the profit rate.

These systems provide the basis for a critique of both alleged inconsistencies and incompleteness in Marx, leading to the conclusion that the attempt to determine values from embodied labour, and prices from values, is logically flawed. In brief, while the value system can usually be solved, the price system has two degrees of freedom (it has n equations, but $n + 2$ unknowns: the n prices, w and r). A solution would require additional restrictions, for example, defining the value of labour power as the value of a fixed bundle, b, of workers' consumption goods (with wages given by $w = pb$), plus one of Marx's aggregate equalities – however, the other aggregate equality would normally not hold, which is allegedly destructive for Marx's analysis. Furthermore, this representation of Marx can scarcely distinguish between the role of labour and other inputs, in which case it cannot be argued that labour creates value and is exploited, rather than any other input, such as corn, iron or energy.

This critique of Marx is insufficient for four reasons. First, it presumes that the production structure is determined exogenously and purely technically while, for Marx, technologies and social forms are mutually constituting (capital accumulation and the development of productive forces do not rest on equilibrium foundations regardless of growth). Second, it assumes that, for values to have conceptual legitimacy, they should be necessary and sufficient for the calculation of the profit rate and the price vector. Since this is not the case in this model (in which, incidentally, the 'value' rate of profit has no significance for economic behaviour), value analysis is allegedly redundant. However, this claim is based on a misrepresentation of Marx's theory, where labour values, direct prices, prices of production and market prices are forms of value belonging to distinct levels of complexity, rather than sequences in deductive calculation. Third, the neoclassical and Sraffian value equation is inconsistent: if l represents concrete labour time, these labours are qualitatively distinct and cannot be aggregated; but if l is a vector of abstract labour values cannot be calculated in practice because abstract labour data are not directly available. Fourth, in this system the social aspect of production is either assumed away or projected upon the sphere of distribution, through the inability of the workers to purchase the entire output with their wages (see Rowthorn, 1980).

(B)   VALUE-FORM THEORIES

Value-form interpretations of Marx draw upon the social division of labour and the production of commodities by 'separate' (independent) producers. Separation brings the need to produce a socially useful commodity, one that can be sold. Consequently, for this tradition, commodities are produced by private labours that are only potentially abstract and social: the conversion to value form only happens when the product is exchanged for money.

Value-form approaches have helped to shift the focus of Marxian studies away from the algebraic calculation of values and prices and towards the analysis of the social relations of production and their forms of appearance. Nevertheless, the claim that 'separation' is the essential feature of commodity production subsumes capitalist relations under simple commodity relations of production. This limitation helps to explain this tradition's stunted contribution to the theory of 'capital(ism)' – including the TVPP, which is frequently bypassed through the direct assimilation of values with market prices.

The 'new interpretation' (NI) of Marx's value theory was developed in the early 1980s, drawing heavily upon value-form analysis (Fine, et al., 2004). It eschews equilibrium analysis, and postulates that money is the immediate and exclusive expression (as well as the measure) of abstract labour. Since this interpretation remains at the aggregate level, it bypasses the relationship between individual prices and values that was normally associated with the TVPP. The NI defines the value of money as the quantity of labour represented by the monetary unit or, conversely, the abstract labour time that adds £1 to the value of the output. The newly produced money value is allocated as price across the net product. Further, the NI defines the value of labour power as the *ex post* wage share of national income (that is, the wage rate times the value of money), while the surplus value is the residual which confirms that profit is merely redistributed surplus value.

The NI has contributed to closer attention to Marx's value analysis, as opposed to imposing equilibrium interpretations of price theory, and it established a channel for empirical and policy studies. Nevertheless, the NI is limited at three levels. First, its focus on the net product short-circuits the production of the means of production (other than the part incorporated into net product for expanded reproduction), rendering invisible a significant proportion of current production and the entire sphere of exchanges between capitalist producers. Second, the NI's concept of value of money short-circuits the real structures, processes and relations mediating the expression of social labour into money, which Marx was at pains to identify across the three volumes of *Capital*. This weakens the NI's ability to examine disequilibrium, conflict and crises logically rather than arbitrarily. Third, the NI definition of value of labour power is limited to one of the effects of exploitation, the inability of the workers to purchase the entire net product. This was also the same aspect of exploitation which the Ricardian socialist and Sraffian economists contemplated. However, for Marx, capitalist exploitation is not due to the unfair distribution of income, and the net product is not 'shared' between the classes at the end of each production cycle. Rather, wages are part of the advance of capital (regardless of when they are paid), whilst profit is the consequence of how much surplus value is extracted. In sum, while addressing crucial issues for value theory, the NI resolves none of them. Rather, it confines value theory to a sequential if not static sociological theory of exploitation in which selective aspects of Marx's transformation are subject to piecemeal (and arbitrary) attention, independently of the structures and processes by which surplus value is produced and distributed competitively through the market.

(C)   DYNAMIC ANALYSIS

Ben Fine (1983) offered a specific dynamic interpretation of the TVPP (see also Saad-Filho 2002, ch. 7). This interpretation departs from (a critique of) conventional views, which tend to focus on the differences in the 'value' composition of capital across different sectors (although often, incorrectly, referring to as differences in OCCs). Paradoxically, nearly all treatments of the TVPP, especially but not exclusively those who reject Marx, deploy the OCC in terminology but the VCC conceptually. However, this is not the case for Marx, who examines the transformation entirely in terms of the OCC, properly conceived and distinguished from the VCC: for him, the TVPP is concerned with the effects on prices of the differing 'rates of increase' at which raw materials are transformed into outputs (rather than the effect of differences in the input values, which are captured by the VCC). This attaches Marx's TVPP to the preceding theory of accumulation and productivity theory of *Capital I*, the circulation of capital from *Capital II* and to the law of the tendency of the rate of profit to fall that immediately follows upon the TVPP in *Capital III*. For standard interpretations of the TVPP, there is no reason why it should not come earlier than *Capital III*, and none why it should have any connection to falling profitability (and, not surprisingly, equilibrium interpretations of the TVPP as transformation problems are heavily associated with denial of Marx's treatment of falling profitability).

For this dynamic view, Marx's problem is the following. If a given amount of living labour employed in sector i (represented by v_i) works up a greater quantity of raw materials (represented by c_i) than in another sector j, 'regardless of their respective costs', the commodities produced in sector i will command a higher price relative to value. That is, the use of a greater quantity of labour in production creates more (surplus) value than a lesser quantity, regardless of the sector, the use value being produced and the cost of the raw materials. This completely general proposition within value theory underpins Marx's explanation of prices and profit. The use of the OCC rather than the VCC in the transformation is significant, because the OCC connects profits with the 'production' of value and surplus value by living labour. In contrast, the VCC links profits with the sphere of 'exchange', where commodities are traded and where the newly established values measure the rate of capital accumulation.

His emphasis on the OCC shows that Marx is mainly concerned with the impact on prices of the different 'quantities' of labour transforming the means of production into the output, regardless of the value of these means of production. This is analytically significant because it pins the source of surplus value and profit down to unpaid labour, substantiating Marx's claims that machines do not create value, that surplus value and profit are not due to unequal exchange, and that industrial profit, interest and rent are shares of the surplus value produced by the productive wage workers. In short, the passage from abstract value to the complex form of prices involves a multiplicity of structures and processes, which need to be ordered in relation to one another and distinctively. This cannot be done by a direct mediation between values and (equilibrium) prices, monetary or otherwise. Furthermore, for this interpretation Marx's own selection of the distinctive role of the TCC, OCC and VCC in the processes of price formation has been seriously misread even by sympathetic interpretations.

CONCLUSION

Commodity values and prices can be analysed at distinct levels. At the most abstract level, value is a social relation of production. Value can also be seen, at increasingly complex levels, as the labour time socially necessary to reproduce each kind of commodity, direct price, price of production, price of production in the presence of commercial capital and market price. The value form is transformed at each one of these levels of analysis; as it becomes increasingly concrete, it encompasses more complex determinations of the value relations of capitalism. The development and implications of these analytical shifts comprise a large part of Marx's work in *Capital*.

In the TVPP, Marx is not addressing the Ricardian (and neoclassical) problem of calculating equilibrium prices from labour magnitudes in the presence of capital and time; rather, Marx is attempting to capture conceptually a relatively complex 'form of social labour'. This approach has a four-fold impact upon the structure of *Capital*: it explains why market exchanges are not directly regulated by labour time; shows that price is a relatively complex form of social labour; allows a more complex understanding of the forms of value; and explains the distribution of labour and surplus value across the economy. Even though it was left incomplete, Marx's procedure is important because it develops further his reconstruction of the capitalist economy, and substantiates the claim that living labour alone, and not the dead labour represented by the means of production, creates value and surplus value.

55. The transition from feudalism to capitalism

David Laibman

Everyone has absorbed, from countless textbooks, treatises and documentaries, the chronicle of the 'Dawn of the Modern Era', or 'Emergence of Our Times'. This parable recounts in broad strokes the history of the rise, from the European 'Middle Ages', of centralized states, markets and trade, and representative political systems. The story is accompanied by a more or less subtle assumption: this Great Transition represents an 'Enlightenment' – the coming of a 'final' form of social, economic and political organization, which may be fine-tuned and amended in minor ways, but never transcended or replaced. In that sense, we have reached the 'end of history' – except for developing countries' need to cross the same threshold into modernity.

Marxist social theory, by contrast, sees the same era in Europe – roughly from the twelfth through the eighteenth centuries – as the transition from feudalism to capitalism: from one exploitative, class-antagonistic mode of production to another. The even more fundamental passage from capitalism to socialism-communism, which is simultaneously the abolition of all forms of surplus extraction, lies ahead.

FEUDALISM AND CAPITALISM

To flesh out this story, and to provide firm grounding for the social movement driving present-day revolutionary challenges to capitalist rule, Marxist scholars have produced a large literature on the transition from feudalism to capitalism. The pioneering contribution to this project in the English-speaking world was the publication in 1947 of Maurice Dobb's *Studies in the Development of Capitalism,* which led to a celebrated debate in *Science & Society,* involving Dobb, Paul Sweezy and others, subsequently published as Hilton (1978). A second wave of debate, largely in *Past and Present,* was occasioned by the work of Robert Brenner on the English Revolution and its source in the agrarian class struggle and capitalist development of the seventeenth century (Brenner, 1976; Aston and Philpin, 1985). A third wave focused on the relation of feudalism-to-capitalism transition to more general themes of determinacy versus contingency and structure versus agency in historical materialist theory (Laibman, 1984, 1987; Amin, 1985; McLennan, 1986; Milonakis, 1993–94). The emergence of the Analytical Marxist School in the mid-1980s produced yet another stream of discussion (Carling, 1991; Wright et al., 1992). Some of this work arose in response to the seminal contribution by G.A. Cohen published in 1978 (with a second edition published as Cohen, 2000), and has led to alternative theories of the driving forces of history, including those that emphasize non-intentional processes at work (Nolan, 1993; Carling, 2006; for a survey and appraisal, see Laibman, 2007, ch. 2).

Early in the development of the debates, it became clear that one's theory of transition out of feudalism would be closely connected to one's conception of the feudal mode of production as such. Dobb's feudalism was defined by a class relation of personal subservience (on the part of serfs) and domination (on the part of lords). He then located the source of tension, and transition, in a 'growing need of the lords for revenue', which prompted them to commute labour services and rent in kind as forms of surplus extraction from the serfs, and replace them with money rent. The three stages – labour services, rent in kind, money rent – are in fact those described by Marx in *Capital III*, chapter 47, 'Genesis of capitalist ground rent', as the foundation for his analysis of the specificity of capitalist forms in agriculture, as these emerged later (see also Fine and Harris, 1979, ch. 7).

The commutation of feudal dues and their replacement by money rent, however, facilitated the growth of markets for consumption necessities and means of production, and weakened the ties of serfs to the feudal manor, thus undermining the feudal system as such – an instance of the role of unintended consequences in social change. Dobb also devoted much attention to the problematic later phase of transition: the transformation of commerce and merchant enrichment into the mature capitalist form of surplus extraction in which producers become propertyless wage labourers, whose subordination to capital is secured by the capitalists' ownership of the means of production and control within the workplace. This passage from 'proto-capitalism' to capitalism-as-such is the object of Marx's attention in *Capital I,* Part VIII, on 'Primitive Accumulation', but also, and importantly in many respects, the work on 'Machinery and modern industry' (ch. 15) and much of the rest of Part IV, 'Production of Relative Surplus Value'.

Paul Sweezy (1978) offered a view with a very different emphasis. Feudalism in his conception was a system of 'production for use'; its demise was sparked by the rise of the market system and trade, which are essentially capitalist in character from the outset. In descriptive terms, either approach will support the grand narrative of the rise of towns, the declining power of the feudal lords faced with the emergence of powerful absolute monarchs, the alliance between king and the merchant class, the growth of trade, and the eventual drive towards devolved sovereignty and representative government. Sweezy's emphasis, however, was on trade (commodity production) as the prime mover, whereas Dobb focused on internal developments within feudal class relations.

Robert Brenner's (1976) theory of the agrarian origins of capitalism, in England, as well as elsewhere, returned to the internal, but centred more generally on class struggle as the source of manorial decline. Some of his critics introduced an additional element: cyclical swings in population, or in population growth, which became evident throughout Europe from the thirteenth century onward (Bois, 1978). Population shifts, of course, were in many cases determined by plagues, an external factor that did not sit well with any attempt at systematic explanation. Both the Dobb-Sweezy exchange and the subsequent Brenner debate evolved into enormously learned but generally inconclusive examinations of empirical evidence emerging out of the complex transitions of the late feudal/early capitalist centuries. Solid theoretical synthesis seemed all but impossible, as the *dei ex machina* of trade, population, plagues and wars crossed swords with the *dei intra machina* of class struggle and the lords' need for revenue. Why did any of these phenomena, all of which are undoubtedly present historically, become significant when and to the extent they did? Why did they have the precise effects they did? What would drive the feudal mode of production into crisis? Why would this crisis eventuate in marketized social relations that increasingly laid foundations for capitalism? (One needs to remember that evidence of trade, markets, money, even finance, goes far back into antiquity, indeed into the earliest records of human existence.) Missing was a robust theory of social formations and transitions in general, which might provide a general structure to synthesize the enormous wealth of information, data and partial insights generated by the debates to this point.

STAGES OF SOCIAL EVOLUTION

A stadial (stages-based) theory of social evolution identifies an abstract set of stages of development. Unlike empirical-descriptive stages, based on apparent commonalities evident within a given period of time, such theoretical stages are interrelated by necessity. A given stage rests upon the preceding one and derives its central character from its predecessor. It has its own 'contradiction', a necessary feature that increasingly undermines it and makes its existence problematic. Finally, it provides a decisive contribution to the succeeding stage, making that stage possible and shaping its defining qualities. Theoretical stages are thus chain-linked. The number of stages, and the order of their succession, are determined by their essential nature and are not arbitrary. Our task is to identify the feudal mode of production as a theoretical stage within this sort of construction.

Resistance to the project of identifying a determinate ladder of modes of production has been widespread. It stems from the perceived multiplicity of paths of development in the historical record, and the role of a host of incalculable contingent factors: geography and climate; warfare; personalities, ideologies and capacities of leaders; and the occurrence of chance events. This objection becomes moot, however, so long as two levels of abstraction are carefully distinguished: the concrete, variegated unfolding of actual history, on the one hand; and the distilled core of that process, embodied in the theoretical stadial model, on the other. The second does not substitute for the first; it only helps organize our thinking about the empirical record, and must receive continuing validation from its usefulness in accomplishing that task. At the level of the stadial model, succession is orderly and determinate, only because that model abstracts from accident and from the fortuitous complexity of the 'real' world. In that world, societies at different stages of development come into contact, usually through trade or conquest, and social formations that combine multiple features of different modes of production develop. Stages are skipped; disease, migration and resource depletion cause regressions to occur; blockages intervene to prevent development; and so on.

FEUDALISM AND STAGES THEORY

Feudalism is not a general term for any sort of pre-capitalist 'tributary' social form (cf. Amin, 1985). It is a precise solution to the defining tension of the slave system of antiquity: the crisis of surplus extraction arising from extensive growth of the productive forces, due in turn to the brutal and primitive slave method of exploitation, and the associated costly and inefficient structures of control (overseers, military forces). Direct physical restraint and confinement of slaves and compulsion of labour based on actual or threatened infliction of pain are ultimately incompatible with productivity-enhancing methods of production, and the potential power such methods would place in the hands of the direct producers. Increased surplus from slave production thus means more slaves, and larger plantations, mining and construction sites. Disproportionate growth in allocations from the surplus to internal and external means of coercion and control make this system increasingly unviable, and vulnerable.

The feudal manorial economy, by contrast, is a small-scale, self-sufficient system, combining partial devolution of control over land, tools and animals to the direct producers with indirect physical constraint (mainly the lack of mobility and alternatives; serfs attached to a manor have 'nowhere else to go', so to speak), an important role for ideology (religion) in the overall system of control, the hierarchy of vassalage masking the source of authority and power, and the advantages of certain shared means of production (common lands, mills, mechanical workshops, irrigation systems). This far more sophisticated complex of incentive, control and coercion makes possible the extraction of a surplus from the labour of serfs, in the form of work on the lord's demesne, rent in kind and other service obligations (including military service). The inherent limitation of scale economies resulting from the parcellization of control combines with enhanced incentives arising from serfs' personal ownership of tools and animals, and vested rights in personal plots of land. This unique combination creates a thrust towards intensive productive development (increase in output per unit of labour): intensive agriculture (crop and field rotation, contouring, irrigation, use of fertilizer, deep ploughing using draft animals, application of wind and water power to threshing and milling and so on), mechanical engineering (clock works, tool-making, weaving) and handicraft industries. Intensive productive forces development, in turn, establishes the possibility – therefore, eventually, the reality – of a significant, dependable surplus in *individual* production (unlike the collective surplus that grounded the earlier emergence of the ancient slave systems). The individual surplus, created in the incubator of the feudal manor, is marketable. Feudal development is thus the foundation for both the possibility and the necessity of markets – with their eventual outcomes: towns, cities, population growth, money, accumulation, polarization – and their shift from the sidelines of social reality to the centre. The entire movement establishes the historic role of feudalism as the specific bridge from the slave empires to capitalism. Capitalist surplus extraction, a still more advanced and sophisticated form, relies on the complete generalization of market relations, which have progressed from accidental, ceremonial and long-distance trade, to trade in luxuries, then to trade in basic consumer and producer goods and, finally, to trade in the capacity to perform labour as such in return for a wage (labour power, the hallmark commodity of capitalist social relations). Surplus extraction now operates by mystifying the social relations of exploitation, which come to appear as something natural and eternal.

Feudalism's contribution to the stadial chain – its necessity as one rung on the ladder of theoretical modes of production – is precisely its capacity to develop the productive forces in an intensive direction, and therefore to ground the later expansion of the market. The 'rise of the market', therefore, is explained; it does not simply fall from the sky. That rise, however, is also the death knell of the very feudal system that made it possible. It shapes the general character of the class struggle, by providing the very exit opportunities for the serfs whose absence in the earlier period of high feudalism was central to feudal surplus extraction. It is also the foundation for the novel capitalist system of coercion that will eventually be consolidated to carry forward productive forces development, within a general framework of class antagonism, in a form that is simultaneously extensive and intensive. Capitalism, with its unique, market-based form of exploitation, occupies the highest rung on the ladder of class-antagonistic modes of production – a claim whose substantiation, however, would take us far beyond the purpose (and space limitations) of this entry.

STAGES AND SOCIAL TRANSFORMATIONS

The story told here may sound teleological; it is not. Teleology is the imputation of will and purpose to objects and processes that do not have these qualities; it is also, in a broader definition, an assumption that social evolution, or any particular step in social evolution, being necessary in some sense, is also inevitable. The necessities and regularities that lie behind the variety and accident of the perceived historical record derive from certain requirements of human existence. There is the obvious: the need to maintain a constant metabolism with the external environment, by means of labour. Increase in productive power is inherent in human symbolic consciousness, even though it emerges irregularly. When it does emerge, it 'requires' a corresponding evolution in social relations. The ladder of class-divided modes of production is the succession of systems of incentive/coercion/control, moving from those that are comparatively crude and work best in connection with lower levels of productive development, to more sophisticated forms that enable, and shape, the higher levels.

'Required' transformations, however, in either methods of production or the social relations surrounding them, do not happen independently of consciousness and will. Nothing is ever done that human beings do not do, acting individually or collectively. And nothing is inevitable. Any given social formation may, for example, stagnate indefinitely, if this is dictated by some stand-off between forces making for change and those making for stasis. Scenarios of collapse, even on a global scale, such as those traced by Jared Diamond (2005), can and must be entertained. Historical materialism can only point to a chain of evolutions that are necessary *if* human potential is to continue to unfold; it cannot assert that humanity *will* survive to witness the higher links along that chain. And the actual choreography – as, for example, the diverse paths of feudalism-to-capitalism transition in Eastern and Western Europe, the unique cases of Japan and Russia, the contrast between the class and state formations propelling and shaped by the English and French revolutions, to take just a few examples – depends on diverse circumstances that the stadial model cannot and should not try to explain.

The stadial model, however, does place feudalism-to-capitalism within a larger explanatory frame. The thinkers of the bourgeois Enlightenment (and their present-day echoes) turn the Great Transition into a one-time apocalyptic event, which in effect elevates capitalism to the status of Grand Terminus, the end of history. Marxist or Marxism-influenced thinkers who make 'the market' central to their definition of capitalism, and the 'rise of trade' the signal (unexplained) event triggering the transition, concede the high ground to the mainstream historians: all roads that are visible to social theory lead to capitalism, and socialism/communism becomes a utopian doctrine with no 'objective' basis. The stadial model, by contrast, suggests that markets are at first engines of social and technical progress, but later become – especially in their capitalist form – a brake on progress. The transition from feudalism to capitalism, then, presages – in theory, not just in wishful thinking – the more profound later transition, to post-capitalist social relations, and beyond. It remains to be seen, of course, whether this subsequent transition will occur successfully, against the resistance of retrograde social forces and facing unprecedented demographic, ecological and cultural challenges, not to mention the threats associated with the destructive potential of present-day technology.

56. Transnational corporations

Hugo Radice

Transnational corporations (TNCs) are widely acknowledged as an important form of capitalist enterprise, defined by the ownership of productive assets in more than one country. In modern times the globally largest and most powerful enterprises, in all sectors of economic activity, are transnational. Their precursors include the remarkable global trading firms of the early era of European colonial domination, the most important of which were chartered corporations established by the rival great powers of France, Britain and the Netherlands; and the banks that financed intra- and extra-European trade from the Middle Ages, with the most developed forms originating in the Italian city-states. The modern TNC dates from the late nineteenth century, and is associated with the forms of mass production and mass consumption that developed from that time on. Typically, the classic TNC has its origin in the concentration and centralization of capital within a particular sector; the few firms that emerge as dominant may then possess technological, financial or other advantages that enable them to go beyond the export of their output to foreign markets, and invest abroad in production facilities. This form of cross-border investment is termed foreign direct investment, or FDI, which is thus intimately related to the emergence and growth of TNCs.

The earliest discussions of FDI and TNCs can be found in the descriptive industrial, economics and business literature of the late nineteenth century, together with contemporary journalistic accounts. At that time one can already distinguish two main varieties of TNC. First, there are those business enterprises, mostly American and German, in the vanguard of the second industrial revolution in sectors such as chemicals, engineering, transport equipment, household durable goods and agricultural machinery: in a period when much industrial activity took place behind tariff barriers in protected markets, FDI was a way to gain access to new markets and thereby generate further increases in sales and profits. The second type of TNC was oriented towards securing natural resources, whether minerals or agricultural products, whose availability was limited in the most dynamic consumer markets for reasons of climate or geology. In the context of growing imperial rivalries in the advanced capitalist countries, the leading traders in raw materials sought to secure supplies through the ownership or control of the most profitable sources: nitrates in Chile or palm oil in West Africa, for example.

In Marx's *Capital* many of the key elements of the organization and business practices of TNCs can already be found: the concentration of capital; the centralization of ownership, especially based on credit and the joint stock system; the subordination of labour within production to the valorization of capital; and the significance of technological development. The first systematic treatment of FDI and TNCs, however, is found in the work of the second-generation classics, in the context of the development of theories of finance capital and imperialism. While Hilferding's (1910 [1994]) *Finance Capital* for the most part abstracts from questions of national location, Part V on the economic policy of finance capital provides a systematic account of the tendency towards capital export and thereby to the development of imperialism. Here, the evolution of competition towards cartels and trusts is seen as favouring policies of tariff protection, and this in turn encourages 'tariff jumping' in the form of setting up production within foreign markets (see ch. 22). Banks are seen as critical, both in funding FDI and in undertaking their own foreign investments to provide support to client firms. In Hilferding's account almost every element of the present-day descriptive analysis of TNCs can be found, notably the lure of cheap foreign labour and land and the weakness of local competition; but especially important is the close link to the systematic colonial annexation that formed a core feature of early twentieth-century imperialism.

It is well known that Hilferding's rich analysis provided much of the material for Lenin's later *Imperialism, the Highest Form of Capitalism*. But Bukharin (1918 [1972]), in *Imperialism and World Economy*, took Hilferding's work and developed a striking new analytical framework which anticipated many later theoretical developments. He identified two interacting dynamics in the capitalism of his day: a trend of 'internationalization', which (in the manner of the *Communist Manifesto*) centred on the boundless and therefore potentially global reach of capital accumulation, through international trade and capital export; and a trend of 'nationalization', centred on the emergence of finance capital, which was organized on a national basis, and had become more and more intertwined with the state. For Bukharin, the relation between the two was that the process of internationalization was 'shaped' by the process of nationalization into imperial expansion, and thus exacerbated the global rivalries of the great colonial powers.

As a result of the innovative work of Hilferding and Bukharin, together with other contributions by Bauer, Kautsky and Lenin, Marxist study of FDI and TNCs very largely took place right up to the 1970s in the context of the political economy of imperialism. It is also important to note that these 'classic' contributions drew heavily on the work of the German historical school and their Anglo-Saxon equivalents such as Hobson (*The Scientific Basis of Imperialism*) in Britain and the institutionalist school in the USA.

The development of TNCs and FDI between the wars shows two contrasting phases. In the 1920s, US enterprises rapidly developed their international production, both in natural resource sectors and in the more market-oriented manufacturing and financial services sectors. UK, French and Japanese businesses concentrated their FDI very much on their colonial possessions, while in Germany, lacking an extensive empire, the focus was on exploiting technological advantage to establish foreign production in industries such as chemicals, electrical and mechanical engineering and machinery. After the 1929 Crash and through the subsequent depression and the collapse of world trade, FDI stagnated and many firms retrenched to their home (including colonial) markets. By 1939, about two-thirds of the world's FDI stocks were investments in less developed regions by businesses headquartered in the leading capitalist countries, especially the USA, the UK, France, Germany and the lesser colonial powers. During this period, there was little sign of any original work by Marxist scholars on these developments, although there were some important contributions by descriptive industrial economists with relatively progressive politics, such as Plummer (1934) on international cartels and combines.

POSTWAR DEVELOPMENTS IN TNCs AND THEIR ANALYSIS

After 1945, both the international environment and the diverse national reconstruction processes in the advanced capitalist countries initially did not favour FDI and TNCs, in particular because of very widespread controls on international capital movements, coupled with equally widespread nationalizations of important businesses, especially across Europe (including whole industries such as coal, railways and so on). But by the 1960s the upward trend of the 1920s was finally resumed. Capital controls were steadily lifted, and the development of offshore capital markets (notably the so-called Eurodollar markets) and cross-border banking investments provided the financial infrastructure for a dramatic acceleration of FDI: first from the USA into Latin America and Europe, then a European response, and finally in the 1980s the even more dramatic growth of Japanese FDI. This growth was very largely focused on cross-investments within the advanced capitalist economies: by the 1970s, the ratio between the stock of FDI in the 'North' and the 'South' had reversed, with two-thirds now in the former. This also meant that natural resource sectors became relatively eclipsed by FDI in manufacturing up to the 1970s, and in services thereafter. By the turn of the century, following widespread privatizations of state enterprises, the demise of Soviet-style socialism and the emergence of new industrial economies in Asia and Latin America, the TNC had become the universal form of the large corporate capitalist firm.

Postwar mainstream economics had great difficulty in coming to terms with the TNC. In part this was simply a variation on the difficulty that neoclassical theory had in dealing with the question of market power (leaving aside the Austrian variant, which rejected the determinist approach that had come to dominate the theory of the firm): market conditions of oligopoly or contestable monopoly were not amenable to the modelling of predictable outcomes. But, in addition, large-scale FDI could not easily be accommodated in the neoclassical theory of international trade, except by making assumptions about the nature of investments, especially the malleability of capital, that were patently at odds with reality. Economists seeking to develop realistic theories of the TNC tended to follow something like J.B. Clark's inductivist method in seeking to understand 'workable competition': they developed stories about the decision mechanisms and managerial practices of TNCs, typically focusing on analytically messy aspects like technological change, product diversity and co-respective behaviour.

By the 1970s, TNCs had emerged as a distinctive area of scholarship, but given the indifference of analytical economics, most scholars gravitated rapidly to the US-style business studies field. The study of TNCs thereby contributed substantively to the training of those who ran them, a new breed of internationally mobile executives, and international business became one of the key fields of teaching and research in business schools. The ideological openness of business studies, as compared with economics, made it easy for Marxists and other heterodox scholars to collaborate in empirical research and analytical enquiry with mainstream scholars whose approach was mostly not dogmatically neoclassical.

But there were other reasons for a significant overlap of interests and scholarly research between Marxists and the mainstream. First, the rapid growth of FDI and TNCs required the development of new areas of government policy and intergovernmental coordination, and this led to vigorous and unusually open debates about the causes and consequences of these phenomena. Second, the theoretical precocity and empirical grounding of the classic Marxist work of Hilferding, Lenin and Bukharin meant that Marxists had something of a head start in coming to grips with TNCs. This was to become increasingly clear when, from the late 1980s, the study of TNCs became a central object in the globalization debates that cut across all the social science disciplines. Notably, Bukharin's dialectic of internationalization and nationalization closely prefigures the market/state dichotomy that became common currency in the field of international political economy in the 1990s.

A third reason was the emergence of the interdisciplinary field of development studies, in close relation to the anti-colonial struggles that brought the old European empires to a close. Although subject to the same ideological divides as other fields, the focus of development studies on long-term postcolonial transformation had a natural attraction for Marxists schooled in a historical approach to socio-economic change and a strong normative commitment to challenge exploitation. Finally, the founding of the European Economic Community in 1958 led to a broader movement for regional integration; again, a historical political economy approach was well suited to the analysis of this trend, focused on the relation between the state and the internationalization of capital.

MARXIST CONTRIBUTIONS TO THE STUDY OF TNCs

Turning to the distinctive contributions of Marxists to the study of TNCs in recent decades, these can be divided into four subject areas. First, a number of important elements of Marxist economic theory have been deployed in the analysis of TNCs. By the 1970s, the latter were being examined under the rubric of the 'internationalization of capital', and in particular Marx's concept of the circuits of capital offered analytical purchase. The different stages in the general circuit M-C. . .P. . .C'-M' could take place in different countries, linking together national patterns of capital accumulation either through trade in inputs (M-C) or outputs (C'-M'), or by the location of production (. . .P. . .) in another country (see especially the paper by Palloix in Radice, 1975). Such an approach has affinities also with the commodity chain approach developed later by Gereffi and other progressive scholars. More broadly, the growth of TNCs and their 'internalization' of trade (that is, flows between their subsidiaries in different countries) intensified the problems long perceived in analysing how the law of value functioned when its scope was tendentially global rather than simply national.

Second, the postwar renaissance of Marxian work on imperialism included attempts to grapple with the consequences of the rise of TNCs for the state and inter-state relations. In the 1960s, the orthodox communist understanding of contemporary capitalism, the theory of state monopoly capitalism, faithfully endorsed the classic Bolshevik position of Lenin and Bukharin, that the locational pattern of global capital accumulation was fundamentally structured by imperial rivalries and close ties between monopoly capitalists and their states of origin. Broadly speaking, this view was shared by Marxists who in other respects strongly criticized the Soviet orthodoxy. The rise of TNCs, however, raised the possibility of a 'denationalization' of the capital-state relation, as a result of what Murray (in Radice, 1975) called 'territorial non-coincidence'; states were choosing to recognize reciprocally the legitimacy of, and benefits from, the presence of foreign-owned business, following in effect the 'most-favoured nation' principle well known in international trade policy. This in turn led some to postulate that at last the 'renegade Kautsky', who had proposed against Lenin that the imperial powers might find common cause in collectively exploiting the globe, had come into his own. European integration could be seen as a first step towards Kautskyan 'ultra-imperialism' (see readings by Mandel and Rowthorn in Radice, 1975).

These two areas of scholarship, on the internationalization of capital and on the role of the state, clearly anticipated some of the key themes of the globalization debates that got under way around 1990. It is important to note, however, that in both periods, Marxists were deeply divided over many of the issues under discussion. These divisions centred, as Jenkins (1987) argued, on the division between classical Marxist and neo-Marxist approaches. In the classical Marxist approach, competition is understood as a dynamic process founded on the extraction of surplus value; capital is seen as intrinsically global, and the state as intrinsically capitalist. An example of this approach would be the 'open Marxist' school, which characterizes the state as a form of the capital relation. In neo-Marxist approaches, present-day capitalism is seen as characterized by monopoly as a market structure, a tendency to stagnation and the pervasive need for state intervention; FDI is a business strategy, and the direction of the 'relatively autonomous' state is contested by competing social interests. The Monthly Review school is an example of this approach and, to a large extent, also the present-day neo-Gramscian school of international political economy.

Third, the analysis of underdevelopment, and especially the approach of the dependency school, identified TNCs as a major agent of international exploitation and the subordination of the Third World. Underdeveloped countries lacked the capital, technology and skills to undertake rapid industrialization and development; TNCs offered all these, plus access to Northern markets, first for natural resources, and from the 1960s for low-cost labour-intensive industrial products. But their financial, technological and political clout meant that TNCs could drive a hard bargain with host countries, something that was equally apparent to many non-Marxist scholars. While dependency theorists often seemed to restrict their critical analyses to conflicts of national interest rather than class relations, Marxist work stressed that dependent capitalism was nevertheless capitalist. The various types of dependent forms of development were shaped very largely by the accumulation dynamics of the advanced industrial economies via the investments of TNCs; but the outcome was the creation of cadres of domestic collaborators in the state and the private sector, as a modern form of Baran's '*comprador* bourgeoisie' (see, for example, Sunkel, 1973).

Fourth, the 1970s also saw a new focus in Marxist scholarship on production and labour, notably focused on the labour process. Given the dominance of TNCs in capitalist enterprise, their transnational organization of production became a significant topic in the field of labour process studies, although in this regard there is little distinctively Marxist scholarship that is specifically concerned with transnationality. More important has been work on the 'new international division of labour' (Fröbel et al., 1980), which provided a new analytical framework that was less contentious than dependency theory. But Marxists also participated in the study of international trade unionism, where their political economy approach proved particularly fruitful.

In conclusion, TNCs have in the last fifty years become increasingly significant as the main organizational vehicle for capital accumulation. As such, they are an important subject of study for the contemporary Marxist critique of political economy. The results of that study not surprisingly reflect the diversity of approaches within the Marxist tradition.

57. Unemployment

Gary Slater

Modern economic theory tends to treat unemployment as the result of individual or market pathologies, where the latter variously involve a range of rigidities or imperfections preventing wages adjusting to a market clearing equilibrium. In sharp contrast, Marx argues that unemployment is inherent within capitalism. Indeed, unemployment is both the condition for, and effect of, capital accumulation and it cannot simply be explained as the outcome of malfunctioning markets. Rather, unemployment plays a crucial role underpinning capitalist development as it variously impacts on the evolution of wages, work effort and poverty. Accordingly, the nature and significance of unemployment in Marxist analysis runs much deeper than within modern economic theory. This is, however, often overlooked in discussions of Marx's contribution. Instead commentators tend to focus on the more polemical passages from the *Communist Manifesto* which suggest rising and relentless immiseration for the working class. In contrast, a much more detailed and mature analysis can be found in the *Grundrisse* and *Capital*. This presents a much more nuanced view, and one which highlights fluctuations in the position of the working class rather than a slide into absolute poverty and worklessness for many.

THE INDUSTRIAL RESERVE ARMY AND ACCUMULATION

For Marx, unemployment presupposes employment under capitalist conditions. That is, unemployment is a historically specific category, intimately related to the nature and dynamics of employment under capitalism. Marx's theory of unemployment is succinctly put in the *Grundrisse*: 'It is a law of capital . . . to create surplus labour, disposable time; it can do this only by setting *necessary labour* in motion – i.e. entering into exchange with the worker . . . It is therefore equally a tendency of capital to increase the labouring population, as well as constantly to posit a part of it as surplus population – population which is useless until such time as capital can utilize it'. But what is the connection between employment and unemployment? To see this it is necessary to unpack the ideas encapsulated in this quotation.

Under capitalism, the source of surplus value is located in the sphere of production. Whilst in the labour market the exchange of labour power for the wage occurs between free agents – the sphere of circulation or commodity exchange, 'within whose boundaries the sale and purchase of labour-power goes on, is in fact a very Eden of the innate rights of man' (Marx, *Capital I*, ch. 6) – production is managed and directed by the capitalist. It is here, in production, that the labour process becomes a valorization process as capitalists employ various strategies that extract more value from workers than the value of the labour power paid for their capacity to work. Marx refers to the capitalist control of the labour process, and the attendant exploitation of workers, as the subjection of labour under capital (Marx, *Capital 1*, ch. 16). There is, however, an important distinction drawn between the formal and real subjection or subsumption of labour (Marx, *The Direct Process of Production of Capital*, 6) The Direct Production Process, Formal Subsumption of Labour under Capital). The former refers to the inclusion of pre-existing processes of production by capitalist relations, corresponding to the emergence and development of capitalism. Here the character of the labour process remains unchanged, but the economic relations between worker and employer have been transformed. Given the inherited mode of labour, at this stage surplus value can only be created by extending the working day, that is, through the creation of absolute surplus value.

In contrast, the real subsumption of labour occurs as the capitalist mode of production proper develops. *Capital I* contains a wealth of theoretical, historical and empirical detail outlining the emergence of large-scale production, mechanization, the changing division of labour and, above all, the way in which the rising social productivity of labour is 'brought about at the cost of the individual labourer; all means for the development of production transform themselves into means of domination over, and exploitation of, the producers' (Marx, *Capital I*, ch. 25, section 4). These developments, entailing the transformation of the labour process, are intimately bound-up with Marx's analysis of unemployment: capital accumulation, based on relative surplus value, gives rise to and, in turn, depends upon a relative surplus population, termed the (industrial) reserve army of labour.

With capital accumulation comes centralization, driven by competition and by the greater availability of credit due to innovations in the financial system (for example, joint-stock companies). Larger, more efficient capitals tend to drive out the smaller in the process of competition, leading to their takeover or elimination and greater centralization. Similarly, the greater availability of credit allows for an increased scale of production. It is this result of the centralization of capital which is the 'starting point for a more comprehensive organisation of the collective work of many, for a wider development of their material motive forces – in other words, for the progressive transformation of isolated processes of production, carried on by customary methods, into processes of production socially combined and scientifically arranged' (Marx, *Capital I*, ch. 25, section 2). This impacts on the demand for labour by intensifying and accelerating the effects of capital accumulation. In particular, from centralization follows more mechanization and the development of new production technologies. As discussed by Marx in the *Resultate* (Marx, *The Direct Process of Production of Capital*, 6) The Direct Production Process, The Real Subsumption of Labour under Capital or the Specifically Capitalist Mode of Production), the greater the use of, refinement and development of machinery, the greater the specialization of the worker and the greater scale of production that allows for these innovations, the higher is productivity, the greater is relative surplus value and the less is the demand for labour power relative to constant capital within these modernizing industries.

Does this mean a secular decline in employment and ever-rising unemployment? Marx is careful to note that the accumulation of capital, and the changes wrought to production, occur unevenly across industries and at a varying pace. Thus, as total social capital expands, there is a dual process by which the absolute number of workers required may rise, but relative to expanding capital they fall, as reflected in a rising organic composition of capital: 'in all spheres, the increase of the variable part of capital, and therefore of the number of labourers employed by it, is always connected with violent fluctuations and transitory production of surplus population, whether this takes the more striking form of the repulsion of labourers already employed, or the less evident but not less real form of the more difficult absorption of the additional labouring population through the usual channels' (Marx, *Capital I*, ch. 25, section 3).

For Marx, then, the generation of a surplus population – the 'industrial reserve army' – constitutes the law of population under capitalism. Contra Malthus, who is roundly criticized for failing to develop a historically specific analysis, this surplus population is independent of any general increase in population. Rather, its size and composition depend upon the rhythm of capital accumulation. As economic activity expands and contracts unevenly over time and between industries and, as new areas emerge, there is a flow of workers between branches of production and into and out of employment. Crucially, however, the reserve army is necessary to allow for growth in expanding areas without damaging others: 'The course characteristic of modern industry . . . depends on the constant formation, the greater or less absorption, and the re-formation of the industrial reserve army or surplus population' (Marx, *Capital I*, ch. 25, section 3).

There is a further step in the argument. Not only is a reserve required to allow for the expansion of production and the emergence of new branches of production, but the very rises in productivity that contribute to the generation of a surplus population are, in turn, underpinned by the reserve army: 'Capital works on both sides at the same time. If its accumulation, on the one hand, increases the demand for labour, it increases on the other the supply of labourers by the "setting free" of them, whilst at the same time the pressure of the unemployed compels those that are employed to furnish more labour, and therefore makes the supply of labour, to a certain extent, independent of the supply of labourers' (Marx, *Capital I*, ch. 25, section 3).

This reserve army has an additional, important role to play – as a short-term regulator of wages. The expansion and contraction of the reserve army over the business cycle acts as a stabilizer to accumulation, preventing wages rising so far as to endanger profitability. During downturns or periods of normal activity the reserve army 'weighs down' the wages of the active workforce whilst, in the boom phases, 'it holds its pretensions in check' (Marx, *Capital I*, ch. 25, section 3).

Again, Marx's approach stands distinct from that of earlier political economy in that total population is, for him, irrelevant to the outcomes for workers or capitalists. Movements in the reserve army overwhelm any longer-term shifts in population; hence only changes in the reserve army serve to regulate wages (Marx, *Capital I*, ch. 25, section 3). Taken together, the above discussion sets out the basis of Marx's theory of unemployment. The reserve army of labour is both a systemic outcome of the capitalist mode of production and a necessary foundation for it; it is both the 'product' and 'lever' of accumulation (Marx, *Capital I*, ch. 25, section 2).

THE COMPOSITION OF THE RESERVE ARMY

So far, the concept of the reserve army of labour has been treated as essentially synonymous with unemployment. However, there is an important distinction between Marx's concept and that of unemployment as it appears in official government statistics or in modern economic theory. In short, Marx's concept runs much more widely and takes as its starting point the potential for the non-employed to be incorporated within capitalist production. To see this, it is instructive to consider the components of the reserve army identified in *Capital*: the floating, latent and stagnant. The floating refers to those with the closest recent experience of capitalist production and, therefore, those for whom periods out of work tend to be temporary. It consists of the workers variously incorporated into and repelled from industrial production with the rhythms of capital accumulation, in terms of both the business cycle and the extension of mechanization. Here Marx suggests a tendency for older workers to be displaced by younger, with the former entering the reserve army or, if successful in securing alternative employment, often seeing a drop in status and wage (Marx, *Capital I*, ch. 25, section 4). Thus, although unemployment is temporary for these workers, the size and composition of this component of the reserve army is predicted to vary across the cycle.

The latent comprises those who are not or who have never been wage-labourers, but who form a potential source of labour power for capitalist expansion. Here Marx discusses the surplus rural population, increasingly struggling to find employment due to the capitalist penetration and industrialization of agriculture, and who must migrate to urban areas in search of work. Finally, Marx identifies a stagnant element which refers to those rendered redundant by technological change and industrial reorganization, but who are able at most to secure only very irregular employment. These workers, expelled from agriculture and independent or small-scale manufacturing, comprise an 'inexhaustible reservoir of disposable labour power'; when they are able to secure work, in domestic service, for example, it is 'characterised by maximum of working-time, and minimum of wages' (Marx, *Capital I*, ch. 25, section 4). For Marx, this segment is predicted to become relatively more important, both as a result of the continual upheaval wrought by accumulation and as a consequence of its relative poverty. This leads the stagnant layer to become both 'a self-reproducing and self-perpetuating element of the working class', not least from rising family sizes which follow from low wages (Marx, *Capital I*, ch. 25, section 4).

Paupers and orphans are also included within the stagnant segment and may similarly join the active army of labour at times of exceptional increases in production. However, there are also those who do not or who cannot. The former are identified as the lumpenproletariat – 'vagabonds, criminals, prostitutes' (Marx, *Capital I*, ch. 25, section 4). The latter comprises the demoralized, injured, sick and old; those who cannot work but whose condition is often the result of their experience in work. It is within this stagnant segment of the reserve army that Marx identifies the source of poverty: '[t]he more extensive, finally, the lazarus layers of the working class, and the industrial reserve army, the greater is official pauperism. *This is the absolute general law of capitalist accumulation*' (Marx, *Capital I*, ch. 25, section 4).

This is not to be interpreted as some 'iron law' leading to the absolute immiseration of the working class as a whole, an idea contained within the younger Marx's *Communist Manifesto*. Indeed, Marx notes immediately after stating this 'law' that its operation is modified in practice by many other tendencies. Rather, for Marx, it encapsulates his analysis of the relation between accumulation, population and poverty (the latter's 'official' proportion alone, derived from one part of the stagnant body of the unemployed, and designated as such to be subject to proportionate increase). Against contemporary political economy, Marx sought to demonstrate that, despite appearances, poverty and worklessness were not a result of over-population, but rather they were a necessary and unavoidable condition of the capitalist system: '[t]he fact that the means of production, and the productiveness of labour, increase more rapidly than the productive population, expresses itself, therefore, capitalistically in the inverse form that the labouring population always increases more rapidly than the conditions under which capital can employ this increase for its own self-expansion' (Marx, *Capital I*, ch. 25, section 4).

As capitalists seek to raise relative surplus value through mechanization and productivity increases, this generates a reserve army of labour and, to a varying degree, generates poverty; the problem is one of capitalism's making, not of some excessive population.

THE CONTINUING SIGNIFICANCE OF MARX'S THEORY OF UNEMPLOYMENT

Clearly much has changed in the structure and operation of capitalism since Marx developed his theory of unemployment. What is the contemporary significance of the reserve army? What light can it shed on the functioning of labour markets? Modifications to the form and function of the reserve army have come variously from the increased role of the state, the rise in organized labour and in the continuing internationalization of capitalism. The role of the state has been twofold. First, the rise of welfarism has removed for most the threat of absolute poverty consequent upon job loss, moderating the depressive function of the reserve army on wage growth (although confirming Marx's absolute general law concerning official 'pauperism'). Second, in the so-called 'golden age' of the 1950s and 1960s, governments committed to policies of full employment, using broadly Keynesian policies, and with some apparent success in eliminating measured unemployment. However, in both cases since the crises of the 1970s and 1980s, capitalist states have executed marked U-turns both in welfare and macroeconomic policy. The slowdown in productivity and squeeze on profits that presaged the end of the golden age led to more or less conscious attempts to replenish the reserve army with restrictive macroeconomic policies. At times, this intention has been explicit, as with the admission by a British Chancellor of the Exchequer that unemployment was a price 'well worth paying' to curb inflationary wage pressures (Lamont, 1991). Similarly on welfare policy, governments have generally sought to restrict the coverage and 'generosity' of payments since the 1980s to create greater pressure on the non-employed to seek work, increasing the compulsion to accept often low-paying and insecure work. Most recently, this pressure has been heightened in parts of Europe by increased migration from new members of the European Union and, as discussed below, this can be seen as replenishing the reserve army and its depressive effect on wages.

It would be naive to map these changes directly onto Marx's original arguments, but they signal the wider role and function of the reserve army, famously highlighted by Kalecki (1943) in his discussion of the political economy of state economic policy. He argued it was a fallacy to assume that what prevented governments from delivering full employment was the absence of the right set of policies. Even were these available, the experience of full employment would lead to overwhelming political pressure to abandon the measures, due to lobbying from big business: "'discipline in the factories" and "political stability" are more appreciated than profits by business leaders. Their class instinct tells them that lasting full employment is unsound from their point of view, and that unemployment is an integral part of the "normal" capitalist system' (Kalecki, 1943, p. 326). Even though full employment would raise profits in the short term, the stronger position of workers would lead to strikes for higher wages and, crucially, erode work effort and discipline as the sack would be no threat with work otherwise easily available elsewhere. In other words, full employment would emasculate the fundamental functions of the reserve army, threatening accumulation and leading to a political revolt among the capitalist class.

Relating to the above, the rise of organized labour has moderated the reserve army function, with unions resisting wage cuts in recession and regulating the intensification of work. The success of unions has been uneven across sectors, not least in the presence of the segmentation of labour markets. Although not the sole preserve of Marxian economists, the argument, in short, is that labour markets in contemporary capitalism are stratified, largely reflecting varying approaches to control of the labour force and differing degrees of industry or firm-specific skill amongst the workforce. In the large-scale, capital-intensive primary segments of the economy, systems of bureaucratic or technical control are used to regulate worker effort, entailing positive incentives within internal labour markets or machine-based monitoring within office or factory-based production, respectively. The significance of this is that it is only in the smaller, more labour-intensive, largely non-unionized firms – the secondary sector – that harsh disciplinary techniques, the threat of the sack and unstable job opportunities regulate work effort. On this argument, in modern capitalism the reserve army effect is felt most keenly in secondary labour markets. Notwithstanding the controversy surrounding segmentation theory within and without Marxist political economy, some support has been found for the proposition that the disciplinary effect of unemployment on work effort is greatest in secondary jobs (see Green, 1991). However, this is not to say that the boundaries are immutable. As union power has declined, not least following deliberate state actions in some countries including the UK, so-called primary employment has declined and secondary conditions have tended to apply to wider sections of employment, reflected in growing non-standard employment, in-work poverty and work intensification (see Green, 2006). This can be seen as enlarging the stagnant section of the reserve army which, in turn, has underpinned the dismantling and restructuring of previous labour market shelters in the primary sector.

These movements are well described by Braverman (1974, ch. 17), who also remarks upon the widening of the latent component of the reserve army in contemporary capitalism. With movements of labour from agriculture to industry largely exhausted in developed capitalist economies (although clearly evident in industrializing economies such as China), the latent reserve army has become international. This is seen most clearly in migration to capitalist economies, from former colonies or neighbouring countries (witness the importance of Mexican labour within the southern United States or the flows between new and old European Union member states) but this is not a process that goes unchecked. Importantly, it is a process that is encouraged or impeded according to the demand for labour and needs of accumulation. This internationalization of the latent reserve is further strengthened by the threat and practice of multinational firms to relocate operations in less developed regions of the world, moves which can be seen as further 'curbing the pretensions' of workers in developed economies.

It could also be said that women have played an important role as a latent reserve in recent decades, with an increasing tendency for married women to return to work over the past few decades. Braverman, however, sees rising female participation as contributing to the floating and stagnant layers of the reserve army, the latter following from women's occupational segregation, tendency to be over-represented in insecure and short-hours jobs and as a result of the continuing female pay gap.

For Marx, then, employment and unemployment cannot be separated and the notion of the reserve army runs much wider and deeper than measured joblessness. This connection can be seen in one final implication of Marx's analysis. The release of workers attendant upon mechanization and the increasing application of science and technology leads to labour piling up in the lower productivity areas associated with services such as sales, caring, hospitality and cleaning. As Braverman notes, this leads to the paradox that periods of rapid scientific and technical advance tend to raise employment in sectors least affected by those advances. This process both creates and depends upon an enlargement of the reserve army, the downward pressure on wages underpinning the profitable expansion of low productivity areas and leading to an expansion of the stagnant component of the reserve army. Although discussed some three decades ago by Braverman, just such a pattern of 'polarized' jobs growth in industrialized economies has recently been remarked upon by some economists. However, in falling back on exogenous technological change and theories of supply and demand in trying to make sense of these outcomes, they miss the essential connections between accumulation, employment and unemployment highlighted by Marx (see Nolan and Slater, 2010).

CONCLUSION

For Marx, unemployment and employment under capitalism are intimately connected. The concept of the reserve army of labour is much broader than the common or official meaning of 'unemployment', in that it incorporates wider categories of potential and underemployed workers. It is also an integral part of the analysis of capitalist accumulation, leading Marxists to point to the impossibility of full employment under capitalism. The dynamics of the reserve army reflect upon the wages and work effort of the employed and, indeed, play an important role in the evolution of the employment structure. Marx's contribution is to establish the inevitability of worklessness for some within capitalism and to demonstrate the unequal distribution of the benefits of rising productivity; rather than increase leisure time under capitalism it tends to expand the surplus population. Despite modifications to the form and function of the reserve army wrought by the changing institutions of capitalism, the concept and Marx's analysis of unemployment remain powerful tools with which to understand contemporary developments in capitalism.

58. Value-form approach

Samuel Knafo

The value-form approach emerged in the 1970s as a reaction against the economistic bias of traditional interpretations of *Capital*. In response, it offered a distinctive reading of Marx's late work which was meant to be more social and philosophical. One of the recurring themes of this approach is that the philosophical early writings are too often ignored when interpreting value theory. By contrast, value-form theorists see in Marx's early works the key to the significance of value theory and, more generally to Marx's later works, especially *Capital*.

The theme of Hegel's influence on Marx is often a central component of the value-form approach. It argues that Marx's Hegelian background imparted a specific logic to his argument about value that is too often missed within more economistic readings of *Capital*. Such interpretations convey the impression that *Capital* is about the production and distribution of wealth in capitalist societies. For those who hold this view, Marx would have shown that workers do not get a fair share of what they produce by contrast to what political economists such as David Ricardo had claimed. However, such economic readings accept the terrain set out by liberal economists too readily. Hence, value-form approaches seek to problematize the specific form wealth takes historically under capitalism and its social purpose. In doing so, they seek to redefine the object of value theory and its purpose.

Underpinning this argument is the contrast established by Hegel between form and content and their articulation through the dialectical method. In the value-form literature, this contrast serves to highlight that, beyond the apparently straightforward discussion about the production and distribution of value, there is a social dimension too often ignored. Hence, the idea of a social form, such as the value form, indicates a level of determination that is more profound and often less easy to perceive. One finds in this argument a direct reproduction of Marx's critique of political economy in the introduction of the *Grundrisse*. There, Marx argues that classical political economists such as Adam Smith and David Ricardo identified important features of capitalist dynamics but naturalized these characteristics by failing to grasp their historical specificity.

In a similar way, value-form approaches criticize both neoclassical economics and Marxist economists for conflating, each in their own way, historical manifestations of capitalism with the specific features of capitalism itself. In light of this problem, the notion of form serves two important purposes. The first is to distinguish what is specific about capitalism. Here, the notion of form is used as a specific abstraction that encapsulates the essential features of capitalism. The second is to reflect on the mediation between the concrete and historical level of analysis (content) and more abstract and theoretical analysis (form). The distinction of form and content is thus often used to link an emphasis on class struggle with a more theoretical appreciation of the distinctive features of capitalism.

PRECURSORS OF THE VALUE-FORM APPROACH

The foundations for the value-form approach were largely established by German and East European scholars, most notably Russian. This explains their belated influence in the Anglo-Saxon world where many of their works were only translated in the 1970s. The basic argument of the approach was first sketched by Hilferding in his reply to Von Böhm-Bawerk (Hilferding, 1975). The latter had criticized Marx's labour theory of value for seeing labour as the common denominator behind commodities. Because many other factors were involved in their production, Böhm-Bawerk considered the focus on labour to be arbitrary and rejected the idea that labour was the main determinant of value. In response, Hilferding argued that Böhm-Bawerk misunderstood the purpose of value theory by assessing it as an economic theory meant to explain how prices are determined. According to Hilferding, the emphasis on labour was not primarily justified on the basis of labour's contribution to the production of value per se. Rather it came from a social perspective based on the importance of labour in society. For him, the contribution of value theory was to highlight the social nature of value as a distinctive product of alienated labour rather than as a natural form of wealth.

Hilferding had a profound influence on Isaac I. Rubin who is often credited for having established the key pillars of the value-form approach. Rubin was a Russian economist who published in the 1920s, most notably his influential book *Essays on Marx's Theory of Value*. His writings explored some of the implications of Marx's Hegelian roots for understanding his theory of value. According to Rubin, value can easily appear as a 'content', that is, a quantity of abstract labour embedded into the commodity. Yet such conceptions of value lend themselves too easily to ahistorical interpretations which cast value as a transhistorical category. For this reason, Rubin insisted that value be taken as a distinctive product of capitalism. It only emerges, he argued, at the intersection of circulation and production, or, more specifically, through the process of exchange which socializes labour. Exchange is thus a necessary moment in the creation of value because it is at this point that different labour processes are compared in order to determine the socially necessary labour time for producing a commodity. This emphasis on the social process through which abstract value comes into being would be a first important contribution. For Rubin, the process through which value emerges as an abstraction is something that cannot be taken for granted and is the focus of value theory.

The attempt to recover value as a distinct and central social form of capitalism required a reworking of accepted notions about *Capital*. According to Rubin, the labour theory of value in the 1920s was too often perceived as the starting point to explain the logic of capitalism. The structure of *Capital* can reinforce, at first, this conception since labour and value appear first in the analysis, as if they represent the means to explain something else that comes later. For this reason, the emphasis is often put on commodities and their prices or the economic crises which result from this logic of capital. Against such a perspective, Rubin inverts the directionality of the argument in *Capital* by putting the emphasis on the beginning rather than the end. In a classic Hegelian move, Rubin sees the starting point as the focus of the analysis, that is, as an object to be further specified as the argument proceeds. Labour thus becomes a central object of analysis, one that is increasingly specified as the analysis of capital unfolds, rather than being slotted as a starting point used to explain the end point (that is, the unsustainability of capitalism). An important consequence is the new conception of value that emerges from this inversion. Indeed, value is no longer seen simply as a product of labour in itself, but becomes more significantly a structure that regulates social labour. In other words, the importance of value as an object of research comes from its impact on labour.

This inversion led Rubin to a third important contribution by shifting the emphasis of value theory towards the alienation of labour rather than the traditional focus on exploitation. Hence, instead of showing that workers do not get their fair share of what is produced, value theory was used by Rubin to examine the consequences for labour from production becoming subjected to the objectified logic of value. Capitalism was thus criticized here from the perspective of the reification of labour. Indeed, more important than the exploitation of labour is that workers are increasingly subjected to imperatives that are alien to their aspirations. It is the inversion between subject and object which becomes emblematic of capitalism as people no longer control their own lives and are increasingly subjected to the impersonal force of capital. In bringing alienation to the forefront of the analysis, Rubin emphasized the continuity in the evolution of Marx's work, seeing *Capital* as a further development of his early works.

Another important foundation for the value-form approach was the rediscovery of Marx's 'rough draft' of *Capital* which provided a crucial bridge between the more philosophical work of the young Marx and the later so-called economic writings. The key figure in the rediscovery of the *Grundrisse* was Roman Rosdolsky, a Ukrainian Marxist who had fled Stalinist persecution and then survived Nazism finally to emigrate to the USA after the Second World War. His book *The Making of Marx's Capital* (1977) became an important classic tracing the Hegelian underpinnings of *Capital*. As Rosdolsky pointed out, the nature of Marx's rough draft, rapidly written in 1857, provided a glimpse of how the Hegelian dialectic had helped him to develop his key insights. According to Rosdolsky, Marx had later removed the traces of this methodological scaffolding from *Capital* as his ideas became more mature and no longer needed the explicit recourse to these philosophical foundations. However, without them, it was too easy for subsequent generations of Marxists to miss the significance of *Capital* and the centrality of Hegel's logic. For this reason, the return to the *Grundrisse* represents for Rosdolsky an important step to grasp the process by which Marx formulated his ideas. It contributed to the growing interest in Marx's method since the 1970s, a theme Rosdolsky considered to be largely ignored in the 1960s.

CONTEMPORARY APPROACHES

In an Anglo-Saxon tradition which had largely been impervious to Hegel's influence on Marx, the value-form approach had to wait until the 1970s to exert a presence. At the time, the growing interest in German debates, notably on the capitalist state, and the translation of authors such as Rubin and Rosdolsky generated significant interest in the idea of social form. It provided various promising ideas for pushing debates in

Marxist theory, notably about value and the state. Geoffrey Pilling mobilized these ideas to recast the debate on value theory which had ensued from the Cambridge controversies of the 1960s. Indeed, in response to Sraffian critiques of Marx's labour theory of value, Pilling published his famous article 'The law of value in Ricardo and Marx' (1972) which established the value-form approach in the English world. In a manner reminiscent of Hilferding's rebuttal of Böhm-Bawerk, Pilling argued that the critiques of Marx's value theory were misguided because they misunderstood its purpose. Theories of value were not to be judged on the basis of their ability to prove the existence of value (Pilling, 1980). Rather, the relevance of this theory was to be assessed in relation to the effects of the law of value on labour. The main contribution of Pilling was to draw a sharp contrast between David Ricardo's and Marx's value theory in order to overcome the Ricardian bias which had plagued Marxist theory. For Pilling, the embodied theory of value, so often targeted by the critiques of Marxism (for example, Paul Samuelson and Joan Robinson), belonged in fact to Ricardo. Marx's contribution, on the contrary, consisted precisely in problematizing the very thing taken for granted by Ricardo: the process by which concrete labour takes the abstract form of value.

Rejecting the embodied labour theory of value generally meant clearly separating value from concrete labour. This solved the problem of reification associated with the Ricardian labour theory of value, but it introduced an indeterminacy regarding the source of value. It was now held that the physical expenditure of labour did not translate directly into abstract labour. But without any obvious quantified magnitudes to start from (for example, labour time), the value-form approach was generally forced away from quantitative considerations. One of the original and rare attempts to bridge this gap was made by Ira Gerstein in 1976. Gerstein argued that the 'transformation problem' was not a mathematical problem that consisted in correctly transforming abstract labour into prices, but rather an analytical step for articulating two different levels of analysis (production and circulation). He used quantitative analysis on the basis that categories such as value, which are associated with circulation, are 'implicitly' present at the level of production. But his goal was not to capture the causal mechanism through which prices are determined. Rather the significance of value theory was analytical. It helped to account for apparently contradictory phenomena. More generally, Gerstein wished to ground structural Marxism within value theory and secure the argument of the autonomy of the state. To this end, he used the distinction between the level of production where one can analyse the extraction of total surplus value, and circulation where one can examine how surplus value is distributed. From this perspective, value theory emphasized the primacy of total surplus value extraction and thus helped to define what was fundamental about capitalist class interests. From there, Gerstein argued that a relatively autonomous state was necessary to guarantee this extraction because individual capitalists were narrowly focused on profits and thus short sighted in their emphasis on how surplus value was distributed.

Gerstein's argument brought to a close a first period in the development of the value-form approach which was prompted by the debates around the transformation problem. Since the late 1970s, this approach has grown significantly to encompass two broad schools of thought. The first remains more firmly anchored in political economy and focuses on the central role of money. It is often linked to the work of Open Marxists (for example, Simon Clarke and Werner Bonefeld). The second is more philosophical and linked to a sustained engagement with Hegel's work and is often associated with the label of systematic dialectics (for example, Chris Arthur, Geert Reuten, Thomas Sekine). For the first group of authors, the notion of the form was initially articulated in relation to the state debate. Seeking to emphasize the centrality and open-ended nature of class struggle, the notion of form became a useful means to theorize the nature of capitalism without prejudging its future trajectory. In other words, it provided a template that could be used to problematize history and which had to be substantiated with a concrete study of class struggle. When theorizing about the form of capitalism, Open Marxists focused on linking different aspects of capitalist reality too often isolated from one another (for example, the political and economic dimensions of capitalism). More importantly, they sought to show how abstract forms of mediations, such as money or the state, appear neutral and apolitical but are rooted in class conflicts.

These ideas were extended most notably to think about money as the key mediator shaping capitalist social relations. Already in the work of Rubin, the idea that abstract labour only emerges through exchange put the emphasis on the pivotal role of money. No longer seen primarily as a commodity, money was conceived by Rubin as the socializing agent of capitalism. In this way, money was identified as a key element of value theory. This analysis was extended by Open Marxists who conceive of money as a social relation. Here, the money form becomes a crucial mediator accounting for both the objective and subjective features of capitalism. On the objective side, Open Marxists examined, for example, how power is exerted through the regulation of money in ways that shape the relations of exploitation. On the subjective side, the money form also helps to explain how capitalist dynamics are experienced by people (alienation), thus accounting for the objectified appearance of capitalism.

Finally, the value-form approach has also been a crucial stepping stone for the development of 'systematic dialectics', a more philosophical trend which insists on the importance of a close study of Hegel's *Logic* as a key for unlocking *Capital*. Whereas Open Marxists use the value form to put class struggle at the heart of all aspects of capitalism, systematic dialectics starts with a critique of empiricism where the main problem is the difficulty in distinguishing necessary from contingent aspects of capitalism. Geert Reuten and Michael Williams (1989), for example, seek to delineate the necessary logic of capital from its concrete historical manifestations. This distinction carves a theoretical space for conceptualizing the inner logic of capital without falling into historical determinism. Hence, the logic of capital is reconstructed by starting from the most fundamental and abstract forms of capitalism which are then further enriched by adding new specifications that progressively ground this concept into history. By reconstructing capitalism on this systematic basis, rather than a historical one, the purpose is precisely to avoid reifying the contingencies of history.

Of particular interest in systematic dialectics is the theme of the inversion of subject and object under capitalism. Reappropriating this central theme of Hegel's work, this approach seeks to show how the requirements of capital lead society to disregard the needs of people or, more specifically, labour. Particularly noteworthy in this tradition is Moishe Postone's (1993) reading of *Capital*. He radicalizes the theme of the subject/object inversion. He reads value as the key structure behind modernity, thus extending the theme of alienation by fusing it with ideas from the Frankfurt School. This enables him to dissociate further the abstract forms of capitalism from their historical concrete manifestations. Value theory is thus cast as a means for examining how capital objectifies social reality, subsuming social reproduction to its own imperatives. One of the notable features of this proposal is that Postone separates the systemic contradiction of capitalism from class struggle, which only represents here a symptom of the former. For Postone, the main contradiction opposes capital as an impersonal objectifying force to the people who are caught in its logic, including the capitalists themselves.

These two broad schools within the value-form approach exemplify how the value form has generated a rich and diverse body of work. In general, it provides an important conceptual space to articulate more philosophical and social reflections in relation to classic and more economic themes of political economy. It has provided a rich avenue for reconsidering debates about value theory and its centrality to Marxism. Although the approach has tended to be confined to a small but dedicated group of scholars, their influence has been greater than might appear at first sight. For, within Marxist scholarship, it has had the effect of sharpening the divisions between Sraffian-type interpretations of value theory that draw entirely upon Ricardian value theory and flirt with orthodox economic methods, and those more conscious of value form itself and true to Marx even if less wedded to the research agenda and positions of the value-form schools themselves. These tend to be seen as salutary in their critique of economistic and deductive methods but too extreme in dividing the logic of capital from its history, and in correspondingly being too unduly preoccupied with form over content.

59. Vladimir I. Lenin

Prabhat Patnaik

Lenin's theoretical contributions to Marxist economics were meant as interventions in the struggle for correct revolutionary practice; they were not dissertations developing Marxist economics as such. The subject matter is far-ranging, but is located within a common perspective that characterized Lenin, namely his view of 'revolution as a concrete project'. This required the delineation of a road map between 'the here and now' and the revolution, an examination of the relationship between the proletariat and other classes in society, and the perception of revolution as a process that unfolds through stages. This approach underlay Lenin's theorization of the revolution in a 'backward' society like Russia. Later, it also enabled him, on the basis of his understanding of imperialism, to theorize a world revolutionary process (which he argued, during World War I, had come on the historical agenda), by unifying the two main revolutionary strands of the twentieth century: the proletarian revolutionary strand of the advanced countries, and the national liberation (or the democratic revolution) strand of the oppressed and 'backward' countries.

Marx's theoretical *opus,* arguing that the development of capitalism created the conditions for its own revolutionary supersession by socialism, had clearly visualized this revolution as occurring in the advanced capitalist world. In their writings on colonialism, Marx and Engels did anticipate the possibility of an anti-colonial revolution in countries like India, but they did not explore the relation of such revolutions in the periphery to the socialist revolution. Late in his life, Marx turned his attention towards Russia, and agreed with Vera Zasulich that a direct transition was possible from the Russian village commune system *(mir)* to socialism, but only if socialism triumphed in Europe to support the process.

Lenin, while also stressing the centrality of the European socialist revolution, visualized an interlinked world revolutionary process where even countries less capitalistically developed could move 'through stages' towards socialism, helped by the European socialist revolution, no matter where the revolution occurred first (the 'chain' in which capitalist imperialism tied the world, he argued, would break at its 'weakest link'). The exact class nature, stage and tasks of the revolution in each country, and how it would progress, had to be worked out, even for countries with underdeveloped capitalism.

For Russia, Lenin believed that the village communes had disintegrated, making way for capitalist development, so that the Zasulich vision of a direct transition from *mir* to socialism had lost relevance. The development of capitalism was proceeding apace in Russia, because of which the working class had emerged as the main revolutionary force. The Russian bourgeoisie, having arrived late on the scene, and threatened by the working class, was incapable of carrying forward the 'democratic' revolution, in particular the overthrow of Tsarism and the seizure of feudal estates, as the bourgeoisie had done in France, for instance, during the French Revolution. Hence, the working class had to take on the job of the bourgeoisie, of leading the democratic revolution, and moving on to socialism, rallying to its cause at each stage substantial sections of the peasantry (the composition of the peasant allies differing from one stage to the next).

PRE-WAR WRITINGS

Much of Lenin's economic writings of the pre-war period were meant to establish these perspectives. Since the Narodnik economists had been arguing that the narrowness of the home market in Russia, arising from the poverty of its people, made capitalist development impossible in that country, Lenin, given his argument that Russia was developing capitalism to the point that the *mir* had been effectively destroyed, engaged in a theoretical debate with them drawing upon Marx's expanded reproduction schemes.

Lenin made three basic points. First, the market was simply the outgrowth of the process of division of labour in the economy. When we move from a situation where the peasant household also engages in craft production to one where peasants specialize in agriculture and a separate group of producers undertake craft production, there necessarily follows the emergence of a market. Second, there may be imbalances in the production undertaken by different branches, some producing in excess of demand and others producing less than demand, but such imbalances giving rise to crises are an inherent feature of capitalism. The system proceeds through crises rather than being rendered an impossibility because of them. Third, the imbalance between production and consumption is a hallmark of capitalism, which keeps the workers at an abysmal standard of living. To argue from this that the system cannot develop at all is illegitimate, since the aim of production in capitalism is not to cater to consumption. Indeed, department I, producing means of production of various kinds, can and does grow quite independently of department II, which produces the means of consumption, by catering to its own internal requirements that keep growing because of the rising organic composition of capital.

Lenin's discussion of the market question was no doubt influenced by Tugan-Baranovski, who had argued that capitalism was characterized by 'production for production's sake' and had believed in Say's Law; but to see Lenin as merely echoing Tugan-Baranovski's argument is erroneous. Lenin remarked that the dynamics of capitalism he sketched, by putting numbers to the reproduction schemes, was not meant to capture 'reality': since the Narodnik economists had argued the 'impossibility of capitalism', it was enough for him to show its 'possibility', which is what he did (in other words, Lenin was producing a counter-example to the Narodniks). It follows that Oskar Lange's later criticism, that the entire Marxist discussion on the market question at the turn of the century was marred by the fact that it simply put numbers to the reproduction schemes, without postulating a 'plausible' investment behaviour, and therefore settled nothing, does not really apply to Lenin, who was interested only in rebutting the Narodnik argument about the impossibility of capitalism. He succeeded in this, and in the process also drew attention, like Tugan-Baranovski, to how capitalism could grow by finding markets for itself through a rise in the organic composition of capital (so that department I largely produced for itself) even as the wage bill, and hence department II, languished (Kalecki was to argue later that state military expenditure could play the same role as the rise in the organic composition in providing a market for department I).

That capitalism was developing in Russia despite the Narodniks' insistence on its impossibility was shown by Lenin in his classic study *The Development of Capitalism in Russia* (1899). The implications of this for the forthcoming Russian Revolution were spelt out in his *Two Tactics of Social Democracy in the Democratic Revolution* (1905, ch. 12), where Lenin argued that 'the bourgeoisie is incapable of carrying the democratic revolution to its consummation, while the peasantry is capable of doing so' (under the leadership of the proletariat). Hence 'the proletariat must carry to completion the democratic revolution, by allying to itself the mass of the peasantry in order to crush by force the resistance of the autocracy and to paralyse the instability of the bourgeoisie. The proletariat must accomplish the socialist revolution, by allying to itself the mass of the semi-proletarian elements of the population in order to crush by force the resistance of the bourgeoisie and to paralyse the instability of the peasantry and the petty bourgeoisie.'

Central to this conception was a distinction between the different agrarian classes, and the role they played in the process of agrarian change. In societies embarking late on capitalist development, the bourgeoisie, though incapable of breaking up the feudal estates, as the consummation of the democratic revolution required, could enter into an alliance with the erstwhile feudal lords to develop what Lenin called a 'semi-feudal capitalism' of which the 'junker capitalism' of Germany was an example; this was in contrast to 'peasant capitalism', which represented a more broad-based, vigorous and less oppressive capitalist development that would ensue with the break-up of the feudal estates. The bourgeoisie's inability to follow the 'peasant capitalist' path meant that the democratic aspirations of the peasantry could be fulfilled only under the leadership of the proletariat.

Lenin, at that time, had argued for the nationalization of land as the sequel to the break-up of feudal property, which would rid the producers of the burden of absolute ground rent and, hence, encourage accumulation. It was only at the time of the Bolshevik Revolution that he changed his position to argue that the break-up of feudal estates should lead to the distribution of land to the peasants, something which the Left Social Revolutionaries, heirs to the Narodnik tradition, had been demanding.

The issue of class differentiation within the peasantry, also central to the conception of the two-stage revolution, was to occupy him much, since the relevance of this conception went far beyond Russia, and it underlay the Comintern's analysis of 'backward' societies. In his *Preliminary Draft Theses to the Second Congress of the Comintern* (1920), Lenin put forward a criterion based on labour-hiring to distinguish between different peasant classes, which was to form the basis of all subsequent analyses of the issue, including the celebrated one by Mao Zedong.

IMPERIALISM AND WAR

Lenin saw World War I as a climacteric for capitalism, which heralded the arrival of the world revolution on the historical agenda. Marx's famous remark that, at a certain stage of the development of a mode of production, the property relations characterizing it become fetters upon the further development of productive forces, had naturally raised the question: how do we know when this 'fetters' stage has arrived? Or, more generally, when can a mode of production be said to have become historically obsolete? The revisionist tradition in German Social Democracy had argued that this obsolescence would manifest itself in a tendency towards the breakdown of the system and, since there were no signs of such a breakdown, the working class had to reconcile itself to capitalism continuing, that it should struggle only to improve its economic lot within the system, and that Marxism accordingly had to be 'revised'. The revolutionary tradition in Germany epitomized by Rosa Luxemburg argued against this that the system did inevitably head for a breakdown but, in the process, it accepted the problematic of the revisionists that the proof of the obsolescence of the system lay in its actual tendency towards breakdown.

Lenin broke with this problematic and saw the war as epitomizing the 'moribund' nature of capitalism. It gave workers a stark choice: they had either to kill fellow workers across trenches or turn their guns against their capitalist exploiters (whence the Bolshevik slogan 'turn the imperialist war into a civil war'). Lenin developed his theory of imperialism both to explain the war and to define the moribund nature of capitalism, of which the war was an expression.

Lenin's theory of imperialism is much misunderstood. The commonest misunderstanding is to attribute to Lenin an underconsumptionist position and the view that imperialism is a device to counteract this tendency. It is because of this interpretation that several authors later argued that Keynesian demand management of the post-World War II period had made Lenin's theory of imperialism obsolete. But Lenin, though intellectually indebted to Hobson, was not an underconsumptionist like the latter. Indeed Lenin's theory is not a 'functional' theory of imperialism at all, that is, imperialism is not perceived by him as providing an antidote to any particular tendency of capitalism.

For Lenin (*Imperialism, the Highest Stage of Capitalism*), imperialism *is* the monopoly stage of capitalism. The process of centralization of capital leads to the emergence of monopolies in the spheres of production and finance, which in turn reinforce each other to the point where a small financial oligarchy, straddling the spheres of finance and industry, decides on the disposal of vast masses of 'finance capital'. These oligarchies are nation-based and integrated with their nation-states, creating a 'personal union' among those presiding over industry, finance and the state in each of the advanced capitalist countries. The competition which always exists between capitals now takes the form of rivalries for the acquisition of 'economic territory' between these powerful oligarchies, each backed by its nation-state. The acquisition of economic territory is not just because of its 'existing' usefulness as markets or sources of raw materials or spheres of financial investment; it is because of its 'potential' usefulness from which rivals have to be excluded. And when the quest for economic territory has succeeded in dividing up the entire world, only redivision remains possible, which can be effected through wars. The era of imperialism, as monopoly capitalism, is characterized by wars.

Lenin's concept of finance capital has been variously criticized: that it is based on a confusion between 'stocks' and 'flows', or that it oscillates between Hobson's notion of 'high finance' (characteristic of Britain where financial and industrial interests were rather distinct) and Hilferding's notion of 'finance capital', or 'capital controlled by banks and employed in industry' (characteristic of Germany where industrial and financial interests coalesced). These criticisms miss the point of Lenin's theory. The 'stocks' and 'flows' distinction assumes significance only within an underconsumptionist perspective, where capital exports in the sense of an export surplus financed through an extension of credit can boost aggregate demand. In short, 'flows' matter from the point of view of aggregate demand, but capital exports as a reflection of portfolio choice, with no accompanying export surplus, do not affect aggregate demand. Once we detach Lenin from underconsumptionism, the criticism that he did not distinguish between stocks and flows ceases to matter. Likewise, since Lenin sought to characterize a whole phase of capitalism, covering the specificities of a number of countries, his use of somewhat elastic and overarching concepts is understandable.

His theory, though extremely simple in its economic conception, and almost unexceptionable within its context (on which more later), was rich in capturing the variety of relationships of domination that imperialism entailed. The attempt at repartitioning an already partitioned world took complex forms (leaving aside war): colonies, semi-colonies, undermining the sovereignty of nominally independent countries and acquiring hegemony over even (apparently hegemonic) colonial powers like Portugal. Lenin's theory opened up the world of international relations to Marxist analysis.

Lenin had attempted in 1908 to explain revisionism in the European working-class movement by suggesting that the influx of petty producers, dispossessed by capitalist competition, into the ranks of the proletariat, brought with it an alien ideology that constituted the soil for revisionism. But in *Imperialism*, taking a cue from some remarks of Engels, he explained revisionism in terms of a section of the working class, and in particular its trade union leadership, being bribed out of the 'superprofits' earned by the monopoly combines. Lenin's position here must be distinguished from later arguments based on unequal exchange, which have gone much further in claiming that the advanced country proletariat is part of the exploiting segment itself: Lenin not only restricted the perceived beneficiaries of imperialist exploitation to a narrow stratum, but linked the phenomenon to 'monopoly'. Theories of unequal exchange that do not invoke monopoly are ill-founded: they lack validity if the metropolis and periphery are not specialized in particular activities, but they cannot explain such specialization in the absence of monopoly. The Leninist emphasis on monopoly is a more fruitful approach to the issue, even if the circle of beneficiaries is sought to be widened beyond the narrow stratum.

In *Imperialism*, Lenin had criticized Karl Kautsky's invoking of the possibility of the joint exploitation of the world through peaceful agreement by internationally united finance capital as 'ultra-imperialism'. Lenin's argument was that any such agreed division of the world among the different finance capitals, assuming it came about, would reflect their relative strengths at the time; but uneven development, endemic to capitalism, would necessarily alter these relative strengths, giving rise to conflicts that would burst into wars. 'Ultra-imperialism' could only be an interlude of truce between wars. Many have argued on the basis of postwar experience that the Kautskyan perception rather than the Leninist one has come to pass, and inter-imperialist rivalries have become less intense under *Pax Americana*.

Two points, however, have to be noted here: first, we have of late 'not a unity among different nation-based and nation-state-aided finance capitals', as Kautsky had visualized, but a new 'international finance capital', and hence a new imperialism, which is a product of further centralization of capital and the removal of restrictions on cross-border capital flows, that is, of the process of globalization of finance. This is a new phenomenon that transcends altogether the Kautsky-Lenin conjuncture. Second, the emergence of international finance capital, while restraining wars 'among imperialist powers', has not prevented wars. The types of wars have changed but wars persist in all their viciousness. The present conjuncture is different from Lenin's, but his *opus* remains the benchmark against which it has to be analysed.

POST-REVOLUTIONARY WRITINGS

Lenin's voluminous post-revolutionary writings remain immensely significant and require separate and more exhaustive treatment. As the Civil War ended, the period of 'War Communism' gave way to the 'New Economic Policy', which opened up the possibility of a capitalist tendency that had to be kept in check through the proletarian state retaining control over the commanding heights of the economy. This emphasis on the centralized state as a bulwark against capitalist restoration has been seen by many as containing the seeds of the subsequent decay of the system. Lenin accordingly has been seen as the conscious progenitor of the centralized system that was perfected in the Stalin era. But this is a misreading of Lenin whose basic libertarian vision of socialism never deserted him, even as the centralized state apparatus was being built to protect the beleaguered Soviet Union after the prospects of a German revolution had faded and Lenin was beginning to look eastwards to China and India.

This libertarian vision, outlined in *The State and Revolution* written in August 1917, visualizing the proletarian state as withering away from the very day of its formation, was reiterated in October 1917 in his remark: 'we can at once set in motion a state apparatus consisting of ten if not twenty million people' (*Can the Bolsheviks Retain State Power?*). Even at critical moments, after circumstances had forced him towards a centralized state apparatus, his interventions, such as against the militarization of trade unions, sprang from this libertarian vision. And even after Soviet democracy had given way to what was effectively a dictatorship of the Party, Lenin was concerned that the Party at least must not become a centralized bureaucratic force, whence his 'last struggle' in attempting to remove Stalin and take steps to prevent the bureaucratization of the Party. He saw with great clarity and prescience that the pursuit of 'democratic centralism' (the organizational principle of the Leninist party) in a society emerging from feudal autocracy can easily degenerate into bureaucratic centralism. The image of Lenin as apotheosizing centralism against the libertarian promise of socialism is a false one.

60. The welfare state

Daniel Ankarloo

When, in the opening sentence of *Capital*, Karl Marx establishes that capitalist wealth emerges 'as "an immense accumulation of commodities"' (*Capital 1*, ch. 1), he is also mindful of the social relations between the individuals who produce these commodities: the process of accumulation entails the social (re)production of the relationships creating labour power as a commodity. The social form of wage labour is both the prerequisite and the chief product of the capitalist production process. The natural and social conditions for the reproduction of capital have been recurring themes in Marxist political economy. This entry examines the role of the welfare state in the reproduction of capitalist social relations, leaving aside other significant aspects including family reproduction, demography and ecology. This is justified not only by the significance of the welfare state for social reproduction today, but also by the centrality of claims that the emergence of the welfare state after World War II refutes some of the central claims of Marx's analysis in *Capital*.

FORERUNNERS

Analyses of the welfare state were, obviously, not present in the works of Marx and Engels nor in the writings of Marxist theorists in the early twentieth century. Nevertheless, the question of social reform was a major challenge to Marxist-inspired movements and in the Second International. In countries with a mass party of social democratic character, like Germany and, later, Sweden, social reform became one of the key differences between (revolutionary) Marxism and (reformist) revisionism. Specifically, should social reform be regarded as a step and even an alternative to social revolution or as an obstacle to it?

Marxist perspectives on the issue were put forward by, among others, Rosa Luxemburg and Anton Pannekoek in Germany and, subsequently, by representatives of the Swedish labour movement, especially Gustav Möller. Their analyses had in common a sharp distinction between those social reforms that were handed down 'from above' (or from the state) – which were viewed as 'hand-outs' to pacify the workers' movement or, even worse, to create reformist illusions of avoiding the necessity of revolution – and those reforms that were imposed on capital through the workers' independent struggles to better their social and economic conditions under capitalism. While the first type of reform was strongly rejected, the second type was of considerable significance for socialist movements. In his *Taktischen Differenzen in der Arbeiterbewegung*, Pannekoek (1909) summarized this viewpoint: '*hard-won* social reforms are stages on the road to the goal [of socialist revolution] *inasmuch* they carry with them a strengthening of our power. Only as such, as the enhancement of our power, they do have value for socialism' (author's translation).

Another influential precursor of Marxist analyses of the welfare state can be traced in the writings of Paul Baran and Paul Sweezy. For them, rising state expenditures emerged, in general, as an attempt to deal with the contradictions of underconsumption in monopoly capitalism, for which welfare spending is a special case. This approach entailed a shift in emphasis away from the contradictions in capitalism and the forces leading to socialism (drawing upon the antagonistic class relation between capital and labour). In its place, (socialist) rationality to fulfil human needs has increasingly been counterposed to (capitalist) waste and degradation. Notwithstanding the critique that Baran and Sweezy's analysis depart significantly from Marxian categories, their analysis is significant in pioneering the Marxist notion that state (welfare) expenditure is related to the contradictions of capitalism.

Worth mentioning is also the work of Herbert Marcuse, who tried to ground the contradictions of postwar welfare state societies not so much in the economic logic of the system as in a contradiction between the drivers of contemporary capitalism and basic human needs and instincts. To Marcuse, the industrial working class is no longer an agent for socialist revolution and transcendence of capitalism. In the end, no such identifiable agent exists, argued Marcuse, but only a new 'sensibility' and 'praxis' in response to (individual) everyday life under capitalism. The Marxist lineage of this approach has been questioned but, again, notwithstanding Marcuse's using Marx as departure rather than starting point, his work predates some of the concerns and themes of subsequent Marxist accounts of the welfare state, not least the integration of the working class into accepting capitalism and the repressive and alienating elements of conformism.

POSTWAR MARXISM AND THE WELFARE STATE

From the Marxian theory of the state, that it is the basis of the class rule of capital, the conclusion is immediately drawn that the welfare state exists to enhance the social reproduction of capital and wage labour. However, in the postwar debate, not least in the work of 'democratic socialist' analysts such as Gösta Esping Andersen and Walter Korpi, the welfare state fulfils the function of 'decommodification' of labour power. In particular, the Scandinavian social democratic welfare regimes are, according to this argument, if not socialism itself, at least a step towards realizing socialist values such as equality and social reproduction beyond the logic of capital. The welfare state is perceived as a countervailing force against the market.

A host of theories of the welfare state under capitalism emerged in neo-Marxist circles in the 1960s and 1970s, partly as a response to the ruling Keynesian paradigm, the notion of a crisis-free capitalism and a 'mixed economy' with full employment, which their advocates attributed, in part, to the benign influence of the 'welfare state'. For the sake of expositional convenience, these theories can be grouped as follows: (1) the welfare state supports the reproduction of capital; (2) the welfare state weakens the reproduction of capital; and (3) the welfare state is contradictory and fulfils both roles simultaneously.

For (1), there is a focus on how welfare state institutions sustain the commodification of labour power. The nationalization and socialization of certain welfare functions such as education and health care, and the socialization of the family by way of childcare and a social security net, are efficient ways to guarantee the availability of a well-trained, healthy and disciplined workforce at the disposal of capital. Hence, capital accrues net gains from the welfare state. Moreover, some of the social costs associated with capitalist production, including unemployment, sickness, the maintenance of the family and the education of future generations of workers, are transferred from capital to the workers themselves, as taxpayers. Since the welfare state socializes the costs of the social repro-duction of the workers, while ensuring that capital's gains remain private, it is ultimately perceived as a creation by capital for capital's interests and, accordingly, against the interests of the working class.

The claim that the welfare state does not redistribute economic and social resources from capital to labour but, rather, redistributes 'costs' and 'benefits' within the working class itself has been put forward by several Marxist analysts, such as Ian Gough (1979) and Anwar Shaikh (2003). Furthermore, so the argument goes, the welfare state recom-modifies labour power in at least two ways. One is that many of the services and social security nets supposedly available to all are conditional on active participation in the labour market; in other words, social security, both in terms of qualification and compen-sation levels, is connected to the commodification of labour power. Hence, the purpose of health care is not good health, and the purpose of education is not the expansion of knowledge per se, but making sure that currently unavailable or 'unemployable' labour power is made available to capital as rapidly as possible. Moreover, the welfare state institutions of education, social services and social security discipline the workforce into a work ethic. This has been stressed in those critiques focusing on the normalizing, stig-matizing and repressive aspects of welfare provision. Finally, welfare provision is carried out by a middle-class stratum of state functionaries and bureaucrats, whose primary function it is to maintain hierarchy, dependency and stigma within the working class and other marginalized groups, weakening their resistance against capitalism through the state regulation of 'the poor'.

A different strand of functionalist Marxist analysis focuses on how the welfare state serves capital through its attempts to pacify the working class: essentially, the economic and social gains from welfare provision 'buy off' the workers in the Western world, legiti-mizing the capitalist system. The most extreme version of this stance is associated with the Danish Maoist, Gotferd Appel, who developed a theory of the 'parasite state' in the 1960s and 1970s. Appel argues that the welfare state is a 'bribe' for the working classes in the Western world, at the expense of marginalized groups and the poor countries. In milder versions, the idea that the welfare state defuses working-class resistance against capitalism stretches far and wide among Marxist circles, without necessarily referring to poor countries.

For (2), by contrast, the welfare state is seen as deriving from the struggle of the working class itself to better its conditions – as 'concessions' from, and weakening of, capital and augmenting the strength of organized labour (Gough, 1979; Sjöström, 1979). These concessions may legitimize and secure capitalist social reproduction, but further concessions to the workers eventually bring costs to capital that slow down its growth and threaten social reproduction. Two aspects of this approach are worth mentioning.

First, presumably, welfare concessions to the working class weaken capitalist growth through rising social wages (at the expense of taxes on capital), incremental decommodification of labour power and services, and a corresponding squeeze on profits. Hence, the welfare state will eventually lead to an accumulation crisis and/ or a fiscal crisis of the state due to excessive borrowing to finance welfare provision (O'Connor, 1973). Second, and more controversially, welfare provision has been linked to Marx's distinction between productive and unproductive labour. The postwar welfare state has entailed the mass expansion of (unproductive) government employment, which squeezes overall profits, hampering the potential for further accumulation.

(3) The mix of analyses across (1) and (2) inevitably induces an implicit synthesis that stresses how welfare expresses the inherent contradictions of capitalism. These contradictions operate at several levels, the most basic being between labour and capital in general. However, the development of postwar welfare states reveals other contradictions both within capital itself (for example, between large corporations and small businesses) and amongst the expanding and, increasingly, socially and culturally fragmented working class. These are significant for the development of the welfare state and the social reproduction of capital, not least in explaining how differentiated welfare states have emerged.

For James O'Connor (1973), welfare state provision fulfils two contradictory functions, accumulation and legitimation. Consequently, social policies can be analysed as a combination of 'social investments' increasing labour productivity and serving the accumulation function, for example, universal education and health care; 'social consumption' supporting the reproduction of labour power through social security, and also serving the accumulation function; and 'social costs' that are not productive for capital but are necessary to serve the legitimation function. Examples of this are retirement benefits and care for the elderly and the disabled. In predicting a fiscal crisis of the state and an accumulation crisis of capital, O'Connor relies on the contradictions inherent in meeting accumulation functions while, at the same time, sustaining legitimacy for capitalist reproduction within the working class.

In Sweden, Kurt Sjöström (1979) also pointed to the double role of the welfare state in the development of the social democratic regime and the postwar boom. Stressing the simultaneous need for the welfare state to guarantee both the reproduction of wage labour at the disposal of capital and the specific social democratic idea of Sweden as a 'People's Home' (of 'common concerns', that is, common class interests), Sjöström further highlighted the role of both inter-class conflicts and conflicts within the state apparatus. In Sweden, collaboration between the working class and capital was achieved by a social accord across union-organized labour, a state governed by social democracy, and the promotion of (export-oriented) big business, at the expense of small businesses. Hence, Swedish social policy was instituted in place of socialism, not as a road towards it.

As regards the Swedish state itself, Sjöström deepened the analysis of its contradictory functions, focusing specifically on the expanding strata of welfare and social workers. These were increasingly recruited from within the working classes, particularly among women. Situated both as members of the working class and as state functionaries whose ultimate role was to secure the social reproduction of labour at the disposal of capital (the repressing and controlling function of the welfare state), social workers found themselves caught in irresolvable contradictions, and increasingly compelled to take sides. Ideological battles between radicalized social workers and the state apparatus were significant contributing factors leading to the progressive social legislation introduced in 1980.

THE WELFARE STATE AFTER NEOLIBERALISM

Marxist analyses of the welfare state lost much of their influence and vitality since the 1980s. Instead of developing specifically Marxist interpretations, more eclectic paths were pursued either in terms of mainstream concerns of typology or in mapping the regulatory move from 'welfare' to 'workfare' as part of more general theories of the state. This is unfortunate since, in the neoliberal era, there have been severe attacks on the levels and forms of state welfare provision calling for a Marxist response. However, these have been overshadowed either by a direct defence of the welfare state within the confines of capitalism, or by postmodernist and post-structuralist critiques of state welfarism as a form of personal and social control (and response).

In retrospect, what are now the classic Marxist critiques of the welfare state can be seen to be in part a product of their own times, when capital and welfare were both expanding on an unprecedented scale, at least in the rich countries. Although some of the predictions and aspirations of these analyses have not withstood the test of time, their virtue was to focus on the accumulation and reproduction of capital at both economic and social levels and to tie these to the contradictions and conflicts engendered by that particular (social democratic) configuration of capitalism. By the same token, in hindsight, it could be argued that these Marxist analyses often exhibit a degree of reductionism to the needs of capital (and in response to class conflict and working-class needs) without sufficient sensitivity to variation across time and place, different elements of provision (health care, education, social security and so on) and other constituencies in social reproduction than class (especially race and gender).

61. World economy

Gong Hoe Gimm

It has been traditional for Marxist political economy in general, and Marx's own value theory in particular, to conceptualize the world economy as such in addressing capitalism both abstractly and concretely, whether they call it empire, commerce, transnational corporations or, most recently, globalization, imperialism and even financialization. Equally frequently, such concepts have either derived loosely from an aggregation across constituent elements (including nation states) or by appeal to generic concepts such as neoliberalism, without these being developed sufficiently in advance. This raises questions about the way in which Marxist political economy should deal with the nature of capitalism as a world economy. Specifically, how should the world economy be located at the most abstract level, as mode(s) of production, whilst also addressing its more concrete and historical forms?

This potential difficulty is most striking in Marx's own value theory. Moreover, increasingly, as the world economy spawned new and more complicated developments, so the concept of world economy experienced a series of transformations both in its meaning and place in theory. For example, during the period of 'actually existing socialism', it was posited that there were two world economies, capitalist and socialist (quite apart from a 'Third World'), requiring different approaches within Marxist political economy. This raises issues over whether the world economy can be confined to capitalism alone and, if not, how account is taken of non-capitalist participation within it (including pre-capitalist modes of production).

MARX ON THE WORLD ECONOMY

For Marx, capitalism had been a world economy from the outset and, based upon this fundamental understanding, he made a number of commentaries on the issue in his personal correspondence, public addresses and newspaper columns. These serve as a vivid record of the development of the world economy, and the world economic crises he witnessed from the 1850s. Also, Marx undertook a formidable amount of empirical research on these crises, which was incorporated into his value theory (Krätke, 2008a, 2008b). Although Marx could not complete this task, he regarded consideration of the world economy as essential to a theory of the capitalist economy. This is not simply a matter of his occasional expressions of intent to devote a whole book to this theme. Even more significant is the imperative to incorporate the world economy for the nature of his value theory itself.

Note first, though, that for Marx capitalism as world 'economy' is often crystallized in the concept of the world 'market'. Selection of this term, on the one hand, reflects the intellectual background from which Marx's conceptualization derived. Long before him, political economists had dealt with the globality of the modern economy, which they observed most immediately in the form of, to employ Sismondi's expression, *'le marché de tout l'univers'* (the market of the universe) (Gimm, 2011). On the other hand, however, especially in Marx, the world market is neither simply a geographical entity nor purely the sphere of circulation, but a concept pertaining to the spatial dimension of the totality of capitalist economic processes, encompassing the production and distribution of value, the accumulation of capital and so on. The world market is both an aggregate and a systemically reproduced totality which, for Marx, can be appropriated in theory only through the movement from relatively abstract to relatively concrete determinants. In this sense, the world market is, theoretically speaking, an abstract concept onto which such categories as value, labour, production and so on are projected. For this reason, these categories themselves can be developed sufficiently, both logically and historically, only at the world level (see below). More technically, whilst the three volumes of *Capital* offer an abstract analysis of the different types of production of (surplus) value, and their forms in circulation and distribution, the world market is constituted logically and historically out of their interaction as a totality – different types of capital, with different modes and levels of development, variously distributed across nation-states.

Second, Marx regards the world market both as a 'precondition' for the capitalist economy to come into existence and as a 'result' that is reproduced through capitalist mechanisms: 'The world-market itself forms the basis for this [capitalist] mode of production' (Marx, *Capital III*, ch. 20). At the same time, '[t]he tendency to create the *world market* is directly given in the concept of capital itself' (Marx, *Grundrisse*). One of the key features of Marx's method is to look upon the basic categories of the capitalist economy both as presuppositions and as results of the specifically capitalist process of production (Marx, *Grundrisse*). This duality also reflects the way capitalism emerged, and how it evolved in relation to economic forms which predate capitalism historically, but survive within it. This is also characteristic of the world market. Marx shows in a number of places how the world market paved the way for the emergence of capitalism, and how the latter, eventually, subsumed the former. For example:

> [W]hen in the 16th, and partially still in the 17th, century the sudden expansion of commerce and emergence of a new world-market overwhelmingly contributed to the fall of the old mode of production and the rise of capitalist production, this was accomplished conversely on the basis of the already existing capitalist mode of production. The world-market itself forms the basis for this mode of production. On the other hand, the immanent necessity of this mode of production to produce on an ever-enlarged scale tends to extend the world-market continually, so that it is not commerce in this case which revolutionises industry, but industry which constantly revolutionises commerce. (Marx, *Capital III*, ch. 20)

This capitalist transformation of the pre-capitalist world is necessarily gradual. Therefore, the coexistence of capitalist and non-capitalist forms within the capitalist world economy is a normal condition, which helps to explain why Marx was so passionate in studying non-European and non-capitalist societies, especially in his later years. Whilst this brings to mind the basic distinction between the mode of production and particular social formations within it, it also points to an essential task for the Marxist theory of the world economy: how to track the interactions between (developing) capitalist relations of production and the non-capitalist elements that are gradually drawn into the orbit of the capitalist world economy (cf. Marx, *Capital I*, ch. 10, section 2).

Third, although the historical precedence of the global over the national is systematically recognized in Marx's value theory, in *Capital* he abstracts from this opposition, simply regarding 'the whole world as one nation':

> We here take no account of export trade . . . In order to examine the object of our investigation in its integrity, free from all disturbing subsidiary circumstances, we must treat the whole world as one nation, and assume that capitalist production is everywhere established and has possessed itself of every branch of industry. (Marx, *Capital I*, ch. 24, note 2).

Abstract as it is, the world economy still has a spatial dimension through which other elementary categories such as value, money, labour and capital are projected. This is why the spatial dimension needs to be held back until these value categories have been developed in the abstract – before they can be attached to a system of nation-states, for example. Accordingly, to extend value theory by developing its 'world' dimension is equivalent to the dual process of locating value in its more complex and concrete historical forms.

MARXIST THEORIES OF THE WORLD ECONOMY: UNDERDEVELOPING MARX'S INSIGHT

Although Marx had a clear conception of the meaning and the place of the world economy in the fabric of his value theory, he did not develop a theory of the global in his work. The first significant step in this direction was taken by the generation of Marxists working in the Second International, including R. Luxemburg, R. Hilferding, N. Bukharin and V.I. Lenin, who developed the 'classical' Marxist theories of imperialism. These theories were mainly, if not exclusively, concerned with the leading capitalist economies at that time, that is, with so-called inter-imperialist rivalry. However, the post-Second World War world looked very different. The political independence of the colonies highlighted aspects of the world economy that had not been significant previously, and the USA emerged as the sole hegemonic power in the West, albeit in rivalry with the USSR, while the former European empires collapsed more or less rapidly. Yet, in the wake of the recovery of those war-stricken economies, the economic relations amongst the leading world economies re-emerged in new forms. From the late 1960s, new theories of the world economy arose, including dependency theory, world-systems theory, theories of US economic and political hegemony, and other theories concerning transnational corporations as the new agents of international economic relations.

These approaches to the world economy reflect, and aspire to incorporate, specific aspects of contemporary capitalism. However, given the significant transformations of the world economy, few amongst these theories were adequately embedded in Marx's value categories. Moreover, some of Marx's works were not even widely available to serve as points of departure, especially the *Grundrisse*.

Despite these limitations, there were significant attempts to construct a 'general' Marxist theory of the world economy grounded on value categories. These include the Marxist 'international value theory' which dates back to Otto Bauer and Henryk Grossmann, in the 1920s, but which was most seriously debated in Japan from the 1940s (Nakagawa, 1999–2003), and the German 'world-market debate' in the 1970s (Nachtwey and ten Brink, 2008). These were attempts to complete the unfinished 'latter half' of Marx's six book plan ('I examine the system of bourgeois economy in the following order: *capital, landed property, wage-labour; the State, foreign trade, world market*', Marx, *A Contribution to the Critique of Political Economy*, Preface), based upon his commentaries on the 'modification' of the law of value in an international context (Marx, *Capital I*, ch. 22). However, these efforts were severely limited both temporally and geographically, and were almost extinguished with the collapse of the Berlin Wall and the emergence of the discourses of neoliberalism and globalization (Gimm, 2011).

CONTINUING ISSUES, EMERGING CHALLENGES

As the globalization debate came of age, it became increasingly necessary to address it through the deployment of value theory, especially in order to examine the material reproduction of global capitalism (Fine, 2004). Thus, it is not surprising that, since the late 1990s, the emergence of theories of the global have claimed to be grounded upon Marx's insights, for example, those developed by Giovanni Arrighi, Robert Brenner, Alex Callinicos, Andrew Glyn and David Harvey.

Whilst a fully developed value theory is a condition for understanding the world economy, this relationship has tended to be overlooked, or at least implicitly set aside in several cases, because of the presumed deficiencies of value theory in addressing the complexities and differentiations of contemporary capitalism. For example, in the discussion of one of the most important topics at the global level in contemporary capitalism, the source of 'development', value theory tends either to be set aside completely or modified beyond recognition. Inevitably, then, especially for those theories focusing upon non- or pre-capitalist forms, these particular elements in the world economy swing between two defective (certainly underdeveloped) extremes. One explains underdevelopment by simply neglecting the 'prior determination' of the world economy as in theories of the (failed) developmental state, with all capable of being successful if only adopting the right policies. The other takes too rigid and determining a role for the world economy as in dependency and world-systems theories (so that none can aspire to break from global constraints). Each in its own way sets aside the unevenness and complexity of capitalist development that necessarily flows from value theory. In any case, it would be wrong, historically and methodologically, to take the individual national economy as the unit or the methodological starting point of the analysis of (part of) the world economy as opposed to vice versa.

It is essential, then, to recognize that the world economy is one of the basic categories in Marx's approach and, accordingly, the categories concerning the national domain are, first and foremost, particular moments of the reproduction of the world economy:

> In Marx's refined framework of analysis in *Capital* . . . national economies . . . are . . . particular moments in the reproduction of a differentiated capitalism . . . on a global scale . . . [T]he existence and persistence of such differentiated societies in the world market requires an abstract theory of capital to be developed, in its different forms in production and exchange, in its

different stages of development, and in the way these mutually coexist. In other words, not least as laid out in *Capital*, value theory provides the constituent elements of a theory of the world economy, but the elements can only be put together through incorporating a historical content. (Fine et al., 2010, p. 73)

Therefore, once the relationship between the global and the national is established in this manner, it follows that other elementary categories should also be viewed from that 'global' perspective. For example, in the early chapters of *Capital*, Marx examines money in its simplest and most abstract forms; at this stage, he regards money as a global as well as a national category, under the heading 'world money'. Note, further, that the precedence of world money is not only logical but also historical: as Marc Bloch (1967) demonstrates, even though money was constituted at the national or local level in mediaeval Europe, it was most frequently used as means of circulation for 'international' transactions, while within national (local) economies its role was largely confined to that of measure of value.

In conclusion, it is not only money but also production, capital, labour and other central categories of Marx's value theory that must be projected onto the canvas of the world economy. This logical conclusion can only be taken forward by incorporating the historical development of global capitalism, which includes a combination of historical and spatial disjunctures. Thus, logically, value theory introduces the category of the state, for instance, to signify the spatial (if not simply physically confined organization of capitals) but, historically, it allows the state to take different forms and to adopt different roles, ranging from imperial to colonial and from 'welfare' to 'developmental', or even 'Chinese'. In this way, the concept of the world economy represents the 'totality' of value, theoretically and historically expressed, from simple to transnational commodity production, and from commodity money through to financial derivatives. The world economy articulates all forms of capital, together with their corresponding logics associated with the production and circulation of (surplus) value. However, the composition and nature of that articulation can only be derived historically. This also requires a periodization of the world economy prior to periodization of its national components.

References

As explained in the Introduction, classic works of Marx and Marxism are not listed, if available on http://www.marxists.org. There they can be consulted as the texts themselves or for quotations in this volume. On occasion, we indicate date of first publication or of drafting prior to bracketed date of edition used.

Agarwal, B. (1997), 'Bargaining and gender relations: within and beyond the household', *Feminist Economics*, **3** (1), 1–51.

Aglietta, M. (1979), *A Theory of Capitalist Regulation*, London: New Left Books.

Aglietta, M. and A. Brender (1984), *Les Metamorphoses de la Societé Salariale*, Paris: Calman-Lévy.

Aglietta, M. and A. Orléan (1982), *La Violence de la Monnaie*, Paris: Presses Universitaires de France.

Althusser, F. and E. Balibar (1965 [1970]), *Reading Capital*, London: New Left Books.

Altvater, E. (1993), *The Future of the Market*, London: Verso.

Amin, S. (1985), 'Modes of production, history, and unequal development', *Science & Society*, **49** (2), 194–207.

Anderson, K.B. (2010), *Marx at the Margins*, Chicago, IL: University of Chicago Press.

Anderson, P. (1974a), *Passages from Antiquity to Feudalism*, London: Verso.

Anderson, P. (1974b), *Lineages of the Absolutist State*, London: Verso.

Anderson, P. (1976), *Considerations on Western Marxism*, London: Verso.

Anievas, A. (ed.) (2010), *Marxism and World Politics: Contesting Global Capitalism*, London and New York: Routledge.

Appelrouth, S. and L.D. Edles (2008), *Classical and Contemporary Sociological Theory: Text and Readings*, London: Pine Forge Press.

Aspromourgos, T. (1986) 'On the origins of the term "neoclassical"', *Cambridge Journal of Economics*, **10** (3), 265–70.

Ashton, T.H. and C.H.E. Philpin (eds) (1985), *The Brenner Debate: Agrarian Class Structure and Economic Development in Pre-Industrial Europe*, Cambridge: Cambridge University Press.

Avineri, S. (ed.) (1969), *On Colonialism and Modernization*, Garden City, NY: Anchor Books.

Bair, J. (2005), 'Global capitalism and commodity chains: looking back, going forward', *Competition and Change*, **9** (2), 153–80.

Ball, M. (1977), 'Differential rent and the role of landed property', *International Journal of Urban and Regional Research*, **1** (3), 380–403.

Ball, M. (1985), 'The urban rent question', *Environment and Planning A*, **17** (4), 503–25.

Banaji, J. (2010), *Theory as History: Essays on Modes of Production and Exploitation*,

Leiden, Netherlands and Boston, MA: Brill, paperback edn. (2011), Haymarket Books.

Banton, M. (1991), 'The race relations problematic', *British Journal of Sociology*, **42** (1), 115–30.

Baran, P.A. (1957), *The Political Economy of Growth*, New York: Monthly Review Press.

Baran, P. and P. Sweezy (1966), *Monopoly Capital*, New York: Modern Reader Paperbacks.

Barratt-Brown, M. (1970), *After Imperialism*, London: Merlin Press.

Barrow, C.W. (2008), 'The intellectual origins of the new political science', *New Political Science*, **30** (2), 215–44.

Belkhir, J. (2001), 'Marxism and class, gender and race: rethinking the trilogy', *Race and Class*, **8** (2), 23–33.

Beneria, L. (1979), 'Reproduction, production and the sexual division of labour', *Cambridge Journal of Economics*, **3** (3), 203–5.

Benkler, Y. (2006), *The Wealth of Networks: How Social Production Transforms Markets and Freedom*, New Haven, CT: Yale University Press.

Bernstein, H. (1996–97), 'Agrarian questions then and now', *Journal of Peasant Studies*, **24** (1–2), 22–59.

Bernstein, H. and L. Campling (2006a), 'Commodity studies and commodity fetishism I: trading down', *Journal of Agrarian Change*, **6** (2), 239–64.

Bernstein, H. and L. Campling (2006b), 'Commodity studies and commodity fetishism II: profits with principles?', *Journal of Agrarian Change*, **6** (3), 414–47.

Bernstein, H. and P. Woodhouse (2001), 'Telling environmental change like it is? Reflections on a study in sub-Saharan Africa', *Journal of Agrarian Change*, **1** (2), 283–324.

Bertram, C. (2008), 'Analytical Marxism', in J. Bidet and S. Kouvelakis (eds), *Critical Companion to Contemporary Marxism*, Leiden, Netherlands: Brill.

Bettelheim, C. (1963), *Economic Calculation and Forms of Property*, London: Routledge.

Bharadwaj, K. and B. Schefold (eds) (1990), *Essays in Honour of Piero Sraffa: Critical Perspectives on the Revival of Classical Theory*, London: Unwin Hyman.

Bisnath, S. and D. Elson (1999), *Women's Empowerment Revisited*, background paper for Progress of the World's Women 2000: A UNIFEM Report.

Bloch, M. (1967), 'Natural economy or money economy: a pseudo-dilema', in *Land and Work in Mediaeval Europe: Selected Papers*, originally published in French in *Annales d'Histoire sociale*, vol V, 1933, translated by J.E. Anderson, London: RKP.

Bois, G. (1978), 'Against the Neo-Malthusian orthodoxy', *Past and Present*, **79**, 60–9, republished in Aston and Philpin, 1985.

Bonacich, E. (1980), 'Class approaches to ethnicity and race', *The Insurgent Sociologist*, **102**, 9–23.

Bonefeld, W. (2003), 'The capitalist state: illusion and critique', accessed 12 August 2011 at http://libcom.org/library/capitalist-state-illusion-critique-werner-bonefeld.

Bonefeld, W., R. Gunn and K. Psychopedis (eds) (1992), *Open Marxism Volume I: Dialectics and History*, London: Pluto Press.

Bonnassie, P. (1991), *From Slavery to Feudalism in South-Western Europe*, Cambridge: Cambridge University Press.

Boyer, R. (1989), 'The eighties: the search for alternatives to Fordism', CEPREMAP discussion paper no. 8909.

Boyer, R. (1990), *The Regulation School*, New York: Columbia University Press.

Braudel, F. (2002), *Civilization and Capitalism 15th–18th Century: The Wheels of Commerce*, London: Phoenix Press.

Braverman, H. (1974), *Labor and Monopoly Capital: The Degradation of Work in the Twentieth Century*, New York: Monthly Review Press.

Brenner, R. (1976), 'Agrarian class structure and economic development in pre-industrial Europe', *Past and Present,* **70**, 30–70, republished in Aston and Philpin, 1985.

Brenner, R. (1977), 'The origins of capitalist development: a critique of neo-Smithian Marxism', *New Left Review*, **104**, 25–92.

Brenner, R. (1998), *The Economics of Global Turbulence*, London: Verso.

Brenner, R. and M. Glick (1991), 'The Regulation Approach: theory and history', *New Left Review*, **188**, 45–119.

Brus, W. (1973), *The Economics and Politics of Socialism*, London: Routledge and Kegan Paul.

Bukharin, N. (1918 [1972]), *Imperialism and World Economy*, London: Merlin Press.

Burkett, P. (2006), *Marxism and Ecology: Towards a Red and Green Political Economy*, Boston, MA: Brill.

Byres, T.J. (1996), *Capitalism from Above and Capitalism from Below: An Essay in Comparative Political Economy*, Basingstoke and London: Macmillan.

Byres, T.J. (2003), 'Structural change, the agrarian question, and the possible impact of globalisation', in J. Ghosh and C.P. Chandrasekhar (eds), *Work and Well-Being in the Age of Finance*, New Delhi: Tulika Press.

Cardoso, F.H. and E. Faletto (1979), *Dependency and Development in Latin America*, Berkeley, CA: University of California Press.

Carling, A. (1990), 'In defence of rational choice: a reply to Ellen Meiksins Wood', *New Left Review*, **184**, 97–109.

Carling, A. (1991), *Social Division*, London: Verso.

Carling, A. (2006), '*Karl Marx's Theory of History* and the recovery of the Marxian tradition', *Science & Society,* **70** (2), 252–74.

Carroll, W.K. (1989), 'Neoliberalism and the recomposition of finance capital in Canada', *Capital & Class*, **13**, 81–113.

Cashmore, E.E. (1988), *Dictionary of Race and Ethnic Relations*, London: Routledge.

Castles, S. and G. Kosack (1973), *Immigrant Workers and Class Structure in Western Europe*, Oxford: Oxford University Press.

Castree, N. (1995), 'The nature of produced nature: materiality and knowledge construction in Marxism', *Antipode*, **27** (1), 12–48.

Castree, N., P. Chatterton, W. Larner and M.W. Wright (eds) (2010), *The Point is to Change It – Geographies of Hope and Survival in an Age of Crisis*, Oxford: Blackwell.

CEPREMAP-CORDES (1977), 'Approches de l'Inflation: l'Exemple Français', CEPREMAP discussion paper no. 22.

Cerni, P. (2007), 'The age of consumer capitalism', *Cultural Logic,* accessed 12 August 2011 at http://clogic.eserver.org/2007/Cerni.pdf.

Chakrabarty, D. (2000), *Provincializing Europe: Postcolonial Thought and Historical Difference*, Princeton, NJ: Princeton University Press.

Clarke, S. (1991), 'The state debate', in S. Clarke (ed.), *The State Debate*, Basingstoke: Palgrave.

Clarke, S. (1994), *Marx's Theory of Crisis*, New York: St Martin's Press.

Cohen, G.A. (2000), *Karl Marx's Theory of History: A Defence*, 2nd edn, Oxford: Oxford University Press (1st edn published in 1978).

Cohen, R. (1987), *The New Helots: Migrants in the International Division of Labour*, Aldershot and Brookfield, VT, USA: Avebury.

Comninel, G.C. (1987), *Rethinking the French Revolution: Marxism and the Revisionist Challenge*, London: Verso.

Comninel, G.C. (2000a), 'English feudalism and the origins of capitalism', *Journal of Peasant Studies*, **27** (4), 1–53.

Comninel, G.C. (2000b), 'Revolution in history: the *Communist Manifesto* in context', in D. Moggach and P. Leduc Browne (eds), *The Revolutions of 1848: A Contested Legacy*, Ottawa: University of Ottawa Press.

Comninel, G.C. (2003), 'Materialist historical sociology and revolutions', in G. Delanty and E. Isin (eds), *Handbook of Historical Sociology*, London: Sage.

Coriat, B. (1979), *L'Atelier et le Chronomètre*, Paris: Christian Bourgois Editeur.

Corsani, A., P. Dieuaide, M. Lazzarato et al. (2001), *Le Capitalisme cognitif comme sortie de la crise du capitalism industriel: Un programme de recherche*, Paris, Colloque de l'école de la régulation, 11–14 October, accessed 12 August 2011 at http://matisse.univ-paris1.fr/doc2/capitalisme.pdf.

Cox, C.O. (1970), *Caste, Class and Race*, New York: Monthly Review Press.

Cox, R.W. (1987), *Production, Power and World Order: Social Forces in the Making of History*, New York: Columbia University Press.

Cracco, G. (1967), *Società e Stato nel Medioevo Veneziano (Secoli xii–xiv)*, Florence, Italy: Olschki.

Davis, H.B. (1967), 'Capital and imperialism. A landmark in Marxist theory', *Monthly Review*, **19** (4), 59–73.

Davies, W. (1996), 'On servile status in the early Middle Ages', in M.L. Bush (ed.), *Serfdom and Slavery: Studies in Legal Bondage*, London: Longman.

Devine, T.M. (1975), *The Tobacco Lords: A Study of the Tobacco Merchants of Glasgow and their Trading Activities c.1740–90*, Edinburgh: John Donald.

Diamond, J. (2005), *Collapse: How Societies Choose to Fail or Succeed*, New York: Viking.

Dickinson, H.D. (1933), 'Price formation in a socialist community', *Economic Journal*, **43** (170), 237–50.

Dobb, M. (1937), *Political Economy of Capitalism*, London: Routledge and Kegan Paul.

Dobb, M. (1947), *Studies in the Development of Capitalism*, New York: International Publishers.

dos Santos, P.L. (2009), 'On the content of banking in contemporary capitalism', *Historical Materialism*, **17**, 180–213.

dos Santos, T. (1978), *Imperialismo y Dependencia*, Mexico City: Ediciones Era.

Draper, H. (1977), *Karl Marx's Theory of Revolution. Part One: State and Bureaucracy*, New York: Monthly Review Press.

Duby, G. (1968), *Rural Economy and Country Life in the Medieval West*, Columbia, SC: University of South Carolina Press.

Dugger, W. (ed.) (1989), *Radical Institutionalism*, New York: Greenwood Press.

Duménil, G. and D. Lévy (1988), 'What can we learn from a century of history of the U.S. economy', Barcelona Conference on Regulation Theory, unpublished manuscript.

Duménil, G. and D. Lévy (1993), *The Economics of the Profit Rate*, Aldershot and Brookfield, VT, USA: Edward Elgar.

Duménil, G. and D. Lévy (2001), 'Costs and benefits of neoliberalism: a class analysis', *Review of International Political Economy*, **8** (4), 578–607.

Duménil, G. and D. Lévy (2004a), *Capital Resurgent: Roots of the Neoliberal Revolution*, Cambridge, MA and London: Harvard University Press.

Duménil, G. and D. Lévy (2004b), 'Production and management: Marx's dual theory of labor', in R. Westra and A. Zuege (eds), *Value and the World Economy Today. Production, Finance and Globalization*, London: Palgrave.

Duménil, G. and D. Lévy (2011), *The Crisis of Neoliberalism*, Cambridge, MA and London: Harvard University Press.

Elson, D. (1979a), 'The value theory of labour', in D. Elson (ed.), *Value, the Representation of Labour in Capitalism*, London: CSE Books.

Elson. D. (ed.) (1979b), *Value, The Representation of Labour in Capitalism*, London: CSE Books.

Elson, D. (1993), 'Gender-aware analysis and development economics', *Journal of International Development,* **5** (2), 237–47.

Elson, D. (1998), 'The economic, the political and the domestic: businesses, states and households in the organisation of production', *New Political Economy*, **3** (2), 189–208.

Emmanuel, A. (1972), *Unequal Exchange*, London: New Left Books.

Fairris, D. (1994), 'Shopfloor relations in the postwar capital-labor accord', in D. Kotz, T. McDonough and M. Reich (eds), *Social Structures of Accumulation: The Political Economy of Growth and Crisis*, Cambridge: Cambridge University Press.

Faith, R.C (1997), *The English Peasantry and the Growth of Lordship*, London: Leicester University Press.

Fanon, F. (1967), *The Wretched of the Earth*, Harmondsworth: Penguin.

Fine, B. (1975), 'The circulation of capital, ideology and crisis', *Bulletin of Conference of Socialist Economist*, **12,** 82–96.

Fine, B. (1979), 'On Marx's theory of agricultural rent', *Economy and Society*, **8** (3), 241–78.

Fine, B. (1980a), 'On Marx's theory of agricultural rent: a rejoinder', *Economy and Society*, **9** (3), 327–31.

Fine, B. (1980b), *Economic Theory and Ideology*, London: Edward Arnold.

Fine, B. (1983), 'A dissenting note on the transformation problem', *Economy and Society*, **12** (4), 520–5.

Fine, B. (ed.) (1986), *The Value Dimension, Marx Versus Ricardo and Sraffa*, London: Routledge and Kegan Paul.

Fine, B. (1992a), *Women's Work and the Capitalist Family*, London: Routledge.

Fine, B. (1992b), 'On the falling rate of profit', in G.A. Caravale (ed.), *Marx and Modern Economic Analysis*, Aldershot, UK and Brookfield, VT, USA: Edward Elgar.

Fine, B. (1998), *Labour Market Theory: A Constructive Reassessment*, London: Routledge.

Fine, B. (2001), 'The continuing imperative of value theory', *Capital & Class*, **75**, 7–18.

Fine, B. (2002), *The World of Consumption: The Material and Cultural Revisited*, London: Routledge.

Fine, B. (2004), 'Examining the ideas of globalisation and development critically: what role for political economy?', *New Political Economy*, **9** (2), 213–31.

Fine, B. (2005), 'Addressing the consumer', in F. Trentmann (ed.), *The Making of the Consumer: Knowledge, Power and Identity in the Modern World*, Oxford: Berg.

Fine, B. (2008), 'Debating Lebowitz: is class conflict the moral and historical element in the value of labour-power?', *Historical Materialism*, **16** (3), 105–14.

Fine, B. (2010) 'Locating financialisation', *Historical Materialism*, **18** (2), 97–116.

Fine, B. and L. Harris (1979), *Rereading 'Capital'*, London: Macmillan.

Fine, B., H.S. Jeon and G.H. Gimm (2010), 'Value is as value does: twixt knowledge and the world economy', *Capital & Class*, **34** (1), 69–83.

Fine, B., C. Lapavitsas and D. Milonakis (1999), 'Addressing the world economy: two steps back', *Capital & Class*, **67**, 47–90.

Fine, B., C. Lapavitsas and A. Saad-Filho (2004), 'Transforming the transformation problem: why the "new interpretation" is a wrong turning', *Review of Radical Political Economics*, **36** (1), January, 3–19.

Fine, B. and E. Leopold (1993), *The World of Consumption*, London: Routledge.

Fine, B. and D. Milonakis (2009), *From Economics Imperialism to Freakonomics: The Shifting Boundaries Between Economics and Other Social Sciences*, London and New York: Routledge.

Fine, B. and A. Saad-Filho (2010), *Marx's 'Capital'*, 5th edn, London: Pluto Press.

Floro, M. (1995), 'Economic restructuring, gender and the allocation of time', *World Development*, **23** (11), 1913–29.

Folbre, N. (1995), 'Holding hands at midnight: the paradox of caring labour', *Feminist Economics*, **1** (1), 73–92.

Foley, D.K. (1983), 'On Marx's theory of money', *Social Concept*, **1** (1), 5–19.

Foley, D.K. (1986), *Understanding Capital*, Cambridge, MA: Harvard University Press.

Foster, J.B. (1986), *The Theory of Monopoly Capitalism*, New York: Monthly Review Press.

Foster, J.B. (1999), 'Marx's theory of metabolic rift: classical foundations for environmental sociology', *American Journal of Sociology*, **105** (2), 366–405.

Foster, J.B. (2000), *Marx's Ecology: Materialism and Nature*, New York: Monthly Review Press.

Foster, J.B. (2008), 'The financialization of capital and the crisis', *Monthly Review*, **59** (11), 1–19.

Frank, A.G. (1967), *Capitalism and Underdevelopment in Latin America*, New York: Monthly Review Press.

Freeman, A. and G. Carchedi (eds) (1996), *Marx and Non-Equilibrium Economics*, Cheltenham, UK and Brookfield, VT, USA: Edward Elgar.

Friedman, A. (1977) 'Responsible autonomy versus direct control over the labour process', *Capital & Class*, **1**, 43–57.

Fröbel, F., J. Heinrichs and O. Kreye (1980), *The New International Division of Labour*, Cambridge: Cambridge University Press.

Fromm, E. (1961), *Marx's Concept of Man*, New York: Frederick Ungar Publishing.

Gereffi, G., J. Humphrey and T. Sturgeon (2005), 'The governance of global value chains', *Review of International Political Economy*, **12** (1), 78–104.

Gereffi, G. and M. Korzeniewicz (eds) (1994), *Commodity Chains and Global Capitalism*, London: Praeger.

Gerschenkron, A. (1962), *Economic Backwardness in Historical Perspective: A Book of Essays*, Cambridge, MA: Harvard University Press.

Gibbon, P. and S. Ponte (2005), *Trading Down: Africa, Value Chains, and the Global Economy*, Philadelphia, PA: Temple University Press.

Gibson-Graham, J.K. S. Resnick and R. Wolff (2001), *Re/presenting Class: Essays in Postmodern Marxism*, Durham, NC: Duke University Press.

Gilpin, R. (1987), *The Political Economy of International Relations*, Princeton, NJ: Princeton University Press.

Gilroy, P. (1987), *There Ain't No Black in The Union Jack*, London: Hutchinson.

Gimm, G.H. (forthcoming), 'Karl Marx's concept of the world market', PhD dissertation in economics, University of London.

Glickman, L.B. (1997), *A Living Wage: American Workers and the Making of Consumer Society*, Ithaca, NY: Cornell University Press.

Glyn, A. and B. Sutcliffe (1972), *British Capitalism, Workers and the Profit Squeeze*, London: Penguin.

Godelier, M. (1966), *Rationality and Irrationality in Economics*, London: New Left Books.

Goodin, R. and H.-D. Klingelman (1996), *A New Handbook of Political Science*, Oxford: Oxford University Press.

Gordon, D., S. Bowles and T. Weisskopf (1998), 'Power, profits and investment: an institutional explanation of the stagnation of US net investment after the mid-1960s', in D. Gordon (ed.) *Economics and Social Justice: Essays on Power, Labor and Institutional Change*, Cheltenham, UK and Lyme, NH, USA: Edward Elgar.

Gordon, D., R. Edwards and M. Reich (1982), *Segmented Work, Divided Workers*, Cambridge: Cambridge University Press.

Gordon, D., R. Edwards and M. Reich (1994), 'Long swings and stages of capitalism', in D. Kotz, T. McDonough and M. Reich (eds), *Social Structures of Accumulation: The Political Economy of Growth and Crisis*, Cambridge: Cambridge University Press.

Gough, I. (1979), *The Political Economy of the Welfare State*, London: Macmillan.

Gowan, P. (1999), *The Global Gamble: Washington's Faustian Bid for World Dominance*, London: Verso.

Gramsci, A. (1971), *Selections from the Prison Notebooks*, New York: International Publishers.

Green, F. (1991), 'The "reserve army hypothesis": a survey of empirical applications', in P. Dunne (ed.), *Quantitative Marxism*, Cambridge: Polity Press.

Green, F. (2006), *Demanding Work: The Paradox of Job Quality in the Affluent Economy*, Princeton, NJ: Princeton University Press.

Habib, I. (2005), *The Agrarian System of Mughal India 1556–1707*, 2nd edn, Delhi: Oxford University Press.

Haila, A. (1990), 'The theory of land rent at the crossroads', *Environment and Planning D: Society and Space*, **8** (3), 275–96.

Haldon, J. (1993), *The State and the Tributary Mode of Production*, London: Verso.

Hall, S. (1980), 'Race, articulation and societies structured in dominance', in UNESCO (ed.), *Sociological Theories: Race and Colonialism*, Paris: UNESCO.

Hardt, M. and A. Negri (2000), *Empire*, Cambridge, MA: Harvard University Press.

Hardt, M. and A. Negri (2004), *Multitude: War and Democracy in the Age of Empire*, New York: Penguin.

Hare, P. (1989), 'The economics of shortage in the centrally planned economies', in C. Davis and W. Charemza (eds), *Models of Disequilibrium and Shortage in Centrally Planned Economies*, London: Chapman and Hall.

Hart, K. (2006), 'Agrarian civilization and world society', in D. Olson and M. Cole (eds), *Technology, Literacy and the Evaluation of Society*, Mahwah, NJ: Lawrence Erlbaum, pp. 29–48.

Hartwell, R. (1966), 'Markets, technology and the structure of enterprise in the development of the eleventh-century Chinese iron and steel industry', *Journal of Economic History*, **26** (1), 29–58.

Harvey, D. (1974), 'Class-monopoly rent, finance capital and the urban revolution', *Regional Studies*, **8** (3), 39–255.

Harvey, D. (1978), 'The urban process under capitalism: a framework for analysis', *International Journal of Urban and Regional Research*, **2** (1–4), 101–31.

Harvey, D. (1996), *Justice, Nature and the Geography of Difference*, Oxford: Blackwell.

Harvey, D. (1999), *The Limits to Capital*, London: Verso.

Harvey, D. (2000), *Spaces of Hope*, Edinburgh: Edinburgh University Press.

Harvey, D. (2005), *A Brief History of Neoliberalism*, New York: Oxford University Press.

Harvey, D. (2006), *Spaces of Global Capitalism: Towards a Theory of Uneven Geographical Development*, London: Verso.

Harvey, D. (2010), *The Enigma of Capital and the Crisis of Capitalism*, London: Profile Books.

Hayek, F.K. (ed.) (1935), *Collectivist Economic Planning*, London: Routledge and Kegan Paul.

Heller, H. (2006), *The Bourgeois Revolution in France, 1789–1815*, Oxford: Berghahn.

Heynen, N., M. Kaika and E. Swyngedouw (eds) (2005), *In the Nature of Cities – The Politics of Urban Metabolism*, London: Routledge.

Hicks, J. (1939), *Value and Capital: An Inquiry into Some Fundamental Principles of Economic Theory*, Oxford: Clarendon Press.

Hilferding, R. (1910 [1994]), *Finance Capital*, London: Routledge.

Hill, C., R. Hilton and E.J. Hobsbawm (1983), 'Past and Present: origins and early years', *Past and Present*, **100**, 3–14.

Hilton, R.H. (ed.) (1978), *The Transition from Feudalism to Capitalism*, London: New Left Books.

Himmelweit, S. (1974), 'The continuing saga of the falling rate of profit – a reply to Mario Cogoy', *Bulletin of the Conference of Socialist Economists*, **9** (Autumn), 105–35.

Hobsbawm, E. (1965), 'Introduction', in K. Marx, *Pre-Capitalist Economic Formations*, New York: International Publishers.

Holloway, J. and S. Picciotto (1982), *Capital and the State*, London: Edward Arnold.

Hopkins, T.K. and I. Wallerstein (eds) (1982), *World-Systems Analysis: Theory and Methodology*, London and New Delhi: Sage Publications.

Hopmann, B., M. Spoerer and B. Weitz (1994), *Zwangsarbeit bei Daimler-Benz*, Stuttgart, Germany: F. Steiner.

Howard, D. (ed.) (1971), *Selected Political Writings of Rosa Luxemburg*, New York: Monthly Review Press.

Hubmann, G. (2005), 'Classici incompiuti. Costellazioni filologico-editoriali in Marx e altri classici delle scienze sociali', in M. Musto (ed.), *Sulle tracce di un fantasma. L'opera di Karl Marx tra filologia et filosofia*, Rome: Manifestolibri.

Hunt, L. (1986), 'French history in the last twenty years: the rise and fall of the annales paradigm', *Journal of Contemporary History*, **21** (2), 209–24.

Itoh, M. (1995), *Political Economy for Socialism*, Houndmill: Macmillan.

Itoh, M. and C. Lapavitsas (1999), *The Political Economy of Money and Finance*, London: Macmillan.

Jeon, H. (2010), 'Cognitive capitalism or cognition in capitalism?: a critique of cognitive capitalism theory', *Spectrum*, **2** (3), 90–117.

Jeon, H. (2011), 'The value and price of information commodities: an assessment of the South Korean controversy', in P. Zarembka and R. Desai (eds), *Revitalizing Marxist Theory for Today's Capitalism (Research in Political Economy)*, vol 27, Emerald Group Publishing, pp. 191–222.

Jenkins, R. (1987), *Transnational Corporations and Uneven Development*, New York: Methuen.

Jessop, B. (1982), *The Capitalist State: Marxist Theories and Methods*, Oxford: Martin Robertson.

Jessop, B. (2001), 'Capitalism, the Regulation Approach and critical realism', in A. Brown, S. Fleetwood and J. Roberts (eds), *Critical Realism and Marxism*, London: Routledge.

Jessop, B. (2002), *The Future of the Capitalist State*, Cambridge: Polity.

Jevons, W.S. (1871 [2001]), *The Theory of Political Economy*, Basingstoke: Macmillan.

Johnson, S.H. (1999), 'An ecofeminist critique of the international economic structure', in M. Mayer and E. Prügl (eds), *Gender Politics in Global Governance*, Lanham, MD: Rowman & Littlefield Publishers.

Kalecki, M. (1943), 'Political aspects of full employment', *Political Quarterly*, **14** (4), 322–31.

Kang, N., S. Kang, D. Rieu et al. (2007), *Debate on the Value of Information Commodities*, Osan, South Korea: Hanshin University Press, in Korean.

Kautsky, Karl (1988), *The Agrarian Question. In Two Volumes*, first published in German 1899, translation by Pete Burgess, London: Zwan Publications.

Kaye, H.J. (1984), *The British Marxist Historians: An Introductory Analysis*, Cambridge: Polity Press.

Keynes, J. (1936 [1973]), *The General Theory of Employment, Interest and Money*, London: Macmillan.

Kiely, R. (2010), *Rethinking Imperialism*, London: Palgrave.

Kiernan, V.G. (1974), *Marxism and Imperialism*, London: Routledge and Kegan Paul.

Kornai, J. (1980), *Economics of Shortage*, Amsterdam, Netherlands: North Holland.
Korsch, K. (1972), *Karl Marx*, Frankfurt, Germany: Europäische Verlagsanstalt.
Kotz, D. (1994a), 'Interpreting the social structure of accumulation theory', in D. Kotz, T. McDonough and M. Reich (eds), *Social Structures of Accumulation: The Political Economy of Growth and Crisis*, Cambridge: Cambridge University Press.
Kotz, D. (1994b), 'The regulation theory and the social structure of accumulation approach', in D. Kotz, T. McDonough and M. Reich (eds), *Social Structures of Accumulation: The Political Economy of Growth and Crisis*, Cambridge: Cambridge University Press.
Kotz, D. (2003), 'Neoliberalism and the US economic expansion of the 1990s', *Monthly Review*, **54** (11), 15–33.
Kotz, D., T. McDonough and M. Reich (1994), *Social Structures of Accumulation*, Cambridge: Cambridge University Press.
Kotz, D., T. McDonough and M. Reich (eds) (2010), *Contemporary Capitalism and its Crises: Social Structure of Accumulation Theory for the 21st Century*, Cambridge: Cambridge University Press.
Krasner, S.D. (1978), *Defending the National Interest: Raw Material Investments and US Foreign Policy*, Princeton, NJ: Princeton University Press.
Krätke, M.R. (2008a), 'The first world economic crisis: Marx as an economic journalist', in M. Musto (ed.), *Karl Marx's Grundrisse: Foundations of the Critique of Political Economy 150 Years Later*, London: Routledge, pp. 161–8.
Krätke, M.R. (2008b), 'Marx's 'Book of Crisis' of 1857–8', in M. Musto (ed.), *Karl Marx's Grundrisse: Foundations of the Critique of Political Economy 150 Years Later*, London: Routledge, pp. 169–75.
Kurz, H.D. and N. Salvadori (eds) (2003), *The Legacy of Piero Sraffa*, Cheltenham, UK and Northampton, MA, USA: Edward Elgar.
Lacher, H. (2008), 'History, structure, and world orders: on the (cross-) purposes of neo-Gramscian theory', in A.J. Ayers (ed.), *Gramsci, Political Economy and International Relations Theory: Modern Princes and Naked Emperors*, New York: Palgrave.
Laibman, D. (1984), 'Modes of production and theories of transition', *Science & Society*, **48** (3), 257–94.
Laibman, D. (1987), 'Modes and transitions', *Science & Society*, **51** (2), 179–88.
Laibman, D. (2007), *Deep History: A Study in Social Evolution and Human Potential*, New York: State University of New York Press.
Lamont, N. (1991), *Parliamentary Debates (House of Commons)*, 6th series, vol. 191 (1990–91), column 413, 16th May.
Lange, O. (1936, 1937), 'On the economic theory of socialism', *Review of Economic Studies,* **4** (1) (October), 53–71 and **4** (2) (February), 123–42.
Lapavitsas, C. (2005), 'The emergence of money in commodity exchange, or money as monopolist of the ability to buy', *Review of Political Economy*, **17** (4), 549–69.
Lapavitsas, C. (2009), 'Financialised capitalism: crisis and financial expropriation', *Historical Materialism*, **17** (2), 114–48.
Lavoie, E. (1985), *Rivalry and Central Planning: The Socialist Calculation Debate Reconsidered*, Cambridge: Cambridge University Press.
Lebowitz, M. (2003), *Beyond 'Capital': Marx's Political Economy of the Working Class*, 2nd edn, Basingstoke: Palgrave Macmillan.

Lebowitz, M. (2010), 'Trapped inside the box?: five questions for Ben Fine', *Historical Materialism*, **18** (1), 131–49.

Lee, F. (2009), *A History of Heterodox Economics: Challenging the Mainstream in the Twentieth Century*, London: Routledge.

Lévi-Strauss, C. (1949), *The Elementary Structures of Kinship*, Boston, MA: Beacon.

Liberman, E.G. (1962 [1966]), 'Plan, profit, and bonus', in K. Nonomura (ed.), *The Soviet Economy and Profit*, Tokyo: Nihonhyoron-sha, in Japanese.

Lipietz, A. (1985), *The Enchanted World*, London: Verso.

Lipietz, A. (1997), 'Warp, woof and regulation: a tool for social science', in G. Benko and U. Strohmayer (eds), *Space and Social Theory*, London: Blackwell.

Löwy, M. (2005), *The Theory of Revolution in the Young Marx*, Chicago, IL: Haymarket Books.

Löwy, M. (2010), *The Politics of Combined and Uneven Development: The Theory of Permanent Revolution*, Chicago, IL: Haymarket Books, first edition London: NLB, 1981.

Luxemburg, R. (1913 [1966]), *Die Akkumulation des Kapitals*, Frankfurt, Germany: Neue Kritik.

Magaline, A.D. (1975), *Lutte de classes et dévalorisation du capital: Contribution à la critique du révisionnisme*, Paris: Maspero, with partial English translation by P. Zarembka in 'Class struggle in production and devalorisation of capital' in '*Revitalising Marxist theory for today's capitalism*', P. Zarembka and R. Desai (eds), *Research in Political Economy*, Vol. 27. Bingley: Emerald Group, pp. 255–68.

Mandel, E. (1968), *Marxist Economic Theory*, London: Merlin Press.

Mandel, E. (1970), 'The laws of uneven development', *New Left Review*, **59**, January/February, 19–38.

Mandel, E. (1975), *Late Capitalism*, London: Verso.

Mandel, E. (1986), 'In defence of socialist planning', *New Left Review*, **159**, September/October, 5–37.

Mandel, E. (1992), *Power and Money: A Marxist Theory of Bureaucracy*, London: Verso.

Mandel, E. and A. Freeman (eds) (1985), *Ricardo, Marx, Sraffa*, London: Verso.

Marglin, S. (1974), 'What do bosses do? The origins and functions of hierarchy in capitalist production', *Review of Radical Political Economics*, **6** (2), 60–112.

Marini, R.M. (1973), *Dialéctica de la Dependencia*, Mexico City: Ediciones Era.

Marshall, A. (1890 [1959]), *Principles of Economics: An Introductory Volume*, 8th edn, London: Macmillan.

Martinez-Alier, J. (2007), 'Social metabolism and environmental conflicts', in L. Panitch and C. Leys (eds), *Socialist Register*, London: Merlin.

Martinez-Alier, J. and K. Schlupmann (1990), *Ecological Economics*, Oxford: Blackwell.

Marx, K. (1857–8 [1953]), *Grundrisse der Kritik der politischen Ökonomie*, Berlin: Dietz Verlag.

Marx, K. (1859 [1980]), 'Zur Kritik der politischen Ökonomie', in *Karl Marx-Friedrich Engels Gesamtausgabe (MEGA)*, Berlin: Dietz Verlag .

Marx, K. (1861–63 [1959]), *Theorien über den Mehrwert*, vol. 2, Berlin: Dietz Verlag.

Marx, K. (1861–63 [1962]), *Theorien über den Mehrwert*, vol. 3, Berlin: Dietz Verlag.

Marx. K. (1861–63 [1976]), 'Zur Kritik der politischen Ökonomie Manuskript' in *MEGA*, II/3, 1, Berlin: Dietz Verlag.

Marx, K. (1863–67 [1988]), 'Ökonomische Manuskripte', in *MEGA*, II/4, 1, Berlin: Dietz Verlag.

Marx, K. (1863–67 [1992]), 'Ökonomische Manuskripte', in *MEGA*, II/4, 2, Berlin: Dietz Verlag.

Marx, K. (1867 [1987]), *Das Kapital,* vol. 1, Berlin: Dietz Verlag.

Marx, K. (1875 [1965]), 'Le Capital', in K. Marx *Œuvres: Economie,* vol. 1, Paris: Gallimard.

Marx, K. (1905 [1956]), *Theorien über den Mehrwert*, vol. 1, Berlin: Dietz Verlag.

Marx, K. (1905–1910 [1959]), *Theorien über den Mehrwert*, vol. 2, Berlin: Dietz Verlag.

Marx, K. (1972), 'Brief an Kugelmann', 28 December 1862, in K. Marx and F. Engels, *Briefe über 'Das Kapital'*, Erlangen: Politladen-Reprint.

Marx, K. (1976), 'Zur Kritik der politischen Ökonomie (Manuskript 1861–1863)', in K. Marx and F. Engels, *Gesamtausgabe*, section 2, vol. 3, part 1, Berlin: Dietz Verlag.

Marx, K. (1980), 'Zur Kritik der politischen Ökonomie (Manuskript 1861–1863)', in K. Marx and F. Engels, *Gesamtausgabe*, section 2, vol. 3, part 5, Berlin: Dietz Verlag.

Marx, K. (1988), 'Value, price and profit', 'Ökonomische Manuskripte (1863–1867)', in K. Marx and F. Engels, *Gesamtausgabe*, section 2, vol. 4, part 1, Berlin: Dietz Verlag.

Marx, K. (1992), 'Ökonomische Manuskripte (1863–1867)', in K. Marx and F. Engels, *Gesamtausgabe,* section 2, vol. 4, part 2, Berlin: Dietz Verlag.

Marx, K. (2008), *Karl Marx/Friedrich Engels Gesamtausgabe (MEGA), Band II/11, Manuskripte zum zweiten Buch des Kapitals, 1868 bis 1881*, Berlin: Akademie Verlag.

Marx, K. and F. Engels (2003), *Karl Marx/Friedrich Engels Gesamtausgabe (MEGA), Band II/14, Manuskripte und redaktionelle Texte zum dritten Buch des 'Kapitals', 1871 bis 1895*, Berlin: Akademie Verlag.

Massey, D.S., J. Arango, G. Hugo, A. Kouaouci, A. Pellegrino and J.E. Taylor (1993), 'Theories of international migration: a review and appraisal', *Population and Development Review*, **19** (3), 431–66.

Mattick, P. (1969), *Marx and Keynes*, London: Merlin.

Mavroudeas, S.D. (1999) 'Regulation theory: the road from creative Marxism to post-modern disintegration', *Science & Society*, **63** (3), 310–37.

Mavroudeas, S.D. (2003), 'Commodities, workers and institutions: analytical and empirical problems in Regulation's consumption theory', *Review of Radical Political Economics*, **35** (4), 485–512.

Mavroudeas, S.D. (2006), 'Social structures of accumulation, regulation approach and stages theory', in T. McDonough, M. Reich, D. Kotz and M. Gonzalez-Perez (eds), *Growth and Crisis: Social Structure of Accumulation Theory and Analysis*, Galway: Centre for Innovation and Structural Change, National University of Ireland.

McDonough, T. (2008), 'Social structures of accumulation: the state of the art', *Review of Radical Political Economics*, **40** (2), 153–73.

McDonough, T., M. Reich and D.M. Kotz (eds) (2010), *Contemporary Capitalism and its Crises: Social Structure of Accumulation Theory for the 21st Century*, Cambridge: Cambridge University Press.

McIntyre, R. and M. Hillard (2008), 'The "limited capital-labor accord": may it rest in peace?', *Review of Radical Political Economics*, **40** (3), 244–9.

McLennan, G. (1986), 'Marxist theory and historical research: between the hard and soft options', *Science & Society*, **50** (1), 85–95.

McMichael, P. (2009), 'Banking on agriculture: a review of the *World Development Report 2008'*, *Journal of Agrarian Change*, **9** (2), 235–46.

Meillassoux, C. (1964), *Anthropologie Economique des Gouro de Côte d'Ivoire*, Paris: Mouton.

Meillassoux, C. (1981), *Maidens, Meals and Money: Capitalism and the Domestic Community*, Cambridge: Cambridge University Press.

Mellon, S. (1958), *The Political Uses of History*, Stanford, CA: Stanford University Press.

Melotti, U. (1977), *Marx and the Third World*, London: Macmillan.

Merrifield, A. (1993), 'Place and space: a Lefebvrian reconciliation', *Transactions of the Institute of British Geographers*, **18** (4), 516–31.

Merrifield, A. (2002), *Metromarxism*, London and New York: Routledge.

Miles, R. (1994), *Racism After 'Race Relations'*, London: Routledge.

Miliband, R (2009), *The State in Capitalist Society*, London: Merlin Press.

Mills, C. Wright (1956), *The Power Elite*, Oxford: Oxford University Press.

Mills, J.S. (1848 [1976]), *Principles of Political Economy*, introduction by Sir William Ashley, first published 1909, New York: Augustus M. Kelley.

Milonakis, D. (1993–94), 'Prelude to the genesis of capitalism: the dynamics of the feudal mode of production', *Science & Society,* **57** (4), 390–419.

Milonakis, D. and B. Fine (2009), *From Political Economy to Economics: Method, the Social and the Historical in the Evolution of Economic Theory*, London: Routledge.

Mohri, K. (1979), 'Marx and "underdevelopment"', *Monthly Review*, **30** (11), 32–42.

Mohun, S. (1994), 'A re(in)statement of the labour theory of value', *Cambridge Journal of Economics*, **18** (4), 391–412.

Mohun, S. (2006), 'Distributive shares in the U.S. economy, 1964–2001', *Cambridge Journal of Economics*, **30** (3), 347–70.

Mohun, S. (2009), 'Aggregate capital productivity in the U.S. economy 1964–2001', *Cambridge Journal of Economics*, **33** (5), 1023–46.

Morgan, L.H. (1877), *Ancient Society*, Cambridge, MA: Belknap Press.

Morishima, M. (1973), *Marx's Economics: A Dual Theory of Value and Growth*, Cambridge: Cambridge University Press.

Moseley, F. (1991), *The Falling Rate of Profit in the Post-War United States Economy*, New York: St. Martin's Press.

Musto, M. (ed.) (2008) *Karl Marx's* Grundisse: *Foundations of the Critique of Political Economy 150 Years Later*. London: Routledge.

Myrdal, G. (1944), *An American Dilemma: The Negro Problem and Modern Democracy*, New York: Harper & Row.

Nachtwey, D. and T. ten Brink (2008), 'Lost in transition: the German world-market debate in the 1970's', *Historical Materialism*, **16** (1), 37–70.

Nakagawa, Nobuyoshi (1999–2003), 'Theories of world-market and universal value (I)–(VI)', *The Quarterly Journal of Economic Studies*, **22** (3), 17–44; **22** (4), 61–102; **24** (1), 27–74; **25** (1), 125–50; **25** (2), 1–26; **25** (3), 25–62, in Japanese.

Nelson, J.A. (1993), 'The study of choice or the study of provisioning? Gender and the definition of economics', in M. Ferber and J. Nelson (eds), *Beyond Economic Man: Feminist Theory and Economics*, Chicago, IL: University of Chicago Press.

Nikolinakos, M. (1975), 'Notes towards a general theory of migration in late capitalism', *Race and Class,* **XVII** (1), 5–17.

Nolan, P. (1993), *Natural Selection and Historical Materialism*, Watford: Glenfield Press.

Nolan, P. and G. Slater (2010), 'Visions of the future, the legacy of the past: demystifying the weightless economy', *Labor History*, **51** (1), 7–27.

Nove, A. (1983), *The Economics of Feasible Socialism*, London: Macmillan.

O'Connor, J. (1973), *The Fiscal Crisis of the State*, New York: St Martin's Press.

O'Connor, J. (1996), 'The second contradiction of capitalism', in T. Benton (ed.), *The Greening of Marxism*, London: Routledge.

O'Leary, B. (1989), *The Asiatic Mode of Production*, Oxford: Oxford University Press.

Ollman, B. (1978), *Social and Sexual Revolution*, Boston, MA: South End Press.

Ollman, B. (2000), 'What is political science? What should it be?', *New Political Science*, **22** (4), 553–62.

Owen, R. and B. Sutcliffe (eds) (1972), *Studies in the Theory of Imperialism*, London: Longman.

Panitch, L. and S. Gindin (2004), *Global Capitalism and American Empire*, London: Merlin Press.

Panitch, L. and C. Leys (eds) (2007), *Coming to Terms with Nature*: Socialist Register *2007*, London: Merlin Press.

Pannekoek, A. (1909), *Die Taktischen Differenzen in der Arbeiterbewegung*, Hamburg, Germany: E. Dubber.

Patnaik, P. (2005), 'Karl Marx as a development economist', in K.S. Jomo (ed.), *The Pioneers of Development Economics*, New Delhi: Tulika Books.

Patnaik, U. (1987), *Peasant Class Differentiation. A Study in Method with Reference to Haryana*, Delhi: Oxford University Press.

Peet, R. (1977), *Radical Geography: Alternative Viewpoints on Contemporary Social Issues*, Chicago, IL: Maaroufa Press.

Pilling, G. (1972), 'The law of value in Ricardo and Marx', *Economy and Soceity*, **1** (3), 281–307.

Pilling, G. (1980), *Marx's 'Capital': Philosophy and Political Economy*, London: Routledge and Kegan Paul.

Plummer, A. (1934), *International Combines in Modern Industry*, London: Pitman.

Portes, R. (1989), 'The theory and measurement of macroeconomic disequilibrium in centrally planned economies', in C. Davis and W. Charemza (eds), *Models of Disequilibrium and Shortage in Centrally Planned Economies*, London: Chapman and Hall.

Post, K. (1978), *Arise Ye Starvelings: The Jamaican Labour Rebellion of 1938 and its Aftermath*, The Hague: Martinus Nijhoff.

Postone, M. (1993), *Time, Labour and Social Domination: A Reinterpretation of Marx's Critical Theory*, Cambridge: Cambridge University Press.

Poulantzas, N. (1974), *Classes in Contemporary Capitalism*, London: New Left Books.

Poulantzas, N. (1978), *State, Power, Socialism*, London: Verso.

Preobrazhensky, E. (1965), *The New Economics*, first published in Russian 1926, translated by Brian Pearce, London: Oxford University Press.

Radice, H. (ed.) (1975), *International Firms and Modern Imperialism*, Harmondsworth: Penguin Education.

Reich, M. (1978), 'Who benefits from racism? The distribution among whites of gains and losses from racial inequality', *Journal of Human Resources*, **13** (4), 524–44.

Reich, M. (1994), 'How social structures of accumulation decline and are built', in D. Kotz, T. McDonough and M. Reich (eds), *Social Structures of Accumulation: The Political Economy of Growth and Crisis*, Cambridge: Cambridge University Press.

Reuten, G. (2004), '"Zirkel Vicieux" or trend fall? The course of the profit rate in Marx's "Capital III"', *History of Political Economy*, **36** (1), 163–86.

Reuten, G. and M. Williams (1989), *Value-Form and the State: The Tendencies of Accumulation and the Determination of Economic Policy in Capitalist Society*, London: Routledge.

Rey, P.-P. (1971), *Colonialisme, Néo-Colonialisme et Transition au Capitalisme*, Paris: Maspero.

Robbins, L. (1935 [2008]), 'The nature and significance of economic science', excerpts from *Essays on the Nature and Significance of Economic Science*, in D. Hausman (ed.), *The Philosophy of Economics: An Anthology*, 2nd edn, Cambridge: Cambridge University Press.

Roberts, M. (1996), *Analytical Marxism. A Critique*, London: Verso.

Robinson, B. (2004), *A Theory of Global Capitalism*, Baltimore, MD: Johns Hopkins University Press.

Rodinson, M. (1977), *Islam and Capitalism*, Harmondsworth: Penguin Books.

Roemer, J.E. (1981), *Analytical Foundations of Marxian Economic Theory*, Cambridge, MA: Harvard University Press.

Roemer, J.E. (ed.) (1986), *Analytical Marxism*, Cambridge: Cambridge University Press.

Roemer, J.E. (1988), *Free to Lose*, Cambridge, MA.: Harvard University Press.

Roemer, J.E. (1994), *A Future for Socialism*, London: Verso.

Rosdolsky, R. (1968 [1977]), *The Making of Marx's 'Capital'*, London: Pluto Press.

Ross, E.B. (1998), *The Malthus Factor: Population, Poverty and Politics in Capitalist Development*, London: Zed Books.

Rousseau, J.-J. (1754 [1984]), *Discourse on the Origins and Foundations of Inequality Among Men*, Harmondsworth: Penguin.

Rowthorn, B. (1974), 'Neo-classicism, Neo-Ricardianism and Marxism', *New Left Review*, **86**, 63–87.

Rowthorn, B. (1980) *Capitalism, Conflict and Inflation*, London: Lawrence and Wishart.

Rubel, M. (1968), 'Introduction', in K. Marx, *Œuvres : Economic* II, Paris: Gallimard.

Rubel, M. (1968 [1982]), 'Introduction', in K. Marx, *Œuvres* III: *Philosophie*, Paris: Gallimard.

Rubel, M. (1995), 'Nach Hundert Jahren: Plädoyer für Friedrich Engels', *Internationale Wissenschaftliche Korrespondenz zur Geschichte der Deutschen Arbeiterbewegung*, **XXXI** (4), 520–30.

Rubin, I.I. (1928 [1973]), *Essays on Marx's Theory of Value*, Montreal, QC: Black Rose Books.

Saad-Filho, A. (2002), *The Value of Marx: Political Economy of Contemporary Capitalism*, London: Routledge.

Saad-Filho, A. (2005), 'The rise and decline of Latin American structuralism and dependency theory', in K.S. Jomo and E.S. Reinert (eds), *The Origins of Development Economics: How Schools of Economic Thought Have Addressed Development*, London and New Delhi: Zed Books and Tulika Books.

Saad-Filho, A. and D. Johnston (eds) (2005), *Neoliberalism: A Critical Reader*, London: Pluto Press.

Samuelson, P. (1947), *Foundations of Economic Analysis*, New York: Harvard University Press.

Sarkar, S. (1999), *Eco-Socialism or Eco-Capitalism? A Critical Analysis of Humanity's Fundamental Choices*, London: Zed Books.

Savran, S. (1979), 'On the theoretical consistency of Sraffa's economics', *Capital & Class*, 7 (Spring), 131–40.

Sayer, A. (1995), *Radical Political Economy: A Critique*, Oxford: Blackwell.

Sayer, D. (1985), 'The critique of politics and political economy: capitalism, communism and the state in Marx's writings of the mid-1840s', *Sociological Review*, 33 (2), 221–53.

Sayer, D. (1987), *The Violence of Abstraction: The Analytic Foundations of Historical Materialism*, Oxford: Blackwell.

Schumpeter, J.A. (1954), *History of Economic Analysis*, New York: Oxford University Press.

Scott, A.J. (1976), 'Land and land rent: an interpretative review of the French literature', *Progress in Geography,* 9, 102–45.

Seddon, D. (ed.) (1978), *Relations of Production: Marxist Approaches to Economic Anthropology*, London: Frank Cass.

Sekine, T. (1997), *An Outline of the Dialectic of Capital*, London: Macmillan.

Sen, A. (1983), 'Economics and the family', *Asian Development Review*, 1 (2), 14–26.

Shaikh, A. (1978), 'An introduction to the history of crisis theories', in *U.S. Capitalism in Crisis*, New York: Union for Radical Political Economics (eds) accessed 12 August 2011 at http://homepage.newschool.edu/~AShaikh/crisis_theories.pdf.

Shaikh, A. (1979–80) 'Foreign trade and the law of value', *Science & Society*, 43 (4) (Winter), 281–302 and 44 (1), 27–57.

Shaikh, A. (2003), 'Who pays for "welfare" in a welfare state? A multi-country study', *Social Research*, 70 (2), 531–50.

Shanin, T. (ed.) (1983), *Late Marx and the Russian Road*, New York: Monthly Review Press.

Sharma, R.S. (2005), *Indian Feudalism,* 3rd edn, Delhi: Macmillan.

Sjöström, K. (1979), *Socialpolitik eller Socialism?*, 2nd edn, Lund, Sweden: Arbetarkultur.

Smedley, A. (1999), *Race in North America: Origin and Evolution of a Worldview*, Oxford: Westview.

Smith, N. (1984), *Uneven Development*, Oxford: Blackwell.

Smith T. (2000), *Technology and Capital in the Age of Lean Production: A Marxian Critique of the 'New Economy'*, Albany, NY: State University of New York Press.

Spencer, D. (2000), 'Braverman and the contribution of labour process analysis to the critique of capitalist production – twenty-five years on', *Work, Employment and Society*, 14 (2), 223–43.

Sraffa, P. (1951), 'Introduction', in *The Works and Correspondence of David Ricardo*, vol. 1, Cambridge: Cambridge University Press.

Sraffa, P. (1960), *Production of Commodities by Means of Commodities*, Cambridge: Cambridge University Press.

Steedman, I. (1977), *Marx After Sraffa*, London: New Left Books.

Steedman, I., P. Sweezy, A. Shaikh et al. (1981), *The Value Controversy*, London: Verso.

Stiglitz, J. (1994), *Whither Socialism?*, Cambridge, MA: MIT Press.

Storper, M. and R. Walker (1989), *The Capitalist Imperative*, Oxford: Blackwell.

Strange, S. (1988), *States and Markets*, Oxford: Blackwell.

Sunkel, O. (1973), 'Transnational capitalism and national disintegration in Latin America', *Social and Economic Studies*, **22** (1), 132–76.

Sweezy, P.M. (1946 [1970]), *The Theory of Capitalist Development*, New York: Monthly Review Press.

Sweezy, P.M. (1949), *Socialism*, New York: McGraw-Hill.

Sweezy, P.M. (1970), *The Theory of Capitalist Development,* New York: Monthly Review Press.

Sweezy, P.M. (1978), 'The transition from feudalism to capitalism', in R.H. Hilton (ed.), *The Transition from Feudalism to Capitalism*, London: New Left Books.

Sweezy, P.M. (1997), 'More (or less) on globalization', *Monthly Review*, **49** (4), 3–4.

Sweezy, P.M., M. Dobb, H.K. Takahashi et al. (1978), *The Transition from Feudalism to Capitalism*, London: Verso.

Swyngedouw, E. (1992), 'Territorial organization and the space/technology nexus', *Transactions, Institute of British Geographers – New Series,* **17** (4), 417–33.

Swyngedouw, E. (2000), 'The Marxian alternative – historical geographical materialism and the political economy of capitalism', in T. Barnes and E. Sheppard (eds), *Reader in Economic Geography*, Oxford: Blackwell.

Swyngedouw, E. (2004), *Social Power and the Urbanization of Water: Flows of Power*, Oxford: Oxford University Press.

Tapscott, D. (1997), *The Digital Economy*, New York: McGraw Hill.

Tarrit, F. (2006), 'A brief history, scope, and peculiarities of "Analytical Marxism"', *Review of Radical Political Economics*, **38** (4), 595–618.

Thompson, E.P. (1968), *The Making of the English Working Class*, Harmondsworth: Penguin.

Thompson, E.P. (1978), *The Poverty of Theory and Other Essays*, London: Merlin Press.

UNCTAD (2002), *Trade and Development Report*, Geneva: UNCTAD.

URPE (1968), 'The Union for Radical Political Economics: a prospectus', conference papers of the Union for Radical Political Economics, December, Ann Arbor, MI, quoted in URPE (n.d.).

URPE (n.d.), 'History of URPE', accessed 12 August 2011 at www.urpe.org/about/history.html.

Veblen, T. (1899), *The Theory of the Leisure Class: An Economic Study in the Evolution of Institutions*, New York and London: Macmillan.

Veneziani, R. (2009), 'The rationality of Analytical Marxism', in A. Chitty and M. McIvor (eds), *Karl Marx and Contemporary Philosophy*, Basingstoke: Palgrave.

Vercellone, C. (2007), 'From formal subsumption to general intellect: elements for a

Marxist reading of the thesis of cognitive capitalism', *Historical Materialism*, **15** (1), 13–36.

Verhulst, A. (2002), *The Carolingian Economy*, Cambridge: Cambridge University Press.

Virdee, S. (2010), 'Racism, class and the dialectics of social transformation', in P. Hill Collins and J. Solomos, *The Sage Handbook of Race and Ethnic Studies*, London: Sage.

Von Böhm-Bawerk, E. and R. Hilferding (1975), *Karl Marx and the Close of His System*, London: Merlin Press.

Vujačić, I. (1988), 'Marx and Engels on development and underdevelopment: the restoration of a certain coherence', *History of Political Economy*, **20** (3), 471–98.

Vygodskij, V. (1976), *Wie das 'Kapital' entstand*, Berlin: Verlag Die Wirtschaft.

Walicki, A. (1969), *The Controversy Over Capitalism: Studies in the Social Philosophy of Russian Populists*, Oxford: Oxford University Press.

Wallerstein, I. (1974a), *The Modern World-System*, 3 volumes, New York: Academic Press.

Wallerstein, I. (1974b), 'The rise and future demise of the world capitalist system: concepts for comparative analysis', *Comparative Studies in Society and History*, **16** (4), 387–415.

Wallerstein, I. (1991 [1985]), 'Marx and underdevelopment', in *Unthinking Social Science: The Limits of Nineteenth-Century Paradigms*, Cambridge: Polity Press.

Walras, L. (1874 [1954]), *Elements of Pure Economics*, London: Augustus M. Kelley.

Warren, B. (1973), 'Imperialism and capitalist industrialization', *New Left Review*, **81**, 3–44.

Warren, B. (1980), *Imperialism: Pioneer of Capitalism*, London: Verso.

Weeks, J. (1981a), *Capital and Exploitation*, Princeton, NJ: Princeton University Press.

Weeks, J. (1981b), 'The differences between materialist theory and dependency theory and why they matter', *Latin American Perspectives*, **8** (3/4), 118–22.

Weeks, J. (2010), *Capital, Exploitation and Crises*, London: Routledge.

Weisskopf, T.E. (1979), 'Marxian crisis theory and the rate of profit in the post-war US economy', *Cambridge Journal of Economics*, **3** (4), 341–78.

Weisskopf, T.E. (1994), 'Alternative social structure of accumulation approaches to the analysis of capitalist booms and crises', in D. Kotz, T. McDonough and M. Reich (eds), *Social Structures of Accumulation: The Political Economy of Growth and Crisis*, Cambridge: Cambridge University Press.

Wickham, C. (2005), *Framing the Early Middle Ages: Europe and the Mediterranean 400–800*, Oxford: Oxford University Press.

Wilson, A. (1993), 'A critical portrait of social history', in A. Wilson (ed.), *Rethinking Social History: English Society 1570–1920 and its Interpretation*, Manchester: Manchester University Press.

Winch, D. (1973), 'Marginalism and the boundaries of economic science', in C. Black, A. Coats and D. Goodwin (eds), *The Marginalist Revolution in Economics*, Durham, NC: Duke University Press.

Wolf, E. (1982), *Europe and the Peoples Without History*, Berkeley, CA: University of California Press.

Wolpe, H. (ed.) (1980), *The Articulation of Modes of Production: Essays from Economy and Society*, London: Routledge and Kegan Paul.

Wood, E.M. (1988), *Peasant-Citizen and Slave: The Foundations of Athenian Democracy*, London: Verso.

Wood, E.M. (1989), 'Rational choice Marxism: is the game worth the candle?', *New Left Review*, **177**, 41–88.

Wood, E.M. (1995), *Democracy Against Capitalism: Renewing Historical Materialism*, Cambridge: Cambridge University Press.

Wood, E.M. (2002), *The Origin of Capitalism: A Longer View*, London: Verso.

Wright, E.O., A. Levine and E. Sober (1992), *Reconstructing Marxism: Essays on Explanation and the Theory of History*, London: Verso.

Young, N. (1977), *An Infantile Disorder? The Crisis and Decline of the New Left*, London: Routledge and Kegan Paul.

Zittrain, J. (2008), *The Future of the Internet*, New Haven, CT: Yale University Press.

Index